For the Record

A DOCUMENTARY HISTORY

OF AMERICA

For the Record

A DOCUMENTARY HISTORY
OF AMERICA

FOURTH EDITION

VOLUME 2

From Reconstruction through Contemporary Times

DAVID E. SHI AND HOLLY A. MAYER

W · W · NORTON & COMPANY   NEW YORK · LONDON

W. W. Norton & Company has been independent since its founding in 1923, when William Warder Norton and Mary D. Herter Norton first published lectures delivered at the People's Institute, the adult education division of New York City's Cooper Union. The firm soon expanded its program beyond the Institute, publishing books by celebrated academics from America and abroad. By mid-century, the two major pillars of Norton's publishing program—trade books and college texts—were firmly established. In the 1950s, the Norton family transferred control of the company to its employees, and today—with a staff of four hundred and a comparable number of trade, college, and professional titles published each year—W. W. Norton & Company stands as the largest and oldest publishing house owned wholly by its employees.

Composition by PennSet, Inc.
Manufacturing by The Courier Companies, Westford.

Library of Congress Cataloging-in-Publication Data

Shi, David E.
    For the record : a documentary history of America / David E. Shi and Holly A. Mayer.— 4th ed.
      p.   cm.
    Includes bibliographical references.
    ISBN: 978-0-393-93403-8 (pbk.: v. 1)
    ISBN: 978-0-393-93404-5 (pbk.: v. 2)
    1. United States—History—Sources.   I. Mayer, Holly A. (Holly Ann), 1956– II. Title.
E173.S487 2010
973—dc22

                                      2009041920

W. W. Norton & Company, Inc., 500 Fifth Avenue, New York, N.Y. 10110
www.wwnorton.com
W. W. Norton & Company Ltd., Castle House, 75/76 Wells Street, London W1T 3QT

2 3 4 5 6 7 8 9 0

DAVID E. SHI is a professor of history and the president of Furman University. He is the author of several books on American cultural history, including *The Simple Life: Plain Living and High Thinking in American Culture* and *Facing Facts: Realism in American Thought and Culture (1850–1920)*.

HOLLY A. MAYER is an associate professor and chair of history at Duquesne University. She is the author of *Belonging to the Army: Camp Followers and Community During the American Revolution*.

For George Tindall

For our students

CONTENTS

CHAPTER 20 ⤾ BIG BUSINESS AND ORGANIZED LABOR   44

CHAPTER 21 ⤾ THE EMERGENCE OF URBAN AMERICA   61

CHAPTER 22   GILDED AGE POLITICS AND AGRARIAN REVOLT   78

CHAPTER 23   AN AMERICAN EMPIRE   104

CHAPTER 24   THE PROGRESSIVE ERA   122

INTERPRETING VISUAL SOURCES: PHOTOGRAPHY AND PROGRESSIVE REFORM   152

CHAPTER 25   AMERICA AND THE GREAT WAR   162

CHAPTER 26 ⤳ THE MODERN TEMPER   179

CHAPTER 27 ⤳ REPUBLICAN RESURGENCE AND DECLINE   201

CHAPTER 28 ⤳ NEW DEAL AMERICA   217

CHAPTER 29   FROM ISOLATION TO GLOBAL WAR   233

CHAPTER 30   THE SECOND WORLD WAR   249

CHAPTER 31   THE FAIR DEAL AND CONTAINMENT   269

CHAPTER **36** ᐁ A CONSERVATIVE INSURGENCY 386

CHAPTER **37** ᐁ TRIUMPH AND TRAGEDY: AMERICA AT THE TURN OF THE CENTURY 402

PREFACE FOR INSTRUCTORS

"The historian, essentially, wants more documents than he can really use."
—Henry James Jr.

The new Fourth Edition of *For the Record* is a substantial revision. A number of new sources have been incorporated into the reader to highlight the new theme on religion in the American experience. We also conducted an extensive user survey to reconsider every primary source included in the reader. The survey suggested that we reduce the number of total selections in the reader to make it handier, more tightly focused, and less expensive. Accordingly, the number of total selections in the new edition has been reduced by twenty-five percent. We have dropped the price by forty percent when purchased alone, and lowered the price to package it with *America: A Narrative History*. If you haven't looked seriously at *For the Record* in awhile, now is a great time to do so, as you think about putting together the lowest-priced main text and companion reader package by far in the marketplace! We know from our own experiences in the classroom that students can benefit greatly from studying the original sources that historians have used to craft their interpretations of the past. And students can use such sources to develop their own perspectives on the past.

In selecting these documents, we have sought to represent the wide spectrum of historical developments by striking a balance among political, diplomatic, economic, social, and cultural perspectives. In general, we have tried to provide entire documents or substantial portions rather than brief snippets, which so often are pedagogically unsound and intellectually unsatisfying. We have edited several of these documents to eliminate extraneous material and make them more accessible to the reader. Ellipses and asterisks indicate where passages or portions have been omitted. In a few cases, we have also modernized spelling and punctuation, taking care not to change the meaning of the original selection.

Chapter introductions set the stage for the accompanying selections by describing each historical period and highlighting its key issues and actors. Each document in turn is introduced by a headnote that places it in the context of the period and suggests its significance. And each document is followed by a list of review questions to stimulate reflections about the material.

One of the unique features of *For the Record* is its recognition that visual artifacts are also important primary sources for the historian. Each volume contains two special sections intended to help students learn how to analyze and interpret visual sources. The four visual features include the following:

- *Picturing Development versus Nature* presents examples of the relationship between words and images that, in turn, describe the relationship between the man-made and natural America.
- *Picturing the Civil War* explores the Civil War as the first "total war" represented through the camera lens of Mathew Brady and his associates.
- *Photography and Progressive Reform* explores the Progressive era through the famous and controversial photos of the immigrant reformer Jacob Riis.
- *Photographs of the Civil Rights Movement* explores the courageous and controversial efforts to gain racial equality and social justice during the twentieth century.

For the Record: A Documentary History of America is primarily a companion reader for *America: A Narrative History*. With a rich collection of 225 primary-source documents, it can also be readily used on its own or in conjunction with other survey texts.

Taken as a whole, *For the Record* reveals the diversity of sources that contribute to our understanding of American history. In the process, it introduces students to important public documents and powerful personal accounts of events and experiences. The result is a more textured and comprehensive understanding of the ways in which we recreate and understand the past.

In compiling *For the Record*, people have benefited from the insights and talents of the editorial and marketing staff at W. W. Norton & Company. Jon Durbin has been our guide and goad for this edition. He has provided wonderful advice in the first role and been properly, thankfully amicably, persistent in the second. Kudos also go to Jason Spears, Melissa Atkin, Christine D'Antonio, and Erin Granville, who did truly fine work in shaping the final product.

WHERE TO BEGIN

This checklist contains a series of questions that can be used to analyze most of the documents in this reader.

✔ What type of document is it?

✔ Why does the document exist? What motives prompted the author to write the material in this form?

✔ Who wrote this document?

✔ Who or what is left out of the document—women, children, other minorities, members of the majority?

✔ In addition to the main subject, what other kinds of information can be obtained from the document?

✔ How do the subjects of the document relate to what we know about broader society?

✔ What was the meaning of the document in its own time? What is its meaning for the reader today?

✔ What does the document tell us about change in society?

For the Record

A DOCUMENTARY HISTORY

OF AMERICA

18 ∽ RECONSTRUCTION: NORTH AND SOUTH

The assassination of Abraham Lincoln in April 1865 brought Vice President Andrew Johnson into the White House. A Tennessee Democrat who served two terms as governor before being elected to the Senate in 1857, he was an ardent Unionist who blamed the slaveholding planter elite for secession and the Civil War. Johnson was the only southern senator who refused to embrace the Confederacy in 1861. Such credentials help explain why Lincoln invited him to be his running mate in 1864.

The Radical Republicans hoped that President Johnson would embrace their comprehensive effort to reconstruct the defeated South. Johnson shared their disdain for the former Confederate leaders and for the planter class, but he also cherished states' rights and feared any effort to expand federal authority. He also retained many of the racial prejudices of his native region. "White men alone must manage the South," Johnson told a journalist. Unlike the Radical Republicans, he balked at putting freed blacks in control of southern politics.

Like Lincoln, Andrew Johnson hoped that middle-class white southern Unionists, along with repentant ex-Confederates, would take control of restoring the South to the Union. He required that the new state constitutional conventions formally abolish slavery, renounce secession, and void all war debts that the state had incurred. The states then could hold elections and officially return to the Union. By April 1866 all of the southern states had fulfilled these requirements, albeit grudgingly, and had formed new governments. At the same time, they steadfastly refused to allow African Americans to vote. Johnson, however, was dismayed that the new political leaders were more often former Confederates than southern Unionists.

The Union victory in the Civil War and the official end of slavery created excited expectations among the freed slaves. Some adopted new names to express their new identity and to make a new beginning. Others discarded the clothes provided by their masters and took up new modes of dress. Many freed people left the plantations and migrated to neighboring towns and cities, where federal troops offered protection.

But freedom itself did not provide security or the resources necessary for meaningful lives. In March 1865 Congress created the Freedmen's Bureau, an agency administered by the War Department, to provide the former slaves with emergency supplies and to help them find employment, procure land, and pursue educational opportunities. By 1870 the Bureau was supervising more than 4,000 schools.

Yet for all of its heroic efforts, the Freedmen's Bureau could help only a small percentage of former slaves. Few freed people were able to acquire land of their own. Most of them were forced to become wage laborers, or sharecroppers or tenant farmers contracting with white landowners to work their land in exchange for food, tools, clothing, and a place to live. This agrarian system, however necessary in the face of the social and economic realities confronting the region, soon placed the freed slaves in a dependent relationship reminiscent of slavery itself.

As the new "lily-white" state governments coalesced in 1865 and 1866, most of them drafted "Black Codes" limiting the rights and freedoms of African Americans. These laws varied from state to state, but all of them restricted the independence of blacks and channeled them into the service of the white-dominated social and economic order.

Some whites decided that such restrictive laws did not sufficiently impress upon blacks their subordinate status. In an effort to promote white supremacy they founded secret organizations such as the Ku Klux Klan. The Klan, organized by former Confederate soldiers, used violence and terror to intimidate blacks and to disrupt the efforts of Radical Republicans to "reconstruct" the South. During one campaign season in Louisiana, over 200 African Americans were killed in one parish alone. Congress passed laws intended to suppress the Klan, but to little avail.

Reconstruction officially ended in 1877 with the withdrawal of the last federal troops from the South. African Americans in the region retained certain constitutional rights, but in practice white supremacy had been reestablished through force and terror. With the loss of federal protection, blacks found themselves not only at the mercy of the southern political elite but also locked into a dependent economic relationship through the sharecrop system as well.

NEW YORK TIMES

FROM The Late Convention of Colored Men (1865)

Freedom did not bring security to many former slaves after the Civil War. They were no longer slaves, but they had no property, no money, and little education. In each state, groups of former slaves met to share their concerns and to request assistance from the federal government. The following message was sent from a convention of freedmen in Alexandria, Virginia, in 1865.

From "The Late Convention of Colored Men," *The New York Times*, 13 August 1865.

We, the undersigned members of a convention of colored citizens of the State of Virginia, would respectfully represent that, although we have been held as slaves, and denied all recognition as a constituent of your nationality for almost the entire period of the duration of your government, and that by your permission we have been denied either home or country, and deprived of the dearest rights of human nature; yet when you and our immediate oppressors met in deadly conflict upon the field of battle, the one to destroy and the other to save your government and nationality, we, with scarce an exception, in our inmost souls espoused your cause, and watched, and prayed, and waited, and labored for your success.

When the contest waxed long, and the result hung doubtfully, you appealed to us for help, and how well we answered is written in the rosters of the two hundred thousand colored troops now enrolled in your service; and as to our undying devotion to your cause, let the uniform acclamation of escaped prisoners, "Whenever we saw a black face we felt sure of a friend," answer.

Well, the war is over, the rebellion is "put down," and we are declared free! Four-fifths of our enemies are paroled or amnestied, and the other fifth are being pardoned, and the President has, in his efforts at the reconstruction of the civil government of the States, late in rebellion, left us

entirely at the mercy of these subjugated but unconverted rebels, in everything save the privilege of bringing us, our wives and little ones, to the auction block. He has, so far as we can understand the tendency and bearing of his action in the case, remitted us for all our civil rights, to men, a majority of whom regard our devotions to your cause and flag as that which decided the contest against them! This we regard as destructive of all we hold dear, and in the name of God, of justice, of humanity, of good faith, of truth and righteousness, we do most solemnly and earnestly protest. Men and brethren, in the hour of your peril you called upon us, and despite all time-honored interpretation of constitutional obligations, we came at your call and you are saved—and now we beg, we pray, we entreat you not to desert us in this the hour of our peril!

We know these men—know them well—and we assure you that, with the majority of them, loyalty is only "lip deep," and that their professions of loyalty are used as a cover to the cherished design of getting restored to their former relation with the Federal Government, and then, by all sorts of "unfriendly legislation," to render the freedom you have given us more intolerable than the slavery they intended for us.

We warn you in time that our only safety is in keeping them under Governors of the military persuasion until you have so amended the Federal

Constitution that it will prohibit the States from making any distinction between citizens on account of race or color. In one word, the only salvation for us besides the power of the Government, is in the possession of the ballot. Give us this, and we will protect ourselves. No class of men relatively as numerous as we were ever oppressed when armed with the ballot. But, 'tis said we are ignorant. Admit it. Yet who denies we know a traitor from a loyal man, a gentleman from a rowdy, a friend from an enemy?

. . . All we ask is an equal chance with the white traitors varnished and japanned with the oath of amnesty. Can you deny us this and still keep faith with us? "But," say some, "the blacks will be overreached by the superior knowledge and cunning of the whites." Trust us for that. We will never be deceived a second time. "But," they continue, "the planters and landowners will have them in their power, and dictate the way their votes shall be cast." We did not know before that we were to be left to the tender mercies of these landed rebels for employment. Verily, we thought the Freedmen's Bureau was organized and clothed with power to protect us from this very thing, by compelling those for whom we labored to pay us, whether they liked our political opinions or not! . . .

We are "sheep in the midst of wolves," and nothing but the military arm of the Government prevents us and all the truly loyal white men from being driven from the land of our birth. Do not then, we beseech you, give to one of these "wayward sisters" the rights they abandoned and forfeited when they rebelled until you have secured our rights by the aforementioned amendment to the Constitution.

Let your action in our behalf be thus clear and emphatic, and our respected President, who, we feel confident, desires only to know your will, to act in harmony therewith, will give you his most earnest and cordial cooperation; and the Southern States, through your enlightened and just legislation, will speedily award us our rights. Thus not only will the arms of the rebellion be surrendered, but the ideas also.

REVIEW QUESTIONS

1. What services had former slaves performed that they believed entitled them to the protection of the federal government?
2. What did the petitioners mean when they said that the white Southerner was "subjugated but unconverted"?
3. What two steps did the freed blacks claim would ensure that their own rights would be guaranteed?

Black Codes of Mississippi (1865)

The so-called Black Codes were enacted by the newly reconstituted southern state legislatures to address the legal status of the freed slaves. Some of the codes, such as Georgia's, were relatively lenient; others, such as those of Louisiana and Mississippi, sought to restore slavery in all but name. Most of the Black Codes were suspended by the federal military governors of the reconstructed states, and both the Civil Rights Act of 1866 and the Fourteenth Amendment were in part a response to these efforts to suppress the rights of blacks. The following sections from the Mississippi code deal with civil rights, apprenticeship, vagrancy, and penal crimes.

From *Laws of the State of Mississippi*, 1865 (Jackson, MS, 1866), pp. 82–90, 165.

1. Civil Rights of Freedmen in Mississippi

Sec. 1. *Be it enacted,* . . . That all freedmen, free negroes, and mulattoes may sue and be sued, implead and be impleaded, in all the courts of law and equity of this State, and may acquire personal property . . . by descent or purchase, and may dispose of the same in the same manner and to the same extent that white persons may: *Provided,* That the provisions of this section shall not be so construed as to allow any freedman, free negro, or mulatto to rent or lease any lands or tenements except in incorporated cities or towns, in which places the corporate authorities shall control the same. . . .

Sec. 3. . . . All freedmen, free negroes, or mulattoes who do now and have herebefore lived and cohabited together as husband and wife shall be taken and held in law as legally married, and the issue shall be taken and held as legitimate for all purposes: that it shall not be lawful for any freedman, free negro, or mulatto to intermarry with any white person; nor for any white person to intermarry with any freedman, free negro, or mulatto: and any person who shall so intermarry, shall be deemed guilty of felony, and on conviction thereof shall be confined in the State penitentiary for life; and those shall be deemed freedmen, free negroes, and mulattoes who are of pure negro blood, and those descended from a negro to the third generation, inclusive, though one ancestor in each generation may have been a white person.

Sec. 4. . . . In addition to cases in which freedmen, free negroes, and mulattoes are now by law competent witnesses, freedmen, free negroes, or mulattoes shall be competent in civil cases, when a party or parties to the suit, either plaintiff or plaintiffs, defendant or defendants, and a white person or white persons, is or are the opposing party or parties, plaintiff or plaintiffs, defendant or defendants. They shall also be competent witnesses in all criminal prosecutions where the crime charged is alleged to have been committed by a white person upon or against the person or property of a freedman, free negro, or mulatto: *Provided,* that in all cases said witnesses shall be examined in open court, on the stand; except, however, they may be examined before the grand jury, and shall in all cases be subject to the rules and tests of the common law as to competency and credibility. . . .

Sec. 6. . . . All contracts for labor made with freedmen, free negroes, and mulattoes for a longer period than one month shall be in writing, and in duplicate, attested and read to said freedman, free negro, or mulatto by a beat, city or county officer, or two disinterested white persons of the county in which the labor is to be performed, of which each party shall have one; and said contracts shall be taken and held as entire contracts, and if the laborer shall quit the service of the employer before the expiration of his term of service, without good cause, he shall forfeit his wages for that year up to the time of quitting.

Sec. 7. . . . Every civil officer shall, and every person may, arrest and carry back to his or her legal employer any freedman, free negro, or mulatto who shall have quit the service of his or her employer before the expiration of his or her term of service without good cause; and said officer and person shall be entitled to receive for arresting and carrying back every deserting employee aforesaid the sum of five dollars, and ten cents per mile from the place of arrest to the place of delivery; and the same shall be paid by the employer, and held as a set-off for so much against the wages of said deserting employee: *Provided,* that said arrested party, after being so returned, may appeal to the justice of the peace or member of the board of police of the county, who, on notice to the alleged employer, shall try summarily whether said appellant is legally employed by the alleged employer, and has good cause to quit said employer; either party shall have the right of appeal to the county court, pending which the alleged deserter shall be remanded to the alleged employer or otherwise disposed of, as shall be right and just; and the decision of the county court shall be final. . . .

Sec. 9. . . . If any person shall persuade or attempt to persuade, entice, or cause any freedman, free negro, or mulatto to desert from the legal employment of any person before the expiration of his or her term of service, or shall knowingly employ any such deserting freedman, free negro, or mulatto, or shall knowingly give or sell to any such deserting freedman, free negro, or mulatto, any food, raiment, or other thing, he or she shall be guilty of a misdemeanor, and, upon conviction, shall be fined not less than twenty-five dollars and not more than two hundred dollars and the costs; and if said fine and costs shall not be immediately paid, the court shall sentence said convict to not exceeding two months' imprisonment in the county jail, and he or she shall moreover be liable to the party injured in damages: *Provided,* if any person shall, or shall attempt to, persuade, entice, or cause any freedman, free negro, or mulatto to desert from any legal employment of any person, with the view to employ said freedman, free negro, or mulatto without the limits of this State, such person, on conviction, shall be fined not less than fifty dollars, and not more than five hundred dollars and costs; and if said fine and costs shall not be immediately paid, the court shall sentence said convict to not exceeding six months imprisonment in the county jail.

*   *   *

Mississippi Vagrant Law

Sec. 1. *Be it enacted, etc.,* . . . That all rogues and vagabonds, idle and dissipated persons, beggars, jugglers, or persons practicing unlawful games or plays, runaways, common drunkards, common night-walkers, pilferers, lewd, wanton, or lascivious persons, in speech or behavior, common railers and brawlers, persons who neglect their calling or employment, misspend what they earn, or do not provide for the support of themselves or their families, or dependents, and all other idle and disorderly persons, including all who neglect all lawful business, habitually misspend their time by frequenting houses of ill-fame, gaming-houses, or tippling shops, shall be deemed and considered vagrants, under the provisions of this act, and upon conviction thereof shall be fined not exceeding one hundred dollars, with all accruing costs, and be

imprisoned at the discretion of the court, not exceeding ten days.

Sec. 2. . . . All freedmen, free negroes and mulattoes in this State, over the age of eighteen years, found on the second Monday in January, 1866, or thereafter, with no lawful employment or business, or found unlawfully assembling themselves together, either in the day or night time, and all white persons so assembling themselves with freedmen, free negroes or mulattoes, or usually associating with freedmen, free negroes or mulattoes, on terms of equality, or living in adultery or fornication with a freed woman, free negro or mulatto, shall be deemed vagrants, and on conviction thereof shall be fined in a sum not exceeding, in the case of a freedman, free negro or mulatto, fifty dollars, and a white man two hundred dollars, and imprisoned at the discretion of the court, the free negro not exceeding ten days, and the white man not exceeding six months. . . .

Sec. 7. . . . If any freedman, free negro, or mulatto shall fail or refuse to pay any tax levied according to the provisions of the sixth section of this act, it shall be *prima facie* evidence of vagrancy, and it shall be the duty of the sheriff to arrest such freedman, free negro, or mulatto or such person refusing or neglecting to pay such tax, and proceed at once to hire for the shortest time such delinquent tax-payer to any one who will pay the said tax, with accruing costs, giving preference to the employer, if there be one.

*   *   *

4. Penal Laws of Mississippi

Sec. 1. *Be it enacted,* . . . That no freedman, free negro or mulatto, not in the military service of the United States government, and not licensed so to do by the board of police of his or her county, shall keep or carry fire-arms of any kind, or any ammunition, dirk or bowie knife, and on conviction thereof in the county court shall be punished by fine, not exceeding ten dollars, and pay the costs of such proceedings, and all such arms or ammunition shall be forfeited to the informer; and it shall be the duty of every civil and military officer to arrest any freedman, free negro, or mulatto found with any such arms or ammunition, and cause him or her to be committed to trial in default of bail.

Sec. 2. . . . Any freedman, free negro, or mulatto committing riots, routs, affrays, trespasses, malicious mischief, cruel treatment to animals, seditious speeches, insulting gestures, language, or acts, or assaults on any person, disturbance of the peace, exercising the function of a minister of the Gospel without a license from some regularly organized church, vending spirituous or intoxicating liquors, or committing any other misdemeanor, the punishment of which is not specifically provided for by law, shall, upon conviction thereof in the county court, be fined not less than ten dollars, and not more than one hundred dollars, and may be imprisoned at the discretion of the court, not exceeding thirty days.

Sec. 3. . . . If any white person shall sell, lend, or give to any freedman, free negro, or mulatto any fire-arms, dirk or bowie knife, or ammunition, or any spirituous or intoxicating liquors, such person or persons so offending, upon conviction thereof

in the county court of his or her county, shall be fined not exceeding fifty dollars, and may be imprisoned, at the discretion of the court, not exceeding thirty days. . . .

Sec. 5. . . . If any freedman, free negro, or mulatto, convicted of any of the misdemeanors provided against in this act, shall fail or refuse for the space of five days, after conviction, to pay the fine and costs imposed, such person shall be hired out by the sheriff or other officer, at public outcry, to any white person who will pay said fine and all costs, and take said convict for the shortest time.

REVIEW QUESTIONS

1. Which "crime" carried the harshest penalty? Why?
2. Summarize the regulations related to employment of freed slaves. How did they represent a form of slavery?
3. The Black Codes were criticized for their vagueness. Cite an example of such vagueness, and note ways in which the codes could be interpreted or manipulated.

HOWELL COBB

An Unreconstructed Southerner (1868)

Many former Confederates resented and resisted both the presence of federal troops in the South after the Civil War and the efforts of the Congress to "reconstruct" the region's political, social, and economic life. Howell Cobb (1815–1868) was a prominent Georgia attorney and Democratic politician who served as Speaker of the United States House of Representatives, governor of Georgia, secretary of the Treasury under President James Buchanan, and as a major general in the Confederate army. In this letter to the federal commander of the third military district, which included Georgia, he expresses the bitter feelings of many white Southerners.

From Howell Cobb to J. D. Hoover, 4 January 1868, in *The Correspondence of Robert Toombs, Alexander H. Stephens, and Howell Cobb*, ed. U. B. Phillips (Washington, DC, 1913), pp. 690–694.

. . . We of the ill-fated South realize only the mournful present whose lesson teaches us to prepare for a still gloomier future. . . . The people of the south, conquered, ruined, impoverished, and oppressed, bear up with patient fortitude under the heavy weight of their burdens. Disarmed and reduced to poverty, they are powerless to protect themselves against wrong and injustice; and can only await with broken spirits that destiny which the future has in store for them. At the bidding of their more powerful conquerors they laid down their arms, abandoned a hopeless struggle, and returned to their quiet homes under the plighted faith of a soldier's honor that they should be protected so long as they observed the obligations imposed upon them of peaceful law-abiding citizens.

Despite the bitter charges and accusations brought against our people, I hesitate not to say that since that hour their bearing and conduct have been marked by a dignified and honorable submission which should command the respect of their bitterest enemy and challenge the admiration of the civilized world. Deprived of our property and ruined in our estates by the results of the war, we have accepted the situation and given the pledge of a faith never yet broken to abide it. Our

conquerors seem to think we should accompany our acquiescence with some exhibition of gratitude for the ruin which they have brought upon us. We cannot see it in that light.

Since the close of the war they have taken our property of various kinds, sometimes by seizure, and sometimes by purchase,—and when we have asked for remuneration have been informed that the claims of rebels are never recognized by the Government. To this decision necessity compels us to submit; but our conquerors express surprise that we do not see in such ruling the evidence of their kindness and forgiving spirit.

They have imposed upon us in our hour of distress and ruin a heavy and burdensome tax, peculiar and limited to our impoverished section. Against such legislation we have ventured to utter an earnest appeal, which to many of their leading spirits indicates a spirit of insubordination which calls for additional burdens. They have deprived us of the protection afforded by our state constitutions and laws, and put life, liberty and property at the disposal of absolute military power. Against this violation of plighted faith and constitutional right we have earnestly and solemnly protested, and our protests have been denounced as insolent;—and our restlessness under the wrong and oppression which have followed these acts has been construed into a rebellious spirit, demanding further and more stringent restrictions of civil and constitutional rights. They have arrested the wheels of State government, paralyzed the arm of industry, engendered a spirit of bitter antagonism on the part of our negro population towards the white people with whom it is the interest of both races they should maintain kind and friendly relations, and are now struggling by all the means in their power both legal and illegal, constitutional and unconstitutional, to make our former slaves *our masters,* bringing these Southern states under the power of *negro supremacy.*

To these efforts we have opposed appeals, protests, and every other means of resistance in our power, and shall continue to do so to the bitter end. If the South is to be made a pandemonium and a howling wilderness, the responsibility shall not rest upon our heads.

Our conquerors regard these efforts on our part to save ourselves and posterity from the terrible results of their policy and conduct as a new rebellion against the constitution of our country, and profess to be amazed that in all this we have failed to see the evidence of their great magnanimity and exceeding generosity. Standing today in the midst of the gloom and suffering which meets the eye in every direction, we can but feel that we are the victims of cruel legislation and the harsh enforcement of unjust laws. . . .

We regarded the close of the war as ending the relationship of enemies and the beginning of a new national brotherhood, and in the light of that conviction felt and spoke of constitutional equality. . . .

We claimed that the result of the war left us a state in the Union, and therefore under the protection of the constitution, rendering in return cheerful obedience to its requirements and bearing in common with the other states of the Union the burdens of government, submitting even as we were compelled to do to *taxation without represen-*

tation; but they tell us that a successful war to keep us in the Union left us out of the Union and that the pretension we put up for constitutional protection evidences bad temper on our part and a want of appreciation of the generous spirit which declares that the constitution is not over us for the purposes of protection. . . .

In such reasoning is found a justification of the policy which seeks to put the South under negro supremacy. Better, they say, to hazard the consequences of negro supremacy in the south with its sure and inevitable results upon Northern prosperity than to put faith in the people of the south who though overwhelmed and conquered have ever showed themselves a brave and generous people, true to their plighted faith in peace and in war, in adversity as in prosperity. . . .

*   *   *

With an Executive[1] who manifests a resolute purpose to defend with all his power the constitution of his country from further aggression, and a Judiciary whose unspotted record has never yet been tarnished with a base subserviency to the unholy demands of passion and hatred, let us indulge the hope that the hour of the country's redemption is at hand, and that even in the wronged and ruined South there is a fair prospect for better days and happier hours when our people can unite again in celebrating the national festivals as in the olden time.

REVIEW QUESTIONS

1. How are white Southerners portrayed in this excerpt?
2. What do you think Cobb meant when he said that "property of various kinds" had been stolen?
3. According to Cobb, what was the motive behind the supposed attempt to create "negro supremacy" in the South?

---

[1] President Andrew Johnson (1808–1875).

Organization and Principles of the Ku Klux Klan (1868)

The Ku Klux Klan was the largest of several white supremacist societies that emerged in the post–Civil War era. Founded in Pulaski, Tennessee, in 1865, it grew rapidly among Confederate veterans across the South. Former Confederate general Nathan Bedford Forrest was the first Grand Wizard. The Klan used terror and violence to defy the efforts of Radical Republicans to "reconstruct" southern society. The following is an early statement of the Klan's principles.

From W. L. Fleming, ed., *The Ku Klux Klan: Its Origin, Growth and Disbandment*, by J. C. Lester and D. L. Wilson (New York: Neale, 1905), pp. 154ff.

Creed

We, the Order of the * * *, reverentially acknowledge the majesty and supremacy of the Divine Being, and recognize the goodness and providence of the same. And we recognize our relation to the United States Government, the supremacy of the Constitution, the Constitutional Laws thereof, and the Union of States thereunder.

Character and Objects of the Order

This is an institution of Chivalry, Humanity, Mercy, and Patriotism; embodying in its genius and its principles all that is chivalric in conduct, noble in sentiment, generous in manhood, and patriotic in purpose; its peculiar objects being

First: To protect the weak, the innocent, and the defenseless, from the indignities, wrongs, and outrages of the lawless, the violent, and the brutal; to relieve the injured and oppressed; to succor the suffering and unfortunate, and especially the widows and orphans of Confederate soldiers.

Second: To protect and defend the Constitution of the United States, and all laws passed in conformity thereto, and to protect the States and the people thereof from all invasion from any source whatever.

Third: To aid and assist in the execution of all constitutional laws, and to protect the people from unlawful seizure, and from trial except by their peers in conformity to the laws of the land.

Titles

Sec. 1. The officers of this Order shall consist of a Grand Wizard of the Empire, and his ten Genii; a Grand Dragon of the Realm, and his eight Hydras; a Grand Titan of the Dominion, and his six Furies; a Grand Giant of the Province, and his four Goblins; a Grand Cyclops of the Den, and his two Night Hawks; a Grand Magi, a Grand Monk, a Grand Scribe, a Grand Exchequer, a Grand Turk, and a Grand Sentinel.

Sec. 2. The body politic of this Order shall be known and designated as "Ghouls."

Territory and its Divisions

Sec. 1. The territory embraced within the jurisdiction of this Order shall be coterminous with the States of Maryland, Virginia, North Carolina, South Carolina, Georgia, Florida, Alabama, Mississippi, Louisiana, Texas, Arkansas, Missouri, Kentucky, and Tennessee; all combined constituting the Empire.

Sec. 2. The Empire shall be divided into four

departments, the first to be styled the Realm, and coterminous with the boundaries of the several States; the second to be styled the Dominion, and to be coterminous with such counties as the Grand Dragons of the several Realms may assign to the charge of the Grand Titan. The third to be styled the Province, and to be coterminous with the several counties; *Provided* the Grand Titan may, when he deems it necessary, assign two Grand Giants to one Province, prescribing, at the same time, the jurisdiction of each. The fourth department to be styled the Den, and shall embrace such part of a Province as the Grand Giant shall assign to the charge of a Grand Cyclops. . . .

Interrogations to be asked

1st. Have you ever been rejected, upon application for membership in the * * * , or have you ever been expelled from the same?

2d. Are you now, or have you ever been, a member of the Radical Republican party, or either of the organizations known as the "Loyal League" and the "Grand Army of the Republic?"

3d. Are you opposed to the principles and policy of the Radical party, and to the Loyal League, and the Grand Army of the Republic, so far as you are informed of the character and purposes of those organizations?

4th. Did you belong to the Federal army during the late war, and fight against the South during the existence of the same?

5th. Are you opposed to negro equality, both social and political?

6th. Are you in favor of a white man's government in this country?

7th. Are you in favor of Constitutional liberty, and a Government of equitable laws instead of a Government of violence and oppression?

8th. Are you in favor of maintaining the Constitutional rights of the South?

9th. Are you in favor of the re-enfranchisement and emancipation of the white men of the South, and the restitution of the Southern people to all their rights, alike proprietary, civil, and political?

10th. Do you believe in the inalienable right of self-preservation of the people against the exercise of arbitrary and unlicensed power? . . .

REVIEW QUESTIONS

1. How could the Klan express such reverence for the Constitution while castigating Union army veterans?
2. Why would poor whites have been attracted to the Klan?
3. How would freed slaves have reacted to the Klan's principles?

LEE GUIDON

Klan Terrorism in South Carolina

During the early 1870s the Congress held hearings to investigate reports that the Ku Klux Klan was engaging in widespread intimidation and violence against blacks in the South. The following three documents relate to a series of racial incidents in York County, South Carolina, in 1871. Throughout the South, where Radical Reconstruction was being implemented, blacks were joining Union Leagues, Republican organizations that also had secret rituals. The first document is an article from the Yorkville Enquirer *describing the rash of violence in the community. The second document is the courtroom testimony of an African American woman, Harriet Postle, whose family was assaulted by Klansmen. The third document is the testimony of Lawson B. Davis, a white Klansman accused of such terrorism.*

From U.S. Congress, *Report of the Joint Select Committee to Inquire into the Condition of Affairs in the Late Insurrectionary States* (Washington, DC, 1872), 3:1540–1541; 1951–1952; 1943–1944.

Whipping and House-Burning.

The state of things which exists in many sections of our country is alarming. Scarcely a night passes but some outrage is perpetrated against the welfare of some community. Houses are burned, persons are whipped, and in some instances killed, by parties unknown, and for causes which no one can decipher. These things are not right; they are not prudent. They are grave crimes against God and the best interest of the country.

By common consent, the house-burning is charged upon the colored race, and the whipping and killing upon the so-called Ku-Klux. This is not certainly known to be the case, but the probability is that the supposition with regard to the perpetrators of these deeds is correct. One thing must be evident to every observing man: there is concert of action both in the house-burning and in the whipping and killing.

For some years there has been, and still is, we are informed by one who claims to know, an organization known as the Union League. Of this we know nothing, save what we have learned by observing its workings. From what we have been able to learn, we are convinced that the Union League is a secret political organization, and on this ground alone, if we knew nothing about its operations and results, we would condemn it. We take the broad ground that all secret political organizations are nothing but conspiracies against the established government of a country, and as such are ruinous to the peace and quiet and prosperity of the people.

Of the Ku-Klux we know even less than we do of the Union League. Sometimes we are disposed to believe that there is no such organization; at other times we think differently. Recent developments rather indicate that there is such an organization, and it is made of no mean material. This is mere conjecture on our part. We do not know one single individual who holds connection with the Ku-Klux. It is evident, however, that there is some sort of complicity of action in the whipping and killing that has recently been perpetrated in this country, and which is going on at present all over the State, and, in fact, all over the South.

We do not believe, from what we know of the

political party which is opposed to the Union League and the political tenets of the dominant party in South Carolina, that the Ku-Klux is a political organization, in the strict sense of that term. Whatever may be its object, we are convinced that the Ku-Klux is doing much harm. To be honest and frank, we charge the Union League with the shameful state of things which now exists. It has placed its members in a predicament which is anything but enviable. The ostensible purpose for which the thing was organized was, we suppose, to protect the freedman; the real purpose, however, was, as is acknowledged by some of its members, to consolidate the votes of the freedman, that designing men might be elevated to positions of honor and profit. There is no doubt but the Union League has done the colored people a great injury. It has been the means of arraying them in hostility against the white man, and the result always has been that in every conflict between the white man and the colored man, the condition of the latter has been materially injured. We do not blame the colored people for joining the League; but we do blame those designing white men who enticed them into this snare of destruction.

However much we may reprobate the Union League, this does not cause us to love or approve of the Ku-Klux. Two wrongs never can make one right. Both the Union League and the Ku-Klux are founded upon dangerous principles, and are working the ruin of this county. We have no disposition to make prediction, especially while so unsettled a state of things continues as exists in this county at present; but we will venture to say that if this house-burning and whipping does not stop soon, it will culminate in a conflict which will be fatal to some party.

What is the duty of every good citizen, under existing circumstances? It is the duty, we believe, of the leading colored people to influence their race to abandon the League and to refrain from acts of violence. On the other hand, it is the duty of the white people, especially the old men, to advise the young men not to engage in whipping and murdering the colored people. So long as the present state of things exists, no one is safe. The minds of

the white people are filled with anxiety lest their houses may be burned down at any time, and no doubt the minds of the colored people are filled with dread lest they be dragged from their beds and taken to the forest and whipped, or, perchance, shot. We have no party purposes to subserve by what we say. All we desire is to assist in restoring peace and quiet to our county. These outrages must stop now, or worse will come. If a few more houses are burned, the public mind will be so exasperated that, in all probability, something will be done that will be very injurious to the public good. It is the imperative duty of every good citizen to discourage house-burning and whipping. We must be permitted to say that it is our impression that, so long as the Union League exists, some kind of an opposing party will also exist. The sooner all such organizations cease to exist, the better it will be for all parties.

Testimony of Harriet Postle.

Examination by Mr. CORBIN:

I live in the eastern part of York County, about four miles from Rock Hill, on Mr. James Smith's plantation; I am about thirty years old; my husband is a preacher; I have a family of six children; the oldest is about fourteen; the Ku-Klux visited me last spring; it was some time in March; I was asleep when they came; they made a great noise and waked me up, and called out for Postle; my husband heard them and jumped up, and I thought he was putting on his clothes, but when I got up I found he was gone; they kept on hallooing for Postle and knocking at the door; I was trying to get on my clothes, but I was so frightened I did not get on my clothes at all; it looked like they were going to knock the door down; then the rest of them began to come into the house, and my oldest child got out and ran under the bed; one of them saw him and said, "There he is; I see him;" and with that three of them pointed their pistols under the bed; I then cried out, "It is my child;" they told him to come out; when my child came out from under the bed, one of them said, "Put it on his neck;" and the child commenced hallooing and crying, and I begged them not to hurt my child; the man did not hurt it, but one of them ran the child back against the wall, and ground a piece of skin off as big as my hand; I then took a chair and sat it back upon a loose plank, and sat down upon it; one of the men stepped up; seeing the plank loose, he just jerked the chair and threw me over, while my babe was in my arms, and I fell with my babe to the floor, when one of them clapped his foot upon the child, and another had his foot on me; I begged him, for the Lord's sake, to save my child; I went and picked up my babe, and when I opened the door and looked I saw they had formed a line; they asked me if Postle was there; I said no; they told me to make up a light, but I was so frightened I could not do it well, and I asked my child to make it up for me; then they asked me where my husband was; I told them he was gone; they said, "He is here somewhere;" I told them he was gone for some meal; they said he was there somewhere, and they called me a damned liar; one of them said: "He is under the house;" then one of them comes to me and says: "I am going to have the truth tonight; you are a damned, lying bitch, and you are telling a lie;" and he had a line, and commenced putting it over my neck; said he: "You are telling a lie; I know it; he is here;" I told them again he was gone; when he had the rope round my head he said, "I want you to tell where your husband is;" and, said he, "The truth I've got to have;" I commenced hallooing, and says he: "We are men of peace, but you are telling me a damned lie, and you are not to tell me any lies to-night;" and the one who had his foot on my body mashed me badly, but not so badly as he might have done, for I was seven or eight months gone in travail; then I got outside of the house and sat down, with my back against the house, and I called the little ones to me, for they were all dreadfully frightened; they said my husband was there, and they would shoot into every crack; and they did shoot all over the place, and there are bullet-holes there and bullet-marks on the hearth yet; at this time there were some in the house and some outside, and says they to me: "We're going to have the truth out of you, you

damned, lying bitch; he is somewhere about here;" said I: "He is gone;" with that he clapped his hands on my neck, and with one hand put the line over my neck; and he says again: "We're going to have the truth out of you, you damned bitch;" and with that he beat my head against the side of the house till I had no sense hardly left; but I still had hold of my babe.

Mr. CORBIN:

Question. Did you recognize anybody?

Answer. Yes, sir; I did; I recognized the first man that came into the house; it was Dr. Avery, [pointing to the accused.] I recognized him by his performance, and when he was entangling the line round my neck; as I lifted my hand to keep the rope off my neck, I caught his lame hand; it was his left hand that I caught, his crippled hand; I felt it in my hand, and I said to myself right then, "I knows you;" and I knew Joe Castle and James Matthews—the old man's son; I didn't know any one else; I suppose there was about a dozen altogether there; Dr. Avery had on a red gown with a blue face, with red about his mouth, and he had two horns on his cap about a foot long; the line that he tried to put over my neck was a buggy-line, not quite so wide as three fingers, but wider than two; they said to me that they rode thirty-eight miles that night to see old Abe Broomfield and preacher Postle; they said that they had heard that preacher Postle had been preaching up fire and corruption; they afterward found my husband under the house, but I had gone to the big house with my children to take them out of the cold, and I did not see them pull him out from the house.

*   *   *

Testimony of Lawson B. Davis.

Witness for the prosecution:

I reside in York County, and have lived there two years. I was initiated as a member of the Ku-Klux Klan. I took the oath at my own house. Three persons were initiated at the same time. I attended one meeting and heard the constitution and by-laws. That was in last January. The contents of the oath, as near as I can remember, were that female friends, widows, and orphans were to be objects of our protection, and that we were to support the Constitution as it was bequeathed to us by our forefathers; and there was to be opposition to the thirteenth, fourteenth, and fifteenth amendments.[1] The fourteenth was particularly specified in the oath I took. The oath was repeated, and I repeated it after them. There was no written document present. The penalty for divulging its secrets was death.

The constitution and by-laws were here handed to the witness by Mr. Corbin.

The witness continued: That is the same oath that I took except the second section, which, as repeated to me, was "opposition to the thirteenth, fourteenth, and fifteenth amendments." The organization, when I joined it, was called the Invisible Empire of the South. After I joined I found it was the same as the Ku-Klux organization. When I found that I determined to leave them. The first meeting I attended there were eight or ten persons sworn in, and a proposition was brought forward to make a raid upon such and such persons. I inquired the reason, and they said they were prominently connected with the Union League. Their object was to discountenance people from joining the League. I heard this from the members. They said that those who belonged to the League were to be visited and warned; that they must discontinue their connection with the League. If they did not, on the second visit they were to leave the country, and if they didn't leave they were to be whipped; and if after this they did not leave, they were to be killed. I know this was how the purposes of the order were to be carried out. I have known of instances of raiding for guns.

They made one raid upon Jerry Adams; Charley Byers told me they had whipped him; he was to be chief of the Klan; he said they had scared the boy very badly—they had fired several guns at him, but didn't mean to hit him. The only charge I ever heard against Jerry Adams was that he was a radical. He was a republican and a colored man. Charley Good, who was whipped very badly by the Klan, came to my house two or three days afterwards. He was a blacksmith, and a very good workman—the best in that part. Charley Good was whipped so badly that he could not follow his trade for several days. Two or three weeks after that he was killed.

Wesley Smith, and William Smith, and William White were among those who killed Charley Good. Smith said he was a member of Smarr's Klan, and some members of that Klan assisted in putting Charley Good's body out of the way. The two Smiths, I know, were members of the Klan. Charley Good was killed because he was a republican. He told me, in the presence of some other persons, that he knew who had whipped him. I told him it would be better for him to keep that to himself. Wesley Smith gave, as the reason for killing him, that Charley Good knew some of the party who had whipped him. I was ordered to assist in disposing of the body of Charley Good. I did not, till then, know that he was missing. They came and summoned me and Mr. Howard to go and secrete the body, which was lying near to where he was murdered.

Wesley Smith said that all who were members of the organization were required to assist, so that they might be connected with it, and that the matter might not get out. I told him that I did not want to go, but he said that all the members had to go. We were ordered to meet at the gate about a quarter of a mile from his house. I left about 9 o'clock and went up to Mr. Howard's, and Wesley Smith had given him the same instructions. He did not feel willing to go, and I said those were my feelings exactly. We waited until the hour had passed, and then when we left we met some ten or fifteen of the party. It was a dark night, and I only recognized Thomas L. Berry, Pinckney Caldwell, Wesley Smith, and Madison Smarr. He is said to be the chief of the Klan. Madison Smarr said I had es-

[1] Amendments to the U.S. Constitution associated with the Civil War. The Thirteenth, ratified in 1865, abolished slavery; the Fourteenth (1866) provided "equal protection under the law"; and the Fifteenth (1870) granted the right to vote to black males.

caped a scouring. He said the body was very heavy to carry. And Pinckney Caldwell told me that "Charley Good is now at the bottom of the river. The body would not sink, and I jumped in upon him," he said, "and fastened him there, as well as I could, with a stake."

Charley Good was at one time a member of a militia company, and, being told it was not to his interest, he left it and returned his gun. He was regarded as a man of republican principles, and was considered a person of some influence in that neighborhood. I never heard him charged with being a member of the Union League.

*   *   *

REVIEW QUESTIONS

1. Based on these testimonies, characterize the methods used by the Klan to intimidate blacks.
2. According to these excerpts, why did the KKK harass certain blacks?
3. How did blacks react to this kind of continuous treatment? What choices did they have?

19 ❧ THE SOUTH AND THE WEST TRANSFORMED

The end of the Civil War found Americans confronting two frontiers of opportunity: the devastated South and the untamed West. The sprawling regions were—and are—the most distinctive sections of the country, and both regions exerted a magnetic attraction for adventurers and entrepreneurs. In the postwar South, people set about rebuilding railroads, mills, stores, barns, and homes. In the process of such renewal, a strenuous debate arose over the nature of the "New South." Should it try to recreate the agrarian culture of the antebellum period? Or should it adopt the northern model of a more diversified economy and urban-industrial society? The debate was never settled completely, and as a result both viewpoints competed for attention throughout the last quarter of the nineteenth century. By 1900, the South remained primarily an agricultural region, but it also had developed a far-flung network of textile mills, railroad lines, and manufacturing plants.

African Americans in the former Confederacy often found themselves at the center of the economic and political debate in the "New South." By the end of the century, black leaders themselves were divided over the best course to follow. For his part, Booker T. Washington counseled southern blacks to focus on economic and educational opportunities at the expense of asserting their political and legal rights. Not so, declared W. E. B. Du Bois. He attacked Washington's "accommodationist" strategy and urged blacks to undertake a program of "ceaseless agitation" for political and social equality.

Controversy also swirled around the frenzied renewal of western settlement after the Civil War. During the century after 1865, fourteen new states were carved out of the western territories. To encourage new settlers, the federal government helped finance the construction of four transcontinental railroads, conquered and displaced the Indians, and sold public land at low prices to farmers and developers. Propelled by a lust for land and profits, millions of Americans headed west across the Mississippi River to establish homesteads, stake out mining claims, and set up shop in the many "boom towns" cropping up across the Great Plains and in the Far West.

This postwar surge of western migration had many of the romantic qualities so often depicted in novels, films, and television. The varied landscape of prairies, rivers, deserts, and mountains was stunning. And the people who braved incredibly harsh conditions to begin new lives in the West were indeed courageous and tenacious. Cowboys and Indians, outlaws and vigilantes, farmers and herders populated the plains, while miners and trappers led nomadic lives in hills and backwoods.

But these familiar images of western life tell only part of the story. Drudgery and tragedy were as commonplace as adventure and success. Droughts, locusts, disease, tornadoes, and the erratic fluctuations of commodity markets made life relentlessly precarious. The people who settled the trans-Mississippi frontier were in fact a diverse lot: they included women as well as men, African Americans, Hispanics, Asians, and European immigrants.

Many of the settlers were also blinded by short-sighted greed and prone to irresponsible behavior. In the process of "removing" the Indians, military forces sometimes exterminated them. By the 1890s there were only 250,000 Native Americans left in the United States. The feverish quest for quick profits also helped fuel a boom/bust economic cycle that injected a chronic instability into the society and politics of the region.

The history of the Old West is thus a much more complicated story than that conveyed through popular culture—or through the accounts of some historians. In 1893 the historian Frederick Jackson Turner announced his so-called frontier thesis. The process of taming and settling an ever-receding frontier, Turner declared, gave American culture its distinctive institutions, values, and energy. The rigors and demands of westward settlement, for example, helped implant in Americans their rugged individualism and hardihood, and such qualities helped reinforce the democratic spirit that set them apart from other peoples. "Up to our day," Turner said, "American history has been in large degree the history of the colonization of the Great West. The existence of an area of free land, its continuous recession, and the advance of American settlement westward, explain American development." He was both right and wrong. The frontier experience explains much about the development of American society, but not all. And while the settling of the West planted seeds of democracy, it also involved the brutal exploitation of the land and its natives.

HENRY W. GRADY

FROM The New South (1886)

*Atlanta newspaper editor Henry W. Grady was one of the most ardent promoters of a
"New South." In numerous speeches during the 1880s, he praised efforts to encourage
industrial development and gave a glowing—and exaggerated—description of improved race relations in his native region. The excerpt below comes from a speech to
the New England Society in New York City.*

From Samuel Harding, ed., *Select Orations Illustrating American Political History* (Indianapo-
lis: Hollenbeck Press, 1908), pp. 490–500.

We[1] have established a thrift in city and
country. We have fallen in love with
work. We have restored comfort to
homes from which culture and elegance never departed. We have let economy take root and spread
among us as rank as the crabgrass which sprung
from Sherman's[2] cavalry camps, until we are ready
to lay odds on the Georgia Yankee as he manufactures relics of the battlefield in a one-story shanty
and squeezes pure olive oil out of his cotton seed,
against any down-easter that ever swapped wooden
nutmegs for flannel sausage in the valleys of Ver-
mont. Above all, we know that we have achieved in
these "piping times of peace" a fuller independence
for the South than that which our fathers sought to
win in the forum by their eloquence or compel in
the field by their swords.

It is a rare privilege, sir, to have had part, however humble, in this work. Never was nobler duty
confided to human hands than the uplifting and
upbuilding of the prostrate and bleeding South—
misguided, perhaps, but beautiful in her suffering,
and honest, brave and generous always. In the
record of her social, industrial and political illustration we await with confidence the verdict of the
world.

But what of the negro? Have we solved the
problem he presents or progressed in honor and
equity toward solution? Let the record speak to the
point. No section shows a more prosperous laboring population than the negroes of the South, none
in fuller sympathy with the employing and land-
owning class. He shares our school fund, has the
fullest protection of our laws and the friendship of
our people.

Self-interest, as well as honor, demand that he
should have this. Our future, our very existence depend upon our working out this problem in full
and exact justice. We understand that when Lincoln signed the emancipation proclamation, your
victory was assured, for he then committed you to
the cause of human liberty, against which the arms
of man cannot prevail—while those of our statesmen who trusted to make slavery the corner-stone
of the Confederacy doomed us to defeat as far as
they could, committing us to a cause that reason
could not defend or the sword maintain in sight of
advancing civilization. . . .

The relations of the southern people with the
negro are close and cordial. We remember with
what fidelity for four years he guarded our defenseless women and children, whose husbands
and fathers were fighting against his freedom. To
his eternal credit be it said that whenever he struck
a blow for his own liberty he fought in open battle,

[1] I.e., Southerners.
[2] Union general William T. Sherman (1820–1891).

and when at last he raised his black and humble hands that the shackles might be struck off, those hands were innocent of wrong against his helpless charges, and worthy to be taken in loving grasp by every man who honors loyalty and devotion.

Ruffians have maltreated him, rascals have misled him, philanthropists established a bank for him, but the South, with the North, protests against injustice to this simple and sincere people. To liberty and enfranchisement is as far as law can carry the negro. The rest must be left to conscience and common sense. It must be left to those among whom his lot is cast, with whom he is indissolubly connected, and whose prosperity depends upon their possessing his intelligent sympathy and confidence. Faith has been kept with him, in spite of calumnious assertions to the contrary by those who assume to speak for us or by frank opponents. Faith will be kept with him in the future, if the South holds her reason and integrity.

But have we kept faith with you? In the fullest sense, yes. When Lee[3] surrendered . . . the South became, and has since been, loyal to this Union. We fought hard enough to know that we were whipped, and in perfect frankness accept as final the arbitrament[4] of the sword to which we had appealed. The South found her jewel in the toad's head of defeat. The shackles that had held her in narrow limitations fell forever when the shackles of the negro slave were broken. Under the old regime the negroes were slaves to the South; the South was a slave to the system. The old plantation, with its simple police regulations and feudal habit, was the only type possible under slavery. Thus was gath-

---

[3] Confederate general Robert E. Lee (1807–1870).
[4] To settle a dispute by force.

ered in the hands of a splendid and chivalric oligarchy the substance that should have been diffused among the people, as the rich blood, under certain artificial conditions, is gathered at the heart, filling that with affluent rapture but leaving the body chill and colorless.

The old South rested everything on slavery and agriculture, unconscious that these could neither give nor maintain healthy growth. The new South presents a perfect democracy, the oligarchs leading in the popular movement—a social system compact and closely knitted, less splendid on the surface, but stronger at the core—a hundred farms for every plantation, fifty homes for every palace—and a diversified industry that meets the complex need of this complex age.

The new South is enamored of her new work. Her soul is stirred with the breath of a new life. The light of a grander day is falling fair on her face. She is thrilling with the consciousness of growing power and prosperity. As she stands upright, full-statured and equal among the people of the earth, breathing the keen air and looking out upon the expanded horizon, she understands that her emancipation came because through the inscrutable wisdom of God her honest purpose was crossed, and her brave armies were beaten.

REVIEW QUESTIONS

1. How does Grady characterize the "negro"?
2. According to Grady, what were the negative effects of slavery on the South?
3. In what respects might Grady have tailored his remarks to his New York audience?

D. AUGUSTUS STRAKER

FROM *The New South Investigated* (1888)

Henry Grady's glowing account of the New South glossed over many unpleasant realities. In 1888 an African-American lawyer named D. Augustus Straker provided his own assessment of the New South.

From D. Augustus Straker, *The New South Investigated* (Detroit: Ferguson Publishing Co., 1888), pp. 26–27, 92–93, 94, 96–97.

The South today has, amid all its troubles, political and otherwise, made great advancement in industry, education and commerce. Our land owners are now ready and willing to utilize their lands and not let them lie uncultivated. Our farmers no longer confine themselves to the growing of cotton only, but are engaged in the more varied industry of planting corn and rice. . . . Manufactories begin to dot the South in all of its principal cities and towns.

*   *   *

Is it true that the progress of the South, which I have shown to have taken place, improved the social condition of the South? Is it true that the Negro of the South, which is known as largely the laboring class, and, therefore, the producing class, has improved in *his* social condition compared with the white class, which is known as largely the capital or non-producing class? Why is it, in plainer terms, that the Negro who was poor at the close the war when made free, is today yet poor when compared to the white man of the South? You may say that this is the result of the ignorance of the one and the knowledge of the other, but while I do not deny that ignorance and knowledge enter largely into the producing and non-producing quality of material advancement, it has not, and should not, have anything to do with the just relationship between capital and labor and the just wages paid as compensation for adequate labor.

*   *   *

As I have said before, it is not only the political change in the administration which is daily causing thousands of colored farm hands, and even mechanics, to migrate from the South to the West, but it is also caused by unjust wages, wages which do not admit of bare living, such as 15 cents a day, and $6 or $8 per month. These low wages are carrying out a plan, said to have been suggested by Calhoun,[1] for the purpose of "keeping the Negro down." And how is this done in the South? Not only by paying him lower wages and giving him poorer rations, but still further denying him the opportunity for further material advancement. A colored man in the South cannot purchase land with the facility of his white brother, not only because of his poor wages as compensation for his services, but because of the general indisposition to sell him land. Since the war, thousands of colored people who have commenced to purchase lands have been unable to do so and have lost what they have already paid, not only because some were defaulters in payment, but because more were the victims of the white man's original design to defraud him by some clause in the mortgage or fee simple deed, which defeated his tenure just at the time when he thought most sure he was the absolute owner. . . .

---

[1] South Carolina statesman John C. Calhoun (1782–1850).

This system of discrimination between labor and capital, as seen in unjust wages and no protection, is also to be found among the few mechanics who perform operative labor in the South. It is not an unusual thing to see a white and black mechanic, who although doing the same work, yet receive different wages. . . . How then can the social condition of the South be other than a dividing and a divergent one between the races? And the question here arises, is the present social condition of the South one of true progress—materially or socially? I unhesitatingly answer, no! The South's progress, socially, is only apparent and shadowy; it is not substantial; it cannot be with a divided and unequal people in condition and opportunity.

The present social condition of the South, as found in its white and black population, arises not so much from the habit of keeping separate these two races on account of race or color, as by reason of the disparity in conditions and the hindrance to industrial pursuits set up by the same powerful whites against their weaker brethren—the blacks. You may say this is equally so with these two classes in the North, East, and West, and yet the social condition is not the same. The principle is not different, but the facts are, and only serve to prove the truth of the principle.

*   *   *

It cannot be denied that the social condition of the South in which it finds itself so far behind the other portions of the country in industry, is owing to the folly of keeping out from engaging in industrial pursuits the class of people largest in numbers in its midst. The folly of trades unions, or the spirit which denies colored persons admissions to the workshops in the South, is the chief cause of Southern depression in trade, and despite the progress it has made, is the reason it has not made greater progress. It is evident that if the South could receive into its midst a large amount of capital, and would then open its avenues of industry for the large quantum of labor it possesses, in the large number of colored people in their midst, it would spring into a powerful, rich and more prosperous portion of our country, with magic and alacrity, and would be the garden spot of the United States. . . .

REVIEW QUESTIONS

1. While stressing the difference between "producers" and "non-producers," how does Straker characterize capitalism in general?
2. In describing some of the hardships faced by African Americans in the South, how does Straker differ from Henry Grady?
3. According to Straker, what prevented poor whites from uniting with impoverished African Americans to promote common concerns?

A Sharecrop Contract (1882)

After the Civil War, farm folk of both races who could not afford to buy their own land were forced to work for others, either as rent-paying tenants or, more often, as sharecroppers. The farm owner would provide the "cropper" with a plot of land, seed, fertilizer, tools, and a line of credit at the general store for other necessities. In exchange, the "cropper" would give the owner a "share" of the crop. The following contract with the Grimes family of North Carolina illustrates the arrangement.

From The Grimes Family Papers (3357), 1882. Southern Historical Collection, University of North Carolina, Chapel Hill.

To every one applying to rent land upon shares, the following conditions must be read, and *agreed to.*

To every 30 or 35 acres, I agree to furnish the team, plow, and farming implements, except cotton planters, and I *do not* agree to furnish a cart to every cropper. The croppers are to have half of the cotton, corn and fodder (and peas and pumpkins and potatoes if any are planted) if the following conditions are complied with, but—if not—they are to have only two fifths. Croppers are to have no part or interest in the cotton seed raised from the crop planted and worked by them. No vine crops of any description, that is, no watermelons, muskmelons, . . . squashes or anything of that kind, except peas and pumpkins, and potatoes are to be planted in the cotton or corn. All must work under my direction. All plantation work to be done by the croppers. My part of the crop to be *housed* by them, and the fodder and oats to be hauled and put in the house. All the cotton must be topped about 1st August. If any cropper fails from any cause to save all the fodder from his crop, I am to have enough fodder to make it equal to one half of the whole if the whole amount of fodder had been saved.

For every mule or horse furnished by me there must be 1000 good sized rails . . . hauled, and the fence repaired as far as they will go, the fence to be torn down and put up from the bottom if I so direct. All croppers to haul rails and work on fence whenever I may order. Rails to be split when I may say. Each cropper to clean out every ditch in his crop, and where a ditch runs between two croppers, the cleaning out of that ditch is to be divided equally between them. Every ditch bank in the crop must be scrubbed down and cleaned off before the crop is planted and must be cut down every time the land is worked with his hoe and when the crop is "laid by," the ditch banks must be left clean of bushes, weeds, and seeds. The cleaning out of all ditches must be done by the first of October. The rails must be split and the fence repaired before corn is planted.

Each cropper must keep in good repair all bridges in his crop or over ditches that he has to clean out and when a bridge needs repairing that is outside of all their crops, then any one that I call on must repair it.

Fence jams to be done as ditch banks. If any cotton is planted on the land outside of the plantation fence, I am to have *three fourths of* all the cotton made in those patches, that is to say, no cotton must be planted by croppers in their home patches.

All croppers must clean out stables and fill them with straw, and haul straw in front of stables whenever I direct. All the cotton must be manured, and enough fertilizer must be brought to manure each crop highly, the croppers to pay for one half of all run in the plantation after crops are gathered.

If the fence should be blown down, or if trees

should fall on the fence outside of the land planted by any of the croppers, any one or all that I may call upon must put it up and repair it. Every cropper must feed, or have fed, the team he works, Saturday nights, Sundays, and every morning before going to work, beginning to feed his team (morning, noon, and night *every day* in the week) on the day he rents and feeding it to and including the 31st day of December. If any cropper shall from any cause fail to repair his fence as far as 1000 rails will go, or shall fail to clean out any part of his ditches, or shall fail to leave his ditch banks, any part of them, well scrubbed and clean when his crop is laid by, or shall fail to clean out stables, fill them up and haul straw in front of them whenever he is told, he shall have only two-fifths of the cotton, corn, fodder, peas and pumpkins made on the land he cultivates.

If any cropper shall fail to feed his team Saturday nights, all day Sunday and all the rest of the week, morning/noon, and night, for every time he so fails he must pay me five cents.

No corn nor cotton stalks must be burned, but must be cut down, cut up and plowed in. Nothing must be burned off the land except when it is *impossible* to plow it in.

Every cropper must be responsible for all gear and farming implements placed in his hands, and if not returned must be paid for unless it is worn out by use.

Croppers must sow & plow in oats and haul them to the crib, but *must have no part of them.* Nothing to be sold from their crops, nor fodder nor corn to be carried out of the fields until my rent is all paid, and all amounts they owe me and for which I am responsible are paid in full.

I am to gin[1] & pack all the cotton and charge every cropper an eighteenth of his part, the cropper to furnish his part of the bagging, ties, & twine.

The sale of every cropper's part of the cotton to be made by me when and where I choose to sell, and after deducting all they owe me and all sums that I may be responsible for on their accounts, to pay them their half of the net proceeds. Work of every description, particularly the work on fences and ditches, to be done to my satisfaction, and must be done over until I am satisfied that it is done as it should be. . . .

REVIEW QUESTIONS

1. Does the sharecrop arrangement seem fair to all parties? Explain.
2. What alternative did landless farmers have?
3. Why was the landowner so determined to prevent croppers from planting cotton and other staple crops in their "home" patches?

---

[1] The process of removing seeds from cotton.

Plessy v. Ferguson (1896)

Augustus Straker alluded to the growing social separation of the races in the South during the 1880s. Practices varied from county to county and state to state, but by the 1890s the trend was clear: white Southerners were determined to mandate a racially segregated society. A Louisiana ordinance of 1890 required that railroads "provide equal but separate accommodations for the white and colored races." A group of New Orleans blacks resolved to test the constitutionality of the law. One of them, Homer Plessy, sat in a "whites only" section of a railcar in 1892 and was arrested. Four years later the United States Supreme Court heard his case when Plessy appealed a ruling by District Judge John H. Ferguson. Seven judges upheld Plessy's conviction and only one, John Marshall Harlan, son of a slaveholder from Kentucky, dissented. Harlan put forth a powerful defense of equal rights.

From *Plessy v. Ferguson*, 163 US 537 (1896).

Justice Henry Brown for the majority: This case turns upon the constitutionality of an act of the general assembly of the state of Louisiana, passed in 1890, providing for separate railway carriages for the white and colored races. . . .

The constitutionality of this act is attacked upon the ground that it conflicts both with the 13th Amendment of the Constitution, abolishing slavery, and the 14th Amendment, which prohibits certain restrictive legislation on the part of the states.

1. That it does not conflict with the 13th Amendment, which abolished slavery and involuntary servitude, except as a punishment for crime, is too clear for argument. . . . Indeed, we do not understand that the 13th Amendment is strenuously relied upon by the plaintiff. . . .

The object of the (14th) amendment was undoubtedly to enforce the absolute equality of the two races before the law, but in the nature of things it could not have been intended to abolish distinctions based upon color, or to enforce social, as distinguished from political, equality or a commingling of the two races upon terms unsatisfactory to either. Laws permitting, and even requiring their separation in places where they are liable to be brought into contact do not necessarily imply the inferiority of either race to the other, and have

been generally, if not universally, recognized as within the competency of the state legislatures in the exercise of their police power. . . .

We consider the underlying fallacy of the plaintiff's argument to consist in the assumption that the enforced separation of the two races stamps the colored race with a badge of inferiority. If this be so, it is not by reason of anything found in the act, but solely because the colored race chooses to put that construction upon it. . . .

The argument also assumes that social prejudice may be overcome by legislation, and that equal rights cannot be secured to the Negro except by an enforced commingling of the two races. We cannot accept this proposition. If the two races are to meet on terms of social equality, it must be the result of natural affinities, a mutual appreciation of each other's merits and a voluntary consent of individuals. . . . Legislation is powerless to eradicate racial instincts or to abolish distinctions based upon physical differences, and the attempt to do so can only result in accentuating the difficulties of the present situation. If the civil and political right of both races be equal, one cannot be inferior to the other civilly or politically. If one race be inferior to the other socially, the Constitution of the United States cannot put them upon the same plane.

———

Justice John Harlan, dissenting: . . . In respect of civil rights, common to all citizens, the Constitution of the United States does not, I think, permit any public authority to know the race of those entitled to be protected in the enjoyment of such rights. . . . I deny that any legislative body or judicial tribunal may have regard to the race of citizens when the civil rights of those citizens are involved. Indeed such legislation as that here in question is inconsistent not only with that equality of rights which pertains to citizenship, national and state, but with the personal liberty enjoyed by everyone within the United States. . . .

The white race deems itself to be the dominant race in this country. And so it is, in prestige, in achievements, in education, in wealth and power. So, I doubt not, it will continue to be for all time, if it remains true to its great heritage and holds fast to the principles of constitutional liberty. Our Constitution is color-blind, and neither knows nor tolerates classes among citizens. In respect to civil rights, all citizens are equal before the law. . . .

The destinies of the two races in this country are indissolubly linked together, and the interests of both require that the common government of all shall not permit the seeds of race hate to be planted under the sanction of law. What can more certainly arouse race hate, what more certainly create and perpetuate a feeling of distrust between these races, than state enactments which in fact proceed on the ground that colored citizens are so inferior and degraded that they cannot be allowed to sit in public coaches occupied by white citizens? That, as all will admit, is the real meaning of such legislation as was enacted in Louisiana. . . .

State enactments regulating the enjoyment of civil rights, upon the basis of race, and cunningly devised to defeat legitimate results of the war,[1] un-

der the pretense of recognizing equality of rights, can have no other result than to render permanent peace impossible, and keep alive a conflict of races, the continuance of which must do harm to all concerned.

We boast of the freedom enjoyed by our people above all other peoples. But it is difficult to reconcile that boast with a state of the law which, practically, puts the brand of servitude and degradation upon a large class of our fellow citizens, our equals before the law. The thin disguise of "equal" accommodations for passengers in railroad coaches will not mislead anyone, or atone for the wrong this day done. . . .

I am of opinion that the state of Louisiana is inconsistent with the personal liberty of citizens, white and black, in that state, and hostile to both the spirit and letter of the Constitution of the United States. If laws of like character should be enacted in the several states of the Union, the effect would be in the highest degree mischievous. . . .

I am constrained to withhold my assent from the opinion and judgment of the majority.

REVIEW QUESTIONS

1. The majority opinion drew a sharp distinction between "political" and "social" equality. How could the justices maintain such a distinction?
2. The majority opinion also insisted that segregation was a symbol of racial inferiority/superiority only if African Americans chose to view it as such. Assess the logic of this argument.
3. Which of Harlan's arguments would be used by later jurists to dismantle segregation? Explain.

---

[1] The Civil War.

BOOKER T. WASHINGTON

The Atlanta Compromise (1895)

How best to improve the plight of blacks in the so-called New South generated intense debate among African American leaders. Booker T. Washington (1856–1915) emerged as the most eloquent advocate of what his critics labeled the "accommodationist" perspective. Born a slave in Virginia, Washington was educated at Hampton Institute, which provided blacks with vocational training. In 1881 Washington created a similar school in Alabama, the Tuskegee Institute. Its success catapulted Washington into the national spotlight. In 1895 he was invited to deliver a speech at the Cotton States Exposition in Atlanta. His remarks seemed to condone social segregation. Journalists later labeled Washington's proposal the "Atlanta Compromise."

From Booker T. Washington, *Up from Slavery: The Autobiography of Booker T. Washington* (Garden City, NY: Doubleday, 1959), pp. 153–158.

One-third of the population of the South is of the Negro race. No enterprise seeking the material, civil, or moral welfare of this section can convey to you, Mr. President and Directors, the sentiment of the masses of my race when I say that in no way have the value and manhood of the American Negro been more fittingly and generously recognized than by the managers of this magnificent Exposition at every stage of its progress. It is a recognition that will do more to cement the friendship of the two races than any occurrence since the dawn of our freedom.

Not only this, but the opportunity here afforded will awaken among us a new era of industrial progress. Ignorant and inexperienced, it is not strange that in the first years of our new life we began at the top instead of at the bottom; that a seat in Congress or the State Legislature was more sought than real estate or industrial skill; that the political convention or stump speaking had more attractions than starting a dairy farm or truck garden.

A ship lost at sea for many days suddenly sighted a friendly vessel. From the mast of the unfortunate vessel was seen a signal: "Water, water, we die of thirst." The answer from the friendly vessel at once came back, "Cast down your bucket where you are." A second time the signal, "Water, water, send us water," ran up from the distressed vessel and was answered, "Cast down your bucket where you are." The captain of the distressed vessel, at last heeding the injunction, cast down his bucket and it came up full of fresh, sparkling water from the mouth of the Amazon River. To those of my race who depend on bettering their condition in a foreign land, or who underestimate the importance of cultivating friendly relations with the Southern white man who is their next-door neighbor, I would say: Cast down your bucket where you are; cast it down in making friends, in every manly way, of the people of all races by whom we are surrounded.

Cast it down in agriculture, mechanics, in commerce, in domestic service, and in the professions. And in this connection it is well to bear in mind that whatever other sins the South may be called upon to bear, when it comes to business pure and simple, it is in the South that the Negro is given a man's chance in the commercial world, and in nothing is this Exposition more eloquent than in emphasizing this chance. Our greatest danger is that, in the great leap from slavery to freedom, we may overlook the fact that the masses of us are to live by the productions of our hands and fail to keep in mind that we shall prosper in the proportion as we learn to dignify and glorify common labor, and put brains and skill into the common occupations of life; shall prosper in proportion as we learn to draw the line between the superficial and the substantial, the ornamental gewgaws[1] of life and the useful. No race can prosper until it learns that there is as much dignity in tilling a field as in writing a poem. It is at the bottom of life we must begin, and not at the top. Nor should we permit our grievances to overshadow our opportunities.

To those of the white race who look to the incoming of those of foreign birth and strange tongue and habits for the prosperity of the South, were I permitted I would repeat what I say to my own race, "Cast down your bucket where you are." Cast it down among the 8,000,000 Negroes whose habits you know, whose fidelity and love you have tested in days when to have proved treacherous meant the ruin of your firesides. Cast down your bucket among these people who have, without strikes and labor wars, tilled your fields, cleared your forests, built your railroads and cities, and brought forth treasures from the bowels of the earth and helped make possible this magnificent representation of the progress of the South. Casting down your bucket among my people, helping and encouraging them as you are doing on these grounds, and, with education of head, hand and heart, you will find that they will buy your surplus land, make blossom the waste places in your fields, and run your factories. While doing this, you can be sure in the future, as in the past, that you and your families will be surrounded by the most patient, faithful, law-abiding and unresentful people that the world has seen. As we have proved our loyalty to you in the past, in nursing your children, watching by the sick-bed of your mothers and fathers, and often following them with tear-dimmed eyes to their graves, so in the future, in our humble way, we shall stand by you with a devotion that

[1] Trinkets.

no foreigner can approach, ready to lay down our lives, if need be, in defense of yours; interlacing our industrial, commercial, civil, and religious life with yours in a way that shall make the interest of both races one. In all things that are purely social we can be as separate as the fingers, yet one as the hand in all things essential to mutual progress.

There is no defense or security for any of us except in the highest intelligence and development of all. If anywhere there are efforts tending to curtail the fullest growth of the Negro, let these efforts be turned into stimulating, encouraging, and making him the most useful and intelligent citizen. Effort or means so invested will pay a thousand per cent interest. These efforts will be twice blessed— "blessing him that gives and him that takes."

There is no escape, through law of man or God, from the inevitable:

The laws of changeless justice bind
Oppressor with oppressed,
And close as sin and suffering joined
We march to fate abreast.

Nearly sixteen million hands will aid you in pulling the load upward, or they will pull against you the load downward. We shall constitute one-third and more of the ignorance and crime of the South, or one-third its intelligence and progress; we shall contribute one-third to the business and industrial prosperity of the South, or we shall prove a veritable body of death, stagnating, depressing, retarding every effort to advance the body politic.

Gentlemen of the Exposition: As we present to you our humble effort at an exhibition of our progress, you must not expect over much. Starting thirty years ago with ownership here and there in a few quilts and pumpkins and chickens (gathered from miscellaneous sources), remember: the path that has led us from these to the invention and production of agricultural implements, buggies, steam engines, newspapers, books, statuary carving, paintings, the management of drugstores and banks, has not been trodden without contact with thorns and thistles. While we take pride in what we exhibit as a result of our independent efforts, we do not for a moment forget that our part in this exhibition would fall far short of your expectations but for the constant help that has come to our educational life, not only from the Southern states, but especially from Northern philanthropists who have made their gifts a constant stream of blessing and encouragement.

The wisest among my race understand that the agitation of questions of social equality is the extremist folly, and that progress in the enjoyment of all the privileges that will come to us must be the result of severe and constant struggle rather than of artificial forcing. No race that has anything to contribute to the markets of the world is long in any degree ostracized. It is important and right that all privileges of the law be ours, but it is vastly more important that we be prepared for the exercise of those privileges. The opportunity to earn a dollar in a factory just now is worth infinitely more than the opportunity to spend a dollar in an opera house.

In conclusion, may I repeat that nothing in thirty years has given us more hope and encouragement, and drawn us so near to you of the white race, as this opportunity offered by the Exposition; and here bending, as it were, over the altar that represents the results of the struggles of your race and mine, both starting practically empty-handed three decades ago, I pledge that, in your effort to work out the great and intricate problem which

God has laid at the door of the South, you shall have at all times the patient, sympathetic help of my race; only let this be constantly in mind that, while from representations in these buildings of the product of field, of forest, or mine, of factory, letters and art, much good will come—yet far above and beyond material benefits, will be that higher good, that let us pray God will come, in a blotting out of sectional difference and racial animosities and suspicions, in a determination to administer absolute justice, in a willing obedience among all classes to the mandates of law. This, coupled with material prosperity, will bring into our beloved South a new heaven and a new earth.

REVIEW QUESTIONS

1. In the previous selection (see pages 25–26), Justice Harlan insisted that the destinies of whites and blacks were "indissolubly linked together." How would Washington have responded to this assertion?
2. Why did many African Americans agree with Washington's statement that it was more important to *earn* a dollar than to *spend* one?
3. Does Washington suggest how long it would take for social equality to develop?

JOHN HOPE

A Critique of the Atlanta Compromise (1896)

Many younger African American activists criticized Washington's accommodationist strategy and advocated a more comprehensive effort to gain civil rights and social equality for all blacks. In a speech to the Colored Debating Society, John Hope (1868–1936), a young professor at Roger Williams University in Nashville, Tennessee, rejected Washington's emphasis on vocational education and called for more militant efforts to improve the status and opportunities of African Americans. Hope was the son of a white father and black mother. He graduated from Brown University in Rhode Island and later would become president of Morehouse College and Atlanta University, the first graduate university for blacks.

From Ridgely Torrence, *The Story of John Hope* (New York: Macmillan, 1948), pp. 114–115.

If we are not striving for equality, in heaven's name for what are we living? I regard it as cowardly and dishonest for any of our colored men to tell white people or colored people that we are not struggling for equality. If money, education, and honesty will not bring to me as much privilege, as much equality as they bring to any American citizens, then they are to me a curse, and not a blessing. God forbid that we should get the implements with which to fashion our freedom, and then be too lazy or pusillanimous to fashion it. Let us not fool ourselves nor be fooled by others. If we cannot do what other freemen do, then we are not free. Yes, my friends, I want equality. Nothing less. I want all that my God-given powers will enable me to get, then why not equality? Now, catch your breath, for I am going to use an adjective: I am going to say we demand *social* equality. In this republic we shall be less than freemen, if we have a whit less than that which thrift, education, and honor afford other freemen. If equality, political, economic, and social, is the boon of other men in this great country of *ours*, then equality, political, economic, and social, is what we demand. Why build a wall to keep me out? I am no wild beast, nor am I an unclean thing.

Rise, Brothers! Come let us possess this land. Never say: "Let well enough alone." Cease to console yourselves with adages that numb the moral sense. Be discontented. Be dissatisfied. "Sweat and grunt" under present conditions. Be as restless as the tempestuous billows on the boundless sea. Let your discontent break mountain-high against the wall of prejudice, and swamp it to the very foundation. Then we shall not have to plead for justice nor on bended knee crave for mercy; for we shall be men. Then and not until then will liberty in its highest sense be the boast of our Republic.

REVIEW QUESTIONS

1. How would Booker T. Washington have responded to Hope's arguments?
2. In what ways does Hope suggest that the lack of social equality would impede the progress of African Americans?
3. If you were a black person living at the turn of the century, whose arguments, Hope's or Washington's, would you find more appealing? Why?

The Life of an Illinois Farmer's Wife (1905)

In 1905 the editors of The Independent *asked an Illinois farmer's wife to write a candid account of her life on the prairie. They granted her request for anonymity.*

From "One Farmer's Wife," *The Independent* 58 (9 February 1905): 294–298. [Editorial insertions appear in square brackets—*Ed.*]

I have been a farmer's wife in one of the States of the Middle West for thirteen years, and everybody knows that the farmer's wife must of necessity be a very practical woman, if she would be a successful one.

I am not a practical woman and consequently have been accounted a failure by practical friends and especially by my husband, who is wholly practical. . . .

I was reared on a farm, was healthy and strong, was ambitious, and the work was not disagreeable, and having no children for the first six years of married life, the habit of going whenever asked to became firmly fixed, and he had no thought of hiring a man to help him, since I could do anything for which he needed help.

I was always religiously inclined; brought up to attend Sunday school . . . every Sunday all the year round. . . .

I was an apt student at school and before I was eighteen I had earned a teacher's certificate of the second grade and would gladly have remained in school a few more years, but I had, unwittingly, agreed to marry the man who is now my husband, and tho I begged to be released, his will was so much the stronger that I was unable to free my self without wounding a loving heart, and could not find it in my heart to do so. . . .

I always had a passion for reading; during girlhood it was along educational lines; in young womanhood it was for love stories, which remained ungratified because my father thought it sinful to read stories of any kind, and especially love stories.

Later, when I was married, I borrowed everything I could find in the line of novels and stories, and read them by stealth still, for my husband thought it a willful waste of time to read anything and that it showed a lack of love for him if I would rather read than to talk to him when I had a few moments of leisure, and, in order to avoid giving offense and still gratify my desire, I would only read when he was not at the house, thereby greatly curtailing my already too limited reading hours. . . .

It is only during the last three years that I have had the news to read, for my husband is so very penurious that he would never consent to subscribing for [news]papers of any kind and that old habit of avoiding that which would give offense was so fixed that I did not dare to break it.

The addition of two children to our family never altered or interfered with the established order of things to any appreciable extent. My strenuous outdoor life agreed with me, and even when my children were born I was splendidly prepared for the ordeal and made rapid recovery. I still hoed and tended the truck [garden] patches and garden, still watered the stock and put out feed for them, still went to the hay field and helped harvest and house the bounteous crops; still helped harvest the golden grain later on when the cereals ripened; often took one team [of horses] and dragged ground to prepare the seed-bed for wheat for weeks at the time, while my husband was using the other team on another farm which he owns several miles away.

While the children were babies they were left at the house, and when they were larger they would go with me to my work; now they are large enough to help a little during the summer and to go to school in winter; they help a great deal during the fruit canning season—in fact, [they] can and do work at almost everything, pretty much as I do. . . .

Any bright morning in the latter part of May I am out of bed at four o'clock [A.M.]; next, after I have dressed and combed my hair, I start a fire in the kitchen stove . . . sweep the floors and then cook breakfast.

While the other members of the family are eating breakfast I strain away the morning's milk (for my husband milks the cows while I get breakfast), and fill my husband's dinner-pail, for he will go to work on our other farm for the day.

By this time it is half-past five o'clock, my husband is gone to his work, and the stock loudly pleading to be turned into the pastures. The younger cattle, a half-dozen steers, are left in the pasture at night, and I now drive the two cows a half-quarter mile and then turn them in with the others, come back, and then there's a horse in the barn that belongs in a field where there is no water, which I take to a spring quite a distance from the barn; bring it back and turn it into a field with the sheep, a dozen in number, which are housed at night.

The young calves are then turned out into the warm sunshine, and the stock hogs, which are kept in a pen, are clamoring for feed, and I carry a pailful of swill to them, and hasten to the house and turn out the chickens and put out feed and water for them, and it is, perhaps, 6:30 A.M.

I have not eaten breakfast yet, but that can wait; I make the beds next and straighten things up in the living room, for I dislike to have the early morning caller find my house topsy-turvy. When this is done I go to the kitchen, which also serves as a dining room, and uncover the table, and take a mouthful of food occasionally as I pass to and fro at my work until my appetite is appeased.

By the time the work is done in the kitchen it is about 7:15 A.M., and the cool morning hours have flown, and no hoeing done in the garden yet, and the children's toilet has to be attended to and churning has to be done.

Finally the children are washed and churning

done, and it is eight o'clock, and the sun getting hot, but no matter, weeds die quickly when cut down in the heat of day, and I use the hoe to a good advantage until the dinner hour, which is 11:30 A.M. We come in, and I comb my hair, and put fresh flowers in it, and eat a cold dinner, put out feed and water for the chickens; set a hen, perhaps, sweep the floors again; sit down and rest and read a few moments, and it is nearly one o'clock, and I sweep the door yard while I am waiting for the clock to strike the hour.

I make and sow a flower bed, dig around some shrubbery, and go back to the garden to hoe until time to do the chores at night. . . .

. . . I hoe in the garden till four o'clock; then I go into the house and get supper . . . when supper is all ready it is set aside, and I pull a few hundred plants of tomato, sweet potato or cabbage for transplanting . . . I then go after the horse, water him, and put him in the barn; call the sheep and house them, and go after the cows and milk them, feed the hogs, put down hay for three horses, and put oats and corn in their troughs, and set those plants and come in and fasten up the chickens. . . . By this time it is 8 o'clock P.M.; my husband has come home, and we are eating supper; when we are through eating I make the beds ready, and the children and their father go to bed, and I wash the dishes and get things in shape to get breakfast quickly next morning. . . .

All the time that I have been going about this work I have been thinking of things I have read . . . and of other things which I have a desire to read, but cannot hope to while the present condition exists.

As a natural consequence, there are, daily, numerous instances of absentmindedness on my part; many things left undone that I really could have done, by leaving off something else of less importance, if I had not forgotten the thing of more importance. My husband never fails to remind me that it is caused by my reading so much; that I would get along much better if I should never see a book or paper, while really I would be distracted if all reading matter was taken from me.

I use an old fashioned [dairy] churn, and the

process of churning occupies from thirty minutes to three hours, according to the condition of the cream, and I always read something while churning, and tho that may look like a poor way to attain self-culture, yet if your reading is of the nature to bring about the desirable result, one will surely be greatly benefited by these daily exercises. . . .

I suppose it is impossible for a woman to do her best at everything which she would like to do, but I really would like to. I almost cut sleep out of my routine in trying to keep up all the rows which I have started in on . . . when the work for the day is over, or at least the most pressing part of it, and the family are all asleep and no one to forbid it, I spend a few hours writing or reading. . . .

I might add that the neighbors among whom I live are illiterate and unmusical, and that my redeeming qualities, in their eyes, are my superior education and musical abilities; they are kind enough to give me more than justice on these qualities because they are poor judges of such matters.

But money is king, and if I might turn my literary bent to account, and surround myself with the evidences of prosperity, I may yet hope fully to redeem myself in their eyes, and I know that I will have attained my ambition in that line.

REVIEW QUESTIONS

1. Do you think this woman's outlook was representative of most farm women? Why or why not?
2. What activities did this woman find most fulfilling? Why?

BENJAMIN SINGLETON

FROM Negro Exodus from the Southern States (1880)

With the return of white supremacy in the post–Reconstruction South, thousands of African Americans migrated to the West in search of economic opportunities and social equality. Most of them flocked to Kansas. Their quest for a new "promised land" on the Great Plains led people to call them "Exodusters." Benjamin Singleton was the foremost promoter of black migration. Born a slave in Tennessee, he escaped and settled in Detroit, where he operated a boardinghouse that became a refuge for other runaway slaves. After the Civil War he returned to Tennessee. To help African Americans free themselves from the surge of racism that accompanied the withdrawal of federal troops from the South in the 1870s, he bought land in Kansas and began recruiting settlers. So many heeded his call that Southerners grew worried about the loss of laborers in their region, and Congress agreed to investigate the matter.

From U.S. Senate, Select Committee Investigating the "Negro Exodus from the Southern States," 17 April 1880 (Washington, DC).

Benjamin Singleton (colored) sworn and examined by Mr. Windom:

Question. Where were you born, Mr. Singleton?

Answer. I was born in the State of Tennessee, sir.

Q. Where do you now live?

A. In Kansas.

Q. What part of Kansas?

A. I have a colony sixty miles from Topeka, sir. . . .

Q. When did you commence the formation of that colony?

A. It was in 1875, perhaps. . . .

Q. When did you change your home from Tennessee to Kansas?

A. I have been going there for the last six or seven years, sir.

Q. Going between Tennessee and Kansas, at different times?

A. Yes, sir; several times.

Q. Well, tell us about it.

A. I have been fetching out people; I believe I fetched out 7,432 people.

Q. You have brought out 7,432 people from the South to Kansas?

A. Yes, sir; brought and sent.

Q. That is, they came out to Kansas under your influence?

A. Yes, sir; I was the cause of it.

Q. How long have you been doing that—ever since 1869?

A. Yes, sir; ever since 1869. . . .

Q. What was the cause of your going out, and in the first place how did you happen to go there, or to send these people there?

A. Well, my people, for the want of land— we needed land for our children—and their disadvantages—that caused my heart to grieve and sorrow; pity for my race, sir, that was coming down, instead of going up—that caused me to go to work for them. I sent out there perhaps in '66—perhaps so; or in '65, any way—my memory don't recollect which; and they brought back tolerable favorable reports; then I jacked up three or four hundred, and went into Southern Kansas, and found it was a good country, and I thought Southern Kansas was congenial to our nature, sir; and I formed a colony there, and bought about a thousand acres of ground—the colony did—my people.

Q. And they went upon it and settled there?

A. Yes, sir; they went and settled there. . . .

Q. Tell us how these people are getting on in Kansas.

A. I am glad to tell you, sir.

Q. Have they any property now?

A. Yes; I have carried some people in there that when they got there they didn't have fifty cents left, and now they have got in my colony—Singleton colony—a house, nice cabins, their milk cows, and pigs, and sheep, perhaps a span of horses, and trees before their yards, and some three or four or ten acres broken up, and all of them has got little houses that I carried there. They didn't go under no relief assistance; they went on their own resources; and when they went in there first the country was not overrun with them; you see they could get good wages; the country was not overstocked with people; they went to work, and I never helped them as soon as I put them on the land.

Q. Well, they have been coming continually, and adding from time to time to your colony these few years past, have they?

A. Yes, sir; I have spent, perhaps, nearly six hundred dollars flooding the country with circulars.

Q. You have sent the circulars yourself, have you?

A. Yes, sir; all over these United States.

Q. Did you send them into other southern states besides Tennessee?

A. O, yes, sir. . . . I then went out to Kansas, and advised them all to go to Kansas; and, sir they are going to leave the Southern country. The Southern country is out of joint. The blood of a white man runs through my veins. That is congenial, you know, to my nature. that is my choice. Right emphatically, I tell you today, I woke up the millions right through me! The great God of glory has worked in me. I have had open air interviews with the living spirit of God for my people; and we are going to leave the South. We are going to leave it if there ain't an alteration and signs of change. I am going to advise the people who left that country (Kansas) to go back. . . .

Q. And you attribute this movement to the information you gave in your circulars?

A. Yes, sir; I am the whole cause of the Kansas immigration!

Q. You take all that responsibility on yourself?

A. I do, and I can prove it; and I think I have done a good deal of good, and I feel relieved!

Q. You are proud of your work?

A. Yes, sir; I am! (Uttered emphatically.)

REVIEW QUESTIONS

1. According to Singleton, what was the primary motive for African American migration to Kansas?
2. How did Singleton entice blacks to leave their homes?
3. Why do you think Congress felt the need to investigate the "Exoduster" movement?

CHIEF JOSEPH

An Indian's Perspective

Chief Joseph was the heroic leader of a large band of Nez Percé (a misnomer, meaning "pierced noses") who had been converted to Christianity in the early nineteenth century. He was born in 1840 in the Wallowa valley of Oregon. Like many other tribes, the Nez Percé negotiated treaties with the American government, only to see the treaties violated, tensions erupt, and conflict ensue. In 1877, after months of ferocious fighting and a spectacular retreat across Idaho and Montana, Chief Joseph's band of some 400 Indians surrendered with the understanding that they would be allowed to return home. Instead, they were taken first to Kansas and then to what is now Oklahoma. Joseph thereafter made repeated appeals to the federal government to let his people return to their native region; he visited Washington, D.C., in 1879 to present his grievances against the federal government to President Rutherford B. Hayes. But it was not until 1885 that he and several others were relocated to Washington State, where he died in 1904.

From Chester Anders Fee, *Chief Joseph: The Biography of a Great Indian* (New York: Wilson-Erickson, 1936), pp. 78–79, 262–263, 281–283.

White men found gold in the mountains around the land of the Winding Water. They stole a great many horses from us and we could not get them back because we were Indians. The white men told lies for each other. They drove off a great many of our cattle. Some white men branded our young cattle so they could claim them. We had no friends who would plead our cause before the law councils. It seemed to me that some of the white men in Wallowa were doing these things on purpose to get up a war. They knew we were not strong enough to fight them. I labored hard to avoid trouble and bloodshed.

We gave up some of our country to the white men, thinking that then we could have peace. We were mistaken. The white men would not let us alone. We could have avenged our wrongs many times, but we did not. Whenever the Government has asked for help against other Indians we have never refused. When the white men were few and we were strong we could have killed them off, but the Nez Percé wishes to live at peace. . . .

We have had a few good friends among the white men, and they have always advised my people to bear these taunts without fighting. Our young men are quick tempered and I have had great trouble in keeping them from doing rash things. I have carried a heavy load on my back ever since I was a boy. I learned then that we were but few while the white men were many, and that we could not hold our own with them. We were like deer. They were like grizzly bears. We had a small country. Their country was large. We were contented to let things remain as the Great Spirit Chief made them. They were not; and would change the mountains and rivers if they did not suit them.

*   *   *

Tell General Howard that I know his heart.[1] What he told me before I have in my heart. I am tired of fighting. Our chiefs are killed. . . . The old men are all dead. . . . It is cold and we have no blankets. The little children are freezing to death. My people— some of them have run away to the hills and have no blankets and no food. No one knows where they are—perhaps freezing to death. I want to have time to look for my children and see how many of them I can find. Maybe I shall find them among the dead. Hear me, my chiefs, my heart is sick and sad. From where the sun now stands I will fight no more against the white man.

*   *   *

At last I was granted permission to come to Washington and bring my friend Yellow Bull and our interpreter with me.[2] I am glad I came. I have shaken hands with a good many friends, but there are

---

[1] This section refers to events after Chief Joseph's surrender in 1877.
[2] This section refers to Chief Joseph's visit to Washington, D.C., in 1879.

some things I want to know which no one seems able to explain. I cannot understand how the Government sends a man out to fight us, as it did General Miles, and then breaks his word. Such a government has something wrong about it. . . .

I have heard talk and talk but nothing is done. Good words do not last long unless they amount to something. Words do not pay for my dead people. They do not pay for my country now overrun by white men. They do not protect my father's grave. They do not pay for my horses and cattle. Good words do not give me back my children. Good words will not make good the promise of your war chief, General Miles. Good words will not give my people a home where they can live in peace and take care of themselves. I am tired of talk that comes to nothing. It makes my heart sick when I remember all the good words and all the broken promises. There has been too much talking by men who had no right to talk. Too many misinterpretations have been made; too many misunderstandings have come up between the white men and the Indians. . . .

I know that my race must change. We cannot hold our own with the white men as we are. We only ask an even chance to live as other men live. We ask to be recognized as men. We ask that the same law shall work alike on all men. If an Indian breaks the law, punish him by the law. If a white man breaks the law, punish him also.

Let me be a free man, free to travel, free to stop, free to work, free to trade where I choose, free to choose my own teachers, free to follow the religion of my fathers, free to talk, think and act for myself—and I will obey every law or submit to the penalty.

Whenever the white man treats the Indian as they treat each other then we shall have no more wars. We shall be all alike—brothers of one father and mother, with one sky above us and one country around us and one government for all. Then the Great Spirit Chief who rules above will smile upon this land and send rain to wash out the bloody spots made by brothers' hands upon the face of the earth. For this time the Indian race is waiting and praying. I hope no more groans of wounded men and women will ever go to the ear of the Great Spirit Chief above, and that all people may be one people.

REVIEW QUESTIONS

1. What initially provoked hostilities between whites and the Nez Percé?
2. What were Chief Joseph's basic demands? Why would whites have balked at meeting them?
3. Analyze Chief Joseph's comments about the historic relationship between whites and Native Americans.

HELEN HUNT JACKSON

FROM *A Century of Dishonor* (1881)

The surge of settlers streaming westward across the Mississippi River after the Civil War brought increasing conflict with Native Americans. Federal troops engaged in a series of frontier wars with the Comanche, the Apache, the Kiowa, the Cheyenne, and the Sioux. At the same time, white hunters devastated the buffalo herds that were essential to the survival of Indian culture. One of the few whites who sympathized with the plight of the Indians was Helen Hunt Jackson. Born in Amherst, Massachusetts, in 1830, she was a childhood friend of the poet Emily Dickinson. After the death in 1863 of Jackson's first husband, a Union army officer, she earned her living by writing poems, stories, and travel accounts. In 1872 she moved to Colorado where she married a financier, grew indignant at the mistreatment of the Indians, and wrote A Century of Dishonor, *published in 1881. Jackson sent the book to every member of Congress with a graphic message printed in red on the cover: "Look upon your hands: they are stained with the blood of your relations." The book had little impact initially, but Jackson's unrelenting crusade for a more enlightened federal Indian policy eventually helped convince Congress to pass the Dawes Act of 1887. She died two years before it was enacted.*

From Helen Hunt Jackson, *A Century of Dishonor* (1881; New York: Indian Head Books, 1994), pp. 335–342.

There are within the limits of the United States between two hundred and fifty and three hundred thousand Indians, exclusive of those in Alaska. The names of the different tribes and bands . . . number nearly three hundred. . . . There is not among these three hundred bands of Indians one which has not suffered cruelly at the hands either of the Government or of white settlers. The poorer, the more insignificant, the more helpless the band, the more certain the cruelty and outrage to which they have been subjected. This is especially true of the bands on the Pacific slope. These Indians found themselves of a sudden surrounded by and caught up in the great influx of gold-seeking settlers, as helpless creatures on a shore are caught up in a tidal wave. There was not time for the Government to make treaties; not even time for communities to make laws. The tale of the wrongs, the oppressions, the murders of the Pacific-slope Indians in the last thirty years would be a volume by itself, and is too monstrous to be believed.

It makes little difference, however, where one opens the record of the history of the Indians; every page and every year has its dark stain. The story of one tribe is the story of all, varied only by differences of time and place; but neither time nor place makes any difference in the main facts. Colorado is as greedy and unjust in 1880 as was Georgia in 1830, and Ohio in 1795; and the United States Government breaks promises now as deftly as then, and with an added ingenuity from long practice.

One of its strongest supports in so doing is the widespread sentiment among the people of dislike to the Indian, of impatience with his presence as a "barrier to civilization" and distrust of it as a possible danger. The old tales of the frontier life, with its horrors of Indian warfare, have gradually, by two or three generations' telling, produced in the average mind something like an hereditary instinct of questioning and unreasoning aversion which it is almost impossible to dislodge or soften. . . .

President after president has appointed commission after commission to inquire into and report upon Indian affairs, and to make suggestions as to the best methods of managing them. The reports are filled with eloquent statements of wrongs done to the Indians, of perfidies on the part of the Government; they counsel, as earnestly as words can, a trial of the simple and unperplexing expedients of telling truth, keeping promises, making fair bargains, dealing justly in all ways and all things. These reports are bound up with the Government's Annual Reports, and that is the end of them. . . .

The history of the Government connections with the Indians is a shameful record of broken treaties and unfulfilled promises. The history of the border white man's connection with the Indians is a sickening record of murder, outrage, robbery, and wrongs committed by the former, as the rule, and occasional savage outbreaks and unspeakably barbarous deeds of retaliation by the latter, as the exception.

Taught by the Government that they had rights entitled to respect, when those rights have been assailed by the rapacity of the white man, the arm which should have been raised to protect them has ever been ready to sustain the aggressor.

The testimony of some of the highest military officers of the United States is on record to the effect that, in our Indian wars, almost without exception, the first aggressions have been made by the white man. . . . Every crime committed by a white man against an Indian is concealed and palliated. Every offense committed by an Indian against a white man is borne on the wings of the post or the telegraph to the remotest corner of the land, clothed with all the horrors which the reality or imagination can throw around it. Against such influences as these are the people of the United States need to be warned.

To assume that it would be easy, or by any one sudden stroke of legislative policy possible, to undo the mischief and hurt of the long past, set the Indian policy of the country right for the future, and make the Indians at once safe and happy, is the blunder of a hasty and uninformed judgment. The notion which seems to be growing more prevalent, that simply to make all Indians at once citizens of the United States would be a sovereign and instantaneous panacea for all their ills and all the Government's perplexities, is a very inconsiderate one. To administer complete citizenship of a sudden, all round, to all Indians, barbarous and civilized alike, would be as grotesque a blunder as to dose them all round with any one medicine, irrespective of the symptoms and needs of their diseases. It would kill more than it would cure. Nevertheless, it is true, as was well stated by one of the superintendents of Indian Affairs in 1857, that, "so long as they are not citizens of the United States, their rights of property must remain insecure against invasion. The doors of the federal tribunals being barred against them while wards and dependents, they can only partially exercise the rights of free government, or give to those who make, execute, and construe the few laws they are allowed to enact, dignity sufficient to make them respectable. While they continue individually to gather the crumbs that fall from the table of the United States, idleness, improvidence, and indebtedness will be the rule, and industry, thrift, and freedom from debt the exception. The utter absence of individual title to particular lands deprives every one among them of the chief incentive to labor and exertion—the very mainspring on which the prosperity of a people depends."

All judicious plans and measures for their safety and salvation must embody provisions for their becoming citizens as fast as they are fit, and must protect them till then in every right and particular in which our laws protect other "persons" who are not citizens. . . .

However great perplexity and difficulty there may be in the details of any and every plan possible for doing at this late day anything like justice to the Indian, however, hard it may be for good statesmen and good men to agree upon the things that

ought to be done, there certainly is, or ought to be, no perplexity whatever, or difficulty whatever, in agreeing upon certain things that ought not to be done, and which must cease to be done before the first steps can be taken toward righting the wrongs, curing the ills, and wiping out the disgrace to us of the present conditions of our Indians.

Cheating, robbing, breaking promises—these three are clearly things which must cease to be done. One more thing, also, and that is the refusal of the protection of the law to the Indian's rights of property, "of life, liberty, and the pursuit of happiness."

When these four things have ceased to be done, time, statesmanship, philanthropy, and Christianity can slowly and surely do the rest. Till these four things have ceased to be done, statesmanship and philanthropy alike must work in vain, and even Christianity can reap but small harvest.

REVIEW QUESTIONS

1. Why did the federal government repeatedly violate its treaties with the various Indian tribes, according to Jackson?
2. Why did Jackson oppose the granting of immediate citizenship to all Indians?

The Dawes Act (1887)

The relentless advance of settlers into the West created constant tensions with Native Americans and sparked numerous wars during the post–Civil War era. President Rutherford B. Hayes acknowledged in 1877 that most "of our Indian wars have had their origin in broken promises and acts of injustice on our part." As a result of such growing concern, federal policy toward the Indians seemingly grew more benevolent. The Dawes Act of 1887, named after its sponsor, Senator Henry L. Dawes of Massachusetts, was intended to improve the lot of the Indians by providing them with private property and opportunities for citizenship. But most of the land grants were inadequate, and the emphasis on individual land ownership eroded tribal unity.

From *United States Statutes at Large*, 24:388–391.

An act to provide for the allotment of lands in severalty to Indians on the various reservations, and to extend the protection of the laws of the United States and Territories over the Indians, and for other purposes.

Be it enacted, that in all cases where any tribe or band of Indians has been, or shall hereafter be, located upon any reservation created for their use, either by treaty stipulation or by virtue of an act of Congress or executive order setting apart the same for their use, the President of the United States be, and he hereby is, authorized . . . to allot the lands in said reservation in severalty to any Indian located thereon in quantities as follows:

To each head of a family, one-quarter of a section;

To each single person over eighteen years of age, one-eighth of a section;

To each orphan child under eighteen years of age, one-eighth of a section; and,

To each other single person under eighteen years now living, or who may be born prior to the date of the order of the President directing an allotment of the lands embraced in any reservation, one-sixteenth of a section. . . .

Sec. 5. That upon the approval of the allotments provided for in the act by the Secretary of the Interior, he shall . . . declare that the United States does and will hold the land thus allotted, for the period of twenty-five years, in trust for the sole use and benefit of the Indian to whom such allotment shall have been made, . . . and that at the expiration of said period the United States will convey the same by patent to said Indian, or his heirs as aforesaid, in fee, discharged of such trust and free of all charge or incumbrance whatsoever. . . .

Sec. 6. That upon the completion of said allotments and the patenting of the lands to said allottees, each and every member of the respective bands or tribes of Indians to whom allotments have been made shall have the benefit of and be subject to the laws, both civil and criminal, of the State or Territory in which they may reside; . . . And every Indian born within the territorial limits of the United States to whom allotments shall have been made under the provisions of this act, or under any law or treaty, and every Indian born within the territorial limits of the United States who has voluntarily taken up, within said limits, his residence separate and apart from any tribe of Indians therein, and has adopted the habits of civilized life, is hereby declared to be a citizen of the United States, and is entitled to all the rights, privileges, and immunities of such citizens, whether said Indian has been or not, by birth or otherwise, a member of any tribe of Indians within the territorial limits of the United States without in any manner impairing or otherwise affecting the right of any such Indian to tribal or other property. . . .

Sec. 10. That nothing in this act contained shall be so construed as to affect the right and power of Congress to grant the right of way through any lands granted to an Indian, or a tribe of Indians, for railroads, or other highways, or telegraph lines, for the public use, or to condemn such lands to public uses, upon making just compensation. . . .

REVIEW QUESTIONS

1. How might the emphasis on private property in the Dawes Act have conflicted with Native American customs?
2. Why did Congress feel the need to retain title to the land allotments for twenty-five years?
3. To qualify for citizenship under the Dawes Act, Native Americans had to adopt "the habits of civilized life." Assess the meaning and implications of such a standard.

FREDERICK JACKSON TURNER

FROM *The Frontier in American History* (1893)

More than any other scholar, historian Frederick Jackson Turner influenced attitudes toward the role of the West in shaping American values and institutions. Born in Portage, Wisconsin, in 1861, he taught at the University of Wisconsin from 1889 until 1910, when he joined Harvard's faculty. In 1893 he presented his "frontier thesis" to the American Historical Society. Turner claimed that the process of western settlement was the defining characteristic of American society. Yet he concluded that at the end of the nineteenth century the frontier era had ended, and he worried that its beneficial effects would be lost to future generations of Americans. His frontier thesis was widely accepted. Today, however, historians criticize him for ignoring the role of women, evading the moral issues associated with the exploitation of the Native Americans, and asserting a simplistic connection between geography and political ideology.

From Frederick Jackson Turner, *The Frontier in American History* (New York: Holt, Rinehart & Winston, 1920), pp. 1–4, 22–23, 29–31, 32, 37–38.

In a recent bulletin of the Superintendent of the Census for 1890 appear these significant words: "Up to and including 1880 the country had a frontier of settlement, but at present the unsettled area has been so broken into by isolated bodies of settlement that there can hardly be said to be a frontier line. In the discussion of its extent, its westward movement, etc., it can not, therefore, any longer have a place in census reports." This brief official statement marks the closing of a great historic movement. Up to our own day American history has been in a large degree the history of the colonization of the Great West. The existence of an area of free land, its continuous recession, and the advance of American settlement westward explain American development.

Behind institutions, behind constitutional forms and modifications, lie the vital forces that call these organs into life and shape them to meet changing conditions. The peculiarity of American institutions is the fact that they have been compelled to adapt themselves to the changes of an expanding people—to the changes involved in crossing a continent, in winning a wilderness, and in developing at each area of this progress out of the primitive economic and political conditions of the frontier into the complexity of city life. Said Calhoun[1] in 1817, "we are great, and rapidly—I was about to say fearfully—growing!" So saying, he touched the distinguishing feature of American life.

* * *

In the case of most nations, however, the development has occurred in a limited area; and if the nation has expanded, it has met other growing peoples whom it has conquered. But in the case of the United States we have a different phenomenon. Limiting our attention to the Atlantic coast, we have the familiar phenomenon of the evolution of institutions in a limited area, such as the rise of representative government; the differentiation of

---

[1] South Carolina statesman John C. Calhoun (1782–1850).

simple colonial governments into complex organs; the progress from primitive industrial society, without division of labor, up to manufacturing civilization. But we have in addition to this a recurrence of the process of evolution in each western area reached in the process of expansion. Thus American development has exhibited not merely advance along a single line, but a return to primitive conditions on a continually advancing frontier line, and a new development for that area.

American social development has been continually beginning over again on the frontier. This perennial rebirth, this fluidity of American life, this expansion westward with its new opportunities, its continuous touch with the simplicity of primitive society, furnish the forces dominating American character. The true point of view in the history of this nation is not the Atlantic coast, it is the Great West. . . .

In this advance, the frontier is the outer edge of the wave—the meeting point between savagery and civilization. . . . The most significant thing about the American frontier is, that it lies at the hither edge of free land.

*   *   *

In the settlement of America we have to observe how European life entered the continent, and how America modified and developed that life and reacted on Europe. Our early history is the study of European germs developing in an American environment. . . . The frontier is the line of most rapid and effective Americanization. The wilderness masters the colonist. It finds him a European in dress, industries, tools, modes of travel, and thought. It takes him from the railroad car and puts him in the birch canoe. It strips off the garments of civilization and arrays him in the hunting shirt and the moccasin. It puts him in the log cabin of the Cherokee and Iroquois and runs an Indian palisade around him. Before long he has gone to planting Indian corn and plowing with a sharp stick; he shouts the war cry and takes the scalp in orthodox Indian fashion. In short, at the frontier the environment is at first too strong for the man. He must accept the conditions which it

furnishes, or perish, and so he fits himself into the Indian clearings and follows the Indian trails. Little by little he transforms the wilderness, but the outcome is not the old Europe. . . .

The fact is, that here is a new product that is American. At first, the frontier was the Atlantic coast. It was the frontier of Europe in a very real sense. Moving westward the frontier becomes more and more American. . . . Thus the advance of the frontier has meant a steady movement away from the influence of Europe, a steady growth of independence on American lines. And to study this advance, the men who grew up under these conditions, and the political, economic, and social results of it, is to study the really American part of our history.

*   *   *

First, we note that the frontier promoted the formation of a composite nationality for the American people. The coast was preponderantly English, but the later tides of continental immigration flowed across to the free lands. . . . In the crucible of the frontier the immigrants were Americanized, liberated, and fused into a mixed race, English in neither nationality nor characteristics. The process has gone on from the early days to our own. . . .

But the most important effect of the frontier has been in the promotion of democracy here and in Europe. As has been indicated, the frontier is productive of individualism. Complex society is precipitated by the wilderness into a kind of primitive organization based on the family. The tendency is anti-social. It produces antipathy to control, and particularly to any direct control.

The frontier States that came into the Union in the first quarter of a century of its existence came in with democratic suffrage provisions, and had reactive effects of the highest importance upon the older States whose peoples were being attracted there. An extension of the franchise became essential. . . .

But the democracy born of free land, strong in selfishness and individualism, intolerant of administrative experience and education, and pressing individual liberty beyond its proper bounds, has its dangers as well as its benefits. Individualism in America has allowed a laxity in regard to governmental affairs which has rendered possible the spoils system and all the manifest evils that follow from a highly developed civil spirit. . . .

The works of travelers along each frontier from colonial days onward describe certain common traits, and these traits have, while softening down, still persisted as survivals in the place of their origin, even when a higher social organization succeeded. The result is that to the frontier the American intellect owes its striking characteristics. The coarseness and strength combined with acuteness and inquisitiveness; that practical, inventive turn of mind, quick to find expedients; that masterful grasp of material things, lacking in the artistic but powerful to effect great ends; that restless nervous energy; that dominant individualism, working for good and for evil, and withal that buoyancy and exuberance which comes with freedom—these are traits of the frontier, or traits called out elsewhere because of the existence of the frontier.

Since the days when the fleet of Columbus sailed into the waters of the New World, America has been another name for opportunity, and the people of the United States have taken their tone from the incessant expansion which has not only been open but has even been forced upon them. He would be a rash prophet who should assert that the expansive character of American life has now entirely ceased. Movement has been its dominant fact, and, unless this training has no effect upon a people, the American energy will continually demand a wider field for its exercise. . . . yet, in spite of environment, and in spite of custom, each frontier did indeed furnish a new field of opportunity. . . . And now, four centuries from the discovery of America, at the end of a hundred years of life under the Constitution, the frontier has gone, and with its going has closed the first period of American history.

REVIEW QUESTIONS

1. What do you think Turner meant by the term "Americanization"?
2. According to Turner, in what crucial respect did western states differ from those on the Atlantic coast?
3. Turner equated the frontier with the American character. Does his set of national characteristics accurately describe Americans today? Explain.
4. In suggesting that the frontier was ultimately synonymous with a "new field of opportunity," what did Turner imply about other living environments in nineteenth-century American life?

20 ⚜ BIG BUSINESS AND ORGANIZED LABOR

During the half century after the Civil War, the United States experienced an economic transformation that catapulted it into the front rank of industrial nations. The reconstruction of the South and the settlement of the West created an unceasing demand for goods and services. At the same time, the growing national economy created job opportunities that served as a powerful magnet luring millions of immigrants from foreign lands. The need to feed, clothe, and shelter such a rapidly growing population added more fuel to industrial expansion, and, in turn, fostered a dramatic increase in the number and size of cities, especially in the East and Midwest. By the end of the nineteenth century, the United States was no longer a decentralized agrarian republic. It was increasingly a nation of cities and factories.

A key development facilitating the urban-industrial revolution was the maturation of a national market. What had been local or regional economies before the Civil War assumed national proportions with the advent of the transcontinental railroad network, the telegraph system, and other innovations that enabled entrepreneurs to manufacture products for distribution across the country. Such a national market helped give rise to larger corporations and huge individual fortunes.

During this turbulent period of industrial expansion and consolidation, many business leaders engaged in unethical and even illegal practices in an effort to gain advantages in the marketplace. Critics charged that some of the most domineering corporate buccaneers, men such as railroad tycoons Jay Gould and Daniel Drew, oil baron John D. Rockefeller, banking magnate J. P. Morgan, and steel giant Andrew Carnegie, were "robber barons" who ruthlessly eliminated their competitors, gouged consumers, and rode roughshod over employees. In their defense, the business leaders pointed out that the new jobs that they were creating, the growing volume of goods and services they were making available to the public, the rising standard of living for the country as a whole, and the philan-

thropic contributions they were making helped improve the general welfare of their communities.

The rise of big business and its attendant excesses helped spawn a new era in the development of an organized labor movement. The first major national union, the Knights of Labor, was founded in 1869. It included all types of laborers, skilled and unskilled, and embraced a wide array of reform initiatives, ranging from the eight-hour working day to the increased use of paper money. Terence Powderly and other leaders of the Knights of Labor sought to gain their objectives through negotiation rather than strikes.

In the 1880s, however, such broad objectives and conciliatory tactics created fissures within the Knights that led to its demise by the end of the century. In its place emerged a new organization, the American Federation of Labor (AFL). Unlike the Knights of Labor, the AFL was a federation of many separate unions, each organized by special craft or skill. Unskilled workers were not allowed in the AFL, nor were women workers. The founder of the AFL, Samuel Gompers, disdained the comprehensive reform agenda of the Knights of Labor in favor of sharply focused "bread-and-butter" issues—higher wages, shorter working hours, and better working conditions. And unlike Powderly, he embraced the strike as the union's most effective weapon in wrenching concessions from recalcitrant corporate leaders. By the turn of the century, the AFL was the largest union in the United States, claiming over 500,000 members.

The AFL did not challenge the basic premises of capitalism. Its aim was simply to gain for its members a larger slice of the economic pie. A few labor leaders, however, grew enamored of the socialist ideas of Karl Marx. In the 1890s a West Indian immigrant, Daniel DeLeon, and a railway union organizer, Eugene Debs, organized separate labor movements grounded in socialist philosophy. Of the two, Debs proved to be the more successful. In 1901 he organized the Socialist Party of America, and three years later he garnered over 400,000 votes as a candidate in the presidential election. Eight years later he ran again and gained over 900,000 votes.

At the same time that Eugene Debs was mobilizing a socialist-based working-class movement, militant labor leaders in the West were forming a parallel organization, the Industrial Workers of the World (IWW). Like the defunct Knights of Labor, the IWW sought to organize all types of workers into "One Big Union." But the "Wobblies," as IWW members were called, sought the complete destruction of the capitalist system and its replacement by autonomous workers' unions ("syndicates"). The IWW used confrontational strikes and tactics to assault the capitalist system. Its efforts, in turn, led to a violent counterattack by the police. During World War I, government officials used emergency powers to crack down on the IWW and arrest its leaders.

ANDREW CARNEGIE

FROM Wealth (1889)

Andrew Carnegie (1835–1919) was a Scottish immigrant who created the world's largest and most efficient steel company; in the process he became one of the wealthiest men in the world. In the following essay, published in the North American Review in 1889, he articulated what came to be known as the "gospel of wealth." Carnegie steadfastly defended the principles of the free enterprise system and the right of individuals to amass huge fortunes, but he stressed that the rich should donate their money for the public good before they died. Carnegie himself gave away $350,000,000. He built thousands of free public libraries, supported scientific research and higher education, and promoted the cause of world peace.

From Andrew Carnegie, "Wealth," *North American Review* 148 (June 1889):653–664. [Editorial insertions appear in square brackets—*Ed.*]

The problem of our age is the proper administration of wealth, so that the ties of brotherhood may still bind together the rich and poor in harmonious relationship. The conditions of human life have not only been changed, but revolutionized, within the past few hundred years. In former days there was little difference between the dwelling, dress, food, and environment of the chief and those of his retainers. . . . The contrast between the palace of the millionaire and the cottage of the laborer with us today measures the change which has come with civilization.

This change, however, is not to be deplored, but welcomed as highly beneficial. It is well, nay, essential for the progress of the race, that the houses of some should be homes for all that is highest and best in literature and the arts, and for all the refinements of civilization, rather than that none should be so. . . . The "good old times" were not good old times. Neither master nor servant was as well situated then as today. A relapse to old conditions would be disastrous to both—not the least so to him who serves—and would sweep away civilization with it. But whether the change be for good or ill, it is upon us, beyond our power to alter, and therefore to be accepted and made the best of. It is a waste of time to criticize the inevitable. . . .

The price we pay for this salutary change, is, no doubt, great. We assemble thousands of operatives in the factory, in the mine, and in the counting-house, of whom the employer can know little or nothing, and to whom the employer is little better than a myth. All intercourse between them is at an end. Rigid castes are formed, and, as usual, mutual ignorance breeds mutual distrust. Each caste is without sympathy for the other, and ready to credit anything disparaging in regard to it. Under the law of competition, the employer of thousands is forced into the strictest economies, among which the rates paid to labor figure prominently, and often there is friction between the employer and the employed, between capital and labor, between rich and poor. Human society loses homogeneity.

The price which society pays for the law of competition, like the price it pays for cheap comforts and luxuries, is also great; but the advantages of this law are also greater still, for it is to this law that we owe our wonderful material development, which brings improved conditions in its train. But, whether the law be benign or not, we . . . cannot evade it; no substitutes for it have been found; and while the law may be sometimes hard for the individual, it is best for the race, because it insures the survival of the fittest in every department. We accept and welcome, therefore, as conditions to which we must accommodate ourselves, great inequality of environment, the concentration of business . . . in the hands of a few, and the law of competition between these, as being not only beneficial, but essential for the future progress of the race. . . .

Objections to the foundations upon which society is based are not in order, because the condition of the race is better with these than it has been with any others which have been tried. Of the effect of any new substitutes proposed we cannot be sure. The Socialist or Anarchist who seeks to overturn present conditions is to be regarded as attacking the foundation upon which civilization itself rests, for civilization took its start from the day that the capable, industrious workman said to his incompetent and lazy fellow, "If thou dost not sow, thou shalt not reap," and thus ended primitive Communism by separating the drones from the bees. One who studies this subject will soon be brought face to face with the conclusion that upon the sacredness of property civilization itself depends—the right of the laborer to his hundred dollars in the savings bank, and equally the legal right of the millionaire to his million. To those who propose to substitute Communism for this intense Individualism the answer, therefore, is: The race has tried that. All progress from that barbarous day to the present time has resulted from its displacement. Not evil, but good, has come to the race from the accumulation of wealth by those who have the ability and energy that produce it.

*   *   *

We start, then, with a condition of affairs under which the best interests of the race are promoted, but which inevitably gives wealth to the few. Thus far, accepting conditions as they exist, the situation can be surveyed and pronounced good. The question then arises—and, if the foregoing be correct, it is the only question with which we have to deal—What is the proper mode of administering

wealth after the laws upon which civilization is founded have thrown it into the hands of the few? And it is of this great question that I believe I offer the true solution. . . .

There are but three modes in which surplus wealth can be disposed of. It can be left to the families of the decedents; or it can be bequeathed for public purposes; or, finally, it can be administered during their lives by its possessors. Under the first and second modes most of the wealth of the world that has reached the few has hitherto been applied. Let us in turn consider each of these modes. The first is the most injudicious. In monarchical countries, the estates and the greatest portion of the wealth are left to the first son, that the vanity of the parent may be gratified by the thought that his name and title are descend to succeeding generations, unimpaired. The condition of this class in Europe today teaches the futility of such hopes or ambitions. . . . Why should men leave great fortunes to their children? If this is done from affection, is it not misguided affection? Observation teaches that, generally speaking, it is not well for the children that they should be so burdened. Neither is it well for the state. . . . It is no longer questionable that great sums bequeathed oftener work more for injury than for the good of the recipients. . . .

As to the second mode, that of leaving wealth at death for public uses, it may be said that this is only a means for the disposal of wealth, provided a man is content to wait until he is dead before it becomes of much good in the world. Knowledge of the results of legacies bequeathed is not calculated to inspire the brightest hopes of much posthumous good being accomplished. . . . Besides this, it may fairly be said that no man is to be extolled for doing what he cannot help doing, nor is he to be thanked by the community to which he only leaves wealth at death. Men who leave vast sums in this way may fairly be thought men who would not have left it at all, had they been able to take it with them. . . .

The growing disposition to tax more and more heavily large estates left at death is a cheering indication of the growth of a salutary change in public opinion. The State of Pennsylvania now takes . . . one-tenth of the property left by its citizens. . . . By taxing estates heavily at death, the state marks its condemnation of the selfish millionaire's unworthy life. . . .

There remains, then, only one mode of using great fortunes; but in this we have the true antidote for the temporary unequal distribution of wealth, the reconciliation of the rich and the poor—a reign of harmony—another ideal, differing indeed, from that of the Communist in requiring only the further evolution of existing conditions, not the total overthrow of our civilization. . . . Under its sway we shall have an ideal state, in which the surplus wealth of the few will become, in the best sense, the property of the many, because it is administered for the common good, and this wealth, passing through the hands of the few, can be made a much more potent force for the elevation of our race than it if had been distributed in small sums to the people themselves. Even the poorest can be made to see this, and to agree that great sums gathered by some of their fellow-citizens and spent for public purposes, from which the masses reap the principal benefit, are more valuable to them than if scattered among them through the course of many years in trifling amounts.

*   *   *

This, then, is held to be the duty of the Man of Wealth: First, to set an example of modest, unostentatious living, shunning display of extravagance; to provide moderately for the legitimate wants of those dependent upon him; and after doing so to consider all surplus revenues which come to him simply as trust funds, which he is called upon to administer . . . in the manner which, in his judgment, is best calculated to produce the most beneficial results for the community—the man of wealth thus becoming the mere agent and trustee for his poorer brethren, bringing to their service his superior wisdom, experience, and ability to administer, doing for them better than they would or could do for themselves. . . .

In bestowing charity, the main consideration should be to help those who will help themselves;

to provide part of the means by which those who desire to improve may do to; to give those who desire to rise the aids by which they may rise. . . . Neither the individual nor the race is improved by alms-giving. . . . The amount which can be wisely given. . . . [to] individuals is necessarily limited, . . . for in alms-giving more injury is probably done by rewarding vice than by relieving virtue. . . .

Thus is the problem of the Rich and Poor to be solved. The laws of accumulation will be left free; the laws of distribution free. Individualism will continue, but the millionaire will be but a trustee for the poor; entrusted for a season with a great part of the increased wealth of the community, but administering it for the community far better than it could or would have done for itself. The best minds will thus have reached a stage in the development of the race in which it is clearly seen that there is no mode of disposing of surplus wealth . . . save by using it year by year for the general good. The day already dawns. But a little while, and . . . the man who dies leaving behind him millions, . . . which was his to administer in life, will pass away "unwept, unhonored, and unsung," no matter to what uses he leave the dross which he cannot take with him. Of such as these the public verdict will then be: "The man who dies thus rich dies disgraced."

Such, in my opinion, is the true Gospel concerning Wealth, obedience to which is destined some day to solve the problem of the Rich and the Poor, and to bring "Peace on earth, among men Good-Will."

REVIEW QUESTIONS

1. How did Carnegie justify the accumulation of wealth?
2. What three ways did Carnegie suggest to dispose of personal wealth?
3. What criteria did Carnegie establish for administering charitable resources? Are his reasons consistent?

Preamble to the Constitution
of the Knights of Labor (1878)

Many disagreed with Andrew Carnegie's defense of unchecked free enterprise. One dissenting group was the Noble Order of the Knights of Labor, the first national union in the United States. Founded in 1869 as a secret fraternal order, it included workers of all types, skilled and unskilled, as well as women and African Americans. The Knights grew slowly until 1879 when Terence V. Powderly assumed leadership of the organization. He brought the Knights into the public arena, advocated an eight-hour working day for all workers, promoted an array of political reforms, and preferred boycotts over strikes. In 1886 the Knights boasted some 800,000 members. Yet their far-flung objectives and their utopian efforts to replace the wage-labor system of competitive free enterprise with a "cooperative" philosophy brought their demise. By 1900 the organization had disappeared. It was displaced by the American Federation of Labor, founded in 1886, which organized only skilled workers and used strikes to gain its objectives. Powderly helped draft the Preamble to the Constitution of the Knights of Labor, excerpted below.

From Terence V. Powderly, *Thirty Years of Labor* (Columbus, OH: Excelsior Publishing House, 1890), pp. 243–246.

The recent alarming development and aggression of aggregated wealth, which, unless checked, will invariably lead to the pauperization and hopeless degradation of the toiling masses, render it imperative, if we desire to enjoy the blessings of life, that a check should be placed upon its power and upon unjust accumulation, and a system adopted which will secure to the laborer the fruits of his toil; and as this much-desired object can only be accomplished by the thorough unification of labor, and the united efforts of those who obey the divine injunction that "In the sweat of thy brow shalt thou eat bread," we have formed the Knights of Labor with a view of securing the organization and direction, by co-operative effort, of the power of the industrial classes; and we submit to the world the object sought to be accomplished by our organization, calling upon all who believe in securing "the greatest good to the greatest number" to aid and assist us:

I. To bring within the folds of organization every department of productive industry, making knowledge a standpoint for action, and industrial and moral worth, not wealth, the true standard of individual and national greatness.

II. To secure to the toilers a proper share of the wealth that they create; more of the leisure that rightfully belongs to them; more societary advantages; more of the benefits, privileges, and emoluments of the world; in a word, all those rights and privileges necessary to make them capable of enjoying, appreciating, defending, and perpetuating the blessing of good government.

III. To arrive at the true condition of the producing masses in their educational, moral, and financial condition, by demanding from the various governments the establishment of bureaus of Labor Statistics.

IV. The establishment of co-operative institutions, productive and distributive.

V. The reserving of the public lands—the heritage of the people—for the actual settler;—not another acre for railroads or speculators.

VI. The abrogation of all laws that do not bear equally upon capital and labor, the removal of unjust technicalities, delays, and discriminations in the administration of justice, and the adopting of measures providing for the health and safety of those engaged in mining, manufacturing, or building pursuits.

VII. The enactment of laws to compel chartered corporations to pay their employees weekly, in full, for labor performed during the preceding week, in the lawful money of the country.

VIII. The enactment of laws giving mechanics and laborers a first lien on their work for their full wages.

IX. The abolishment of the contract system on national, state, and municipal work.

X. The substitution of arbitration for strikes, whenever and wherever employers and employees are willing to meet on equitable grounds.

XI. The prohibition of the employment of children in workshops, mines, and factories before attaining their fourteenth year.

XII. To abolish the system of letting out by contract the labor of convicts in our prisons and reformatory institutions.

XIII. To secure for both sexes equal pay for equal work.

XIV. The reduction of the hours of labor to eight per day, so that the laborers may have more time for social enjoyment and intellectual improvement, and be enabled to reap the advantages conferred by the labor-saving machinery which their brains have created.

XV. To prevail upon governments to establish a purely national circulating medium,[1] based upon the faith and resources of the nation, and issued directly to the people, without the intervention of any system of banking corporations, which money shall be a legal tender in payment of all debts, public or private.

REVIEW QUESTIONS

1. Whom did the Preamble identify as enemies of social and economic equality? Explain.
2. How did the Preamble characterize the impact of labor-saving machines?
3. How do you think Carnegie might have reacted to this document?

---

[1] Currency.

LEONORA M. BARRY

Organizing Women Workers

Women workers during the nineteenth century suffered discrimination in hiring and pay. The Knights of Labor sought to organize women workers into unions on a national scale. The organization accepted women both in "mixed" assemblies and gender-segregated locals. The Knights hired Leonora M. Barry, a former mill worker herself, to work as an organizer. During her first year she visited numerous factories and mills across the country, documenting the conditions and prejudice she encountered. The following excerpt from her report reveals the special difficulties that women workers faced and helps explain why the Knights were generally unsuccessful in organizing them.

From Pamphlet. Sophia Smith Collection, Smith College, Northampton, MA. [Editorial insertions appear in square brackets—*Ed.*]

General Master Workman and Members of the General Assembly:

One year ago the Knights of Labor, in convention assembled at Richmond, Va., elected me to a position of honor and trust—the servant and representative of thousands of toiling women. . . .

Having no legal authority I have been unable to make as thorough an investigation in many places as I would like . . . consequently the facts stated in my report are not all from actual observation but from authority which I have every reason to believe truthful and reliable.

Upon the strength of my observation and experience I would ask of officers and members of this Order that more consideration be given, and more thorough educational measures be adopted on behalf of the working-women of our land, the majority of whom are entirely ignorant of the economic and industrial question which is to them of such vital importance; and they must ever remain so while the selfishness of their brothers in toil is carried to such an extent as I find it to be among those who have sworn to demand equal pay for equal work. Thus far in the history of our Order that part of our platform has been but a mockery of the principles intended. . . .

Men! ye whose earnings count from nine to fifteen dollars a week and upward, cease, in the name of God and humanity, cease your demands and grievances and give us your assistance for a time to bring some relief to the poor unfortunate, whose week's work of eighty-four hours brings her but $2.50 or $3 per week.

*　　*　　*

December 10 went to Newark to investigate the matter concerning the sewing-women of that city, which was referred to our committee at the General Assembly at Richmond. Found, after a careful study of the matter, that . . . in general the working-women of Newark were very poorly paid, and the system of fines in many industries were severe and unjust. Instance: a corset factory where a fine is imposed for eating, laughing, singing or talking of 10 cents each. If not inside the gate in the morning when the whistle stops blowing, an employee is locked out until half past seven; then she can go to work, but is docked two hours for waste power; and many other rules equally slavish and unjust. Other industries closely follow these rules, while the sewing-women receive wages which are only one remove from actual starvation. In answer to all my inquiries of employer and employed why this state of affairs exists, the reply was, monopoly and competition. . . .

Went to Auburn, N.Y., Feb. 20. I found the working-women of this city in a deplorable state, there being none of them organized. There were long hours, poor wages, and the usual results consequent upon such a condition. Not among male employers alone in this city, but women in whose heart we would expect to find a little pity and compassion for the suffering of her own sex. To the contrary, on this occasion, however, I found one who, for cruelty and injustice toward employees, has not an equal on the pages of labor's history—one who owns and conducts an establishment in which is manufactured women's and children's wear. Upon accepting a position in her factory an employee is compelled to purchase a sewing machine from the proprietress, who is agent for the S. M. Co. This must be paid for in weekly payments of 50 cents, provided the operative makes $3. Should she make $4 the weekly payment is 75 cents. At any time before the machine is paid for, through a reduction of the already meagre wages, or the enforcement of some petty tyrannical rule—sickness, anger, or any cause, the operative leaves her employ, she forfeits the machine and all the money paid upon it, and to the next applicant the machine is resold. She must also purchase the thread for doing the work, as she is an agent for a thread company. It takes four spools of thread at 50 cents a spool to do $5 worth of work, and when $2 is paid for thread, and 50 cents for the machine, the unfortunate victim has $2.50 wherewith to board, clothe and care for herself generally; and it is only experts who can make even this. . . .

I succeeded in organizing two Local Assemblies in this city, one of woodworkers, and one women's Local Assembly, numbering at organization 107 members, which has grown rapidly and is now one of the most flourishing Local Assemblies in the State. Here it was that Sister Annie Conboy was

discharged from the silk mill for having taken me through the mill, although she had received permission from her foreman to take a friend through, yet, when the proprietor found out I was a Knight of Labor she was discharged without a moment's warning.

March 14 was sent to Paterson to look into the condition of the women and children employed in the Linen-thread Works of that city. There are some fourteen or fifteen hundred persons employed in this industry, who were at that time out of employment for this reason: Children who work at what is called doffing[1] were receiving $2.70 per week, and asked for an increase of 5 cents per day. They were refused, and they struck, whereupon all the other employees were locked out. . . . The abuse, injustice and suffering which the women of this industry endure from the tyranny, cruelty and slave-driving propensities of the employers is [sic] something terrible to be allowed existence in free America. In one branch of this industry women are compelled to stand on a stone floor in water the year round, most of the time barefoot, with a spray of water from a revolving cylinder flying constantly against the breast; and the coldest night in winter as well as the warmest in summer those poor creatures must go to their homes with water dripping from their underclothing along their path, because there could not be space or a few moments allowed them wherein to change their clothing. A constant supply of recruits is always on hand to take the places of any who dare rebel against the ironclad authority of those in charge.

*   *   *

In submitting my report to the members of the Order and the public at large, I ask only one favor, namely, a careful perusal and just criticism. . . . I can only hope that my labor will yet bear good fruit, and that in the near future fair consideration and justice will be meted out to the oppressed women of our nation. . . .

---

[1] Removing a bobbin from a spinning frame.

REVIEW QUESTIONS

1. Compare the data given for men's wages and women's wages. Were women receiving equal pay for equal work? What kinds of costs were often deducted from women's wages?

2. Describe the kinds of conditions that women faced at work.

3. Why was it easy to fire women workers? What does this suggest about the dynamics of nineteenth-century supply and demand for labor?

SAMUEL GOMPERS

The American Federation of Labor (1883)

The American Federation of Labor supplanted the Knights of Labor, and it developed a quite different philosophy. Rather than trying to abolish the wage-labor system, it sought to use strikes to gain higher wages, lower working hours, and better working conditions for its members. Unlike the Knights of Labor, the AFL organized only skilled workers into unions defined by particular trades. The AFL also emphasized relatively high dues in order to create a treasury large enough to sustain the members during a prolonged strike. Under the leadership of Samuel Gompers (1850–1924), a London-born cigarmaker, the AFL became not only a powerful force serving the interests of its members but also a conservative defender of capitalism against the appeal of socialism and communism. In 1883 Gompers testified before a Congressional committee about his organization.

From U.S. Senate, Testimony of Samuel Gompers, August 1883, *Report of the Committee of the Senate upon the Relations between Labor and Capital* (Washington, DC, 1885), 1:365–370.

. . . There is nothing in the labor movement that employers who have had unorganized workers dread so much as organization; but organization alone will not do much unless the organization provides itself with a good fund, so that the operatives may be in a good position, in the event of a struggle with their employers, to hold out. . . .

Modern industry evolves these organizations out of the existing conditions where there are two classes in society, one incessantly striving to obtain the labor of the other class for as little as possible, and to obtain the largest amount or number of hours of labor; and the members of the other class, being as individuals utterly helpless in a contest with their employers, naturally resort to combinations to improve their condition, and, in fact, they are forced by the conditions which surround them to organize for self-protection. Hence trades unions. Trade unions are not barbarous, nor are they the outgrowth of barbarism. On the contrary they are only possible where civilization exists. Trade unions cannot exist in China; they cannot exist in Russia; and in all those semi-barbarous countries they can hardly exist, if they can exist at all. But they have been formed successfully in this country, in Germany, in England, and they are gradually gaining strength in France. . . .

Wherever trades unions have organized and are most firmly organized, there are the rights of the people most respected. A people may be educated, but to me it appears that the greatest amount of intelligence exists in that country or that state where the people are best able to defend their rights, and their liberties as against those who are desirous of undermining them. Trades unions are organizations that instill into men a higher motive-power and give them a higher goal to look to. . . .

The trades unions are by no means an outgrowth of socialistic or communistic ideas or principles, but the socialistic and communistic notions are evolved from the trades unions' movements. As to the question of the principles of communism or socialism prevailing in trades unions, there are a number of men who connect themselves as workingmen with the trades unions who may have socialistic convictions, yet who never gave them currency. . . . On the other hand, there are men— not so numerous now as they have been in the past—who are endeavoring to conquer the trades-union movement and subordinate it to those doctrines, and in a measure, in a few such organizations that condition of things exists, but by no means does it exist in the largest, most powerful, and best organized trades unions. There the view of which I spoke just now, the desire to improve the condition of the workingmen by and through the efforts of the trades union, is fully lived up to. . . . I believe that the existence of the trades-union movement, more especially where the unionists are better organized, has evoked a spirit and a demand for reform, but has held in check the more radical elements in society.

REVIEW QUESTIONS

1. Why did Gompers believe that unions were necessary?
2. Why did Gompers claim that trade unions did not exist in China or Russia?
3. What were the advantages of Gompers's explicit rejection of socialism and communism?

EDWARD O'DONNELL

FROM Women as Bread Winners— The Error of the Age (1887)

The AFL excluded not only unskilled workers, but also blacks, women, and recent immigrants. In 1900 only 3 percent of working women were represented by unions. At times the arguments against admitting women into unions grew hysterical, as illustrated by the AFL pamphlet.

From Edward O'Donnell, "Women as Bread Winners—The Error of the Age," *American Federationist* 48 (October 1887):167–168.

The invasion of the crafts by women has been developing for years amid irritation and injury to the workman. The right of the woman to win honest bread is accorded on all sides, but with craftsmen it is an open question whether this manifestation is of a healthy social growth or not.

The rapid displacement of men by women in the factory and workshop has to be met sooner or later, and the question is forcing itself upon the leaders and thinkers among the labor organizations of the land.

Is it a pleasing indication of progress to see the father, the brother and the son displaced as the bread winner by the mother, sister and daughter?

Is not this evolutionary backslide, which certainly modernizes the present wage system in vogue, a menace to prosperity—a foe to our civilized pretensions? . . .

The growing demand for female labor is not founded upon philanthropy, as those who encourage it would have sentimentalists believe; it does not spring from the milk of human kindness. It is an insidious assault upon the home; it is the knife of the assassin, aimed at the family circle—the divine injunction. It debars the man through financial embarrassment from family responsibility, and physically, mentally and socially excludes the woman equally from nature's dearest impulse. Is this the demand of civilized progress; is it the desire of Christian dogma? . . .

Capital thrives not upon the peaceful, united, contented family circle; rather are its palaces, pleasures and vices fostered and increased upon the disruption, ruin or abolition of the home, because with its decay and ever glaring privation, manhood loses is dignity, its backbone, its aspirations. . . .

To combat these impertinent inclinations, dangerous to the few, the old and well-tried policy of divide and conquer is invoked, and to our own shame, it must be said, one too often renders blind aid to capital in its warfare upon us. The employer in the magnanimity of his generosity will give employment to the daughter, while her two brothers are weary because of their daily tramp in quest of work. The father, who has a fair, steady job, sees not the infamous policy back of the flattering propositions. Somebody else's daughter is called in the same manner, by and by, and very soon the shop or factory are full of women, while their fathers have the option of working for the same wages or a few cents more, or take their places in the large army of unemployed. . . .

College professors and graduates tell us that this is the natural sequence of industrial development, an integral part of economic claim.

Never was a greater fallacy uttered of more poisonous import. It is false and wholly illogical. The great demand for women and their preference over men does not spring from a desire to elevate humanity; at any rate that is not its trend.

The wholesale employment of women in the various handicrafts must gradually unsex them, as it most assuredly is demoralizing them, or stripping them of that mode's demeanor that lends a charm to their kind, while it numerically strengthens the multitudinous army of loafers, paupers, tramps and policemen, for no man who desires honest employment, and can secure it, cares to throw his life away upon such a wretched occupation as the latter.

The employment of women in the mechanical departments is encouraged because of its cheapness and easy manipulation, regardless of the consequent perils; and for no other reason. The generous sentiment enveloping this inducement is criminal design, since it comes from a thirst to build riches upon the dismemberment of the family or the hearthstone cruelly dishonored. . . .

But somebody will say, would you have women pursue lives of shame rather than work? Certainly not; it is to the alarming introduction of women into the mechanical industries, hitherto enjoyed by the sterner sex, at a wage uncommandable by them, that leads so many into that deplorable pursuit. . . .

REVIEW QUESTIONS

1. What did O'Donnell mean by female employment constituting an "insidious assault upon the home"?
2. According to the pamphlet, how did employment "unsex" women?

PHILIP HUBERT

The Business of a Factory (1897)

The late nineteenth century saw the spread of gigantic factories and mills. In 1897,
Scribner's Magazine *published a series of articles on "The Conduct of Great Business." This article by Philip Hubert focused on a New England textile mill. He described the mill more from the perspective of the owners than the workers, but his observations do provide insight into the changing nature of the workplace during the Gilded Age.*

From Philip G. Hubert, Jr., "The Business of a Factory," *Scribner's Magazine* 21 (January–June 1897):306–331. [Editorial insertions appear in square brackets—*Ed.*]

One hot evening in July last I stood on the brink of a little canal that skirts a row of noble buildings constituting the largest textile mill in New England and perhaps in the world, and watched hundreds and thousands of mill-hands pour over the bridge that connects the mills with the town of which they are the chief support and pride. As the great bell clanged forth its six peals, one could hear the cessation of toil for the day. The mighty turbines, fed by this canal from the Merrimac [River], ceased to revolve, the great Corliss engines that in recent years have come to the aid of water-power in all big mills, came to a stop; the three hundred thousand spindles, the eight thousand looms, and the thousands of other ponderous machines, ingenious and effective almost past belief, for picking, cleaning, roving, bleaching, printing, drying, and finishing the one hundred million yards of cotton and woolen goods turned out from these mills every year—all this vast mass of machinery, scattered over sixty acres of flooring, came to a stop. Bell-time, as six o'clock in the afternoon is called in all New England mill-towns, had come. In place of the hum and clatter of machinery, the patter of innumerable feet made itself heard. Then the first of the army of five thousand operatives began to come, first by driblets, comprising those who did not need to wash, or did not care to, then the larger streams as the doors of

some great room were thrown open, each operative having to go and come by a special staircase in order to avoid the gorging of any particular exit in case of fire, and finally the dense stream of humanity, male and female, big and little, until the broad iron bridge was packed and shook under the strain. . . .

There were men and women, boys and girls, of all ages and colors—even green, and blue, and yellow, and striped—for the operatives in the printing and dyeing shops are as apt to be covered with color as the miller is powdered with flour; here were the fat and the lean, the tall and the short, pretty women and women—less pretty; dark and fair, neat and sloven. And it should be said here that no such squalid poverty saddens the visitor to these mills as can be seen in every manufacturing town in England. Every woman and girl wore shoes; the poor slattern, barefooted, and with a ragged shawl thrown over her head, that one finds by the thousand coming from the cotton-mills of England, was conspicuous by her absence. The women and girls of our manufacturing towns, especially where the native American stock still holds its own, retain a vivid appreciation of pretty things in dress and adornment. In some of the cotton towns, such as Fall River, where the French Canadian and the Irish have driven the Yankee girl from the spindles and the loom, there is less concern for personal appearance than in Lynn, for instance, with its American shoe operatives, or in Manchester with its American thread-makers. Among the more recent recruits to the mills are the Armenians and Polish Jews, of whom there are some in almost all the New England manufacturing towns.

Watching the privates of this army of workers pour forth from the mills where they have been at work since half past six in the morning, with an hour's rest at noon, and bearing in mind the fact that these mills have been in steady and profitable operation for nearly half a century, the management of this vast machine for turning out and selling one hundred million yards of goods a year will impress any one as possessing as much general interest, and far more human interest, than the processes of manufacture themselves. How is the business conducted, whether the product be cotton-yarn, printed calico, watches, shoes, or bicycles? What are the principles governing the art of making money by the manufacture and sale of articles requiring an army of operatives? . . .

It is commonly admitted that while a man or woman who does some small thing in the manufacture of an article—whether it is piecing the broken yarns of a spinning machine, or cutting the eye of a needle, or gathering matches for boxing—may become marvelously expert, the operator runs the risk of becoming more or less of a machine. The girl who stands at the end of a frame of one hundred spindles and sees a broken thread, catches it with lightning-like rapidity and joins it with a touch; the one who cuts the eyes in needles can do the same thing with a human hair; and the girls who pack matches pick up the requisite number for the box, whether it is one hundred, more or less, without counting them, judging simply by touch whether or not the right number is there, and doing it as fast as the eye can follow the hand. Mr. [John] Ruskin contends, probably with reason, that the minute division of labor that makes such wonders possible brutalizes the laborer, and that if the girl made the whole article instead of doing one operation out of fifty, she would gain in intelligence if not in expertness. From an economic, or rather an industrial point of view, however, manu-

facturing has to be carried on at present with the greatest subdivision of labor possible. Fierce competition and a small margin of profit demand it. Mr. Ruskin's dream of a manufacturing community in which the same person shall shear the sheep, clean the wool, dye it, card, spin, and weave it, doing all this in country homes made beautiful with flowers, working but six hours a day, and devoting the rest of the time to reading good books, raising flowers, and singing songs, is a very pretty dream to be made possible only when some philanthropist provides a market at good profit as well as the pleasant conditions for this labor. For the present steam-power is the only power suitable for the work of manufacturing, and this compels the work to be done at one spot. . . .

The discipline of such mills is by no means military. In visiting several of the largest of them I was impressed with the friendly relations between superintendents and men. "We never scold," said the agent of a big mill. "If a man or girl proves to be habitually careless or idle, a discharge follows; but for small infractions of rules we trust the various foremen to look after their own people. In the sixteen years I have been here we have had no strikes." At half-past six in the morning the bell rings for work to begin; there is an hour's intermission at noon, and then from one to six it goes on again. On Saturdays all work in most cotton-mills stops for the day at noon. The law limits factory work in Massachusetts to fifty-eight hours a week. . . .

Opinions differ as to whether or not the growth of the factory system is a blessing to a community, but, as a rule, it is conceded that the standard of intelligence and of living among the mill-hands of New England is not so high now as it was forty years ago. And this, notwithstanding higher wages and shorter hours. In 1850, the average mill-hand earned $175 a year, as against $300 at present, and worked thirteen hours a day as against ten hours to-day. The American farmer's daughter who worked in the cotton mills fifty years ago has been almost wholly displaced, first by women of Irish and English birth, and more recently by the French Canadian, all representing lower types. The very growth of the mills has tended to do away with certain features of factory life, that worked for good in smaller communities. In the old days, say in 1850, the American girls who made cotton cloth in Lowell, or shoes in Lynn, or thread in Manchester, had their own singing and reading societies, their benevolent clubs, and church sociables. The owner or agent of a small mill in a small town was able to exercise something of a paternal supervision over the few hundred girls or men who might work for him. With the immense increase in mill plants, the force now numbering thousands where it was hundreds fifty years ago, this is impossible. Yet, whether it be as a matter of self-interest or not, the visitor to Lowell, Manchester, Lawrence, Fall River, and other factory centers will find an attempt on the part of mill owners to help the hands after they leave the buildings. Saving societies, libraries, and hospitals are common. In Lawrence there are no less than three flourishing co-operative stores patronized exclusively by mill-hands. The rise in power of the unions seems to have made the mill-hands suspicious of all interference with matters outside the mill. One is apt to find a dozen unions in a cotton-mill, and in the shoe shops there are unions for every one of the score or more of operations through which a shoe passes. The factory law of Massachusetts prescribes that wages shall be paid weekly. This rule has been found to work rather disadvantageously so far as saving by the mill-hand goes, for, receiving no large sum of money in a lump, he finds it difficult to spare from the comparatively small weekly wage. Efforts are made almost periodically by many mill corporations to render the homes of the hands more sanitary than they were in earlier years, and attractive with gardens and flowers. In some towns, notably in Manchester, where the mill operatives number many native Americans, some success in this direction has been met with; in other towns, notably the larger centres—Lowell, Nashua, Fall River, Lawrence—where the population is either foreign-born or but one generation removed from it, not much has been effected. The hands live mostly in tenements unadorned with gardens or even grass-plats. A large number of the hands in every factory are young people who have to board, necessitating the existence in all mill towns of large rows of tenements known as boarding-houses, as a rule dreary homes inside and out. The people who live in them, looking upon themselves as temporary inmates or tenants only, cannot be induced to better their surroundings, and will decline to care for the vines and flowers offered to them by their employers. . . .

REVIEW QUESTIONS

1. In what ways does the author reveal ethnic prejudices and stereotypes?
2. What evidence does the author use to claim that discipline at the mill is lenient?
3. Are the workers described as better or worse off than their pre–Civil War predecessors?

EUGENE V. DEBS

FROM Outlook for Socialism in the United States (1900)

By the end of the nineteenth century some labor activists insisted that capitalism itself must give way to a socialist system. Eugene Debs (1855–1926) was a railroad union organizer who converted to socialism during a stint in jail. He later would run as the Socialist Party candidate for president in several elections.

From Eugene V. Debs, "Outlook for Socialism in the United States," *International Socialist Review* 1 (September 1900):129–135.

The sun of the passing century is setting upon scenes of extraordinary activity in almost every part of our capitalistic, old planet. Wars and rumors of wars are of universal prevalence . . . and through all the flame and furor of the fray can be heard the savage snarlings of the Christian "dogs of war" as they fiercely glare about them, and with jealous fury threaten to fly at one another's throats to settle the question of supremacy and the spoil and plunder of conquest. . . .

Cheerless indeed would be the contemplation of such sanguinary scenes were the light of Socialism not breaking upon mankind. . . . From out of the midnight of superstition, ignorance and slavery the disenthralling, emancipating sun is rising. I am not gifted with prophetic vision, and yet I see the shadows vanishing. I behold near and far prostrate men lifting their bowed forms from the dust. I see thrones in the grasp of decay; despots relaxing their hold upon scepters, and shackles falling, not only from the limbs, but also from the souls of men. . . .

Socialists generally will agree that the past year has been marked with a propaganda of unprecedented activity and that the sentiment of the American people in respect to Socialism has undergone a most remarkable change. It would be difficult to imagine a more ignorant, bitter and unreasoning prejudice than that of the American people against Socialism during the early years of its introduction. . . .

Socialism was cunningly associated with "anarchy and bloodshed," and denounced as a "foul foreign importation" to pollute the fair, free soil of America, and every outrage to which the early agitators were subjected won the plaudits of the people. But they persevered in their task; they could not be silenced or suppressed. Slowly they increased in number and gradually the movement began to take root and spread over the country. . . .

The subject has passed entirely beyond the domain of sneer and ridicule and now commands serious treatment. Of course, Socialism is violently denounced by the capitalist press and by all the brood of subsidized contributors to magazine literature, but this only confirms the view that the advance of Socialism is very properly recognized by the capitalist class as the one cloud upon the horizon which portends an end to the system in which they have waxed fat, insolent and despotic through the exploitation of their countless wage-working slaves.

In school and college and church, in clubs and public halls everywhere, Socialism is the central theme of discussion, and its advocates, inspired by its noble principles, are to be found here, there and in all places ready to give or accept challenge to battle. In the cities the corner meetings are popular and effective. But rarely is such a gathering now molested by the "authorities," and then only where they have just been inaugurated. They are too numerously attended by serious, intelligent and self-reliant men and women to invite interference. . . .

Needless is it for me to say to the thinking workingman that he has no choice between these two capitalist parties,[1] that they are both pledged to the same system and that whether the one or the other succeeds, he will still remain the wage-working slave he is today.

What but meaningless phrases are "imperialism," "expansion," "free silver," "gold standard," etc., to the wage-worker? The large capitalists represented by Mr. McKinley and the small capitalists represented by Mr. Bryan[2] are interested in these "issues," but they do not concern the working class.

What the workingmen of the country are profoundly interested in is the private ownership of the means of production and distribution, the enslaving and degrading wage-system in which they toil for a pittance at the pleasure of their masters and are bludgeoned, jailed or shot when they protest—this is the central, controlling, vital issue of the hour, and neither of the old party platforms has a word or even a hint about it. . . .

Whether the means of production—that is to say, the land, mines, factories, machinery, etc.—are owned by a few large Republican capitalists, who organize a trust, or whether they be owned by a lot of small Democratic capitalists, who are opposed to the trust, is all the same to the working class. Let the capitalists, large and small, fight this out among themselves.

The working class must get rid of the whole brook of masters and exploiters, and put themselves in possession and control the means of production, that they may have steady employment without consulting a capitalist employer, large or small, and that they may get the wealth their labor produces, all of it, and enjoy with their families the

fruits of their industry in comfortable and happy homes, abundant and wholesome food, proper clothing and all other things necessary to "life, liberty and the pursuit of happiness." It is therefore a question not of "reform," the mask of fraud, but of revolution. The capitalist system must be overthrown, class-rule abolished and wage-slavery supplanted by cooperative industry.

We hear it frequently urged that the Democratic Party is the "poor man's party," "the friend of labor." There is but one way to relieve poverty and to free labor, and that is by making common property of the tools of labor. . . .

The differences between the Republican and Democratic parties involve no issue, no principle in which the working class has any interest. . . . For a time the Populist Party had a mission, but it is practically ended. The Democratic Party has "fused" it out of existence. The "middle-of-the-road" element will be sorely disappointed when the votes are counted, and they will probably never figure in another national campaign. Not many of them will go back to the old parties. Many of them have already come to Socialism, and the rest are sure to follow.

There is no longer any room for a Populist Party, and progressive Populists realize it, and hence the "strongholds of Populism" are becoming the "hot-beds" of Socialism.

It is simply a question of capitalism or Socialism, of despotism or democracy, and they who are not wholly with us are wholly against us. . . . Oh, that all the working class could and would use their eyes and see; their ears and hear; their brains and think. How soon this earth could be transformed and by the alchemy of social order made to blossom with beauty and joy.

REVIEW QUESTIONS

1. Why did Debs say that Socialists should shun both Republicans and Democrats?
2. By what means did Socialists gain power?
3. Critics then and since dismissed Socialists as utopians. Do you agree?

---

[1] Republican and Democratic.

[2] The 1896 presidential candidates, William Jennings Bryan (1860–1925) and William McKinley (1843–1901).

21 ✎ THE EMERGENCE OF URBAN AMERICA

During the second half of the nineteenth century, two revolutions—the scientific and the urban-industrial—transformed social and intellectual life. The prestige of science increased enormously as researchers announced a dazzling array of new discoveries. Remarkable new technological developments—the telegraph, railroad, and electric dynamos and lights—and spectacular achievements in industrial engineering such as the Brooklyn Bridge and majestic skyscrapers provided conspicuous physical evidence of the transforming effects of science and engineering.

Modern scientists opened up a gulf of doubt about many inherited truths and spiritual convictions. When the English biologist Charles Darwin published On the Origin of Species *in 1859, the* New York Times *reported that the book contained "arguments and inferences so revolutionary" that they promised "a radical reconstruction of the fundamental doctrines of natural history." Darwin's provocative thesis argued that the "modification" of species occurred through a ceaseless process of "natural selection." This challenged the biblical story of all animal species originating in an act of divine creation that forever fixed their forms. In Darwin's world, new species were not "special creations" of God; they emerged randomly from the struggle for existence. Natural selection, he implied, was arbitrary, capricious, and devoid of ultimate meaning—a long, gradual process of intense competition and hereditary development without divine plan or purpose.*

Darwin's concept of evolutionary change challenged established beliefs about nature and about providential design and life processes. "If this be truth," growled one college president, "let me live in ignorance." As time passed, however, more and more people accepted many aspects of evolutionary naturalism. "This scientific current," a writer in the North American Review *concluded, "is moving more or less all schools of thought." Sociologists such as William Graham Sumner promoted what came to be called social Darwinism, arguing that just as "survival of the fittest" was the balancing mechanism in the natural world, so, too, should unfettered competition and free enterprise determine the fate of human society.*

While Darwinism and modern science were overturning traditional beliefs, an ever-accelerating urban-industrial revolution was transforming social life. In 1860 there were but sixteen cities in the United States with populations over 50,000; in 1910 there were well over eighty. Between 1870 and 1920 almost 11 million Americans left farms and rural villages for the excitement and energy of the cities, and even more urban newcomers arrived from abroad. Wave after wave of foreigners flowed into American cities, and the immigrants tended to come from eastern and southern Europe and Asia rather than Britain and western Europe. This so-called new immigration generated ethnic and religious tensions that prompted efforts to restrict the flow of "strange" newcomers.

By the end of the nineteenth century, commentators were expressing concerns not only about the influx of "aliens," but also about the debilitating effects of rapid urban development and rising prosperity. The industrial revolution had brought spreading material comforts, yet it also fostered moral complacency and even "decadence." Many observers feared that city-dwelling men, who now worked in offices rather than on farms, were losing their virility. As "the rich become effeminate, weak, and immoral," a prominent doctor claimed, the "lower classes, taking advantage of this moral lassitude, and led on by their savage inclinations, undertake strikes, boycotts and riots." Another concerned observer claimed that most middle-class businessmen "have bodies that disgrace them. Everywhere you see fat, clumsy, unsightly bodies; stooped, flabby, feeble bodies."

Theodore Roosevelt shared such anxieties and led a national movement promoting a "strenuous life" for Americans in an effort to revive masculine virtues. He and others touted vigorous exercise and combative sports as an especially powerful antidote to urban ills. "Physical exercise," declared the publisher of Physical Culture Magazine, "is destined to effect the regeneration of the Caucasian race." Through athletic participation, another sports advocate insisted, young men develop "all the 'manly' attributes—glorious strength and skill and endurance."

Football became an especially popular instrument of revived manhood. The novelist Willa Cather observed that intercollegiate athletics were "the one resisting force that curbs the growing tendencies toward effeminacy" among young American men. Football, she added, was especially rejuvenating because it "is a game of blood and muscle and fresh air." By the end of the nineteenth century, virtually all high schools and colleges sponsored football teams.

JOSIAH STRONG

FROM *Our Country* (1885)

During the so-called Gilded Age, many social commentators worried about the effects of unchecked urban development. Josiah Strong, a prominent Congregationalist minister from Ohio, was among the most concerned. In 1885 he published Our Country, *a comprehensive critique of modern developments. Strong viewed large cities as a menace to morals and to the social order. He also feared that the tenor of urban culture warred against the teachings of Christianity.*

From Josiah Strong, *Our Country: Its Possible Future and Its Present Crisis* (New York: The American Home Missionary Society, 1885), pp. 128–143.

The city is the nerve center of our civilization. It is also the storm center. The fact, therefore, that it is growing much more rapidly than the whole population is full of significance. In 1790, one-thirtieth of the population of the United States lived in cities of 8,000 inhabitants and over; in 1800, one twenty-fifth; in 1810, and also in 1820, one-twentieth; in 1830, one sixteenth; in 1840, one-twelfth; in 1850, one-eighth; in 1860, one-sixth; in 1870, a little over one-fifth; and in 1880, 22.5 per cent, or nearly one-fourth. From 1790 to 1880 the whole population increased a little less than four fold, the urban population thirteen fold. . . . In 1790 there were only six cities in the United States which had a population of 8,000 or more. In 1880 there were 286.

The city has become a serious menace to our civilization. . . . It has a peculiar attraction for the immigrant. Our fifty principal cities contain 39.3 per cent of our entire German population, and 45.8 per cent of the Irish. Our ten larger cities only nine per cent of the entire population, but 23 per cent of the foreign. While a little less than one-third of the population of the United States is foreign by birth or parentage, sixty-two per cent of the population of Cincinnati are foreign, eighty-three per cent of Cleveland, sixty-three per cent of Boston, eighty-eight per cent of New York, and ninety-one per cent of Chicago.

Because our cities are so largely foreign, Romanism[1] finds in them its chief strength. For the same reason the saloon, together with the intemperance and the liquor power which it represents, is multiplied in the city. East of the Mississippi there was, in 1880, one saloon to every 438 of the population; in Boston, one to every 329; in Cleveland, one to every 192; in Chicago, one to every 179; in New York, one to every 171; in Cincinnati, one to every 124. Of course the demoralizing and pauperizing power of the saloons and their debauching influence in politics increase with their numerical strength.

It is the city where wealth is massed; and here are the tangible evidences of it piled many stories high. Here the sway of Mammon[2] is widest, and his worship the most constant and eager. Here are luxuries gathered—everything that dazzles the eye, or tempts the appetite; here is the most extravagant expenditure. Here, also, is the *congestion* of wealth severest. Dives and Lazarus[3] are brought face to

---

[1] Roman Catholicism.

[2] The false god of riches in the New Testament.

[3] Dives was the rich man in the biblical parable of Lazarus, the diseased beggar.

face; here, in sharp contrast, are the *ennui* of sur-
feit and the desperation of starvation. The rich are
richer, and the poor are poorer, in the city than
elsewhere; and, as a rule, the greater are the riches
of the rich and the poverty of the poor. Not only
does the proportion of the poor increase with the
growth of the city, but their condition becomes
more wretched. The poor of a city with 8,000 inhabitants are well off compared with many in New
York; and there are no such depths of woe, such utter and heart-wringing wretchedness in New York
as in London. . . .

Socialism not only centers in the city, but is
almost confined to it; and the materials of its
growth are multiplied with the growth of the city.
Here is heaped the social dynamite; here roughs,
gamblers, thieves, robbers, lawless and desperate
men of all sorts, congregate; men who are ready
on any pretext to raise riots for the purpose of
destruction and plunder; here gather foreigners
and wage-workers; here skepticism and irreligion
abound; here inequality is the greatest and most
obvious, and the contrast between opulence and
penury the most striking; here is suffering the sor-
est. As the greatest wickedness in the world is to
be found not among the cannibals of some far
off coast, but in Christian lands where the light
of truth is diffused and rejected, so the utmost
depth of wretchedness exists not among savages,
who have few wants, but in great cities, where, in
the presence of plenty and of every luxury men
starve. . . .

"During the past three years, 220,976 persons
in New York have asked for outside aid in one form
or another." Said a New York Supreme judge, not
long since: "There is a large class—I was about to
say a majority—of the population of New York
area Brooklyn, who just live, and to whom the rearing of two or more children means inevitably a boy
for the penitentiary, and a girl for the brothel." Under such conditions smolder the volcanic fires of a
deep discontent.

As a rule, our largest cities are the worst governed. It is natural, therefore, to infer that, as our
cities grow larger and more dangerous, the government will become more corrupt, and control will

pass more completely into the hands of those
who themselves most need to be controlled. If we
would appreciate the significance of these facts and
tendencies, we must bear in mind that the disproportionate growth of the city is undoubtedly to
continue, and the number of great cities to be
largely increased. . . .

But the supreme peril, which will certainly
come, eventually, and must probably be faced by
multitudes now living, will arise, when, the conditions having been fully prepared, some great industrial or other crisis precipitates an open
struggle between the destructive and the conservative elements of society. As civilization advances,
and society becomes more highly organized, commercial transactions will be more complex and
immense. As a result, all business relations and
industries will be more sensitive. Commercial distress in any great business center will the more
surely create widespread disaster. Under such conditions, industrial paralysis is likely to occur from
time to time, more general and more prostrating
than any heretofore known. When such a commercial crisis has closed factories by the ten thousand, and wageworkers have been thrown out of
employment by the million; when the public lands,
which hitherto at such times have afforded relief,
are all exhausted; when our urban population has
been multiplied several fold; and our Cincinnatis
have become Chicagos, our Chicagos and our New
Yorks, Londons; when class antipathies are deepened; when socialistic organizations, armed and
drilled, are in every city, and the ignorant and vicious power of crowded populations has fully
found itself; when the corruption of city governments is grown apace; when crops fail, or some gigantic "corner" doubles the price of bread; with
starvation in home; with idle workingmen gathered, sullen and desperate, in the saloons with un-
protected wealth at hand; with the tremendous
forces of chemistry within easy reach; then with *the
opportunity, the means, the fit agents; the motive, the
temptation to destroy, all brought into evil conjunction,* THEN will come the real test of our institutions, then will appear whether we are capable of
self-government.

REVIEW QUESTIONS

1. Why do you think Strong was concerned that immigrants comprised such a high percentage of urban dwellers?

2. What kinds of problems did the disparity of wealth create in cities?

3. What forces did Strong overlook as possible causes for urban woes?

ADNA FERRIN WEBER

FROM *The Growth of Cities in the Nineteenth Century* (1899)

The modern city had its defenders during the nineteenth century. The following excerpt, from a pioneering study in urban sociology, applied Charles Darwin's concept of natural selection to "document" the advantages of urban life over rural life.

From Adna Ferrin Weber, *The Growth of Cities in the Nineteenth Century: A Study in Statistics* (New York: Macmillan, 1899), pp. 218–222, 439–442, 444–445.

. . . SOCIAL CAUSES—To enumerate the social advantages that the cities possess as compared with the country would demand too much space, but most of them will be found to be embraced in the following classification:

1) Educational. The city alone must be the residence of those who study art, medicine, music, etc. Even in the matter of primary education, city advantages are superior to those of the rural districts, though not to those of the villages. . . .

2) Amusements. The opera, philharmonic concerts, art exhibits, etc., may be classed as educational advantages or mere amusements, but there are many other forms of recreation afforded by the city and not by the country, which come under the head of amusements alone.

3) The standard of living. The desire for a higher standard of life, for purely material comforts and luxuries, brings many people to the city. Food is to be procured at prices almost as low as in the country, and in vastly greater variety; while everything else is cheaper. The buyer enjoys a larger consumer's rent, as the economists say; that is, he can buy at prices much below those he would be willing to give if pressed, thus deriving a surplus of enjoyment. Then there are conveniences to be had, in the city which in many cases could not be obtained in the country, on account of the small numbers to bear the heavy expenses.

4) Intellectual Associations. The village is dull not only to the man pursuing light amusements, but to him who seeks cultivated associations, for in these days the cities are the centers of intellect as of wealth. Even the

college town with its intellectual atmosphere is to many high-minded people less stimulating than the city, where intellectual ability is much more varied.

Such are some of the advantages of city life; some of them are modern, and some are as old as civilization. Not the least important factor in city growth is gregariousness or the social instinct itself, which appears to be stronger than ever before in these days of restlessness. . . . Another thing to be reckoned with is the passion for "the crowd, the hum, the shock of men," among those who have once lived in the city. One of the trying difficulties of social workers in their efforts to improve the housing conditions of the tenement population is the strong desire of these poor people to be among their associates, and their absolute refusal to settle in more comfortable homes in the country or in the suburbs.

*   *   *

Finally, we have to take into consideration the forces which in recent times have spread a knowledge of the advantages of city life among all classes of the community. Education has a great deal to do with it, especially the half-education which prevails in the rural districts and gives the farmers' boys a glimpse of a more attractive life, without teaching them how to attain such a life at home. Then the newspaper comes in to complete the enchantment, with its gibes against the "hayseed" and "country bumpkin." Thus the spread of information, made possible by nineteenth-century improvements in communication, creates a distaste for country life, and more especially for rural life; while easier travel enables young men lightly to abandon the distasteful life. . . .

Socially, the influence of the cities is similarly exerted in favor of liberal and progressive thought. The variety of occupation, interests and opinions in the city produces an intellectual friction, which leads to a broader and freer judgment and a great inclination to and appreciation of new thought, manners, and ideals. City life may not have produced genius, but it has brought thinkers into touch

with one another, and has stimulated the divine impulse to originate by sympathy or antagonism. As the seat of political power, as the nursery of the arts and sciences, as the center of industry and commerce, the city represents the highest achievements of political, intellectual and industrial life.

The rural population is not merely conservative; it is full of error and prejudice; it receives what enlightenment it possesses from the city. Nor is the small city free from the same reproach; while it performs the useful function of an intermediary between the progressivism, liberalism, radicalism of the great city, and the conservatism, bigotry, of the country, it is the chief seat of the pseudo-bourgeois Philistine. . . . Americans of the present generation are destined to see this provincialism vanish before the powerful influences of large cities, which the introduction of manufactures and commerce on a large scale will in a short time produce. The South will be brought into contact with the current of world-thought. To the negro, race justice will at length be accorded, and a stronger feeling of fraternity toward the North will grow up, strengthening the bonds of patriotism.

*   *   *

The city is the spectroscope of society; it analyzes and sifts the population, separating and classifying the diverse elements. The entire progress of civilization is a process of differentiation, and the city is the greatest differentiator. The mediocrity of the country is transformed by the city into the highest talent or the lowest criminal. Genius is often born in the country, but it is brought to light and developed by the city. On the other hand, the opportunities of the city work just as powerfully in the opposite direction upon the countrymen of an ignoble cast; the boy thief of the village becomes the daring bank robber of the metropolis. . . .

. . . . Even if the "fittest" members of society did perish earlier in the struggle for existence in the city than in the country, it would be open to doubt if society would not gain more by their residence in the city where they can find scope for their abilities than in the country without opportunities for performing the highest social service of which they are capable. But with the modern combination of city business life and rural residence, or at least open-air holidays and recreation periods, and the opportunities that cities alone offer for the carrying on of athletic sports and games, the best blood of the race is not liable to extinction.

REVIEW QUESTIONS

1. Describe some of the "social advantages" offered by cities.
2. What did Weber mean when he wrote that the "rural population" is "full of error and prejudice"?
3. Why did Weber claim that some of the implicit dangers of city life were not really serious concerns?

THEODORE DREISER

The Lure of the City (1900)

The migration of millions of Americans from farms and villages to large cities prompted many writers to center their novels on the process of urbanization. Theodore Dreiser, for instance, believed that "going to the city" is one of the most powerful desires in human experience. "To join in the great, hurrying throng; to see the endless lights, the great shops and stores, the towering structures and palatial mansions, becomes a desire which the mind can scarcely resist." In Sister Carrie *(1900), Dreiser described the powerful lure of city life and urban pleasures to young people from the countryside. As the novel opens, eighteen-year-old Carrie Meeber leaves Columbia City, her small rural hometown, to pursue her fortune in Chicago and later in New York City.*

From Theodore Dreiser, *Sister Carrie* (1900; New York: W. W. Norton, 1970), pp. 6–7, 11–13. [Editorial insertions appear in square brackets—*Ed.*]

To the child, the genius with imagination, or the wholly untravelled, the approach to a great city for the first time is a wonderful thing. Particularly if it be evening—that mystic period between the glare and gloom of the world when life is changing from one sphere or condition to another. Ah, the promise of the night. What does it not hold for the weary! What old illusion of hope is not here forever repeated! Says the soul of the toiler to itself, "I shall soon be free. I shall be in the ways and the hosts of the merry. The streets, the lamps, the lighted chamber set for dining, are for me. The theatre, the halls, the parties, the ways of rest and the paths of song—these are mine in the night." Though all humanity be still enclosed in the shops, the thrill runs abroad. It is in the air. The dullest feel something which they may not always express or describe. It is the lifting of the burden of toil. . . .

Before following her in her round of seeking [a job], let us look at the sphere in which her future was to lie. In 1889 Chicago had the peculiar qualifications of growth which made such adventuresome pilgrimages even on the part of young girls plausible. Its many and growing commercial opportunities gave it widespread fame, which made of it a giant magnet, drawing to itself, from all quarters, the hopeful and the hopeless—those who had their fortune yet to make and those whose fortunes and affairs had reached a disastrous climax elsewhere. It was a city of over 500,000, with the ambition, the daring, [and] the activity of a metropolis of a million. Its streets and houses were already scattered over an area of seventy-five square miles. Its population was not so much thriving upon established commerce as upon the industries which prepared for the arrival of others. The sound of the hammer engaged upon the erection of new structures was everywhere heard. Great industries were moving in. The huge railroad corporations which had long before recognized the prospects of the place had seized upon vast tracts of land for transfer and shipping purposes. Street-car lines had been extended far out into the open country in anticipation of rapid growth. The city had laid miles and miles of streets and sewers through regions where, perhaps, one solitary house stood out alone—a pioneer of the populous ways to be. There were regions open to the sweeping winds and rain, which were yet lighted throughout the night with long, blinking lines of gas-lamps, fluttering in the wind. Narrow board walks extended out, passing here a house, and there a store, at far intervals, eventually ending on the open prairie.

In the central portion was the vast wholesale and shopping district, to which the uninformed seeker for work usually drifted. It was a characteristic of Chicago then, and one not generally shared by other cities, that individual firms of any pretension occupied individual buildings. The presence of ample ground made this possible. It gave an imposing appearance to most of the wholesale houses, whose offices were upon the ground floor and in plain view of the street. The large plates of window glass, now so common, were then rapidly coming into use, and gave to the ground floor offices a distinguished and prosperous look. The casual wanderer could see as he passed a polished array of office fixtures, much frosted glass, clerks hard at work, and genteel businessmen in "nobby" suits and clean linen lounging about or sitting in groups. Polished brass or nickel signs at the square stone entrances announced the firm and the nature of the business in rather neat and reserved terms. The entire metropolitan centre possessed a high and mighty air calculated to overawe and abash the common applicant, and to make the gulf between poverty and success seem both wide and deep.

Into this important commercial region the timid Carrie went. She walked east along Van Buren Street through a region of lessening importance, until it deteriorated into a mass of shanties and coal-yards, and finally verged upon the river. She walked bravely forward, led by an honest desire to find employment and delayed at every step by the interest of the unfolding scene, and a sense of helplessness amid so much evidence of power and force which she did not understand. These vast buildings, what were they? These strange energies and huge interests, for what purposes were they there? She could have understood the meaning of a little stone-cutter's yard at Columbia City, carving little pieces of marble for individual use, but when the yards of some huge stone corporation came into view, filled with spur tracks and flat cars, transpierced by docks from the river and traversed overhead by immense trundling cranes of wood and steel, it lost all significance in her little world.

It was so with the vast railroad yards, with the crowded array of vessels she saw at the river, and the huge factories over the way, lining the water's edge. Through the open windows she could see the figures of men and women in working aprons, moving busily about. The great streets were wall-lined mysteries to her; the vast offices, strange mazes which concerned far-off individuals of importance. She could only think of people connected with them as counting money, dressing magnificently, and riding in carriages. What they dealt in, how they labored, to what end it all came, she had only the vaguest conception. It was all wonderful, all vast, all far removed, and she sank in spirit inwardly and fluttered feebly at the heart as she thought of entering any one of these mighty concerns and asking for something to do—something that she could do—anything.

1. How does Dreiser describe the lure of the city that Carrie and other migrants from the countryside felt?
2. In what ways does Dreiser suggest that the appeal of urban culture is superficial?

ROYAL MELENDY

Saloon Culture (1900)

During the second half of the nineteenth century, the most popular places for working-class Americans to spend their free time were saloons and dance halls. Saloons were the poor man's social clubs. By the end of the nineteenth century, there were more saloons in the United States than there were grocery stores and meat markets. New York City alone had ten thousand saloons in 1900, or one for every five hundred residents. Critics claimed that saloons aggravated an array of social problems such as alcoholism, family abuse, and absenteeism. Researchers, however, reported that saloons served important social roles. They were in effect public homes, offering haven and fellowship to people who often worked ten hours a day, six days a week. The following article by sociologist Royal Melendy reveals how the saloons in Chicago met a range of social, economic, and cultural needs.

From Royal Melendy, from "The Saloon in Chicago," *The American Journal of Sociology,* 6 (November 1900):289–306.

The popular conception of the saloon as a "place where men and women revel in drunkenness and shame," or "where the sotted beasts gather nightly at the bar," is due to exaggerated pictures, drawn by temperance lecturers and evangelists, intended to excite the imagination with a view to arousing public sentiment. I am not charging them with intended falsehood, but with placing in combination things which never so exist in real life; with blending into one picture hideous incidents taken here and there from the lives of those whom the saloon has wrecked; with

portraying vividly the dark side of saloon life and calling this picture "the saloon."

. . . The term "saloon" is too general to admit of concise definition. It is an institution grown up among the people, not only in answer to their demand for its wares, but to their demand for certain necessities and conveniences, which it supplies, either alone or better than any other agency. It is a part of the neighborhood, which must change with the neighborhood; it fulfills in it the social functions which unfortunately have been left to it to exercise. With keen insight into human nature and into the wants of the people, it anticipates all other agencies in supplying them, and thus claims its right to existence. In some sections of the city it has the appearance of accomplishing more for the laboring classes from business interests than we from philanthropic motives. The almost complete absence of those things with which the uninitiated are accustomed to associate the drinking of liquor, and the presence of much that is in itself beneficial, often turns them into advocates of the saloon as a social necessity—an equally false position.

Hedged in on every side by law, opposed by every contrivance the mind of man could invent, the saloon persists in existing and flourishing—"it spreadeth like a green bay tree." The very fact of its persistence ought to cause us to realize that we have not yet struck at the root. The saloon in Chicago is restricted by every kind of law, yet it sells liquor to minors, keeps open door all night and Sundays, from January 1 to January 1. True, some of the down-town saloons close at 12 o'clock. But why? In obedience to the ordinance filed away in the archives of the city hall? Not so; but in obedience to another law—the law of demand. Those who in the daytime patronize the down-town saloons have returned to their homes and have joined the patrons of the saloons of their immediate neighborhoods. This is the law—and almost the only law that they will obey, and it is this law that we must face and deal with unflinchingly.

THE SALOON IN WORKINGMEN'S DISTRICTS.

When the poor, underpaid, and unskilled laborer returns from his day's work, go with him, if you will, into the room or rooms he calls "home." Eat with him there, in the midst of those squalid surroundings and to the music of crying children, a scanty, poorly cooked meal served by an unkempt wife. Ask yourself if this is just the place where he would want to spend his evenings, night after night; if here he will find the mental stimulus as necessary to his life as to your life. Is there no escape from the inevitable despair that must come to him whose long hours of heavy physical labor preclude any mental enjoyment, if his few leisure hours are to be spent in the wretched surroundings

of a home, or, worse yet, of the ordinary cheap lodging-house, either of which must constantly remind him of his poverty? Are there not places in the neighborhood where the surroundings will be more congenial; where his mental, yes, his moral, nature will have a better chance for development? Are there not some in the neighborhood who have recognized and sought to satisfy the social cravings of these men, which the home at best does not wholly satisfy?

Yes, business interests have occupied this field. With a shrewd foresight, partially due to the fierce competition between the great brewing companies, they have seen and met these needs. The following table, made by a careful investigation of each of the 163 saloons of the seventeenth ward—a fairly representative ward of the working people—shows some of the attractions offered by these saloons:

Number of saloons 163
Number offering free lunches 111
Number offering business lunches 24
Number offering newspapers 139
Number offering music 8
Number offering billiard tables 44
Number offering stalls 56
Number offering dance halls 6
Number allowing gambling 3

In the statement, now current among those who have studied the saloon "at first hand," that it is the workingman's club, lies the secret of its hold upon the vast working and voting populace of Chicago. . . . As you step in, you find a few men standing at the bar, a few drinking, and farther back men are seated about the tables, reading, playing cards, eating, and discussing, over a glass of beer, subjects varying from the political and sociological problems of the day to the sporting news and the lighter chat of the immediate neighborhood. Untrammeled by rules and restrictions, it surpasses in spirit the organized club. That general atmosphere of freedom, that spirit of democracy, which men crave, is here realized; that men seek it and that the saloon tries to cultivate it is blazoned forth in such titles as "The Freedom," "The Social,"

"The Club," etc. Here men "shake out their hearts together." Intercourse quickens the thought, feeling, and action. . . .

This is the workingman's school. He is both scholar and teacher. The problems of national welfare are solved here. Many as patriotic men as our country produces learn here their lessons in patriotism and brotherhood. Here the masses receive their lessons in civil government, learning less of our ideals, but more of the practical workings than the public schools teach. It is the most cosmopolitan institution in the most cosmopolitan of cities. One saloon advertises its cosmopolitanism by this title, "Everybody's Exchange." Men of all nationalities meet and mingle, and by the interchange of views and opinions their own are modified. Nothing short of travel could exert so broadening an influence upon these men. It does much to assimilate the heterogeneous crowds that are constantly pouring into our city from foreign shores. But here, too, they learn their lessons in corruption and vice. It is their school for good and evil.

The saloonkeeper, usually a man their superior in intelligence, often directs their thought. He has in his possession the latest political and sporting news. Here in argument each has fair play. He who can win and tell the best story is, not by election, but by virtue of fitness, the leader. The saloon is, in short, the clearing-house for the common intelligence—the social and intellectual center of the neighborhood.

Again, some saloons offer rooms furnished, heated, and lighted, free to certain men's clubs and organizations. For example, a certain German musical society, occupying one of these rooms, fully compensates the saloonkeeper with the money that passes over the bar as the members go in and out of the club-room. In like manner some trade unions and fraternal organizations are supplied with meeting-places. A saloon on Armitage Avenue has a bowling-alley, billiard tables, and club-rooms, in which nonpartisan political meetings were held during last spring's campaign. It is also offered to the people for various neighborhood meetings. In such a room a gay wedding party celebrated the

marriage vow. It is, in very truth, a part of the life of the people of this district.

But the young man, where does he spend his evenings? Leaving the supper table he takes his hat and sets out from home, to go where? Let us follow the boy in the crowded districts—in the river wards of Chicago. As he comes out of the house into the street he is surrounded for miles with brick and mortar; not a blade of grass or a leaf of green to be seen. Placing his fingers to his mouth he gives a shrill whistle, which is answered by one and another of the boys, till the little crowd—their club—has gathered. Seeking to join informally such a crowd of the older young men, the only question asked on eligibility was: "Can you run?" Short words, but of tremendous significance. It is this: As soon as a small crowd of boys collects it is dispersed by the police. Having been arrested once or twice, these young men learned the lesson, and I was told "to scatter" at the word "jiggers," the warning note given at the sight of an approaching "cop." Driven about the streets like dogs by the civil authorities (whether it be necessary I am not now discussing); provided with no place for the healthy exercise of their physical natures, or even an opportunity to meet and tell stories, they have recourse to but one of two alternatives: to dodge the police, hiding in underground caves and under sidewalks until they become hardened against the law; or to enter the places the saloon has provided for them.

Thus again business interests have seized the opportunity that has been let slip, and have taken advantage of boys' necessities. Rooms, well lighted, furnished with billiard and pool tables, tables for cards and other games, are placed at the disposal of these boys. Five cents is charged for a game of billiards and a check which entitles the holder to a glass of beer, a five-cent cigar, a box of cigarettes, or a soft drink. The table shows 27 per cent of these saloons thus equipped. Much less numerous are the saloons furnishing handball courts. These courts, models of attractiveness when compared with the neighborhood in which they are located, are used by young and old. Shower-baths are provided free. The boys must pass out by the bar of the adjoining saloon, where, heated by the game and feeling somewhat under obligations, they patronize the saloonkeeper. Some saloons have gymnasiums, more or less fully equipped. Bowling-alleys and shuffle-board are among the attractions offered.

For the large floating population of these districts, and for the thousands of men whose only home is in the street or the cheap lodging-house, where they are herded together like cattle, the saloon is practically the basis of food supply. The table shows that 68 per cent furnish free lunches, and 15 per cent business lunches. On the free-lunch counters are dishes containing bread, several kinds of meats, vegetables, cheeses, etc., to which the men freely help themselves. Red-hots (Frankfurters), clams, and egg sandwiches are dispensed with equal freedom to those who drink and to those who do not. For those desiring a hot lunch, clam chowder, hot potatoes, several kinds of meat, and vegetables are served at tables, nearly always with a glass of beer. . . .

While it is true that a vast army of the laboring men and boys find the saloon the best place in their neighborhood for the development of their social, intellectual, and physical natures, they find there also things which appeal to their lower natures. Almost without exception the saloons exhibit pictures of the nude; in the higher-class saloons by costly paintings, in the smaller saloons by cards furnished by the brewing companies. As the saloon is "no respecter of persons," even in the best of them vile persons find entrance. That the youths are here corrupted is too well known. . . .

REVIEW QUESTIONS

1. In addition to alcohol, what services did saloons provide their patrons?
2. What roles did the saloonkeeper play in addition to bartender?
3. Why have saloons declined in importance?

WILLIAM GRAHAM SUMNER

FROM The Absurd Effort to Make the World Over (1883)

The concept of the survival of the fittest as embodied in Darwinism captured the imagination of a new generation of social scientists after the Civil War. Led by Yale sociologist William Graham Sumner (1840–1910), these "social Darwinists" applied evolutionary theory to the operations of human society. In the following selection, Sumner invokes Darwin's ideas in order to criticize efforts by reformers to intervene in the social process. To Sumner, modern industrial development represented the "natural" evolution of society, and any effort to intervene in this process was therefore misguided.

From William Graham Sumner, *War and Other Essays* (New Haven, CT: 1911), pp. 195–210.

The burden of proof is on those who affirm that our social condition is utterly diseased and in need of radical regeneration! My task at present, therefore, is entirely negative and critical: to examine the allegations of fact and the doctrines which are put forward to prove the correctness of the diagnosis and to warrant the use of the remedies proposed.

The propositions put forward by social reformers nowadays are chiefly of two kinds. There are assertions in historical form, chiefly in regard to the comparison of existing with earlier social states, which are plainly based on defective historical knowledge, or at most on current stock historical dicta which are uncritical and incorrect. Writers very often assert that something never existed before because they do not know that it ever existed before, or that something is worse than ever before because they are not possessed of detailed information about what has existed before.

The other class of propositions consists of dogmatic statements which, whether true or not, are unverifiable. This class of propositions is the pest and bane of current economic and social discussion. Upon a more or less superficial view of some phenomenon a suggestion arises which is embodied in a philosophical proposition and promulgated as a truth. From the form and nature of such propositions they can always be brought under the head of "ethics." This word at least gives them an air of elevated sentiment and purpose, which is the only warrant they possess. It is impossible to test or verify them by any investigation or logical process whatsoever. It is therefore very difficult for anyone who feels a high responsibility for historical statements, and who absolutely rejects any statement which is unverifiable, to find a common platform for discussion or to join issue satisfactorily in taking the negative.

When anyone asserts that the class of skilled and unskilled manual laborers of the United States is worse off now in respect to diet, clothing, lodgings, furniture, fuel, and lights; in respect to the age at which they can marry; the number of children they can provide for; the start in life which they can give to their children, and their chances of ac-cumulating capital, than they ever have been at any former time, he makes a reckless assertion for which no facts have been offered in proof. Upon an appeal to facts, the contrary of this assertion would be clearly established. It suffices, therefore, to challenge those who are responsible for the assertion to make it good.

If it is said that the employed class are under much more stringent discipline than they were thirty years ago or earlier, it is true. It is not true that there has been any qualitative change in this respect within thirty years, but it is true that a movement which began at the first settlement of the country has been advancing with constant acceleration and has become a noticeable feature within our time.

This movement is the advance in the industrial organization. The first settlement was made by agriculturists, and for a long time there was scarcely any organization. There were scattered farmers, each working for himself, and some small towns with only rudimentary commerce and handicrafts. As the country has filled up, the arts and professions have been differentiated and the industrial organization has been advancing.

This fact and its significance has hardly been noticed at all; but the stage of the industrial organization existing at any time, and the rate of advance in its development, are the absolutely controlling social facts. Nine-tenths of the socialistic and semi-socialistic, and sentimental or ethical, suggestions by which we are overwhelmed come from failure to understand the phenomena of the industrial organization and its expansion. It controls us all because we are all in it. It creates the conditions of our existence, sets the limits of our social activity, regulates the bonds of our social relations, determines our conceptions of good and evil, suggests our life-philosophy, molds our inherited political institutions, and reforms the oldest and toughest customs, like marriage and property.

I repeat that the turmoil of heterogeneous and antagonistic social whims and speculations in which we live is due to the failure to understand what the industrial organization is and its all-pervading control over human life, while the traditions of our school of philosophy lead us always to approach the industrial organization, not from the side of objective study, but from that of philosophical doctrine. Hence it is that we find that the method of measuring what we see happening by what are called ethical standards, and of proposing to attack the phenomena by methods thence deduced, is so popular.

*   *   *

All organization implies restriction of liberty. The gain of power is won by narrowing individual range. The methods of business in colonial days were loose and slack to an inconceivable degree. The movement of industry has been all the time toward promptitude, punctuality, and reliability. It has been attended all the way by lamentations about the good old times; about the decline of small industries; about the lost spirit of comradeship between employer and employee; about the narrowing of the interests of the workman; about his conversion into a machine or into a "ware," and about industrial war.

These lamentations have all had reference to unquestionable phenomena attendant on advancing organization. In all occupations the same movement is discernible—in the learned professions, in schools, in trade, commerce, and transportation. It is to go on faster than ever, now that the continent is filled up by the first superficial layer of population over its whole extent and the intensification of industry has begun. The great inventions both make the intention of the organization possible and make it inevitable, with all its consequences, whatever they may be.

I must expect to be told here, according to the current fashions of thinking, that we ought to control the development of the organization. The first instinct of the modern man is to get a law passed to forbid or prevent what, in his wisdom, he disapproves. A thing which is inevitable, however, is one which we cannot control. We have to make up our minds to it, adjust ourselves to it, and sit down to live with it. Its inevitableness may be disputed, in which case we must re-examine it; but if our analysis is correct, when we reach what is inevitable

we reach the end, and our regulations must apply to ourselves, not to the social facts.

Now the intensification of the social organization is what gives us greater social power. It is to it that we owe our increased comfort and abundance. We are none of us ready to sacrifice this. On the contrary, we want more of it. We would not return to the colonial simplicity and the colonial exiguity if we could. If not, then we must pay the price. Our life is bounded on every side by conditions. We can have this if we will agree to submit to that. In the case of industrial power and product the great condition is combination of force under discipline and strict coordination. Hence the wild language about wage-slavery and capitalistic tyranny.

In any state of society no great achievements can be produced without great force. Formerly great force was attainable only by slavery aggregating the power of great numbers of men. Roman civilization was built on this. Ours has been built on steam. It is to be built on electricity. Then we are all forced into an organization around these natural forces and adapted to the methods or their application; and although we indulge in rhetoric about political liberty, nevertheless we find ourselves bound tight in a new set of conditions, which control the modes of our existence and determine the directions in which alone economic and social liberty can go.

If it is said that there are some persons in our time who have become rapidly and in a great degree rich, it is true; it if is said that large aggregations of wealth in the control of individuals is a social danger, it is not true. . . .

If this poor old world is as bad as they say, one more reflection may check the zeal of the headlong reformer. It is at any rate a tough old world. It has taken its trend and curvature and all its twists and tangles from a long course of formation. All its wry and crooked gnarls and knobs are therefore stiff and stubborn. If we puny men by our arts can do anything at all to straighten them, it will only be by modifying the tendencies of some of the forces at work, so that, after a sufficient time, their action may be changed a little and slowly the lines of movement may be modified. This effort, however, can at most be only slight, and it will take a long time. In the meantime spontaneous forces will be at work, compared with which our efforts are like those of a man trying to deflect a river, and these forces will have changed the whole problem before our interferences have time to make themselves felt.

The great stream of time and earthly things will sweep on just the same in spite of us. It bears with it now all the errors and follies of the past, the wreckage of all the philosophies, the fragments of all the civilizations, the wisdom of all the abandoned ethical systems, the debris of all the institutions, and the penalties of all the mistakes. It is only in imagination that we stand by and look at and criticize it and plan to change it. Everyone of us is a child of his age and cannot get out of it. He is in the stream and is swept along with it. All his sciences and philosophy come to him out of it.

Therefore the tide will not be changed by us. It will swallow up both us and our experiments. It will absorb the efforts at change and take them into itself as new but trivial components, and the great movement of tradition and work will go on unchanged by our fads and schemes. The things which will change it are the great discoveries and inventions, the new reactions inside the social organism, and then changes in the earth itself on account of changes in the cosmical forces.

These causes will make of it just what, in fidelity to them, it ought to be. The men will be carried along with it and be made by it. The utmost they can do by their cleverness will be to note and record their course as they are carried along, which is what we do now, and is that which leads us to the vain fancy that we can make or guide the movement. That is why it is the greatest folly of which a man can be capable, to sit down with a slate and pencil to plan out a new social world.

REVIEW QUESTIONS

1. Why was Sumner critical of the two kinds of "propositions" put forward by social reformers?
2. Explain what Sumner meant by his statement that all "organization implies restriction of liberty".
3. Do Sumner's views reflect a sense of predestination? Explain.

The Athletic Craze (1893)

During the latter half of the nineteenth century, Americans began pursuing a variety of new leisure and recreational activities. In cities, industrial wage-earners took advantage of playgrounds, dance halls, and amusement parks. In more rural areas, "base-ball," bicycle riding, and "foot-ball" matches became favorite pastimes. While civic, religious, and business interests often sanctioned and regulated these activities, some commentators nevertheless worried that these recreations fostered inappropriate behavior and attitudes. In the excerpt below, the editors of The Nation *magazine expressed their concerns about the growing influence of team sports, especially football, on college campuses.*

From "The Athletic Craze," *The Nation* (7 December 1893):422–423.

We are glad that the Harvard Overseers have appointed a committee to investigate the game of football in its various aspects. We are also glad to learn that there is to be this winter a convention of the deities of the football world, to revise the rules, and probably abolish the "flying wedge" and other dangerous features of the present game. So far so good. But we would respectfully ask the college faculties whether they propose this winter to take any action looking to the reform of the game, and indeed all college games, on the moral side.

We refer them to some paragraphs in *Harper's Weekly* on Phillips Exeter Academy, which show the effect that the inordinate attention given to athletics in college is having on young boys in the preparatory schools. How many of them who have the size and weight qualifying to row or play football now think of the college to which they are going as a seat of learning? The practice, on the part of the athletic element in the colleges, of seeking them out, and bribing them by offers of a free education to come to one college rather than another, has become unhappily common, and has ceased to seem discreditable; that is, very young boys are invited to become professionals, and to take what is in reality a salary for acting as football players in the guise of students.

That the faculties play into the hands of these debauchers of youth by being easy with these young professionals in examinations and recitations is at least generally believed. Can nothing be done to suppress or make disgraceful this abuse of allowing professional athletes to haunt the college buildings as sham students? Is not the presence of such men at all in colleges highly demoralizing, and likely to confuse the minds of freshmen as to the ends for which colleges exist?

We are informed on good authority that Yale spent last year about $47,000 on athletics, and the team went to Springfield the other day with three drawing-room cars and fifty men as substitutes, doctors, trainers, rubbers, and cooks. The receipts from the gate-money in New York cannot have fallen far short of $50,000. It was earned by exhibiting feats of strength and agility by scholars and gentlemen before an enormous city crowd, in which the gambling fraternity and the prostitutes were very prominent.

We are not inveighing against athletic games. If the colleges were to-morrow to make football compulsory for every man in them, we should not say a word in objection. We are simply asking for moderation and decency. It seems to be the weakness of the American people to take nearly everything in "crazes." There was the greenback craze, and the silver craze, and the granger craze, and the cholera craze, and now there is the athletic craze, and the leading colleges are becoming huge training-grounds for young gladiators, around whom nearly as many spectators roar as roared in the Flavian amphitheater.

One of its worst results is, however, that it frightens "the plain people" away from the colleges. The modest father who is willing to pinch himself and wife and daughters in order to give a son a college education, is appalled by what he hears and sees of the results of a football match. Debt, drink, debauchery rise up before his mind's eye as a probable concomitant of "college training," and he decides to keep his pet lamb at home. The colleges are not drawing as they ought for this class. The wealthy men are going to them in greater and greater numbers, but it is not they who keep alive the traditions of American scholarship, or show the world what a college education can do by way of preparation for life. Of the effect on the members of the various teams of the conspicuousness in which they pass some months of every year, of the interviews, the newspaper gossip, and portraits, we will not speak, as nothing definite can be known about it. But if much remains of "the modest stillness and humility"[1] which is, the poet says, so becoming in time of peace, after training for two or three matches, they must be almost more than human.

---

[1] From William Shakespeare, *King Henry V*, 3.1.

REVIEW QUESTIONS

1. According to this excerpt, what were some of the negative aspects of college athletic programs? What do you think was meant by the plea for "moderation and decency"?

2. This selection contains gender and class assumptions about the types of individuals who were supposedly suited to attend college. What were these assumptions, and how have they changed over time?

3. Reflect on the current role of athletic programs in university life. Does this excerpt contain criticisms that are still relevant today? Explain your response.

22 ∽ GILDED AGE POLITICS AND AGRARIAN REVOLT

American political life during the last quarter of the nineteenth century has long been viewed in negative terms. Novelist Mark Twain labeled the era "The Gilded Age" because of the corrupt connections between business tycoons and political leaders. Political life during the period was preoccupied with patronage, the long-established pattern of rewarding loyal supporters with government jobs. Prominent senators such as Roscoe Conkling of New York and Benjamin Butler of Massachusetts, as well as urban bosses like New York City's William Marcy Tweed and George Washington Plunkitt, were masters of the so-called spoils system, a term derived from the saying, "To the victor belongs the spoils." They and other political "bosses" used the patronage system to reward supporters and to maintain powerful political "machines."

Eventually, however, the abuses of the spoils system sparked protests and legislation. In 1881 concerned citizens founded the National Civil Service Reform League, and in 1883 they helped push through Congress the Pendleton Civil Service Act. It created a federal civil service commission to establish job qualifications and competitive exams for a variety of government positions, thereby removing them from the patronage system.

While Republicans controlled the White House, the two major political parties were evenly balanced in the Congress. Tariff and monetary policies dominated public debate. Republicans generally supported high tariffs (taxes on imported goods) as a means of protecting American farmers and manufacturers from foreign competition. Republicans also tended to promote a conservative monetary policy based on the gold standard. To maintain its base of support among northern voters, the Grand Old Party (GOP) also consistently supported generous government pensions for Union war veterans. For their part, Democrats were more divided on such issues, with factions on opposite sides. This reflected the geographic diversity of the party. The Democrats found their reliable base of support in two contrasting regions: the rural South and the northern cities with large immigrant populations.

Unlike today, voter participation during the Gilded Age was remarkably high. Elections aroused enormous interest. Of course, women could not yet vote in national elections, and most African-American males were prevented from voting in the former Confederacy as the century came to a close. Indians and Asians were also the subjects of racial prejudice and legal discrimination. Both Native Americans and Chinese Americans were denied citizenship. The white men who did vote across the country were most keenly interested in local concerns rooted in ethnic and cultural issues such as Sunday closing laws, liquor prohibition, and immigration restriction.

The phenomenal economic development after the Civil War fostered a massive wave of foreign immigration to the United States. Europeans and Asians flocked to America in search of jobs and freedom. The massive influx eventually provoked a rising nativist sentiment to limit immigration. During the mid-nineteenth century, for instance, thousands of Chinese began streaming into the United States, most of them settling in California. Although initially encouraged to migrate to the United States, they soon found themselves the victims of violent harassment. A new California constitution drafted in 1879 included numerous anti-Chinese provisions, prohibiting them from owning land or engaging in particular professions. Courts also refused to accept testimony from Chinese. Anti-Chinese riots killed dozens of the newcomers.

By 1880 there were over 100,000 Chinese on the West Coast, and the rising numbers prompted efforts to prohibit further immigration. This culminated in the Chinese Exclusion Act of 1882, the first significant law restricting immigration into the United States. Although President Chester A. Arthur vetoed the bill, Congress passed it to protect "American" jobs and to maintain white "racial purity." The new restrictions provided a precedent for a series of laws thereafter limiting foreign access.

Perhaps the most salient political issue during the last quarter of the nineteenth century was a tension between city and country, industry and agriculture. Millions of distressed farmers during the late nineteenth century felt ignored or betrayed by the city-dominated political process. While the industrial economy and urban culture witnessed unprecedented expansion, farmers confronted a chronic boom-bust cycle characterized by falling prices, growing indebtedness and dependence on local merchants and middlemen, and the high cost of credit. In the rural South and in the Midwest, discontented farmers first formed grassroots Granges or Alliances that provided opportunities for both social recreation and political action. By the 1890s these regional efforts had combined to form a third national political party, the Populists. The new party promoted a variety of reforms and policies, but it soon fastened upon a seeming panacea: the free and unlimited coinage of silver. A massive coinage of silver, they argued, would inflate the money supply and thereby increase the prices for farm commodities, make credit cheaper, and relieve debtors of their paralyzing burdens.

In 1892 Populists participated in their first presidential elections, with candidate James B. Weaver garnering nine percent of the popular vote. A year later a sharp financial panic triggered what became the onset of the worst depression in American history up to that time. This prolonged crisis gave sudden credibility to many Populist ideas, and the free-silver crusade made inroads into the Democratic party, especially in the West and South. In 1896 the Democrats and the Populists nominated Congressman William Jennings Bryan of Nebraska to run against Republican William McKinley, thus setting the stage for one of the most important presidential elections in American history. The Republicans and McKinley emerged triumphant, but Populists succeeded in creating momentum for a more activist government in the early twentieth century.

George W. Plunkitt

A Defense of Political Graft (1905)

The most powerful political machine during the Gilded Age was Tammany Hall, an Irish-based organization that dominated New York City politics throughout the nineteenth century. It involved a network of Democratic politicians and party workers in alliance with various contractors who provided kickbacks in exchange for government favors. George Washington Plunkitt was district leader of Tammany Hall who took for granted the patronage system. In 1905 he participated in a series of interviews with a local reporter in which he defended the political machine against the criticisms of reformers.

From William Riordan, ed., *Plunkitt of Tammany Hall* (1905; New York: E. P. Dutton, 1963), pp. 3–4, 11, 12–13.

Everybody is talkin' these days about Tammany men growin' rich on graft, but nobody thinks of drawin' the distinction between honest graft and dishonest graft. There's all the difference in the world between the two. Yes, many of our men have grown rich in politics. I have myself. I've made a big fortune out of the game, and I'm gettin' richer every day, but I've not gone in for dishonest graft—blackmailin' gamblers, saloonkeepers, disorderly people, etc.—and neither has any of the men who have made big fortunes in politics.

There's an honest graft, and I'm an example of how it works. I might sum up the whole thing by sayin': "I seen my opportunities and I took 'em."

Just let me explain by examples. My party's in power in the city, and it's goin' to undertake a lot of public improvements. Well, I'm tipped off, say, that they're going to lay out a park at a certain place.

I see my opportunity and I take it. I go to that place and I buy up all the land I can in the neighborhood. Then the board of this or that makes its plan public, and there is a rush to get my land, which nobody cared particular for before.

Ain't it perfectly honest to charge a good price and make a profit on my investment and foresight? Of course, it is. Well, that's honest graft.

*   *   *

. . . This civil service law is the biggest fraud of the age. It is the curse of the nation. There can't be no real patriotism while it lasts. How are you goin' to interest our young men in their country if you have no offices to give them when they work for their party? Just look at things in this city today. There are ten thousand good offices, but we can't get at more than a few hundred of them. How are we goin' to provide for the thousands of men who worked for the Tammany ticket? It can't be done. These men were full of patriotism a short time ago. They expected to be servin' their city, but when we tell them that we can't place them [in government jobs], do you think their patriotism is goin' to last? Not much. They say: "What's the use workin' for your country anyhow? There's nothin' in the game [for us]." And what can they do? I don't know, but I'll tell you what I do know. I know more than one young man in past years who worked for the ticket and was overflowin' with patriotism, but when he was knocked out by the civil service humbug he got to hate his country and became an Anarchist.

*   *   *

When the people elected Tammany, they knew just what they were doin'. We didn't put up any false pretenses. We didn't go in for humbug civil service and all that rot. We stood as we always have stood, for rewardin' the men that won the victory. They call that the spoils system. All right: Tammany is for the spoils system, and when we go in we fire every anti-Tammany man from office that can be fired under the law. It's an elastic sort of law and you can bet it will be stretched to the limit. . . .

The civil service humbug is undermin' our institutions and if a halt ain't called soon this great republic will tumble down like a Park Avenue house when they were buildin' the subway, and on its ruins will rise another Russian government.

REVIEW QUESTIONS

1. How does Plunkitt distinguish between "honest" and "dishonest" graft? Is his distinction persuasive?
2. According to Plunkitt, what is the primary motivation behind political involvement?

Chinese Exclusion Act (1882)

The Chinese Exclusion Act of 1882 suspended all Chinese immigration for ten years and declared the Chinese ineligible for citizenship. Chinese workers already in the country challenged the constitutionality of the law, but their efforts failed. The act was renewed in 1892 for another ten years, and in 1902 Chinese immigration was permanently prohibited. Not until 1943 did Congress grant Chinese Americans eligibility for citizenship.

From *United States Statutes at Large,* 22:58ff.

An act to execute certain treaty stipulations relating to Chinese:

WHEREAS, in the opinion of the Government of the United States the coming of Chinese laborers to this country endangers the good order of certain localities within the territory thereof: Therefore, Be it enacted, That from and after the expiration of ninety days next after the passage of this act, and until the expiration of ten years next after the passage of this act, the coming of Chinese laborers to the United States be . . . suspended; and during such suspension it shall not be lawful for any Chinese laborer to come, or, having so come after the expiration of said ninety days, to remain within the United States.

* * *

SEC. 2. That the master of any vessel who shall knowingly bring within the United States on such vessel, and land or permit to be landed, any Chinese laborer, from any foreign port or place, shall be deemed guilty of a misdemeanor, and on conviction thereof shall be punished by a fine of not more than five hundred dollars for each and every such Chinese laborer so brought, and may be also imprisoned for a term not exceeding one year.

SEC. 3. That the two foregoing sections shall not apply to Chinese laborers who were in the United States on the seventeenth day of November, eighteen hundred and eighty, or who shall have come into the same before the expiration of ninety days next after the passage of this act, . . .

* * *

SEC. 6. That in order to the faithful execution of articles one and two of the treaty in this act before mentioned, every Chinese person other than a laborer who may be entitled by said treaty and this act to come within the United States, and who shall be about to come to the United States, shall be identified as so entitled by the Chinese Government in each case, such identity to be evidenced by a certificate issued under the authority of said government, which certificate shall be in the English language or (if not in the English language) accompanied by a translation into English, stating such right to come, and which certificate shall state the name, title, or official rank, if any, the age, height, and all physical peculiarities former and present occupation or profession and place of residence in China of the person to whom the certificate is issued and that such person is entitled conformably to the treaty in this act mentioned to come within the United States. . . .

* * *

SEC. 12. That no Chinese person shall be permitted to enter the United States by land without producing to the proper office of customs the certificate in this act required of Chinese persons seeking to land from a vessel. Any Chinese person found unlawfully within the United States shall be caused to be removed therefrom to the country from whence he came, by direction of the President of the United States, and at the cost of the United States, after being brought before some justice, judge, or commissioner of a court of the United States and found to be one not lawfully entitled to be or remain in the United States.

SEC. 13. That this act shall not apply to diplomatic and other officers of the Chinese Government traveling upon the business of that government, whose credentials shall be taken as equivalent to the certificate in this act mentioned, and shall exempt them and their body and household servants from the provisions of this act as to other Chinese persons.

SEC. 14. That hereafter no State court or court of the United States shall admit Chinese to citizenship; and all laws in conflict with this act are hereby repealed.

SEC. 15. That the words "Chinese laborers," whenever used in this act, shall be construed to mean both skilled and unskilled laborers and Chinese employed in mining.

REVIEW QUESTIONS

1. What do you think the phrase "endangers the good order of certain localities" meant? Do you think its vagueness was intentional?

2. What types of penalties did the act prescribe?
3. Who would have supported this legislation? Who would have opposed it?

ROBERT G. INGERSOLL

FROM Should the Chinese Be Excluded? (1893)

Among the critics of the anti-Chinese legislation, the most articulate was Illinois attorney Robert G. Ingersoll (1833–1899). The era's most eloquent orator and an outspoken agnostic, he addressed more people than any other public figure in the nineteenth century. Ingersoll was a Civil War veteran who after 1865 promoted civil rights for the freed slaves and equal rights for women. He once declared that there was "but one use for law, but one excuse for government—the preservation of liberty." In the following speech he condemned the racist attitudes that lay behind the legislation renewing the Exclusion Act in 1892, known as the Geary Act.

From Robert G. Ingersoll, "Should the Chinese Be Excluded?" *North American Review* 157 (July 1893):52–58.

The average American, like the average man of any country, has but little imagination. People who speak a different language, or worship some other god, or wear clothing unlike his own, are beyond the horizon of his sympathy. He cares but little or nothing for the sufferings or misfortunes of those who are of a different complexion or of another race. His imagination is not powerful enough to recognize the human being, in spite of peculiarities.

Instead of this he looks upon every difference as an evidence of inferiority, and for the inferior he has but little if any feeling. If these "inferior people" claim equal rights he feels insulted, and for the purpose of establishing his own superiority tramples on the rights of the so-called inferior.

In our own country the native has always considered himself as much better than the immigrant, and as far superior to all people of a different complexion. At one time our people hated the Irish, then the Germans, then the Italians, and now the Chinese. The Irish and Germans, however, became numerous. They became citizens, and, most important of all, they had votes. They combined, became powerful, and the political parties sought their aid. They had something to give in exchange for protection—in exchange for political rights. In consequence of this, they were flattered by candidates, praised by the political press, and became powerful enough not only to protect themselves, but at last to govern the principal cities in the United States. As a matter of fact the Irish and the Germans drove the native Americans out of the trades and from the lower forms of labor. They built the railways and canals. They became servants. Afterward the Irish and the Germans were driven from the canals and railways by the Italians.

The Irish and Germans improved their condition. They went into other businesses, into the higher and more lucrative trades. They entered the professions, turned their attention to politics, became merchants, brokers, and professors in colleges. They are not now building railroads or digging on public works. They are contractors, legislators, holders of office, and the Italians and Chinese are doing the old work.

If matters had been allowed to work in a natural way, without the interference of mobs or legislators, the Chinese would have driven the Italians to better employments, and all menial labor would, in time, be done by the Mongolians. . . .

In our country, as a matter of fact, there is but little prejudice against emigrants coming from Europe, except among naturalized citizens; but nearly all foreign-born citizens are united in their prejudice against the Chinese. The truth is that the Chinese came to this country by invitation. . . .

These Chinese laborers are inoffensive, peaceable and law-abiding. They are honest, keeping their contracts, doing as they agree. They are exceedingly industrious, always ready to work and always giving satisfaction to their employers. They do not interfere with other people. They cannot become citizens. They have no voice in the making or the execution of the laws. They attend to their own business. They have their own ideas, customs, religion and ceremonies—about as foolish as our own; but they do not try to make converts or to force their dogmas on others. They are patient, uncomplaining, stoical and philosophical. They earn what they can, giving reasonable value for the money they receive, and as a rule, when they have amassed a few thousand dollars, they go back to their own country. They do not interfere with our ideas, our ways or customs. They are silent workers, toiling without any object, except to do their work and get their pay. They do not establish saloons and run for Congress. Neither do they combine for the purpose of governing others. Of all the people on our soil they are the least meddlesome. Some of them smoke opium, but the opium-smoker does not beat his wife. Some of them play games of chance, but they are not members of the Stock Exchange. They eat the bread that they earn; they neither beg nor steal, but they are of no use to parties or politicians except as they become fuel to supply the flame of prejudice. They are not citizens and they cannot vote.

Their employers are about the only friends they have. In the Pacific States the lowest became their enemies and asked for their expulsion. They denounced the Chinese and those who gave them work. The patient followers of Confucius were treated as outcasts—stoned by boys in the streets and mobbed by the fathers. Few seemed to have any respect for their rights or their feelings. They were unlike us. They wore different clothes. They dressed their hair in a peculiar way, and therefore they were beyond our sympathies. These ideas, these practices, demoralized many communities; the laboring people became cruel and the small politicians infamous.

When the rights of even one human being are held in contempt the rights of all are in danger. We cannot destroy the liberties of others without losing our own. By exciting the prejudices of the ignorant we at last produce a contempt for law and justice, and sow the seeds of violence and crime. . . .

Both of the great parties ratified the outrages committed by the mobs, and proceeded with alacrity to violate the treaties and solemn obligations of the Government. These treaties were violated, these obligations were denied, and thousands of Chinamen were deprived of their rights, of their property, and hundreds were maimed or murdered. They were driven from their homes. They were hunted like wild beasts. All this was done in a country that sends missionaries to China to tell the benighted savages of the blessed religion of the United States. . . .

The idea of imprisoning a man at hard labor for a year, and this man a citizen of a friendly nation, for the crime of being found in this country without a certificate of residence, must be abhorrent to the mind of every enlightened man. Such punishment for such an "offense" is barbarous and belongs to the earliest times of which we know.

This law makes industry a crime and puts one who works for his bread on a level with thieves and the lowest criminals, treats him as a felon, and clothes him in the stripes of a convict,—and all this is done at the demand of the ignorant, of the prejudiced, of the heartless, and because the Chinese are not voters and have no political power.

The Chinese are not driven away because there is no room for them. Our country is not crowded. There are many millions of acres waiting for the plow. There is plenty of room here under our flag for five hundred millions of people. These Chinese that we wish to oppress and imprison are people who understand the art of irrigation. They can redeem the deserts. They are the best of gardeners. They are modest and willing to occupy the lowest seats.

They only ask to be day-laborers, washers and ironers. They are willing to sweep and scrub. They are good cooks. They can clear lands and build railroads. They do not ask to be masters—they wish only to serve. In every capacity they are faithful; but in this country their virtues have made enemies, and they are hated because of their patience, their honesty and their industry. . . .

*   *   *

This law is contrary to the laws and customs of nations. The punishment is unusual, severe, and contrary to our Constitution, and under its provisions aliens—citizens of a friendly nation—can be imprisoned without due process of law. The law is barbarous, contrary to the spirit and genius of American institutions, and was passed in violation of solemn treaty stipulations.

The Congress that passed it is the same that closed the gates of the World's Fair on the "blessed Sabbath," thinking it wicked to look at statues and pictures on that day. These representatives of the people seem to have had more piety than principle.

After the passage of such a law by the United States is it not indecent for us to send missionaries to China? Is there not work enough for them at home? We send ministers to China to convert the heathen; but when we find a Chinaman on our soil, where he can be saved by our example, we treat him as a criminal. It is to the interest of this country to maintain friendly relations with China. We want the trade of nearly one-fourth of the human race. . . .

After all, it pays to do right. This is a hard truth to learn—especially for a nation. A great nation should be bound by the highest conception of justice and honor. Above all things it should be true to its treaties, its contracts, its obligations. It should remember that its responsibilities are in accordance with its power and intelligence.

Our Government is founded on the equality of human rights—on the idea, the sacred truth, that all are entitled to life, liberty and the pursuit of happiness. Our country is an asylum for the oppressed of all nations—of all races. Here, the Government gets its power from the consent of the governed. After the abolition of slavery these great truths were not only admitted, but they found expression in our Constitution and laws. Shall we now go back to barbarism? . . .

Let us retrace our steps, repeal the law and accomplish what we justly desire by civilized means. Let us treat China as we would England; and, above all, let us respect the rights of Men.

REVIEW QUESTIONS

1. Why did Ingersoll believe that the differences among people led to charges of racial inferiority?
2. What were some of the positive characteristics that Ingersoll attributed to the Chinese?
3. Why did Ingersoll think that the exclusion law contradicted American principles?

FRANCES ELLEN WATKINS HARPER

A Black Woman's Appeal for Civil Rights (1891)

In the 1890s, as the southern states began to pass new legislation restricting the voting and civil rights of blacks, few people spoke out against the rising tide of racism. One courageous voice of protest was that of Frances Ellen Watkins Harper (1825–1911), a poet and organizer of African American women. In the following speech before a national gathering of women's clubs in 1891, she made an impassioned appeal for equal rights.

From Rachel F. Avery, ed., *Transactions of the National Council of Women of the United States, Assembled in Washington, DC, on February 22–25, 1891* (New York: J. B. Lippincott, 1891), pp. 86–91.

I deem it a privilege to present the negro, not as a mere dependent asking for Northern sympathy or Southern compassion, but as a member of the body politic who has a claim upon the nation for justice, simple justice, which is the right of every race, upon the government for protection, which is the rightful claim of every citizen, and upon our common Christianity for the best influences which can be exerted for peace on earth and good-will to man.

Our first claim upon the nation and government is the claim for protection to human life. That claim should lie at the basis of our civilization, not simply in theory but in fact. Outside of America, I know of no other civilized country, Catholic, Protestant, or even Mahometan, where men are still lynched, murdered, and even burned for real or supposed crimes. . . . A government which has power to tax a man in peace, and draft him in war, should have power to defend his life in the hour of peril. A government which can protect and defend its citizens from wrong and outrage and does not is vicious. A government which would do it and cannot is weak; and where human life is insecure through either weakness or viciousness in the administration of law, there must be a lack of justice, and where this is wanting nothing can make up the deficiency.

The strongest nation on earth cannot afford to deal unjustly towards its weakest and feeblest members. . . . I claim for the negro protection in every right with which the government has invested him. Whether it was wise or unwise, the government has exchanged the fetters on his wrist for the ballot in his right hand, and men cannot vitiate his vote by fraud, or intimidate the voter by violence, without being untrue to the genius and spirit of our government, and bringing demoralization into their own political life and ranks. Am I here met with the objection that the negro is poor and ignorant, and the greatest amount of land, capital, and intelligence is possessed by the white race, and that in a number of States negro suffrage means negro supremacy? . . .

It is said the negro is ignorant. But why is he ignorant? It comes, with ill grace from a man who has put out my eyes to make a parade of my blindness—to reproach me for my poverty when he has wronged me of my money. If the negro is ignorant, he has lived under the shadow of an institution which, at least in part of the country, made it a crime to teach him to read the name of the ever-blessed Christ. If he is poor, what has become of the money he has been earning for the last two hundred and fifty years? Years ago it was said cotton fights and cotton conquers for American slavery. The negro helped build up that great cotton power in the South, and in the North his sigh was in the whir of its machinery, and his blood and tears upon the warp and woof of its manufactures.

But there are some rights more precious than the rights of property or the claims of superior intelligence: they are the rights of life and liberty, and to these the poorest and humblest man has just as much right as the richest and most influential man in the country. Ignorance and poverty are conditions which men outgrow. Since the sealed volume was opened by the crimson hand of war, in spite of entailed ignorance, poverty, opposition, and a heritage of scorn, schools have sprung like wells in the desert dust. It has been estimated that about two millions have learned to read. Colored men and women have gone into journalism. Some of the first magazines in the country have received contributions from them. Learned professions have given them diplomas. Universities have granted them professorships. Colored women have combined to shelter orphaned children. Tens of thousands have been contributed by colored persons for the care of the aged and infirm. . . . Millions of dollars have flowed into the pockets of the race, and freed people have not only been able to provide for themselves, but reach out their hands to impoverished owners. . . .

Instead of taking the ballot from his hands, teach him how to use it, and to add his quota to the progress, strength, and durability of the nation. . . . Underlying this racial question, if I understand it aright, is one controlling idea, not simply that the negro is ignorant; *that* he is outgrowing; not that he is incapable of valor in war or adaptation in peace. On fields all drenched with blood he made his record in war, abstained from lawless violence when left on the plantation, and received his freedom in peace with moderation. But he holds in this Republic the position of an alien race among a people impatient of a rival. And in the eyes of some it seems that no valor redeems him, no social advancement nor individual development wipes off the ban which clings to him. It is the pride of Caste which opposed the spirit of Christ, and the great work to which American Christianity is called is a work of Christly reconciliation. . . .

REVIEW QUESTIONS

1. What essential protection did Harper ask the government to provide? What larger issue did her plea underscore?
2. How does Harper counter claims that African Americans were ignorant?
3. Harper implies that Americans displayed religious hypocrisy. How might southern whites have responded to this charge?

A BLACK WOMAN

Racism in the South (1902)

The era of Progressive reform was fraught with contradictions. At the same time that social idealists were assaulting political corruption and promoting laws protecting women and children in the workplace, racial prejudice was flourishing. During the 1890s, state after state in the South passed "Jim Crow" laws mandating racial segregation of public facilities and schools. Efforts to use fraud and intimidation to reduce black voting continued unabated. The following article, written by a black woman from Alabama who felt the need to withhold her name, describes the racial abuses suffered by blacks at the turn of the century.

From "The Negro Problem: How It Appears to a Southern Colored Woman," *The Independent* 54 (September 18, 1902):2221–2224. [Editorial insertions appear in square brackets—*Ed.*]

I am a colored woman, wife and mother. I have lived all my life in the South, and have often thought what a peculiar fact it is that the more ignorant the Southern whites are of us, the more vehement they are in their denunciation of us. They boast that they have little intercourse with us, never see us in our homes, churches or places of amusement, but still they know us thoroughly.

They also admit that they know us in no capacity except as servants, yet they say we are at our best in that single capacity. What philosophers they are! The Southerners say we negroes are a happy, laughing set of people, with no thought of tomorrow. How mistaken they are! The educated, thinking Negro is just the opposite. There is a feeling of unrest, insecurity, almost panic among the best class of negroes in the South. In our homes, in our churches, wherever two or three are gathered together, there is a discussion of what is best to do. Must we remain in the South or go elsewhere? Where can we go to feel that security which other people feel? Is it best to go in great numbers or only in several families? These and many other things are discussed over and over.

People who have security in their homes, whose children can go on the street unmolested, whose wives and daughters are treated as women, cannot, perhaps, sympathize with the Southern negro's anxieties and complaints. I ask forebearance of such people.

It is asserted that we are dying more rapidly than other people in the South. It is not remarkable when the houses built for sale or rent to colored people are usually placed in the lowest and most unhealthy spots. I know of houses occupied by poor negroes in which a respectable farmer would not keep his cattle. It is impossible for them to rent elsewhere. All Southern real estate agents have "white property" and "colored property." In one of the largest Southern cities there is a colored minister, a graduate of Harvard, whose wife is an educated, Christian woman, who lived for weeks in a tumble-down rookery because he could neither rent nor buy in a respectable locality.

Many colored women who wash, iron, scrub, cook or sew all the week to help pay the rent for these miserable hovels and help fill the many small mouths, would deny themselves some of the necessaries of life if they could take their little children and teething babies on the cars to the parks of a Sunday afternoon and sit under trees, enjoy the cool breezes and breathe God's pure air for only two or three hours; but this is denied them. Some of the parks have signs, "No negroes allowed on these grounds except as servants." Pitiful, pitiful customs and laws that make war on women and babes! There is no wonder that we die; the wonder is that we persist in living.

Fourteen years ago I had just married. My husband had saved sufficient money to buy a small home. On account of our limited means we went to the suburbs, on unpaved streets, to look for a home, only asking for a high, healthy locality. Some real estate agents were "sorry, but had nothing to suit," some had "just the thing," but we discovered on investigation that they had "just the thing" for an unhealthy pigsty. Others had no "colored property." One agent said that he had what we wanted, but we should have to go to see the lot after dark, or walk by and give the place a casual look; for, he said, "all the white people in the neighborhood would be down on me." Finally, we bought this lot. When the house was being built we went to see it. Consternation reigned. We had ruined this [all-white] neighborhood of poor people; poor as we, poorer in manners at least. The people who lived next door received the sympathy of their friends. When we walked on the street (there were no sidewalks) we were embarrassed by the stare of many unfriendly eyes.

Two years passed before a single woman spoke to me, and only then because I helped one of them when a little sudden trouble came to her. Such was the reception, I a happy young woman, just married, received from people among whom I wanted to make a home. Fourteen years have now passed, four children have been born to us, and one has died in this same home, among these same neighbors. Although the neighbors speak to us, and occasionally one will send a child to borrow the morning's paper or ask the loan of a pattern, not one woman has ever been inside of my house, not even at the times when a woman would doubly appreciate the slightest attention of a neighbor. . . .

. . . A colored woman, however respectable, is lower [in status] than the white prostitute. The Southern white woman will declare that no Negro women are virtuous, yet she placed her innocent children in their care. . . .

White agents and other chance visitors who come into our homes ask questions that we must not dare ask their wives. They express surprise that our children have clean faces and that their hair is combed. . . .

. . . We were delighted to know that some of our Spanish-American [War] heroes were coming where we could get a glimpse of them. Had not black men helped in a small way to give them their honors? In the cities of the South, where these heroes went, the white school children were assembled, flags waved, flowers strewn, speeches made, and "My Country, 'Tis of Thee, Sweet Land of Liberty," was sung. Our children, who need to be taught so much, were not assembled, their hands

waved no flags, they threw no flowers, heard no thrilling speech, sang no song of their country. And this is the South's idea of justice. Is it surprising that [racist] feeling grows more bitter, when the white mother teaches her boy to hate my boy, not because he is mean, but because his skin is dark? I have seen very small white children hang their black dolls. It is not the child's fault, he is simply an apt pupil. . . .

Why does not the mistreatment of thousands of the [black] citizens of our country call forth a strong, influential champion? It seems to me that the very weakness of the negro should cause at least a few of our great men to come to the rescue. Is it because an espousal of our cause would make any white man unpopular, or do most of our great men think that we are worthless? Are there greater things to do than to "champion the rights of human beings and to mitigate human suffering?"

The way seems dark, and the future almost hopeless, but let us not despair, "For right is right, since God is God, and right the day must win." Some one will at last arise who will champion our cause and compel the world to see that we deserve justice, as other heroes compelled it to see that we deserved freedom.

REVIEW QUESTIONS

1. To what extent are racist prejudices the result of ignorance and stereotypes?
2. Are patterns of racial segregation still visible in American society? Explain.

GROVER CLEVELAND

Veto of Pension Legislation (1886)

A popular form of political patronage during the Gilded Age was federal pensions paid to military veterans and their widows. After the Civil War thousands of Union veterans and their relatives applied individually for federal pensions. Many of their claims were fraudulent, but congressmen and presidents used such pensions as political rewards. By 1880 pensions represented 21 percent of all federal government expenses. In 1886 Democratic president Grover Cleveland vetoed a pension bill, only to see the Republican Congress pass more sweeping legislation in 1890.

From James D. Richardson, ed., *A Compilation of the Messages and Papers of the Presidents* (New York: Bureau of National Literature, 1897), 11:5022–23.

To the Senate:

... I am so thoroughly tired of disapproving gifts of public money to individuals who in my view have no right or claim to the same, notwithstanding apparent Congressional sanction, that I interpose with a feeling of relief a veto in a case where I find it unnecessary to determine the merits of the application. In speaking of the promiscuous and ill-advised grants of pensions which have lately been presented to me for approval, I have spoken of their "Apparent Congressional sanction" in recognition of the fact that a large proportion of these bills have never been submitted to a majority of either branch of Congress, but are the result of nominal sessions held for the express purpose of their consideration and attended by a small minority of the members of the respective Houses of the legislative branch of Government. ...

I have not been insensible to the suggestions which should influence every citizen, either in private station or official place, to exhibit not only a just but a generous appreciation of the services of our country's defenders. In reviewing the pension legislation presented to me, many bills have been approved upon the theory that every doubt should be resolved in favor of the proposed beneficiary. I have not, however, been able to entirely divest myself of the idea that the public money appropriated for pensions is the soldiers' fund, which should be devoted to the indemnification of those who in the defense of the Union and in the nation's service have worthily suffered, and who in the day of their dependence resulting from such suffering are entitled to the benefactions of their Government. This reflection lends to the bestowal of pensions a kind of sacredness which invites the adoption of such principles and regulations as will exclude perversion as well as insure a liberal and generous application of grateful and benevolent designs. Heedlessness and a disregard of the principle which underlies the granting of pensions is unfair to the wounded, crippled soldier who is honored in the just recognition of his Government. Such a man should never find himself side by side on the pension roll with those who have been tempted to attribute the natural ills to which humanity is heir to service in the Army. Every relaxation of principle in the granting of pensions invites applications without merit and encourages those who for gain urge honest men to become dishonest. This is the demoralizing lesson taught the people that as against the public Treasury the most questionable expedients are allowable. ...

I have now more than 130 of these bills before me awaiting Executive action. It will be impossible to bestow upon them the examination they deserve, and many will probably become operative which should be rejected. In the meantime I venture to suggest the significance of the startling increase in this kind of legislation and the consequences involved in its continuance.

REVIEW QUESTIONS

1. Why did Cleveland claim that the pension bills had "apparent" Congressional approval?
2. Why did Cleveland believe people were being tempted to submit fraudulent pension claims?

Populist Party Platform (1892)

The People's Party, more commonly known as the Populist Party, was organized in St. Louis in 1892 to represent the common folk—especially farmers—against the entrenched interests of railroads, bankers, processors, corporations, and the politicians in league with such interests. At its first national convention in Omaha in July 1892, the party nominated James K. Weaver for president and ratified the so-called Omaha Platform, drafted by Ignatius Donnelly of Minnesota.

From "People's Party Platform," *Omaha Morning World–Herald*, 5 July 1892. [Editorial insertions appear in square brackets—*Ed.*]

Assembled upon the 116th anniversary of the Declaration of Independence, the People's Party of America, in their first national convention, invoking upon their action the blessing of Almighty God, put forth in the name and on behalf of the people of this country, the following preamble and declaration of principles:

Preamble

The conditions which surround us best justify our cooperation; we meet in the midst of a nation brought to the verge of moral, political, and material ruin. Corruption dominates the ballot-box, the Legislatures, the Congress, and touches even the ermine of the bench.[1] The people are demoralized; most of the States have been compelled to isolate the voters at the polling places to prevent universal intimidation and bribery. The newspapers are largely subsidized or muzzled, public opinion silenced, business prostrated, homes covered with mortgages, labor impoverished, and the land concentrating in the hands of capitalists. The urban workmen are denied the right to organize for self-protection, imported pauperized labor beats down their wages, a hireling standing army, unrecognized by our laws, is established to shoot them down, and they are rapidly degenerating into European conditions. The fruits of the toil of millions are badly stolen to build up colossal fortunes for a few, unprecedented in the history of mankind; and the possessors of these, in turn, despise the Republic and endanger liberty. From the same prolific womb of governmental injustice we breed the two great classes—tramps and millionaires. The national power to create money is appropriated to enrich bond-holders; a vast public debt payable in legal-tender currency has been funded into gold-bearing bonds, thereby adding millions to the burdens of the people.

---

[1] A valuable white fur adorning the robes of some judges.

Silver, which has been accepted as coin since the dawn of history, has been demonetized to add to the purchasing power of gold by decreasing the value of all forms of property as well as human labor, and the supply of currency is purposely abridged to fatten usurers, bankrupt enterprise, and enslave industry. A vast conspiracy against mankind has been organized on two continents, and it is rapidly taking possession of the world. If not met and overthrown at once it forebodes terrible social convulsions, the destruction of civilization, or the establishment of an absolute despotism.

We have witnessed for more than a quarter of a century the struggles of the two great political parties for power and plunder, while grievous wrongs have been inflicted upon the suffering people. We charge that the controlling influences dominating both these parties have permitted the existing dreadful conditions to develop without serious effort to prevent or restrain them. Neither do they now promise us any substantial reform. They have agreed together to ignore, in the coming campaign, ever issue but one. They propose to drown the outcries of a plundered people with the uproar of a sham battle over the tariff, so that capitalists, corporations, national banks, rings, trusts, watered stock, the demonetization of silver and the oppressions of the usurers may all be lost sight of. They propose to sacrifice our homes, lives, and children on the altar of mammon; to destroy the multitude in order to secure corruption funds from the millionaires.

Assembled on the anniversary of the birthday of the nation, and filled with the spirit of the grand general and chief who established our independence, we seek to restore the government of the Republic to the hands of the "plain people," with which class it originated. We assert our purposes to be identical with the purposes of the National Constitution; to form a more perfect union and establish justice, insure domestic tranquillity, provide for the common defense, promote the general welfare, and secure the blessings of liberty for ourselves and our posterity. . . .

Our country finds itself confronted by conditions for which there is not precedent in the history of the world; our annual agricultural productions amount to billions of dollars in value, which must, within a few weeks or months, be exchanged for billions of dollars' worth of commodities consumed in their production; the existing currency supply is wholly inadequate to make this exchange; the results are falling prices, the formation of combines and rings, the impoverishment of the producing class. We pledge ourselves that if given power we will labor to correct these evils by wise and reasonable legislation, in accordance with the terms of our platform.

We believe that the power of government—in other words, of the people—should be expanded (as in the case of the postal service) as rapidly and as far as the good sense of an intelligent people and the teaching of experience shall justify, to the end that oppression, injustice, and poverty shall eventually cease in the land. . . .

Platform

We declare, therefore—

First.—That the union of the labor forces of the United States this day consummated shall be permanent and perpetual; may its spirit enter into all hearts for the salvation of the republic and the uplifting of mankind.

Second.—Wealth belongs to him who creates it, and every dollar taken from industry without an equivalent is robbery. "If any will not work, neither shall he eat." The interests of rural and civil labor are the same; their enemies are identical.

Third.—We believe that the time has come when the railroad corporations will either own the people or the people must own the railroads; and should the government enter upon the work of owning and managing all railroads, we should favor an amendment to the constitution by which all persons engaged in the government service shall be placed under a civil-service regulation of the most rigid character, so as to prevent the increase of the power of the national administration by the use of such additional government employees.

FINANCE.—We demand a national currency, safe, sound, and flexible issued by the general government only, a full legal tender for all debts, public and private, and that without the use of banking corporations; a just, equitable, and efficient means of distribution direct to the people, at a tax not to exceed 2 per cent, per annum, to be provided as set forth in the sub-treasury plan of the Farmers' Alliance, or a better system; also by payments in discharge of its obligations for public improvements.

1. We demand free and unlimited coinage of silver and gold at the present legal ratio of 16 to 1.
2. We demand that the amount of circulating medium[1] be speedily increased to not less than $50 per capita.
3. We demand a graduated income tax.
4. We believe that the money of the country should be kept as much as possible in the hands of the people, and hence we demand that all State and national revenues shall be limited to the necessary expenses of the government, economically and honestly administered.

We demand that postal savings banks be established by the government for the safe deposit of the earnings of the people and to facilitate exchange.

TRANSPORTATION.—Transportation being a means of exchange and a public necessity, the government should own and operate the railroads in the interest of the people. The telegraph and telephone, like the post-office system, being a necessity for the transmission of news, should be owned and operated by the government in the interest of the people.

LAND.—The land, including all the natural sources of wealth, is the heritage of the people, and should not be monopolized for speculative purposes, and alien ownership of land should be prohibited. All land now held by railroads and other corporations in excess of their actual needs, and all lands now owned by aliens should be reclaimed by the government and held for actual settlers only.

---

[1] Currency and/or coin.

Expressions of Sentiments

Your Committee on Platform and Resolutions beg leave unanimously to report the following:

Whereas, Other questions have been presented for our consideration, we hereby submit the following, not as a part of the Platform of the People's Party, but as resolutions expressive of the sentiment of this Convention.

1. RESOLVED, That we demand a free ballot and a fair count in all elections and pledge ourselves to secure it to every legal voter without Federal Intervention, through the adoption by the States of the unperverted Australian or secret ballot system.
2. RESOLVED, That the revenue derived from a graduated income tax should be applied to the reduction of the burden of taxation now levied upon the domestic industries of this country.
3. RESOLVED, That we pledge our support to fair and liberal pensions to ex-Union soldiers and sailors.
4. RESOLVED, That we condemn the fallacy of protecting American labor under the present system, which opens our ports to the pauper and criminal classes of the world and crowds out our wage-earners; and we denounce the present ineffective laws against [foreign] contract labor, and demand the further restriction of undesirable emigration.
5. RESOLVED, That we cordially sympathize with the efforts of organized workingmen to shorten the hours of labor, and demand a rigid enforcement of the existing eight-hour law on Government work, and ask that a penalty clause be added to the said law.
6. RESOLVED, That we regard the maintenance of a large standing army of mercenaries, known as the Pinkerton system, as a menace to our liberties, and we demand its abolition. . . .
7. RESOLVED, That we commend to the favorable consideration of the people and

the reform press the legislative system known as the initiative and referendum.

8. RESOLVED, That we favor a constitutional provision limiting the office of President and Vice-President to one term, and providing for the election of Senators of the United States by a direct vote of the people.

9. RESOLVED, That we oppose any subsidy or national aid to any private corporation for any purpose.

10. RESOLVED, That this convention sympathizes with the Knights of Labor and their righteous contest with the tyrannical combine of clothing manufacturers of Rochester, and declare it to be a duty of all who hate tyranny and oppression to refuse to purchase the goods made by the said manufacturers, or to patronize any merchants who sell such goods.

REVIEW QUESTIONS

1. In what ways did the Populists present a class-based interpretation of American politics? Who comprised the social classes described by the Populists?

2. What were some of the Populists' specific demands? What groups would have opposed these demands?

3. Compare Populist proposals with those advocated by Democrats and Republicans. Were Populists truly radical?

MARY E. LEASE

The Money Question (1892)

The Populist movement provided unprecedented opportunities for women to participate in politics. Among the most active and impassioned was Mary Elizabeth Lease. Born in Pennsylvania in 1853, she moved to Kansas at the age of twenty. There she married, had four children, practiced law, and became a fiery orator on behalf of Populism. She urged farmers to "raise less corn and more hell!" The following excerpt from one of her speeches reveals her impassioned style.

From Elizabeth N. Barr, "The Populist Uprising," in W. E. Connelly, ed., *History of Kansas, State, and People* (Topeka: Lewis Publishing, 1928), 2:1167.

This is a nation of inconsistencies. The Puritans fleeing from oppression [in England] became oppressors [in New England]. We fought England for our liberty and put chains on four million of blacks. We wiped out slavery and by our tariff laws and national banks began a system of white wage slavery worse than the first.

Wall Street owns the country. It is no longer a government of the people, by the people, and for the people, but a government of Wall Street, by Wall Street, and for Wall Street.

The great common people of this country are slaves, and monopoly is the master. The West and South are bound and prostrate before the manufacturing East.

Money rules. . . . The parties lie to us and the political speakers mislead us. We were told two years ago to go to work and raise a big crop, that was all we needed. We went to work and plowed and planted; the rains fell, the sun shone, nature smiled, and we raised the big crop that they told us to; and what came of it? Eight-cent corn, ten-cent oats, two-cent beef, and no price at all for butter and eggs—that's what came of it.

Then the politicians said we suffered from overproduction. Overproduction, when 10,000 little children, so statistics tell us, starve to death every year in the United States, and over 100,000 shopgirls in New York are forced to sell their virtue for the bread that niggardly wages deny them.

Tariff is not the paramount question. The main question is the money question. . . . Kansas suffers from two great robbers, the Santa Fe Railroad and the loan companies. The common people are robbed to enrich their masters. . . .

*   *   *

We want money, land, and transportation. We want the abolition of the national banks, and we want the power to make loans direct from the government. We want the accursed foreclosure system wiped out. . . .

We will stand by our homes and stay by our fireside by force if necessary, and we will not pay our debts to the loan-shark companies until the government pays its debt to us. The people are at bay; let the bloodhounds of money who have dogged us thus far beware.

REVIEW QUESTIONS

1. What did Lease mean when she wrote, "Wall Street owns the country"?
2. How did Lease interpret the conflict in geographic terms? How might such a regional outlook inhibit the effort to build political coalitions?
3. Characterize Lease's attitude toward the federal government. Explain your response.

EVA MCDONALD-VALESH

FROM The Strength and Weakness of the People's Movement (1892)

The emergence of the People's Party (Populism) generated great interest within social and political reform circles across the country. The following article in the Boston-based Arena *magazine focused on the need for the agrarian-based organization to make common cause with the urban working class. Its insights and warnings proved to be quite astute.*

From Eva McDonald-Valesh, "The Strength and Weakness of the People's Movement," *Arena* 5 (May 1892):726–731.

The rapid growth and popularity of the political movement known as the People's Party invest it with an importance that leads the general public to scan it closely for those indices which mark all truly great industrial movements. If it has not certain characteristics, it may excite those momentary outbursts of discontent emanating from a single class, only to die of inanition or be buried under a storm of well-directed ridicule.

A political movement, to be an instrument of real industrial progress, ought to be general enough in its scope to embrace all classes of workers whose conditions are affected by the same general causes. Today there is the agricultural population, on one hand, producing more than enough to feed the world; on the other, the city workmen; producing, in their many occupations, more than enough to clothe and supply all other civilized needs of the race. The two classes are quite distinct, so far as environment is concerned; yet consuming each other's products and supplying both necessities and luxuries to all other classes, there is between them a bond of common interest, stronger than either realizes.

Both classes, while conceding the immeasurable superiority of their present condition over that of their ancestors of any time, still feel that many differences are yet to be adjusted before industry attains the dignity warranted by the achievements and progress of the nineteenth century. Each division of the industrial body has various grades of expressed discontent with the present and hope for the future. . . .

The two great bodies of organized discontent[1] are working independently and by different methods on the same problem—the distribution of wealth. In the past, having observed so little their relations to each other, or the local conditions seeming to form a barrier between them, they now appear to have but faint sympathy or community of interest.

It is of vast significance that the two organizations have the same reason for existing, and are trying to solve the same problem. Some combination of circumstances must soon reveal its community of purpose, and from that moment the workers of the farm and the factory will be bound by that strongest of ties, self-interest. The industrial world is becoming convinced that the People's Party will be this agent.

The recent conference at St. Louis showed that a surprisingly large number of reform elements already agree on the general principles, leaving details to the future. . . . Still, to those familiar with industrial organization in cities, this conference revealed that the mass of city workers was unrepresented. Did this silence mean antagonism, even indifference, it might prove fatal to the success of the new movement. For if the People's Party, in its ultimate development, only represents a class, no matter how large that class, its work must necessarily partake of a sectional character, and from a lack of breadth and depth, fail to accomplish those great reforms which mark epochs of civilization. . . .

A promising field of work open to view, although it still needs cultivation. Workingmen understand the value of the right of suffrage and its importance in securing industrial reform. They cannot fail to be keenly dissatisfied with the prospect held out by existing parties.[2] The agricultural classes equally need just the elements that the cities could contribute. Each organization would be the gainer from close contact and interchange of views with the other.

There is still an element wanting to insure harmonious action. It is a peculiarity of the People's movement that it has not yet produced a leader. It has teachers—earnest, thoughtful, and progressive. It has statesmen of good parts. But a leader, in the true sense, is yet wanting. . . . A true leader can unite them in so irresistible a force that by a peaceful revolution of ballots, great abuses will be swept away and replaced by more equitable conditions inuring to the benefit of all society.

Nor should such a coalition of the forces of farm and factory be feared by the most conservative. The *world will advance*, in spite of the

---

[1] Farmers and laborers.

[2] I.e., national political parties.

remonstrances from those who are perfectly satisfied with the existing order. Reforms, working in
peaceful and legitimate channels, are a sure guarantee against the violence which, in preceding eras,
has so often accompanied popular movements.

REVIEW QUESTIONS

1. Why didn't the urban workers support the Populists?
2. What did McDonald-Valesh believe could unite
agricultural and industrial workers? Is her perspective credible?

J. STERLING MORTON

What Farm Problem? (1896)

*The People's Party and its reform agenda aroused intense opposition. Democrat
J. Sterling Morton of Nebraska served as secretary of agriculture under Grover Cleveland from 1893 to 1897. He vigorously denied that there was a serious "farm problem" and staunchly opposed the Populist movement's efforts to gain government
benefits for farmers.*

From *The Report of Secretary of Agriculture, 1896* (Washington, DC, 1896), pp. xlv–xlvi.

Out of each thousand farms in the United
States only 282 are mortgaged, and three-
fourths of the money represented by the
mortgages upon the 282 farms was for the purchase of those farms or for money borrowed to
improve those farms. And the prevalent idea that
the West and the South are more heavily burdened
with farm mortgages than the East and North-
east sections of the United States is entirely erro-
neous. . . .

The constant complaint by the alleged friends
of farmers, and by some farmers themselves, is that
the Government does nothing for agriculture. In
conventions and congresses it has been proclaimed
that the farmers of the country are almost universally in debt, despondent, and suffering. Largely
these declarations are without foundation. Their
utterance is a belittlement of agriculture and an indignity to every intelligent and practical farmer of

the United States. The free and independent farmers of this country are not impoverished; they are
not mendicants; they are not wards of the Government to be treated to annuities, like Indians upon
reservations. On the other hand, they are the representatives of the oldest, most honorable, and
most essential occupation of the human race.
Upon it all other vocations depend for subsistence
and prosperity. The farmer is the copartner of the
elements. His intelligently directed efforts are in
unison with the light and heat of the sun, and the
success of his labors represents the commingling of
the raindrops and his own sweat.

Legislation can neither plow nor plant. The intelligent, practical, and successful farmer needs no
aid from the Government. The ignorant, impractical, and indolent farmer deserves none. It is not the
business of Government to legislate in behalf of
any class of citizens because they are engaged in

any specific calling, no matter how essential the calling may be to the needs and comforts of civilization. Lawmakers can not erase natural laws nor restrict or efface the operation of economic laws. It is a beneficent arrangement of the order of things and the conditions of human life that legislators are not permitted to repeal, amend, or revise the laws of production and distribution.

REVIEW QUESTIONS

1. What did Morton mean by "practical" farmers and "impractical" farmers?
2. What did Morton mean when he wrote that the farmer was the "copartner of the elements"? What important factor did he omit in this context?
3. What relationship, if any, did the government have with "natural" or "economic" laws? How does this reflect late-nineteenth-century notions about governance?

The Republican Party Platform of 1896

In 1896 the Republican Party National Convention convened in St. Louis. The delegates nominated William McKinley of Ohio as their standard bearer, and they adopted a conservative platform reaffirming the sanctity of the gold standard and the benefits of high tariffs, thus setting the stage for a climactic election contest.

From Donald Bruce Johnson and Kirk H. Porter, eds., *National Party Platforms, 1840–1972* (Urbana: University of Illinois Press, 1973), pp. 107–108.

. . . For the first time since the civil war the American people have witnessed the calamitous consequence of full and unrestricted Democratic control of the government. It has been a record of unparalleled incapacity, dishonor, and disaster. In administrative management it has ruthlessly sacrificed indispensable revenue, entailed an unceasing deficit, eked out ordinary current expenses with borrowed money, piled up the public debt by $262,000,000, in time of peace, forced an adverse balance of trade, kept a perpetual menace hanging over the redemption fund, pawned American credit to alien syndicates and reversed all the measures and results of successful Republican rule. In the broad effect of its policy it has precipitated panic, blighted industry and trade with prolonged depression, closed factories, reduced work and wages, halted enterprise and crippled American production, while stimulating foreign production for the American market. Every consideration of public safety and individual interest demands that the government shall be wrested from the hands of those who have shown themselves incapable of conducting it without disaster at home and dishonor abroad and shall be restored to the party which for thirty years administered it with unequaled success and prosperity. And in this connection, we heartily endorse the wisdom, patriotism and success of the administration of Benjamin Harrison.

We renew and emphasize our allegiance to the policy of [tariff] protection as the bulwark of American industrial independence and the foundation of American development and prosperity. This true American policy taxes foreign products and encourages home industry. It puts the burden of revenue on foreign goods; it secures the American market for the American producer. It upholds the American standard of wages for the American workingman; it puts the factory by the side of the farm, and makes the American farmer less dependent on foreign demand and price; it diffuses general thrift, and founds the strength of each. In its reasonable application it is just, fair and impartial, equally opposed to foreign control and domestic monopoly, to sectional discrimination and individual favoritism. . . .

We demand such an equitable tariff on foreign imports which come into competition with the American products as will not only furnish adequate revenue for the necessary expense of the Government, but will protect American labor from degradation and the wage level of other lands. We are not pledged to any particular schedules. The question of rates is a practical question, to be governed by the condition of time and of production. The ruling and uncompromising principle is the protection and development of American labor and industries. . . .

The Republican party is unreservedly for sound money. It caused the enactment of a law providing for the resumption of specie payments in 1879. Since then every dollar has been as good as gold. We are unalterably opposed to every measure calculated to debase our currency or impair the credit of our country. We are therefore opposed to the free coinage of silver. . . . All of our silver and paper currency must be maintained at parity with gold, and we favor all measures designated to maintain inviolable the obligations of the United States, of all our money, whether coin or paper, at the present standard, the standard of most enlightened nations of the world. . . .

REVIEW QUESTIONS

1. What were some of the "calamitous consequences" linked to Democratic policies?
2. In discussing tariff protection for American industries, which aspect of the production process did the platform emphasize? Whose political support was being courted?
3. How might a Populist have responded to the Republican platform?

WILLIAM JENNINGS BRYAN

FROM The "Cross of Gold" Speech (1896)

The 1896 presidential election was one of the most significant in American history. Having suffered a humiliating defeat in the 1894 congressional elections, the Democratic party faced a turning point: either embrace the "free silver" issue promoted by the Populists or echo the Republican platform by reaffirming the "gold standard" and "sound money" principles. At the party's national convention in Chicago in 1896, the silverites prevailed during the platform debate. What turned the tide was a rousing address to the 15,000 delegates by William Jennings Bryan of Nebraska. The thirty-six-year-old reformer was one of the greatest orators of his day, and his dramatic speech propelled the convention to nominate him as the Democratic presidential can-

didate. His references to "bimetallism" refer to proposals to allow for the coining of both gold and silver.

From William J. Bryan, *The First Battle: A Story of the Campaign of 1896* (Chicago: W. B. Conkey, 1896), pp. 199–206.

Mr. Chairman and Gentlemen of the Convention:

I would be presumptuous, indeed, to present myself against the distinguished gentlemen to whom you have listened if this were a mere measuring of abilities; but this is not a contest between persons. The humblest citizen in all the land, when clad in the armor of a righteous cause, is stronger than all the hosts of error. I come to speak to you in defense of a cause as holy as the cause of liberty—the cause of humanity. . . .

Never before in the history of this country has there been witnessed such a contest as that through which we have just passed. Never before in the history of American politics has a great issue been fought out as this issue has been, by the voters of a great party. On the fourth of March, 1895, a few Democrats, most of them members of Congress, issued an address to the Democrats of the nation, asserting that the money question was the paramount issue of the hour; declaring that a majority of the Democratic party had the right to control the action of the party on this paramount issue; and concluding with the request that the believers in the free coinage of silver in the Democratic party should organize, take charge of, and control the policy of the Democratic party.

Three months later, at Memphis, an organization was perfected, and the silver Democrats went forth openly and courageously proclaiming their belief, and declaring that, if successful, they would crystallize into a platform the declaration which they had made. Then began the conflict. With a zeal approaching the zeal which inspired the Crusaders who followed Peter the Hermit, our silver Democrats went forth from victory unto victory until they are now assembled, not to discuss, not to debate, but to enter up the judgment already rendered by the plain people of this country. In this contest brother has been arrayed against brother, father against son. The warmest ties of love, acquaintance, and association have been disregarded; old leaders have been cast aside when they have refused to give expression to the sentiments of those whom they would lead, and new leaders have sprung up to give direction to this cause of truth. Thus has the contest been waged, and we have assembled here under as binding and solemn instructions as were ever imposed upon representatives of the people. . . .

When you[1] come before us and tell us that we are about to disturb your business interests, we reply that you have disturbed our business interests by your course. We say to you that you have made the definition of a business man too limited in its application. The man who is employed for wages is as much a business man as his employer; the attorney in a country town is as much a business man as the corporation counsel in a great metropolis; the merchant at the cross-roads store is as much a business man as the merchant of New York; the farmer who goes forth in the morning and toils all day, who begins in spring and toils all summer, and who by the application of brain and muscle to the natural resources of the country creates wealth, is as much a business man as the man who goes upon the Board of Trade and bets upon the price of grain; the miners who go down a thousand feet into the earth, or climb two thousand feet upon the cliffs, and bring forth from their hiding places the precious metals to be poured into the channels of trade are as much businessmen as the few financial magnates who, in a back room, corner the money of the world. We come to speak of this broader class of business men.

---

[1] Bryan is referring to the delegates committed to a gold-only currency.

Ah, my friends, we say not one word against those who live upon the Atlantic Coast, but the hardy pioneers who have braved all the dangers of the wilderness, who have made the desert to blossom as the rose—the pioneers away out there,[2] who rear their children near to Nature's heart, where they can mingle their voices with the voices of the birds—out there where they have erected schoolhouses for the education of their young, churches where they praise their creator, and cemeteries where rest the ashes of their dead—these people, we say, are as deserving of the consideration of our party as any people in this country. It is for these that we speak. We do not come as aggressors. Our war is not a war of conquest; we are fighting in the defense of our homes, our families, and posterity. We have petitioned, and our petitions have been scorned; we have entreated, and our entreaties have been disregarded; we have begged, and they have mocked when our calamity came. We beg no longer; we entreat no more; we petition no more. We defy them!

The gentleman from Wisconsin has said that he fears a Robespierre.[3] My friends, in this land of the free you need not fear that a tyrant will spring up from among the people. What we need is an Andrew Jackson to stand, as Jackson stood, against the encroachments of organized wealth.

They tell us that this platform was made to catch votes. We reply to them that changing conditions make new issues; that the principles upon which Democracy rests are as everlasting as the hills, but that they must be applied to new conditions as they arise. Conditions have arisen, and we are here to meet those conditions. They tell us that the income tax ought not to be brought in here; that it is a new idea. They criticize us for our criticism of the Supreme Court of the United States. My friends, we have not criticized; we have simply called attention to what you already know. If you want criticisms, read the dissenting opinions of the court. There you will find criticisms. They say that

we passed an unconstitutional law; we deny it. The income tax law was not unconstitutional when it was passed; it was not unconstitutional when it went before the Supreme Court for the first time; it did not become unconstitutional until one of the judges changed his mind, and we cannot be expected to know when a judge will change his mind. The income tax is just. It simply intends to put the burdens of government justly upon the backs of the people. I am in favor of an income tax. When I find a man who is not willing to bear his share of the burdens of the government which protects him, I find a man who is unworthy to enjoy the blessings of a government like ours.

They say that we are opposing national bank currency; it is true. . . . We say in our platform that we believe that the right to coin and issue money is a function of government. We believe it. We believe that it is a part of sovereignty, and can no more with safety be delegated to private individuals than we could afford to delegate to private individuals the power to make penal statutes or levy taxes. Mr. Jefferson, who was once regarded as good Democratic authority, seems to have differed in opinion from the gentleman who has addressed us on the part of the minority. Those who are opposed to this proposition tell us that the issue of paper money is a function of the bank, and that the government ought to go out of the banking business. I stand with Jefferson rather than with them, and tell them, as he did that the issue of money is a function of government, and that the banks ought to go out of the governing business. . . .

And now, my friends, let me come to the paramount issue. If they ask us why it is that we say more on the money question than we say upon the tariff question, I reply that, if protection has slain its thousands, the gold standard has slain its tens of thousands. If they ask us why we do not embody in our platform all the things that we believe in, we reply that when we have restored the money of the Constitution all other necessary reforms will be possible; but that until this is done there is no other reform that can be accomplished.

Why is it that within three months such a change has come over the country? Three months

---

[2] The West.

[3] The ruthless leader of the French Revolution who was himself guillotined in 1794.

ago when it was confidently asserted that those who believe in the gold standard would frame our platform and nominate our candidates, even the advocates of the gold standard did not think that we could elect a President. And they had good reason for their doubt, because there is scarcely a state here today asking for the gold standard which is not in the absolute control of the Republican party.

But note the change. Mr. McKinley was nominated at St. Louis upon a platform which declared for the maintenance of the gold standard until it can be changed into bimetallism by international agreement. Mr. McKinley was the most popular man among the Republicans, and three months ago everybody in the Republican party prophesied his election. How is it to-day? Why, the man who was once pleased to think that he looked like Napoleon—that man shudders today when he remembers that he was nominated on the anniversary of the battle of Waterloo. . . .

Why this change? Ah, my friends, is not the reason for the change evident to any one who will look at the matter? No private character, however pure, no personal popularity, however great, can protect from the avenging wrath of an indignant people a man who will declare that he is in favor of fastening the gold standard upon this country, or who is willing to surrender the right of self-government and place the legislative control of our affairs in the hands of foreign potentates and powers.

We go forth confident that we shall win. Why? Because upon the paramount issue of this campaign there is not a spot of ground upon which the enemy will dare to challenge battle. If they tell us that the gold standard is a good thing, we shall point to their platform and tell them that their platform pledges the party to get rid of the gold standard and substitute bimetallism.

If the gold standard is a good thing, why try to get rid of it? I call your attention to the fact that some of the very people who are in this Convention today and who tell us that we ought to declare in favor of international bimetallism—thereby declaring that the gold standard is wrong and that the principle of bimetallism is better—these very people four months ago were open and avowed advocates of the gold standard, and were then telling us that we could not legislate two metals together, even with the aid of all the world. If the gold standard is a good thing, we ought to declare in favor of its retention and not in favor of abandoning it; and if the gold standard is a bad thing why should we wait until other nations are willing to help us to let go?

Here is the line of battle, and we care not upon which issue they force the fight; we are prepared to meet them on either issue or on both. If they tell us that the gold standard is the standard of civilization, we reply to them that this, the most enlightened of all the nations of the earth, has never declared for a gold standard and that both the great parties this year are declaring against it. If the gold standard is the standard of civilization, why, my friends, should we not have it? If they come to meet us on that issue we can present the history of our nation. More than that; we can tell them that they will search the pages of history in vain to find a single instance where the common people of any land have ever declared themselves in favor of the gold standard. They can find where the holders of fixed investments have declared for a gold standard, but not where the masses have. . . .

My friends, the question we are to decide is: Upon which side will the Democratic party fight; upon the side of "the idle holders of idle capital" or upon the side of "the struggling masses"? That is the question which the party must answer first, and then it must be answered by each individual hereafter. The sympathies of the Democratic party, as shown by the platform, are on the side of the struggling masses who have ever been the foundation of the Democratic party.

There are two ideas of government. There are those who believe that, if you will only legislate to make the well-to-do prosperous, their prosperity will leak through on those below. The Democratic idea, however, has been that if you legislate to make the masses prosperous, their prosperity will find its way up through every class which rests upon them.

You come to us and tell us that the great cities are in favor of the gold standard; we reply that the great cities rest upon our broad and fertile prairies.

Burn down your cities and leave our farms, and your cities will spring up again as if by magic; but destroy our farms and the grass will grow in the streets of every city in the country.

My friends, we declare that this nation is able to legislate for its own people on every question, without waiting for the aid or consent of any other nation on earth; and upon that issue we expect to carry every state in the Union. I shall not slander the inhabitants of the fair state of Massachusetts nor the inhabitants of the state of New York by saying that, when they are confronted with the proposition, they will declare that this nation is not able to attend to its own business.

It is the issue of 1776 over again. Our ancestors, when but three millions in number, had the courage to declare their political independence of every other nation; shall we, their descendants, when we have grown to seventy millions, declare that we are less independent than our forefathers?

No, my friends, that will never be the verdict of our people. Therefore, we care not upon what lines the battle is fought. If they say bimetallism is good, but that we cannot have it until other nations help us, we reply that, instead of having a gold standard because England has, we will restore bimetallism, and then let England have bimetallism because the United States has it.

If they dare to come out in the open field and defend the gold standard as a good thing, we will fight them to the uttermost. Having behind us the producing masses of this nation and the world, supported by the commercial interests, the laboring interests and the toilers everywhere, we will answer their demand for a gold standard by saying to them: You shall not press down upon the brow of labor this crown of thorns, you shall not crucify mankind upon a cross of gold.

REVIEW QUESTIONS

1. Why did Bryan profess such a distaste for banks?
2. Why did Bryan support an income tax?
3. Bryan claimed that the cities' survival depended on the farms, and therefore the urban dwellers should support the silverite position. Do you find this argument convincing? Explain.

23 ⌘ AN AMERICAN EMPIRE

In 1889 the prominent Massachusetts Congressman Henry Cabot Lodge observed that "our relations with foreign nations today fill but a slight place in American politics, and excite generally only a languid interest." Indeed, Americans after the Civil War gave scant attention to world affairs. They instead focused their energies on the domestic concerns associated with industrial development and the settling of the western frontier. At the same time, presidents and the Congress steadfastly refused to entangle the nation in foreign crises and controversies.

During the 1890s, however, this period of "splendid isolationism" abruptly ended as the United States rushed to join European nations in competing for overseas empires. By 1900 U.S. army and naval forces had won an easy victory over Spain, acquired far-flung possessions in the Pacific and Caribbean, and assumed a significant new role in world affairs.

How did this happen? How was it that a nation long committed to a non-interventionist foreign policy had become an expansionist imperial power and world leader? The reasons are many and complex, involving long-developing commercial and strategic interests, missionary impulses, and a quest for international prestige, but the catalytic event was the Spanish-American War in 1898.

Elected president in 1896, William McKinley pursued a diplomatic solution to the protracted war in Cuba between Spanish forces and Cuban rebels seeking independence. But after the mysterious sinking of the American battleship Maine *in Havana harbor on 15 February 1898, Republican leaders such as Theodore Roosevelt and Henry Cabot Lodge urged immediate military action against Spain. Even the pacifist Democrat William Jennings Bryan argued that "the time for intervention has arrived. Humanity demands that we shall act." But President McKinley counseled caution and asked the nation to withhold judgment until an investigation of the tragic event could be undertaken.*

On 27 March 1898, the investigating board reported that an external explosion caused the sinking of the Maine. Most people assumed the culprits were the

Spanish, but skeptics asked why they would do something to provoke American intervention. McKinley used the report as an excuse to send the Spanish government an ultimatum: either accept American efforts to mediate the dispute and allow for Cuban independence or risk war. When the Spanish refused, McKinley succumbed to public pressure and asked for a declaration of war.

The "splendid little war" against Spain, as Republican John Hay called it, lasted only 113 days. During the summer of 1898, American forces defeated the Spanish army and navy, and on 12 August, Spanish officials signed a preliminary peace treaty. Some 5,500 Americans had died in the Spanish-American War, but only 379 of them were killed in battle. The rest fell victim to a variety of accidents and diseases: yellow fever, malaria, and typhoid.

Although the United States officially declared war against Spain on behalf of the Cuban struggle for independence, America in the end took control of Puerto Rico, the Philippine Islands, Guam, and Wake Island, completed the annexation of Hawaii, and established a protectorate over Cuba. Soon thereafter, the United States "acquired" the right to build an inter-oceanic canal in Panama, repeatedly used military force to intervene in the internal affairs of Central American nations, and undertook a major diplomatic initiative in Asia known as the Open Door policy.

By 1900 the United States had thus become a great world power with global responsibilities. While advocates of American expansionism rejoiced in such developments, others lamented the abandonment of many of the principles and policies that had served the nation well since 1776. "Mr. Dooley," the popular cartoon character created by Finley Peter Dunne, looked back to "th' good old days befur we became . . . a wurrld power." He recalled that "our favrite sport was playin' solytare," but now that the nation had become a participant in the game of power politics, "be Hivens we have no peace iv mind."

Under President Theodore Roosevelt (1901–1909), the United States asserted its right to intervene in the internal affairs of Latin American nations. In perhaps his most controversial action, Roosevelt helped Panama break away from Colombia in order to facilitate the building of an American canal across the isthmus. In 1904 a financial crisis in the debt-ridden Dominican Republic led Roosevelt to announce his "corollary" modifying the Monroe Doctrine: it allowed for American intervention in other countries in the Western Hemisphere in order to preempt such actions by European governments eager to collect debts. However well-intentioned, such interventionist policies helped generate among Latin Americans an intense resentment of the United States and "Yankee imperialism." Roosevelt's swaggering rhetoric and bold actions led one Argentine writer to lament the bullying tactics of the "Colossus of the North."

NEW YORK WORLD

The War Must Be Ended (1897)

In trying to suppress the Cuban revolt, the Spanish commander, General Valeriano ("Butcher") Weyler, established concentration camps for rebels and their families. Atrocities occurred on both sides, but the United States heard little of Cuban misdeeds. Locked in an intense competition for newspaper subscribers, Joseph Pulitzer's New York World *and William Randolph Hearst's* New York Journal *engaged in sensational reporting that came to be called "yellow journalism." The phrase derived from the first color newspaper cartoon, "Hogan's Alley." It was enormously popular and featured the Yellow Kid. Hence, "yellow journalism" was born when two competing New York newspapers fought over rival versions of this cartoon. Stories highlighted horrifying tales of Spanish cruelty and atrocities. A* World *reporter claimed that slaughtered Cuban rebels were fed to dogs, and that children of high-ranking Spanish families used ears from dead Cubans as playthings. The following editorial in Pulitzer's* World *urged the American government to take direct action to end the fighting in Cuba.*

From "The War Must Be Ended," *New York World*, 13 February 1897. [Editorial insertions appear in square brackets—*Ed.*]

How long are the Spaniards to drench Cuba with the blood and tears of her people?

How long is the peasantry of Spain to be drafted away to Cuba to die miserably in a hopeless war, that Spanish nobles and Spanish officers may get medals and honors?

How long shall old [Cuban] men and women and children be murdered by the score, the innocent victims of Spanish rage against the patriot armies they cannot conquer?

How long shall the sound of rifles in Castle Morro at sunrise proclaim that bound and helpless prisoners of war have been murdered in cold blood?

How long shall Cuban women be the victims of Spanish outrages and lie sobbing and bruised in loathsome prisons?

How long shall women passengers on vessels flying the American flag be unlawfully seized and stripped and searched by brutal, jeering Spanish officers, in violation of the laws of nations and of the honor of the United States?

How long shall American citizens, arbitrarily arrested while on peaceful and legitimate errands, be immured in foul Spanish prisons without trial?

How long shall the navy of the United States be used as the sea police of barbarous Spain?

How long shall the United States sit idle and indifferent within sound and hearing of rapine and murder? How long?

REVIEW QUESTIONS

1. What techniques did the *World* editorial use to heighten the impact of its theme?
2. If you were writing an opposing editorial to the *New York World*'s position, what would be your key arguments?

William McKinley

Declaration of War (1898)

President William McKinley found it impossible to resist the mounting public and political pressure for war against Spain. In requesting a declaration of war from the Senate on 11 April 1898, he listed several concerns but stressed the nation's humanitarian sympathy for the Cuban independence movement. He said little about the long-range implications of war.

From James D. Richardson, ed., *Messages and Papers of the Presidents* (Washington, DC, 1899), 10:139–150.

To the Congress of the United States:

. . . The present revolution is but the successor of other similar insurrections which have occurred in Cuba against the dominion of Spain, extending over a period of nearly half a century, each of which during its progress has subjected the United States to great effort and expense in enforcing its neutrality laws, caused enormous losses to American trade and commerce, caused irritation, annoyance, and disturbance among our citizens, and, by the exercise of cruel, barbarous, and uncivilized practices of warfare, shocked the sensibilities and offended the human sympathies of our people. . . .

Our trade has suffered, the capital invested by our citizens in Cuba has been largely lost, and the temper and forbearance of our people have been so sorely tried as to beget a perilous unrest among our own citizens, which has inevitably found its expression from time to time in the National Legislature, so that issues wholly external to our own body politic engross attention and stand in the way of that close devotion to domestic advancement that becomes a selfcontained commonwealth whose primal maxim has been the avoidance of all foreign entanglements.

All this must needs awaken, and has, indeed, aroused, the utmost concern on the part of this Government, as well during my predecessor's term as in my own. . . . The overtures of this Government [to the Spanish government] . . . were met by assurances that home rule in an advanced phase would be forthwith offered to Cuba, without waiting for the war to end, and that more humane methods should thenceforth prevail in the conduct of hostilities.

*   *   *

The war in Cuba is of such a nature that, short of subjugation or extermination, a final military victory for either side seems impracticable. The alternative lies in the physical exhaustion of the one or the other party, or perhaps of both. . . . The prospect of such a protraction and conclusion of the present strife is a contingency hardly to be contemplated with equanimity by the civilized world, and least of all by the United States, affected and injured as we are, deeply and intimately, by its very existence. . . .

The spirit of all our acts hitherto has been an earnest, unselfish desire for peace and prosperity in Cuba, untarnished by differences between us and Spain and unstained by the blood of American citizens. The forcible intervention of the United States as a neutral to stop the war . . . is justifiable on rational grounds . . . [which] may be briefly summarized as follows:

First. In the cause of humanity and to put an end to the barbarities, bloodshed, starvation, and horrible miseries now existing there, and which the parties to the conflict are either unable or unwilling to stop or mitigate. It is no answer to say this is all in another country, belonging to another nation, and is therefore none of our business. It is specially our duty, for it is right at our door.

Second. We owe it to our citizens in Cuba to afford them that protection and indemnity for life and property which no government there can or will afford, and to that end to terminate the conditions that deprive them of legal protection.

Third. The right to intervene may be justified by the very serious injury to the commerce, trade, and business of our people and by the wanton destruction of property and devastation of the island.

Fourth, and which is of the utmost importance. The present condition of affairs in Cuba is a constant menace to our peace and entails upon this Government an enormous expense. With such a conflict waged for years in an island so near us and with which our people have such trade and business relations; when the lives and liberty of our citizens are in constant danger and their property destroyed and themselves ruined; where our trading vessels are liable to seizure and are seized at our very door by war ships of a foreign nation; the expeditions of filibustering that we are powerless to prevent altogether, and the irritating questions and entanglements thus arising—all these and others that I need not mention, with the resulting strained relations, are a constant menace to our peace and compel us to keep on a semiwar footing with a nation with which we are at peace.

These elements of danger and disorder already pointed out have been strikingly illustrated by a tragic event which has deeply and justly moved the American people. I have already transmitted to Congress the report of the naval court of inquiry on the destruction of the battleship *Maine* in the harbor of Havana during the night of the l5th of February. The destruction of that noble vessel has filled the national heart with inexpressible horror.

*   *   *

The naval court of inquiry, which, it is needless to say, commands the unqualified confidence of the Government, was unanimous in its conclusion that

the destruction of the *Maine* was caused by an exterior explosion—that of a submarine mine. It did not assume to place the responsibility. That remains to be fixed. In any event, the destruction of the *Maine*, by whatever exterior cause, is a patent and impressive proof of a state of things in Cuba that is intolerable. That condition is thus shown to be such that the Spanish Government can not assure safety and security to a vessel of the American Navy in the harbor of Havana on a mission of peace, and rightfully there. . . .

The long trial has proved that the object for which Spain has waged the war can not be attained. The fire of insurrection may flame or may smolder with varying seasons, but it has not been and it is plain that it can not be extinguished by present methods. The only hope of relief and repose from a condition which can no longer be endured is the enforced pacification of Cuba. In the name of humanity, in the name of civilization, in behalf of endangered American interests which give us the right and the duty to speak and to act, the war in Cuba must stop.

In view of these facts and of these considerations I ask the Congress to authorize and empower the President to take measures to secure a full and final termination of hostilities between the Government of Spain and the people of Cuba, and to secure in the island the establishment of a stable government, capable of maintaining order and observing its international obligations, insuring peace and tranquility and the security of its citizens as well as our own, and to use the military and naval forces of the United States as may be necessary for these purposes. . . .

REVIEW QUESTIONS

1. What were the specific interests of the United States in Cuba? Were they legitimate and significant enough to warrant intervention?
2. How did President McKinley justify going to war against Spain over events in Cuba?
3. Had McKinley indeed "exhausted every effort" short of war, as he claimed in his statement to Congress?

ALBERT J. BEVERIDGE

FROM The March of the Flag

Although the ostensible reason for declaring war against Spain was to stop the oppression of Cubans, the McKinley administration decided to dispatch Commodore George Dewey's Pacific naval task force to Manila Bay, where on 1 May 1898, it destroyed the Spanish Pacific fleet and took control of the Philippines. Spain ceded the Philippines to the United States in the Treaty of Paris, which officially ended the war on 10 December 1898. This posed an unexpected dilemma. What was to be done with the Philippines now that they were in American hands? Those supporting annexation were led by a small but prominent group of imperialists that included Theodore Roosevelt, senators Henry Cabot Lodge and Albert Beveridge, and John Hay, soon to become secretary of state. In the following selection, Beveridge articulated why he supported annexation of the Philippines—and perhaps other areas in the future.

From Albert Beveridge, "The March of the Flag," in *Congressional Record*, 56th Cong., 1st sess., 9 January 1900, pp. 4–12.

Fellow citizens, It is a noble land that God has given us; a land that can feed and clothe the world; a land whose coast lines would enclose half the countries of Europe; a land set like a sentinel between the two imperial oceans of the globe, a greater England with a nobler destiny. It is a mighty people that He has planted on this soil; a people sprung from the most masterful blood of history; a people perpetually revitalized by the virile, man-producing working folk of all the earth; a people imperial by virtue of their power, by right of their institutions, by authority of their Heaven directed purposes—the propagandists and not the misers of liberty.

It is a glorious history our God has bestowed upon His chosen people; a history whose keynote was struck by Liberty Bell; a history heroic with faith in our mission and our future; a history of statesmen who flung the boundaries of the Republic out into unexplored lands and savage wildernesses; a history of soldiers who carried the flag across the blazing deserts and through the ranks of hostile mountains, even to the gates of sunset; a history of a multiplying people who overran a continent in half a century; a history of prophets who saw the consequences of evils inherited from the past and of martyrs who died to save us from them; a history divinely logical, in the process of whose tremendous reasoning we find ourselves today. . . .

Shall the American people continue their resistless march toward the commercial supremacy of the world? Shall free institutions broaden their blessed reign as the children of liberty wax in strength, until the empire of our principles is established over the hearts of all mankind?

Have we no mission to perform, no duty to discharge to our fellowman? Has the Almighty Father endowed us with gifts beyond our deserts and marked us as the people of His peculiar favor, merely to rot in our own selfishness, as men and nations must, who take cowardice for their companion and self for their deity—as China has, as India has, as Egypt has?

Shall we be as the man who had one talent and hid it, or as he who had ten talents and used them until they grew to riches? And shall we reap the reward that waits on our discharge of our high duty as the sovereign power of earth; shall we occupy new markets for what our farmers raise, new markets for what our factories make, new markets for what our merchants sell—aye, and, please God, new markets for what our ships shall carry?

*   *   *

Hawaii is ours; Porto Rico is to be ours; at the prayer of her people Cuba will finally be ours; in the islands of the East, even to the gates of Asia, coaling-stations are to be ours at the very least; the flag of a liberal government is to float over the Philippines, and I pray God it may be the banner that Taylor unfurled in Texas and Frémont[1] carried to the coast—the Stars and Stripes of glory. . . .

The Opposition tells us that we ought not to govern a people without their consent. I answer, The rule of liberty that all just government derives its authority from the consent of the governed, applies only to those who are capable of self-government. I answer, We govern the Indians without their consent, we govern our territories without their consent, we govern our children without their consent. I answer, How do you assume that our government would be without their consent? Would not the people of the Philippines prefer the just, humane, civilizing government of this Republic to the savage, bloody rule of pillage and extortion from which we have rescued them? . . .

Today, we are raising more than we can consume. Today, we are making more than we can use. Today, our industrial society is congested; there are more workers than there is work; there is more capital than there is investment. We do not need more money—we need more circulation, more employment. Therefore we must find new markets for our produce, new occupation for our capital, new work for our labor. And so, while we did not need the territory taken during the past century at the time it was acquired, we do need what we have taken in 1898, and we need it now. . . .

Think of the tens of thousands of Americans who will invade mine and field and forest in the Philippines when a liberal government, protected and controlled by this republic, if not the government of the republic itself, shall establish order and equity there! Think of the hundreds of thousands of Americans who will build a soap-and-water, common-school civilization of energy and industry in Cuba, when a government of law replaces the double reign of anarchy and tyranny!—think of the prosperous millions that Empress of Islands will support when, obedient to the law of political gravitation, her people ask for the highest honor liberty can bestow, the sacred Order of the Stars and Stripes, the citizenship of the Great Republic!

What does all this mean for every one of us? It means opportunity for all the glorious young manhood of the republic—the most virile, ambitious, impatient, militant manhood the world has ever seen. It means that the resources and the commerce of these immensely rich dominions will be increased as much as American energy is greater than Spanish sloth; for Americans henceforth will monopolize those resources and that commerce. . . .

Fellow Americans, we are God's chosen people. . . . His power . . . delivered the Spanish fleet into our hands on the eve of Liberty's natal day, as he delivered the elder Armada[2] into the hands of our English sires two centuries ago. His great purposes are revealed in the progress of the flag, which surpasses the intentions of Congresses and Cabinets, and leads us like a holier pillar of cloud by day and pillar of fire by night into situations unforeseen by finite wisdom, and duties unexpected by the unprophetic heart of selfishness. The American people cannot use a dishonest medium of exchange; it is ours to set the world its example of right and honor. We cannot fly from our world duties; it is ours to execute the purpose of a fate that has driven us to be greater than our small intentions. We cannot retreat from any soil where Providence has unfurled our banner; it is ours to save that soil for Liberty and Civilization. . . .

---

[1] John Charles Frémont was an American soldier and explorer who seized California for the United States during the Mexican War in the mid-ninteenth century. General Zachary Taylor led American troops in the Mexican War.

[2] The Spanish Armada was a naval fleet sent to attack England in 1588. It fell victim to powerful storms.

REVIEW QUESTIONS

1. How did Beveridge justify American acquisition of new territories? Does one country have the right to control another country, without "the consent of the governed"?
2. What did he mean by asserting that Americans were "God's chosen people"?
3. Do you share his belief that it was the "manifest destiny" of the United States to bring the blessings of its civilization to other peoples?
4. How did Beveridge imply that domestic economic concerns were dictating American foreign policy?

Platform of the American Anti-Imperialist League (1899)

Those opposed to the new expansionism included Republicans and Democrats, business leaders such as Andrew Carnegie, the philosopher William James, prominent scholars such as William Graham Sumner, and literary figures such as Mark Twain and William Dean Howells. Many of them joined the Anti-Imperialist League, formed in Boston in 1898 for the purpose of galvanizing public opinion against the Philippine War and the evils of imperialism. Anti-imperialists almost prevented the annexation of the Philippines through their lobbying efforts against the Treaty of Paris, which the Senate ultimately ratified by only one vote on 6 February 1899. The following excerpt outlines the anti-imperialist critique of American foreign policy.

"Platform of the American Anti-Imperialist League," in *Speeches, Correspondence, and Political Papers of Carl Schurz*, vol. 6, ed. Frederick Bancroft (New York: G. P. Putnam's Sons, 1913), p. 77, n. 1.

We hold that the policy known as imperialism is hostile to liberty and tends toward militarism, an evil from which it has been our glory to be free. We regret that it has become necessary in the land of Washington and Lincoln to reaffirm that all men, of whatever race or color, are entitled to life, liberty, and the pursuit of happiness. We maintain that governments derive their just powers from the consent of the governed. We insist that the subjugation of any people is "criminal aggression" and open disloyalty to the distinctive principles of our Government.

We earnestly condemn the policy of the present National Administration in the Philippines. It seeks to extinguish the spirit of 1776 in those is-

lands. We deplore the sacrifice of our soldiers and sailors, whose bravery deserves admiration even in an unjust war. We denounce the slaughter of the Filipinos as a needless horror. We protest against the extension of American sovereignty by Spanish methods.

We demand the immediate cessation of the war against liberty, begun by Spain and continued by us. We urge that Congress be promptly convened to announce to the Filipinos our purpose to concede to them the independence for which they have so long fought and which of right is theirs.

The United States have always protested against the doctrine of international law which permits the subjugation of the weak by the strong. A selfgoverning state cannot accept sovereignty over an unwilling people. The United States cannot act upon the ancient heresy that might makes right.

Imperialists assume that with the destruction of selfgovernment in the Philippines by American hands, all opposition here will cease. This is a grievous error. Much as we abhor the war of "criminal aggression" in the Philippines, greatly as we regret that the blood of the Filipinos is on American hands, we more deeply resent the betrayal of American institutions at home. The real firing line is not in the suburbs of Manila. The foe is of our own household. The attempt of 1861 was to divide the country. That of 1899 is to destroy its fundamental principles and noblest ideals.

Whether the ruthless slaughter of the Filipinos shall end next month or next year is but an incident in a contest that must go on until the Declaration of Independence and the Constitution of the United States are rescued from the hands of their betrayers. Those who dispute about standards of value while the Republic is undermined will be listened to as little as those who would wrangle about the small economies of the household while the house is on fire. The training of a great people for a century, the aspiration for liberty of a vast immigration are forces that will hurl aside those who in the delirium of conquest seek to destroy the character of our institutions.

We deny that the obligation of all citizens to support their Government in times of grave na-tional peril applies to the present situation. If an Administration may with impunity ignore the issues upon which it was chosen, deliberately create a condition of war anywhere on the face of the globe, debauch the civil service for spoils to promote the adventure, organize a truthsuppressing censorship and demand of all citizens a suspension of judgment and their unanimous support while it chooses to continue the fighting, representative government itself is imperiled.

We propose to contribute to the defeat of any person or party that stands for the forcible subjugation of any people. We shall oppose for reelection all who in the White House or in Congress betray American liberty in pursuit of unAmerican gains. We still hope that both of our great political parties will support and defend the Declaration of Independence in the closing campaign of the century. . . .

REVIEW QUESTIONS

1. What arguments did the Anti-Imperialist League offer against the annexation of any new territories?
2. What did they plan to do to oppose annexation efforts?
3. How would you have felt about these issues?

ALICE BYRAM CONDICT

American Christianity in the Philippines (1902)

Christian missionaries were among the first Americans to travel to the Philippines after the war with Spain ended in 1898. Most of them were Protestants, eager to convert both Catholic Filipinos and those committed to indigenous religions. Among the missionaries was Dr. Alice Byram Condict. She first went to India to assist those suffering from famine. In 1899 Condict arrived in Manila, the capital of the Philippines. After months traveling across the newly "liberated" country, she wrote a book about the Filipinos and their opportunity to embrace American democracy and American Christianity—whether they wanted to or not.

From Alice Byram Condict, *Old Glory and the Gospel in the Philippines* (New York: Revell, 1902), pp. 14–16, 18, 23–24, 46–47, 111–115, 118–120, 124. [Editorial insertions appear in square brackets—*Ed.*]

Salvation from super-civilization lies in the restless Anglo-Saxon blood that always moves on, guided by the unseen Almighty God. We were prompted in 1898 by sympathy and education to rescue those of our less fortunate neighbors from oppression and tyranny. In doing this we are led further than we dreamed. Even the oppressors forge a link in the chain of circumstances that stirred the American nation to deeds of valor in the sinking of the *Maine.* From the North to the South, from the Atlantic to the Pacific, the excitement aroused by the indignity done to our navy was intense. The people's cry of agony was in the high key of the infuriated. President [William] McKinley, in his calm attitude of waiting to obtain absolute evidence of the murderous intents of our host, for whose land we had only the most benevolent intentions, was urged to plunge at once into war. Can we forget those days of suspense? But our statesman at the helm could not be hurried. How characteristic of our late and much lamented President McKinley was his attitude in those days of waiting. The silence in the White House was golden. Full time was given to investigate before our nation was allowed to become involved in war. Mr. McKinley coolly weighed every detail. He seemed to be thinking of his duty to the Spaniards while the impulse of the people was their annihilation. Every test, however, failed to exonerate the cowardly government that alike crushed its own subjects and murdered those who came to pour balm on their wounds. The great Republic that had such fathers as Washington and Lincoln could not in the name of humanity prevent the will of the people from being carried out.

War was inevitable. First, to satisfy our responsibility to those crying to us for aid and to show that dishonor done our navy could not remain unpunished, war was declared. When once launched into war, we were bound to finish what had been begun. As has already been said, to protect our shores from invasion by the reputed powerful Spanish navy, the order was given to destroy the Spanish-Philippine ships which might menace our seaports. The command was carried out; and in doing so, instead of sinking a few Spanish ships, the chain of events ended in the taking of Manila, and eventually the islands whose capital had already surrendered. Thus it has come about that in point of center of area, our Pacific Coast becomes the center of dominion. The Atlantic Ocean, whose waters have for the past four hundred years been fulfilling the high edicts of the Almighty God in carrying civilization from the East to the West, is still in its zenith of usefulness. The "ocean greyhounds" and massive freight vessels are increasing year by year, but still there is a moving westward. Now the Pacific Ocean, whose extent is possibly double that of the Atlantic, is about to take its part, as never before, in the world-civilization that still remains to be accomplished. . . .

The new century is inaugurated in its mission of enlightening the Far East, as China and Thibet are often called; and we of the United States have become a factor in the working out of problems so rapidly to be solved. Surely Old Glory should feel quite in its element in the East, standing always for liberty of conscience and advancement of civilization.

Our United States, with the two greatest oceans of the world as its highway for commerce and civilization, is on the threshold of its greatest era of prosperity.

This little book goes on its mission of love—clothed in the simplest dress—having no literary merit, but with the endeavor to show who our wards are, something of their past history, and why Old Glory has a mission to meet their necessities, the first fruits having already ripened. All matters relating to business possibilities, or information regarding trade, have been utterly ignored, as others are treating of these important matters most comprehensively.

*　　*　　*

When driving about this tropical city [Manila], one is impressed by its cosmopolitan character.

There are Spanish families still living in their old houses, with lovely gardens partly enclosed in high walls. On the street we meet the "Mestizo," or Filipino of the plains, with his flowing white dress. Here are found, too, the German and English merchants or shipowners, the Parsee or educated Hindu who has come from India for business. The omnipresent Chinaman, however, is seen in every grade and class. Possibly the first to encounter will be the Chinese peddler who is sure to want to sell you something from the huge pack he carries all day on his shoulders. . . .

One is struck by the large number of children. If it were not for the fact that four out of five children die before ten years of age, the population would be like China or Japan.

*　　*　　*

"The Christian churches of the United States have no more important task before them than to give at once to the people of the Philippine Islands the Living Word of God. Spanish Romanism [Catholicism], in all its three hundred years of rule in these regions, neither translated the Bible into the languages of the people nor distributed its own versions among them. If we have any right in these islands, we have the high duty of bringing to these naturally favored regions the first essentials of Christian civilization. The spirit of Bible liberty brought our forefathers to American shores, and shaped our Government and institutions. The millions now looking for the first time to the Stars and Stripes for protection can be civilized most thoroughly and most in harmony with our own ideas by the gift of the Bible. Schools, churches, trade, and self-government *follow* its lead."

The hour for the deliverance of these people has come. Even this old walled city of Manila can no longer resist the edict of the Almighty. It is no longer necessary to shut the gates and pull up the draw-bridges at dark. This is the first hour of the dawn of a day when we hope to have a Bible institute and training school for Filipinos, that they may read their Bibles, know their God, and rejoice in religious liberty.

*　　*　　*

Many pages of this modest little book are necessarily filled with the recital of the agonies of a people who, for centuries, had blindly groped for deliverance from oppression. How delightful, in these closing pages, to be able to record the changed conditions, and give the reader a glimpse of a new order of things, that with leaps and bounds carries us on to see the probabilities in the near future of a new Filipino race.

In the policy of President McKinley toward the Philippine Islands, "the gospel of kindliness" has gendered faith in America and Americans, but death, in its most dramatic form, has suddenly removed him from us. "In the twinkling of an eye he has been placed beside Washington and Lincoln, the greatest of his predecessors. He has been canonized by the united love of all the people."

The world began to realize that the United States has become a first-class power, when in the Spanish-American war, as well as in the episode in Pekin, "our President had been able to pitch the world's concert in a higher key, and to make the United States the moral leader of the nations."

His successor, President [Theodore] Roosevelt, immediately made public his intention to continue, "absolutely unbroken, the policies of President McKinley." These policies were distinctly outlined in President McKinley's last speech, the scope of which leads on to new ventures of magnificent magnitude.

"America's exclusiveness is to be a thing of the

past." The American nation has entered its majority. Our statesman outlined the work of the new century, when he said, "We must encourage our merchant marine. We must have more ships under the American flag, built and manned and owned by Americans."

With our long line of frontage on the two great oceans, and the possibility of leading ocean traffic for 2,000 miles into the interior of our continent, through the St. Lawrence river and the Great Lakes, that Merchant Marine would be able to carry exports, directly from the sources of production, to any part of the world.

The coal of the Philippines will be needed by that Merchant Marine as it sails to the Far East. The rich treasures of lumber, and still more varied and valuable agricultural products of the Philippines, can be carried by our ships to the center of our continent. Thus does the prophetic speech of our statesman, in his last utterance, vividly outline our near future.

*   *   *

It was so ordained that our present leader in Washington [President Theodore Roosevelt] had outlined the Philippine policy months before the reins of government were put in his hands. He says, "In the Philippine Islands we have brought peace, and we are giving them freedom and self-government as they could never, under any conceivable conditions, have obtained, had we left them to sink into a welter of blood and confusion, or to become the prey of some strong tyranny, without or within. *We are not trying to subjugate a people, we are trying to develop them*, and make them a law-abiding, industrious and educated people, and eventually we hope a self-governing people."

*   *   *

The American public school teacher has trodden closely on the heels of the departing army. When has the world had put before it such an object lesson of kindly purpose in a victorious power? The call for 1,000 of these American public school teachers is already under way of fulfillment, thus placing some of our own best trained educators in the cities of these islands.

That the Filipino needs teaching more than shooting is being rapidly proven, for these public school teachers are a more convincing proposition to the Filipino than any proclamation or assurance that American sovereignty is the best thing that ever came to their islands. They were never so cared for in the past. The English language is rapidly becoming their pride. They seize every opportunity to study it and use it in conversation, and while our Government decided to retain the Spanish language for five years as the language of governmental instruments, there is little doubt but that in that time great numbers of the Filipinos will have thoroughly mastered the English and be as much rejoiced as ourselves to replace Spanish by English in all governmental papers.

While the United States Government, as such, has no direct influence in the forming of the people into a national church, yet the presence of our flag promoted such liberty of action that the Filipinos themselves have been able to unite with our missionaries of Protestant Evangelical Christianity and have formed the nucleus of an Evangelical Church.

A large proportion of the Filipino people have left the church of their fathers, but it was still their desire to worship God. They had never known but one form of worship. Denominational differences they could not comprehend. Our Protestant missionaries realized that a comprehensive and simple creed was a necessity to bind these Filipino Christians into one church. God planned the time and place for the forming of this infant Filipino Evangelical Church, without any preconcerted efforts of men. The missionaries who were needed to represent seven different religious organizations were in Manila, and easily drawn together in conference in April, 1901. In that conference, the power of the Holy Spirit was so markedly present that all felt that there was but one possible outcome to the discussions, and that a "union." All felt that it was not Church, but Christ, they had come to serve.

The organizations represented in that conference were Presbyterian, Methodist, United

Brethren, Christian Alliance, the American Bible Society, the Baptist, the British and Foreign Bible Society and the Y. M. C. A. Denominational differences were not mentioned. The Evangelical Union of the Philippine Islands was organized, and embraces all the denominations mentioned.

This is without doubt the most important and progressive missionary movement of the age. Its value cannot be overstated. While each missionary society, naturally, still has its separate organization, dependent on a different source for support, and each society also has its own polity, yet the body, as a whole, is one in name and unity of purpose. "La Iglesia Evangelica" represents all evangelical efforts to bring the Filipino people to Christ.

*   *   *

With better sanitation and medical skill the Filipino people will rapidly increase in numbers. With advanced education they will surprise the world with their material progress, even as much as the Japanese have done. With characteristic, warm-hearted enthusiasm, the prosperous Filipino will never disappoint us in his want of appreciative gratitude. God grant that we may be true to President Roosevelt's forecast of their future. "We are not trying to subjugate a people; we are trying to develop them, and make them a law-abiding, industrious and educated people; with God's help we hope a truly Christian and self-governing people."

REVIEW QUESTIONS

1. How does Condit explain the motives for the United States declaring war against Spain?
2. How does Condit justify American expansion into the Pacific Ocean and Asia? What role does religion play in her view?
3. Summarize the elements comprising Condit's paternalistic attitude toward the Filipinos.

JOHN HAY

The Open Door in China (1899–1900)

Having extended American control over the Philippines, the McKinley administration next turned its attention to the most coveted economic market in Asia—China. In 1899 Secretary of State John Hay issued the first "Open Door Note," a letter sent to each of the nations engaged in commercial activity in China—Great Britain, France, Germany, Italy, Japan, and Russia. In an effort to thwart the efforts of Japan and Russia to carve out exclusive economic spheres of interest in China, the letter affirmed the commercial equality of all nations trading in China. Although most major powers ignored or evaded the Open Door Note, Hay announced their acceptance on 20 March 1900.

From U.S. Department of State, *Papers Relating to Foreign Relations of the United States, 1899* (Washington, DC, 1901), pp. 129–130.

At the time when the Government of the United States was informed by that of Germany that it had leased from His Majesty the Emperor of China the port of Kiaochao and the adjacent territory in the province of Shantung, assurances were given to the ambassador of the United States at Berlin by the Imperial German minister for foreign affairs that the rights and privileges insured by treaties with China to citizens of the United States would not thereby suffer or be in anywise impaired within the area over which Germany had thus obtained control.

More recently, however, the British Government recognized by a formal agreement with Germany the exclusive right of the latter country to enjoy in said leased area and the contiguous "sphere of influence or interest" certain privileges, more especially those relating to railroads and mining enterprises; but, as the exact nature and extent of the rights thus recognized have not been clearly defined, it is possible that serious conflicts of interest may at any time arise, not only between British and German subjects within said area, but that the interests of our citizens may also be jeopardized thereby.

Earnestly desirous to remove any cause of irritation and to insure at the same time to the commerce of all nations in China the undoubted benefits which should accrue from a formal recognition by the various powers claiming "spheres of interest" that they shall enjoy perfect equality of treatment for their commerce and navigation within such "spheres," the Government of the United States would be pleased to see His German Majesty's Government give formal assurances and lend its cooperation in securing like assurances from the other interested powers that each within its respective sphere of whatever influence—

First. Will in no way interfere with any treaty port or any vested interest within any socalled "sphere of interest" or leased territory it may have in China.

Second. That the Chinese treaty tariff of the time being shall apply to all merchandise landed or shipped to all such ports as are within said "sphere of interest" (unless they be "free ports"), no matter to what nationality it may belong, and that duties so leviable shall be collected by the Chinese Government.

Third. That it will levy no higher harbor dues on vessels of another nationality frequenting any port in such "sphere" than shall be levied on vessels of its own nationality, and no higher railroad charges over lines built, controlled, or operated within its "sphere" on merchandise belonging to citizens or subjects of other nationalities transported through such "sphere" than shall be levied on similar merchandise belonging to its own nationals transported over equal distances. . . .

The commercial interests of Great Britain and Japan will be so clearly served by the desired declaration of intentions, and the views of the Governments of these countries as to the desirability of the adoption of measures insuring the benefits of equality of treatment of all foreign trade throughout China are so similar to those entertained by the United States, that their acceptance of the propositions herein outlined and their cooperation in advocating their adoption by the other powers can be confidently expected. . . .

REVIEW QUESTIONS

1. How did the United States justify an "open door policy"?
2. What did it ask the other foreign powers in China to do?
3. What do you think was the primary motive for such a policy?

JOSIAH QUINCY

FROM China and Russia (1900)

When the Boxer Rebellion erupted against the presence of foreign nations on Chinese soil, England, France, Germany, Russia, and the United States dispatched a rescue expedition (including 2,500 American troops) to protect their citizens living in China. Fearing that some of the competing Western powers might take advantage of the volatile situation to seize Chinese territory, Hay decided to expand America's commitment to China to include the preservation of Chinese territorial and administrative integrity as well as commercial equality. He failed to realize the long-range significance of such a commitment. In 1900 Josiah Quincy, formerly first assistant United States secretary of state, criticized Hay and McKinley for committing the United States to policies it could not enforce.

From Josiah Quincy, "China and Russia," *North American Review* 171 (October 1900): 529–542.

. . . The action of our own Government for the last year in connection with Chinese affairs, beginning with the circular note of Secretary Hay relative to the "open door" policy, in September, 1899, has certainly, in the main, been wise and conservative, and it may well be conceded that if the record closes equally well, a creditable chapter will have been added to the annals of American diplomacy. But the critical period of the real difficulties is just upon us, and this may last even for years before any final settlement is effected—if, indeed, the Chinese puzzle is to be solved at all in our day, which is by no means certain. It may not, therefore, be out of place to point out, in a spirit of considerate criticism, two mistakes, perhaps not unnatural ones, and fortunately not of the gravest importance or incapable of correction, which the present Administration seems to have made.

In the first place, the program outlined in Secretary Hay's note of July 3rd, while excellent ideally, was too ambitious and comprehensive in its scope, and too political in its character, differing radically in the latter respect from the policy embodied in his negotiations for the maintenance of the "open door" for commerce. His promise to hold the responsible authors of wrongs to American citizens to "the uttermost accountability" can easily be seen, in the light of recent developments, to have been somewhat too sweeping, and a more intimate knowledge of existing conditions in China would, doubtless, have prevented it from being made. It is never wise to threaten punishment which cannot be inflicted; and even on July 3rd it should have been sufficiently evident that the difficulties in the way of even ascertaining, to say nothing of punishing, the "responsible authors" of outrages would be so great as to make threats worse that idle; and a great nation cannot but suffer some loss of dignity if unable to make good its solemn words. . . .

In further declaring it to be the policy of the United States to seek a solution of the existing troubles which should "prevent a recurrence of such disasters, bring about permanent safety and peace in China," Secretary Hay plainly implied the intention of our Government to join in political action for the radical reconstruction of Chinese administration. Fortunately, his language is general and does not hold us to any specific program, and when it suits our convenience we can dismiss it as a mere expression of pious good will toward the Chinese people; but taking the then existing conditions in connection with the context, it is sufficiently clear that the intention was to commit the United States to political action for the reform of Chinese government—an object quite outside the scope of previous American policy in the Far East, impossible of attainment by our own independent action and, if pursued in common with other Powers, fraught with the gravest possibilities of those international entanglements with European nations, which it is our historical policy to keep out of.

The Chinese government is, indeed, in the most crying need of reconstruction, whether from within or from without. But if this reform is to come from within, we have no more right to interfere with the internal politics of China than she has to take sides in our Presidential election; if from without, we had much better leave this huge, if not impossible, task to such nations as Russia or Japan, which could alone attempt it with any hope of success. It is not the mission of the United States to set right everything that is amiss all over the world, even if we have interests involved, or to take part in remodeling the government of some four hundred millions of people who deeply resent foreign interference with their affairs.

The idea of joining a syndicate of nations for the establishment of a political trust to regulate the affairs of the world may be a dazzling one, but when it seriously appeals to the United States, the whole character of our government and of our institutions will have to be changed; for world-empire and democracy are inconsistent with each other and cannot coexist. Fortunately, the territory and power of the whole eastern hemisphere have already been so far divided up or preempted among the older nations that the share which a new political partner would now receive would not be a very tempting one, in comparison with their great empires and dependencies—and perhaps we have our share in the political hegemony of the whole American hemisphere under the Monroe doctrine, to say nothing of our newly acquired islands.

The second mistake of the Administration was its assent to the appointment of a Commander-in-Chief of the forces of the allied Powers. A willingness to place American troops under any foreign officer implied a closer alliance with other Powers in China than was consistent with the independent attitude of the United States in Asiatic affairs in the past, and involved unknown risks of entangling us in political complications.

*   *   *

We should never lose sight of the cardinal fact in the Chinese situation, so far as we are concerned—namely, that we have no present or prospective territorial or political interests, "spheres of influence," or "leases" of ports, in China, and that we do not want any—in which respects we are in a radically different position from all the other Powers represented in the concert. If we have joined with other nations in forcing our missionaries and our trade on China, we have not, at least, participated in the exaction of those cessions of territory and comprehensive privileges which seem to have been the direct cause of the present outbreak. We may, therefore, well leave the main task of quelling the storm to those Powers which have raised it, merely safeguarding our own special interests, so far as that is possible.

In another respect, also, the position of the United States in China is fundamentally different from that of the other allied Powers. Every one of these has such important interests at stake or such political alliances in Europe, that it must unfortunately consider becoming involved in war over the issues to be settled in Asia as at least a possibility—and each is at present practically on a war footing, though this can only be said of Great Britain owing to the conflict in South Africa.

Doubtless, the tremendous disasters which would be involved in any war carried on between two great Powers under modern conditions—disasters which would fall only less heavily upon the victors than upon the vanquished—are fully realized by responsible statesmen and rulers, and this knowledge makes their action most careful and conservative. Yet to the European Powers and

Japan the dread possibility of armed conflict is always present in the background. Fortunately for the United States, in spite of our large army in the Philippines and our troops now in China, no sane American thinks that we will fight with any other member of the concert, whatever may be our policy or our interests, either to prevent the dismemberment of China or to secure any share in the partition for ourselves, or to reform the Chinese government, or even to maintain the "open door" for our trade. This certainly affords another cogent consideration in favor of keeping out of the threatening complications which may lead to war between the Powers; for, if we do not mean to fight, neither do we want to suffer any loss of dignity or prestige. . . .

REVIEW QUESTIONS

1. What was the basis of Quincy's critique of Hay's Open Door Notes and policies?
2. How did Quincy define American interests in China?
3. Do you find Quincy or Hay more convincing? Why?

The Roosevelt Corollary to the Monroe Doctrine (1904)

When he became president in 1901, Theodore Roosevelt brought with him to the White House a candid assumption of American superiority in the affairs of the Western Hemisphere. Within a few years, he grew concerned about the chronic instability of Latin American governments and economies. He especially worried that European powers might intervene in order to collect overdue debts. In 1904 a financial crisis in the Dominican Republic provoked him to formulate a new policy that came to be known as the Roosevelt Corollary to the Monroe Doctrine. His reasoning rested on the assumption that nations are not equal in stature. Those states unable to manage their affairs must submit to outside supervision by "first-class" powers.

From James D. Richardson, ed., *Messages and Papers of the Presidents* (Washington, DC, 1905), 14:6923ff.

. . . It is not true that the United States feels any land hunger or entertains any projects as regards the other nations of the Western Hemisphere save such as are for their welfare. All that this country desires is to see the neighboring countries stable, orderly, and prosperous. Any country whose people conduct themselves well can count upon our hearty friendship. If a nation shows that it knows how to act with reasonable efficiency and decency in social and political matters, if it keeps order and pays its obligations, it need fear no interference from the United States.

Chronic wrongdoing, or an impotence which results in a general loosening of the ties of civilized society, may in America, as elsewhere, ultimately require intervention by some civilized nation, and in the Western Hemisphere the adherence of the United States to the Monroe Doctrine may force the United States, however reluctantly, in flagrant cases of such wrongdoing or impotence, to the exercise of an international police power. If every country washed by the Caribbean Sea would show the progress in stable and just civilization which with the aid of the Platt amendment Cuba has shown since our troops left the island, and which so many of the republics in both Americas are constantly and brilliantly showing, all question of interference by this Nation with their affairs would be at an end.

Our interests and those of our southern neighbors are in reality identical. They have great natural riches, and if within their borders the reign of law and justice obtains, prosperity is sure to come to them. While they thus obey the primary laws of civilized society they may rest assured that they will be treated by us in a spirit of cordial and helpful sympathy. We would interfere with them only in the last resort, and then only if it became evident that their inability or unwillingness to do justice at home and abroad had violated the rights of the United States or had invited foreign aggression to the detriment of the entire body of American nations. It is a mere truism to say that every nation, whether in America or anywhere else, which desires to maintain its freedom, its independence, must ultimately realize that the right of such independence can not be separated from the responsibility of making good use of it.

In asserting the Monroe Doctrine, in taking such steps as we have taken in regard to Cuba, Venezuela, and Panama, and in endeavoring to cir-cumscribe the theater of war in the Far East, and to secure the open door in China, we have acted in our own interest as well as in the interest of humanity at large. There are, however, cases in which, while our own interests are not greatly involved, strong appeal is made to our sympathies. . . . But in extreme cases action may be justifiable and proper. What form the action shall take must depend upon the circumstances of the case; that is, upon the degree of the atrocity and upon our power to remedy it. The cases in which we could interfere by force of arms as we interfered to put a stop to intolerable conditions in Cuba are necessarily very few.

REVIEW QUESTIONS

1. Why did Roosevelt claim that the United States should interfere in the internal affairs of nations in Central and South America?
2. What factors contributed to Roosevelt's Corollary? Do you agree with his reasoning? Why?
3. In reflecting upon the expansion of American power around the world at the turn of the century, do you think it was motivated more by moral idealism or by power politics? Why?

24 ✑ THE PROGRESSIVE ERA

The capitalists and entrepreneurs who built the United States into one of the world's leading economies took full advantage of America's free-enterprise culture to launch an industrial revolution of unprecedented scope. With few state or federal laws to hinder them, many business leaders used questionable tactics to drive out competitors and establish monopolies or near-monopolies in their respective industries. Along the way they cajoled, bribed, or blackmailed political leaders to facilitate their efforts.

To address such excesses, a diverse group of reformers set about trying to gain political power and public support at the end of the nineteenth century. Progressivism, as historians have come to label this reform movement, found its support primarily in urban areas among the middle and upper-middle classes—business executives, professionals, teachers, and government workers. They promoted greater efficiency in the workplace and greater honesty in government. Their fervent hope was to restore democratic control of the economic and political sectors.

There was no all-encompassing "progressive" organization, agenda, or motive. The movement cut across both political parties, appeared in every geographic region, and contained many conflicting elements. Some activists were spurred by strong religious convictions while others were animated by secular ideals. Some were earnest humanitarians and others were more concerned with issues of efficiency and productivity. Prominent men such as Robert La Follette, Theodore Roosevelt, and Woodrow Wilson are most often associated with the Progressive movement, yet women were disproportionately involved in the array of "progressive" causes and issues.

While varied in motivation and mission, Progressives believed that government should take a more active role in promoting the general welfare. More specifically, this meant the passage of laws breaking up the huge corporate trusts, regulating child and female labor, promoting better working conditions, and conserving the environment. In addition, Progressives supported voluntary associa-

tions such as settlement houses and other charitable organizations intended to help immigrants, the poor, and the disabled.

Progressivism changed the social and political landscape of American life by enlarging the sphere of government action. New laws, regulations, and attitudes resulted from the efforts of self-styled progressives to deal with many persistent social ills. The glaring failure of the Progressive movement was its unwillingness to address racial injustice. For the most part, progressivism was for whites only. African Americans in the South were increasingly victims of disfranchisement, Jim Crow laws, vigilante assaults, and poverty.

WASHINGTON GLADDEN

The Social Gospel (1902)

During the last quarter of the nineteenth century, many Protestants began to promote what came to be called the social gospel. They sought to apply Christian ethics in an effort to ameliorate the many problems spawned by rapid urbanization and industrialization: poverty, unsanitary living conditions, racial and ethnic tensions, and labor strife. Among the early champions of the social gospel was Washington Gladden, a prominent Congregational minister who pastored large churches in Springfield, Massachusetts, and Columbus, Ohio. Gladden was the first minister to endorse the labor union movement. He also spoke out against anti-Catholicism and racial segregation. In the following selection from his book Social Salvation, *he explains why Christians need to become social reformers.*

From, Washington Gladden, *Social Salvation* (Boston: Houghton Mifflin, 1902), pp. 14–15, 25–28, 206–8, 226.

Any treatment of social questions which failed to bring the responsibility for right social actions home to individuals would, indeed, be defective treatment; on the other hand, any discussion of the problems of the individual life which did not keep the social environment steadily in view would be utterly inadequate.

I am therefore unable to understand how Christianity, whether as a law or as a gospel, can be intelligently or adequately preached or lived in these days without a constant reference to social questions. No individual is soundly converted until he comprehends his social relations and strives to fulfill them; and the work of growth and sanctification largely consists in a clearer apprehension of these relations and a more earnest effort to fill them with the life of the divine Spirit. The kingdom of heaven is *within* us and *among* us; the preposition, in Christ's saying, seems to have the double meaning. It cannot be among us unless it is within us, and it cannot be within us without being among us.

It would seem, therefore, that the minister's work, in these days, must lie, very largely, along the lines of social amelioration. He is bound to understand the laws of social structure. It is just as needful that he should understand the constitution of human society as that he should understand the constitution of the human soul; the one comes under his purview no less directly than the other. He does not know definitely what sin is, unless he understands the nature of the social bond; he does not surely know what salvation means until he has comprehended the reciprocal action of society upon the individual and of the individual upon society. The men who are working out their own salvation are doing it largely through the establishment of right relations between themselves and their neighbors, and he cannot help them in this unless he has some clear idea of what these right relations are.

*   *   *

. . . The minister who has become merely or mainly political, or sociological, or economical, or scientific, has abandoned his vocation. The minister to whom religion is not the central and culminating power in all his teaching has no right in any Christian pulpit. It is *the religion* of politics, of economics, of sociology that we are to teach,—nothing else. We are to bring the truths and the powers of the spiritual world, the eternal world, to bear upon all these themes. This is what we have to do with these social questions, and we have nothing else to do with them.

The first thing for us to understand is that God is in his world, and that we are workers together with him. In all this industrial struggle he is present in every part of it, working according to the counsel of his perfect will. In the gleams of light which sometimes break forth from the darkness of the conflict we discern his inspiration; in the stirrings of goodwill which temper the wasting strife we behold the evidence of his presence; in the sufferings and losses and degradations which wait

upon every violation of his law of love we witness the retributions with which that law goes armed. In the weltering masses of poverty; in the giddy throngs that tread the paths of vice; in the multitudes distressed and scattered as sheep having no shepherd; in the brutalized ranks marching in lock-step through the prison yard; in the groups of politicians scheming for place and plunder,—in all the most forlorn and untoward and degrading human associations, the One who is never absent is that divine Spirit which brooded over the chaos at the beginning, nursing it to life and beauty, and which is

> nearer to every creature he hath made,
> Than anything unto itself can be.

Nay, there is not one of these hapless, sinning multitudes in whose spirit he is not present to will and to work according to his good pleasure; never overpowering the will, but gently pressing in, by every avenue open to him, his gifts of love and truth. As he has for every man's life a plan, so has he for the common life a perfect social order into which he seeks to lead his children, that he may give them plenty and blessedness and abundance of peace as long as the moon endureth. Surely he has a way for men to live in society; he has a way of organizing industry; he has a way of life for the family, and for the school, and for the shop, and for the city, and for the state; he has a way for preventing poverty, and a way for helping and saving the poor and the sick and the sinful; and it is his way that we are to seek and point out and follow. We cannot know it perfectly, but if we are humble and faithful and obedient, we shall come to understand it better and better as the years go by. The one thing for us to be sure of is that God has a way for human beings to live and work together, just as truly as he has a way for the stars over our heads and the crystals under our feet; and that it is man's chief end to find this way and follow it.

*   *   *

No one who has lived and labored for many years in ill-governed cities, in the interests of virtue, can fail to be aware of the evil influence which bad government exerts upon the characters of those who live under it. The tone of public morality is affected; the convictions of the youth are blurred; the standards of honor and fidelity are lowered. That which in the family and in the Sunday-school and in the day-school and in the pulpit we are teaching our children to regard as sacred, the bad city government, by the whole tenor of its administration, openly despises; the things which we tell them are detestable and infamous, the bad city government, by its open connivance or inaction, proclaims to be honorable. The whole weight of the moral influence of a municipal government like that which has existed until recently in New York, like that which exists to-day in Philadelphia, and in many other cities, is hostile to honesty, honor, purity, and decency. The preacher of righteousness finds, therefore, in bad municipal government, one of the deadliest of the evil forces with which he is called to contend. The problem of the city is a problem in which he has a vital interest, a question on which he has an undoubted right to speak.

The American city of the nineteenth century has been notable for two things, the rapidity of its growth and the corruptness of its civic administration. The population of the whole land has been growing apace, but the cities have grown at the expense of the rural districts. . . .

*　　*　　*

Let us not underrate our problem. These people of the cities—many of them ignorant, depraved, superstitious, unsocial in their tempers and habits; many of them ignorant of the language in which our laws are written, and unable freely to communicate with those who wish to influence them for good; having no conception of government but that of an enemy to be eluded or an unkind providence from which dole may be extorted; and no idea of a vote higher than that of a commodity which can be sold for money—these are the "powers that be" who must give us good government in our cities, if we are ever to get it.

REVIEW QUESTIONS

1. How convincing is Gladden's argument for a social gospel? Explain.
2. Should ministers be social activists and political reformers? Why or why not?
3. How does Gladden characterize the foreign immigrants streaming into American cities in the late nineteenth century?

JANE ADDAMS

FROM The Subjective Necessity for Social Settlements (1892)

Women provided much of the energy, idealism, and leadership during the Progressive era. Jane Addams (1860–1935) was one of the most prominent and tireless social reformers. After graduating from Rockford College in Illinois in 1881 and studying medicine in Philadelphia, she toured Europe and England several times, examining their efforts to deal with spreading urban poverty. After her return she and Ellen Gates Starr formed Hull House in Chicago's West Side in 1889. Modeled after Toynbee Hall in London, it served as a "halfway" settlement house and social center for immigrants streaming into the city. It was staffed by middle- and upper-class young men and women animated by a desire to "do" something about social problems.

From Jane Addams, *Philanthropy and Social Progress* (New York: Thomas Y. Crowell, 1893), pp. 1–26.

Hull House, which was Chicago's first Settlement, was established in September, 1889 . . . in the belief that the mere foothold of a house, easily accessible, ample in space, hospitable and tolerant in spirit, situated in the midst of the large foreign colonies which so easily isolate themselves in American cities, would be in itself a serviceable thing for Chicago. Hull House endeavors to make social intercourse express the growing sense of the economic unity of society. It is an effort to add the social function to democracy. It was opened on the theory that the dependence of classes on each other is reciprocal; and that as "the social relation is essentially a reciprocal relation, it gave a form of expression that has peculiar value."

This paper is an attempt to treat of the subjective necessity for Social Settlements, to analyze the motives which underlie a movement based not only upon conviction, but genuine emotion. Hull House of Chicago is used as an illustration, but so far as the analysis is faithful, it obtains wherever educated young people are seeking an outlet for that sentiment of universal brotherhood which the best spirit of our times is forcing from an emotion into a motive.

I have divided the motives which constitute the subjective pressure toward Social Settlements into three great lines: the first contains the desire to make the entire social organism democratic, to extend democracy beyond its political expression; the second is the impulse to share the race life, and to bring as much as possible of social energy and the accumulation of civilization to those portions of the race which have little; the third springs from a certain renaissance of Christianity, a movement toward its early humanitarian aspects.

It is not difficult to see that although America is pledged to the democratic ideal, the view of democracy has been partial, and that its best achievement thus far has been pushed along the line of the franchise. Democracy has made little attempt to assert itself in social affairs. We have refused to move beyond the position of its eighteenth-century leaders, who believed that political equality alone would secure all good to all men. We conscientiously followed the gift of the ballot hard upon the gift of freedom to the negro, but we are quite unmoved by the fact that he lives among us in a practical social ostracism. We hasten to give the franchise to the immigrant from a sense of justice, from a tradition that he ought to have it, while we dub him with epithets deriding his past life or present occupation, and feel no duty to invite him to our houses. We are forced to acknowledge that it is only in our local and national politics that we try very hard for the ideal so dear to those who were enthusiasts when the century was young. We have almost given it up as our ideal in social intercourse.

*   *   *

The social organism has broken down through large districts of our great cities. Many of the people living there are very poor, the majority of them without leisure or energy for anything but the gain of subsistence. They move often from one wretched lodging to another. They live for the moment side by side, many of them without knowledge of each other, without fellowship, without local tradition or public spirit, without social organization of any kind.

Practically nothing is done to remedy this. The people who might do it, who have the social tact and training, the large houses, and the traditions and custom of hospitality, live in other parts of the city. The clubhouses, libraries, galleries, and semi-public conveniences for social life are also blocks away. We find working-men organized into armies of producers because men of executive ability and business sagacity have found it to their interests thus to organize them. But these working-men are not organized socially; although living in crowded tenement-houses, they are living without a corresponding social contact. The chaos is as great as it would be were they working in huge factories without foreman or superintendent. Their ideas and resources are cramped. The desire for higher social pleasure is extinct. They have no share in the traditions and social energy which make for progress.

Too often their only place of meeting is a saloon, their only host a bartender; a local demagogue forms their public opinion. Men of ability

and refinement, of social power and university cultivation, stay away from them. Personally, I believe the men who lose most are those who thus stay away. But the paradox is here: when cultivated people do stay away from a certain portion of the population, when all social advantages are persistently withheld, it may be for years, the result itself is pointed at as a reason, is used as an argument, for the continued withholding.

It is constantly said that because the masses have never had social advantages they do not want them, that they are heavy and dull, and that it will take political or philanthropic machinery to change them. This divides a city into rich and poor; into the favored, who express their sense of the social obligation by gifts of money, and into the unfavored, who express it by clamoring for a "share"—both of them actuated by a vague sense of justice. This division of the city would be more justifiable, however, if the people who thus isolate themselves in certain streets and use their social ability for each other gained enough thereby and added sufficient to the sum total of social progress to justify the withholding of the pleasures and results of that progress from so many people who ought to have them. But they cannot accomplish this. "The social spirit discharges itself in many forms, and no one form is adequate to its total expression." We are all uncomfortable in regard to the sincerity of our best phrases, because we hesitate to translate our philosophy into the deed.

It is inevitable that those who feel most keenly this insincerity and partial living should be our young people, our so-called educated young people who accomplish little toward the solution of this social problem, and who bear the brunt of being cultivated into unnourished, oversensitive lives. They have been shut off from the common labor by which they live and which is a great source of moral and physical health. They feel a fatal want of harmony between their theory and their lives, a lack of coordination between thought and action. I think it is hard for us to realize how seriously many of them are taking to the notion of human brotherhood, how eagerly they long to give tangible expression to the democratic ideal. These young men and women, longing to socialize their democracy, are animated by certain hopes.

These hopes may be loosely formulated thus: that if in a democratic country nothing can he permanently achieved save through the masses of the people, it will be impossible to establish a higher political life than the people themselves crave; that it is difficult to see how the notion of a higher civic life can be fostered save through common intercourse; that the blessings which we associate with a life of refinement and cultivation can be made universal and must be made universal if they are to be permanent; that the good we secure for ourselves is precarious and uncertain, is floating in mid-air, until it is secured for all of us and incorporated into our common life.

These hopes are responsible for results in various directions, pre-eminently in the extension of educational advantages. We find that all educational matters are more democratic in their political than in their social aspects. The public schools in the poorest and most crowded wards of the city are inadequate to the number of children, and many of the teachers are ill-prepared and overworked; but in each ward there is an effort to secure public education. The schoolhouse itself stands as a pledge that the city recognizes and endeavors to fulfill the duty of educating its children. But what becomes of these children when they are no longer in public schools? Many of them never come under the influence of a professional teacher nor a cultivated friend after they are twelve. Society at large does little for their intellectual development. The dream of transcendentalists that each New England village would be a university, that every child taken from the common school would be put into definite lines of study and mental development, had its unfulfilled beginning in the village lyceum and lecture courses, and has its feeble representative now in the multitude of clubs for study which are so sadly restricted to educators, to the leisure class, or only to the advanced and progressive wage-workers.

*   *   *

I find it somewhat difficult to formulate the second line of motives which I believe to constitute the trend of the subjective pressure toward the Settlement. There is something primordial about these motives, but I am perhaps over-bold in designating them as a great desire to share the race life. We all bear traces of the starvation struggle which for so long made up the life of the race. Our very organism holds memories and glimpses of that long life of our ancestors which still goes on among so many of our contemporaries. Nothing so deadens the sympathies and shrivels the power of enjoyment as the . . . continual ignoring of the starvation struggle which makes up the life of at least half the race. To shut one's self away from that half of the race life is to shut one's self away from the most vital part of it; it is to live out but half the humanity which we have been born heir to and to use but half our faculties. We have all had longings for a fuller life which should include the use of these faculties. . . .

You may remember the forlorn feeling which occasionally seizes you when you arrive early in the morning a stranger in a great city. The stream of laboring people goes past you as you gaze through the plate-glass window of your hotel. You see hardworking men lifting great burdens; You hear the driving and jostling of huge carts. Your heart sinks with a sudden sense of futility. The door opens behind you and you turn to the man who brings you in your breakfast with a quick sense of human fellowship. You find yourself praying that you may never lose your hold on it at all. A more poetic prayer would be that the great mother breasts of our common humanity, with its labor and suffering and its homely comforts, may never be withheld from you. You turn helplessly to the waiter. You feel that it would be almost grotesque to claim from him the sympathy you crave. Civilization has placed you far apart, but you resent your position with a sudden sense of snobbery.

*   *   *

We have in America a fast-growing number of cultivated young people who have no recognized outlet for their active faculties. They bear constantly of the great social maladjustment, but no way is provided for them to change it, and their uselessness bangs about them heavily. . . . These young people have had advantages of college, of European travel and economic study, but they are sustaining this shock of inaction. They have pet phrases, and they tell you that the things that make us all alike are stronger than the things that make us different. They say that all men are united by needs and sympathies far more permanent and radical than anything that temporarily divides them and sets them in opposition to each other. . . . Our young people feel nervously the need of putting theory into action, and respond quickly to the Settlement form of activity.

The third division of motives which I believe make toward the Settlement is the result of a certain renaissance going forward in Christianity. The impulse to share the lives of the poor, the desire to make social service, irrespective of propaganda, express the spirit of Christ, is as old as Christianity itself. . . .

I believe that there is a distinct turning among many young men and women toward this simple acceptance of Christ's message. They resent the assumption that Christianity is a set of ideas which belong to the religious consciousness, whatever that may be, that it is a thing to be proclaimed and instituted apart from the social life of the community. They insist that it shall seek a sim-

ple and natural expression in the social organism itself. The Settlement movement is only one manifestation of that wider humanitarian movement which throughout Christendom, but preeminently in England, is endeavoring to embody itself, not in a sect, but in society itself. . . .

Certain it is that spiritual force is found in the Settlement movement, and it is also true that this force must be evoked and must be called into play before the success of any Settlement is assured. There must be the overmastering belief that all that is noblest in life is common to men as men, in order to accentuate the likenesses and ignore the differences which are found among the people whom the Settlement constantly brings into juxtaposition. . . .

REVIEW QUESTIONS

1. What were the three motives that Addams identified with social settlements?
2. What were some of the serious social problems that Addams discussed?
3. Addams's emphasis on the role of the well-educated as reform leaders suggested what about her view of social change?

UPTON SINCLAIR

FROM *The Jungle* (1906)

Muckraking (investigative) journalists and novelists were the shock troops of progressive efforts to promote government regulation of corporate America. One of the most powerful of these reform-minded writers was Upton Sinclair. In 1906 he published The Jungle, *a novel set in Chicago's horrific meat-packing district. With graphic detail, it tells the story of Jurgis Rudkus, a Lithuanian immigrant, and his travails in Dunham's, a fictional meat-packing plant. Soon after the book appeared Congress passed the Meat Inspection Act in an effort to address the abuses cited by Sinclair and others.*

From Upton Sinclair, *The Jungle* (1906; New York: Signet, 1960), pp. 100–102.

There was another interesting set of statistics that a person might have gathered in Packingtown—those of the various afflictions of the workers. When Jurgis had first inspected the packing plants . . . he had marveled while he listened to the tale of all the things that were made out of the carcasses of animals, and of all the lesser industries that were maintained there; now he found that each one of these lesser industries was a separate little inferno, in its way as horrible as the killing-beds, the source and fountain of them all. The workers in each of them had their own peculiar diseases. And the wandering visitor might be sceptical about all the swindles, but he could not be sceptical about these, for the worker bore the evidences of them about his own person—generally he had only to hold out his hand.

There were the men in the pickle rooms, for instance, where old Antanas had gotten his death; scarce a one of these that had not some spot of horror on his person. Let a man so much as scrape his finger pushing a truck in the pickle rooms, and he might have a sore that would put him out of the world; all the joints in his fingers would be eaten by the acid one by one. Of the butchers and floorsmen, the beef boners and trimmers, and all those who used knives, you could scarcely find a person who had the use of his thumb; time and time again the base of it had been slashed, till it was a mere lump of flesh against which the man pressed the knife to hold it. The hands of these men would be crisscrossed with cuts, until you could no longer pretend to count them or trace them. They would have no nails,—they had worn them off pulling hides; their knuckles were swollen so that their fingers spread out like a fan. There were men who had worked in the cooking rooms, in the midst of steam and sickening odors, by artificial light; in these rooms the germs of tuberculosis might live for two years, but the supply was renewed every hour. There were the beef luggers, who carried two-hundred-pound quarters into the refrigerator cars, a fearful kind of work, that began at four o'clock in the morning, and that wore out the most powerful men in two years. There were those who worked in the chilling rooms, and whose special disease was rheumatism, the time limit that a man could work in the chilling rooms was said to be five years. There were the wool pluckers, whose hands went to pieces even sooner than the hands of the pickle men; for the pelts of sheep had to be painted with acid to loosen the wool, and then the pluckers had to pull out this wool with their bare hands, till the acid had eaten their fingers off. There were those who made tile tins for the canned meat, and their hands, too, were a maze of cuts, and each cut represented a chance for blood poisoning. Some worked at the stamping machines, and it was very seldom that one could work long there at the pace that was set, and not give out and forget himself, and have a part of his hand chopped off. There were the "hoisters," as they were called, whose task it was to press the level which lifted the dead cattle off the floor. They ran along upon a rafter, peering down through the damp and the steam, and as old Dunham's architects had not built the killing room for the convenience of the hoisters, at every few feet they would have to stop under a beam, say four feet above the one they ran on, which got them into the habit of stooping, so that in a few years they were walking like chimpanzees. Worst of any, however, were the fertilizer men, and those who served in the cooking rooms. These men could not be shown to the visitor—for the odor of a fertilizer man would scare any ordinary visitor at a hundred yards, and as for the other men, who worked in the tank rooms full of steam, and in some of which there were open vats near the level of the floor, their peculiar trouble was that they fell into the vats; and when they were fished out, there was never enough of them left to be worth exhibiting— sometimes they would be overlooked for days, till all but the bones of them had gone out to the world as Dunham's Pure Beef Lard!

REVIEW QUESTIONS

1. Why would such a description of working conditions prompt calls for regulation?
2. Why did workers have to endure such working conditions?

Muller v. Oregon (1908)

Dangerous and unhealthy working conditions prevailed in American industry at the turn of the century, and regulating them became a major concern of Progressive re-formers. The Oregon state legislature passed a law mandating that women employed in laundries could be required to work no more than ten hours a day. It was chal-lenged by conservatives as a violation of the right of contract and an infringement of free enterprise. They cited the Court's ruling in Lochner v. New York *(1905) disal-lowing a law regulating the hours of bakers. Yet the Supreme Court ruled in favor of the Oregon statute. Evidence presented by attorney Louis Brandeis (who later would become a Supreme Court justice) that documented the sociological and medical effects of long working hours on women proved persuasive to the Court.*

From *Muller v. Oregon,* 208 U.S. 412 (1908).

BREWER, J. . . . The single question is the con-stitutionality of the statute under which the defendant was convicted so far as affects the work of a female in a laundry. . . .

It is the law of Oregon that women, whether married or single, have equal contractual and per-sonal rights with men. . . .

It thus appears that, putting to one side the elective franchise, in the matter of personal and contractual rights they stand on the same plane as the other sex. Their rights in these respects can no more be infringed than the equal rights of their brothers. We held in *Lochner v. New York,* 198 U.S. 45, that a law providing that no laborer shall be re-quired or permitted to work in a bakery more than sixty hours in a week or ten hours in a day was not as to men a legitimate exercise of the police power of the State, but an unreasonable, unnecessary and arbitrary interference with the right and liberty of the individual to contract in relation to his labor, and as such was in conflict with, and void under, the Federal Constitution. That decision is invoked by plaintiff in error as decisive of the question be-fore us. But this assumes that the difference be-tween the sexes does not justify a different rule respecting a restriction of the hours of labor.

It may not be amiss, in the present case, before examining the constitutional question, to notice the course of legislation as well as expressions of opinion from other than judicial sources. In the brief filed by Mr. Louis D. Brandeis, for the defen-dant in error is a very copious collection of all these matters. . . .

The legislation and opinions referred to[1] . . . may not be, technically speaking, authorities, and in them is little or no discussion of the constitu-tional question presented to us for determination, yet they are significant of a widespread belief that woman's physical structure, and the functions she performs in consequence thereof, justify special legislation restricting or qualifying the conditions under which she should be permitted to toil. Con-stitutional questions, it is true, are not settled by even a consensus of present public opinion, for it is the peculiar value of a written constitution that it places in unchanging form limitations upon leg-islative action, and thus gives a permanence and stability to popular government which other-wise would be lacking. At the same time, when a question of fact is debated and debatable, and the extent to which a special constitutional limitation goes is affected by the truth in respect to that fact, a widespread and long-continued be-lief concerning it is worthy of consideration. We

---

[1] I.e., in Brandeis's brief.

take judicial cognizance of all matters of general knowledge. . .

That woman's physical structure and the performance of maternal functions place her at a disadvantage in the struggle for subsistence is obvious. This is especially true when the burdens of motherhood are upon her. Even when they are not, by abundant testimony of the medical fraternity continuance for a long time on her feet at work, repeating this from day to day, tends to injurious effects upon the body, and as healthy mothers are essential to vigorous offspring, the physical well-being of woman becomes an object of public interest and care in order to preserve the strength and vigor of the race. . . .

Differentiated by these matters from the other sex, she is properly placed in a class by herself, and legislation designed for her protection may be sustained, even when like legislation is not necessary for men and could not be sustained. It is impossible to close one's eyes to the fact that she still looks to her brother and depends upon him. Even though all restrictions on political, personal and contractual rights were taken away, and she stood, so far as statutes are concerned, upon an absolutely equal plane with him, it would still be true that she is so constituted that she will rest upon and look to him for protection; that her physical structure and a proper discharge of her maternal functions—having in view not merely her own health, but the well-being of the race—justify legislation to protect her from the greed as well as the passion of man. The limitations which this statute places upon her contractual powers, upon her right to agree with her employer as to the time she shall labor, are not imposed solely for her benefit, but also largely for the benefit of all. Many words cannot make this plainer. The two sexes differ in structure of body, in the functions to be performed by each, in the amount of physical strength, in the capacity for long-continued labor, particularly when done standing, the influence of vigorous health upon the future well-being of the race, the self-reliance which enables one to assert full rights, and in the capacity to maintain the struggle for subsistence. This difference justifies a difference in legislation and upholds that which is designed to compensate for some of the burdens which rest upon her. . . .

For these reasons, and without questioning in any respect the decision in *Lochner* v. *New York*, we are of the opinion that it cannot be adjudged that the act in question is in conflict with the federal Constitution, so far as it respects the work of a female in a laundry. . . .

REVIEW QUESTIONS

1. According to Justice Brewer, why didn't the decision in *Lochner* invalidate the Oregon statute?
2. What role did women perform that was vital to maintaining the "vigor of the race"? How might harsh working conditions interfere with this role?
3. In the eyes of some feminists how might the Court's opinion that women required special legislation produce negative consequences?

ROSE SCHNEIDERMAN

Working Women and the Vote (1912)

The efforts to gain voting rights for women reached a crescendo during the early twentieth century. In New York a state senator sought to deflect such efforts by claiming that women were not suited for the rough-and-tumble tactics of the political arena: "Get women into the arena of politics with its alliances and distressing contests—the delicacy is gone, the charm is gone, and you emasculize women." His incendiary comments outraged proponents of female suffrage and prompted a meeting with New York legislators at the Cooper Union on 22 April 1912. Several working women spoke on behalf of voting rights. Among them was Rose Schneiderman (1884–1972), a Polish immigrant who worked in a cap factory and served as the chief organizer of the women's trade union movement. She concluded that women needed the vote in order to force legislators to pass laws improving the most exploitative labor conditions.

From *Miss Rose Schneiderman, Cap Maker, Replies to New York Senator on Delicacy and Charm of Women* (New York: Wage Earners' Suffrage League, 1912), pp. 1–8. [Editorial insertions appear in square brackets—*Ed.*]

Fellow-workers, it already has been whispered to you that there is a possibility that our New York Senators don't know what they are talking about. I am here to voice the same sentiment. It seems to me that if our Senators really represented the people of New York State, they ought to know the conditions under which the majority of the people live. Perhaps, working women are not regarded as women, because it seems to me, when they talk all this strash of theirs about [women's] finer qualities and "man's admiration and devotion to the sex." . . . "Preserving Motherhood"—"The delicacy and charm of women being gone," they cannot mean the working women. We have 800,000 women in New York State who go out into the industrial world, not through any choice of their own, but because necessity forces them out to earn their daily bread.

I am inclined to think if we were sent home now we would not go home. We want to work, that is the thing. We are not afraid of work, and we are not ashamed to work, but we do decline to be driven; we want to work like human beings; we want to work for the welfare of the community and not for the welfare of a few.

Can it be that our Senators do not realize that we have women working in every trade but nine? We have women working in the foundries, stripped to the waist, if you please, because of the heat. *Yet the Senator says nothing about these women losing their charm.* They have got to retain their charm and delicacy and work in foundries. Of course, you know the reason they are employed in foundries is that they are cheaper and work longer hours than men.

Women in the laundries, for instance, stand for 13 or 14 hours in the terrible steam and heat with their hands in hot starch. Surely these women won't lose any more of their beauty and charm by putting a ballot in a ballot box once a year than they are likely to lose standing in foundries or laundries all year round.

There is no harder contest than the contest for

bread, let me tell you that. Women have got to meet it and in a good many instances they contest for the job with their brother workman. When the woman is preferred, it is because of her weakness, because she is frail, because she will sell her labor for less money than man will sell his.

When our Senators acknowledge that our political life has *alliances and distressing contests* which would take the charm away from women if she got into them, let me reassure the gentlemen that women's great charm has always been that when she found things going wrong she has set to work to make them go right. Do our Senators fear that when women get the vote they will demand clean polling places, etc.? It seems to me that this rather gives them away. Is it their wish to keep the voters in such a condition that it is a disgrace for anybody to come in contact with them?

Is not this Senator's talk about political contests and alliances an insult to all honest voters? What about the delicacy and charm of women who have to live with men in the condition of a good many male voters on election day? Perhaps the Senators would like them to keep that condition all year round; they would not demand much of their political bosses, and he could be sure that they would cast their votes for the man who gave them the most booze.

I did some lobbying work last year for the 54-hour [workweek] bill, and I can tell you how courteous our Senators and Assemblymen are when a disenfranchised citizen tries to convince them of the necessity of shorter hours for working women. *I assure you chivalry is dead.*

During the hearing at Albany our learned Senators listened to the opposition very carefully; they wanted to be able to justify themselves afterwards when they voted against our bill. But when the Committee, who spoke for the working women came to plead for the bill, there was only one Senator left in the room—he was the chairman—he couldn't very well get out; we had to make our arguments to the chairman of the Committee, all the other Senators had left. Mind you, we were pleading for a shorter work week for working-women. We had our evidence to show that physical ex-

haustion leads to moral exhaustion, and the physical and moral exhaustion of women will lead to the deterioration of the human species. What did these men care? We were voteless working women—no matter what we felt or thought we could not come back at them.

When you ask these gentlemen why they oppose the bill so shamefully, they will tell you it is the fault of the Republican Assembly; that the Democrats would have passed it, only that the Republicans held up the bill to consider the canning industry. That is what they say this year, but when you ask them what was the matter last year, when both houses were Democratic, they don't know what to say.

It seems to me that the working women ought to wake up to the truth of the situation; all this talk about women's charm does not mean working women. Working women are expected to work and produce their kind [children] so that they, too, may work until they die of some industrial disease.

We hear our anti-suffragettes saying, "Why, when you get the vote it will hinder you from doing welfare work, doing uplift work." Who are they going to uplift? Is it you and I they want to uplift? I think if they would lift themselves off our shoulders they would be doing a better bit of useful work. I think you know by now that if the workers got what they earn there would be no need of uplift work and welfare work or anything of that kind.

We want to tell our Senators that the working women of our State demand the vote as an economic necessity. We need it because we are workers and because the workers are the ones that have to carry civilization on their backs.

What does all this talk about becoming mannish signify? I wonder if it will add to my height when I get the vote. I might work for it all the harder if it did. It is too ridiculous, this talk of becoming less womanly, just as if a woman could be anything else except a woman.

This vote that she is going to cast is going to work this marvelous change in her all of a sudden. Just by beginning to think of how the laws are made and using such intelligence as she has to put good men in office with her vote she will be made over into a creature without delicacy or charm.

Poor Mr. Senator, you don't expect us to put any faith in you when we have seen women working in electric works, working all day with sleeves rolled up until they had developed the muscles of their arms as strong and hard as a strong man's; yet these women were intelligent and charming.

No man need be ashamed of the working-women. They do more than their share of the world's work. Our Senators do not think *long hours* is making them mannish or less delicate or less womanly. Not at all. If you tell these men "Those women ought to work only eight hours a day," they will answer, "No, a woman is a free American citizen; you must not hinder her, let her work as many hours as she pleases."

I honestly believe that it is fear of the enfranchisement of working-women that prompts the Senators to oppose us. They do not want the working-women enfranchised because politicians know that a woman who works will use her ballot intelligently; she will make the politician do things which he may not find so profitable; therefore, they come out with all these subterfuges.

Senators and legislators are not blind to the horrible conditions around them, especially among women workers. Some of these Senators come from the canning district where women and children may be working 24 hours a day, the canning districts *where little children fall asleep while at work in the pens. Others of these Senators come from the textile district, where the whole family goes to work and there is no one to do the administrating of the so-called home; again, others of these Senators come from the New York district where women have to sew* 37 SEAMS FOR ONE CENT *and where a woman has to* IRON 70 DOZEN SKIRTS A DAY TO EARN $1.25! It does not speak well for the intelligence of our Senators to come out with state-ments about women losing their charm and attractiveness, when they begin to use their intelligence in the face of facts like these. If these men really were representatives of the people, if they knew how the people lived, then they would think and act differently. They have a few women in mind, to whom they think it would be a bad thing to give the vote—these are some of the well-to-do women—they are afraid that these women, instead of going down to the settlements to teach a girl how to use her knife and fork, how to be lady-like, etc., might turn their energy into political house-cleaning. And what would the Senator do then, poor thing?

Those Senators who have opposed the enfranchisement of women will be ashamed of themselves in a few years. The vote has got to come whether they like it or not. It is the next step. This republic has got to come to it, and it is going to before long.

Every working woman ought to work to hasten the day. I assure you we are not going to sit down on our job; we are going to push "Votes for Women" among working women everywhere. Those of you who want to be on the winning side of this abolition movement better join right now.

Let us demonstrate to our Senators and Assemblymen and all other anti-suffragettes everywhere, that the citizens of New York, the voting citizens of New York, stand by this democratic demand for "Votes for Women."

REVIEW QUESTIONS

1. Why were women workers paid less than male workers?
2. How did opponents of the vote for women justify their opposition?
3. What does Schneiderman claim were the real motives behind legislators' opposition to female suffrage?

IDA B. WELLS

FROM Lynch Law in America (1900)

While Progressives helped improve the lives of immigrants, convince Congress to provide the vote to women, and establish national parks, they did little to address the surge of racism that welled up at the turn of the century. Throughout the South, state after state passed laws effectively disenfranchising African Americans and instituting statutory segregation of public facilities. The most vicious manifestation of this new racism was the vigilante lynching of blacks accused of various crimes. On average, over one hundred African Americans were lynched each year, most of them in the South. An investigative journalist, Ida Wells, born a slave in 1862, organized in the early twentieth century a national crusade against lynching. Despite her efforts it would be another generation before Congress addressed the issue.

From Ida B. Wells, "Lynch Law in America," *Arena* 23 (January 1900):15–24.

Our country's national crime is *lynching*. It is not the creature of an hour, the sudden outburst of uncontrolled fury, or the unspeakable brutality of an insane mob. It represents the cool, calculating deliberation of an intelligent people who openly avow that there is an "unwritten law" that justifies them in putting to death without complaint under oath, without trial by jury, without opportunity to make defense, without right of appeal. . . .

The alleged menace of universal suffrage having been avoided by the absolute suppression of the negro vote, the spirit of mob murder should have been satisfied and the butchery of negroes should have ceased. But men, women, and children were the victims of murder by individuals and murder by mobs, just as they had been when killed at the demands of the "unwritten law" to prevent "negro domination." Negroes were killed for disputing over terms of contracts with their employers. If a few barns were burned some colored man was killed to stop it. If a colored man resented the imposition of a white man and the two come to blows, the colored man had to die, either at the hands of the white man then and there or later at the hands of the mob that speedily gathered. If he showed a spirit of courageous manhood he was hanged for his pains, and the killing was justified by the declaration that he was a "saucy nigger." Colored women have been murdered because they refused to tell the mobs where relatives could be found for "lynching bees." Boys of fourteen years have been lynched by white representatives of American civilization. In fact, for all kinds of offenses—and for no offenses—from murders to misdemeanors, men and women are put to death without judge or jury; so that, although the political excuse was no longer necessary, the wholesale murder of human beings went on just the same. A new name was given to the killings and a new excuse was invented for doing so.

Again the aid of the "unwritten law" is invoked, and again it comes to the rescue. During the last ten years a new statute has been added to the "unwritten law." This statute proclaims that for certain crimes or alleged crimes no negro shall be allowed a trial; that no white woman shall be compelled to charge an assault under oath or to submit any such charge to the investigation of a court of law. The result is that many men have been put to death whose innocence was afterward established; and today, under the reign of the "unwritten law," no colored man, no matter what his reputation, is safe from lynching if a white woman, no matter what her standing or motive, cares to charge him with insult or assault.

It is considered a sufficient excuse and reasonable justification to put a prisoner to death under this "unwritten law" for the frequently repeated charge that these lynching horrors are necessary to prevent crimes against women. The sentiment of the country has been appealed to, in describing the isolated condition of white families in thickly populated negro districts; and the charge is made that these homes are in as great danger as if they were surrounded by wild beasts. And the world has accepted this theory without let or hindrance. In many cases there has been open expression that the fate meted out to the victim was only what he deserved. In many other instances there has been a silence that says more forcibly than words can proclaim it that it is right and proper that a human being should be seized by a mob and burned to death upon the unsworn and the uncorroborated charge of his accuser. No matter that our laws presume every man innocent until he is proved guilty; no matter that it encourages those criminally disposed to blacken their faces and commit any crime in the calendar so long as they can throw suspicion on some negro as is frequently done, and then lead a mob to take his life; no matter that mobs make a farce of the law and a mockery of justice; no matter that hundreds of boys are being hardened in crime and schooled in vice by the repetition of such scenes before their eyes—if a white woman declares herself insulted or assaulted, some life must pay the penalty, with all the horrors of the Spanish Inquisition and all the barbarism of the Middle Ages. The world looks on and says it is well.

*   *   *

Quite a number of the one-third alleged cases of assault that have been personally investigated by the writer have shown that there was no foundation in fact for the charges; yet the claim is not made that there were no real culprits among them. The negro has been too long associated with the white man not to have copied his vices as well as his virtues. But the negro resents and utterly repudiates the effort to blacken his good name by asserting that assaults suffered far more from the commission of this crime against the women of his race by white men than the white race has ever suffered through his crimes. Very scant notice is taken of the matter when this is the condition of affairs. What becomes a crime deserving capital punishment when the tables are turned is a matter of small moment when the negro woman is the accusing party. . . .

REVIEW QUESTIONS

1. According to Wells, what rights were denied to accused blacks?
2. What was one of the most common charges leveled against black men? In what way did this reveal a double standard?

BENJAMIN R. TILLMAN

The Use of Violence against Southern Blacks (1900)

During the last quarter of the nineteenth century, southern whites brazenly acceler-
ated their efforts to restore "all-white" rule in the region's social, economic, and politi-
cal life. Senator Benjamin R. Tillman, whose nickname was "Pitchfork Ben" (because
he once threatened to stick a pitchfork in President Grover Cleveland because of his
conservative financial policies) played a leading role in the efforts to disenfranchise
blacks and enforce racial segregation. A vocal white supremacist from Edgefield
County, South Carolina, Tillman recruited and inspired racist white militias and vig-
ilantes. He served as governor of South Carolina from 1890 to 1894. Elected to the
Senate in 1895, he promoted the interests of small farmers and greater regulation of
railroads. He also continued to promote white supremacy—by any means necessary.
In the following speeches to the Senate, Tillman defended the use of violence to intim-
idate African Americans.

From "Speech of Senator Benjamin R. Tillman, March 23, 1900," *Congressional Record,* 56th
Cong., 1st sess., pp. 3223–3224. [Editorial insertions appear in square brackets—*Ed.*]

[I]t can not be denied that the slaves of the South were a superior set of men and women to the freedmen of today, and that the poison in their minds—the race hatred of the whites—is the result of the teachings of Northern fanatics. Ravishing a woman, white or black, was never known to occur in the South till after the Reconstruction era. So much for that phase of the subject. . . .

. . . And he [Senator John C. Spooner of Wisconsin] said we had taken their [blacks'] rights away from them. He asked me was it right to murder them in order to carry the elections. I never saw one murdered. I never saw one shot at an election. It was the riots before the elections, precipitated by their own hot-headedness in attempting to hold the government, that brought on conflicts between the races and caused the shotgun to be used. That is what I meant by saying we used the shotgun.

I want to call the Senator's attention to one fact. He said that the Republican Party [during Reconstruction] gave the negroes the ballot in order to protect themselves against the indignities and wrongs that were attempted to be heaped upon them by the enactment of the black code. I say it was because the Republicans of that day, led by [Congressman] Thad Stevens, wanted to put white necks under black heels and to get revenge. There is a difference of opinion. You have your opinion about it, and I have mine, and we can never agree.

I want to ask the Senator this proposition in arithmetic: In my State there were 135,000 negro voters, or negroes of voting age, and some 90,000 or 95,000 white voters. General [Edward] Canby set up a carpetbag government there [after the Civil War] and turned our State over to this majority. Now, I want to ask you, with a free vote and a fair count, how are you going to beat 135,000 by 95,000? How are you going to do it? You had set us an impossible task. You had handcuffed us and thrown away the key, and you propped your carpetbag negro government with [federal] bayonets. Whenever it was necessary to sustain the [Reconstruction] government you held it up by the Army.

Mr. President, I have not the facts and figures here, but I want the country to get the full view of the Southern side of this question and the justification for anything we did. We were sorry we had the necessity forced upon us, but we could not help it, and as white men we are not sorry for it, and we do not propose to apologize for anything we have done in connection with it. We took the government away from them [blacks] in 1876. We did take it. If no other Senator has come here previous to this time who would acknowledge it, more is the pity. We have had no fraud in our elections in South Carolina since 1884. There has been no organized Republican party in the State.

We did not disfranchise the negroes until 1895. Then we had a constitutional convention convened which took the matter up calmly, deliberately, and avowedly with the purpose of disfranchising as many of them as we could under the fourteenth and fifteenth amendments. We adopted the educational qualification [for voting] as the only means left to us, and the negro is as contented and as prosperous and as well protected in South Carolina today as in any State of the Union south of the Potomac. He is not meddling with politics, for he found that the more he meddled with them the worse off he got. As to his "rights"—I will not discuss them now. We of the South have never recognized the right of the negro to govern white men, and we never will. We have never believed him to be equal to the white man, and we will not submit to his gratifying his lust on our wives and daughters without lynching him. I would to God the last one of them was in Africa and that none of them had ever been brought to our shores. . . .

REVIEW QUESTIONS

1. What is Tillman's underlying premise for justifying the forceful restoration of all-white rule in South Carolina?
2. How does Tillman justify the benefits of slavery to slaves?

THE NIAGARA MOVEMENT

Declaration of Principles (1905)

The progressive reform impulse at the turn of the century fostered efforts by black activists to promote the interests of African Americans. Dr. W. E. B. Du Bois, the first African American to earn a doctoral degree from Harvard University, emerged as a powerful counter force to the accommodationist stance promoted by Booker T. Washington. Du Bois insisted that African Americans focus on obtaining full political rights and social equality, not simply vocational opportunities. In 1905 Du Bois and twenty-eight other black activists met at Niagara Falls (on the Canadian side because no American hotel would host them), where they drafted a list of political and social demands. The Niagara Movement provided the foundation for the formation of the National Association for the Advancement of Colored People (NAACP) in 1910.

From Joanne Grant, ed., *Black Protest: History, Documents, and Analyses, 1619 to the Present* (New York: Fawcett, 1968), pp. 206–209. [Editorial insertions appear in square brackets—*Ed.*]

*P*rogress: The members of the conference, known as the Niagara Movement . . . congratulate the Negro-Americans on certain undoubted evidences of progress in the last decade, particularly the increase of intelligence, the buying of property, the checking of crime, the uplift in home life, the advance in literature and art, and the demonstration of constructive and executive ability in the conduct of great religious, economic and educational institutions.

Suffrage: At the same time, we believe that this class of American citizens should protest emphatically and continually against the curtailment of their political rights. We believe in manhood suffrage; we believe that no man is so good, intelligent or wealthy as to be entrusted wholly with the welfare of his neighbor.

Civil Liberty: We believe also in protest against the curtailment of our civil rights. All American citizens have the right to equal treatment in places of public entertainment according to their behavior and deserts.

Economic Opportunity: We especially complain against the denial of equal opportunities to us in economic life; in the rural districts of the South this amounts to peonage and virtual slavery; all over the South it tends to crush labor and small business enterprises; and everywhere American prejudice, helped often by iniquitous laws, is making it more difficult for Negro-Americans to earn a decent living.

Education: Common school education should be free to all American children and compulsory. High school training should be adequately provided for all, and college training should be the monopoly of no class or race in any section of our common country. We believe that, in defense of our own institutions, the United States should aid common school education, particularly in the South, and we especially recommend concerted agitation to this end. We urge an increase in public high school facilities in the South, where the Negro-Americans are almost wholly without such provisions. We favor well-equipped trade and technical schools for the training of artisans, and the need of adequate and liberal endowment for a few

institutions of higher education must be patent to sincere well-wishers of the race.

Courts: We demand upright judges in courts, juries selected without discrimination on account of color and the same measure of punishment and the same efforts at reformation for black as for white offenders. We need orphanages and farm schools for dependent children, juvenile reformatories for delinquents, and the abolition of the dehumanizing convict-lease system.[1]

Public Opinion: We note with alarm the evident retrogression in this land of sound public opinion on the subject of manhood rights, republican government and human brotherhood, and we pray God that this nation will not degenerate into a mob of boasters and oppressors, but rather will return to the faith of the fathers, that all men were created free and equal, with certain unalienable rights.

Health: We plead for health—for an opportunity to live in decent houses and localities, for a chance to rear our children in physical and moral cleanliness.

Employers and Labor Unions: We hold up for public execration the conduct of two opposite classes of men: The practice among employers of importing ignorant Negro-American laborers in emergencies, and then affording them neither protection nor permanent employment; and the practice of labor unions in proscribing and boycotting and oppressing thousands of their fellow-toilers, simply because they are black. These methods have accentuated and will accentuate the war of labor and capital, and they are disgraceful to both sides.

Protest: We refuse to allow the impression to remain that the Negro-American assents to inferiority, is submissive under oppression and apologetic before insults. Through helplessness we may submit, but the voice of protest of ten million Americans must never cease to assail the ears of their fellows, so long as America is unjust.

Color-Line: Any discrimination based simply on race or color is barbarous, we care not how hal-

---

[1] After the Civil War, southern governments rented convicts, mostly African Americans, to landowners.

lowed it be by custom, expediency or prejudice. Difference made on account of ignorance, immorality, or disease are legitimate methods of fighting evil, and against them we have no word of protest; but discriminations based simply and solely on physical peculiarities, place of birth, color of skin, are relics of that unreasoning human savagery of which the world is and ought to be thoroughly ashamed.

"Jim Crow Cars": We protest against the "Jim Crow" [railroad] car, since its effect is and must be to make us pay first-class fare for third-class accommodations, render us open to insults and discomfort and to crucify wantonly our manhood, womanhood and self-respect.

Soldiers: We regret that this nation has never seen fit adequately to reward the black soldiers who, in its five wars, have defended their country with their blood, and yet have been systematically denied the promotions which their abilities deserve. And we regard as unjust, the exclusion of black boys from the military and naval training schools.

War Amendments: We urge upon Congress the enactment of appropriate legislation for securing the proper enforcement of those articles of freedom, the thirteenth, fourteenth and fifteenth amendments of the Constitution of the United States.

Oppression: We repudiate the monstrous doctrine that the oppressor should be the sole authority as to the rights of the oppressed. The Negro race in America stolen, ravished and degraded, struggling up through difficulties and oppression, needs sympathy and receives criticism; needs help and is given hindrance, needs protection and is given mob-violence, needs justice and is given charity; needs leadership and is given cowardice and apology, needs bread and is given a stone. This nation will never stand justified before God until these things are changes.

The Church: Especially are we surprised and astonished at the recent attitude of the church of Christ—of an increase of desire to bow to racial prejudice, to narrow the bounds of human brotherhood, and to segregate black men to some outer sanctuary. This is wrong, unchristian and disgraceful to the twentieth-century civilization.

Agitation: Of the above grievances we do not hesitate to complain, and to complain loudly and insistently. To ignore, overlook, or apologize for these wrongs is to prove ourselves unworthy of freedom. Persistent agitation is the way to liberty, and toward this goal the Niagara Movement has started and asks the cooperation of all men of all races.

Help: At the same time we want to acknowledge with deep thankfulness the help of our fellowmen from the Abolitionist down to those who today still stand for equal opportunity and who have given and still give of their wealth and of their poverty for our advancement.

Duties: And while we are demanding and ought to demand, and will continue to demand the rights enumerated above, God forbid that we should ever forget to urge corresponding duties upon our people:

> The duty to vote.
> The duty to respect the rights of others
> The duty to obey the laws.
> The duty to be clean and orderly.
> The duty to send our children to school.
> The duty to respect ourselves, even as we respect others.

This statement, complaint and prayer we submit to the American people, and Almighty God.

REVIEW QUESTIONS

1. Summarize the rights that Du Bois demanded for African Americans.
2. Why do you think Du Bois included a list of "duties" for African Americans? What was the significance of each?
3. How might whites have claimed that Du Bois was demanding social as well as political equality?

THEODORE ROOSEVELT

FROM Message to Congress (1901)

Although the Sherman Anti-Trust Act of 1890 ostensibly dealt with the problem of corporate monopolies, in practice it left much to be desired, as least so far as Progressives were concerned. Its phrasing was vague. It never defined what a "trust" or "monopoly" involved. And the Supreme Court threw out many of the government's efforts to prosecute trusts under the Sherman Act. When Theodore Roosevelt assumed the presidency in 1901, he recognized that the trust issue remained an acute economic and political problem. In his first message to Congress he distinguished between good and bad trusts, with the good ones led by executives of sterling character who promoted the public interest and the bad ones led by rascals pursuing selfish motives.

From First Annual Message to Congress, December 3, 1901, in *The Works of Theodore Roosevelt* (New York: Charles Scribner's Sons, 1926), 15:87–93.

. . . The tremendous and highly complex industrial development which went on with everaccelerated rapidity during the latter half of the nineteenth century brings us face to face, at the beginning of the twentieth, with very serious social problems. The old laws, and the old customs which had almost the binding force of law, were once quite sufficient to regulate the accumulation and distribution of wealth. Since the industrial changes which have so enormously increased the productive power of mankind, they are no longer sufficient.

The growth of cities has gone on beyond comparison faster than the growth of the country, and the upbuilding of the great industrial centers has meant a startling increase, not merely in the aggregate of wealth, but in the number of very large individual, and especially of very large corporate, fortunes. The creation of these great corporate fortunes has not been due to the tariff nor to any other governmental action, but to natural causes in the business world, operating in other countries as they operate in our own.

The process has aroused much antagonism, a great part of which is wholly without warrant. . . . The captains of industry who have driven the rail-way systems across this continent, who have built up our commerce, who have developed our manufactures, have on the whole done great good to our people. Without them the material development of which we are so justly proud could never have taken place.

Moreover, we should recognize the immense importance of this material development by leaving as unhampered as is compatible with the public good the strong and forceful men upon whom the success of business operations inevitably rests. The slightest study of business conditions will satisfy any one capable of forming a judgment that the personal equation is the most important factor in a business operation; that the business ability of the man at the head of any business concern, big or little, is usually the factor which fixes the gulf between striking success and hopeless failure.

An additional reason for caution in dealing with corporations is to be found in the international commercial conditions of today. The same business conditions which have produced the great aggregations of corporate and individual wealth have made them very potent factors in international commercial competition. Business concerns which have the largest means at their disposal and are managed by the ablest men are naturally those which take the lead in the strife for commercial supremacy among the nations of the world. America has only just begun to assume that commanding position in the international business world which we believe will more and more be hers. It is of the utmost importance that this position be not jeopardized, especially at a time when the overflowing abundance of our own natural resources and the skill, business energy, and mechanical aptitude of our people make foreign markets essential. Under such conditions it would be most unwise to cramp or to fetter the youthful strength of our nation.

Moreover, it cannot too often be pointed out that to strike with ignorant violence at the interests of one set of men almost inevitably endangers the interests of all. The fundamental rule in our national life—the rule which underlies all others—is that, on the whole, and in the long run, we shall go up or down together.

*   *   *

The mechanism of modern business is so delicate that extreme care must be taken not to interfere with it in a spirit of rashness or ignorance. Many of those who have made it their vocation to denounce the great industrial combinations which are popularly, although with technical inaccuracy, known as "trusts," appeal especially to hatred and fear. These are precisely the two emotions, particularly when combined with ignorance, which unfit men for the exercise of cool and steady judgment. In facing new industrial conditions, the whole history of the world shows that legislation will generally be both unwise and ineffective unless undertaken after calm inquiry and with sober self-restraint. . . .

All this is true; and yet it is also true that there are real and grave evils, one of the chief being over-capitalization because of its many baleful consequences; and a resolute and practical effort must be made to correct these evils.

There is a widespread conviction in the minds of the American people that the great corporations known as trusts are in certain of their features and tendencies hurtful to the general welfare. This . . .

is based upon sincere conviction that combination and concentration should be, not prohibited, but, supervised and within reasonable limits controlled; and in my judgment this conviction, is right.

It is no limitation upon property rights or freedom of contract to require that when men receive from government the privilege of doing business under corporate form, which frees them from individual responsibility, and enables them to call into their enterprises the capital of the public, they shall do so upon absolutely truthful representations as to the value of the property in which the capital is to be invested.

Corporations engaged in interstate commerce should be regulated if they are found to exercise a license working to the public injury. It should be as much the aim of those who seek for social betterment to rid the business world of crimes of cunning as to rid the entire body politic of crimes of violence. Great corporations exist only because they are created and safeguarded by our institutions; and it is therefore our right and our duty to see that they work in harmony with these institutions.

The first essential in determining how to deal with the great industrial combinations is knowledge of the facts—publicity. In the interest of the public, the government should have the right to inspect and examine the workings of the great corporations engaged in interstate business. Publicity is the only sure remedy which we can now invoke. What further remedies are needed in the way of governmental regulation, or taxation, can only be determined after publicity has been obtained, by process of law, and in the course of administration. The first requisite is knowledge, full and complete—knowledge which may be made public to the world.

*   *   *

The large corporations, commonly called trusts, though organized in one State, always do business in many States, often doing very little business in the State where they are incorporated. There is utter lack of uniformity in the State laws about them; and as no State has any exclusive interest in or power over their acts, it has in practice proved impossible to get adequate regulation through State action.

Therefore, in the interest of the whole people, the nation should, without interfering with the power of the States in the matter itself, also assume power of supervision and regulation over all corporations doing an interstate business. This is especially true where the corporation derives a portion of its wealth from the existence of some monopolistic element or tendency in its business. There would be no hardship in such supervision; banks are subject to it, and in their case it is now accepted as a simple matter of course. . . .

When the Constitution was adopted, at the end of the eighteenth century, no human wisdom could foretell the sweeping changes, alike in industrial and political conditions, which were to take place by the beginning of the twentieth century. At that time it was accepted as a matter of course that the several States were the proper authorities to regulate, so far as was then necessary, the comparatively insignificant and strictly localized corporate bodies of the day.

The conditions are now wholly different and wholly different action is called for. I believe that a law can be framed which will enable the National Government to exercise control along the lines above indicated; profiting by the experience gained through the passage and administration of the Interstate Commerce Act. If, however, the judgment of the Congress is that it lacks the constitutional power to pass such an act, then a constitutional amendment should be submitted to confer the power.

REVIEW QUESTIONS

1. According to Roosevelt, were the "captains of industry" contributing to the public good?
2. What specific recommendations did Roosevelt make with respect to corporations?
3. Did Roosevelt's views imply an expansion or reduction of government powers?

THEODORE ROOSEVELT

The Conservation of Natural Resources (1908)

During the early twentieth century, Theodore Roosevelt was the most prominent promoter of government programs to protect natural resources. In 1908 he convened a meeting of state governors at the White House to explore better ways to preserve the nation's natural resources.

Theodore Roosevelt, "Opening Address by the President," *Proceedings of a Conference of Governors in the White House*, ed. Newton C. Blanchard (Washington, DC, 1909), pp. 3–12.

White House, Washington, D.C., May 13, 1908
Governors of the several States; and Gentlemen:

I welcome you to this conference at the White House. You have come hither at my request so that we may join together to consider the question of the conservation and use of the great fundamental sources of wealth of this nation. . . .

This conference on the conservation of natural resources is in effect a meeting of the representatives of all the people of the United States called to consider the weightiest problem now before the nation; and the occasion for the meeting lies in the fact that the natural resources of our country are in danger of exhaustion if we permit the old wasteful methods of exploiting them longer to continue.

With the rise of peoples from savagery to civilization, and with the consequent growth in the extent and variety of the needs of the average man, there comes a steadily increasing growth of the amount demanded by this average man from the actual resources of the country. And yet, rather curiously, at the same time that there comes that increase in what the average man demands from the resources, he is apt to grow to lose the sense of his dependence upon nature. He lives in big cities. He deals in industries that do not bring him in close touch with nature. He does not realize the demands he is making upon nature.

Savages, and very primitive peoples generally, concern themselves only with superficial natural resources; with those which they obtain from the actual surface of the ground. As peoples become a little less primitive, their industries, although in a rude manner, are extended to resources below the surface; then, with what we call civilization and the extension of knowledge, more resources come into use, industries are multiplied, and foresight begins to become a necessary and prominent factor in life. Crops are cultivated; animals are domesticated; and metals are mastered.

Every step of the progress of mankind is marked by the discovery and use of natural resources previously unused. Without such progressive knowledge and utilization of natural resources, population could not grow, nor industries multi-ply, nor the hidden wealth of the earth be developed for the benefit of mankind.

From the first beginnings of civilization, on the banks of the Nile and the Euphrates, the industrial progress of the world has gone on slowly, with occasional setbacks, but on the whole steadily, through tens of centuries to the present day. But of late the rapidity of the process has increased at such a rate that more space has been actually covered during the century and a quarter occupied by our national life than during the preceding six thousand years that take us back to the earliest monuments of Egypt, to the earliest cities of the Babylonian plain.

When the founders of this nation met at Independence Hall in Philadelphia, the conditions of commerce had not fundamentally changed from what they were when the Phoenician keels first furrowed the lonely waters of the Mediterranean. The differences were those of degree, not of kind, and they were not in all cases even those of degree. Mining was carried on fundamentally as it had been carried on by the pharaohs in the countries adjacent to the Red Sea. The wares of the merchants of Boston, of Charleston, like the wares of the merchants of Nineveh and Sidon, if they went by water, were carried by boats propelled by sails or oars; if they went by land they were carried in wagons drawn by beasts of draft or in packs on the backs of beasts of burden. The ships that crossed the high seas were better than the ships that had once crossed the Aegean, but they were of the same type, after all—they were wooden ships propelled by sails; and on land, the roads were not as good as the roads of the Roman Empire, while the service of the posts was probably inferior.

In [George] Washington's time anthracite coal was known only as a useless black stone; and the great fields of bituminous coal were undiscovered. As steam was unknown, the use of coal for power production was undreamed of. Water was practically the only source of power, save the labor of men and animals; and this power was used only in the most primitive fashion. But a few small iron deposits had been found in this country, but the use of iron by our countrymen was very small.

Wood was practically the only fuel, and what lumber was sawed was consumed locally, while the forests were regarded chiefly as obstructions to settlement and cultivation. The man who cut down a tree was held to have conferred a service upon his fellows.

Such was the degree of progress to which civilized mankind had attained when this nation began its career. It is almost impossible for us in this day to realize how little our Revolutionary ancestors knew of the great store of natural resources whose discovery and use have been such vital factors in the growth and greatness of this nation, and how little they required to take from this store in order to satisfy their needs.

Since then our knowledge and use of the resources of the present territory of the United States have increased a hundred-fold. Indeed, the growth of this nation by leaps and bounds makes one of the most striking and important chapters in the history of the world. Its growth has been due to the rapid development, and alas that it should be said, to the rapid destruction of our natural resources. Nature has supplied to us in the United States, and still supplies to us, more kinds of resources in more lavish degree than has ever been the case at any other time or with any other people. Our position in the world has been attained by the extent and thoroughness of the control we have achieved over nature; but we are more, and not less, dependent upon what she furnishes than at any previous point of history since the days of primitive man. . . .

The wise use of all of our natural resources, which are our natural resources as well, is the great material question of today. I have asked you to come together now because the enormous consumption of these resources, and the threat of imminent exhaustion of some of them, due to reckless and wasteful use, . . . calls for common effort, common action.

We want to take action that will prevent the advent of a woodless age, and defer as long as possible the advent of an ironless age. . . .

Disregarding for the moment the question of moral purpose, it is safe to say that the prosperity of our people depends directly on the energy and intelligence with which our natural resources are used. It is equally clear that these resources are the final basis of national power and perpetuity. Finally, it is ominously evident that these resources are in the course of rapid exhaustion.

This nation began with the belief that its landed possessions were illimitable and capable of supporting all the people who might care to make our country their home; but already the limit of unsettled land is in sight, and indeed but little land fitted for agriculture now remains unoccupied save what can be reclaimed by irrigation and drainage. We began with an unapproached heritage of forests; more than half of the timber is gone. We began with coal fields more extensive than those of any other nation and with iron ores regarded as inexhaustible, and many experts now declare that the end of both iron and coal is in sight. . . . In a word, we have thoughtlessly, and to a large degree unnecessarily, diminished the resources upon which not only our prosperity but the prosperity of our children must always depend.

We have become great because of the lavish use of our resources, and we have just reason to be proud of our growth. But the time has come to inquire seriously what will happen when our forests are gone, when the coal, the iron, the oil, and the gas are exhausted, when the soils shall have been still further impoverished and washed into the streams, polluting the rivers, denuding the fields, and obstructing navigation. These questions do not relate only to the next century or to the next generation. It is time for us now as a nation to exercise the same reasonable foresight in dealing with our great natural resources that would be shown by any prudent man in conserving and widely using the property which contains the assurance of well-being for himself and his children. . . .

The natural resources I have enumerated can be divided into two sharply distinguished classes accordingly as they are or are not capable of renewal. Mines if used must necessarily be exhausted. The minerals do not and cannot renew themselves. Therefore in dealing with the coal, the oil, the gas, the iron, metals generally, all that we can do is to try to see that they are wisely used. The exhaustion is certain to come in time. We can trust that it will be deferred long enough to enable the extraordinarily inventive genius of our people to devise means and methods for more or less adequately replacing what is lost; but the exhaustion is sure to come.

The second class of resources consists of those which cannot only be used in such manner as to leave them undiminished for our children, but can actually be improved by wise use. The soil, the forests, the waterways come in this category. In dealing with mineral resources, man is able to improve on nature only by putting the resources to a beneficial use which in the end exhausts them; but in dealing with the soil and its products man can improve on nature by compelling the resources to renew and even reconstruct themselves in such manner as to serve increasingly beneficial uses—while the living waters can be so controlled as to multiply their benefits. . . .

We are coming to recognize as never before the right of the nation to guard its own future in the essential matter of natural resources. In the past we have admitted the right of the individual to injure the future of the Republic for his own present profit. The time has come for a change. As a people we have the right and the duty, second to none other but the right and duty of obeying the moral law, of requiring and doing justice, to protect our-selves and our children against the wasteful development of our natural resources, whether that waste is caused by the actual destruction of such resources or by making them impossible of development hereafter. . . .

Finally, let us remember that the conservation of our natural resources, though the gravest problem of today, is yet but part of another and greater problem to which this nation is not yet awake, but to which it will awake in time, and with which it must hereafter grapple if it is to live—the problem of national efficiency, the patriotic duty of insuring the safety and continuance of the nation. When the people of the United States consciously undertake to raise themselves as citizens, and the nation and the states in their several spheres, to the highest pitch of excellence in private, state, and national life, and to do this because it is the first of all the duties of true patriotism, then and not till then the future of this nation, in quality and in time, will be assured.

REVIEW QUESTIONS

1. Why did Roosevelt consider conservation to be the "weightiest issue" facing the nation?
2. What actions did Roosevelt want to replace the unlimited private exploitation of natural resources?

GEORGE L. KNAPP

The Other Side of Conservation (1910)

Not all Americans were as supportive of conservation efforts as Theodore Roosevelt. Writing in 1910, business executive George Knapp saw no need for government protection of natural resources.

The North American Review 191 (April 1910):465–481.

For some years past, the reading public has been treated to fervid and extended eulogies of a policy which the eulogists call the "conservation of our natural resources." In behalf of this so-called "conservation," the finest press bureau in the world has labored with a zeal quite unhampered by any considerations of fact or logic; and has shown its understanding of practical psychology by appealing, not to popular reason, but to popular fears. We are told by this press bureau that our natural resources are being wasted in the most wanton and criminal style; wasted, apparently, for the sheer joy of wasting. We are told that our forests are being cut at a rate which will soon leave us a land without trees. . . . We are told that our coal mines would be exhausted within a century; that our iron ores are going to the blast-furnace at a rate which will send us back to the stone age within the lifetime of men who read the fearsome prophecy. . . .

For all these evils which make the future a thing to dread, the remedy is "conservation." The "government" . . . must stint its natural and proper tasks to engage in the regulation of this, that or the other industry, to "conserve" our resources. To "conserve" our timber, the wooded areas of the public domain, together with all lands touching on and appertaining to the wooded areas, and all other lands that might, could, would or should bear trees and don't, must be segregated from ordinary use and put under despotic control as "National Forests." To "conserve" our coal supply, the coal lands must be kept from passing into individual ownership, and operated, if at all, by persons who lease the privilege from the national government. To "conserve" our water-power, the power sites must be treated as the coal lands, and developed, if at all, as leaseholds. In a word, the Federal Government must constitute itself a gigantic feudal land lord, ruling over unwilling tenants by the agency of irresponsible bureaus; traversing every local right, meddling with every private enterprise, which seems to stand in the way of the sacred fetish of "conservation." Only by such drastic means, we are told, can the rights of the people be protected, and the continued prosperity of the nation be assured. So persistently and

adroitly has this view been urged by this press bureau, that millions of people wonder, in their innocence, why any one should object to so needful and righteous a work. . . .

I propose to speak for those exiles in sin who hold that a large part of the present "conservation" movement is unadulterated humbug. That the modern Jeremiahs are as sincere as was the older one, I do not question. But I count their prophecies to be baseless vaporings, and their vaunted remedy worse than the fancied disease. I am one who can see no warrant of law, of justice, nor of necessity for that wholesale reversal of our traditional policy which the advocates of "conservation" demand. I am one who does not shiver for the future at the sight of a load of coal, nor view a steel mill as the arch-robber of posterity. I am one who does not believe in a power trust, past, present or to come; and who, if he were a capitalist seeking to form such a trust, would ask nothing better than just the present conservation scheme to help him. I believe that a government bureau is the worst imaginable landlord; and that its essential nature is not changed by giving it a high-sounding name, and decking it with home-made haloes. I hold that the present forest policy ceases to be a nuisance only when it becomes a curse. . . .

We have a policy [government conservation of forests] which is an absolute reversal of more than one hundred years of national habit and tradition; a policy which holds barrenness a blessing and settlement a sin; which fines, instead of encouraging, the man who would develop a natural resource; which looks forward to a population of tenants instead of to a population of proprietors; which seeks to replace the individual initiative that has made our land great by a bureaucratic control that has made many another land small. Surely, the danger must be imminent and terrible which is held to justify such a course.

The danger is said to be imminent, indeed. The conservation press bureau is strong on asserting. The picture of the lost and forlorn condition of the land ground under the iron heel of the coming power trust is calculated to move the faithful to tears; and the picture of the desolation which will follow the wasting of our natural resources is yet more harrowing. But somehow the details of these panoramas of terror are not quite convincing.

Just one of all the scares adduced to justify the freaks of "conservation" has any basis in fact, and that basis rests on a legislative folly against which no disciple of "conservation" protests. The rest of the terrors are the unreal fabric of a bureaucratic dream. And if they were real the worst possible method of meeting them would be that scheme which is touted by the conservation press bureau as a piece of statesmanship so profound that its authors are appalled afresh each day at their own supernal wisdom. If the power trust were a real menace, how could its coming be hastened more surely than by cutting off from use the supply of power sites? If a coal famine were impending, what could be worse folly than to put in charge of the coal mines an agency which cannot even run a monopolistic post office without a deficit? If the timber famine were as near and as fearsome as we have been told, who shall measure the criminal folly of taxing the people to "conserve" one-fifth of their timber-supply and taxing them again to provide bounties to hasten the destruction of the other four-fifths?

The terrors from which "conservation" is to save us are phantoms. The evils which "conservation" brings us are very real. Mining discouraged, homesteading brought to a practical standstill, power development fined as criminal and, worst of all, a Federal bureaucracy arrogantly meddling with every public question in a dozen great States—these are some of the things which result from the efforts of a few well-meaning zealots to install themselves as official prophets and saviors of the future, and from that exalted station to regulate the course of evolution.

It is no more a part of the Federal Government's business to enter upon the commercial production of lumber than to enter upon the commercial production of wheat, or breakfast bacon, or hand-saws. . . .

Our natural resources have been used, not wasted. Waste in one sense there has been, to be sure; in that a given resource has not always been put to its best use as we now see that use. But from Eden down,

knowledge has been the costliest thing that man could covet: and the knowledge of how to make the earth best serve him seems well-nigh the most expensive of all. But I think we have made a fair start at the lesson; and considering how well we have already done for ourselves, the intrusion of a Government schoolmaster at this stage seems scarcely needed. The pine woods of Michigan have vanished to make the homes of Kansas; the coal and iron which we have failed—thank Heaven!—to "conserve" have carried meat and wheat to the hungry hives of men and gladdened life with an abundance which no previous age could know. We have turned forests into villages, mines into ships and skyscrapers, scenery into work. Our success in doing the things already accomplished has been exactly proportioned to our freedom from governmental "guidance," and I know no reason to believe that a different formula will hold good in the tasks that lie before. If we can stop the governmental encouragement of destruction, conservation will take care of itself.

To me the future has many problems but no terrors. I belong to the generation which has seen the birth of the electric transformer, the internal-combustion engine, the navigation of the air and the commercial use of aluminum, and I quite decline to worry about what may happen "when the world busts through." There is just one heritage which I am anxious to transmit to my children and to their children's children—the heritage of personal liberty, of free individual action, of "leave to live by no man's leave underneath the law." And I know of no way to secure that heritage save to sharply challenge and relentlessly fight every bureaucratic invasion of local and individual rights, no matter how friendly the mottoes on the invading banners.

REVIEW QUESTIONS

1. Why is Knapp unconcerned with the need to conserve natural resources?
2. Why is Knapp skeptical of placing the federal government in charge of protecting the nation's natural resources?

WOODROW WILSON

FROM *The New Freedom* (1913)

Unlike Theodore Roosevelt, who distinguished between "good" and "bad"
trusts, Democrat Woodrow Wilson believed that all trusts were inherently "bad."
The federal government, he felt, had the responsibility to dismantle them in order to
restore competition and to allow individual enterprise and small businesses to flourish
again. The following selection includes extracts from Wilson's 1912 campaign
speeches.

From Woodrow Wilson, *The New Freedom* (New York: Doubleday, Page, 1913), pp. 163–191.

I admit the popularity of the theory that the trusts have come about through the natural development of business conditions in the United States, and that it is a mistake to try to oppose the processes by which they have been built up, because those processes belong to the very nature of business in our time, and that therefore the only thing we can do, and the only thing we ought to attempt to do, is to accept them as inevitable arrangements and make the best out of it that we can by regulation.

I answer, nevertheless, that this attitude rests upon a confusion of thought. Big business is no doubt to a large extent necessary and natural. The development of business upon a great scale, upon a great scale of cooperation, is inevitable, and, let me add, is probably desirable. But that is a very different matter from the development of trusts, because the trusts have not grown. They have been artificially created; they have been put together, not by natural processes, but by the will, the deliberate planning will, of men who were more powerful than their neighbors in the business world, and who wished to make their power secure against competition.

* * *

Did you ever look into the way a trust was made? It is very natural, in one sense, in the same sense in which human greed is natural. If I haven't efficiency enough to beat my rivals, then the thing I am inclined to do is to get together with my rivals and say: "Don't let's cut each other's throats; let's combine and determine prices for ourselves; determine the output, and thereby determine the prices: and dominate and control the market."

That is very natural. That has been done ever since freebooting was established. That has been done ever since power was used to establish control. The reason that the masters of combination have sought to shut out competition is that the basis of control under competition is brains and efficiency. I admit that any large corporation built up by the legitimate processes of business, by economy, by efficiency, is natural; and I am not afraid of it, no matter how big it grows. It can stay big only by doing its work more thoroughly than anybody else. And there is a point of bigness, as every business man in this country knows, though some of them will not admit it, where you pass the limit of efficiency and get into the region of clumsiness and unwieldiness.

* * *

I take my stand absolutely, where every progressive ought to take his stand, on the proposition that private monopoly is indefensible and intolerable. And there I will fight my battle. And I know how to fight it. . . . What these gentlemen do not want is this: they do not want to be compelled to meet all comers on equal terms. I am perfectly willing that they should beat any competitor by fair means; but I know the foul means they have adopted, and I know that they can be stopped by law. . . .

I have been told by a great many men that the idea I have, that by restoring competition you can restore industrial freedom, is based upon a failure to observe the actual happenings of the last decades in this country; because, they say, it is just free competition that has made it possible for the big to crush the little. I reply, it is not free competition that has done that; it is illicit competition. It is competition of the kind that the law ought to stop, and can stop,—this crushing of the little man.

You know, of course, how the little man is crushed by the trusts. He gets a local market. The big concerns come in and undersell him in his local market, and that is the only market he has; if he cannot make a profit there, he is killed. They can make a profit all through the rest of the Union, while they are underselling him in his locality, and recouping themselves by what they can earn elsewhere. Thus their competitors can be put out of business, one by one, wherever they dare to show a head. Inasmuch as they rise up only one by one, these big concerns can see to it that new competitors never come into the larger field. . . .

But unless you have unlimited capital (which of course you wouldn't have when you were beginning) or unlimited credit (which these gentlemen can see to it that you shan't get), they can kill you out in your local market any time they try. . . .

That is the difference between a big business and a trust. A trust is an arrangement to get rid of competition, and a big business is a business that survived competition by conquering in the field of intelligence and economy. A trust does not bring efficiency to the aid of business; it buys efficiency out of business. I am for big business, and I am against the trusts.

*   *   *

You know that Mr. Roosevelt long ago classified trusts for us as good and bad, and he said that he was afraid only of the bad ones. Now he does not desire that there be any more bad ones, but proposes that they should all be made good by discipline, directly applied by a commission of executive appointment. All he explicitly complains of is a lack of publicity and lack of fairness; not the exercise of power, for throughout that plank the power of the great corporations is accepted as the inevitable consequence of the modern organization of industry.

*   *   *

We are at a parting of the ways. We have, not one or two or three, but many established and formidable monopolies in the United States. We have, not one or two, but many fields of endeavor into which it is difficult, if not impossible, for the independent man to enter. We have restricted credit, we have restricted opportunity, we have controlled development, and we have come to be . . . no longer a government by free opinion . . . but a government by the opinion and duress of small groups of dominant men. . . .

America stands for opportunity. America stands for a free field and no favor. . . . Our purpose is restoration of freedom. We propose to prevent private monopoly by law, to see to it that the methods by which monopolies have been built up are legally made impossible. We design that the limitations on private enterprise shall be removed, so that the next generation of youngsters, as they come along, will not have to become proteges of benevolent trusts, but will be free to go about making their own lives what they will. . . .

REVIEW QUESTIONS

1. Why did Wilson consider "local markets" so important?
2. What did Wilson mean when he said that he was "for big business, and I am against the trusts"?
3. Which social groups would have been most supportive of Wilson's position?

INTERPRETING VISUAL SOURCES: PHOTOGRAPHY AND PROGRESSIVE REFORM

Progressive reformers eager to improve the living and working conditions of the urban poor found a powerful weapon in the new medium of documentary photography. Like the muckraking writers who exposed political corruption and corporate excesses, talented journalists began to use cameras to shed light on the miseries of contemporary social life. Photographs not only served as witnesses to reality, they also served as agents of reform. Compelling visual evidence of the wretchedness of life in the city tenements and of the exploitation of children and adult poor in the workplace captured the attention of the public and helped provoke remedial legislation.

The pioneer of documentary journalism was Jacob Riis (pronounced Reese), a Danish immigrant turned reporter and reformer who used photojournalism to excite public concern for the hidden poor. His book, How the Other Half Lives, *remains a classic example of documentary photography, and his career epitomizes the fact-worshipping approach of progressive reform. "Ours is an age of facts," Riis once insisted. "It wants facts, not theories, and facts I have endeavored to put down on these pages."*

Soon after arriving in the United States from Denmark in 1870, Riis found himself jobless and homeless. He wandered the streets of Manhattan, sleeping in police station lodging houses and rummaging for scraps outside restaurants. Filthy and unkempt, he "was too shabby to get work, even if there had been any to get." Riis finally made his way to Philadelphia, where the Danish consul helped him find work as a lumberjack, hunter, and trapper in upstate New York. But his "desire to roam" kept him moving, and in 1877 he became a reporter for the New York Tribune.

As a journalist Riis developed a passion for human interest stories drawn from the back alleys and tenements of Manhattan's congested Lower East Side. There he saw throngs of poor Irish, Italians, Bohemians, African Americans, and Jews crammed into unsanitary hovels that bred disease, ignorance, and crime. His

*own encounters with the pinch of poverty and the sting of discrimination sea-
soned his observations and ignited his fervor for reform. Convinced that a bad
environment was the primary cause of poverty, Riis began writing graphic ex-
posés of the miserable conditions in the slums. "The power of fact," he decided, "is
the mightiest lever of this or of any day."*

*Yet merely printing the "facts" about urban squalor failed to summon much
public outcry. "I wrote, but it seemed to make no impression," Riis recalled in his
autobiography. To heighten the impact of his written testimony, he began to use
photographs of crowded streets, decrepit tenements, and poorly clothed slum
dwellers. The camera, he realized, had a special evidentiary power to lay bare
hidden truths, and few facts were as visually compelling as poverty.*

*In 1887 Riis and his colleagues began taking photographs to accompany his
articles, and their exhausting efforts provided the first graphic images of the
seamy underside of New York life. They lugged around cumbersome cameras on
tripods and used flash-lit photography—a dangerous new process requiring a pis-
tol lamp that fired magnesium flash-powder cartridges with a flaming bang.
"Twice I set fire to the house with my apparatus," Riis admitted, "and once to
myself."*

*Through such explosive illumination, Riis literally brought light into some of
the darkest corners of American society. His intriguing pictures of tenement life
helped people see that poverty was not simply an evil to be condemned as it was
a condition to be remedied. Eager to go beyond mere reportage and to promote
concrete reforms, Riis began giving slide lectures to church and civic groups
throughout the city and across the nation. "Neighbors," he would say at the end
of his presentation, go out and "find your neighbors." Many found this a compelling challenge. A midwestern journalist reported that to those of "us who are
unfamiliar with life in a large city," Riis's slide presentation "was a revelation."
His photographs "were certainly more realistic than any words could be."*

Riis's graphic account of bitter poverty so impressed the editor of Scribner's
Monthly *that he invited Riis to write an illustrated article for the popular
middle-class magazine. "How the Other Half Lives" appeared in the Christmas
1889 issue accompanied by nineteen photographs transformed into line drawings.
The article described sordid tenements "nurtured in the greed and avarice" of ra-
pacious slumlords, disease-ridden ghettos where people were shoehorned into
windowless warrens. In one thirteen-square-foot Bayard Street room, Riis found
twelve male and female lodgers. Another two-room apartment on Essex Street
hosted a family of fourteen plus six boarders.*

*Riis's shocking revelations excited so much interest that he agreed to expand
his article into a book. Published in 1890,* How the Other Half Lives: Studies
among the Tenements of New York *created an immediate sensation and went
through eleven editions in the next five years. "No book of the year," proclaimed
the* Dial, *"has aroused a deeper interest or wider discussion than Mr. Riis's*

earnest study of the poor and outcast." In spirited prose, Riis detailed the crowded life of the "unventilated and fever-breeding" tenements, the ravages of disease and alcohol, the tragedy of homeless street urchins, the violence of "gangs," the sound of tubercular coughs, the oppressive atmosphere of sweatshops, and the "queer, conglomerate mass of heterogeneous elements" forming New York's diverse ethnic tapestry.

Forty-three illustrations and fifteen halftone reproductions authenticated Riis's narrative. Riis, however, refused to let his pictures speak for themselves. He combined preaching prose with his photographs. "What then are the bald facts with which we have to deal in New York?" he asked. "That we have a tremendous, even swelling crowd of wage-earners which it is our business to house decently. . . . This is the fact from which we cannot get away, however we deplore it." Riis offered neither easy solutions nor the salve of consolation to bruised consciences. "We know now," he wrote, "that there is no way out; that the 'system' that was the awful offspring of public neglect and private greed has come to stay, a storm center forever of our civilization. Nothing is left but to make the best of a bad bargain." His own plan of action called for rigorous enforcement of building codes and the construction of new, sanitary, well-ventilated, and affordable housing, more city parks, and better playgrounds. Riis goaded the hesitant: "What are you going to do about it?" Some readers were moved to take action. Theodore Roosevelt, then serving as president of the board of New York City's police commissioners, visited Riis's office and left a note: "I have read your book, and I have come to help."

Riis rarely asked people for permission to enter their hovels and take their pictures. Many of the destitute and powerless resented the uninvited efforts of Riis's "raiding party," however noble their intentions. Some people pelted Riis and his associates with rocks, others fled their hovels or demanded to be paid for their cooperation. Such reactions reveal again the fine line separating well-intentioned reform from intrusive manipulation.

Despite the intrusive nature of his methods, the crusading Riis revealed to Americans how much of their contemporary social reality had been overlooked. From his pictures, he asserted, "there was no appeal." The poor of the inner city "compelled recognition." They were "dangerous less because of their own crimes than because of the criminal ignorance of those who are not of their kind." Riis's photographs revealed more than the degradations of slum life; they illuminated the dark side of the American dream, and in the process they startled many into a keener sense of social responsibility. The muckraking journalist and novelist Ernest Poole remembered how "hungrily" he read How the Other Half Lives because it revealed to him "a tremendous new field, scarcely touched by American writers."

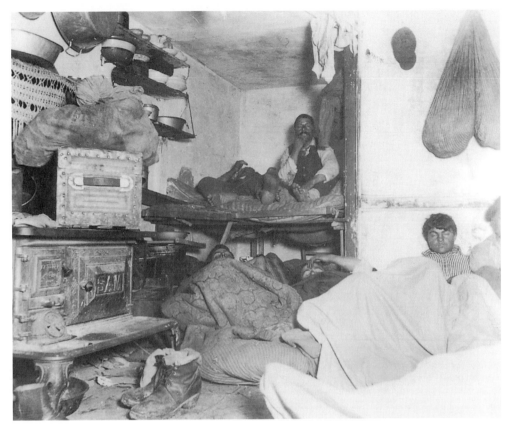

FIVE CENTS A SPOT   Museum of the City of New York

A typical example of Riis's photographic technique is Lodgers in a Crowded Bayard Street Tenement: Five Cents a Spot. *It exposes a catacomb-like room, only thirteen square feet, clogged with twelve immigrant "lodgers" and their motley possessions. Awakened by Riis at midnight in their wretched roost, the bleary-eyed tenants stare at the camera in the midst of pots, pans, boots, caps, clothes, trunks, duffel bags, and firewood. The precise details of such a mundane scene heighten its emphatic immediacy, but its strength derives from its stark contrast with the norms of middle-class domesticity. The room's filth and claustrophobia pricked the consciences of well-to-do suburbanites preoccupied with clean homes and wholesome families.*

A BLACK-AND-TAN DIVE   Museum of the City of New York

Riis revealed the ethical ambiguities embedded in his brand of documentary photography in A Black-and-Tan Dive, *a photograph of two white women and a black man in a darkened cellar saloon where a fastidious Riis witnessed the "commingling of the utterly depraved of both sexes." The sudden flash of illumination invades the secret sanctuary and catches the patrons off guard. Seated on a keg, the black man betrays both surprise and perhaps anger. The white woman on his left, face smudged with grime, looks down with a visage suggesting sullen resentment or embarrassment. The hand of another black man (off camera) rests on her shoulder, providing a controversial nuance in an age when racial mixing was deemed an abomination. Most striking is the third figure, a woman with her back turned to the camera and a shawl draped over her head in a spontaneous effort to shield her eyes from the glare and protect her privacy from the invasive lens. The photograph gave Riis's middle-class audience voyeuristic access into an alluring world of sensual gratification and forbidden behavior.*

DENS OF DEATH   Museum of the City of New York

The relentless stream of immigrants arriving in New York prompted landowners to erect ramshackle shanties. They were often built so hastily and carelessly that they soon collapsed. In this picture of immigrant housing on Baxter Street, Riis revealed how crowded and unsafe the living quarters were. He also learned that a chronic foul odor in the neighborhood prompted a visit from a sanitary inspector. Upon investigation he discovered that the sewage pipe from the buildings was not connected to the sewer drain. It simply poured its contents directly into the ground under the buildings.

POLICE STATION LODGER   Museum of the City of New York

In the late nineteenth century the homeless had few options. During the winter months, police stations allowed people to come in at night and sleep on the floor. This photograph shows a vagrant suffering from typhus, lying on the bare floor near the stove for warmth. Sockless and sick, he offered poignant testimony to the plight of the downtrodden.

TENEMENT YARD   Museum of the City of New York

Riis was particularly concerned about the fate of children consigned to life in the congested tenements. Here he encountered a group of urchins forced to play in a confined space. "There was about as much light in this 'yard,' " he observed, "as in the average cellar." He counted 128 children living among the forty families in the building.

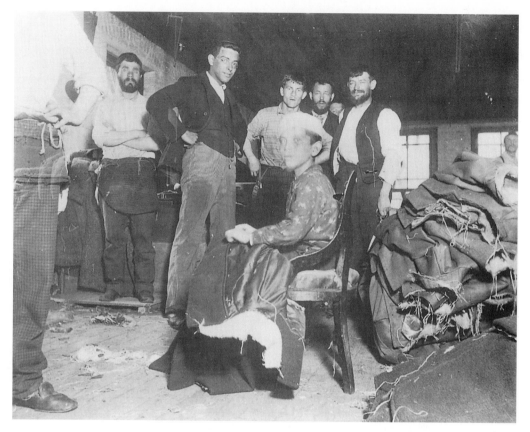

IN A SWEAT SHOP   Museum of the City of New York

Child labor was one of the chief targets of progressive reformers. Riis visited numerous sweatshops in New York, where he witnessed children as young as six years old working ten to twelve hours each day. They were given no time off for meals; they kept working while eating. In this photograph of an East Side sweatshop, he shows a boy at work pulling threads. The state law in New York said that children under sixteen could not be employed unless they could read and write English; and none could be employed under fourteen. Riis found that this boy had a certificate claiming he was sixteen, but he confessed to being only twelve.

REVIEW QUESTIONS

1. Why might photographs have been a more powerful medium for social documentary than sketches or drawings?
2. Was Riis practicing a form of "yellow journalism"? Why or why not?
3. Taken as a whole, what do these photographs suggest about urban growth during this period?
4. What is your reaction to the fact that Riis frequently "staged" his photographs, positioning people and their possessions for dramatic effect?

25 ❧ AMERICA AND THE GREAT WAR

*Woodrow Wilson and Secretary of State William J. Bryan were diplomatic ideal-
ists who hoped that international tensions could always be settled peaceably. To
this end they negotiated "cooling off" treaties with thirty nations, whereby disputes between two countries would be handed over to an international arbitration commission. However logical such agreements might have seemed in theory,
they ignored the fact that international disputes often involved emotional issues
and self-interests that were non-negotiable.*

*Nowhere was this truer than in Europe. There the great powers had divided
themselves into two large interlocking military alliances. Germany and Austria-
Hungary formed the Triple Alliance, and Britain, France, and Russia formed the
Triple Entente. Intended to maintain a rough balance of power, these alliances
also ensured that when conflict erupted it would rapidly escalate into a major
war. In 1914 the unthinkable occurred when a Serbian nationalist assassinated
Archduke Franz Ferdinand, heir to the Austro-Hungarian empire. The archduke
and his wife were gunned down in Sarajevo, the capital of Bosnia in the Balkans.
The Austrians resolved to punish the Serbs for the killings, triggering Russia to
mobilize its army in defense of Serbia's large population of Slavs. Germany
rushed to support Austria-Hungary, preemptively declaring war on Russia and
France. When Germany invaded Belgium (thereby violating its neutrality) in order to attack France, the British declared war on Germany. The First World War
had begun.*

*Americans were stunned by the sudden outbreak of European war, but were
quickly reassured by the beliefs—mistaken, as it turned out—that the United
States had no vital interests at stake in the conflict and that the Atlantic Ocean
would insulate America from the conflagration. But it soon became obvious that
Americans could not long remain neutral or uninvolved in an expanding world
war. By virtue of their own ethnic background, political ideals, and economic
interests, most Americans supported the Allies (as Britain, France, and Russia*

became known). Wilson, as it turns out, also sought to support the Allies behind the scenes while calling publicly for neutrality. By insisting on the American right to maintain trade with the belligerent nations, he was in effect aiding the Allies, for they received the vast majority of supplies.

Germany sought to cut off the pipeline of American shipments to Great Britain. In 1915 the German navy unleashed its submarines against transatlantic shipping and announced a blockade of the British Isles. Wilson warned the German government that he would hold them to "strict accountability" if any American lives were lost. The sinking of the huge British passenger liner Lusitania *in May 1915 killed nearly 1,200 people, including over one hundred Americans. The loss of the* Lusitania *horrified Americans. Some commentators called for a declaration of war. Wilson instead sent strident protests to the German government, demanding payment for the lost lives and a pledge not to sink passenger vessels. The Germans agreed and tensions eased. But Wilson predicted that the fragile peace would not last. As he confided to an aide in 1916, "I can't keep the country out of war. . . . Any little German lieutenant (submarine commander) can put us into war at any time by some calculated outrage."*

On 31 January 1917, the Germans announced the renewal of unrestricted submarine attacks on Atlantic shipping. A few days later the United States broke off diplomatic relations with Germany. Soon thereafter, on 1 March, an intercepted telegram from the German foreign secretary, Arthur Zimmermann, to the German ambassador in Mexico inflamed public opinion in the United States. The Zimmermann telegram promised Mexico the restoration of Texas, New Mexico, and Arizona if Mexico supported Germany in a war against the United States.

More immediately, however, American officials in early 1917 were preoccupied with the escalating number of ships sunk by German submarines. Between 12 and 21 March, five American ships were lost. This was the last straw. On 2 April, Wilson asked Congress to declare war. The war resolution swept through the Senate by a vote of 82 to 6 and the House by 373 to 50.

No sooner had the United States officially entered the war than President Wilson began to turn the conflict into a crusade—not only to transform the nature of international relations but also to create a permanent peace. On 8 January 1918, in part to counter the Bolshevik claim that the Allies were fighting for imperialist aims, Wilson announced his Fourteen Point peace plan outlining allied intentions.

By the end of 1918 the war was winding down. American intervention proved decisive in turning the tide against the Germans and their allies. In December Wilson made the controversial decision for the American delegation to join the peace conference convening in Paris. This proved to be a political disaster because the Republican-controlled Senate felt that President Wilson was purposely ignoring its historic role in shaping foreign policy. When Wilson presented the peace plan—with its controversial provision for a League of Nations to police world affairs—to the American public, it aroused intense debate. Critics led by powerful Republican senator Henry Cabot Lodge balked at American participation in the League, arguing that it would transfer war-making authority to an outside body.

Worn down by a public speaking tour intended to arouse public support for the Versailles Treaty, Wilson suffered a stroke in the summer of 1919 that left him bedridden for months. Wilson's absence proved fatal to his hopes to gain Senate support. After much maneuvering and many votes, the Senate refused to ratify the Versailles Treaty in March 1920.

American involvement in the so-called Great War signaled the arrival of the United States on the center stage of world affairs. Yet in the immediate aftermath of the war, most Americans returned to their earlier stance of isolation from the turmoil of international events. Little did they know that the United States was more intertwined than ever in the fate of other nations.

The Zimmermann Note (1917)

One of the incidents inflaming American public opinion against Germany was the disclosure of the so-called Zimmermann Note. It was in fact a secret telegram sent in January 1917 from the German foreign secretary, Arthur Zimmermann, to the German ambassador in Mexico. British intelligence officers intercepted the message and excitedly informed the United States of its provocative contents.

From James B. Scott, ed., *Diplomatic Correspondence between the United States and Germany, August 1, 1914–April 6, 1917* (New York: Oxford University Press, 1918), p. 338.

Berlin, January 19, 1917

On the first of February we intend to begin submarine warfare unrestricted. In spite of this it is our intention to keep neutral the United States of America.

If this attempt is not successful we propose an alliance on the following basis with Mexico: That we shall make war together and together make peace. We shall give general financial support, and it is understood that Mexico is to reconquer the lost territory in New Mexico, Texas, and Arizona. The details are left for your settlement.

You are instructed to inform the President of Mexico of the above in the greatest confidence as soon as it is certain there will be an outbreak of war with the United States, and we suggest that the President of Mexico on his own initiative should communicate with Japan suggesting adherence at once to this plan; at the same time offer to mediate between Germany and Japan.

Please call to the attention of the President of Mexico that the employment of ruthless submarine warfare now promises to compel England to make peace in a few months.

Zimmermann

REVIEW QUESTIONS

1. What in this message would have most angered Americans? Why?
2. What did the Germans believe that unrestricted submarine warfare would cause the British to do?
3. If you were a newspaper editor in 1917, what headline would you choose for the discovery of the Zimmermann telegram?

WOODROW WILSON

Declaration of War against Germany (1917)

On 2 April 1917, Wilson spoke to a joint session of Congress and summarized his two-year effort to maintain American neutrality in the face of the German submarine campaign. He called for a war not only to punish the Germans and reaffirm neutral rights, but also to make the world "safe for democracy." In this sense he viewed the war as a "great crusade" to establish legal and moral principles for all nations to follow.

From "Address by the President of the United States," *Congressional Record*, 65th Cong., 1st sess., 1917, 55:102–104.

I have called the Congress into extraordinary session because there are serious, very serious, choices of policy to be made, and made immediately, which it was neither right nor constitutionally permissible that I should assume the responsibility of making.

On the third of February last I officially laid before you the extraordinary announcement of the Imperial German Government that on and after the first day of February it was its purpose to put aside all restraints of law or of humanity and use its submarines to sink every vessel that sought to approach either the ports of Great Britain and Ireland or the western coasts of Europe or any of the ports controlled by the enemies of Germany within the Mediterranean. . . .

I was for a little while unable to believe that such things would in fact be done by any government that had hitherto subscribed to the humane practices of civilized nations. International law had its origin in the attempt to set up some law which would be respected and observed upon the seas, where no nation had right of dominion and where lay the free highways of the world. . . .

This minimum of right the German Government has swept aside under the plea of retaliation and necessity and because it had no weapons which it could use at sea except these which it is impossible to employ as it is employing them without throwing to the winds all scruples of humanity or of respect for the understandings that were supposed to underlie the intercourse of the world.

I am not now thinking of the loss of property involved, immense and serious as that is, but only of the wanton and wholesale destruction of the lives of non-combatants, men, women, and children, engaged in pursuits which have always, even in the darkest periods of modern history, been deemed innocent and legitimate. Property can be paid for; the lives of peaceful and innocent people cannot be. The present German submarine warfare against commerce is a warfare against mankind.

It is a war against all nations. American ships have been sunk, American lives taken, in ways which it has stirred us very deeply to learn of, but the ships and people of other neutral and friendly nations have been sunk and overwhelmed in the waters in the same way. There has been no discrimination. The challenge is to all mankind. Each nation must decide for itself how it will meet it. The choice we make for ourselves must be made with a moderation of counsel and a temperateness of judgment befitting our character and our motives as a nation. We must put excited feeling away. Our motive will not be revenge or the victorious assertion of the physical might of the nation, but only the vindication of right, of human right, of which we are only a single champion. . . .

With a profound sense of the solemn and even tragic character of the step I am taking and of the grave responsibilities which it involves, but in unhesitating obedience to what I deem my constitutional duty, I advise that the Congress declare the recent course of the Imperial German Government to be in fact nothing less than war against the government and people of the Unites States; that it formally accept the status of belligerent which has thus been thrust upon it; and that it take immediately steps not only to put the country in a more thorough state of defense but also to exert all its power and employ all its resources to bring the Government of the German Empire to terms and end the war. . . .

We have no quarrel with the German people. We have no feeling towards them but one of sympathy and friendship. It was not upon their impulse that their government acted in entering this war. It was not with their previous knowledge or approval. It was a war determined upon as wars used to be determined upon in the old, unhappy days when peoples were nowhere consulted by their rulers and wars were provoked and waged in the interest of dynasties or of little groups of ambitious men who were accustomed to use their fellow men as pawns and tools. . . .

The world must be made safe for democracy. Its peace must be planted upon the tested foundations of political liberty. We have no selfish ends to serve. We desire no conquest no dominion. We seek no indemnities for ourselves, no material compensation for the sacrifices we shall freely make. We are but one of the champions of the rights of mankind. We shall be satisfied when those rights have been made as secure as the faith and the freedom of nations can make them. . . .

Just because we fight without rancor and without selfish object, seeking nothing for ourselves but what we shall wish to share with all free peoples, we shall, I feel confident, conduct our operations as belligerents without passion and ourselves observe with proud punctilio[1] the principles of right and of fair play we profess to be fighting for. We enter this war only where we are clearly forced into it because there are no other means of defending our rights. It will be all the easier for us to conduct ourselves as belligerents in a high spirit of right and fairness because we act without animus, not in enmity towards a people or with the desire to bring any injury or disadvantage upon them, but only in armed opposition to an irresponsible government which has thrown aside all considerations of humanity and of right and is running amuck.

We are, let me say again, the sincere friends of the German people, and shall desire nothing so much as the early reestablishment of intimate relations of mutual advantage between us,—however hard it may be for them, for the time being, to believe that this is spoken from our hearts. We have borne with their present Government through all these bitter months because of that friendship,—exercising a patience and forbearance which would otherwise have been impossible.

We shall, happily, still have an opportunity to prove that friendship in our daily attitude and actions towards the millions of men and women of German birth and native sympathy who live amongst us and share our life, and we shall be proud to prove it towards all who are in fact loyal

---

[1] A scrupulous adherence to laws or rules.

to their neighbors and to the Government in the hour of test. They are, most of them, as true and loyal Americans as if they had never known any other fealty or allegiance. They will be prompt to stand with us in rebuking and restraining the few who may be of a different mind and purpose. If there should be disloyalty, it will be dealt with a firm hand of stern repression; but, if it lifts its head at all, it will lift it only here and there and without countenance except from a lawless and malignant few.

It is a distressing and oppressive duty, Gentlemen of the Congress, which I have performed in thus addressing you. There are, it may be, many months of fiery trial and sacrifice ahead of us. It is a fearful thing to lead this great peaceful people into war, into the most terrible and disastrous of all wars, civilization itself seeming to be in the balance.

But the right is more precious than peace, and we shall fight for the things which we have always carried nearest our hearts,—for democracy, for the right of those who submit to authority to have a voice in their own Governments, for the rights and liberties of small nations, for a universal dominion of right by such a concert of free peoples as shall bring peace and safety to all nations and make the world itself at last free.

To such a task we can dedicate our lives and our fortunes, everything that we are and everything that we have, with the pride of those who know that the day has come when America is privileged to spend her blood and her might for the principles that gave her birth and happiness and the peace which she has treasured. God helping her, she can do no other.

REVIEW QUESTIONS

1. What did Wilson mean when he claimed, "We have no quarrel with the German people"?
2. How did Wilson deal with the topic of German-Americans?
3. Were Wilson's ultimate war goals realistic? Explain.

RANDOLPH BOURNE

The War and the Intellectuals (1917)

Support for American intervention in World War I was not universal. Randolph Bourne, a brilliant young New York literary critic and pacifist, criticized the sentiment for war. He feared that intervention would cost many lives, stifle progressive social reforms, and unleash a wave of anti-German hysteria.

From Randolph Bourne, "The War and the Intellectuals," *Seven Arts* 2 (1917):133–136. [Editorial insertions appear in square brackets—*Ed.*]

To those of us who still retain an irreconcilable animus against war, it has been a bitter experience to see the unanimity with which the American intellectuals have thrown their support to the use of war-technique in the crisis in which America found herself. Socialists, college professors, publicists, new-republicans, practitioners of literature, have vied with each other in confirming with their intellectual faith the collapse of neutrality and the riveting of the war-mind on a hundred million more of the world's people. And the intellectuals are not content with confirming our belligerent gesture. They are now complacently asserting that it was they who effectively willed it, against the hesitation and dim perceptions of the American democratic masses. A war made deliberately by the intellectuals! . . .

Those intellectuals who have felt themselves totally out of sympathy with this drag toward war will seek some explanation for this joyful leadership. They will want to understand this willingness of the American intellect to open the sluices and flood us with the sewage of the war spirit. . . . To the American academic mind of 1914 defense of war was inconceivable. . . . They would have thought anyone mad who talked of shipping American men by the hundreds of thousands—conscripts—to die on the fields of France. Such a spiritual change seems catastrophic when we shoot our minds back to those days when neutrality was a proud thing.

But the intellectual progress has been so gradual that the country retains little sense of the irony. The war sentiment, begun so gradually but so perseveringly by the preparedness advocates who came from the ranks of big business, caught hold of one after another of the intellectual groups. With the aid of [Theodore] Roosevelt the murmurs became a monotonous chant and finally a chorus so mighty that to be out of it was at first to be disreputable and finally almost obscene. And slowly a strident rant was worked up against Germany which compared very creditably with the German fulminations against the greedy power of England.

The nerve of the war-feeling centered, of course, in the richer and older classes of the Atlantic seaboard and was keenest where there were French or English businesses and particularly social connections. The sentiment then spread over the country as a class-phenomenon, touching everywhere those upper-class elements in each section who identified themselves with this Eastern ruling group. It must never be forgotten that in every community it was the least liberal and least democratic elements among whom the preparedness and later the war sentiment was found. The farmers were apathetic, the small businessmen and workingman are still apathetic towards the war. The election [of 1916] was a vote of confidence of these latter classes in a President [Wilson] who would keep the faith of neutrality. The intellectuals, in other words, have identified themselves with the least democratic forces in American life. They have assumed the leadership for war of those very classes whom the American democracy has been immemorially fighting. Only in a world where irony was dead could an intellectual class enter war at the head of such illiberal cohorts in the avowed cause of world-liberalism and world-democracy. No one is left to point out the undemocratic nature of this war-liberalism. In a time of faith skepticism is the most intolerable of all insults.

Our intellectual class might have been occupied during the last two years of war in studying and clarifying the ideals and aspirations of the American democracy, in discovering a true Americanism which would not have been merely nebulous but might have federated the different ethnic groups and traditions. They might have spent the time in endeavoring to clear the public mind of the cant of war, to get rid of old mystical notions that clog our thinking. We might have used the time for a great wave of education, for setting our house in spiritual order. We could at least have set the problem before ourselves. If our intellectuals were going to lead the administration, they might conceivably have tried to find some way of securing peace by making neutrality effective. They might have turned their intellectual energy not to the problem of jockeying the nation into war but to the problem of using our vast neutral power to attain democratic ends for the rest of the world and ourselves without the use of the malevolent technique of war. They might have failed. The point is that they scarcely tried. The time was spent not in clarification and education but in a mulling over of nebulous ideals of democracy and liberalism and civilization, which had never meant anything fruitful to those ruling classes who now so glibly use them, and in giving free rein to the elementary instinct of self-defense.

The whole era has been spiritually wasted. The outstanding feature has been not its Americanism but its intense colonialism. The offense of our intellectuals was not so much that they were colonial—for what could we expect of a nation composed of so many national elements?—but that it was so one-sidedly and partisanly colonial. The official reputable expression of the intellectual class has been that of the English colonial. Certain portions of it have been even more loyalist than the King, more British even than Australia. Other colonial attitudes have been vulgar. The colonialism of the other American stocks [ethnic groups] was denied a hearing from the start. America might have been made a meeting-ground for the different national attitudes. An intellectual class, cultural colonists of the different European nations, might have threshed out the issues here as they could not be threshed out in Europe. Instead of this, the English colonials in university and press took command at the start. . . . The reputable opinion of the American intellectuals became more and more either what could be read pleasantly in London or what was written in an earnest effort to put Englishmen straight on their war-aims and war-technique. . . . The great masses, the other ethnic groups, were inarticulate. American public opinion was almost as little prepared for war in 1917 as it was in 1914. . . .

We have had to watch, therefore, in this country the same process which so shocked us abroad —the coalescence of the intellectual classes in support of the military program. In this country, indeed, the socialist intellectuals did not even have the grace of their German brothers to wait for the declaration of war before they broke for cover. And when they declared for war they showed how thin was the intellectual veneer of their socialism. For they called us in terms that might have emanated from any bourgeois journal to defend democracy and civilization, just as if it were not exactly against those very bourgeois democracies and capitalist civilizations that socialists had been fighting for decades. But so subtle is the spiritual chemistry of the "inside" that all this intellectual cohesion—herd-instinct become herd-intellect—which seemed abroad so hysterical and so servile comes to us here in highly rational terms. We go to war to save the world from subjugation! But the German intellectuals went to war to save their culture from barbarization! And the French went to war to save their beautiful France! And the English to save international honor! And Russia, most altruistic and self-sacrificing of all, to save a small State from destruction. Whence is our miraculous intuition of our moral spotlessness? Whence our confidence that history will not unravel huge economic and imperialist forces upon which our rationalizations float like bubbles? The Jew often marvels that his race alone should have been chosen as the true people of the cosmic God. Are not our intellectuals equally fatuous when they tell us that our war of all wars is stainless and thrillingly achieving for good?

An intellectual class that was wholly rational would have called insistently for peace and not for war. For months the crying need has been for a negotiated peace in order to avoid the ruin of a deadlock. Would not the same amount of resolute statesmanship thrown into intervention have secured a peace that would have been a subjugation for neither side? Was the terrific bargaining power of a great neutral ever really used? Our war followed, as all wars follow, a monstrous failure of diplomacy. Shamefacedness should now be our intellectual's attitude, because the American play for peace was made so little more than a polite play. The intellectuals have still to explain why, willing as they now are to use force to continue the war to absolute exhaustion, they were not willing to use force to coerce the world to a speedy peace. . . .

The results of war on the intellectual class are already apparent. Their thought becomes little more than a description and justification of what is going on. They turn upon any rash one who continues idly to speculate. Once the war is on, the conviction spreads that individual thought is helpless, that the only way one can count is as a cog in the great wheel. There is no good holding back. We are told to dry our unnoticed and ineffective tears and plunge into the great work [of winning the war]. Not only is everyone forced into line but the new certitude becomes idealized. It is a noble realism which opposes itself to futile obstruction and the cowardly refusal to face facts. This realistic boast is so loud and sonorous that one wonders whether realism is always a stern and intelligent grappling with realities. May it not be sometimes a mere surrender to the actual, an abdication of the ideal through a sheer fatigue from intellectual suspense? The pacifist is roundly scolded for refusing to face the facts and for retiring into his own world of sentimental desire. But is the realist, who refuses to challenge or criticize facts, entitled to any more credit than that which comes from following the line of least resistance? The realist thinks he at least can control events by linking himself to the forces that are moving. Perhaps he can. But, if it is a question of controlling war, it is difficult to see how the child on the back of a mad elephant is to be any more effective in stopping the beast than is the child who tries to stop him from the ground. The ex-humanitarian, turned realist, sneers at the snobbish neutrality, colossal conceit, crooked thinking, dazed sensibilities, of those who are still unable to find any balm of consolation for this war. We manufacture consolations here in America while there are probably not a dozen men fighting in Europe who did not long ago give up every reason for their being there except that nobody knew how to get them away.

But the intellectuals whom the crisis has crystallized into an acceptance of war have put themselves into a terrifyingly strategic position. It is only on the craft, in the stream, they say, that one has any chance of controlling the current forces for liberal purposes. If we obstruct, we surrender all power for influence. If we responsibly approve, we then retain our power for guiding. We will be listened to as responsible thinkers, while those who obstructed the coming of war have committed intellectual suicide and shall be cast into outer darkness. Criticism by the ruling powers will only be accepted from those intellectuals who are in sympathy with the general tendency of the war. Well, it is true that they may guide, but if their stream leads to disaster and the frustration of national life, is their guiding any more than a preference whether they shall go over the right-hand or the left-hand side of the precipice? Meanwhile, however, there is comfort on board. Be with us, they call, or be negligible, irrelevant. Dissenters are already excommunicated. Irreconcilable radicals, wringing their hands among the debris, become the most despicable and impotent of men. There seems no choice for the intellectual but to join the mass of acceptance. But again the terrible dilemma arises—either support what is going on, in which case you count for nothing because you are swallowed in the mass and great incalculable forces bear you on, or remain aloof, passively resistant, in which case you count for nothing because you are outside the machinery of reality.

Is there no place left, then, for the intellectual who cannot yet crystallize, who does not dread suspense, and is not yet drugged with fatigue? The American intellectuals, in their preoccupation with reality, seem to have forgotten that the real enemy is War rather than imperial Germany. There is work to be done to prevent this war of ours from passing into popular mythology as a holy crusade. What shall we do with leaders who tell us that we go to war in moral spotlessness or who make "democracy" synonymous with a republican form of government? There is work to be done in still shouting that all the revolutionary by-products will not justify the war or make war anything else than the most noxious complex of all the evils that afflict men. There must be some to find no consolation whatever and some to sneer at those who buy the cheap emotion of sacrifice. There must be some irreconcilables left who will not even accept the war with walrus tears. There must be some to call unceasingly for peace and some to insist that the terms of settlement shall be not only liberal but democratic. There must be some intellectuals who are not willing to use the old discredited counters again and to support a peace which would leave all the old inflammable materials of armament lying about the world. There must still be opposition to any contemplated "liberal" world-order founded on military coalitions. The "irreconcilable" need not be disloyal. He need not even be "impossi-bilist." His apathy towards war should take the form of a heightened energy and enthusiasm for the education, the art, the interpretation that make for life in the midst of the world of death. The intellectual who retains his animus against war will push out more boldly than ever to make his case solid against it. The old ideals crumble; new ideals must be forged. His mind will continue to roam widely and ceaselessly. The thing he will fear most is premature crystallization. If the American intellectual class rivets itself to a "liberal" philosophy that perpetuates the old errors, there will then be need for "democrats" whose task will be to divide, confuse, disturb, keep the intellectual waters constantly in motion to prevent any such ice from ever forming.

REVIEW QUESTIONS

1. According to Bourne, is pacifism a compelling ideal? What are its strengths and weaknesses?
2. Bourne charges that support for war originated in the "ruling classes" and from business interests. Is this a convincing argument? Explain.
3. Why is dissent so difficult once war is declared?

GEORGE NORRIS

The Profits of War (1917)

Support for the declaration of war in 1917 was overwhelming but by no means unanimous. Several prominent legislators, most of them from the Midwest, criticized President Woodrow Wilson's actions, claiming that American national interests were not at risk and that the impetus for war was coming from the selfish interests of American munitions makers and bankers eager to maintain a lucrative war trade with the British and French. Republican senator George Norris of Nebraska led the opposition in the Senate.

From *Congressional Record*, 65th Cong., 1st sess., 1917, 55:213–214.

. . . We have loaned many hundreds of millions of dollars to the allies in this controversy. While such action was legal and countenanced by international law, there is no doubt in my mind but the enormous amount of money loaned to the allies in this country has been instrumental in bringing about a public sentiment in favor of our country taking a course that would make every bond worth a hundred cents on the dollar and making the payment of every debt certain and sure.

Through this instrumentality and also through the instrumentality of others who have not only made millions out of the war in the manufacture of munitions, etc., and who would expect to make millions more if our country can be drawn into the catastrophe, a large number of the great newspapers and news agencies of the country have been controlled and enlisted in the greatest propaganda that the world has ever know, to manufacture sentiment in favor of war.

It is now demanded that the American citizens shall be used as insurance policies to guarantee the safe delivery of munitions of war to belligerent nations. The enormous profits of munitions manufacturers, stockbrokers, and bond dealers must be still further increased by our entrance into the war. This has brought us to the present moment, when Congress, urged by the President and backed by the artificial sentiment, is about to declare war and engulf our country in the greatest holocaust that the world has ever known.

*   *   *

To whom does war bring prosperity? Not to the soldier who for the munificent compensation of $16 per month shoulders his musket and goes into the trench, there to shed his blood and to die if necessary; not to the broken-hearted widow who waits for the return of the mangled body of her husband; not to the mother who weeps at the death of her brave boy; not to the little children who shiver with cold; not to the babe who suffers from hunger; nor to the millions of mothers and daughters who carry broken hearts to their graves.

War brings no prosperity to the great mass of common and patriotic citizens. It increases the cost of living of those who toil and those who already must strain every effort to keep soul and body together. War brings prosperity to the stock gambler on Wall Street—to those who are already in possession of more wealth than can be realized or enjoyed. Again this writer says that if we can not get war, "it is nevertheless good opinion that the preparedness program will compensate in good measure for the loss of the stimulus of actual war." That is, if we can not get war, let us go as far in that direction as possible. If we can not get war, let us cry for additional ships, additional guns, additional munitions, and everything else that will have a tendency to bring us as near as possible to the verge of war. And if war comes do such men as these shoulder the musket and go into the trenches?

Their object in having war and in preparing for war is to make money. Human suffering and the sacrifice of human life are necessary, but Wall Street considers only the dollars and the cents. The men who do the fighting, the people who make the sacrifices, are the ones who will not be counted in the measure of this great prosperity that he depicts.

The stockbrokers would not, of course, go to war, because the very object they have in bringing on the war is profit, and therefore they must remain in their Wall Street offices in order to share in that great prosperity which they say war will bring. The volunteer officer, even the drafting officer, will not find them. They will be concealed in their palatial offices on Wall Street, sitting behind mahogany desks, covered up with clipped coupons—coupons soiled with the sweat of honest toil, coupons stained with mothers' tears, coupons dyed in the lifeblood of their fellow men.

We are taking a step today that is fraught with untold danger. We are going into war upon the command of gold. We are going to run the risk of sacrificing millions of our countrymen's lives in order that other countrymen may coin their lifeblood into money. And even if we do not cross the Atlantic and go into the trenches, we are going to pile up a debt that the toiling masses that shall come many generations after us will have to pay. Unborn millions will bend their backs in toil in order to pay for the terrible step we are now about to take. We are about to do the bidding of wealth's terrible mandate. By our act we will make millions of our countrymen suffer, and the consequences of it may well be that millions of our brethren must shed their lifeblood, millions of broken-hearted women must weep, millions of children must suffer with cold, and millions of babes must die from hunger, and all because we want to preserve the commercial right of American citizens to deliver munitions of war to belligerent nations.

REVIEW QUESTIONS

1. Explain what Norris meant by "artificial sentiment."
2. According to Norris, who really suffered during wartime? How?
3. What did this speech suggest about the influences on foreign policy decisions? Do you agree?

HIRAM JOHNSON

Why Not a Dollar Draft? (1919)

The spirit of progressive liberalism manifested itself during the war years in many different ways. Hiram Johnson, the former reform governor of California who served in the Senate during World War I, spoke for many who feared that American involvement in the Great War might generate obscene profits for munitions makers. To ensure that corporate interests did not reap unfair gains from the war taxes imposed on the citizenry, Johnson proposed that the government make the defense industry contribute toward the expenses of the war. Although his proposed legislation failed, it reflected the effort by Progressives to regulate economic activity so as to serve the public interest.

From Hiram W. Johnson, "Why Not a Dollar Draft?" *Independent* (8 September 1919):386. [Editorial insertions appear in square brackets—*Ed.*]

The design that I believe the Congress should have in mind in relation to the taxation of war profits is that ultimately we may do that which is best for all the people of the nation, and that behind the line of trenches, which will be ours in the near future, we may have a contented people, a people not irritated by any sense of injustice or inequality in taxation, and that finally we may not only conscript the blood of the nation, but we may conscript a part of the wealth of this nation that is coined out of its blood.

With a boundless enthusiasm we conscripted, in a very brief period, the youth of this land. With an enthusiasm that would brook no delay, we took our youth and sent that forth to fight for this nation, and to die, if necessary, upon a foreign soil. I ask that same enthusiasm for conscripting the wealth of the nation today to stand behind the lads that have gone forth to fight our battle over the seas. In asking this I ask nought that interferes with legitimate [business] enterprise or with going business concerns. I ask the conscription of war profits, and I ask a response as ready to the experience of Britain as was given in conscripting our youth.

Those who coin the blood of war are the ones best able to pay the expense of war. Those who make swollen war profits out of this particular exigency are those who ought to pay for the cost of this war. It is, indeed, to me quite a trivial thing to take from the swollen fortunes that have come from war in the last couple of years the little moiety that this bill, by the majority, takes. We are staggered when we think of the amount of money thus far required, this year, in the undertaking—$20,000,000,000. I confess that it is infinite to me. All this our people are willing to do. But in doing it, in accepting not alone the burdens placed on them, a burden greater than was ever placed upon any other people, but also with responding with their best beloved, and their blood, they ask that burden, as much of it as possible, be taken from those who make profits out of this war.

The war profits are derived from the war and the war alone. Let the war cease the first day of December next, or within the next year, and the war profits then cease. Is it wise statesmanship to look to a time in the future when there may be no war profits, to tax these particular swollen fortunes?

I submit there can be no future as to these war profits, because they are fleeting, ephemeral at best, lasting alone with the war, with the exigency, with the strife, and with the conflict, ceasing the very moment that the war ceases. So I insist that we proceed to take the largest possible share of the war profits that it is possible to take in this conjuncture of affairs and to devote those war profits to the prosecution of the particular enterprise which itself makes the war profits.

England today takes 80 per cent of the war profits there to run the war. Do you realize how much we take based on the minimum of $3,000,000,000 for the last year? We take additionally under this bill, less than 20 per cent and England takes 80 per cent of war profits. I would not follow blindly, of course, the advice, either of allies or of neutral nations. I would not, of course, ask the Senate under any other circumstances to follow another nation in taking an undue proportion of war profits merely because that other nation did it. But, oh, how persuasive indeed, how convincing were the arguments of what England did when we dealt with our blood and how little con-

vincing those arguments are when we deal with our wealth. . . .

I insist that these taxes should be raised so that practically every dollar under this bill may be raised by war profits taxes, by income taxes, and by the taxes upon alcoholic beverages and the like, and that every consumer's tax that is in the bill, whether it be little or whether it be big, whether it touch one source or one class or another class, shall be eliminated, and we take the money from where we ought to take it—from the war profits made out of this great conflict!

REVIEW QUESTIONS

1. Was Johnson's argument persuasive? Why or why not?
2. Why did Johnson compare the United States to England?
3. How would a munitions manufacturer have responded to Johnson's assertions?

WOODROW WILSON

The League of Nations (1919)

When the Paris Peace Conference convened in 1919, Woodrow Wilson lobbied strenuously for inclusion of a League of Nations covenant in the final peace settlement. He was convinced that such a multilateral organization was essential to the maintenance of peace. In June he returned to the United States, confident that the Senate would ratify the treaty and thereby commit the United States to membership in the new League of Nations. He greatly underestimated the issues at stake and the opposition they would arouse. Soon he found himself struggling to defend many of the treaty's provisions.

From *Senate Documents*, No. 76, 66th Cong., 1st sess., 1919, 13:6–19.

To the Senate Committee on Foreign Relations

MR. CHAIRMAN: I have taken the liberty of writing out a little statement in the hope that it might facilitate discussion by speaking directly on some points that I know have been points of controversy and upon which I thought an expression of opinion would not be unwelcome. . . .

Nothing, I am led to believe, stands in the way of ratification of the treaty except certain doubts with regard to the meaning and implication of certain articles of the Covenant of the League of Nations; and I must frankly say that I am unable to understand why such doubts should be entertained. . . . It was pointed out that . . . it was not expressly provided that the League should have no authority to act or to express a judgment of matters of domestic policy; that the right to withdraw from the League was not expressly recognized; and that the constitutional right of the Congress to determine all questions of peace and war was not sufficiently safeguarded.

On my return to Paris all these matters were taken up again by the Commission on the League of Nations and every suggestion of the United States was accepted.

The views of the United States with regard to the questions I have mentioned had, in fact, already been accepted by the commission and there was supposed to be nothing inconsistent with them in the draft of the Covenant first adopted— the draft which was the subject of our discussion in March—but no objection was made to saying explicitly in the text what all had supposed to be implicit in it. There was absolutely no doubt as to the meaning of any one of the resulting provisions of the Covenant in the minds of those who participated in drafting them, and I respectfully submit that there is nothing vague or doubtful in their wording.

The Monroe Doctrine is expressly mentioned as an understanding which is in no way to be impaired or interfered with by anything contained in the Covenant and the expression "regional understandings like the Monroe Doctrine" was used, not be-

cause any one of the conferees thought there was any comparable agreement anywhere else in existence or in contemplation, but only because it was thought best to avoid the appearance of dealing in such a document with the policy of a single nation. Absolutely nothing is concealed in the phrase.

With regard to domestic questions, Article 16 of the Covenant expressly provides that, if in case of any dispute arising between members of the League, the matter involved is claimed by one of the parties "and is found by the council to arise out of a matter which by international law is solely within the domestic jurisdiction of that party, the council shall so report, and shall make no recommendation as to its settlement." The United States was by no means the only Government interested in the explicit adoption of this provision, and there is no doubt in the mind of any authoritative student of international law that such matters as immigration, tariffs, and naturalization are incontestably domestic questions with which no international body could deal without express authority to do so. No enumeration of domestic questions was undertaken because to undertake it, even by sample, would have involved the danger of seeming to exclude those not mentioned.

The right of any sovereign State to withdraw[1] had been taken for granted, but no objection was made to making it explicit. Indeed, so soon as the views expressed at the White House conference were laid before the commission it was at once conceded that it was best not to leave the answer to so important a question to inference. No proposal was made to set up any tribunal to pass judgment upon the question whether a withdrawing nation had in fact fulfilled "all its international obligations and all its obligations under the covenant." It was recognized that that question must be left to be resolved by the conscience of the Nation proposing to withdraw; and I must say that it did not seem to me worthwhile to propose that the article be made more explicit, because I knew that the United States would never itself propose to withdraw from

---

[1] I.e., from the League.

the League if its conscience was not entirely clear as to the fulfillment of all its international obligations. It has never failed to fulfill them and never will. . . .

The United States will, indeed, undertake under Article 10 to "respect and preserve as against external aggression the territorial integrity and existing political independence of all members of the League," and that engagement constitutes a very grave and solemn moral obligation. But it is a moral, not a legal, obligation, and leaves our Congress absolutely free to put its own interpretation upon it in all cases that call for action. It is binding in conscience only, not in law.

Article 10 seems to me to constitute the very backbone of the whole Covenant. Without it the League would be hardly more than an influential debating society. . . .

If the United States were to qualify the document in any way, moreover, I am confident from what I know of the many conferences and debates which accompanied the formulation of the treaty that our example would immediately be followed in many quarters, in some instances with very serious reservations, and that the meaning and operative force of the treaty would presently be clouded from one end of its clauses to the other.

Pardon me, Mr. Chairman, if I have been entirely unreserved and plainspoken in speaking of the great matters we all have so much at heart. If excuse is needed, I trust that the critical situation of affairs may serve as my justification. The issues that manifestly hang upon the conclusions of the Senate with regard to peace and upon the time of its action are so grave and so clearly insusceptible of being thrust on one side or postponed that I have felt it necessary in the public interest to make this urgent plea, and to make it as simply and as unreservedly as possible.

REVIEW QUESTIONS

1. What specific objections did Wilson address in this speech?
2. Did Wilson expect the League to be a strong or weak organization? Explain.
3. Do you believe that American participation in the League would have represented a sharp break with American tradition? Why or why not?

HENRY CABOT LODGE

The League of Nations Must Be Revised (1919)

Republican senator Henry Cabot Lodge of Massachusetts led the opposition to Woodrow Wilson's promotion of America's membership in a League of Nations. As the powerful leader of the Senate Foreign Relations Committee, he emerged as the pivotal figure in the protracted debate over the League. Lodge offered to support it only if substantial revisions were made in its key provisions, especially Article X, which in his view transferred from the Senate to the League of Nations the authority to wage war. In an August 1919 speech Lodge summarized his objections.

From *Congressional Record*, 66th Cong., 1st sess., 1919, 3779–84.

For ourselves we asked absolutely nothing. We have not asked any government or governments to guarantee our boundaries or our political independence. We have no fear in regard to either. We have sought no territory, no privileges, no advantages, for ourselves. That is the fact. It is apparent on the face of the treaty. I do not mean to reflect upon a single one of the powers with which we have been associated in the war against Germany, but there is not one of them which has not sought individual advantages for their own national benefit. I do not criticize their desires at all. The services and sacrifices of England and France and Belgium and Italy are beyond estimate and beyond praise. I am glad they should have what they desire for their own welfare and safety. But they all receive under the peace territorial and commercial benefits. We are asked to give, and we in no way seek to take. Surely it is not too much to insist that when we are offered nothing but the opportunity to give and to aid others we should have the right to say what sacrifices we shall make and what the magnitude of our gifts shall be. In the prosecution of the war we have unstintedly given American lives and American treasure. When the war closed we had 3,000,000 men under arms. We were turning the country into a vast workshop for war. We advanced ten billions to our allies. We refused no assistance that we could possibly render. All the great energy and power of the Republic were put at the service of the good cause. We have not been ungenerous. We have been devoted to the cause of freedom, humanity, and civilization everywhere. Now we are asked, in the making of peace, to sacrifice our sovereignty in important respects, to involve ourselves almost without limit in the affairs of other nations and to yield up policies and rights which we have maintained throughout our history. We are asked to incur liabilities to an unlimited extent and furnish assets at the same time which no man can measure. I think it is not only our right but our duty to determine how far we shall go. Not only must we look carefully to see where we are being led into endless disputes and entanglements, but we must not forget that we have in this country millions of people of foreign birth and parentage.

Our one great object is to make all these people Americans so that we may call on them to place America first and serve America as they have done in the war just closed. We can not Americanize them if we are continually thrusting them back into the quarrels and difficulties of the countries from which they came to us. We shall fill this land with political disputes about the troubles and quarrels of other countries. We shall have a large portion of our people voting not on American questions and not on what concerns the United States but dividing on issues which concern foreign countries alone. That is an unwholesome and perilous condition to force upon this country. We must avoid it. We ought to reduce to the lowest possible point the foreign questions in which we involve ourselves. Never forget that this league is primarily—I might say overwhelmingly—a political organization, and I object strongly to having the policies of the United States turn upon disputes where deep feeling is aroused but in which we have no direct interest. It will all tend to delay the Americanization of our great population, and it is more important not only to the United States but to the peace of the world to make all these people good Americans than it is to determine that some piece of territory should belong to one European country rather than to another. For this reason I wish to limit strictly our interference in the affairs of Europe and of Africa. We have interests of our own in Asia and in the Pacific which we must guard upon our own account, but the less we undertake to play the part of umpire and thrust ourselves into European conflicts the better for the United States and for the world.

It has been reiterated here on this floor, and reiterated to the point of weariness, that in every treaty there is some sacrifice of sovereignty we are justified in sacrificing. In what I have already said about other nations putting us into war I have covered one point of sovereignty which ought never to be yielded—the power to send American soldiers and sailors everywhere, which ought never to be taken from the American people or impaired in the slightest degree. Let us beware how we palter with our independence. We have not reached the great position from which we were able to come down into the field of battle and help to save the world from tyranny by being guided by others. Our vast power has all been built up and gathered together by ourselves alone. We forced our way upward from the days of the Revolution, through a world often hostile and always indifferent. We owe no debt to anyone except to France in that Revolution, and those policies and those rights on which our power has been founded should never be lessened or weakened. It will be no service to the world to do so and it will be of intolerable injury to the United States. We will do our share. We are ready and anxious to help in all ways to preserve the world's peace. But we can do it best by not crippling ourselves. . . .

. . . I am thinking of what is best for the world, for if the United States fails the best hopes of mankind fail with it. I have never had but one allegiance—I can not divide it now. I have loved but one flag and I can not share that devotion and give affection to the mongrel banner invented by a league. Internationalism, illustrated by the Bolshevik and by the man to whom all countries are alike provided they can make money out of them, is to me repulsive. National I must remain, and in that way I like all other Americans can render the amplest service to the world. The United States is the world's best hope, but if you fetter her in the interests and quarrels of other nations, if you tangle her in the intrigues of Europe, you will destroy her power for good and endanger her very existence. . . .

We are told that we shall "break the heart of the world" if we do not take this league just as it stands. I fear that the hearts of the vast majority of mankind would beat on strongly and steadily and without any quickening if the league were to perish altogether. . . .

No doubt many excellent and patriotic people see a coming fulfillment of noble ideals in the word "League for Peace." We all respect and share these aspirations and desires, but some of us see no hope, but rather defeat, for them in this murky covenant. For we, too, have our ideals, even if we differ from those who have tried to establish a monopoly of idealism. Out first ideal is our country, and we see her in the future, as in the past, giving service to all her people and to the world. Our ideal of the future is that she should continue to render that service of her own free will. She has great problems of her own to solve, very grim and perilous problems, and a right solution, if we can attain to it, would largely benefit mankind. We would have our country strong to resist a peril from the West, as she has flung back the German menace from the East. We would not have our politics distracted and embittered by the dissensions of other lands. We would not have our country's vigor exhausted, or her moral force abated, by everlasting meddling and muddling in every quarrel, great and small, which afflicts the world. Our ideal is to make her ever stronger and better and finer because in that way alone, as we believe, can she be of the greatest service to the world's peace and to the welfare of mankind.

REVIEW QUESTIONS

1. Why did Lodge emphasize that America has "millions" of foreign-born residents?
2. Why did Lodge call the League primarily a "political organization"? Do you agree?
3. In what respects could Lodge's remarks have been interpreted as a partisan campaign speech aimed at undermining the Democratic presidential hopes for 1920?

26 ✦ THE MODERN TEMPER

World War I unleashed forces that caused severe social strains in the United States. In 1920 the American economy suffered a brief but sharp recession as factories and businesses shifted back to peacetime production. At the same time, returning soldiers and sailors swamped the labor market. Prices soared as consumers sought to buy the goods and services they had sacrificed during the war. Frustration over scarce jobs and high prices led to violent labor disputes fanned by socialist and communist agitators. In 1919 a flurry of mail bombs addressed to government officials led many Americans to fear that something akin to Russia's Bolshevik Revolution was erupting in the United States.

This "Red Scare" prompted Attorney General A. Mitchell Palmer, whose front porch was destroyed by a mail bomb, to launch a series of raids directed at labor radicals and alien activists across the country. Over 5,000 people were arrested, some 250 of whom were convicted without the benefit of a court hearing, loaded onto a ship, and deported to the Soviet Union. These "witch hunts" were conducted by the FBI under the direction of a young official named J. Edgar Hoover.

These powerful anti-immigrant and anti-radical sentiments surfaced in the most sensational criminal trial of the decade. In 1920 robbers shot and killed the paymaster and guard at a shoe factory in Braintree, Massachusetts. The police later arrested two Italian immigrants who were avowed anarchists, Nicola Sacco and Bartolomeo Vanzetti, and charged them with the murders. A jury found them guilty in 1921, and numerous appeals supported by prominent liberals kept the case in court until 1927, when they both were executed.

During the summer of 1919 the same social tensions that ignited the Red Scare fueled a new round of race riots. The war had disrupted the patterns of race relations. Blacks from the rural South who served in the military were less willing to tolerate racial abuse and "Jim Crow" segregation laws once they returned home. Thousands of southern blacks also migrated north and west in search of higher wages and racial equality, only to discover that racism was not limited to the deep South. White mobs in communities across the nation assaulted blacks for various reasons or for no reason at all. In a Chicago riot thirty-eight people were killed and hundreds injured; troops had to be called in to restore order.

By the end of 1920 the race riots and the Red Scare had dissipated, but they left in their wake an atmosphere of venomous racism and xenophobia and a latent tension that repeatedly erupted in violence over the next two decades. During the early 1920s the Ku Klux Klan witnessed a dramatic revival, and anti-immigration sentiment culminated in new laws intended specifically to restrict the number of newcomers from southern and eastern Europe.

The nativism and racism that surfaced after World War I revealed fissures that repeatedly sent tremors through American society and culture during the 1920s. The social fault lines tended to occur between rural and urban values. Large cities increasingly represented centers of modernism. The residents were more affluent, more secular, and more "liberated" about values and manners than their rural counterparts. Many young adults—especially affluent college students—discarded old prohibitions. They engaged in sensual dancing, public kissing and swimming, cigarette smoking, and alcohol consumption that shocked and angered moral guardians. Drawing upon manipulated theories of the Viennese psychiatrist Sigmund Freud, young rebels engaged in what amounted to a sexual revolution during the 1920s. Many modernists joined Margaret Sanger in promoting the use of birth control to free mothers of the burden of supporting unwanted children. In the face of such cosmopolitan challenges, many rural traditionalists countered with an aggressive conservatism that coupled religious and cultural fundamentalism.

Traditionalists focused much of their energy on an old crusade: the prohibition of alcoholic beverages. Throughout the nineteenth century, moral reformers had tried to outlaw the production and sale of alcoholic beverages, but not until 1919 did they succeed on the national level. With the ratification of the Eighteenth Amendment, the federal government prohibited the manufacture, sale, or transport of all intoxicating liquors, and the Volstead Act, enacted the same year, defined as "intoxicating" any beverage with an alcohol content of 0.5 percent or more.

The clash between rural and urban values reached a theatrical climax during the famous "monkey trial" in the town of Dayton, Tennessee, in 1925. A state law prohibiting the teaching of Charles Darwin's theory of evolution was challenged by a high-school biology teacher named John Scopes, and the resulting trial pitted the forces of fundamentalism against liberalism. The court ruled against Scopes, but the widely publicized trial helped generate a nationwide assault against fundamentalism that further eroded the foundations of biblical and social orthodoxy. Liberal Protestants and advocates of modern scientific methods heaped scorn upon fundamentalists, initiating a cultural civil war that persists today.

A. MITCHELL PALMER

FROM The Case against the Reds (1920)

After the outbreak of strikes and riots in 1919, Attorney General A. Mitchell Palmer organized a carefully coordinated series of raids against communists and anarchists on 3 January 1920. He was a Quaker attorney from Pennsylvania who had served three terms in Congress. Driven by hatred of foreign radicals and a desire to gain the Democratic presidential nomination in 1920, he often acted on his own without informing or consulting President Wilson. In the article below, he sought to counter the many critics of the "Palmer raids."

From A. Mitchell Palmer, "The Case against the Reds," *The Forum* 63 (February 1920): 63–75. [Editorial insertions appear in square brackets—*Ed.*]

Like a prairie-fire, the blaze of revolution was sweeping over every American institution of law and order a year ago. It was eating its way into the homes of the American workman, its sharp tongues of revolutionary heat were licking into the altars of the churches, leaping into the belfry of the school bell, crawling into the sacred corners of American homes, seeking to replace marriage vows with libertine laws, burning up the foundations of society.

Robbery, not war, is the ideal of communism. This has been demonstrated in Russia, Germany, and in America. As a foe, the anarchist is fearless in his own life, for his creed is a fanaticism that admits no respect for any other creed. Obviously it is the creed of any criminal mind, which reasons always from motives impossible to clean thought. Crime is the degenerate factor in society.

Upon these two basic certainties, first that the "Reds" were criminal aliens, and secondly that the American Government must prevent crime, it was decided that there could be no nice distinctions drawn between the theoretical ideals of the radicals and their actual violations of our national laws. An assassin may have brilliant intellectuality, he may be able to excuse his murder or robbery with fine oratory, but any theory which excuses crime is not wanted in America. This is no place for the criminal to flourish, nor will he do so, so long as the rights of common citizenship can be exerted to prevent him. . . .

By stealing, murder and lies, Bolshevism has looted Russia not only of its material strength, but of its moral force. A small clique of outcasts from the East Side of New York has attempted this, with what success we all know. Because a disreputable alien—Leon Bronstein, the man who now calls himself Trotzky—can inaugurate a reign of terror from his throne room in the Kremlin: because this lowest of all types known to New York can sleep in the Czar's bed, while hundreds of thousands in Russia are without food or shelter, should Americans be swayed by such doctrines? . . .

My information showed that communism in this country was an organization of thousands of aliens, who were direct allies of Trotzky. Aliens of the same misshapen cast of mind and indecencies of character, and it showed that they were making the same glittering promises of lawlessness, of criminal autocracy to Americans, that they had made to the Russian peasants. How the Department of Justice discovered upwards of 60,000 of these organized agitators of the Trotzky doctrine in the United States, is the confidential information upon which the Government is now sweeping the nation clean of such alien filth. . . .

One of the chief incentives for the present activity of the Department of Justice against the "Reds" has been the hope that American citizens will, themselves, become voluntary agents for us, in a vast organization for mutual defense against the sinister agitation of men and women aliens, who appear to be either in the pay or under the spell of Trotzky and Lenine [*sic*] . . . .

The whole purpose of communism appears to be a mass formation of the criminals of the world to overthrow the decencies of private life, to usurp property that they have not earned, to disrupt the present order of life regardless of health, sex, or religious rights. By a literature that promises the wildest dreams of such low aspirations, that can occur to only the criminal minds, communism distorts our social law. . . .

These are the revolutionary tenets of Trotzky and the Communist Internationale. Their manifesto further embraces the various organizations in this country of men and women obsessed with discontent, having disorganized relations to American society. These include the I. W. W.'s, the most radical socialists, the misguided anarchists, the agitators who oppose the limitations of unionism, the moral perverts and the hysterical neurasthenic women who abound in communism. The phraseology of their manifesto is practically the same wording as was used by the Bolsheviks for their International Communist Congress.

. . . The Department of Justice will pursue the attack of these "Reds" upon the Government of the United States with vigilance, and no alien, advocating the overthrow of existing law and order in this country, shall escape arrest and prompt deportation.

It is my belief that while they have stirred discontent in our midst, while they have caused irritating strikes, and while they have infected our social ideas with the disease of their own minds and their unclean morals, we can get rid of them! And not until we have done so shall we have removed the menace of Bolshevism for good.

REVIEW QUESTIONS

1. What crimes did Palmer accuse the "Reds" of committing?
2. How did Palmer address the legal rights of aliens?
3. What would be the public response to such a statement today? Explain.

WILLIAM ALLEN WHITE

The Red Scare Is Un-American (1920)

The majority of Americans supported the actions of Attorney General A. Mitchell Palmer and shared his fears of communist conspiracies. A few people, however, raised concerns about the arbitrary use of police powers to deal with aliens. William Allen White, the crusading editor of the Emporia Gazette *in Kansas and a prominent Republican progressive, criticized Palmer's crusade.*

From William Allen White, "The Red Scare Is Un-American," *Emporia Gazette* (Kansas), 8 January 1920.

The Attorney General [A. Mitchell Palmer] seems to be seeing red. He is rounding up every manner of radical in the country; every man who hopes for a better world is in danger of deportation by the Attorney General. The whole business is un-American. There are certain rules which should govern in the treason cases.

First, it should be agreed that a man may believe what he chooses.

Second, it should be agreed that when he preaches violence he is disturbing the peace and should be put in jail. Whether he preaches violence in politics, business, or religion, whether he advocates murder and arson and pillage for gain or for political ends, he is violating the common law and should be squelched—jailed until he is willing to quit advocating force in a democracy.

Third, he should be allowed to say what he pleases so long as he advocates legal constitutional methods of procedure. Just because a man does not believe this government is good is no reason why he should be deported.

Abraham Lincoln did not believe this government was all right seventy-five years ago. He advocated changes, but he advocated constitutional means, and he had a war with those who advocated force to maintain the government as it was.

Ten years ago Roosevelt[1] advocated great changes in our American life—in our Constitution, in our social and economic life. Most of the changes he advocated have been made, but they were made in the regular legal way. He preached no force. And if a man desires to preach any doctrine under the shining sun, and to advocate the realization of his vision by lawful, orderly, constitutional means—let him alone. If he is Socialist, anarchist, or Mormon, and merely preaches his creed and does not preach violence, he can do no harm. For the folly of his doctrine will be its answer.

The deportation business is going to make martyrs of a lot of idiots whose cause is not worth it.

REVIEW QUESTIONS

1. Was White concerned that the views of socialists might be true? Explain.
2. How did White suggest social change could be promoted?
3. What did White mean when he wrote that the "deportation business" would create martyrs?

---

[1] Theodore Roosevelt (1858–1919).

MARGARET SANGER

The Need for Birth Control (1922)

During the 1920s New Yorker Margaret Sanger (1883–1966) became the crusading champion for a woman's right to birth control devices. Her mother was a devout Roman Catholic who went through eighteen pregnancies before dying of tuberculosis, and Margaret was determined to give women access to contraceptives to free them from such child-bearing burdens. Her tireless efforts ignited fierce opposition from the Catholic Church and other religious organizations.

From Margaret Sanger, *The Pivot of Civilization* (New York, 1922), pp. 196–219.

Religious propaganda against Birth Control is crammed with contradiction and fallacy. It refutes itself. Yet it brings the opposing views into vivid contrast. In stating these differences we should make clear that advocates of Birth Control are not seeking to attack the Catholic Church. We quarrel with that church, however, when it seeks to assume authority over non-Catholics and to dub their behavior immoral because they do not conform to the dictatorship of Rome. The question of bearing and rearing children we hold is the concern of the mother and the potential mother. If she delegates the responsibility, the ethical education, to an external authority, that is her affair. We object, however, to the State or the Church which appoints itself as arbiter and dictator in this sphere and attempts to force unwilling women into compulsory maternity. . . .

The sex instinct in the human race is too strong to be bound by the dictates of any church. The Church's failure, its century after century of failure, is now evident on every side: for, having convinced men and women that only in its baldly propagative phase is sexual expression legitimate, the teachings of the Church have driven sex underground, into secret channels, strengthened the conspiracy of silence, concentrated men's thoughts upon the "lusts of the body," have sown, cultivated and reaped a crop of bodily and mental diseases, and developed a society congenitally and almost hopelessly unbalanced. How is any progress to be made, how is any human expression or education possible when women and men are taught to combat and resist their natural impulses and to despise their bodily functions? . . .

Humanity, we are glad to realize, is rapidly freeing itself from this "morality" imposed upon it by its self-appointed and self-perpetuating masters. From a hundred different points the imposing edifice of this "morality" has been and is being attacked. Sincere and thoughtful defenders and exponents of the teachings of Christ now acknowledge the falsity of the traditional codes and their malignant influence upon the moral and physical well-being of humanity. . . .

Psychology and the outlook of modern life are

stressing the growth of independent responsibility and discrimination as the true basis of ethics. The old traditional morality, with its train of vice, disease, promiscuity and prostitution, is in reality dying out, killing itself off because it is too irresponsible and too dangerous to individual and social well-being. The transition from the old to the new, like all fundamental changes, is fraught with many dangers. But it is a revolution that cannot be stopped.

The smaller family, with its lower infant mortality rate, is, in more definite and concrete manner than many actions outwardly deemed "moral," the expression of moral judgment and responsibility. It is the assertion of a standard of living, inspired by the wish to obtain a fuller and more expressive life for the children than the parents have enjoyed. If the morality or immorality of any course of conduct is to be determined by the motives which inspire it, there is evidently at the present day no higher morality than the intelligent practice of Birth Control.

The immorality of many who practice Birth Control lies in not daring to preach what they practice. What is the secret of the hypocrisy of the well-to-do, who are willing to contribute generously to charities and philanthropies, who spend thousands annually in the upkeep and sustenance of the delinquent, the defective and the dependent; and yet join the conspiracy of silence that prevents the poorer classes from learning how to improve their conditions, and elevate their standards of living? It is as though they were to cry: "We'll give you anything except the thing you ask for—the means whereby you may become responsible and self-reliant in your own lives."

The brunt of this injustice falls on women, because the old traditional morality is the invention of men. . . . In the moral code developed by the Church, women have been so degraded that they have been habituated to look upon themselves through the eyes of men. Very imperfectly have women developed their own self-consciousness, the realization of their tremendous and supreme position in civilization. Women can develop this power only in one way; by the exercise of responsibility, by the exercise of judgment, reason or discrimination. They need ask for no "rights." They need only assert power. Only by the exercise of self-guidance and intelligent self-direction can that inalienable, supreme, pivotal power be expressed. More than ever in history women need to realize that nothing can ever come to us from another. Everything we attain we must owe to ourselves. Our own spirit must vitalize it. Our own heart must feel it. For we are not passive machines. We are not to be lectured, guided and molded this way or that. We are alive and intelligent, we women, no less than men, and we must awaken to the essential realization that we are living beings, endowed with will, choice, comprehension, and that every step in life must be taken at our own initiative.

Moral and sexual balance in civilization will only be established by the assertion and expression of power on the part of women. This power will not be found in any futile seeking for economic independence or in the aping of men in industrial and business pursuits, nor by joining battle for the so-called "single standard." Woman's power can only be expressed and make itself felt when she refuses the task of bringing unwanted children into the world to be exploited in industry and slaughtered in wars. When we refuse to produce battalions of babies to be exploited; when we declare to the nation; "Show us that the best possible chance in life is given to every child now brought into the world, before you cry for more! At present our children are a glut on the market. You hold infant life cheap. Help us to make the world a fit place for children. When you have done this, we will bear you children,—then we shall be true women." . . .

Moreover, woman shall further assert her power by refusing to remain the passive instrument of sensual self-gratification on the part of men. Birth Control, in philosophy and practice, is the destroyer of that dualism of the old sexual code. It denies that the sole purpose of sexual activity is procreation; it also denies that sex should be reduced to the level of sensual lust, or that woman should permit herself to be the instrument of its satisfaction. In increasing and differentiating her love demands, woman must elevate sex into

another sphere, whereby it may subserve and enhance the possibility of individual and human expression. Man will gain in this no less than woman; for in the age-old enslavement of woman he has enslaved himself; and in the liberation of womankind, all of humanity will experience the joys of a new and fuller freedom. . . .

To the foregoing contentions, it might be objected, you are encouraging passion. My reply would be, passion is a worthy possession—most men, who are any good, are capable of passion. You all enjoy ardent and passionate love in art and literature. Why not give it a place in real life? Why some people look askance at passion is because they are confusing it with sensuality. Sex love without passion is a poor, lifeless thing. Sensuality, on the other hand, is on a level with gluttony—a physical excess—detached from sentiment, chivalry, or tenderness. It is just as important to give sex love its place as to avoid its over-emphasis. Its real and effective restraints are those imposed by a loving and sympathetic companionship, by the privileges of parenthood, the exacting claims of career and that civic sense which prompts men to do social service. . . .

. . . Birth Control is an ethical necessity for humanity today because it places in our hands a new instrument of self-expression and self-realization. It gives us control over one of the primordial forces of nature, to which in the past the majority of mankind have been enslaved, and by which it has been cheapened and debased. It arouses us to the possibility of newer and greater freedom. It develops the power, the responsibility and intelligence to use this freedom in living a liberated and abundant life. It permits us to enjoy this liberty without danger of infringing upon the similar liberty of our fellow men, or of injuring and curtailing the freedom of the next generation. It shows us that we need not seek in the amassing of worldly wealth, nor in the illusion of some extra-terrestrial Heaven or earthly Utopia of a remote future the road to human development. The Kingdom of Heaven is in a very definite sense within us. Not by leaving our body and our fundamental humanity behind us, not by aiming to be anything but what we are, shall we become ennobled or immortal. By knowing ourselves, by expressing ourselves, by realizing ourselves more completely than has ever before been possible, not only shall we attain the kingdom ourselves but we shall hand on the torch of life undimmed to our children and the children of our children.

REVIEW QUESTIONS

1. Why, according to Sanger, was the "traditional morality" related to sexual intercourse dying out?
2. What did Sanger say were the advantages of smaller families?
3. Why did she believe that birth control was an "ethical necessity"?

HIRAM W. EVANS

FROM The Klan's Fight for Americanism (1926)

The backlash against "alien" groups "infesting" American life after World War I assumed its most virulent form in a revival of the Ku Klux Klan. The organization had first emerged in the rural South after the Civil War, seeking to intimidate blacks from voting or holding office, and had pretty much died out by 1900. The zealous patriotism fostered by American intervention in World War I helped revive the Klan. In its new form it was more of an urban than a rural phenomenon. It adopted a broader agenda than the original organization, and its membership grew across the nation. By 1926 it boasted over 3 million members. Klan intolerance now went beyond blacks to include Jews, Catholics, communists, and labor unionists. Texas dentist Hiram Evans assumed leadership of the organization in 1926. In this speech he reveals that the Klan was fundamentally a protest against all of the ills associated with modern culture.

From Hiram W. Evans, "The Klan's Fight for Americanism," *North American Review* 223 (March 1926):38–39.

. . . The Klan, therefore, has now come to speak for the great mass of Americans of the old pioneer stock. We believe that it does fairly and faithfully represent them, and our proof lies in their support. To understand the Klan, then, it is necessary to understand the character and present mind of the mass of old-stock Americans. The mass, it must be remembered, as distinguished from the intellectually mongrelized "Liberals."

These are, in the first place, a blend of various peoples of the so-called Nordic race, the race which, with all its faults, has given the world almost the whole of modern civilization. The Klan does not try to represent any people but these. . . .

These Nordic Americans for the last generation have found themselves increasingly uncomfortable, and finally deeply distressed. There appeared first confusion in thought and opinion, a groping and hesitancy about national affairs and private life alike, in sharp contrast to the clear, straightforward purposes of our earlier years. There was futility in religion, too, which was in many ways even more distressing. Presently we began to find that we were dealing with strange ideas; policies that always sounded well but somehow always made us still more uncomfortable.

Finally came the moral breakdown that has been going on for two decades. One by one all our traditional moral standards went by the boards or were so disregarded that they ceased to be binding. The sacredness of our Sabbath, of our homes, of chastity, and finally even of our right to teach our own children in our own schools fundamental facts and truths were torn away from us. Those who maintained the old standards did so only in the face of constant ridicule. . . .

The old-stock Americans are learning, however. They have begun to arm themselves for this new type of warfare. Most important, they have broken away from the fetters of the false ideals and philanthropy which put aliens ahead of their own children and their own race. . . .

One more point about the present attitude of the old-stock American: he has revived and increased his long-standing distrust of the Roman Catholic Church. It is for this that the native Americans, and the Klan as their leader, are most often denounced as intolerant and prejudiced. . . .

The Ku Klux Klan, in short, is an organization which gives expression, direction and purpose to the most vital instincts, hopes, and resentments of the old-stock Americans, provides them with leadership, and is enlisting and preparing them for militant, constructive action toward fulfilling their racial and national destiny. . . . The Klan literally is once more the embattled American farmer and artisan, coordinated into a disciplined and growing army, and launched upon a definite crusade for Americanism! . . .

Thus the Klan goes back to the American racial instincts, and to the common sense which is their first product, as the basis of its beliefs and methods. . . .

There are three of these great racial instincts, vital elements in both the historic and the present attempts to build an America which shall fulfill the aspirations and justify the heroism of the men who made the nation. These are the instincts of loyalty to the white race, to the traditions of America, and to the spirit of Protestantism, which has been an essential part of Americanism ever since the days of Roanoke and Plymouth Rock. They are condensed into the Klan slogan: "Native, white, Protestant supremacy."

REVIEW QUESTIONS

1. What "evils" did Evans claim were infecting modern American society?
2. According to Evans, what were the implied objectives of the Klan?
3. To what extent do you think the Klan's philosophy was consistent with other American ideals and principles? Explain.

The Need for Immigration Restriction (1923)

The Red Scare after World War I helped generate pervasive fears of "foreign" radicals streaming into the United States. The postwar depression also fueled concerns that a wave of new immigrants would take jobs away from Americans. At the same time, people continued to worry that "alien" peoples from eastern Europe and Asia could not be assimilated into American culture. These concerns took legislative form in the passage of restrictive immigration laws in 1921 and 1924. The 1921 act limited the number of immigrants from any country to 3 percent of that nation's proportion of the American population as of 1910. The 1924 act was even more restrictive. In the following selection, the federal official in charge of immigration policy explains the context for these new laws.

From U.S. Department of Labor, *Annual Report of the Commissioner-General of Immigration to the Secretary of Labor* (Washington, DC, 1923), pp. 3–4.

Even a casual survey of congressional discussions of the immigration problem during the past quarter of a century demonstrates very clearly that while the law makers were deeply concerned with the mental, moral, and physical quality of immigrants, there developed as time went on an even greater concern as to the fundamental racial character of the constantly increasing numbers who came.

The record of alien arrivals year by year had shown a gradual falling off in the immigration of northwest European peoples, representing racial stocks which were common to America even in colonial days, and a rapid and remarkably large increase in the movement from southern and eastern European countries and Asiatic Turkey. Immigration from the last-named sources reached an annual average of about 750,000 and in some years nearly a million came, and there seems to have been a general belief in Congress that it would increase rather than diminish. At the same time no one seems to have anticipated a revival of the formerly large influx from the "old sources," as the countries of northwest Europe came to be known.

This remarkable change in the sources and racial character of our immigrants led to an almost continuous agitation of the immigration problem both in and out of Congress, and there was a steadily growing demand for restriction, particularly of the newer movement from the south and east of Europe. During the greater part of this period of agitation the so-called literacy test for aliens was the favorite weapon of the restrictionists, and its widespread popularity appears to have been based quite largely on a belief, or at least a hope, that it would reduce to some extent the stream of "new" immigration, about one-third of which was illiterate, without seriously interfering with the coming of the older type, among whom illiteracy was at a minimum.

Presidents Cleveland and Taft vetoed immigration bills because they contained a literacy test provision, and President Wilson vetoed two bills largely for the same reason. In 1917, however, Congress passed a general immigration bill which included the literacy provision over the President's veto, and, with certain exceptions, aliens who are unable to read are no longer admitted to the United States. At that time, however, the World War had already had the effect of reducing immigration from Europe to a low level, and our own entry into the conflict a few days before the law in question went into effect practically stopped it altogether. Consequently, the value of the literacy provision as a means of restricting European immigration was never fairly tested under normal conditions.

The Congress, however, seemingly realized that even the comprehensive immigration law of 1917, including the literacy test, would afford only a frail barrier against the promised rush from the war-stricken countries of Europe, and in December, 1920, the House of Representatives, with little opposition, passed a bill to suspend practically all immigration for the time being. The per centum limit plan was substituted by the Senate, however, and the substitute prevailed in Congress, but it failed to become a law at the time because President Wilson withheld executive approval. Nevertheless, favorable action was not long delayed, for at the special session called at the beginning of the present administration the measure was quickly enacted, and, with President Harding's approval, became a law on May 19, 1921. This law expired by limitation June 30, 1922, but by the act of May 11, 1922, its life was extended to June 30, 1924, and some strengthening amendments were added.

The principal provisions of the per centum limit act, or the "quota," as it is popularly known, are as follows:

The number of aliens of any nationality who may be admitted to the United States in any fiscal year shall not exceed 3 per cent of the number of persons of such nationality who were resident in the United States according to the census of 1910. Monthly quotas are limited to 20 per cent of the annual quota. For the purposes of the act, "nationality" is determined by country of birth.

The law does not apply to the following classes of aliens: Government officials; aliens in transit; aliens visiting the United States as tourists or temporarily for business or pleasure; aliens from countries immigration from which is regulated in accordance with treaties or agreement relating solely to immigration, otherwise China and Japan; aliens from the so-called Asiatic barred zone; aliens who have resided continuously for at least five years in Canada, Newfoundland, Cuba, Mexico, Central or South America, or adjacent islands; aliens under the age of 18 who are children of citizens of the United States.

Certain other classes of aliens who are counted against quotas are admissible after a quota is exhausted. The following are included in this category: Aliens returning from a temporary visit abroad; aliens who are professional actors, artists, lecturers, singers, ministers of any religious denomination, professors for colleges or seminaries, members of any recognized learned profession, or aliens employed as domestic servants.

So far as possible preference is given to the wives and certain near relatives of citizens of the United States, applicants for citizenship and honorably discharged soldiers, eligible to citizenship, who served in the United States military or naval forces at any time between April 6, 1917, and November 11, 1918.

Transportation companies are liable to a fine of $200 for each alien brought to a United States port in excess of the quota and where such fine is imposed the amount paid for passage must be returned to the rejected alien.

The quota limit law is in addition to and not in substitution for the provisions of the immigration laws.

REVIEW QUESTIONS

1. What did the distinction between "new" and "old" immigrants suggest about the ethnic and religious tensions of the era?
2. Why did support for a literacy test skyrocket during this period?
3. How would members of the Klan have responded to these immigration restrictions?

ROBERT H. CLANCY

The Immigration Act of 1924

The new immigration quota law of 1921 substantially reduced immigration from southern and eastern Europe. Even more restrictive was the Immigration Act of 1924 (Johnson-Reed Act). Only six representatives in Congress voted against this act. One of the dissenters was Robert H. Clancy, a Republican congressman from Detroit, a city with a large immigrant population. In a speech to Congress on 8 April 1924, he criticized the quota provisions of the new Immigration Act for being racially discriminatory and "un-American."

From a speech by Robert H. Clancy, April 8, 1924, *Congressional Record*, 68th Cong., 1st sess. (Washington, DC, 1924), 65:5929–5932. [Editorial insertions appear in square brackets—*Ed.*]

Since the foundations of the American commonwealth were laid in colonial times over 300 years ago, vigorous complaint and more or less bitter persecution have been aimed at newcomers to our shores. . . . Old citizens in Detroit of Irish and German descent have told me of the fierce tirades and propaganda directed against the great waves of Irish and Germans who came over from 1840 on for a few decades to escape civil, racial, and religious persecution in their native lands.

The "Know-Nothings," lineal ancestors of the Ku-Klux Klan, bitterly denounced the Irish and Germans as mongrels, scum, foreigners, and a menace to our institutions, much as other great branches of the Caucasian race of glorious history and antecedents are berated to-day. All are riff-raff, unassimilables, "foreign devils," swine not fit to associate with the great chosen people—a form of national pride and hallucination as old as the division of races and nations.

But today it is the Italians, Spanish, Poles, Jews, Greeks, Russians, Balkanians, and so forth, who are [considered] the racial lepers. And it is eminently fitting and proper that so many Members of this House with names as Irish as Paddy's pig, are taking the floor these days to attack once more as their kind has attacked for seven bloody centuries the fearful fallacy of chosen peoples and inferior peoples. The fearful fallacy is that one is made to rule and the other to be abominated. . . .

In this bill we find racial discrimination at its worst—a deliberate attempt to go back 84 years in our census taken every 10 years so that a blow may be aimed at peoples of eastern and southern Europe, particularly at our recent allies in the Great War—Poland and Italy.

Jews in Detroit Are Good Citizens

Of course the Jews too are aimed at, not directly, because they have no country in Europe they can call their own, but they are set down among the inferior peoples. Much of the animus against Poland and Russia, old and new, with the countries that have arisen from the ruins of the dead Czar's European dominions, is directed against the Jew.

We have many American citizens of Jewish descent in Detroit, tens of thousands of them—active in every profession and every walk of life. They are particularly active in charities and merchandising. One of our greatest judges, if not the greatest, is a Jew. Surely no fair-minded person with a knowledge of the facts can say the Jews or Detroit are a menace to the city's or the country's well-being. . . .

Forty or fifty thousand Italian-Americans live in my district in Detroit. They are found in all walks and classes of life—common hard labor, the trades, business, law, medicine, dentistry, art, literature, banking, and so forth. They rapidly become Americanized, build homes, and make themselves into good citizens. They brought hardihood, physique, hope, and good humor with them from their outdoor life in Sunny Italy, and they bear up under the terrific strain of life and work in busy Detroit.

One finds them by the thousands digging streets, sewers, and building foundations, and in the automobile and iron and steel fabric factories of various sorts. They do the hard work that the native-born American dislikes. Rapidly they rise in life and join the so-called middle and upper classes. . . .

The Italian-Americans of Detroit played a glorious part in the Great War. They showed themselves as patriotic as the native born in offering the supreme sacrifice. In all, I am informed, over 300,000 Italian-speaking soldiers enlisted in the American Army, almost 10 percent of our total fighting force. Italians formed about 4 percent of the population of the United States and they formed 10 percent of the American military force. Their casualties were 12 percent. . . .

Detroit Satisfied with the Poles

I wish to take the liberty of informing the House that from my personal knowledge and observation of tens of thousands of Polish-Americans living in my district in Detroit that their Americanism and patriotism are unassailable from any fair or just standpoint.

The Polish-Americans are as industrious and as frugal and as loyal to our institutions as any class of people who have come to the shores of this country in the past 300 years. They are essentially home builders, and they have come to this country to stay. They learn the English language as quickly as possible, and take pride in the rapidity with which they become assimilated and adopt our in-

stitutions. Figures available to all show that in Detroit in the World War the proportion of American volunteers of Polish blood was greater than the proportion of Americans of any other racial descent. . . . Polish-Americans do not merit slander nor defamation. If not granted charitable or sympathetic judgment, they are at least entitled to justice and to the high place they have won in American and European history and citizenship.

The force behind the Johnson bill and some of its champions in Congress charge that opposition to the racial discrimination feature of the 1800 quota basis arises from "foreign blocs." They would give the impression that 100 percent of Americans are for it and that the sympathies of its opponents are of the "foreign-bloc" variety, and bear stigma of being "hyphenates." I meet that challenge willingly. I feel my Americanism will stand any test.

Every American Has Foreign Ancestors

The foreign born of my district writhe under the charge of being called "hyphenates." The people of my own family were all hyphenates—English-Americans, German-Americans, Irish-Americans. They began to come in the first ship or so after the *Mayflower*. But they did not come too early to miss the charge of anti-Americanism. Roger Williams was driven out of the Puritan colony of Salem to die in the wilderness because he objected "violently" to blue laws and the burning or hanging of rheumatic old women on witchcraft charges. He would not "assimilate" and was "a grave menace to American Institutions and democratic government."

My family put 11 men and boys into the Revolutionary War, and I am sure they and their women and children did not suffer so bitterly and sacrifice until it hurt to establish the autocracy of bigotry and intolerance which exists in many quarters to-day in this country. Some of these men and boys shed their blood and left their bodies to rot on American battle fields. To me real Americanism and the American flag are the product of the blood of men and of the tears of women and children of a different type than the rampant "Americanizers" of to-day.

My mother's father fought in the Civil War,

leaving his six small children in Detroit when he marched away to the southern battle fields to fight against racial distinctions and protect his country. My mother's little brother, about 14 years old, and the eldest child, fired by the traditions of his family, plodded off to the battle fields to do his bit. He aspired to be a drummer boy and inspire the men in battle, but he was found too small to carry a drum and was put at the ignominious task of driving army mules, hauling cannons and wagons. I learned more of the spirit of American history at my mother's knee than I ever learned in my four years of high school study of American history and in my five and a half years of study at the great University of Michigan. All that study convinces me that the racial discriminations of this bill are un-American. . . .

It must never be forgotten also that the Johnson bill, although it claims to favor the northern and western European peoples only, does so on a basis of comparison with the southern and western European peoples. The Johnson bill cuts down materially the number of immigrants allowed to come from northern and western Europe, the so-called Nordic peoples. . . .

Then I would be true to the principles for which my forefathers fought and true to the real spirit of the magnificent United States of today. I can not stultify myself by voting for the present bill and overwhelm my country with racial hatreds and racial lines and antagonisms drawn even tighter than they are to-day. [Applause.]

REVIEW QUESTIONS

1. Why did Congress seek to use the Immigration Act of 1924 to discriminate against immigrants from southern and western Europe?
2. Why did the United States restrict immigration at all?

The Great Black Migration (1917)

One of the most important social developments triggered by World War I was a massive migration of African Americans from the rural South to other regions of the country. Over a half million men, women, and children relocated between 1915 and 1920, and thousands more followed during the 1920s. They left in search of better paying jobs and the hope of greater social equality and political participation. Black newspapers such as the Chicago Defender *actively encouraged the exodus. Most of the migrants settled in cities such as New York, Philadelphia, and Chicago, forming African American neighborhoods that became fertile centers of black culture. The following letters from southern blacks requesting information about life in the North poignantly reveal the challenges for those wishing to migrate.*

From Emmet J. Scott, ed., "Letters of Negro Migrants of 1916–1918," *Journal of Negro History* 4 (1 July 1919):290–340.

Palestine, Tex. 1/2/1917—Sir: I hereby enclose you a few lines to find out some things if you will be so kind to word them to me. I am a southerner lad and has never been in the north no further than Texas and I has heard much talk about the north and how much better the colard people are treated up there than down here and I has ben striving so hard in my coming up and now I see that I cannot get up there without the ade of some one and I wants to ask you Dear Sir to please direct me in your best manner the step that I shall take to get there and if there are any way that you can help me to get there I am kindly asking for your ade. And if you will ade me please notify me by return mail because I am sure ancious to make it in the north because these southern white people ar so mean and they seems to be getting worse and I wants to get away and they wont pay me in getting up there please give me information how I can get there I would like to get there in the early spring, if I can get there if possible. Our southern white people are so cruel we collard people are almost afraid to walke the streets after night. So please let me hear from you by return mail. I will not say very much in this letter I will tell you more about it when I hear from you please ans. soon.

Newbern, Ala. 4/17/1917—Sir: . . . Doubtless you have learned of the great exodus of our people to the north and west from this and other states. I wish to say that we are forced to go when one thinks of a grown man wages is only fifty to seventy cents per day for all grades of work. He is compelled to go where there is better wages and sociable conditions, believe me. When I say that [at] many places here in this state the only thing that the black man gets is a peck of meal and from three to four lbs. of bacon per week, and he is treated as a slave. As leaders we are powerless for we dare not resent such or to show even the slightest disapproval. Only a few days ago more than 1,000 people left here for the North and West. They cannot stay here. The white man is saying that you must not go, but they are not doing anything by way of assisting the black man to stay. As a minister of the Methodist Episcopal Church I am on the verge of starvation simply because of the above conditions. I shall be glad to know if there is any possible way by which I could be of real service to you as director of your society. Thanking you in advance for an early reply, and for any suggestions that you might be able to offer.

Dapne, Ala., 4/20/17—Sir: I am writing you to let you know that there is 15 or 20 familys wants to come up there at once but cant come on account of money to come with and we cant phone you here we will be killed they dont want us to leave here & say if we dont go to war and fight for our country they are going to kill us and wants to get away if we can if you send 20 passes there is no doubt that every one of us will com at once. we are not doing any thing here we cant get a living out of what we do now some of these people are farmers and som are cooks barbers and black smiths but the greater part are farmers & good worker & honest people & up to date the trash pile dont want to go no where These are nice people and respectable find a place like that & send passes & we all will come at once we all wants to leave here out of this hard luck place if you cant use us find some place that does need this kind of people we are called Negroes here. I am a reader of the Defender and am delighted to know how times are there & was to glad to, know if we could get some one to pass us away from here to a better land. We work but cant get scarcely any thing for it & they dont want us to go away & there is not much of anything here to do & nothing for it Please find some one that need this kind of a people & send at once for us. We dont want anything but our wareing and bed clothes & have not got no money to get away from here with & beging to get away before we are killed and hope to here from you at once. We cant talk to you over the phone here we are afraid to they dont want to hear one say that he or she wants to leave here if we do we are apt to be killed. They say if we dont go to war they are not going to let us stay here with their folks and it is not any thing that we have done to them.

REVIEW QUESTIONS

1. According to these accounts, what role did racial discrimination play in provoking southern blacks to migrate to the North?
2. Describe some of the economic hardships faced by blacks in the South.
3. Why might southern elites have wanted blacks to remain in the South?

HARRY EMERSON FOSDICK

FROM Shall the Fundamentalists Win? (1922)

The reactionary temper of the 1920s sparked a resurgence of Protestant fundamental-
ism. So-called liberal Protestants sought to reconcile religion and reason, faith and
science, and to challenge the backward tendencies of fundamentalism. Reverend
Harry Emerson Fosdick exemplified such liberal Protestantism. His influential 1922
sermon, excerpted below, enraged fundamentalists and eventually forced his resigna-
tion from New York City's First Presbyterian Church. Fosdick went on to become one
of the nation's most influential clergymen.

From Harry Emerson Fosdick, "Shall the Fundamentalists Win?" *Christian Work* 102 (June 10, 1922):716–22.

This morning we are to think of the funda-mentalist controversy which threatens to divide the American churches as though al-ready they were not sufficiently split and riven. . . . Already all of us must have heard about the people who call themselves the Fundamentalists. Their apparent intention is to drive out of the evangelical churches men and women of liberal opinions. I speak of them the more freely because there are no two denominations more affected by them than the Baptist and the Presbyterian. We should not identify the Fundamentalists with the conservatives. All Fundamentalists are conserva-tives, but not all conservatives are Fundamentalists. The best conservatives can often give lessons to the liberals in true liberality of spirit, but the Funda-mentalist program is essentially illiberal and intol-erant.

The Fundamentalists see, and they see truly, that in this last generation there have been strange new movements in Christian thought. A great mass of new knowledge has come into man's possession —new knowledge about the physical universe, its origin, its forces, its laws; new knowledge about human history and in particular about the ways in which the ancient peoples used to think in matters of religion and the methods by which they phrased and explained their spiritual experiences; and new knowledge, also, about other religions and the strangely similar ways in which men's faiths and re-ligious practices have developed everywhere. . . .

Now, there are multitudes of reverent Chris-tians who have been unable to keep this new knowledge in one compartment of their minds and the Christian faith in another. They have been sure that all truth comes from the one God and is His revelation. Not, therefore, from irreverence or caprice or destructive zeal but for the sake of intel-lectual and spiritual integrity, that they might re-ally love the Lord their God, not only with all their heart and soul and strength but with all their mind, they have been trying to see this new knowl-edge in terms of the Christian faith and to see the Christian faith in terms of this new knowledge.

Doubtless they have made many mistakes. Doubtless there have been among them reckless radicals gifted with intellectual ingenuity but lack-ing spiritual depth. Yet the enterprise itself seems to them indispensable to the Christian Church. The new knowledge and the old faith cannot be left antagonistic or even disparate, as though a man on Saturday could use one set of regulative ideas for his life and on Sunday could change gear to an-other altogether. We must be able to think our modern life clear through in Christian terms, and to do that we also must be able to think our Christian faith clear through in modern terms.

There is nothing new about the situation. It has happened again and again in history, as, for example, when the stationary earth suddenly began to move and the universe that had been centered in this planet was centered in the sun around which the planets whirled. Whenever such a situation has arisen, there has been only one way out—the new knowledge and the old faith had to be blended in a new combination. Now, the people in this generation who are trying to do this are the liberals, and the Fundamentalists are out on a campaign to shut against them the doors of the Christian fellowship. Shall they be allowed to succeed?

It is interesting to note where the Fundamentalists are driving in their stakes to mark out the deadline of doctrine around the church, across which no one is to pass except on terms of agreement. They insist that we must all believe in the historicity of certain special miracles, preeminently the virgin birth of our Lord; that we must believe in a special theory of inspiration—that the original documents of the Scripture, which of course we no longer possess, were inerrantly dictated to men a good deal as a man might dictate to a stenographer; that we must believe in a special theory of the Atonement—that the blood of our Lord, shed in a substitutionary death, placates an alienated Deity and makes possible welcome for the returning sinner; and that we must believe in the second coming of our Lord upon the clouds of heaven to set up a millennium here, as the only way in which God can bring history to a worthy denouement.

Such are some of the stakes which are being driven to mark a deadline of doctrine around the church. If a man is a genuine liberal, his primary protest is not against holding these opinions, although he may well protest against their being considered the fundamentals of Christianity. This is a free country and anybody has a right to hold these opinions or any others if he is sincerely convinced of them. The question is—Has anybody a right to deny the Christian name to those who differ with him on such points and to shut against

them the doors of the Christian fellowship? The Fundamentalists say that this must be done. In this country and on the foreign field they are trying to do it. They have actually endeavored to put on the statute books of a whole state binding laws against teaching modern biology. If they had their way, within the church, they would set up in Protestantism a doctrinal tribunal more rigid than the pope's. In such an hour, delicate and dangerous, when feelings are bound to run high, I plead this morning the cause of magnanimity and liberality and tolerance of spirit. . . .

Here in the Christian churches are these two groups of people and the question which the Fundamentalists raise is this—Shall one of them throw the other out? Has intolerance any contribution to make to this situation? Will it persuade anybody of anything? Is not the Christian Church large enough to hold within her hospitable fellowship people who differ on points like this and agree to differ until the fuller truth be manifested? The Fundamentalists say not. They say the liberals must go. Well, if the Fundamentalists should succeed, then out of the Christian Church would go some of the best Christian life and consecration of this generation—multitudes of men and women, devout and reverent Christians, who need the church and whom the church needs. . . .

I do not believe for one moment that the Fundamentalists are going to succeed. Nobody's intolerance can contribute anything to the solution of the situation which we have described. If, then, the Fundamentalists have no solution of the problem, where may we expect to find it? In two concluding comments let us consider our reply to that inquiry.

The first element that is necessary is a spirit of tolerance and Christian liberty. When will the world learn that intolerance solves no problems? This is not a lesson which the Fundamentalists alone need to learn; the liberals also need to learn it. . . .

Nevertheless, it is true that just now the Fundamentalists are giving us one of the worst exhibitions of bitter intolerance that the churches of this country have ever seen. As one watches them and listens to them he remembers the remark of General Armstrong of Hampton Institute, "Cantankerousness is worse than heterodoxy." There are many opinions in the field of modern controversy concerning which I am not sure whether they are right or wrong, but there is one thing I am sure of: courtesy and kindliness and tolerance and humility and fairness are right. Opinions may be mistaken; love never is.

As I plead thus for an intellectually hospitable, tolerant, liberty-loving church, I am, of course, thinking primarily about this new generation. We have boys and girls growing up in our homes and schools, and because we love them we may well wonder about the church which will be waiting to receive them. Now, the worst kind of church that can possibly be offered to the allegiance of the new generation is an intolerant church. . . .

My friends, nothing in all the world is so much worth thinking of as God, Christ, the Bible, sin and salvation, the divine purposes for humankind, life everlasting. But you cannot challenge the dedicated thinking of this generation to these sublime themes upon any such terms as are laid down by an intolerant church.

The second element which is needed if we are to reach a happy solution of this problem is a clear insight into the main issues of modern Christianity and a sense of penitent shame that the Christian Church should be quarreling over little matters when the world is dying of great needs. If, during the war, when the nations were wrestling upon the very brink of hell and at times all seemed lost, you chanced to hear two men in an altercation about some minor matter of sectarian denominationalism, could you restrain your indignation? You said, "What can you do with folks like this who, in the face of colossal issues, play with the tiddledywinks and peccadillos of religion?" . . .

The present world situation smells to heaven! And now, in the presence of colossal problems, which must be solved in Christ's name and for Christ's sake, the Fundamentalists propose to drive out from the Christian churches all the consecrated souls who do not agree with their theory of inspiration. What immeasurable folly!

Well, they are not going to do it; certainly not in this vicinity. I do not even know in this congregation whether anybody has been tempted to be a Fundamentalist. Never in this church have I caught one accent of intolerance. God keep us always so and ever increasing areas of the Christian fellowship; intellectually hospitable, open-minded, liberty-loving, fair, tolerant, not with the tolerance of indifference, as though we did not care about the faith, but because always our major emphasis is upon the weightier matters of the spirit.

REVIEW QUESTIONS

1. Do you agree that religious fundamentalists are "illiberal and intolerant"? Why or why not?
2. Why did fundamentalists feel threatened by new scientific knowledge?

WILLIAM JENNINGS BRYAN

FROM *In His Image* (1922)

William Jennings Bryan (1860–1925) ran as the Democratic nominee for president three times. He never won, but he remained famous for his theatrical speeches. During the 1920s, Bryan, a lifelong Presbyterian, emerged as the foremost spokesman for the fundamentalist Christian movement. He became a powerful crusader against Darwinism and the inroads of "modernism" in schools and in society. During the famous trial of Tennessee teacher John Scopes, accused of teaching Darwinism in his science classes in violation of state law, Bryan served as one of the prosecuting attorneys. Bryan died five days after the controversial trial ended.

From William Jennings Bryan, *In His Image* (New York: Revell, 1922), pp. 120–123. [Editorial insertions appear in square brackets—*Ed.*]

The Origin of Man

Is any other proof needed to show the irreligious influence exerted by Darwinism applied to man? At the University of Wisconsin (so a Methodist preacher told me) a teacher told his class that the Bible was a collection of myths. When I brought the matter to the attention of the President of the University, he criticized me but avoided all reference to the professor. At Ann Arbor [University of Michigan] a professor argued with students against religion and asserted that no thinking man could believe in God or the Bible. At Columbia (I learned this from a Baptist preacher) a professor began his course in geology by telling his class to throw away all that they had learned in the Sunday school. There is a professor in Yale of whom it is said that no one leaves his class a believer in God. (This came from a young man who told me that his brother was being led away from the Christian faith by this professor.) A father (a Congressman) tells me that a daughter on her return from Wellesley [College] told him that nobody believed in the Bible stories now. Another father (a Congressman) tells me of a son whose faith was undermined by this doctrine in a Divinity School. Three preachers told me of having their interest in the subject aroused by the return of their children from college with their faith shaken. The Northern Baptists have recently, after a spirited contest, secured the adoption of a Confession of Faith: it was opposed by the evolutionists.

In Kentucky the fight is on among the Disciples, and it is becoming more and more acute in the Northern branches of the Methodist and Presbyterian Churches. A young preacher, just out of a theological seminary, who did not believe in the virgin birth of Christ, was recently ordained in Western New York. Last April I met a young man who was made an atheist by two teachers in a Christian college.

These are only a few illustrations that have come under my own observation—nearly all of them within a year. What is to be done? Are the members of the various Christian churches willing to have the power of the pulpit paralyzed by a false, absurd and ridiculous doctrine which is without support in the written Word of God and without support also in nature? Is "thus saith the Lord" to be supplanted by guesses and speculations and assumptions? I submit three propositions for the consideration of the Christians of the nation:

First, the preachers who are to break the bread of life to the lay members should believe that man has in him the breath of the Almighty, as the Bible declares, and not the blood of the brute, as the evolutionists affirm. He should also believe in the virgin birth of the Saviour.

Second, none but Christians in good standing and with a spiritual conception of life should be allowed to teach in Christian schools. Church schools are worse than useless if they bring students under the influence of those who do not believe in the religion upon which the Church and church schools are built. Atheism and Agnosticism are more dangerous when hidden under the cloak of religion than when they are exposed to view.

Third, in schools supported by taxation we should have a real neutrality wherever neutrality in religion is desired. If the Bible cannot be defended in these schools it should not be attacked, either directly or under the guise of philosophy or science. The neutrality which we now have is often but a sham; it carefully excludes the Christian religion but permits the use of the schoolrooms for the destruction of faith and for the teaching of materialistic doctrines.

It is not sufficient to say that *some* believers in Darwinism retain their belief in Christianity; some survive smallpox. As we avoid smallpox because *many* die of it, so we should avoid Darwinism because it *leads many astray*.

If it is contended that an instructor has a right to teach anything he likes, I reply that the parents who pay the salary have a right to decide what shall be taught. To continue the illustration used above, a person can expose himself to the smallpox if he desires to do so, but he has no right to communicate it to others. So a man can believe anything he pleases but he has no right to teach it against the protest of his employers.

Acceptance of Darwin's doctrine tends to destroy one's belief in immortality as taught by the Bible. If there has been no break in the line between man and the beasts—no time when by the act of the Heavenly Father man became "a living Soul," at what period in man's development was he endowed with the hope of a future life? And, if the brute theory leads to the abandonment of belief in a future life with its rewards and punishments, what stimulus to righteous living is offered in its place?

Darwinism leads to a denial of God. Nietzsche carried Darwinism to its logical conclusion and it made him the most extreme of anti-Christians. I had read extracts from his writings—enough to acquaint me with his sweeping denial of God and of the Saviour—but not enough to make me familiar with his philosophy.

REVIEW QUESTIONS

1. On what basis does Bryan dismiss evolution? Do you find his arguments convincing? Explain.
2. In your view, how should educational institutions address the topic of Charles Darwin's theory of evolution?
3. Do you agree with Bryan's assertion that "righteous living" depends upon belief in an afterlife?

The Scopes Trial (1925)

In the 1920s the Tennessee legislature passed a law forbidding teachers in the state-supported (but not private) schools to teach the Darwinian theory of evolution. John T. Scopes, a young biology teacher, defied the law and was brought to trial in the backwoods hamlet of Dayton. The case drew the attention of the nation. Scopes's defense team was buttressed by the celebrated attorney and agnostic, Clarence G. Darrow; aiding the prosecution was the famed orator and fundamentalist William J. Bryan, who had long spearheaded the nationwide crusade against evolution. Bryan was induced to take the stand as an expert witness on the Bible, and Darrow proceeded to skewer him and his "fool religion."

From *The World's Most Famous Court Trial: Tennessee Evolution Case* (Cincinnati: National Book Club, 1925), pp. 303–304.

DARROW: Do you believe the story of the temptation of Eve by the serpent?

BRYAN: I do.

DARROW: Do you believe that after Eve ate the apple, or gave it to Adam, whichever way it was, that God cursed Eve, and at that time decreed that all womankind thenceforth and forever should suffer the pains of childbirth in the reproduction of the earth?

BRYAN: I believe what it says, and I believe the fact as fully—

DARROW: That is what it says, doesn't it?

BRYAN: Yes.

DARROW: And for that reason, every woman born of woman, who has to carry on the race, the reason they have childbirth pains is because Eve tempted Adam in the Garden of Eden?

BRYAN: I will believe just what the Bible says. I ask to put that in the language of the Bible, for I prefer that to your language. Read the Bible and I will answer.

DARROW: All right, I will do that.

[*Darrow reads from Genesis 3:15–16.*]

BRYAN: I accept it as it is.

DARROW: And you believe that came about because Eve tempted Adam to eat the fruit?

BRYAN: Just as it says.

DARROW: And you believe that is the reason that God made the serpent to go on his belly after he tempted Eve?

BRYAN: I believe the Bible as it is, and I do not permit you to put your language in the place of the language of the Almighty. You read that Bible and ask me questions, and I will answer them. I will not answer your questions in your language.

DARROW: I will read it to you from the Bible: "And the Lord God said unto the serpent, because thou hast done this, thou art cursed above all cattle, and above every beast of the field; upon thy belly shalt thou go and dust shalt thou eat all the days of thy life." Do you think that is why the serpent is compelled to crawl upon its belly?

BRYAN: I believe that.

DARROW: Have you any idea how the snake went before that time?

BRYAN: No, sir.

DARROW: Do you know whether he walked on his tail or not?

BRYAN: No, sir. I have no way to know. (Laughter in audience.)

DARROW: Now, you refer to the cloud that was put in the heaven after the flood, the rainbow. Do you believe in that?

BRYAN: Read it.

DARROW: All right, I will read it for you.

BRYAN: Your Honor, I think I can shorten this testimony. The only purpose Mr. Darrow has is to slander the Bible, but I will answer his question. I will answer it all at once, and I have no objection in the world, I want the world to know that this man, who does not believe in a God, is trying to use a court in Tennessee—

DARROW: I object to that.

BRYAN: (continuing) —to slur at it, and while it will require time, I am willing to take it.

DARROW: I object to your statement. I am examining you on your fool ideas that no intelligent Christian on earth believes.

REVIEW QUESTIONS

1. How did Bryan indicate his belief that the Bible is the literal word of God?
2. What do you think Darrow meant by an "intelligent Christian"?
3. Why do you think Bryan became the hero of biblical fundamentalists?

27 ✑ REPUBLICAN RESURGENCE AND DECLINE

In the aftermath of World War I and the collapse of Woodrow Wilson's health and his presidency, the Republican party regained control of the White House and the Congress. President Warren G. Harding promised the nation a "return to normalcy." This meant abandoning the efforts of Wilson and Theodore Roosevelt to promote political reform and economic regulation. Instead, the Republicans would revive the pro-business orientation that had served the party so well during the Gilded Age. Harding's successors, Calvin Coolidge and Herbert Hoover, shared this philosophy. Coolidge, who assumed office in 1923 upon the death of Harding, proclaimed that the "business of America is business."

To foster the growth of business, the Republicans emphasized reduced government spending, lower taxes, and higher tariffs. Secretary of the Treasury Andrew Mellon, a wealthy Pittsburgh banker and industrialist, slashed personal income and estate tax rates and sharply reduced federal government spending. Coolidge once remarked that if the federal government disappeared, few would notice and even fewer would regret it. At the same time, Secretary of Commerce Herbert Hoover worked closely with business leaders to create benefits for workers so as to reduce the appeal of trade unions. He also established new government initiatives to help mediate disputes between labor and management and thereby avert strikes and boycotts.

The Democrats, meanwhile, fragmented along sectional lines that reflected the cultural civil wars of the decade. The rural faction, rooted in the South and West, sustained a commitment to cultural populism. This meant support for Prohibition, fundamentalism, the Klan, and government programs for farmers. The urban faction of the party, centered in the growing cities of the East and Midwest, depended for its support on immigrant groups that were largely Catholic or Jewish. They tended to oppose Prohibition and recoil from the Protestant orthodoxy of their rural counterparts.

The split within the Democratic party turned into a chasm at the 1924 national convention in New York. Efforts to unify the divided party proved fruitless. Urban delegates dismissed the "rubes and hicks" from "the sticks" while populist spokesmen charged that metropolitan Democrats were "rooted in corruption, directed by greed and dominated by selfishness." A northern effort to pass a resolution condemning the Ku Klux Klan aroused bitter opposition from the southern delegates, and failed by one vote.

Progressives in both parties felt alienated by the conservative spirit of the times. In the 1924 election they rallied their support behind the third-party candidacy of Robert La Follette of Wisconsin, who headed a revived Progressive Party. La Follette and the Progressives adopted a pro-labor and pro-farm platform that echoed the Populists: it called for federal ownership of railroads and utilities, higher taxes on the wealthy, the end of child labor, and conservation of natural resources. La Follette received the endorsement of the Socialist Party and the American Federation of Labor (AFL), and he drew nearly 5 million votes, mostly from disaffected Democrats. Nevertheless, he still finished a distant third behind Coolidge and Davis.

Four years later Herbert Hoover rode the wave of economic prosperity into the White House. In his acceptance speech he predicted the "final triumph over poverty," and in his inaugural address he declared that he "had no fears for the future of our country. It is bright with hope." Hoover embodied the principles of rugged individualism and equal opportunity embedded in the American experience. Although a staunch supporter of corporate interests and an ardent defender of Prohibition, he was a more progressive thinker than either Harding or Coolidge. Hoover believed that capitalism had advanced beyond the initial stage of cutthroat competition and was entering a period of rational cooperation in marketing, wage policies, and product standardization. He also argued that it was in the best interests of corporate America for businesses to engage in voluntary acts of welfare capitalism, extending benefits to workers in order to eliminate the need for trade unions and to blunt the appeal of socialism.

The prevailing political and economic conservatism during the 1920s stunted the growth of organized labor. Antiunion sentiment was fiercest in the South where only a small percentage of workers were unionized. The southern tradition of rugged individualism and employer paternalism impeded efforts to organize workers. When unorganized southern workers tried to strike, or when northern activists tried to arouse union interest in the region, they were met with fierce hostility.

In 1929 a wave of violent strikes swept across the South. Most of the unrest centered in the large textile mills that had come to dominate the southern economy since the 1880s. During World War I, the desperate need for military clothing brought rapid expansion and high profits to the textile industry. Wages rose with the increases in production. After the war, however, demand for cotton cloth sagged and prices and wages plummeted. Military demobilization, changing women's fashions—rising hemlines—and foreign competition combined to erode the profit margins of the textile companies. In response, owners closed mills, slashed wages, raised production quotas, and operated the mills "around-the-clock." They installed faster machinery and adopted new production techniques to improve efficiency and reduce the number of employees.

This onerous "stretch-out" system finally provoked workers to rebel. Many of them joined the AFL's United Textile Workers (UTW). Strikes and work stoppages followed, and the powerful mill owners, supported by security guards, local police, and state militia, forcefully suppressed union efforts. Few of the strikes lasted more than a week, but the 1929 walkout at the huge Loray Mill in Gastonia, North Carolina, escalated into a prolonged conflict that involved two deaths and captured the attention of the world.

Herbert Hoover was by far the best qualified and most able of all the Republican presidents during the twenties, but he assumed office in 1929, the year in which the Great Bull Market collapsed and the nation began to spiral downward into the worst economic depression in its history. To be sure, Hoover did not cause the Great Depression, but he failed to recognize the ominous warning signals.

The Great Depression deepened quickly after October 1929 and spread across the country. In 1930 alone almost 1,300 banks closed their doors. During 1931 another 2,300 collapsed. Unemployment rose from 3 percent in 1929 to 25 percent in 1933, meaning that almost 13 million people found themselves jobless.

Statistics hardly convey the human costs of the depression. Prolonged unemployment led people to lose their homes and farms. By the thousands, the displaced and dispossessed began to roam the streets and byways looking for work, begging for money, and sleeping on benches or the ground. Suicides increased by 30 percent between 1929 and 1932, and marriage and birth rates plummeted.

Those already living on the margin of society were especially hard hit: African Americans, Mexican Americans, and recent immigrants. Yet for all of the depression's devastating effects, most Americans refused to succumb to fatalism. They refused to let hard times break their spirits or corrupt their dignity. As Ma Joad declares in John Steinbeck's The Grapes of Wrath *(1936), "They ain't gonna wipe us out. Why, we're the people—we go on."*

EDWARD PURINTON

Big Ideas from Big Business (1921)

The prosperity generated by the American economy during the 1920s became the marvel of the world and a source of great pride. Among the most active celebrants of free enterprise and its blessings was Edward Earle Purinton, dean of the American Efficiency Foundation and a prolific author.

From Edward Purinton, "Big Ideas from Big Business," *The Independent* 105 (16 April 1921): 395–396.

Among the nations of the earth today America stands for one idea: *Business.* . . . For in this fact lies, potentially, the salvation of the world.

Through business, properly conceived, managed and conducted, the human race is finally to be redeemed. How and why a man works foretells what he will do, think, have, give and be. And real salvation is in doing, thinking, having, giving and being—not in sermonizing and theorizing. . . .

What is the finest game? Business. The soundest science? Business. The truest art? Business. The fullest education? Business. The fairest opportunity? Business. The cleanest philanthropy? Business. The sanest religion? Business.

You may not agree. That is because you judge business by the crude, mean, stupid, false imitation of business that happens to be located near you.

The finest game is business. The rewards are for everybody, and all can win. There are no favorites—Providence always crowns the career of the man who is worthy. And in this game there is no "luck"—you have the fun of taking chances but the sobriety of guaranteeing certainties. The speed and size of your winnings are for you alone to determine; you needn't wait for the other fellow in the game—it is always your move. And your slogan is not "Down the Other Fellow!" but rather "Beat Your Own Record!" or "Do It Better Today!" or "Make Every Job a Masterpiece!" The great sportsmen of the world are the great business men. . . .

The fullest education is business. A proper blend of study, work and life is essential to advancement. The whole man is educated. Human nature itself is the open book that all business men study; and the mastery of a page of this educates you more than the memorizing of a dusty tome from a library shelf. In the school of business, moreover, you teach yourself and learn most from your own mistakes. What you learn here you live out, the only real test.

The fairest opportunity is business. You can find more, better, quicker chances to get ahead in a large business house than anywhere else on earth. The biographies of champion business men show how they climbed, and how you can climb. Recognition of better work, of keener and quicker thought, of deeper and finer feeling, is gladly offered by the men higher up, with early promotion the rule for the man who justifies it. There is, and can be, no such thing as buried talent in a modern business organization.

The cleanest philanthropy is business. By "clean" philanthropy I mean that devoid of graft, inefficiency and professionalism, also of condolence, hysterics and paternalism. Nearly everything that goes by the name of Charity was born a triplet, the other two members of the trio being Frailty and Cruelty. Not so in the welfare departments of leading corporations. Savings and loan funds; pension and insurance provisions; health precautions, instructions and safeguards; medical attention and hospital care; libraries, lectures and classes; musical, athletic and social features of all kinds; recreational facilities and financial opportunities—these types of "charitable institutions" for employees add to the worker's self-respect, self-knowledge and self-improvement, by making him an active partner in the welfare program, a producer of benefits for his employer and associates quite as much as a recipient of bounty from the company. I wish every "charity" organization would send its officials to school to the heads of the welfare departments of the big corporations; the charity would mostly be transformed into capability, and the minimum of irreducible charity left would not be called by that name.

The sanest religion is business. Any relationship that forces a man to follow the Golden Rule rightfully belongs amid the ceremonials of the church. A great business enterprise includes and presupposes this relationship. I have seen more Christianity to the square inch as a regular part of

the office equipment of famous corporation presidents than may ordinarily be found on Sunday in a verbalized but not vitalized church congregation. A man is not wholly religious until he is better on weekdays than he is on Sunday. The only ripened fruits of creeds are deeds. You can fool your preacher with a silky sprout or a wormy semblance of character, but you can't fool your employer. I would make every business house a consultation bureau for the guidance of the church whose members were employees of the house. . . .

REVIEW QUESTIONS

1. Did luck or chance play any role in Purinton's view of "business"? Explain.
2. Why did Purinton call business the "sanest religion"? Do you agree?
3. What negative effects of free market capitalism did Purinton ignore?

CALVIN COOLIDGE

FROM Government and Business (1925)

President Calvin Coolidge was an outspoken champion of America's free enterprise system. He was convinced that America's postwar domination of the world economy and the growing size of American corporations were compatible with American ideals. In this 1925 speech to the New York State Chamber of Commerce, he outlined his faith in American economic values and international leadership.

From Calvin Coolidge, "Government and Business," in *Foundations of the Republic: Speeches and Addresses* (New York, 1926), pp. 317–332. [Editorial insertions appear in square brackets —Ed.]

This time and place naturally suggest some consideration of commerce in its relation to Government and society. We are finishing a year which can justly be said to surpass all others

in the overwhelming success of general business. We are met not only in the greatest American metropolis [New York City], but in the greatest center of population and business that the world has ever known. If any one wishes to gauge the power which is represented by the genius of the American spirit, let him contemplate the wonders which have been wrought in this region in the short space of 200 years. Not only does it stand unequaled by any other place on earth, but it is impossible to conceive of any other place where it could be equaled. . . .

The foundation of this enormous development rests upon commerce. New York is an imperial city, but it is not a seat of government. The empire over which it rules is not political, but commercial. The great cities of the ancient world were the seats of both government and industrial power. The Middle Ages furnished a few exceptions. The great capitals of former times were not only seats of government but they actually governed. In the modern world government is inclined to be merely a tenant of the city. Political life and industrial life flow on side by side, but practically separated from each other. When we contemplate the enormous power, autocratic and uncontrolled, which would have been created by joining the authority of government with the influence of business, we can better appreciate the wisdom of the [founding] fathers in their wise dispensation which made Washington the political center of the country and left New York to develop into its business center. . . .

Everyone knows that it was our resources that saved Europe from a complete collapse immediately following the armistice [ending World War I]. Without the benefit of our credit, an appalling famine would have prevailed over great areas. In accordance with the light of all past history, disorder and revolution, with the utter breaking down of all legal restraints and the loosing of all the passions which had been aroused by four years of conflict, would have rapidly followed. Others did what they could, and no doubt made larger proportionate sacrifices, but it was the credits and food which we supplied that saved the situation.

When the work of restoring the fiscal condition of Europe began, it was accomplished again with our assistance. When Austria determined to put her financial house in order, we furnished a part of the capital. When Germany sought to establish a

sound fiscal condition, we again contributed a large portion of the necessary gold loan. Without this, the reparations plan would have utterly failed. Germany could not otherwise have paid. The armies of occupation would have gone on increasing international irritation and ill will. It was our large guarantee of credit that assisted Great Britain to return to a gold basis. What we have done for France, Italy, Belgium, Czechoslovakia, Poland, and other countries, is all a piece of the same endeavor. These efforts and accomplishments, whether they be appreciated at home or received with gratitude abroad, which have been brought about by the business interests of our country, constitute an enormous world service. Others have made plans and adopted agreements for future action which hold a rank of great importance. But when we come to the consideration of what has been done, when we turn aside from what has been promised, to examine what has been performed, no positive and constructive accomplishment of the past five years compares with the support which America has contributed to the financial stability of the world. It clearly marks a new epoch.

This holds a distinctly higher rank than a mere barter and sale. It reaches above the ordinary business transaction into a broader realm. America has disbanded her huge armies and reduced her powerful fleet, but in attempting to deal justly through the sharing of our financial resources we have done more for peace than we could have done with all our military power. Peace, we know, rests to a great extent upon justice, but it is very difficult for the public mind to divorce justice from economic opportunity. The problem for which we have been attempting a solution is in the first instance to place the people of the earth back into avenues of profitable employment. It was necessary to restore hope, to renew courage. A great contribution to this end has been made with American money. The work is not all done yet. No doubt it will develop that this has not been accomplished without some mistakes, but the important fact remains that when the world needed to be revived we did respond. As nations see their way to a safer economic existence, they will see their way to a more peaceful existence.

Possessed of the means to meet personal and public obligations, people are reestablishing their self-respect. The financial strength of America has contributed to the spiritual restoration of the world. It has risen into the domain of true business.

The working out of these problems of regulation, government economy, the elimination of waste in the use of human effort and of materials, conservation and the proper investment of our savings both at home and abroad, is all a part of the mighty task which was imposed upon mankind of subduing the earth. America must either perform her full share in the accomplishment of this great world destiny or fail. For almost three centuries we were intent upon our domestic development. We sought the help of the people and the wealth of other lands by which to increase our numerical strength and augment our national fortune. We have grown exceedingly great in population and in riches. This power and this prosperity we can continue for ourselves if we will but proceed with moderation. If our people will but use those resources which have been entrusted to them, whether of command over large numbers of men or of command over large investments of capital, not selfishly but generously, not to exploit others but to serve others, there will be no doubt of an increasing production and distribution of wealth.

All of these efforts represent the processes of reducing our domestic and foreign relations to a system of law. They consist of a determination of clear and definite rules of action. It is a civilizing and humanizing method adopted by means of conference, discussion, deliberation, and determination. If it is to have any continuing success, or any permanent value, it will be because it has not been brought about by one will compelling another by force, but has resulted from men reasoning together. It has sought to remove compulsion from the business life of the country and from our relationship with other nations. It has sought to bestow a greater freedom upon our own people and upon the people of the world. We have worshipped the ideals of force long enough. We have turned to worship at the true shrine of understanding and reason. . . .

This is the land of George Washington. We can do no less than work toward the realization of his hope. It ought to be our ambition to see the institutions which he founded grow in the blessings which they bestow upon our own citizens and increase in the good which their influence casts upon all the world. He did not hesitate to meet peril or encounter danger or make sacrifices. There is no cause which can be supported by any other methods. We cannot listen to the counsels of perfection; we cannot pursue a timorous policy; we cannot avoid the obligations of a common humanity. We must meet our perils; we must encounter our dangers; we must make our sacrifices; or history will recount that the works of Washington have failed. I do not believe the future is to be dismayed by that record. The truth and faith and justice of the ancient days have not departed from us.

REVIEW QUESTIONS

1. Why did the United States provide financial credits and loans to the European nations after World War I?
2. How might a working-class American respond to Coolidge's speech?

HERBERT HOOVER

FROM The "New York City" Speech (1928)

Herbert Hoover positioned himself somewhere between the conservative orthodoxy of Calvin Coolidge and the progressive Republican tradition of Theodore Roosevelt and Robert La Follette. Born in Iowa and raised in a Quaker family, he pursued a successful career as a mining engineer before being asked by Woodrow Wilson to head the Food Administration during World War I. He then served with distinction as secretary of commerce under Harding and Coolidge, expanding American markets abroad and nurturing the infant airline and radio industries. In the excerpt below, he described the American system of individualism and free enterprise.

From Herbert Hoover, "New York City," in *The New Day: Campaign Speeches of Herbert Hoover, 1928* (Palo Alto, CA: Stanford University Press, 1928), pp. 149–176. [Editorial insertions appear in square brackets—*Ed.*]

. . . During one hundred and fifty years we have builded [*sic*] up a form of self-government and a social system which is peculiarly our own. It differs essentially from all others in the world. It is the American system. It is just as definite and positive a political and social system as has ever been developed on earth. It is founded upon a particular conception of self-government in which decentralized local responsibility is the very base. Further than this, it is founded upon the conception that only through ordered liberty, freedom and equal opportunity to the individual will his initiative and enterprise spur on the march of progress. And in our insistence upon equality of opportunity has our system advanced beyond all the world.

During the war we necessarily turned to the government to solve every difficult economic problem. The government having absorbed every energy of our people for war, there was no other solution. For the preservation of the State, the Federal Government became a centralized despotism which undertook unprecedented responsibilities, assumed autocratic powers, and took over the business of citizens. To a large degree we regimented our whole people temporarily into a socialistic state. However justified in time of war if

continued in peace time it would destroy not only our American system but with it our progress and freedom as well.

When the war closed, the most vital of all issues both in our own country and throughout the world was whether Governments should continue their wartime ownership and operation of many instrumentalities of production and distribution. We were challenged with a peace-time choice between the American system of rugged individualism and a European philosophy of diametrically opposed doctrines—doctrines of paternalism and state socialism. The acceptance of these ideas would have meant the destruction of self-government through centralization of government. It would have meant the undermining of the individual initiative and enterprise through which our people have grown to unparalleled greatness.

*   *   *

When the Republican party came into full power it went at once resolutely back to our fundamental conception of the State and the rights and responsibilities of the individual. Thereby it restored confidence and hope in the American people, it freed and stimulated enterprise, it restored the Government to its position as an umpire instead of a player in the economic game. For these reasons the American people have gone forward in progress while the rest of the world has halted, and some countries have even gone backwards. If anyone will study the causes of retarded recuperation in Europe, he will find much of it due to the stifling of private initiative on one hand, and overloading of the Government with business on the other.

There has been revived in this campaign, however, a series of proposals which, if adopted, would be a long step toward the abandonment of our American system and a surrender to the destructive operation of governmental conduct of commercial business. Because the country is faced with difficulty and doubt over certain national problems—that is, prohibition, farm relief and electrical power—our opponents propose that we must thrust government a long way into the business which gave rise to these problems. In effect, they abandon the tenets of their own party and turn to State socialism as a solution for the difficulties presented by all three.

It is proposed that we shall change from prohibition to the State purchase and sale of liquor. If their agricultural relief program means anything, it means that the Government shall directly or indirectly buy and sell and fix prices of agricultural products. And we are to go into the hydro-electric-power business. In other words, we are confronted with a huge program of government in business.

There is, therefore, submitted to the American people a question of fundamental principle. That is: shall we depart from the principles of our American political and economic system, upon which we have advanced beyond all the rest of the world, in order to adopt methods based on principles destructive to its very foundations?

*   *   *

I should like to state to you the effect that this projection of government in business would have upon our system of self-government and our economic system. That effect would reach to the daily life of every man and woman. It would impair the very basis of liberty and freedom not only for those left outside the fold of expanded bureaucracy but for those embraced within it. . . .

It is a false liberalism that interprets itself into the government operation of commercial business. Every step of bureaucratizing of the business of our country poisons the very roots of liberalism—that is, political equality, free speech, free assembly, free press, and equality of opportunity. It is the road not to more liberty, but to less liberty. Liberalism should be found not striving to spread bureaucracy but striving to set bounds to it. True liberalism seeks all legitimate freedom, first in the confident belief that without such freedom the pursuit of all other blessings and benefits is vain. That belief is the foundation of all American progress, political as well as economic.

Liberalism is a force truly of the spirit, a force proceeding from the deep realization that economic freedom cannot be sacrificed if political freedom is to be preserved. Even if Governmental conduct of business could give us more efficiency instead of less efficiency, the fundamental objection to it would remain unaltered an unabated. It would destroy political equality. It would increase rather than decrease abuse and corruption. It would stifle initiative and invention. It would undermine the development of leadership. It would cramp and cripple the mental and spiritual energies of our people. It would extinguish equality and opportunity. It would dry up the spirit of liberty and progress. For these reasons primarily it must be resisted. For a hundred and fifty years liberalism has found its true spirit in the American system, not in the European systems.

I do not wish to be misunderstood in this statement. I am defining a general policy. It does not mean that our Government is to part with one iota of its national resources without complete protection to the public interest. . . .

Nor do I wish to be misinterpreted as believing that the United States is free-for-all and devil-take-the-hind-most. The very essence of equality of opportunity and of American individualism is that there shall be no domination by any group or combination in this Republic, whether it be business or political. On the contrary, it demands economic justice as well as political and social justice. It is no system of laissez faire.

I feel deeply on this subject because during the war I had some practical experience with governmental operation and control. I have witnessed not only at home but abroad the many failures of Government in business. I have seen its tyrannies, its injustices, its destruction of self-government, its undermining of the very instincts which carry our people forward to progress. I have witnessed the lack of advance, the lowered standards of living, the depressed spirits of people working under such a system. My objection is based not upon theory or upon a failure to recognize wrong or abuse, but I know the adoption of such methods would strike at the very roots of American life and would destroy the very basis of American progress.

*   *   *

And what have been the results of our American system? Our country has become the land of opportunity to those born without inheritance, not merely because of the wealth of its resources and industry, but because of this freedom of initiative and enterprise. Russia has natural resources equal to ours. Her people are equally industrious, but she has not had the blessings of 150 years of our form of government and of our social system. . . .

The greatness of America has grown out of a political and social system and a method of control of economic forces distinctly its own—our American system—which has carried this great experiment in human welfare further than ever before in all history. We are nearer today to the ideal of the abolition of poverty and fear from the lives of men and women than ever before in any land. And I again repeat that the departure from our American system by injecting principles will jeopardize the very liberty and freedom of our people, will destroy equality of opportunity, not alone to ourselves but to our children. . . .

REVIEW QUESTIONS

1. For Hoover, what were some of the problems of "government in business"?
2. Even if government involvement could produce greater business efficiency, why did Hoover oppose it?
3. Based on the views expressed here, how might Hoover have responded to an economic crisis?

FREDERICK NELSON

North Carolina Justice (1929)

In 1929 Gaston County, North Carolina, had more textile plants than any other county in the nation. The Loray Mill was the largest in the South. At its peak, the mill employed 3,500 workers, almost half of them women. During 1927 and 1928, however, the workforce was slashed. Those who kept their jobs were required to work longer hours (11 hours a day, 6 days a week) and tend more machines for lower wages (averaging about $15 a week for men; $6 a week for women). On 1 April 1929, over one thousand exhausted Loray workers walked off the job. They were encouraged to do so by the Communist Party–led National Textile Workers Union (NTWU). Local officials were outraged that mill workers were collaborating with "northern" communists. Equally shocking was the large number of young women *among the strikers. In the fall of 1929 the strike at the Loray Mill turned violent. A vigilante group assaulted a group of strikers and killed twenty-nine-year-old Ella May Wiggins, a longtime labor activist, poet, and folk singer. Northern journalists who covered the trial of the murder suspects insisted that the trial was a farce; the North Carolina authorities were prejudiced against the strikers. The following article from the* New Republic *condemns the state's legal system for failing to bring the murderers to justice.*

From Frederick Nelson, "North Carolina Justice," *New Republic* 60 (6 November 1929): 314–316. [Editorial insertions appear in square brackets—*Ed.*]

Nobody is to be indicted for the murder of Ella May Wiggins, the "poet laureate of the union," who was shot down on the highway between Gastonia and South Gastonia, N.C., on September 14. I hardly imagine there is anybody who expected that the Grand Jury of Gaston County would return a true bill [of indictment] for the wanton assassination of this unfortunate woman. Certainly I did not expect any such result as I sat in the little courtroom last month and listened to the coroner's inquest into the affair. County Solicitor Carpenter himself made it clear enough what the ultimate result would be. His examination of the men charged with pursuing the truckload of Union organizers, forcing it off the road and then shooting into the crowded truck, was distinguished by such sharp and remorseless questions as "You didn't have a gun with you, did you?" or "Weren't lookin' for any trouble, were you?"

One of the International Labor Defense lawyers, who tried to interject a little real cross-examination of the men, was told to "keep out of this." The manager of the Manville-Jenckes Company went bail for all. Everybody was happy. The unionites, however, postponed the funeral of Ella May for fear of another shooting. Murder is sometimes a crime in North Carolina. A "speakin' " by union organizers always is.

This strange lack of proportion pervades the whole attitude of North Carolina toward this labor disturbance. . . . The Charlotte newspaper man who told me that there was going to be a whipping every time there was speakin' [on behalf of the union] had

substantially the right information. "The people over there in Gastonia aren't going to tolerate these Red bastards and you can put that in your paper," he told me. "And nobody is going to be convicted for these whipping parties," he added. "You might as well have all the fun you can get out of these hearings because that's all there'll be to it." It is unreasonable to demand moral indignation in a journalist, but I wish I could report that this was said at least with regret over the state of mind of a community which has so succumbed to a frenzy that it has come to regard soapbox oratory as a high crime, and murder as a misdemeanor which can be forgotten when "everything blows over." But my journalistic friend wasn't horrified at all. He was like most of the people you meet down there, who talk to you superciliously on this question just as they talk about the Negro question—as if an outsider couldn't understand their "peculiar local problem."

. . . Another newspaper man, also a North Carolinian, ran squarely against Gastonia respectability when he tried to provide a bail for a girl among the unionists who had been arrested on the charge of possessing liquor. The bail bond was for $100, and the scribe was willing to provide it. However, although everybody in the town knew him and his responsibility was unquestioned, he was not allowed to write a check to accompany the bond. The court had to have the money. And when he told people what he wanted a check cashed for, several refused to cash it and accused him of being a Red himself. . . .

Sometimes I wish I could believe that the North Carolina mob was really out of hand. Mob spirit is fearful to contemplate, but it is passionate and uncalculating. The bourgeoisie of Gaston County tell you the population is so inflamed with hatred toward the Communists that "anything may happen." I don't believe it. I have seen the proletariat of Gastonia, and I doubt if they are ever inflamed on any subject more serious than the number of flapjacks necessary for breakfast. It has required some healthy blow-torches to set those embers glowing.

The *Gastonia Gazette*, with its constant references to the Christ-like patience of Gastonia in the face of provocations [by striking workers and union leaders], which it then proceeded to describe in incendiary fashion, doubtless contributed to the continuation of mob rage, and some of the gentry who told me with long faces how hard it was to "hold the boys in" had their fingers crossed. One such reminded me, after Ella May [Wiggins] had been killed, "how much worse a thing like that looks in the paper than what it really was." He said that in the courtroom, which was full of his fellow-citizens who were accused of wantonly shooting down a helpless woman. He might have said, "What's all this fuss about a striker?" He chuckled and said, "You can't tell what the boys'll do when they get all rared up," as if they had stolen the front gate off the parsonage fence.

It was Samuel Butler, I believe, who wanted to know why sexual immorality in English fiction is so much more seriously condemned than homicide. North Carolina might ask herself by what processes of mind has she come to consider a ragged little Union meeting so much more criminal than murder, kidnapping, flogging, false arrest and arson. I don't see how her citizens can ask themselves such a question without seeing the necessity of a quick march out of the bog of ethical confusion in which these labor troubles have mired them.

REVIEW QUESTIONS

1. In such a charged atmosphere, was it possible to prosecute the murderers of Ella May Wiggins? Explain.
2. In what respects does the trial resemble the famous Sacco-Vanzetti case?

MERIDEL LE SUEUR

FROM Women on the Breadlines (1932)

The human misery caused by the Great Depression is hard to fathom. Widespread unemployment and homelessness forced millions of people to the very edge of survival. The following account describes daily life for unemployed women in Minneapolis.

From Meridel Le Sueur, "Women on the Breadlines," *New Masses*, 7, January 1932, pp. 5–7. Reprinted in *Harvest: Collected Stories*. Copyright 1932, © 1977 by Meridel Le Sueur. Reprinted by permission of West End Press.

I am sitting in the city free employment bureau. It's the woman's section. We have been sitting here now for four hours. We sit here every day, waiting for a job. There are no jobs. Most of us have had no breakfast. Some have had scant rations for over a year. Hunger makes a human being lapse into a state of lethargy, especially city hunger. Is there any place else in the world where a human being is supposed to go hungry amidst plenty without an outcry, without protest, where only the boldest steal or kill for bread, and the timid crawl the streets, hunger like the beak of a terrible bird at the vitals?

We sit looking at the floor. No one dares think of the coming winter. There are only a few more days of summer. Everyone is anxious to get work to lay up something for that long siege of bitter cold. But there is no work. Sitting in the room we all know it. That is why we don't talk much. We look at the floor dreading to see that knowledge in each other's eyes. There is a kind of humiliation in it. We look away from each other. We look at the floor. It's too terrible to see this animal terror in each other's eyes.

So we sit hour after hour, day after day, waiting for a job to come in. There are many women for a single job. A thin sharp woman sits inside the wire cage looking at the book. For four hours we have watched her looking at that book. She has a hard little eye. In the small bare room there are half a dozen women sitting on the benches waiting. Many come and go. Our faces are all familiar to each other, for we wait here everyday.

This is a domestic employment bureau. Most of the women who come here are middle aged, some have families, some raised their families and are now alone, some have men who are out of work. Hard times and the man leaves to hunt for work. He doesn't find it. He drifts on. The woman probably doesn't hear from him for a long time. She expects it. She isn't surprised. She struggles alone to feed the many mouths. Sometimes she gets help from the charities. If she's clever she can get herself a good living from the charities, if she's naturally a lick spittle,[1] naturally a little docile and cunning. If she's proud then she starves silently, leaving her children to find work, coming home after a day's searching to wrestle with her house, her children.

Some such story is written on the faces of all these women. There are young girls too, fresh from the country. Some are made brazen too soon by the city. There is a great exodus of girls from the farms into the city now. Thousands of farms have been vacated completely in Minnesota. The girls are trying to get work. The prettier ones can get jobs in the stores when there are any, or waiting on tables but these jobs are only for the attractive and the adroit, the others, the real peasants have a more difficult time. . . .

It's one of the great mysteries of the city where women go when they are out of work and hungry. There are not many women in the bread line. There are no flop houses for women as there are for men, where a bed can be had for a quarter or less. You don't see women lying on the floor at the mission in the free flops. They obviously don't sleep in the jungle or under newspapers in the park. There is no law I suppose against their being in these places but the fact is they rarely are.

Yet there must be as many women out of jobs in cities and suffering extreme poverty as there are men. What happens to them? Where do they go? Try to get into the Y.W.[2] without any money or looking down at the heel. Charities take care of very few and only those that are called "deserving." The lone girl is under suspicion by the virgin women who dispense charity.

I've lived in cities for many months broke, without help, too timid to get in bread lines. I've known many women to live like this until they simply faint on the street from privations, without saying a word to anyone. A woman will shut herself up in a room until it is taken away from her, and eat a cracker a day and be as quiet as a mouse so there are no social statistics concerning her.

I don't know why it is, but a woman will do this unless she has dependents, will go for weeks, verging on starvation, crawling in some hole, going through the streets ashamed, sitting in libraries, parks, going for days without speaking to a living soul like some exiled beast, keeping the runs mended in her stockings, shut up in terror in her own misery, until she becomes too super sensitive and timid to even ask for a job. . . .

---

[1] Someone who seeks favor by fawning over superiors.

[2] I.e., Young Women's Christian Association (Y.W.C.A.)

It is no wonder these young girls refuse to marry, refuse to rear children. They are like certain savage tribes, who, when they have been conquered, refuse to breed.

REVIEW QUESTIONS

1. In Meridel Le Sueur's opinion, what kinds of women had the best chance to overcome financial difficulties?

2. Why were most of the women she observed unemployed?

3. How did the activities of poor men differ from those of poor women?

Two Views of the Great Depression (1932)

For those already living at barely a subsistence level, the onset of the Great Depression had an impact different from its effect on those enjoying affluence. The following accounts convey the difficulties of surviving the economic downturn. The first interview is with a retired black worker named Clifford Burke, living in Chicago. The second is the recollection of Jane Yoder, whose immigrant father was a blacksmith in a small Illinois mining town. The Yoders had seven children. In 1929 the mines closed down, and her father was forced to move from town to town in search of work. Take note of their references to New Deal programs, such as the Works Progress Administration, intended to relieve the distress of prolonged unemployment by providing government jobs.

From Studs Terkel, "Two Views of the Great Depression," *Hard Times*, pp. 82–83. Reprinted by permission of Donadio & Olson, Inc. Copyright 1970 Studs Terkel.

A Black Man's Perspective

The Negro was born in depression. It didn't mean too much to him, The Great American Depression, as you call it. There was no such thing. The best he could be is a janitor or a porter or a shoeshine boy. It only became official when it hit the white man. If you can tell me the difference between the depression today and the Depression of 1932 for a black man, I'd like to know it. Now, it's worse, because of the prices. Know the rents they're payin' out here? I hate to tell ya. . . .

We had one big advantage. Our wives, they could go to the store and get a bag of beans or a sack of flour and a piece of fat meat, and they could cook this. And we could eat it. Steak? A steak would kick in my stomach like a mule in a tin stable. Now you take the white fella, he couldn't do this. His wife would tell him: Look, if you can't do any better than this, I'm gonna leave you. I seen it happen. He couldn't stand bringing home beans instead of steak and capon. And he couldn't stand the idea of going on relief like a Negro.

You take a fella had a job paying him $60, and here I am making $25. If I go home taking beans to my wife, we'll eat it. It isn't exactly what we want, but we'll eat it. The white man that's making big money, he's taking beans home, his wife'll say: Get out. (Laughs.)

Why did these big wheels kill themselves? They weren't able to live up to the standards they were accustomed to, and they got ashamed in front of their women. You see, you can tell anybody a lie, and he'll agree with you. But you start layin' down the facts of real life, he won't accept it. The American white man has been superior so long, he can't figure out why he should come down.

I remember a friend of mine, he didn't know he was a Negro. I mean he acted like he never knew it. He got tied downtown with some stock. He blew about twenty thousand. He came home and drank a bottle of poison. A bottle of iodine or something like that. It was a rarity to hear a Negro killing himself over a financial situation. He might have killed himself over some woman. Or getting in a fight. But when it came to the financial end of it, there were so few who had anything. (Laughs).

I made out during that . . . *Great* Depression. (Laughs.) Worked as a teamster for a lumber yard. Forty cents an hour. Monday we'd have a little work. They'd say come back Friday. There wasn't no need to look for another job. The few people working, most all of them were white.

So I had another little hustle. I used to play pool pretty good. And I'd ride from poolroom to poolroom on this bicycle. I used to beat these guys, gamble what we had. I'd leave home with a dollar. First couple of games I could beat this guy, I'd put that money in my pocket. I'd take the rest of what I beat him out of and hustle the day on that. Sometimes I'd come home with a dollar and a half extra. That was a whole lot of money. Everybody was out trying to beat the other guy, so he could make it. It was pathetic.

I never applied to the PWA (Public Works Administration) or WPA (Works Progress Administration), 'cause as long as I could hustle, there was no point in beating the other fellow out of a job, cuttin' some other guy out.

A Woman's Account

We were struggling, just desperate to be warm. No blankets, no coats. At this time I was in fourth grade. Katie[1] went to Chicago and bought an Indian blanket coat. . . .

Before that I had one coat. It must have been a terrible lightweight coat or what, but I can remember being cold, just shivering. And came home, and nothing to do but go to bed, then you put the coat on the bed and you got warm.

The cold that I've known. I never had boots. I think when I got married, I had my first set of boots. In rainy weather, you just ran for it, you ran between the raindrops or whatever. This was luxuriating to have boots. You simply wore your old shoes if it was raining. Save the others. You always polished them and put shoe trees in them. You didn't have unlimited shoe trees, either. When the shoes were worn out, they're used around the house. And of the high heels, you cut the heels down and they're more comfortable. . . .

If we had a cold or we threw up, nobody ever took your temperature. We had no thermometer. But if you threw up and were hot, my mother felt your head. She somehow felt that by bringing you oranges and bananas and these things you never had—there's nothing wrong with you, this is what she'd always say in Croatian; you'll be all right. Then she gave you all these good things. Oh, gee, you almost looked forward to the day you could throw up. I could remember dreaming about oranges and bananas, dreaming about them. . . .

I can think of the WPA . . . my father got immediately employed in this WPA. This was a godsend. This was the greatest thing. It meant food, you know. Survival, just survival.

How stark it was for me to come into nurses' training and have the girls . . . give their impressions of the WPA. How it struck me. Before I could ever say that my father was employed in the WPA, discussions in the bull sessions in our rooms immediately was: these lazy people, the shovel lean-

---

[1] An older sister.

ers. I'd just sit there and listen to them. I'd look around and realize: sure, Susan Stewart was talking this way, but her father was a doctor, and her mother was a nurse. Well, how nice. They had respectable employment. In my family, there was no respectable employment. I thought, you don't know what it's like.

How can I defend them? I was never a person who could control this. It just had to come out or I think I'd just blow up. So I would say, "I wonder how much we know until we go through it. Just like the patients we take care of. None of them are in the hospital by choice." I would relate it in abstractions. I think it saved me from just blowing up.

I would come back after that and I'd just say: Gee, these are just two separate, separate worlds.

REVIEW QUESTIONS

1. What did Burke mean when he asserted that the "Negro was born in depression"?
2. Why did Burke feel so many whites committed suicide as a result of the economic collapse? What stereotypes did he hold about whites?
3. Describe some of the hardships that Yoder endured as a child. What did she consider to be luxuries that many people now take for granted?
4. What seemed to cause the differences in opinion regarding government relief programs?

28 ❧ NEW DEAL AMERICA

During the 1932 election campaign, Democrat Franklin D. Roosevelt promised the American people a "new deal" and "bold persistent experimentation" to help pull the nation out of the Great Depression. His charismatic personality and infectious energy struck a resonant chord. Roosevelt bested Herbert Hoover in a landslide, and he brought with him large Democratic majorities in both houses of Congress. On 4 March 1933, millions of Americans huddled around their radios to hear Roosevelt deliver his inaugural address. He promised them immediate action—and he delivered. No sooner did the former New York governor move into the White House than he began making an unprecedented series of executive decisions and signing new legislation that served to transform the very nature of the federal government.

During the "First Hundred Days" of his presidency, Roosevelt and the Democratic Congress repealed the Eighteenth Amendment, ending the thirteen-year experiment with prohibition of alcoholic beverages, intervened to shore up the banking industry, drafted new regulations for the stock market, and created an array of new federal agencies and programs designed to reopen factories, raise farm prices, put people back to work, conserve natural resources, and relieve the distress created by chronic unemployment.

The flurry of governmental activity and Roosevelt's uplifting rhetoric helped restore hope to many among the desperate and destitute, but the depression persisted. The honeymoon of expectation that Roosevelt enjoyed immediately after his election gave way to strident criticism from both ends of the political spectrum. Conservatives accused him of assaulting the freedoms undergirding capitalism. In 1934 disgruntled conservative Democrats formed the American Liberty League to organize opposition to Roosevelt's "socialistic" programs. Roosevelt denounced the Liberty League as a group of "economic royalists" indifferent to the misery of the masses. "I welcome their hatred," he declared.

Other critics lambasted Roosevelt for not doing enough to help the poor and unemployed. The desperate economic conditions gave new life to the Socialist and Communist parties, both of which had fielded candidates in the 1932 presidential election. Many prominent writers, artists, and academics gravitated to the radical Left, and several labor unions began to witness the effects of communist agitators.

The volatile social tensions of the 1930s also helped spawn a diverse array of "neo-populist" demagogues. The most prominent of these independent operators was Democratic Senator Huey P. Long of Louisiana. In late 1934 he launched his "Share Our Wealth" program as an alternative to the New Deal. Using rabble-rousing techniques that he had refined as governor, Long called for a 100 percent tax on all personal income over $1 million and all fortunes over $5 million. He promised to use the revenue from these new taxes to provide every American with a home, a car, retirement benefits, and free educational opportunities. By 1935 Long boasted almost 8 million followers around the country and was preparing to launch a challenge to Roosevelt's reelection. In September, however, he was gunned down in Louisiana by the relative of a disgruntled political opponent.

Another landslide victory in 1936 emboldened Roosevelt to broaden the scope of his New Deal initiatives. He launched new programs for the unemployed, created the first minimum wage, reorganized the executive branch, and began urban redevelopment programs that included public housing for the homeless. Still, millions of Americans continued to live in squalor, especially in the rural South, where tenants and sharecroppers rarely benefited from the new government programs. By 1938, amid a new recession, the momentum of the New Deal began to wane. Roosevelt had expended most of his creativity and political capital. In the November congressional elections, the Republicans made deep inroads into the Democratic majorities in both houses. Foreign crises began to distract the attention of the administration and the nation, and Roosevelt began to focus on international diplomacy and military preparedness.

Even more so than her husband, Eleanor Roosevelt understood the human impact of the depression, and she used her platform as First Lady to minister to the needs of the destitute and to reach out to disadvantaged minorities. She broke precedent to hold her own weekly press conferences, traveled throughout the country to meet with people of all walks of life, gave numerous lectures and radio addresses, and expressed her candid opinions in a daily syndicated newspaper column entitled "My Day." In the process of such ceaseless agitation, Eleanor Roosevelt became a beloved symbol of the New Deal's concern for common folk and their daily distress.

FRANKLIN D. ROOSEVELT

First Inaugural Address (1933)

As Roosevelt took office the nation faced a banking crisis as well as a deepening depression. He had yet to formulate the specific programs that would comprise the New Deal, but he knew that the nation expected quick action and bold leadership. In his inaugural address he sought to provide both.

From "Text of the Inaugural Address: President for Vigorous Action," *The New York Times,* 5 March 1933.

This is a day of national consecration, and I am certain that my fellow Americans expect that on my induction into the Presidency I will address them with a candor and a decision which the present situation of our Nation impels.

This is pre-eminently the time to speak the truth, the whole truth, frankly and boldly. Nor need we shrink from honestly facing conditions in our country today. This great nation will endure as it has endured, will revive and will prosper.

So first of all let me assert my firm belief that the only thing we have to fear is fear itself— nameless, unreasoning, unjustified terror which paralyzes needed efforts to convert retreat into advance.

In every dark hour of our national life a leadership of frankness and vigor has met with that understanding and support of the people themselves which is essential to victory. I am convinced that you will again give the support to leadership in these critical days.

In such a spirit on my part and on yours we face our common difficulties. They concern, thank God, only material things. Values have shrunken to fantastic levels; taxes have risen; our ability to pay has fallen; government of all kinds is faced by serious curtailment of income; the means of exchange are frozen in the currents of trade; the withered leaves of industrial enterprise lie on every side; farmers find no markets for their produce; the savings of many years in thousands of families are gone.

More important, a host of unemployed citizens face the grim problem of existence, and an equally great number toil with little return. Only a foolish optimist can deny the dark realities of the moment.

Yet our distress comes from no failure of substance. We are stricken by no plague of locusts. Compared with the perils which our forefathers conquered because they believed and were not afraid, we have still much to be thankful for. Nature still offers her bounty and human efforts have multiplied it. Plenty is at our doorsteps, but a generous use of it languishes in the very sight of the supply. Primarily this is because the rulers of the exchange of mankind's goods have failed, through their own stubbornness and their own incompetence, have admitted their failure, and abdicated. Practices of the unscrupulous money changers stand indicted in the court of public opinion, rejected by the hearts and minds of men. . . .

Our greatest primary task is to put people to work. This is no unsolvable problem if we face it wisely and courageously.

It can be accomplished in part by direct recruiting by the Government itself, treating the task as we would treat the emergency of a war, but at the same time, through this employment, accomplishing greatly needed projects to stimulate and reorganize the use of our natural resources.

Hand in hand with this we must frankly recognize the overbalance of population in our industrial centers and, by engaging on a national scale in a redistribution, endeavor to provide a better use of the land for those best fitted for the land.

The task can be helped by definite efforts to raise the values of agricultural products and with this the power to purchase the output of our cities.

It can be helped by preventing realistically the tragedy of the growing loss through foreclosure of our small homes and our farms.

It can be helped by insistence that the Federal, State, and local governments act forthwith on the demand that their cost be drastically reduced. It can be helped by the unifying of relief activities which to-day are often scattered, uneconomical, and unequal. It can be helped by national planning for and supervision of all forms of transportation and of communications and other utilities which have a definitely public character.

There are many ways in which it can be helped, but it can never be helped merely by talking about it. We must act and act quickly.

Finally, in our progress toward a resumption of work we require two safeguards against a return of the evils of the old order; there must be a strict supervision of all banking and credits and investments; there must be an end to speculation with other people's money, and there must be provision for an adequate but sound currency.

There are the lines of attack. I shall presently urge upon a new Congress in special session detailed measures for their fulfillment, and I shall seek the immediate assistance of the several States.

Through this program of action we address ourselves to putting our own national house in order and making income balance outgo. . . .

In the field of world policy I would dedicate this Nation to the policy of the good neighbor— the neighbor who resolutely respects himself and, because he does so, respects the rights of others— the neighbor who respects his obligations and respects the sanctity of his agreements in and with a world of neighbors.

If I read the temper of our people correctly, we now realize as we have never realized before our interdependence on each other; that we can not merely take but we must give as well; that if we are to go forward, we must move as a trained

and loyal army willing to sacrifice for the good of a common discipline, because without such discipline no progress is made, no leadership becomes effective.

We are, I know, ready and willing to submit our lives and property to such discipline, because it makes possible a leadership which aims at a larger good. This I propose to offer, pledging that the larger purposes will bind upon us all as a sacred obligation with a unity of duty hitherto evoked only in time of armed strife.

With this pledge taken, I assume unhesitatingly the leadership of this great army of our people dedicated to a disciplined attack upon our common problems.

Action in this image and to this end is feasible under the form of government which we have inherited from our ancestors. Our Constitution is so simple and practical that it is possible always to meet extraordinary needs by changes in emphasis and arrangement without loss of essential form. That is why our constitutional system has proved itself the most superbly enduring political mechanism the modern world has produced. It has met every stress of vast expansion of territory, of foreign wars, of bitter internal strife, of world relations.

It is to be hoped that the normal balance of executive and legislative authority may be wholly adequate to meet the unprecedented task before us. But it may be that an unprecedented demand and need for undelayed action may call for temporary departure from that normal balance of public procedure.

I am prepared under my constitutional duty to recommend the measures that a stricken nation in the midst of a stricken world may require. These measures, or such other measures as the Congress may build out of its experience and wisdom, I shall seek, within my constitutional authority, to bring to speedy adoption.

But in the event that the congress shall fail to take one of these two courses, and in the event that the national emergency is still critical, I shall not evade the clear course of duty that will then confront me. I shall ask the congress for the one remaining instrument to meet the crisis—broad Executive power to wage a war against the emergency, as great as the power that would be given to me if we were in fact invaded by a foreign foe.

For the trust reposed in me I will return the courage and the devotion that befit the time. I can do no less.

We face the arduous days that lie before us in the warm courage of national unity; with the clear consciousness of seeking old and precious moral values; with the clean satisfaction that comes from the stern performance of duty by young and old alike. . . .

In this dedication of a nation we humbly ask the blessing of God. May He protect each and every one of us! May He guide me in the days to come!

REVIEW QUESTIONS

1. What measures did Roosevelt pledge to put before the Congress?
2. How was Roosevelt prepared to govern if Congress blocked his initiatives?
3. Give examples of Roosevelt's efforts to bolster morale and instill hope among the public.

Letters to the Roosevelts during the Depression

As the human consequences of the prolonged depression unfolded, people grew desperate. Many of them looked to Franklin and Eleanor Roosevelt for help. Indeed, the Roosevelts received over 15 million letters from struggling Americans. Two such letters are excerpted below.

Goff, Kansas
May 10, 1935
Mrs. Franklin D. Roosevelt:
My Dear Friend:

For the first time of my lifetime I am asking a favor and this one I am needing very badly and I am coming to you for help.

Among your friends do you know of one who is discarding a spring coat for a new one. If so could you beg the old one for me. I wear a size 40 to 42 I have not had a spring coat for six years and last Sunday when getting ready to go to church I see my winter coat had several very thin places in the back that is very noticeable My clothes are very plain so I could wear only something plain. we were hit very hard by the drought and every penny we can save goes for feed to put in crop.

Hoping for a favorable reply.

Your friend Mrs. J. T.

Mr. and Mrs. Roosevelt
Wash. D.C.
February 1936

Dear Mr. President,

I am a boy of 12 years. I want to tell you about my family. My father hasn't worked for 5 months. He went plenty times to relief, he filed out application. They won't give us anything. I don't know why. Please you do something. We haven't paid 4 months rent, Everyday the landlord rings the bell, we don't open the door for him. We are afraid that will be put out, been put out before, and don't want to happen again. We haven't paid the gas bill, and the electric bill, haven't paid grocery bill for 3 months. My bother goes to Lane Tech. High School. He's eighteen years old, hasn't gone to school for 2 weeks because he got no carfare. I have a sister she's twenty years, she can't find work. My father he staying home. All the time he's crying because he can't find work. I told him why are you crying daddy, and daddy said why shouldn't I cry when there is nothing in the house. I feel sorry for him. That night I couldn't sleep. The next morning I wrote this letter to you. in my room. Were American citizens and were born in Chicago, Ill. and I

don't know why they don't help us Please answer right away because we need it. Will starve. Thank you.

God bless you.

[Anonymous]
Chicago, Ill.

REVIEW QUESTIONS

1. In the first letter what was the source of the writer's economic difficulties?
2. How did the economic circumstance of the second writer differ from the first?
3. What did the letters imply about attitudes toward the office of the presidency? toward the Roosevelts?

REINHOLD NIEBUHR

Communist Efforts to Organize a Steel Union (1936)

The crisis of the Great Depression provided a surge of momentum for the Communist Party in the United States (CPUSA). In the midst of labor strife, communists sought to penetrate the trade unions and convert them to their ideology. The following letter from a communist agitator outlines some of their tactics.

From Max Gordan, "The Communists and the Drive to Organize Steel, 1936," in *Labor History* 23 (Spring 1982):260–265.

Youngstown, Ohio
August 31, 1936

Dear Comrade Stachel:

. . . The drive[1] in the Youngstown steel district like throughout the country has not yet assumed a mass character. However, this does not express the real sentiment of the steel workers, meeting hundreds of them every week, both American and foreign-born, I have yet to find one case of real

hostility towards the union. On the contrary, I am met with open arms and the steel workers are keenly interested in the drive and are anxiously hoping to see the drive go over big. I am absolutely convinced that the greatest majority of the steel workers will join the union in the next few months to come.

Why then is there this great discrepancy between the favorable sentiment and the actual growth of the union? The way I see it, these are some of the reasons:

---

[1] I.e., to organize a union.

1. The open warning of the companies to fire the men who join the union, still constitute the greatest obstacle. Although we can already observe a definite break down of this fear.

2. Many old foreign-born workers are still bitter against the American steel workers who didn't back them in the 1919 strike and want to see the Americans come in first.

3. The self-satisfaction of the SWOC[2] on the top with the progress of the drive. This results in a failure to press the field organizers to produce better results. . . . These people on the top (SWOC) also picture the steel drive as a mere series of mass meetings and a mechanical signing up of members without developing any partial struggles and obtain certain initial victories for the workers, without necessarily calling local strikes. . . .

4. The work of the organizers, especially the UMWA[3] organizers, is perhaps one of the weakest links in the whole drive. . . .

This is so important a question that I therefore must deal with it in detail. The organizers' staff in Youngstown can be divided into two categories: The UMWA organizers and the Party forces. There is a vast difference between the two. It is amazing how people can be so long in the labor movement and know so little! Not only are they political babies, they are not even good union organizers. . . . Our forces that are on the staff are the best organizers and produce more results than any of them. I, personally, have established myself as the best recruiter and on the average I recruit close to fifty percent of the total recruits. Our youth organizer and the other comrades are also doing fine. . . .

*   *   *

A few words on the method of recruiting. Of course we are using Comrade Foster's[4] three point theory of organization as our starting point. On the basis of this theory, I have developed a method which has been proven and tested to be the best and the whole crew in Youngstown is now practicing it. I call it the "chain form of recruiting." In brief, it works like this—when I sign up a worker, I ask him to recommend three or five other men from his department. Then I ask him to talk to these workers in the mill and prepare the ground for me. Then two days later I visit these workers, most of them already expect me and when I come to their house and present my credential, they already know who I am and I find no difficulty in signing them up. These men in turn recommend others and the chain is endless. Right now, for example, over a hundred workers are expecting me at their homes. This week, every house that I went to, as soon as I present my credential, the reply was, "Come in, I have been waiting for you." My list is already so big that another organizer will be attached to me so that the workers will not be kept waiting too long. Those organizers that begun to practice this chain form of organizing are also meeting with similar success. . . .

While it is absolutely correct to discourage local strikes at this stage of the game and even be on guard against any strikes that may be contemplated by the steel companies, yet, the union must already begin to develop certain partial struggles that will result in some immediate victories for the workers. These can be developed through progressive company union representatives, through committees and petitions. The companies are terribly nervous and it is possible to obtain all kinds of concessions that in turn will help to build the union. It is unfortunate that the SWOC don't realize the importance of such actions. Then, there is another aspect to the same problem: when a worker joins the union he expects some kind of help and if this is not forthcoming he will fall for the company propaganda of "Why pay dues?" I think that our forces on the staff should raise this question everywhere and bring it to the attention of the CIO. . . .

Present Policies of Steel Corporations

Our secret method of recruiting and organization created a very difficult situation for the companies. They are really not aware of the degree of progress we have made so far. The decentralized form of or-

---

[2] Steel Worker Organizing Committee.

[3] United Mine Workers of America.

[4] William Z. Foster (1881–1961).

ganization is an additional obstacle to them. However, we know that they are careful in firing union men. Sixteen of our people were uncovered . . . including many of our comrades. But so far only the YCL[5] organizer was fired out of the Sheet & Tube. All the others were called in, warned but not yet fired.

Through a friendly federal man we have also learned that the companies have brought in a lot of ammunition inside the mills. Sheet & Tube has deputized 151 men, Republic 50 men. We have also learned that when the first public meeting is held, they will provoke a fight and open a barrage of tear gas.

Meanwhile, they are publishing every Sunday a full page ad. I will send you a sample of this Sunday ad. They are also circulating a petition among wives of steel workers against the CIO. The spies continue to shadow the organizers and all our wires are tapped. Recently I moved to a new house hoping to keep it secret, several days later two cars with the stool pigeons were in front early in the morning. I figure it is no use to move again, I have arranged for another sleeping place in case of emergencies. I have also learned from the same source that they are especially out to get us and to link us up with the CIO and then make a big splash in the papers. We are now expecting it to break soon and we are prepared for it. . . .

On the Party

. . . The functioning of the Party is very unsatisfactory. . . . At present I devote all my time to the drive. However, as soon as I personally recruit 500 into the union (I have already reached the 200 mark) and the other comrades recruit another 500 steel workers, it will no longer be necessary for me to devote my time on individual recruiting and I will have more time for direct Party work. However, I have already established dozens of splendid contacts for the Party. I look forward that within six months from now the bulk of the Party will be composed of powerful nuclei inside the mills. We have already made a start by recruiting one of the organizers into the Party. . . . I am now working on several other leading people in the drive and I am sure we will soon have them in the Party.

The Party comrades inside the mills are doing splendid work and they are coming forward very nicely. Up to now the active comrades were busy with putting the Party on the ballot, now we're through with this work, we will get busy on stabilizing the units and involve our Party forces in the steel drive. . . .

Comradely yours,
Steuben

REVIEW QUESTIONS

1. Describe "chain recruiting." What might have been its advantages and disadvantages?
2. Why did communist recruiters work in secrecy? Did this help or hurt them? Explain.
3. According to this account, did the activities of the communists represent a threat to American democracy? Why or why not?

---

[5] Young Communist League.

HUEY LONG

Share Our Wealth (1935)

Huey Long cemented his control as governor of Louisiana by using state power and state funds to improve social services; to build roads, bridges, and schools; and to reform tax codes. In 1932 he was elected to the U.S. Senate. Initially he supported Roosevelt's New Deal measures, but by 1935 he had broken with the president and launched his own "Share Our Wealth" movement as an alternative to the New Deal. He developed a large grassroots following across the country before being assassinated in 1935.

From *Congressional Record*, 74th Cong., 1st sess., 7 May 1935, pp. 7049–7050.

. . . Here is what we stand for in a nutshell:

1. We propose that every family in America shall at least own a homestead equal in value to not less than one-third the average family wealth. The average family wealth of America, at normal values, is approximately $16,000. So our first proposition means that every family shall have a home and the comforts of a home up to a value of not less than $5,000.

2. We propose that no family shall own more than 300 times the average family wealth, which means that no family shall possess more than a wealth of $5,000,000. And we think that is too much. The two propositions together mean that no family shall own less than one-third of the average family wealth, nor shall any family own more than 300 times the average family wealth. That is to say that none should be so poor as to have less than one-third of the average, and none should be so rich as to have more than 300 times the average.

3. We next propose that every family shall have an income equal to at least one-third of the average family income in America. If all were allowed to work, according to our statistics, there would be an average family income of from $5,000 to $10,000 per year. So, therefore, in addition to the home which every family would own and the comforts of life which every family would enjoy,

every family would make not less than $2,000 to $3,000 per year upon which to live and educate their children.

4. We propose that no family shall have an income of more than 300 times the average family income. Less the income taxes, this would mean an annual income of $1,000,000 would be the maximum allowed any one family in 1 year. The third and fourth propositions simply mean that no family should earn less than one-third the average, and no family should earn more than 300 times the average; none to make too much, none to make too little. Everyone to have the things required for life; every man a king.

5. We propose a pension to the old people. Under our proposal taxes would not be levied upon the sons and daughters, nor the working people to support their aged fathers and mothers. But on the contrary, such support as would be given for old-age pensions would be borne solely by the surplus money which the Government would rake off the big fortunes and big inheritances.

6. We propose to care for the veterans of our wars, including the immediate cash payment of the soldiers' bonus, and last, but not least, we propose that every child in America have a right to education and training, not only through grammar and high school, but also through colleges and univer-

sities. And this education and training would be of such extent as will equip each child to battle on fair terms in the work which it is compelled to perform throughout life. We would not have it that a child could go to college or university provided his parents had the money on which to send him, but it would be the right of every child under our plan to the costs, including living expenses of college and university training, which could be done by our country at a cost considerably less than is required for the military training which has been given our youth in the past. . . .

Let no one tell you that it is difficult to redistribute the wealth of this land; it matters not how rich or great one may be, when he dies his wealth must be redistributed anyway. The law of God shows how it has been throughout time. Nothing is more sensible or better understood than the redistribution of property. The laws of God command it. It is required of all nations that live. . . .

So let us be about our work. It is simple. Why lie ye here idle? There is enough for all. Let there be peace in the land. Let our children be happy. . . .

How wonderful, how great, how fruitful to all this great land of ours can be. We only have to eliminate useless greed, provide that none shall be too big and none too small. Beautiful America can rise to the opportunity before it. It means to us all:

Every man a king.

REVIEW QUESTIONS

1. What did the "Share Our Wealth" program seek to accomplish with regard to personal incomes?
2. Where did Long propose to find the revenue to fund his proposed programs? How realistic was this notion?
3. How accurate were those who charged that Long's program represented an American version of socialism?

Republican Party Platform (1936)

By 1936 Roosevelt's sweeping New Deal legislation had provoked spirited criticism across the country. The Republican Party platform of 1936 encapsulates many of the conservative complaints.

From Donald Bruce Johnson and Kirk H. Porter, eds., *National Party Platforms, 1840–1972* (Urbana: University of Illinois Press, 1973), pp. 365–370.

America is in peril. The welfare of American men and women and the future of our youth are at stake. We dedicate ourselves to the preservation of their political liberty, their individual opportunity and their character as free citizens, which today for the first time are threatened by Government itself.

For three long years the New Deal Administration has dishonored American traditions and flagrantly betrayed the pledges upon which the Democratic Party sought and received public support.

The powers of Congress have been usurped by the President.

The integrity and authority of the Supreme Court have been flouted.

The rights and liberties of American citizens have been violated.

Regulated monopoly has displaced free enterprise.

The New Deal Administration constantly seeks to usurp the rights reserved to the States and to the people.

It has insisted on the passage of laws contrary to the Constitution.

It has intimidated witnesses and interfered with the right of petition.

It has dishonored our country by repudiating its most sacred obligations.

It has been guilty of frightful waste and extravagance, using public funds for partisan political purposes.

It has promoted investigations to harass and intimidate American citizens, at the same time denying investigations into its own improper expenditures.

It has created a vast multitude of new offices, filled them with its favorites, set up a centralized bureaucracy, and sent out swarms of inspectors to harass our people.

It has bred fear and hesitation in commerce and industry, thus discouraging new enterprises, preventing employment and prolonging the depression.

It secretly has made tariff agreements with our foreign competitors, flooding our markets with foreign commodities.

It has coerced and intimidated voters by withholding relief from those opposing its tyrannical policies.

It has destroyed the morale of many of our people and made them dependent upon Government.

Appeals to passion and class prejudice have replaced reason and tolerance.

To a free people these actions are insufferable. This campaign cannot be waged on the traditional differences between the Republican and Democratic parties. The responsibility of this election transcends all previous political divisions. We invite all Americans, irrespective of party, to join us in defense of American institutions.

Constitutional Government and Free Enterprise

We Pledge Ourselves:

1. To maintain the American system of constitutional and local self government, and to resist all attempts to impair the authority of the Supreme Court of the United States, the final protector of the rights of our citizens against the arbitrary encroachments of the legislative and executive branches of Government. There can be no individual liberty without an independent judiciary.
2. To preserve the American system of free enterprise, private competition, and equality of opportunity, and to seek its constant betterment in the interests of all.

Reemployment

The only permanent solution of the unemployment problem is the absorption of the unemployed by industry and agriculture. To that end, we advocate:

Removal of restrictions on production.

Abandonment of all New Deal policies that raise production costs, increase the cost of living, and thereby restrict buying, reduce volume and prevent reemployment.

Encouragement instead of hindrance to legitimate business.

Withdrawal of Government from competition with private payrolls.

Elimination of unnecessary and hampering regulations.

Adoption of such policies as will furnish a chance for individual enterprise, industrial expansion, and the restoration of jobs.

Relief

The necessities of life must be provided for the needy, and hope must be restored pending recovery. The administration of relief is a major failure of the New Deal. It has been faithless to those who most deserve our sympathy. To end confusion, partisanship, waste and incompetence,

We Pledge:

1. The return of responsibility for relief administration to non-political local agencies familiar with community problems.
2. Federal grants-in-aid to the States and Territories while the need exists, upon compliance with these conditions: (a) a fair proportion of the total relief burden to be provided from the revenues of States and local governments; (b) all engaged in relief administration to be selected on the basis of merit and fitness; (c) adequate provision to be made for the encouragement of those persons who are trying to become self-supporting.
3. Undertaking of Federal public works only on their merits and separate from the administration of relief.
4. A prompt determination of the facts concerning relief and unemployment.

Security

Real security will be possible only when our productive capacity is sufficient to furnish a decent standard of living for all American families and to provide a surplus for future needs and contingencies. For the attainment of that ultimate objective, we look to the energy, self-reliance and character of our people, and to our system of free enterprise.

Society has an obligation to promote the security of the people, by affording some measure of protection against involuntary unemployment and dependency in old age. The New Deal policies, while purporting to provide social security, have, in fact, endangered it.

We propose a system of old age security, . . .

We propose to encourage adoption by the

States and Territories of honest and practical measures for meeting the problems of unemployment insurance.

The unemployment insurance and old age annuity sections of the present Social Security Act are unworkable and deny benefits to about two-thirds of our adult population, including professional men and women and all those engaged in agriculture and domestic service, and the self employed, while imposing heavy tax burdens upon all. The so-called reserve fund estimated at forty-seven billion dollars for old age insurance is no reserve at all, because the fund will contain nothing but the Government's promise to pay, while the taxes collected in the guise of premiums will be wasted by the Government in reckless and extravagant political schemes.

Labor

The welfare of labor rests upon increased production and the prevention of exploitation. We pledge ourselves to:

Protect the right of labor to organize and to bargain collectively through representatives of its own choosing without interference from any source.

Prevent governmental job holders from exercising autocratic powers over labor.

Support the adoption of State laws and interstate compacts to abolish sweatshops and child labor, and to protect women and children with respect to maximum hours, minimum wages and working conditions. We believe that this can be done within the Constitution as it now stands.

Agriculture

The farm problem is an economic and social, not a partisan problem, and we propose to treat it accordingly. . . . Our paramount object is to protect and foster the family type of farm, traditional in American life, and to promote policies which will bring about an adjustment of agriculture to meet the needs of domestic and foreign markets. As an emergency measure, during the agricultural depression, Federal benefit payments or grants-in-aid when administered within the means of the Federal Government are consistent with a balanced budget.

We Propose:

1. To facilitate economical production and increased consumption on a basis of abundance instead of scarcity.
2. A national land-use program, including the acquisition of abandoned and non-productive farm lands by voluntary sale or lease, subject to approval of the legislative and executive branches of the States concerned, and the devotion of such land to appropriate public use, such as watershed protection and flood prevention, reforestation, recreation, and conservation of wild life.
3. That an agricultural policy be pursued for the protection and restoration of the land resources, designed to bring about such a balance between soil-building and soil-depleting crops as will permanently insure productivity, with reasonable benefits to co-operating farmers on family-type farms, but so regulated as to eliminate the New Deal's destructive policy towards the dairy and live-stock industries.
4. To extend experimental aid to farmers developing new crops suited to our soil and climate. . . .

Regulation of Business

We recognize the existence of a field within which governmental regulation is desirable and salutary. The authority to regulate should be vested in an independent tribunal acting under clear and specific laws establishing definite standards. Their determinations on law and facts should be subject to review by the Courts. We favor Federal regulation, within the Constitution, of the marketing of securities to protect investors. We favor also Federal regulation of the interstate activities of public utilities. . . .

Government Finance

The New Deal Administration has been characterized by shameful waste and general financial irresponsibility. It has piled deficit upon deficit. It threatens national bankruptcy and the destruction through inflation of insurance policies and savings bank deposits.

We Pledge Ourselves To:

Stop the folly of uncontrolled spending.

Balance the budget—not by increasing taxes but by cutting expenditures, drastically and immediately.

Revise the Federal tax system and coordinate it with State and local tax systems.

Use the taxing power for raising revenue and not for punitive or political purposes.

Money and Banking

We advocate a sound currency to be preserved at all hazards.

The first requisite to a sound and stable currency is a balanced budget.

We oppose further devaluation of the dollar.

We will restore to the Congress the authority lodged with it by the Constitution to coin money and regulate the value thereof by repealing all the laws delegating this authority to the Executive.

We will cooperate with other countries toward stabilization of currencies as soon as we can do so with due regard for our national interests and as soon as other nations have sufficient stability to justify such action.

Conclusion

We assume the obligations and duties imposed upon Government by modern conditions. We affirm our unalterable conviction that, in the future as in the past, the fate of the nation will depend, not so much on the wisdom and power of Government, as on the character and virtue, self-reliance, industry and thrift of the people and on their willingness to meet the responsibilities essential to the preservation of a free society.

Finally, as our party affirmed in its first Platform in 1856: "Believing that the spirit of our institutions as well as the Constitution of our country guarantees liberty of conscience and equality of rights among our citizens, we oppose all legislation tending to impair them," and "we invite the affiliation and cooperation of the men of all parties, however differing from us in other respects, in support of the principles herein declared."

The acceptance of the nomination tendered by this Convention carries with it, as a matter of private honor and public faith, an undertaking by each candidate to be true to the principles and program herein set forth.

REVIEW QUESTIONS

1. What were some of the accusations made by the Republicans against the New Deal?
2. What kinds of economic assistance did Republicans advocate for the disadvantaged? Did they differ from the New Deal initiatives?
3. Why do you think Republicans specifically targeted the New Deal in their rhetoric?

DOROTHY THOMPSON

Roosevelt's "Court-Packing" Plan (1937)

President Franklin Roosevelt's 1937 attempt to restructure the Supreme Court, which critics labeled his "court-packing plan," aroused intense opposition in Congress, even among Democrats. Dorothy Thompson, the distinguished journalist and one of the earliest enemies of Nazism, lambasted Roosevelt's efforts to reshape the Supreme Court.

If the American people accept this last audacity of the President without letting out a yell to high heaven, they have ceased to be jealous of their liberties and are ripe for ruin. This is the beginning of pure personal government. Do you want it? Do you like it? Look around about the world—there are plenty of examples—and make up your mind.

The Executive [President Roosevelt] is already powerful by reason of his overwhelming victory in November [1936], and will be strengthened even more if the reorganization plan for the administration, presented some weeks ago, is adopted. We have, to all intents and purposes, a one party Congress, dominated by the President. Although nearly 40 percent of the voters repudiated the New Deal at the polls, they have less than 20 percent representation in both houses of Congress. And now the Supreme Court is to have a majority determined by the President and by a Senate which he dominates. When that happens we will have a one-man Government. It will all be constitutional. So, he claims, is Herr [Adolf] Hitler.

Leave the personality and the intentions of the President out of the picture. They are not the crux of this issue. . . . He may have the liberties of the American people deeply at heart. But he will have a successor who may be none of these things. There have been benevolent dictatorships and benevolent tyrannies. They have even, at times in history, worked for the popular welfare. But that is not the welfare, which up to now, the American people have chosen.

And let us not be confused by the words "liberal" and "conservative" or misled into thinking that the expressed will of the majority is the essence of democracy. By that definition Hitler, Stalin and Mussolini are all great democratic leaders. The essence of democracy is the protection of minorities. Nor has a majority of this generation the right to mortgage a majority of the next. In the Constitution of the United States is incorporated the rights of the people, rights enjoyed by every American citizen in perpetuity, which cannot be voted away by any majority, ever. Majorities are temporary things. The Supreme Court is there to protect the fundamental law even against the momentary "will of the people." That is its function. And it is precisely because nine men can walk out and say: "You can't do that!" that our liberties are protected against the mob urge that occasionally the Court has been traditionally divorced from momentary majorities. . . .

This is no proposal to change the Constitution. This is no proposal to limit the powers of the Supreme Court. This is a proposal to capture the Supreme Court. . . .

Don't talk of liberalism! The liberal does not

believe that the end justifies the means. Long experience has taught him that the means usually determine the end. No human being can believe in the sincerity of this proposal. It is clever, in a world sick of cleverness and longing for plain talk and simple honesty. Must we begin to examine every message from the President to see whether there is a trick in it somewhere?

Are the opposition in Washington phonographs or are they men? If they are men we shall see another little "willful group." They are a handful, but they can do one thing: They can see that this measure is not rushed through without debate, they can see to it that the country has time to think about this, to talk about it, to debate it on every forum platform, to act upon it, individually and in groups, regardless of party.

REVIEW QUESTIONS

1. Do you agree with Thompson that Roosevelt's attempt to restructure the Supreme Court resembled fascism? Explain.
2. Do you agree that the "essence of democracy is the protection of minorities"? Why or why not?

29 ∾ FROM ISOLATION TO GLOBAL WAR

In the aftermath of World War I many Americans sought to distance the United States from further international involvement and commitments. The American refusal to join the League of Nations signaled a return to the isolationist sentiment that had governed the nation's foreign policy during the nineteenth century. Woodrow Wilson's liberal internationalism was deemed bankrupt by his Republican opponents. "We seek no part in directing the destiny of the world," President Warren G. Harding announced in 1924.

Yet in reality the United States could no longer isolate itself from world affairs. The nation's economy and its interests were now global in nature. Indeed, the proportion of total international exports belonging to the United States steadily increased throughout the interwar period. American investments abroad increased sevenfold during the 1920s, and the rapidly industrializing American economy grew dependent on raw materials imported from abroad.

The history of American foreign relations between 1920 and the mid-1930s thus seems paradoxical in hindsight: at the same time that the United States was becoming more dependent on international trade, its statesmen were disdaining the use of force in international affairs to ensure free trade. They instead placed their faith in democratic principles and international treaties to preserve the peace and protect American economic interests abroad.

U.S. diplomats in the 1920s believed that a global arms race threatened both international stability and free trade. They therefore advocated a series of multinational arms limitations agreements. Such goals led the United States to convene the Washington Naval Conference in 1921–1922. It produced a series of agreements limiting warships and armaments, reaffirming the principles of free trade and the "Open Door" in China, and creating a diplomatic mechanism for dealing with international crises. In theory the American role in negotiating these treaties was a great diplomatic success. Each major power accepted some reductions in its navy, but there was no way to enforce the treaties when violated.

"While armed conflict has cooled off," the Japanese prime minister observed, "economic competition is becoming more and more intense."

The capstone of this reliance on international agreements to preserve world peace was the Kellogg-Briand Pact of 1928 (also known as the Pact of Paris). The French foreign minister, Aristide Briand, proposed that the United States and France sign a treaty disavowing war as a method of settling disputes between the two countries. The American secretary of state, Frank Kellogg, embraced the concept but insisted that it be a multilateral pact. The two diplomats then convinced Great Britain, Japan, Italy, Belgium, Poland, Germany, Czechoslovakia, and six other countries to join them in signing the treaty. The U.S. Senate ratified it in 1929.

The Kellogg-Briand Pact condemned "recourse to war" and renounced it "as an instrument of national policy." The fifteen nations agreed "that the settlement or solution of all disputes or conflicts . . . shall never be sought except by pacific means." But the authors of the pact refused to recognize that it was not treaties or idealistic rhetoric that sustained world peace but individual national interests mediated by the balance of power—a mechanism that would require the timely use of force to ensure its survival. One critic dismissed the treaty as a hollow cluster of pious phrases representing nothing more than "an international kiss."

The inability of the Kellogg-Briand Pact to maintain global peace was vividly revealed in the world's response to the Japanese invasion of Manchuria in 1931. In direct violation of both the Nine-Power Treaty signed at Washington in 1922 and the Kellogg-Briand Pact, the Japanese army took control of the northeastern Chinese province and set up their own puppet state of Manchukuo. When China turned to the League of Nations for assistance, it received nothing but rhetorical support. President Hoover and Secretary of State Henry L. Stimson condemned the Japanese actions and refused to recognize the new regime in Manchukuo. The Japanese paid no attention and consolidated their control over Chinese territory.

The unwillingness of Europe and the United States to use economic or military force against Japan mirrored their response to aggression by Nazi Germany and Fascist Italy during the 1930s. Preoccupied with the ravages of the Great Depression and paralyzed by the prospect of another world war, the Western democracies proved unable or unwilling to act collectively against Japanese expansionism in East Asia, German militancy in Europe, and Italian aggression in North Africa.

In 1935 Adolf Hitler defied the provisions of the Versailles Treaty and announced the rearming of the German military. The following year German troops occupied the Rhineland. Such rising international tensions ignited a surge of isolationist activity in the United States. Whatever the provocation, whatever the strategic interests, isolationist leaders insisted there was no excuse for American involvement in another world war.

Congress responded to public pressure by passing a "neutrality act" in 1935 that was intended to prevent the munitions industry and other interests from *leading the nation into another war. The Neutrality Act of 1935 gave the president authority to prohibit American ships from carrying weapons and munitions to nations involved in war. It also deprived government protection to Americans who traveled on belligerent vessels, and it imposed an embargo on loans and arms shipments to countries at war. All of this was intended to avoid drawing the United States into a European war, as isolationists believed had happened in 1917. President Roosevelt reluctantly signed the measure, noting that its "inflexible provisions . . . might have exactly the opposite effect from that which is intended."*

As Roosevelt feared the pace of events in Europe and Asia quickly put the neutrality legislation to the test. In the fall of 1935 Benito Mussolini's Italian troops invaded Ethiopia. In July 1936 civil war erupted in Spain as fascists led by General Francisco Franco and aided by Hitler and Mussolini sought to overthrow the democratic government. A year later the Japanese provoked an incident with the Chinese at the Marco Polo bridge near Beijing that was then used as an excuse to mount a massive invasion. Japanese troops occupied Beijing while their planes unleashed bombing raids on Shanghai that killed thousands of civilians.

The assault outraged public opinion in the West, called into question the passive stance of the United States, and heightened the sense of international urgency. Secretary of State Cordell Hull, who like Stimson grounded his diplomatic philosophy on the moral authority of international law, denounced the Japanese invasion, but his strong words fell on deaf ears. The Japanese were convinced that Western democracies were not willing to use force to stop their conquest of China.

Roosevelt found himself wracked with ambivalence. Keenly aware of the strength of isolationist sentiment among the American public, he was wary of responding too militantly to totalitarianism. Yet privately he began to worry that only military force could blunt the aggressive designs of the fascists. To test the national mood, he delivered a speech in Chicago on 5 October 1937, in which he said that the "spreading epidemic of world lawlessness" required that the Western democracies isolate or "quarantine" the aggressors. The forceful rhetoric of the so-called quarantine speech, however, did not translate into concrete action. The United States endorsed the League of Nations' condemnation of Japanese aggression but opposed any economic sanctions. By 1938 Japan had assumed effective control over China.

Meanwhile, events in Europe seemingly careened out of control. In 1938 Hitler forced Austria to merge with Germany and began threatening Czechoslovakia. The British and French responded by signing the Munich Agreement, which forced Czechoslovakia to cede strategic frontier provinces to Germany. However, Hitler violated the Munich accords only a few months later and took control of all of Czechoslovakia in March 1939. Poland was next. Yet this time the British and the French pledged to go to war if Hitler attacked.

Roosevelt decided that world war was imminent and that the only way for the United States to stay out of the conflict was to provide all possible assistance to the British and the French. To that end he called for a rearmament program in the United States and also asked Congress to revise the neutrality legislation to enable him to sell arms and munitions to belligerents on a cash-and-carry basis. The isolationist bloc in Congress defeated the proposal, but Roosevelt's effort gained new support after Germany invaded Poland in September 1939. In November Congress repealed the arms embargo and approved the cash-and-carry concept. The British and the French now could benefit from American military supplies, but they had to transport them across the Atlantic in their own ships. For the time being, this distinction protected the United States from actual military involvement.

In 1940–1941, as war raged in Europe, a debate erupted between Roosevelt and other internationalists promoting assistance to the Allies and isolationists concerned about America edging toward intervention. Roosevelt devoted his 1941 State of the Union address to an ambitious "lend-lease" program that would extend credit to the British to buy more military supplies. He insisted that the United States could no longer remain isolated from the consequences of the European war. America's values and ideals were being directly assailed in every part of the world. None of his arguments swayed the committed isolationists. The America First Committee coordinated the isolationist effort, and its leadership included prominent figures such as Herbert Hoover and Charles Lindbergh. They argued that a Nazi victory in Europe, while distasteful, would not challenge America's national security. Therefore, the United States should not risk involvement by becoming the military depot for the Allies.

The debate between isolationism and interventionism suddenly shifted focus on 7 December 1941, when the Japanese unleashed a surprise air raid on American air and naval bases in Hawaii. The next day President Roosevelt asked Congress for a declaration of war against Japan. Soon thereafter Germany declared war on the United States. The world war that Americans had struggled to keep at bay had arrived at last. British Prime Minister Winston Churchill spoke for his besieged nation when he said that he "slept the sleep of the saved and thankful" on learning of the American entry into the war. He knew that bringing American industrial and military power to bear on the battlefields would grind the Axis "to powder."

Henry Cabot Lodge Jr.

FROM The Meaning of the Kellogg-Briand Treaty (1928)

*Among the most articulate critics of the Kellogg-Briand Pact was Henry Cabot
Lodge, Jr. He graduated from Harvard in 1924 and began a career in journalism. In
this 1928 article he invokes many of the same principles and concerns voiced by his
father, Senator Henry Cabot Lodge, who once led the fight against the Versailles
Treaty and the League of Nations.*

[The Kellogg-Briand Pact] . . . is so loosely worded
as to be nothing more than a "moral" pledge and
so as to mean very little in international law. . . .
The sole value of the treaty lay not in its binding
effect—which admittedly is practically nil—but in
the "moral" effect which the knowledge of its existence would have on public opinion—which, it was
hoped, would be very great. . . .

[Lodge then analyzed "the two principal reservations" made by the signers of the Kellogg-Briand
Pact]—that which excepts wars of "self-defense"
and which makes each nation its own judge of
what constitutes "self-defense" and that which excepts from the scope of the treaty all questions
pertaining to the chief danger spots of the world.
There are others—notably Great Britain's representation enunciating in effect a British Monroe
Doctrine zone, where no interference is to be tolerated. This adds to the exceptions to the treaty; it
removes from its scope another wide area whence
international complications might spring; and
seems to help reduce the pact to nonentity. . . .

I have tried to show that the Kellogg treaty has
no binding force, and this is admitted even by its
strongest supporters; that it is so surrounded by
exceptions as to be robbed of its value; and that
connected with it are reservations, such as that
pertaining to self-defense, which are sources of
danger and provide official, international loop-
holes for waging wars of conquest. Why, then, is it
desired?

The nations of Europe seem to desire it most,
in spite of the fact that their representatives in this
country realize the impossibility of its fulfilling its
purpose. They want it because to them it means
American participation in their affairs. This has
been shouted from the house-tops; it has been proclaimed in many public ways; it really needs no
proof. . . .

The *New York Herald Tribune*, in an editorial
on July 19th, charged that the treaty involved us in
the quarrels of Europe and entailed great sacrifices
on our part without bringing us anything in return. On July 21st Secretary [of State] Kellogg, in a
press interview, indicated that it did not such
thing, arguing that since it is without sanctions it
is similarly free of legal commitments. Is this not a
plain *non sequitur* in view of his belief that the importance of the treaty is not legal but moral? . . .

Europe has given us clear and unmistakable
proof that she regards the Kellogg treaty as oblig-
ing us to interfere [in the internal affairs of other
nations to ensure peace] and that her interpretation of it [the treaty] is totally different from ours.
And interpretations, where so vague a pact is concerned, are of prime importance. Formally to agree
to such a pact, when opinions on both sides of the
water are so wholly different, is not really to agree

at all, but to sow the seeds of more trouble and misunderstanding. . . .

If the question of ratification [of the proposed treaty] be considered solely from the standpoint of incurring European anger, must it not be set down that it would be better to refuse to ratify now rather than wait till later? And from the standpoint of historic American foreign policy, does not rejection seem the one intelligent course to follow?

The treaty may be good enough for Europe; but it cannot be repeated too often that the position of the United States in world affairs is wholly different from that of the individual European state. This statement does not seek to deny the assertion that we have an interest in what happens in Europe. But our interest is bound to be peculiar, and our actions are certain to be different. We are so happily situated by geography that what happens in Asia or South America is of nearly equal interest to us with what happens in Europe. Being so far away and remote from strife, we can apply ourselves to improving our civilization and, perhaps, setting a real example to mankind. In any case, our influence in the affairs of others should not be fettered and predetermined. On the contrary, should we not adhere strictly to the simple rule that the United States should never agree in advance to support or oppose any Power or group of Powers? . . .

An active, growing state collides with its neighbors. The vast ferment of life and of human activity brings war on—not the neatly worded understandings of diplomatists. To have pointed this out would have been realistic and courageous.

I do not suggest that any attempt should have been made actually to cut down on those activities which make for economic pressure and so often result in hostilities. Such an attempt, at this stage, would have been doomed to failure. Education is necessary, but the government could have called attention to the situation, and so have paved the way for reducing the activities of our growing nation if it saw fit to do so. Instead, they gave us the Kellogg treaty which is an attempt to get some-

thing for nothing—and that, as every child knows, is impossible.

In the meantime hundreds of newspapers are hailing the treaty as a great step towards permanent peace, and thousands of persons are being made to believe that something really has been done, when, of course, nothing has or can be until a price is paid. A sense of false security is thus created and official sanction is thereby given to a most portentous misconception.

The conception of renouncing war by governmental fiat seems inherently absurd. The great forces in modern society—and especially American society—are quite independent of the government. We are in great measure our own masters. The banks, the newspapers, the great organizations of business—that whole body of influences which affect our thoughts, our food, our clothes, and our incomes are forging along no matter what Washington says. We, as individuals, cannot dodge the responsibility of war; we cannot put it off on a few office holders, no matter how conscientious or well-meaning they may be. That may have been possible once; it is no longer possible today.

It seems to me that this attempt to get something for nothing, which is actually a program to give something for nothing, entrenches war more solidly than ever. War fears truth and realism; only understanding and mutual sacrifice can end it. Is it not apparent that the Kellogg treaty, and its many textual dangers, only thickens the haze, deepens the pitfalls, and once again postpones the day when some really clear thinking is done? . . .

REVIEW QUESTIONS

1. Was the Kellogg-Briand Pact interpreted differently in the European nations than in the United States? How?
2. Do you agree that the treaty was "patently absurd"? Explain your answer.
3. According to Lodge, was there any way to prevent war? If so, how?

HENRY L. STIMSON

FROM War Is an Illegal Thing (1932)

*In 1931 Japanese forces invaded and took control of Manchuria, renaming it
Manchukuo. This action violated the Kellogg-Briand Pact, several of the treaties
Japan had signed at the Washington Conference in 1921–1922, and the Covenant of
the League of Nations. On 7 January 1932, Secretary of State Henry L. Stimson sent
a dispatch to Japan and China condemning the Japanese invasion and announcing
that the United States refused to recognize the legitimacy of the Japanese action in
Manchuria. On 11 March 1932, the League of Nations, which the United States
never joined, approved Stimson's non-recognition principle. In August, Stimson delivered a speech to the Council of Foreign Relations in which he explained the logic of
his "non-recognition" stance and expressed his faith in the Kellogg-Briand Pact as a
peacekeeping mechanism.*

From Henry Stimson, "War Is an Illegal Thing." Reprinted by permission of *Foreign Affairs*,
Vol. 11, 1932. © 1932 by the Council on Foreign Relations, Inc. www.ForeignAffairs.com.

When the American Government took the responsibility of sending its note of January 7, it was a pioneer. It was appealing to a new common sentiment and to the provisions of a Treaty as yet untested. Its own refusal to recognize the fruits of aggression might be of comparatively little moment to an aggressor. But when the entire group of civilized nations took their stand beside the position of the American Government, the situation was revealed in its true sense. Moral disapproval, when it becomes the disapproval of the whole world, takes on a significance hitherto unknown in international law. For never before has international opinion been so organized and mobilized.

Another consequence which follows the development of the Briand-Kellogg Treaty . . . is that consultation between the signatories of the Pact when faced with the threat of its violation becomes inevitable. Any effective invocation of the power of world opinion involves discussion and consultation. As long as the signatories of the Pact of Paris support the policy which the American Government has endeavored to establish during the past three years of arousing a united and living spirit of public opinion as a sanction to the Pact, as long as this course is adopted and endorsed by the great nations of the world who are signatories of that Treaty, consultations will take place as an incident to the unification of that opinion. The course which was followed in the Sino-Japanese controversy last winter conclusively proves that fact. The moment a situation arose which threatened the effectiveness of this Treaty, which the peoples of the world have come to regard as so vital to the protection of their interests, practically all the nations consulted in an effort to make effective the great peaceful purposes of the Treaty. . . .

I believe that this view of the Briand-Kellogg Treaty which I have been discussing will become one of the great and permanent policies of our nation. It is founded upon conceptions of law and ideals of peace which are among our most cherished faiths. It is a policy which combines the readiness to cooperate for peace and justice in the world, which Americans have always manifested, while at the same time it preserves the independence of judgment and the flexibility of action upon which we have always insisted. I believe that this policy must strike a chord of sympathy in the conscience of other nations. We all feel that the dreadful lessons taught by the World War must not be forgotten. The determination to abolish war which emerged from that calamity must not be relaxed. These aspirations of the world are expressed in this great Treaty. It is only by continued vigilance that it can be built into an effective living reality. The American people are serious in their support and evaluation of the Treaty. They will not fail to do their share in this endeavor.

REVIEW QUESTIONS

1. Is moral indignation an effective response to international aggression? Explain.
2. What assumptions about the behavior of nations led to the belief that reliance upon moral indignation and legal requirements could ensure peace and stability?

JOSEPH GREW

A More Forceful Response to Japan Is Needed (1937)

The American ambassador to Japan during the 1930s was a penetrating thinker and veteran Asian specialist named Joseph Grew. His analysis of the situation in East Asia increasingly differed from that animating the policies of Secretary of State Henry Stimson and his successor, Cordell Hull. In a diary entry in October 1937, Grew recorded his doubts about the effectiveness of moral suasion in blunting Japanese imperialism.

From Joseph C. Grew, *Turbulent Era: A Diplomatic Record of Forty Years, 1904–1945*, Joseph C. Grew, edited by Walter Johnson. Copyright 1952 by Joseph C. Grew, © renewed 1980 by Elizabeth Lyon, Anita J. English and Lilla Levitt. Reprinted by permission of Houghton Mifflin Harcourt Publishing Company. All rights reserved.

I have no right, as a representative of the Government, to criticize the Government's policy and actions, but that doesn't make me feel any less sorry about the way things have turned. An architect who has spent five years slowly building what he hoped was going to be a solid and permanent edifice and has then seen that edifice suddenly crumble about his ears might feel similarly. Or a doctor who has worked hard over a patient and then has lost his case. Our country came to a fork in the road and, paradoxical as it may seem to a peace loving nation, chose the fork which leads not to peace but potentially to war. Our primary and fundamental concept was to avoid involvement in the Far Eastern mess; we have chosen the road which might lead directly to involvement.

If this sudden turnabout in policy could possibly help the situation either now or in the future, if our branding of Japan as an aggressor and our appeal to the Nine Power Treaty and the Kellogg Pact and our support of the League of Nations, could serve to stop the fighting in China or limit its sphere or prevent similar aggression in the future, my accord with this step would be complete and wholehearted. But, alas, history and experience have shown that Realpolitik and not ethereal idealism should govern our policy and our acts today. With Manchuria, Ethiopia, and Spain written in big letters across the pages of history, how can we ignore the practical experience of those events and the hopelessness of deterring them *unless we are willing to fight*? Moral suasion is ineffective; economic and financial sanctions have been shown to be ineffective and dangerous to boot. Once again I fear that we shall crawl out on a limb—and be left there—to reap the odium and practical disadvantages of our course from which other countries will then hasten to profit. Such is internationalism today. Why, oh why, do we disregard the experience and facts of history which stare us in the face?

REVIEW QUESTIONS

1. Why did American statesmen oppose the kind of aggressive stance toward Japan that Grew advocated?
2. How might a World War I veteran have responded to Grew's perspective?
3. Why did so many Americans consider domestic concerns more important than foreign ones in the 1930s?

FRANKLIN D. ROOSEVELT

Quarantine the Aggressors (1937)

President Roosevelt used the occasion of a speech in Chicago to gauge the limits of American isolationism. In his remarks, he suggested that the cancer of totalitarian aggression warranted more forceful actions on the part of the Western democracies.

From U.S. Department of State, *Addresses and Messages of Franklin D. Roosevelt*, Senate Document No. 188, 77th Cong., 2d sess., pp. 21–24.

It is because the people of the United States under modern conditions must, for the sake of their own future, give thought to the rest of the world, that I, as the responsible executive head of the nation, have chosen this great inland city and this gala occasion to speak to you on a subject of definite national importance.

The political situation in the world, which of late has been growing progressively worse, is such as to cause grave concern and anxiety to all the peoples and nations who wish to live in peace and amity with their neighbors.

Some fifteen years ago the hopes of mankind for a continuing era of international peace were raised to great heights when more than sixty nations solemnly pledged themselves not to resort to arms in furtherance of their national aims and policies. The high aspirations expressed in the Briand-Kellogg Pact and the hopes for peace thus raised have of late given way to a haunting fear of calamity. The present reign of terror and international lawlessness began a few years ago.

It began through unjustified interference in the internal affairs of other nations or the invasion of alien territory in violation of treaties. It has now reached the stage where the very foundations of civilization are seriously threatened. The landmarks and traditions which have marked the progress of civilization toward a condition of law and order and justice are being wiped away.

Without a declaration of war and without warning or justification of any kind, civilians, including vast numbers of women and children, are being ruthlessly murdered with bombs from the air. In times of so-called peace, ships are being attacked and sunk by submarines without cause or notice. Nations are fomenting and taking sides in civil warfare in nations that have never done them any harm. Nations claiming freedom for themselves deny it to others.

Innocent people, innocent nations are being cruelly sacrificed to a greed for power and supremacy which is devoid of all sense of justice and humane considerations. . . .

If those things come to pass in other parts of the world, let no one imagine that America will escape, that America may expect mercy, that this Western hemisphere will not be attacked and that it will continue tranquilly and peacefully to carry on the ethics and the arts of civilization.

No, if those days come, "there will be no safety by arms, no help from authority, no answer in science. The storm will rage until every flower of culture is trampled and all human beings are leveled in a vast chaos."

If those days are not to come to pass—if we are to have a world in which we can breathe freely and live in amity without fear—then the peace-loving nations must make a concerted effort to uphold laws and principles on which alone peace can rest secure.

The peace-loving nations must make a concerted effort in opposition to those violations of treaties and those ignorings of human instincts which today are creating a state of international anarchy and instability from which there is no escape through mere isolation or neutrality.

Those who cherish their freedom and recognize and respect the equal right of their neighbors to be free and live in peace, must work together for the triumph of law and moral principles in order that peace, justice, and confidence may prevail throughout the world. There must be a return to a belief in the pledged word, in the value of a signed treaty. There must be recognition of the fact that national morality is as vital as private morality. . . .

There is a solidarity and interdependence about the modern world, both technically and morally, which makes it impossible for any nation completely to isolate itself from economic and political upheavals in the rest of the world, especially when such upheavals appear to be spreading and not declining. There can be no stability or peace either within nations or between nations except under laws and moral standards adhered to by all. International anarchy destroys every foundation for peace. It jeopardizes either the immediate or the future security of every nation, large or small. It is, therefore, a matter of vital interest and concern to the people of the United States that the sanctity of international treaties and the maintenance of international morality be restored.

The overwhelming majority of the peoples and nations of the world today want to live in peace. They seek the removal of barriers against trade. They want to exert themselves in industry, in agriculture and in business, that they may increase their wealth through the production of wealth-producing goods rather than striving to produce military planes and bombs and machine guns and cannon for the destruction of human lives and useful property.

In those nations of the world which seem to be piling armament on armament for purposes of aggression, and those other nations which fear acts of aggression against them and their security, a very high proportion of their national income is being spent directly for armaments. It runs from 30 to as high as 50 per cent. The proportion that we in the United States spend is far less—11 or 12 per cent.

How happy we are that the circumstances of the moment permit us to put our money into bridges and boulevards, dams and reforestation, the conservation of our soil, and many other kinds of useful works rather than into huge standing armies and vast supplies of implements of war.

Nevertheless, my friends, I am compelled, as you are compelled, to look ahead. The peace, the freedom, and the security of 90 per cent of the population of the world is being jeopardized by the remaining 10 per cent who are threatening a breakdown of all international order and law. Surely the 90 per cent who want to live in peace under law and in accordance with moral standards that have received almost universal acceptance through the centuries, can and must find some way to make their will prevail.

The situation is definitely of universal concern. The questions involved relate not merely to violations of specific provisions of particular treaties; they are questions of war and of peace, of international law and especially of principles of humanity. It is true that they involve definite violations of agreements, and especially of the Covenant of the League of Nations, the Briand-Kellogg Pact and the Nine Power Treaty. But they also involve problems of world economy, world security and world humanity.

It is true that the moral consciousness of the world must recognize the importance of removing injustices and well-founded grievances; but at the same time it must be aroused to the cardinal necessity of honoring sanctity of treaties, of respecting the rights and liberties of others and of putting an end to acts of international aggression.

It seems to be unfortunately true that the epidemic of world lawlessness is spreading.

AND MARK THIS WELL: When an epidemic of physical disease starts to spread, the community approves and joins in a quarantine of the patients in order to protect the health of the community against the spread of the disease.

It is my determination to pursue a policy of peace and to adopt every practicable measure to avoid involvement in war. It ought to be inconceivable that in this modern era, and in the face of experience, any nation could be so foolish and ruthless as to run the risk of plunging the whole world into war by invading and violating, in contravention of solemn treaties, the territory of other nations that have done them no real harm and are too weak to protect themselves adequately. Yet the peace of the world and the welfare and security of every nation are today being threatened by that very thing.

No nation which refuses to exercise forbearance and to respect the freedom and rights of others can long remain strong and retain the confidence and respect of other nations. No nation ever loses its dignity or its good standing by conciliating its differences, and by exercising great patience with, and consideration for, the rights of other nations.

War is a contagion, whether it be declared or undeclared. It can engulf states and peoples remote from the original scene of hostilities. We are determined to keep out of war, yet we cannot insure ourselves against the disastrous effects of war and the dangers of involvement. We are adopting such measures as will minimize our risk of involvement, but we cannot have complete protection in a world of disorder in which confidence and security have broken down.

If civilization is to survive, the principles of the Prince of Peace must be restored. Shattered trust between nations must be revived. Most important of all, the will for peace on the part of peace-loving nations must express itself to the end that nations that may be tempted to violate their agreements and the rights of others will desist from such a course. There must be positive endeavors to preserve peace.

America hates war. America hopes for peace. Therefore, America actively engages in the search for peace.

REVIEW QUESTIONS

1. This speech was intended to be a trial balloon to test the willingness of Americans to support a more forceful stance against Japan and Germany. What specifically did Roosevelt propose doing?
2. Which passages from Roosevelt's speech suggested the potency of isolationist sentiment?
3. Did you find Roosevelt's analogy linking war with disease persuasive? Why or why not?

FRANKLIN D. ROOSEVELT

The Four Freedoms (1941)

By early 1941 President Roosevelt was openly committed to helping the Allies win the war against Hitler's Germany. In his annual message to the Congress in 1941 he suggested why it was so important that the United States ensure an allied victory, and he outlined a creative way to enable cash-poor England to buy American supplies. Two months later Congress passed the Lend-Lease Act which authorized the "lease or loan" of military supplies to "any country whose defense the President deems vital to the defense of the United States."

From *Congressional Record*, 77th Cong., 1st sess., 6 January 1941, 87:44ff.

. . . I suppose that every realist knows that the democratic way of life is at this moment being directly assailed in every part of the world—assailed either by arms or by secret spreading of poisonous propaganda by those who seek to destroy unity and promote discord in nations that are still at peace. . . .

There is much loose talk of our immunity from immediate and direct invasion from across the seas. Obviously, as long as the British Navy retains its power, no such danger exists. Even if there were no British Navy, it is not probable that any enemy would be stupid enough to attack us by landing troops in the United States from across thousands of miles of ocean, until it acquired strategic bases from which to operate.

But . . . as long as the aggressor nations maintain the offensive, they, not we, will choose the time and place and the method of their attack.

That is why the future of all American Republics is today in serious danger. . . .

Just as our national policy in internal affairs has been based upon a decent respect for the rights and dignity of all our fellow-men within our gates, so our national policy in foreign affairs has been based on a decent respect for the rights and dignity of all nations, large and small. And the justice of morality must and will win in the end.

Our national policy is this:

First, by an impressive expression of the public will and without regard to partisanship, we are committed to all-inclusive national defense.

Second, by an impressive expression of the public will and without regard to partisanship, we are committed to full support of all those resolute people everywhere who are resisting aggression and are thereby keeping war away from our hemisphere. By this support we express our determination that the democratic cause shall prevail, and we strengthen the defense and the security of our own nation.

Third, by an impressive expression of the public will and without regard to partisanship, we are committed to the proposition that principles of morality and considerations for our own security will never permit us to acquiesce in a peace dictated by aggressors and sponsored by appeasers. We know that enduring peace cannot be bought at the cost of other people's freedom. . . .

Our most immediate and useful role is to act as an arsenal for them[1] as well as for ourselves. They do not need man-power. They do need billions of dollars worth of the weapons of defense. . . .

As men do not live by bread alone, they do

---

[1] I.e., the Allies.

not fight by armaments alone. Those who man our defenses and those behind them who build our defenses must have the stamina and the courage which come from an unshakable belief in the manner of life which they are defending. The mighty action that we are calling for cannot be based on a disregard of all the things worth fighting for.

The nation takes great satisfaction and much strength from the things which have been done to make its people conscious of their individual stake in the preservation of democratic life in America. Those things have toughened the fibre of our people, have renewed their faith and strengthened their devotion to the institutions we make ready to protect. . . .

In the future days which we seek to make secure, we look forward to a world founded upon four essential human freedoms.

The first is freedom of speech and expression—everywhere in the world.

The second is freedom of every person to worship God in his own way—everywhere in the world.

The third is freedom from want—which, translated into world terms, means economic understandings which will secure to every nation a healthy peacetime life for its inhabitants—everywhere in the world.

The fourth is freedom from fear, which, translated into world terms means a world-wide reduction of armaments to such a point and in such a thorough manner that no nation will be in a position to commit an act of physical aggression against any neighbor—anywhere in the world.

That is no vision of a distant millennium. It is a definite basis for a kind of world attainable in our own time and generation. That kind of world is the very antithesis of the so-called "new order" of tyranny which the dictators seek to create with the crash of a bomb.

To that new order we oppose the greater conception—the moral order. A good society is able to face schemes of world domination and foreign revolutions alike without fear.

Since the beginning of our American history we have been engaged in change, in a perpetual, peaceful revolution, a revolution which goes on steadily, quietly, adjusting itself to changing conditions without the concentration camp or the quick-lime in the ditch. The world order which we seek is the co-operation of free countries, working together in a friendly, civilized society.

This nation has placed its destiny in the hands, heads, and hearts of its millions of free men and women, and its faith in freedom under the guidance of God. Freedom means the supremacy of human rights everywhere. Our support goes to those who struggle to gain those rights and keep them. Our strength is in our unity of purpose.

To the high concept there can be no end save victory.

REVIEW QUESTIONS

1. How does this message differ from Roosevelt's quarantine speech?
2. Were Roosevelt's remarks about democracy meant to apply to European colonies?
3. If you were to add a fifth "freedom" to Roosevelt's list of four, what would it be?

CHARLES A. LINDBERGH

Address to America First Rally (1941)

Charles Lindbergh was the young aviator who electrified the world in 1927 when he flew alone nonstop from New York to Paris in thirty-three hours. After his historic flight, he became an international celebrity. During the late 1930s he emerged as a leading spokesman for isolationism. The largest of the isolationist groups was the America First organization. When war did erupt, however, Lindbergh participated, secretly flying some fifty combat missions in Asia, shooting down one Japanese fighter.

From "The Text of Colonel Lindbergh's Address to the America First Committee Here," *The New York Times*, 24 April 1941.

. . . I know I will be severely criticized by the interventionists in America when I say we should not enter a war unless we have a reasonable chance of winning. . . . But I do not believe that our American ideals, and our way of life, will gain through an unsuccessful war. And I know that the United States is not prepared to wage war in Europe successfully at this time. . . .

I have said before, and I will say again, that I believe it will be a tragedy to the entire world if the British Empire collapses. That is one of the main reasons why I opposed this war before it was declared, and why I have constantly advocated a negotiated peace. I did not feel that England and France had a reasonable chance of winning. France has now been defeated; and, despite the propaganda and confusion of recent months, it is now obvious that England is losing the war. I believe this is realized even by the British government. But they have one last desperate plan remaining. They hope that they may be able to persuade us to send another American Expeditionary Force to Europe, and to share with England militarily, as well as financially, the fiasco of this war. . . .

*   *   *

. . . There is a policy open to this nation that will lead to success—a policy that leaves us free to follow our way of life, and to develop our own civilization. It is not a new and untried idea. It was advocated by Washington.[1] It was incorporated in the Monroe Doctrine. Under its guidance the United States became the greatest nation in the world.

It is based upon the belief that the security of the nation lies in the strength and character of its own people. It recommends the maintenance of armed forces sufficient to defend this hemisphere from attack by any combination of foreign powers. It demands faith in an independent American destiny. This is the policy of the America First Committee today. It is a policy not of isolation, but of independence; not of defeat, but of courage. It is a policy that led this nation to success during the most trying years of our history, and it is a policy that will lead us to success again. . . .

War is not inevitable for this country. Such a claim is defeatism in the true sense. No one can make us fight abroad unless we are willing ourselves to do so. No one will attempt to fight us here if we are ourselves as a great nation should be armed. Over a hundred million people in this nation are opposed to entering the war. If the principles of democracy mean anything at all, that is reason enough for us to stay out. If we are forced into a war against the wishes of an overwhelming

---

[1] George Washington (1732–1799).

majority of our people, we will have proved democracy such a failure at home that there will be little use of fighting for it abroad.

The time has when those of us who believe in an independent American destiny must band together and organize for strength. We have been led toward war by a minority of our people. This minority has power. It has influence. It has a loud voice. But it does not represent the American people. During the last several years I have traveled over this country from one end to the other. I have talked to many hundreds of men and women, and I have letters from tens of thousands more, who feel the same way as you and I.

Most of these people have no influence or power. Most of them have no means of expressing their convictions, except by their vote which has always been against this war. They are the citizens who have had to work too hard at their daily jobs to organize political meetings. Hitherto, they have relied upon their vote to express their feelings; but

now they find that it is hardly remembered except in the oratory of a political campaign. These people—the majority of hardworking American citizens, are with us. They are the true strength of our country. And they are beginning to realize, as you and I, that there are times when we must sacrifice our normal interests in life in order to insure the safety and the welfare of our nation. . . .

REVIEW QUESTIONS

1. Contrast Lindbergh's arguments against helping the Allies with Roosevelt's proposals.
2. Assess the viability of Lindbergh's defensive military strategy.
3. Assess Lindbergh's distinction between isolation and independence.
4. To whom was Lindbergh referring when he said that a "minority" had led the United States toward war?

FRANKLIN D. ROOSEVELT

War Message to Congress (1941)

The morning after the Japanese attack on Pearl Harbor, President Franklin Roosevelt appeared before Congress to request an immediate declaration of war against Japan. On the same day, Congress—with only one dissenting vote cast by Montana representative Jeannette Rankin, a dedicated pacifist—declared war.

From *Congressional Record*, 77th Cong., 1st sess., 8 December 1941, p. 9519.

Yesterday, December 7, 1941—a date which will live in infamy—the United States of America was suddenly and deliberately attacked by naval and air forces of the empire of Japan.

The United States was at peace with that nation and, at the solicitation of Japan, was still in conversation with its government and its emperor looking toward the maintenance of peace in the Pacific.

Indeed, one hour after Japanese air squadrons had commenced bombing in the American Island of Oahu the Japanese Ambassador to the United States and his colleague delivered to our Secretary of State a formal reply to a recent American message. And, while this reply stated that it seemed useless to continue the existing diplomatic negotiations, it contained no threat or hint of war or of armed attack.

It will be recorded that the distance of Hawaii from Japan makes it obvious that the attack was deliberately planned many days or even weeks ago. During the intervening time the Japanese Government has deliberately sought to deceive the United States by false statements and expressions of hope for continued peace.

The attack yesterday on the Hawaiian Islands has caused severe damage to American naval and military forces. I regret to tell you that very many American lives have been lost. In addition American ships have been reported torpedoed on the high seas between San Francisco and Honolulu.

Yesterday the Japanese Government also launched an attack against Malaya. Last night Japanese forces attacked Guam. Last night Japanese forces attacked the Philippine Islands. Last night the Japanese attacked Wake Island. And this morning the Japanese attacked Midway Island.

Japan has therefore undertaken a surprise offensive extending throughout the Pacific area. The facts of yesterday and today speak for themselves. The people of the United States have already formed their opinions and well understand the implications to the very life and safety of our nation.

As Commander in Chief of the Army and Navy I have directed that all measures be taken for our defense. Always will our whole nation remember the character of the onslaught against us.

No matter how long it may take us to overcome this premeditated invasion, the American people in their righteous might, will win through to absolute victory.

I believe that I interpret the will of the Congress and of the people when I assert that we will not only defend ourselves to the uttermost but will make it very certain that this form of treachery shall never again endanger us.

Hostilities exist. There is no blinking at the fact that our people, our territory and our interests are in grave danger.

With confidence in our armed forces, with the unbounding determination of our people, we will gain the inevitable triumph. So help us God.

I ask that the Congress declare that since the unprovoked and dastardly attack by Japan on Sunday, Dec. 7, 1941, a state of war has existed between the United States and the Japanese Empire.

REVIEW QUESTIONS

1. Why did Roosevelt consider it so important to highlight the "dastardly" nature of Japanese attacks?
2. Why did Roosevelt emphasize that Japan had also attacked areas other than Hawaii?

30 ✥ THE SECOND WORLD WAR

The Japanese attack on Pearl Harbor on 7 December 1941, unified Americans as nothing had done before. Men and women rushed to join the armed forces. Eventually over 16.4 million people would serve in the military, including 350,000 women who performed various noncombat roles. To direct this vast military enterprise, Roosevelt formed the Joint Chiefs of Staff, bringing together the leaders of the army, navy, and army air force. In 1942 they and their staff of 35,000 military and civilian personnel moved into the newly opened Pentagon, the largest building in the world.

World War II was the most significant event of the twentieth century. The conflict eventually engulfed five continents, leaving few people untouched and over 50 million dead, most of them civilians. Almost 300,000 Americans would lose their lives in the conflict. This was total war on a nightmarish scale. Whole cities were destroyed, nations dismembered, and societies transformed. Devilish new instruments of destruction were invented—plastic explosives, proximity fuses, rockets, jet airplanes, and atomic weapons—and systematic genocide emerged as an explicit war aim of the Germans and Japanese.

The war also led to an unprecedented expansion of the federal government. The number of civilian government employees more than tripled during the war, from 1.1 million to 3.8 million. And nationwide mobilization created an alliance between the defense industry and the federal government that became known as the military-industrial complex.

While the war raged in Asia and in Europe, its massive requirements served to transform social and economic life at home, changing the way Americans worked and lived. Total war required massive government spending that provided a powerful catalyst for industry and manufacturing. This created 17 million new jobs which, along with military service, led to full employment of the nation's workforce. The war economy thus pulled the nation out of its prolonged depression and set in motion a massive internal migration. Some 6 million people left farms to take up work in the cities. California, speckled with defense plants, was an especially powerful magnet, adding some 2 million residents during the war. Several million whites and blacks left the rural South, lured by jobs in defense plants in the North and West.

Women were aggressively recruited for defense-related jobs. Between 1940 and 1945, 6.3 million women entered the work force, and for the first time in history working women who were married outnumbered those who were single. By 1945 women constituted 37 percent of the work force. African Americans participated in the wartime migration into the service and into new job opportunities. Nearly one million blacks served in the armed forces, but mostly in segregated units usually led by white officers. Millions more found their way into the civilian workforce. In the process, they encountered even more obstacles than did women. Prejudice against blacks in the workplace remained rampant; they continued to be the last hired and first fired.

While millions of people were migrating across the country in search of new and better jobs during the war, one group of Americans was being forcibly moved and quarantined. In the aftermath of the attack on Pearl Harbor, anti-Japanese hysteria and racial prejudice ran high, especially on the West Coast. Exaggerated fears of possible Japanese attacks on the mainland and sabotage efforts led Roosevelt to approve an army order in 1942 requiring that some 110,000 Japanese Americans, including 40,000 children, be "relocated" from their homes and "interned" in barbed-wire enclosed prison camps in seven southern and western states.

By the spring of 1945 the war in Europe was essentially over, but fighting in the Pacific persisted. The desperate Japanese launched kamikaze (suicide) air assaults on British and American ships. Such determined—even fanatical—defensive measures gravely concerned Allied strategists as they planned the invasion of Japan for late 1945. They estimated that 35 percent of the allied assault force, some 250,000 men, would be killed or wounded. Some analysts predicted that the figure would be twice that high. This sobering prospect combined with the death of President Roosevelt in April to dull the celebrations of the German surrender on 8 May.

Two months later, the new president, Harry S. Truman, learned of an alternative way to end the war with Japan. In July an American team of scientists successfully detonated an atomic bomb in the New Mexico desert. A few days later, while meeting with Winston Churchill and Josef Stalin in Germany, Truman issued what has become known as the Potsdam Declaration: if the Japanese did not offer unconditional surrender, they would face "prompt and utter destruction." When Japan rejected the ultimatum, Truman ordered the bomb dropped. On 6 August a B-29 bomber named the Enola Gay *took off from the island of Tinian and at 8:16 a.m. dropped a five-ton uranium bomb on the port city of Hiroshima, subjecting the residents to what one called "a hell of unspeakable torments."*

More than 80,000 people were killed immediately by the bomb blast. Thou-sands more died months and years later as a result of radiation poisoning. Four square miles of the city were flattened. Three days later, on 9 August, another bomb was dropped on Nagasaki—with similar results. On 14 August Japan surrendered.

On 2 September 1945, the most devastating conflict in world history was of-ficially over, but it left in its wake power vacuums in Europe and Asia that a re-juvenated Soviet Union and a newly "internationalist" United States sought to fill in order to protect their military, economic, and political interests. Instead of peace resulting from the end of the Second World War, a new and protracted "cold war" between the Soviet Union and the United States came to dominate world affairs.

The changes wrought by World War II led the United States to discard the deeply embedded tradition of isolationism. The destruction of the traditional bal-ance of power in Europe thrust the United States into the lead role on the stage of world affairs. As the New Yorker *magazine asked, "If you do not know that your country is now entangled beyond recall with the rest of the world, what do you know?"*

FRANKLIN D. ROOSEVELT AND WINSTON CHURCHILL

The Atlantic Charter (1941)

In August 1941, several months before the attack on Pearl Harbor, President Roo-sevelt met with Winston Churchill aboard a warship off Newfoundland to discuss American efforts to help Britain stave off German attacks. In the process the two Western leaders articulated the basic principles and high ideals upon which their alliance was based. The Atlantic Charter echoed many of the themes of Woodrow Wilson's Fourteen Points. It condemned aggression, affirmed the right of self-determination, and endorsed the principles of collective security and arms reduction. As such it provided the foundation upon which the United States, Great Britain, and later, albeit ambivalently, the Soviet Union, established their military strategy and political objectives.

From U.S. Department of State, *Peace and War: United States Foreign Policy, 1931–1941* (Washington, DC, 1943), pp. 718–719.

The President of the United States of America and the Prime Minister, Mr. Churchill, representing His Majesty's Government in the United Kingdom, being met together, deem it right to make known certain common principles in the national policies of their respective countries on which they base their hopes for a better future for the world.

FIRST, their countries seek no aggrandizement, territorial or other;

SECOND, they desire to see no territorial changes that do not accord with the freely expressed wishes of the peoples concerned;

THIRD, they respect the right of all peoples to choose the form of government under which they will live; and they wish to see sovereign rights and self-government restored to those who have been forcibly deprived of them;

FOURTH, they will endeavor, with due respect for their existing obligations, to further the enjoyment by all States, great or small, victor or vanquished, of access, on equal terms, to the trade and to the raw materials of the world which are needed for their economic prosperity;

FIFTH, they desire to bring about the fullest collaboration between all nations in the economic field with the object of securing, for all, improved labor standards, economic adjustment and social security;

SIXTH, after the final destruction of the Nazi tyranny, they hope to see established a peace which will afford to all nations the means of dwelling in safety within their own boundaries, and which will afford assurance that all the men in all the lands may live out their lives in freedom from fear and want;

SEVENTH, such a peace should enable all men to traverse the high seas and oceans without hindrance;

EIGHTH, they believe that all of the nations of the world, for realistic as well as spiritual reasons, must come to the abandonment of the use of force. Since no future peace can be maintained if land, sea or air armaments continue to be employed by nations which threaten, or may threaten, aggression outside of their frontiers, they believe, pending the establishment of a wider and permanent system of general security, that the disarmament of such nations is essential. They will likewise aid and encourage all other practicable measures which will lighten for peace-loving peoples the crushing burden of armaments.

REVIEW QUESTIONS

1. In affirming "sovereign rights" and "self-government," the Atlantic Charter created what kind of dilemma for European nations that possessed colonies?
2. Why did economic issues play such an important role in the Atlantic Charter?
3. Do you think the eighth point was realistic? Explain.

FRANKLIN D. ROOSEVELT

FROM The Casablanca Conference Radio Address (1943)

In 1943 President Roosevelt met with British Prime Minister Winston Churchill at Casablanca, Morocco, on the coast of North Africa. They agreed to continue the Anglo-American offensive against German-Italian forces in the Mediterranean by invading Sicily, and they decided to postpone a landing in western Europe until 1944. The Allied leaders also fastened upon the "island-hopping" strategy in the Pacific against the Japanese. But the most significant decision resulting from the Casablanca Conference was the announcement that the war would continue until Germany and Japan offered unconditional surrender. In a radio address excerpted below, Roosevelt explained his reasoning.

From Samuel I. Rosenman, ed., *The Public Papers and Addresses of Franklin Delano Roosevelt* (1950; New York: Russell and Russell, 1969), 12:78, 79–80.

The decisions reached and the actual plans made at Casablanca were not confined to any one theater of war or to any one continent or ocean or sea. Before this year is out, it will be made known to the world—in actions rather than words—that the Casablanca Conference produced plenty of news; and it will be bad news for the Germans and Italians—and the Japanese. . . .

We do not expect to spend the time it would take to bring Japan to final defeat merely by inching our way forward from island to island across the vast expanse of the Pacific.

Great and decisive actions against the Japanese will be taken to drive the invader from the soil of China. Important actions will be taken in the skies over China—and over Japan itself. . . . There are many roads which lead right to Tokyo. We shall neglect none of them.

In an attempt to ward off the inevitable disaster, the Axis propagandists are trying all of their old tricks in order to divide the United Nations.[1] They seek to create the idea that if we win this war, Russia, England, China, and the United States are going to get into a cat-and-dog fight.

This is their final effort to turn one nation against another, in the vain hope that they may settle with one or two at a time—that any of us may be so gullible and so forgetful as to be duped into making "deals" at the expense of our Allies.

To these panicky attempts to escape the consequences of their crimes we say—all the United Nations say—that the only terms on which we shall deal with an Axis government or any Axis factions are the terms proclaimed at Casablanca: "Unconditional Surrender." In our uncompromising policy we mean no harm to the common people of the Axis nations. But we do mean to impose punishment and retribution in full upon their guilty, barbaric leaders.

*   *   *

In the years of the American and French revolutions the fundamental principle guiding our

---

[1] I.e., the Allies.

democracies was established. The cornerstone of our whole democratic edifice was the principle that from the people and the people alone flows the authority of government.

It is one of our war aims, as expressed in the Atlantic Charter, that the conquered populations of today be again the masters of their destiny. There must be no doubt anywhere that it is the unalterable purpose of the United Nations to restore to conquered peoples their sacred rights.

REVIEW QUESTIONS

1. What special challenges did the United States face in deciding not to limit its actions to "any one theater of war"?
2. Why was unconditional surrender so important to the Allies?
3. What was the reasoning behind the distinction between the "common people of the Axis nations" and their leaders?

A. PHILIP RANDOLPH

FROM Call to Negro America to March on Washington (1941)

In May 1941, A. Philip Randolph (1889–1979), the African American head of the Brotherhood of Sleeping Car Porters, threatened a "thundering march" on Washington of 150,000 blacks "to wake up and shock white America as it has never been shocked before." Such a dramatic public event, he decided, was the only way to convince President Roosevelt to ensure that minorities had equal access to jobs in the rapidly expanding defense industries and government agencies. Just before the scheduled march, President Roosevelt issued Executive Order 8802, which created a Fair Employment Practices Committee (FEPC) to eliminate racial discrimination in government hiring. Randolph thereupon canceled the march. But the mere creation of a new federal agency did not ensure justice. Randolph therefore kept the pressure on the administration to provide adequate funding and staffing for the FEPC. Although black employment in federal jobs increased from 60,000 in 1941 to 200,000 in 1945, the FEPC could not directly regulate private employers or labor unions. Moreover, despite these limitations, attempts to make the FEPC a permanent government agency never generated broad-based political support.

From A. Philip Randolph, "Call to Negro America to March on Washington for Jobs and Equal Participation in National Defense," *Black Worker* 14 (May 1941):n.p.

We call upon you to fight for jobs in National Defense. We call upon you to struggle for the integration of Negroes in the armed forces. . . .

We call upon you to demonstrate for the abolition of Jim-Crowism in all Government departments and defense employment.

This is an hour of crisis. It is a crisis of

democracy. It is a crisis of minority groups. It is a crisis of Negro Americans.

What is this crisis?

To American Negroes, it is the denial of jobs in Government defense projects. It is racial discrimination in Government departments. It is widespread Jim-Crowism in the armed forces of the Nation.

While billions of the taxpayers' money are being spent for war weapons, Negro workers are finally being turned away from the gates of factories, mines and mills—being flatly told, "NOTHING DOING." Some employers refuse to give Negroes jobs when they are without "union cards," and some unions refuse Negro workers union cards when they are "without jobs."

What shall we do?

What a dilemma!

What a runaround!

What a disgrace!

What a blow below the belt!

Though dark, doubtful and discouraging, all is not lost, all is not hopeless. Though battered and bruised, we are not beaten, broken, or bewildered.

Verily, the Negroes' deepest disappointments and direst defeats, their tragic trials and outrageous oppressions in these dreadful days of destruction and disaster to democracy and freedom, and the rights of minority peoples, and the dignity and independence of the human spirit, is the Negroes' greatest opportunity to rise to the highest heights of struggle for freedom and justice in Government, in industry, in labor unions, education, social service, religion, and culture.

With faith and confidence of the Negro people in their own power for self-liberation, Negroes can break down that barriers of discrimination against employment in National Defense. Negroes can kill the deadly serpent of race hatred in the Army, Navy, Air and Marine Corps, and smash through and blast the Government, business and labor-union red tape to win the right to equal opportunity in vocational training and re-training in defense employment.

Most important and vital of all, Negroes, by the mobilization and coordination of their mass power, can cause PRESIDENT ROOSEVELT TO ISSUE AN EXECUTIVE ORDER ABOLISHING DISCRIMINATIONS IN ALL GOVERNMENT DEPARTMENT, ARMY, NAVY, AIR CORPS AND NATIONAL DEFENSE JOBS.

Of course, the task is not easy. In very truth, it is big, tremendous and difficult.

It will cost money.

It will require sacrifice.

It will tax the Negroes' courage, determination and will to struggle. But we can, must and will triumph.

The Negroes' stake in national defense is big. It consists of jobs, thousands of jobs. It may represent millions, yes hundreds of millions of dollars in wages. It consists of new industrial opportunities and hope. This is worth fighting for.

But to win our stakes, it will require an "all-out," bold and total effort and demonstration of colossal proportions.

Negroes can build a mammoth machine of mass action with a terrific and tremendous driving and striking power that can shatter and crush the evil fortress of race prejudice and hate, if they will only resolve to do so and never stop, until victory comes.

Dear fellow Negro Americans, be not dismayed by these terrible times. You possess power, great power. Our problem is to harness and hitch it up for action on the broadest, daring and most gigantic scale.

In this period of power politics, nothing counts but pressure, more pressure, and still more pressure, through the tactic and strategy of broad, organized, aggressive mass action behind the vital and important issues of the Negro. To this end, we propose that ten thousand Negroes MARCH ON WASHINGTON FOR JOBS IN NATIONAL DEFENSE AND EQUAL INTEGRATION IN THE FIGHTING FORCES OF THE UNITED STATES.

An "all-out" thundering march on Washington, ending in a monster and huge demonstration at Lincoln's Monument will shake up white America.

It will shake up official Washington.

It will give encouragement to our white friends

to fight all the harder by our side, with us, for our righteous cause.

It will gain respect for the Negro people.

It will create a new sense of self-respect among Negroes.

But what of national unity?

We believe in national unity which recognizes equal opportunity of black and white citizens to jobs in national defense and the armed forces, and in all other institutions and endeavors in America. We condemn all dictatorships, Fascist, Nazi and Communist. We are loyal, patriotic Americans all.

But if American democracy will not defend its defenders; if American democracy will not protect its protectors; if American democracy will not give jobs to its toilers because of race or color; if American democracy will not insure equality of opportunity, freedom and justice to its citizens, black and white, it is a hollow mockery and belies the principles for which it is supposed to stand. . . .

Today we call on President Roosevelt, a great humanitarian and idealist, to . . . free American Ne-

gro citizens of the stigma, humiliation and insult of discrimination and Jim-Crowism in Government departments and national defense.

The Federal Government cannot with clear conscience call upon private industry and labor unions to abolish discrimination based on race and color as long as it practices discrimination itself against Negro Americans.

REVIEW QUESTIONS

1. What kind of equality did Randolph advocate? How does his outlook compare with that of Booker T. Washington?
2. Why did Randolph focus on a protest march as his preferred tactic? What other options might have been available?
3. Assess the advantages and disadvantages of Randolph's linking of domestic racial equality and global freedom.

Women in War Industries

Encouraged by government recruiting campaigns, some 6 million women took jobs in defense plants during the first three years of the war. Many of them left conventional domestic jobs—as maids, cooks, waitresses—to join industrial assembly lines. Others had never worked outside the home. Not surprisingly, they encountered prejudice among their male co-workers. Yet the overall experience was quite positive for many women, and it created long-lasting changes in outlook and perspective. The two following accounts are representative of the experiences of wartime working women.

From *The Homefront* by Mark Jonathan Harris, Franklin D. Mitchell, and Steven J. Schechter. Copyright © 1984 by Mark Jonathan Harris, Franklin D. Mitchell, and Steven J. Schechter. Used by permission of Putman Berkley, a division of Penguin Putnam Inc.

Inez Sauer, Chief Clerk, Tool Room

I was thirty-one when the war started and I had never worked in my life before. I had a six-year-old daughter and two boys, twelve and

thirteen. We were living in Norwalk, Ohio, in a large home in which we could fit about 200 people playing bridge, and once in a while we filled it.

I remember my husband saying to me, "You've lived through a depression and you weren't even aware it was here." It was true. I knew that people were without work and having a hard time, but it never seemed to affect us or our friends. They were all of the same ilk—all college people and all golfing and bridge-playing companions. I suppose you'd call it a life of ease. We always kept a live-in maid, and we never had to go without anything.

Before the war my life was bridge and golf and clubs and children. . . . When the war broke out, my husband's rubber-matting business in Ohio had to close due to the war restrictions on rubber. We also lost our live-in maid, and I could see there was no way I could possibly live the way I was accustomed to doing. So I took my children home to my parents in Seattle.

The Seattle papers were full of ads for women workers needed to help the war effort. "Do your part, free a man for service." Being a D. A. R.,[1] I really wanted to help the war effort. I could have worked for the Red Cross and rolled bandages, but I wanted to do something that I thought was really vital. Building bombers was, so I answered an ad for Boeing.

My mother was horrified. She said no one in our family had ever worked in a factory. "You don't know what kind of people you're going to be associated with." My father was horrified too, no matter how I tried to impress on him that this was a war effort on my part. He said, "You'll never get along with the people you'll meet there." My husband thought it was utterly ridiculous. I had never worked. I didn't know how to handle money, as he put it. I was nineteen when I was married. My husband was ten years older, and he always made me feel like a child, so he didn't think I would last very long at the job, but he was wrong.

They started me as a clerk in this huge tool room. I had never handled a tool in my life outside of a hammer. Some man came in and asked for a bastard file. I said to him, "If you don't control your language, you won't get any service here." I went to my supervisor and said, "You'll have to cor-

---

[1] Daughter of the American Revolution.

rect this man. I won't tolerate that kind of language." He laughed and laughed and said, "Don't you know what a bastard file is? It's the name of a very coarse file." He went over and took one out and showed me.

*   *   *

The first year, I worked seven days a week. We didn't have any time off. They did allow us Christmas off, but Thanksgiving we had to work. That was a hard thing to do. The children didn't understand. My mother and father didn't understand, but I worked. I think that put a little iron in my spine too. I did something that was against my grain, but I did it and I'm glad. . . .

Because I was working late one night I had a chance to see President Roosevelt. They said he was coming on the swing shift, after four o'clock, so I waited to see him. They cleared out all the aisles of the main plant, and he went through in a big, open limousine. He smiled and he had his long cigarette holder, and he was very, very pleasant. "Hello there, how are you? Keep up the war effort. Oh, you women are doing a wonderful job." We were all thrilled to think the President could take time out of the war effort to visit us factory workers. It gave us a lift, and I think we worked harder.

Boeing was a real education for me. It taught me a different way of life. I had never been around uneducated people before, people that worked with their hands. I was prudish and had never been with people that used coarse language. Since I hadn't worked before, I didn't know there was such a thing as the typical male ego. My contact with my first supervisor was one of animosity, in which he stated, "The happiest duty of my life will be when I say goodbye to each of you women as I usher you out the front door." I didn't understand that kind of resentment, but it was prevalent throughout the plant. Many of the men felt that no woman could come in and run a lathe, but they did. I learned that just because you're a woman and have never worked is no reason you can't learn.

The job really broadened me. I had led a very sheltered life. I had had no contact with Negroes except as maids or gardeners. My mother was a

Virginian, and we were brought up to think that colored people were not of the same economic or social level. I learned differently at Boeing. I learned that because a girl is a Negro she's not necessarily a maid, and because a man is a Negro doesn't mean that all he can do is dig. In fact, I found that some of the black people I got to know there were very superior—and certainly equal to me—equal to anyone I ever knew.

Before I worked at Boeing I also had had no exposure to unions. After I was there for awhile, I joined the machinists union. We had a contract dispute, and we had a one-day walkout to show Boeing our strength. We went on this march through the financial district in downtown Seattle.

My mother happened to be down there seeing the president of the Seattle First National Bank at the time. Seeing this long stream of Boeing people, he interrupted her and said, "Mrs. Ely, they seem to be having a labor walkout. Let's go out and see what's going on." So my mother and a number of people from the bank walked outside to see what was happening. And we came down the middle of the street—I think there were probably five thousand of us. I saw my mother, I could recognize her—she was tall and stately—and I waved and said, "Hello, mother." That night when I got home, I thought she was never going to honor my name again. She said, "To think my daughter was marching in that labor demonstration. How could you do that to the family?" But I could see that it was a new, new world.

My mother warned me when I took the job that I would never be the same. She said, "You will never want to go back to being a housewife." At that time I didn't think it would change a thing. But she was right, it definitely did.

I had always been in a shell; I'd always been protected. But at Boeing I found a freedom and an independence that I had never known. After the war I could never go back to playing bridge again, being a club woman and listening to a lot of inanities when I knew there were things you could use your mind for. The war changed my life completely. I guess you could say, at thirty-one, I finally grew up.

*　　*　　*

Sybil Lewis, Riveter

When I first arrived in Los Angeles, I began to look for a job. I decided I didn't want to do maid work anymore, so I got a job as a waitress in a small black restaurant. I was making pretty good money, more than I had in Sapulpa, Oklahoma, but I didn't like the job that much; I didn't have the knack for getting good tips. Then I saw an ad in the newspaper offering to train women for defense work. I went to Lockheed Aircraft and applied. They said they'd call me, but I never got a response, so I went back and applied again. You had to be pretty persistent. Finally they accepted me. They gave me a short training program and taught me how to rivet. Then they put me to work in the plant riveting small airplane parts, mainly gasoline tanks.

The women worked in pairs. I was the riveter and this big, strong white girl from a cotton farm in Arkansas worked as the bucker. The riveter used a gun to shoot rivets through the metal and fasten it together. The bucker used a bucking bar on the other side of the metal to smooth out the rivets. Bucking was harder than shooting rivets; it required more muscle. Riveting required more skill.

I worked for a while as a riveter with this white girl when the boss came around one day and said, "We've decided to make some changes." At this point he assigned her to do the riveting and me to do the bucking. I wanted to know why. He said, "Well, we just interchange once in a while." But I was never given the riveting job back. This was the first encounter I had with segregation in California, and it didn't sit too well with me. It brought back some of my experiences in Sapulpa—you're a Negro, so you do the hard work. I wasn't failing as a riveter—in fact, the other girl learned to rivet from me—but I felt they gave me the job of bucker because I was black. . . .

The war years had a tremendous impact on women. I know for myself it was the first time I had a chance to get out of the kitchen and work in industry and make a few bucks. This was something I had never dreamed would happen. In Sapulpa all that women had to look forward to was keeping house and raising families. The war years offered new possibilities. You came out to California, put on your pants, and took your lunch pail to a man's job. This was the beginning of women's feeling that they could do something more. We were trained to do this kind of work because of the war, but there was no question that this was just an interim period. We were all told that when the war was over, we would not be needed anymore.

REVIEW QUESTIONS

1. Assess whether factory work for women offered more sacrifices or opportunities.
2. What racial or gender stereotypes emerged in these accounts? What did such attitudes suggest about the prospects for social progress in the postwar era?
3. How do you think these women would educate their own children about their vocational futures?

FROM *Korematsu v. United States* (1944)

In the aftermath of the Japanese attack on Pearl Harbor, Lt. Gen. John L. DeWitt grew concerned about the prospect of saboteurs being among the West Coast's large population of Japanese Americans. To deal with this threat, which he and others greatly exaggerated, General DeWitt ordered that all Japanese and Japanese Americans on the Pacific coast be transferred to inland detention camps where they were placed behind barbed-wire fences and under the scrutiny of armed guards. President Roosevelt and Congress supported the detention program. In 1944 the issue gained a hearing before the Supreme Court when Fred Korematsu appealed his conviction for violating the detention order. Justice Hugo Black delivered the majority opinion upholding the detention program on the grounds of military necessity. Three justices dissented. The internment program understandably embittered many Japanese Americans. Some 5,000 decided to renounce their American citizenship and to move to Japan at the end of the war. Not until 1988 did the Congress finally admit the injustice of the internment program and award $20,000 to each of the 62,000 surviving detainees.

From U.S. Supreme Court, *Korematsu* v. *U.S.* (1944) in *Supreme Court Reporter* (St. Paul, MN: West Publishing, 1946), 65:194–195, 197–198, 201–202, 203–206. [Editorial insertions appear in square brackets—*Ed.*]

MR. JUSTICE BLACK delivered the opinion of the Court:
. . . It should be noted, to begin with, that all legal restrictions which curtail the civil rights of a single racial group are immediately suspect. That is not to say that all such restrictions are unconstitutional. It is to say that courts must subject them to the most rigid scrutiny. Pressing public necessity may sometimes justify the existence of such restrictions; racial antagonism never can. . . .

Exclusion Order No. 34, which the petitioner knowingly and admittedly violated, was one of a number of military orders and proclamations, all of which were substantially based upon Executive Order No. 9066. That order, issued after we were at war with Japan, declared that the successful prosecution of the war requires every possible protection against espionage and against sabotage to national defense material, national defense premises, and national defense utilities. . . .

We uphold the exclusion order as of the time it was made and when the petitioner violated it. . . . In doing so, we are not unmindful of the hardships imposed by it upon a large group of American citizens. But hardships are part of war, and war is an aggregation of hardships. All citizens alike, both in and out of uniform, feel the impact of war in greater or lesser measure. Citizenship has its responsibilities, as well as its privileges, and, in time of war, the burden is always heavier.

Compulsory exclusion of large groups of citizens from their homes, except under circumstances of direst emergency and peril, is inconsistent with our basic governmental institutions. But when, under conditions of modern warfare, our shores are threatened by hostile forces, the power to protect must be commensurate with the threatened danger.

* * *

It is said that we are dealing here with the case of imprisonment of a citizen in a concentration camp solely because of his ancestry, without evidence or inquiry concerning his loyalty and good disposition towards the United States. Our task would be simple, our duty clear, were this a case involving the imprisonment of a loyal citizen in a concentration camp because of racial prejudice. Regardless of the true nature of the assembly and relocation centers—and we deem it unjustifiable to call them concentration camps, with all the ugly connotations that term implies—we are dealing specifically with nothing but an exclusion order. To cast this case into outlines of racial prejudice, without reference to the real military dangers which were presented, merely confuses the issue.

Korematsu was not excluded from the Military Area because of hostility to him or his race. He was excluded because we are at war with the Japanese Empire, because the properly constituted military authorities feared an invasion of our West Coast and felt constrained to take proper security measures, because they decided that the military urgency of the situation demanded that all citizens of Japanese ancestry be segregated from the West Coast temporarily, and, finally, because Congress, reposing its confidence in this time of war in our military leaders—as inevitably it must—determined that they should have the power to do just this. There was evidence of disloyalty on the part of some, the military authorities considered that the need for action was great, and time was short. We cannot—by availing ourselves of the calm perspective of hindsight—now say that, at that time, these actions were unjustified.

* * *

MR. JUSTICE ROBERTS, dissenting:

I dissent, because I think the indisputable facts exhibit a clear violation of Constitutional rights.

This is not a case of keeping people off the streets at night . . . nor a case of temporary exclusion of a citizen from an area for his own safety or that of the community, nor a case of offering him an opportunity to go temporarily out of an area where his presence might cause danger to himself or to his fellows.

On the contrary, it is the case of convicting a citizen as a punishment for not submitting to imprisonment in a concentration camp, based on his ancestry, and solely because of his ancestry, without evidence or inquiry concerning his loyalty and good disposition towards the United States. If this be a correct statement of the facts disclosed by this record, and facts of which we take judicial notice, I need hardly labor the conclusion that Constitutional rights have been violated.

* * *

MR. JUSTICE MURPHY, dissenting:

This exclusion of "all persons of Japanese ancestry, both alien and non-alien," from the Pacific Coast area on a plea of military necessity in the absence of martial law ought not to be approved. Such exclusion goes over "the very brink of constitutional power," and falls into the ugly abyss of racism.

In dealing with matters relating to the prosecution and progress of a war, we must accord great respect and consideration to the judgments of the military authorities who are on the scene and who have full knowledge of the military facts. The scope of their discretion must, as a matter of necessity and common sense, be wide. And their judgments ought not to be overruled lightly by those whose training and duties ill-equip them to deal intelligently with matters so vital to the physical security of the nation.

At the same time, however, it is essential that there be definite limits to military discretion, especially where martial law has not been declared. Individuals must not be left impoverished of their constitutional rights on a plea of military necessity that has neither substance nor support. Thus, like other claims conflicting with the asserted constitutional rights of the individual, the military claim must subject itself to the judicial process of having its reasonableness determined and its conflicts with other interests reconciled. What are the allowable limits of military discretion, and whether or not they have been overstepped in a particular case, are judicial questions.

The judicial test of whether the Government, on a plea of military necessity, can validly deprive an individual of any of his constitutional rights is whether the deprivation is reasonably related to a public danger that is so "immediate, imminent, and impending" as not to admit of delay and not to permit the intervention of ordinary constitutional processes to alleviate the danger.

*　　*　　*

[This relocation order] clearly does not meet that test. Being an obvious racial discrimination, the order deprives all those within its scope of the equal protection of the laws as guaranteed by the Fifth Amendment. It further deprives these individuals of their constitutional rights to live and work where they will, to establish a home where they choose and to move about freely. In excommunicating them without benefit of hearings, this order also deprives

them of all their constitutional rights to procedural due process. Yet no reasonable relation to an "immediate, imminent, and impending" public danger is evident to support this racial restriction, which is one of the most sweeping and complete deprivations of constitutional rights in the history of this nation in the absence of martial law. . . .

Justification for the exclusion is sought, instead, mainly upon questionable racial and sociological grounds not ordinarily within the realm of expert military judgment, supplemented by certain semi-military conclusions drawn from an unwarranted use of circumstantial evidence. Individuals of Japanese ancestry are condemned because they are said to be "a large, unassimilated, tightly knit racial group, bound to an enemy nation by strong ties of race, culture, custom and religion." They are claimed to be given to "emperor worshipping ceremonies," and to "dual citizenship." Japanese language schools and allegedly pro-Japanese organizations are cited as evidence of possible group disloyalty, together with facts as to certain persons being educated and residing at length in Japan. It is intimated that many of these individuals deliberately resided "adjacent to strategic points," thus enabling them to carry into execution a tremendous program of sabotage on a mass scale should any considerable number of them have been inclined to do so.

The need for protective custody is also asserted. The report refers, without identity, to "numerous incidents of violence," as well as to other admittedly unverified or cumulative incidents. From this, plus certain other events not shown to have been connected with the Japanese Americans, it is concluded that the "situation was fraught with danger to the Japanese population itself," and that the general public "was ready to take matters into its own hands." Finally, it is intimated, though not directly charged or proved, that persons of Japanese ancestry were responsible for three minor isolated shellings and bombings of the Pacific Coast area, as well as for unidentified radio transmissions and night signaling.

The main reasons relied upon by those responsible for the forced evacuation, therefore, do not prove a reasonable relation between the group characteristics of Japanese Americans and the dangers of invasion, sabotage and espionage. The reasons appear, instead, to be largely an accumulation of much of the misinformation, half-truths and insinuations that for years have been directed against Japanese Americans by people with racial and economic prejudices—the same people who have been among the foremost advocates of the evacuation. A military judgment based upon such racial and sociological considerations is not entitled to the great weight ordinarily given the judgments based upon strictly military considerations. Especially is this so when every charge relative to race, religion, culture, geographical location, and legal and economic status has been substantially discredited by independent studies made by experts in these matters. . . .

No one denies, of course, that there were some disloyal persons of Japanese descent on the Pacific Coast who did all in their power to aid their ancestral land. Similar disloyal activities have been engaged in by many persons of German, Italian and even more pioneer stock in our country. But to infer that examples of individual disloyalty prove group disloyalty and justify discriminatory action against the entire group is to deny that, under our system of law, individual guilt is the sole basis for deprivation of rights.

Moreover, this inference, which is at the very heart of the evacuation orders, has been used in support of the abhorrent and despicable treatment of minority groups by the dictatorial tyrannies which this nation is now pledged to destroy. To give constitutional sanction to that inference in this case, however well intentioned may have been the military command on the Pacific Coast, is to adopt one of the cruelest of the rationales used by our enemies to destroy the dignity of the individual and to encourage and open the door to discriminatory actions against other minority groups in the passions of tomorrow.

*   *   *

I dissent, therefore, from this legalization of racism. Racial discrimination in any form and in any degree has no justifiable part whatever in our democratic way of life. It is unattractive in any setting, but it is utterly revolting among a free people who have embraced the principles set forth in the Constitution of the United States. All residents of this nation are kin in some way by blood or culture to a foreign land. Yet they are primarily and necessarily a part of the new and distinct civilization of the United States. They must, accordingly, be treated at all times as the heirs of the American experiment, and as entitled to all the rights and freedoms guaranteed by the Constitution.

*   *   *

MR. JUSTICE JACKSON, dissenting:

Korematsu was born on our soil, of parents born in Japan. The Constitution makes him a citizen of the United States by nativity, and a citizen of California by residence. No claim is made that he is not loyal to this country. There is no suggestion that, apart from the matter involved here, he is not law-abiding and well disposed. Korematsu, however, has been convicted of an act not commonly a crime. It consists merely of being present in the state whereof he is a citizen, near the place where he was born, and where all his life he has lived.

Even more unusual is the series of military orders which made this conduct a crime. They forbid such a one to remain, and they also forbid him to leave. They were so drawn that the only way Korematsu could avoid violation was to give himself up to the military authority. This meant submission to custody, examination, and transportation out of the territory, to be followed by indeterminate confinement in detention camps.

A citizen's presence in the locality, however, was made a crime only if his parents were of Japanese birth. Had Korematsu been one of four—the others being, say, a German alien enemy, an Italian alien enemy, and a citizen of American-born ancestors, convicted of treason but out on parole—only Korematsu's presence would have violated the order. The difference between their innocence and his crime would result, not from anything he did, said, or thought, different than they, but only in that he was born of different racial stock.

Now, if any fundamental assumption underlies our system, it is that guilt is personal and not inheritable. Even if all of one's antecedents had been convicted of treason, the Constitution forbids its penalties to be visited upon him, for it provides that "no attainder of treason shall work corruption of blood, or forfeiture except during the life of the person attainted." But here is an attempt to make an otherwise innocent act a crime merely because this prisoner is the son of parents as to whom he had no choice, and belongs to a race from which there is no way to resign.

REVIEW QUESTIONS

1. Why did Justice Black object to calling relocation centers concentration camps?
2. What did Justice Murphy mean when he stated that "individual guilt is the sole basis for deprivation of rights"? Do you agree?

HARRY S. TRUMAN

The Atomic Bombing of Hiroshima— The Public Explanation (1945)

The following selection is President Truman's public announcement on 6 August 1945, of the dropping of the atomic bomb. His comments were directed as much to the political and military leaders in Japan as they were to the American people.

From U.S. Department of State, Publication No. 2702, *The International Control of Atomic Energy: Growth of a Policy* (Washington, D.C., n.d. [1947]), pp. 95–97.

Sixteen hours ago an American airplane dropped one bomb on Hiroshima, an important Japanese Army base. That bomb had more power than 20,000 tons of T.N.T. It had more than two thousand times the blast power of the British "Grand Slam," which is the largest bomb ever yet used in the history of warfare.

The Japanese began the war from the air at Pearl Harbor. They have been repaid many fold. And the end is not yet. With this bomb we have now added a new and revolutionary increase in destruction to supplement the growing power of our armed forces. In their present forms these bombs are now in production and even more powerful forms are in development. It is an atomic bomb. It is a harnessing of the basic power of the universe.

The force from which the sun draws its power has been loosed against those who brought war to the Far East. Before 1939, it was the accepted belief of scientists that it was theoretically possible to release atomic energy. But no one knew any practical method of doing it. By 1942, however, we knew that the Germans were working feverishly to find a way to add atomic energy to the other engines of war with which they hoped to enslave the world.

But they failed. . . . The battle of the laboratories held fateful risks for us as well as the battles of the air, land, and sea, and we have now won the battle of the laboratories as we have won the other battles. . . .

With American and British scientists working together we entered the race of discovery against the Germans. The United States had available the large number of scientists of distinction in the many needed areas of knowledge. It had the tremendous industrial and financial resources necessary for the project and they could be devoted to it without undue impairment of other vital war work. In the United States the laboratory work and the production plants, on which a substantial start had already been made, would be out of reach of enemy bombing, while at that time Britain was exposed to constant air attack and was still threatened with the possibility of invasion.

For these reasons Prime Minister Churchill and President Roosevelt agreed that it was wise to carry on the project here. We now have two great plants and many lesser works devoted to the production of atomic power. Employment during peak construction numbered 125,000 and over 65,000 individuals are even now engaged in operating the plants. Many have worked there for two and a half years. Few know what they have been producing. . . .

What has been done is the greatest achievement of organized science in history. It was done under high pressure and without failure. We are now prepared to obliterate more rapidly and completely every productive enterprise the Japanese have above ground in any city. We shall destroy their docks, their factories, and their communications. Let there be no mistakes; we shall completely destroy Japan's power to make war.

It was to spare the Japanese people from utter destruction that the ultimatum of July 26 was is-

sued at Potsdam. Their leaders promptly rejected that ultimatum. If they do not now accept our terms, they may expect a rain of ruin from the air, the like of which has never been seen on this earth. Behind this air attack will follow sea and land forces in such numbers and power as they have not yet seen and with the fighting skill of which they are already well aware. . . .

The fact that we can release atomic energy ushers in a new era in man's understanding of nature's forces. Atomic energy may in the future supplement the power that now comes from coal, oil, and falling water, but at present it cannot be produced on a basis to compete with them commercially. Before that comes, there must be a long period of intensive research. . . .

I shall recommend that the Congress of the United States consider promptly the establishment of an appropriate commission to control the production and use of atomic power within the United States. I shall give further consideration and make further recommendations to the Congress as to how atomic power can become a powerful and forceful influence towards the maintenance of world peace.

REVIEW QUESTIONS

1. According to Truman, why had production of atomic bombs taken place in the United States rather than elsewhere?
2. Why did Truman omit any reference to the thousands of Japanese killed by the atomic bomb?
3. What was Truman's attitude toward sharing nuclear technology with other countries after the war?

KARL T. COMPTON

If the Atomic Bomb Had Not Been Used (1946)

Winston Churchill declared that the atomic bomb was "a miracle of deliverance" that ended the war and thereby saved over a million lives. Not everyone agreed. In fact, wartime documents reveal that some military analysts predicted that an amphibious invasion of Japan would have resulted in approximately 46,000 deaths—slightly more than those suffered during the Normandy invasion. Thus, critics then and since have argued that Allied casualties during an invasion of Japan would have been high but acceptable and that the atomic bombs were unnecessary because the Japanese would have soon surrendered anyway. In 1946 physicist Karl T. Compton, who had worked on various scientific projects during World War II, defended the use of the atomic bomb. After reading Compton's article, President Truman wrote him a letter in which he agreed with his account. "The Japanese," he stressed, "were given fair warning and were offered the terms, which they finally accepted, well in advance of the dropping of the bomb. I imagine the bomb caused them to accept the terms."

From Karl T. Compton, "If the Atomic Bomb Had Not Been Used," *Atlantic Monthly*, 178, Dec. 1946, pp. 54–56. Reprinted by permission of Charles A. Compton.

About a week after V-J Day I was one of a small group of scientists and engineers interrogating an intelligent, well-informed Japanese Army officer in Yokohama. We asked him what, in his opinion, would have been the next major move if the war had continued. He replied: "You would probably have tried to invade our homeland with a landing operation on Kyushu about November 1. I think the attack would have been made on such and such beaches."

"Could you have repelled this landing?" we asked, and he answered: "It would have been a very desperate fight, but I do not think we could have stopped you."

"What would have happened then?" we asked.

He replied: "We would have kept on fighting until all Japanese were killed, but we would not have been defeated," by which he meant that they would not have been disgraced by surrender.

It is easy now, after the event, to look back and say that Japan was already a beaten nation, and to ask what therefore was the justification for the use of the atomic bomb to kill so many thousands of helpless Japanese in this inhuman way; furthermore, should we not better have kept it to ourselves as a secret weapon for future use, if necessary? This argument has been advanced often, but it seems to me utterly fallacious.

I had, perhaps, an unusual opportunity to know the pertinent facts from several angles, yet I was without responsibility for any of the decisions. I can therefore speak without doing so defensively. While my role in the atomic bomb development was a very minor one, I was a member of the group called together by Secretary of War Stimson[1] to assist him in plans for its test, use, and subsequent handling. Then, shortly before Hiroshima, I became attached to General MacArthur[2] in Manila, and lived for two months with his staff. In this way

---

[1] Henry L. Stimson (1867–1950).

[2] General Douglas MacArthur (1880–1964).

I learned something of the invasion plans and of the sincere conviction of these best-informed officers that a desperate and costly struggle was still ahead. Finally, I spent the first month after V-J Day in Japan, where I could ascertain at first hand both the physical and the psychological state of that country. Some of the Japanese whom I consulted were my scientific and personal friends of long standing.

From this background I believe, with complete conviction, that the use of the atomic bomb saved hundreds of thousands—perhaps several millions—of lives, both American and Japanese; that without its use the war would have continued for many months; that no one of good conscience knowing, as Secretary Stimson and the Chiefs of Staff did, what was probably ahead and what the atomic bomb might accomplish could have made any different decision. Let some of the facts speak for themselves.

Was the use of the atomic bomb inhuman? All war is inhuman. Here are some comparisons of the atomic bombing with conventional bombing. At Hiroshima the atomic bomb killed about 80,000 people, pulverized about five square miles, and wrecked an additional ten square miles of the city, with decreasing damage out to seven or eight miles from the center. At Nagasaki the fatal casualties were 45,000 and the area wrecked was considerably smaller than at Hiroshima because of the configuration of the city.

Compare this with the results of two B-29 incendiary raids over Tokyo. One of these raids killed about 125,000 people, the other nearly 100,000.

Of the 210 square miles of greater Tokyo, 85 square miles of the densest part was destroyed as completely, for all practical purposes, as were the centers of Hiroshima and Nagasaki; about half the buildings were destroyed in the remaining 125 square miles; the number of people driven homeless out of Tokyo was considerably larger than the population of greater Chicago. These figures are based on information given us in Tokyo and on a detailed study of the air reconnaissance maps. They may be somewhat in error but are certainly of the right order of magnitude.

Was Japan already beaten before the atomic bomb? The answer is certainly "yes" in the sense that the fortunes of war had turned against her. The answer is "no" in the sense that she was still fighting desperately and there was every reason to believe that she would continue to do so; and this is the only answer that has any practical significance.

General MacArthur's staff anticipated about 50,000 American casualties and several times that number of Japanese casualties in the November 1 operation to establish the initial beachheads on Kyushu. After that they expected a far more costly struggle before the Japanese homeland was subdued. There was every reason to think that the Japanese would defend their homeland with even greater fanaticism than when they fought to the death on Iwo Jima and Okinawa. No American soldier who survived the bloody struggles on these islands has much sympathy with the view that battle with the Japanese was over as soon as it was clear that their ultimate situation was hopeless. No, there was every reason to expect a terrible struggle long after the point at which some people can now look back and say, "Japan was already beaten."

A month after our occupation I heard General MacArthur say that even then, if the Japanese government lost control over its people and the millions of former Japanese soldiers took to guerrilla warfare in the mountains, it could take a million American troops ten years to master the situation.

That this was not an impossibility is shown by the following fact, which I have not seen reported. We recall the long period of nearly three weeks between the Japanese offer to surrender and the actual surrender on September 2. This was needed in order to arrange details of the surrender and occupation and to permit the Japanese government to prepare its people to accept the capitulation. It is not generally realized that there was threat of a revolt against the government, led by an Army group supported by the peasants, to seize control and continue the war. For several days it was touch and go as to whether the people would follow their government in surrender.

The bulk of the Japanese people did not consider themselves beaten; in fact they believed they were winning in spite of the terrible punishment they had taken. They watched the paper balloons take off and float eastward in the wind, confident that these were carrying a terrible retribution to the United States in revenge for our air raids.

We gained a vivid insight into the state of knowledge and morale of the ordinary Japanese soldier from a young private who had served through the war in the Japanese Army. He had lived since babyhood in America, and had graduated in 1940 from Massachusetts Institute of Technology. This lad, thoroughly American in outlook, had gone with his family to visit relatives shortly after his graduation. They were caught in the mobilization and he was drafted into the Army.

This young Japanese told us that all his fellow soldiers believed that Japan was winning the war. To them the losses of Iwo Jima and Okinawa were parts of a grand strategy to lure the American forces closer and closer to the homeland, until they could be pounced upon and utterly annihilated. He himself had come to have some doubts as a result of various inconsistencies in official reports. Also he had seen the Ford assembly line in operation and knew that Japan could not match America in war production. But none of the soldiers had any inkling of the true situation until one night, at ten-thirty, his regiment was called to hear the reading of the surrender proclamation.

Did the atomic bomb bring about the end of the war? That it would do so was the calculated gamble and hope of Mr. Stimson, General Marshall,[3] and their associates. The facts are these. On July 26, 1945, the Potsdam Ultimatum called on Japan to surrender unconditionally. On July 29 Premier Suzuki issued a statement, purportedly at a cabinet press conference, scorning as unworthy of official notice the surrender ultimatum, and emphasizing the increasing rate of Japanese aircraft production. Eight days later, on August 6, the first atomic bomb was dropped on Hiroshima; the second was dropped on August 9 on Nagasaki; on the following day, August 10, Japan declared its intention to surrender, and on August 14 accepted the Potsdam terms.

On the basis of these facts, I cannot believe that, without the atomic bomb, the surrender would have come without a great deal more of costly struggle and bloodshed.

Exactly what role the atomic bomb played will always allow some scope for conjecture. A survey has shown that it did not have much immediate effect on the common people far from the two bombed cities; they knew little or nothing of it. The even more disastrous conventional bombing of Tokyo and other cities had not brought the people into the mood to surrender.

The evidence points to a combination of factors. (1) Some of the more informed and intelligent elements in Japanese official circles realized that they were fighting a losing battle and that complete destruction lay ahead if the war continued. These elements, however, were not powerful enough to sway the situation against the dominating Army organization, backed by the profiteering industrialists, the peasants, and the ignorant masses. (2) The atomic bomb introduced a dramatic new element into the situation, which strengthened the hands of those who sought peace and provided a face-saving argument for those who had hitherto advocated continued war. (3) When the second atomic bomb was dropped, it became clear that this was not an isolated weapon, but that there were others to follow. With dread prospect of a deluge of these terrible bombs and no possibility of preventing them, the argument for surrender was made convincing. This I believe to be the true picture of the effect of the atomic bomb in bringing the war to a sudden end, with Japan's unconditional surrender.

If the atomic bomb had not been used, evidence like that I have cited points to the practical certainty that there would have been many more months of death and destruction on an enormous scale. Also the early timing of its use was fortunate for a reason which could not have been anticipated. If the invasion plans had proceeded as scheduled, October, 1945, would have seen Okinawa covered with airplanes and its harbors

---

[3] General George Marshall (1880–1959).

crowded with landing craft poised for the attack. The typhoon which struck Okinawa in that month would have wrecked the invasion plans with a military disaster comparable to Pearl Harbor.

These are some of the facts which led those who know them, and especially those who had to base decisions on them, to feel that there is much delusion and wishful thinking among those after-the-event strategists who now deplore the use of the atomic bomb on the ground that its use was inhuman or that it was unnecessary because Japan was already beaten. And it was not one atomic bomb, or two, which brought surrender; it was the experience of what an atomic bomb will actually do to a community, plus the *dread of many more*, that was effective.

If 500 bombers could wreak such destruction on Tokyo, what will 500 bombers, each carrying an atomic bomb, do to the City of Tomorrow? It is this deadly prospect which now lends such force to the two basic policies of our nation on this Subject: (1) We must strive generously and with all our ability to promote the United Nations' effort to assure future peace between nations; but we must not lightly surrender the atomic bomb as a means for our own defense. (2) We should surrender or share it only when there is adopted an international plan to enforce peace in which we can have great confidence.

REVIEW QUESTIONS

1. Do you agree that there was no fundamental difference between firebombing Tokyo and dropping atomic bombs on Hiroshima and Nagasaki? Why or why not?
2. Should the United States have shared the technical information about atomic bombs with other nations or kept it a secret?

31 ~ THE FAIR DEAL AND CONTAINMENT

On 12 April 1945, an inexperienced Harry S. Truman became president as a result of Franklin Roosevelt's death. Truman immediately confronted issues of bewildering magnitude and complexity. The protracted world war had altered the balance of power in Europe, dislodged colonial empires, and created social and political turbulence within nations. Of immediate concern was the disintegration of the wartime alliance with the Soviet Union. Having "liberated" eastern Europe from Nazi control, the Soviets were imposing their political and military will upon the region, determined to absorb the area into their own sphere of influence. While the United States insisted that the peoples of eastern Europe should determine their own postwar status through democratic elections and free trade, the Soviets were even more determined to create a buffer of "friendly states" along their western border so as to prevent another invasion of their homeland (Russia had been invaded three times since the early nineteenth century).

Throughout 1946 and 1947 political leaders subservient to Soviet desires consolidated their control over eastern Europe, especially Poland. At the same time, the Soviets established a puppet regime in newly created East Germany. Former British prime minister Winston Churchill warned that the Soviets had pulled an "iron curtain" of repression across the eastern half of Europe.

In the process of pursuing such conflicting objectives in eastern Europe, both sides helped escalate tensions and intensify an emerging "cold war" (a phrase popularized by the prominent American journalist Walter Lippmann). By 1947 American officials had become convinced that Soviet foreign policy was not pursuing legitimate security concerns; instead, they had come to view Josef Stalin as a paranoid dictator driven by an uncompromising communist ideology that envisioned world domination.

In early 1947 Truman's key foreign policy aides—Secretary of State and former army chief of staff George C. Marshall, Undersecretary of State Dean G. Acheson, and career foreign service officer George F. Kennan—fashioned a new diplomatic strategy to deal with the burgeoning cold war. Truman was tired of "babying the Russians" and wanted a tougher stance. The lesson that he and others had drawn from the failed statesmanship of the 1930s was that appeasing aggressive dictators was disastrous. His advisors responded with what became known as the "containment policy."

The first application of this containment doctrine focused on the eastern Mediterranean. Since 1946 the Greek government had been locked in a civil war with communist guerrillas. At the same time, its neighbor Turkey was facing unrelenting pressure from the Soviet Union to gain naval access to the Mediterranean. The British had provided financial and military support to the Greeks and Turks, but in early 1947 they informed the United States that they could no longer provide such assistance because of their own economic distress.

Truman acted swiftly. On 12 March 1947, he asked a joint session of Congress to provide $400 million worth of military and economic assistance to Greece and Turkey. He portrayed the situation in stark terms: failure to act would encourage further Soviet expansion around the world. In stating the case for such assistance, the president outlined what became known as the Truman Doctrine. The United States, he said, must be willing to support free peoples everywhere in order to resist the cancer of "totalitarian regimes." Failure to do so would "endanger the peace of the world" and the "welfare of our own nation."

The Truman Doctrine laid the foundation for American foreign policy during the next forty years. It committed the United States to the role of a worldwide policeman. Critics, including George Kennan, warned that the United States could not alone suppress every communist insurgency around the world. The prominent journalist Walter Lippmann derided the new containment doctrine as a "strategic monstrosity" that would entangle the United States in endless international disputes.

Truman's policies could not keep pace with the dynamic changes reshaping the world order. In 1949 the Chinese Communists led by Mao Zedong won a civil war against the "nationalist" forces of Generalissimo Jiang Jieshi (Chiang Kai-shek) and forced the nationalists off the mainland onto the island of Formosa (Taiwan). Dean Acheson, who became secretary of state in 1949, quickly asserted that "the Communist regime serves not [Chinese] interests but those of Soviet Russia." The victory of Mao's forces prompted Truman's critics to ask "Who lost China?" Republicans believed that the United States should have acted more aggressively to support Jiang's nationalist cause.

Truman faced new problems as well. The global competition between the United States and the Soviet Union forced Americans to confront the deeply embedded racism that still governed social relations. It was difficult for American diplomats in Africa to convince new nations on that continent that the United States was their friend when so many vestiges of racism still existed in American society. As a result, the cold war served as a stimulus to the civil rights move-

ment. At the same time, the discovery that the Soviet Union had detonated an atomic bomb in 1949, years in advance of American predictions, gave Republicans another weapon in their fight with the administration. The Soviets, they reasoned, must have gained access to secret American documents through their espionage network in the United States. Scattered evidence of successful Soviet espionage in North America gave fuel to the partisan claim that the Truman administration was "soft on Communism" and helped launch the anticommunist crusade led by Republican senator Joseph McCarthy.

The invasion of South Korea in June 1950 by 75,000 Soviet-equipped North Korean troops surprised the world and heightened fears of possible communist infiltration at home. Senator McCarthy stepped up his campaign of accusations and half-truths. Truman first pushed through the United Nations a resolution of condemnation. He then ordered General Douglas MacArthur to send military equipment to the South Koreans and to use American airpower to blunt the North Korean advance. Truman never asked Congress for a declaration of war. Officially, the Korean conflict was a police action supported by the United Nations. Critics labeled it "Mr. Truman's War."

In September General MacArthur assumed the offensive with a brilliant maneuver that outflanked the North Koreans and sent them reeling. Sensing a great victory, MacArthur and Truman convinced the United Nations to allow the allied forces to cross the thirty-eighth parallel, "liberate" North Korea from communist control, and unify the country under democratic rule. A policy of containment now gave way to a policy of liberation. The plan was working to perfection by mid-October as the American-dominated U.N. forces pushed across North Korea toward the Yalu River border with China. Concerned about Chinese entry into the conflict, Truman flew to Midway Island to consult with MacArthur. The American general dismissed concerns about the Chinese, arguing that they could not mount significant opposition and that American airpower would neutralize them in any event. Truman remained skeptical and ordered MacArthur to use only South Korean forces in the vanguard of the coalition as it approached the border.

But MacArthur refused to be bridled by his civilian commander-in-chief. He disobeyed the president, and moved American and British troops close to the Yalu River on 24 November. Two days later 300,000 Chinese "volunteers" streamed across the border, attacking in waves inspired by blaring bugles. The U.N. forces fell back in the most brutal fighting of the war. Three weeks later they recrossed the thirty-eighth parallel. In the midst of the retreat, MacArthur asked permission to bomb bridges on the Yalu River as well as Chinese bases across the border. He also asked for a naval blockade of the Chinese coast and suggested the possible use of Nationalist Chinese forces in Korea.

Truman feared that such measures would provoke World War III with China and possibly the Soviet Union. His assessment of the situation was bleak: the best that could be achieved was a negotiated restoration of the dividing line at the thirty-eighth parallel. To MacArthur this smacked of appeasement, and he publicly criticized Truman, saying that "there is no substitute for victory." Truman now had no choice but to relieve the popular but erratic and insubordinate MacArthur. The cashiered general returned to a hero's welcome in the United States, including a ticker-tape parade down New York City's Fifth Avenue. His Republican supporters called for Truman's impeachment and urged MacArthur to run for president. But the congressional testimony of General Omar Bradley, chairman of the Joint Chiefs of Staff, blunted MacArthur's case. Expanding the fighting into China, Bradley asserted, would be "the wrong war, at the wrong place, at the wrong time, and with the wrong enemy."

As the months passed and the war raged on, public opinion soured on Truman and the American commitment in Korea. By the onset of the 1952 election campaign, the battlefront in Korea had stabilized at the thirty-eighth parallel and voters simply wanted the conflict ended. Negotiations begun in July 1951 dragged on for two years while intense but sporadic fighting continued. When an armistice agreement was finally concluded by the Eisenhower administration in 1953, the Korean conflict had cost over $20 billion and 33,000 American lives. Over 2 million Koreans had been killed. Communism had been contained, but at a high cost.

Mr. X [George F. Kennan]

FROM The Sources of Soviet Conduct (1947)

George F. Kennan was a career diplomat with extensive service abroad as well as in Washington. In 1947 he was tapped to head the state department's new policy-planning staff, which was to provide long-range analyses and plans for the conduct of American foreign relations. This article was a distillation of a long cable message that Kennan had prepared a year before while serving in the American embassy in Moscow. Published in the July 1947 issue of the prestigious journal Foreign Affairs *under the pseudonym "Mr. X," it offered an unofficial summary of administration assessments of the Soviet threat. As he himself later admitted, Kennan failed to specify what he meant by containment—economic? political? military? Kennan's vague language also implied a global commitment to contain communism militarily anywhere and everywhere in the world. Policymakers in later years would fail to distinguish between areas vital to American interests and regions of less significance.*

The political personality of Soviet power as we know it today is the product of ideology and circumstances: ideology inherited by the present Soviet leaders from the movement in which they had their political origin, and circumstances of the power which they have exercised for nearly three decades in Russia. . . . The main concern [of the Kremlin] is to make sure that it has filled every nook and cranny available to it in the basin of world power. But if it finds unassailable barriers in its path, it accepts these philosophically and accommodates itself to them. The main thing is that there should always be pressure, increasing constant pressure, toward the desired goal. There is no trace of any feeling in Soviet psychology that the goal must be reached at any given time.

These considerations make Soviet diplomacy at once easier and more difficult to deal with than the diplomacy of individual aggressive leaders like Napoleon and Hitler. On the one hand it is more sensitive to contrary force, more ready to yield on individual sectors of the diplomatic front when that force is felt to be too strong, and thus more rational in the logic and rhetoric of power.

On the other hand it cannot be easily defeated or discouraged by a single victory on the part of its opponents. And the patient persistence by which it is animated means that it can be effectively countered not by sporadic acts which represent the momentary whims of democratic opinion but only by intelligent long-range policies on the part of Russia's adversaries—policies no less steady in their purpose, and no less variegated and resourceful in their application, than those of the Soviet Union itself.

In these circumstances it is clear that the main element of any United States policy toward the Soviet Union must be that of a long-term, patient but firm and vigilant containment of Russian expansionist tendencies. It is important to note, however, that such policy has nothing to do with outward histrionics: with threats or blustering or superfluous gestures of outward "toughness." . . . The Russian leaders are keen judges of human psychology, and as such they are highly conscious that loss of temper and self-control is never a source of

strength in political affairs. They are quick to exploit such evidences of weakness. For these reasons, it is the *sine qua non* of successful dealing with Russia that the foreign government in question should remain at all times cool and collected and that its demands on Russian policy should be put forward in such a manner as to leave the way open for a compliance not too detrimental to Russian prestige.

In the light of the above, it will be clearly seen that the Soviet pressure against the free institutions of the Western world is something that can be contained by the adroit and vigilant application of counter-force at a series of constantly shifting geographical and political points, corresponding to the shifts and maneuvers of Soviet policy, but which cannot be charmed or talked out of existence. The Russians look forward to a duel of infinite duration, and they see that already they have scored great successes. . . .

It is clear that the United States cannot expect in the foreseeable future to enjoy political intimacy with the Soviet regime. It must continue to regard the Soviet Union as a rival, not a partner, in the political arena. It must continue to expect that Soviet policies will reflect no abstract love of peace and stability, no real faith in the possibility of a permanent happy coexistence of the Socialist and capitalist worlds, but rather a cautious, persistent pressure toward the disruption and weakening of all rival influence and rival power.

Balanced against this are the facts that Russia, as opposed to the Western world in general, is still by far the weaker party, that Soviet policy is highly flexible, and that Soviet society may well contain deficiencies which will eventually weaken its own total potential. This would of itself warrant the United States entering with reasonable confidence upon a policy of firm containment, designed to confront the Russians with unalterable counter-force at every point where they show signs of encroaching upon the interests of a peaceful and stable world. . . .

It would be an exaggeration to say that American behavior unassisted and alone could exercise a power of life and death over the Communist movement and bring about the early fall of Soviet power in Russia. But the United States has it in its power to increase enormously the strains under which Soviet policy must operate, to force upon the Kremlin a far greater degree of moderation and circumspection than it has had to observe in recent years, and in this way to promote tendencies which must eventually find their outlet in either the break-up or the gradual mellowing of Soviet power. . . .

REVIEW QUESTIONS

1. According to Kennan, what did Soviet leaders value or respect?
2. How did Kennan propose that the United States increase the "strains" within the Soviet system?
3. How do you think Soviet officials would have responded to Kennan's analysis?

WALTER LIPPMANN

A Critique of Containment (1947)

Kennan's "containment doctrine" elicited a spirited critique from Walter Lippmann, a Pulitzer Prize–winning journalist widely recognized as one of the most authoritative commentators on political and diplomatic affairs.

. . . My objection, then, to the policy of containment is not that it seeks to confront the Soviet power with American power, but that the policy is misconceived, and must result in a misuse of American power. For as I have sought to show, it commits this country to a struggle which has for its objective nothing more substantial than the hope that in ten or fifteen years the Soviet power will, as the result of long frustration, "break up" or "mellow." In this prolonged struggle the role of the United States is, according to Mr. X, to react "at a series of constantly shifting geographical and political points" to the encroachments of the Soviet power.

The policy, therefore, concedes to the Kremlin the strategic initiative as to when, where and under what local circumstances the issue is to be joined. It compels the United States to meet the Soviet pressure at these shifting geographical and political points by using satellite states, puppet governments and agents which have been subsidized and supported, though their effectiveness is meager and their reliability uncertain. By forcing us to expend our energies and our substance upon these dubious and unnatural allies on the perimeter of the Soviet Union, the effect of the policy is to neglect our natural allies in the Atlantic community, and to alienate them.

*   *   *

All the other pressures of the Soviet Union at the "constantly shifting geographical and political points," which Mr. X is so concerned about—in the Middle East and in Asia—are, I contend, secondary and subsidiary to the fact that its armed forces are in the heart of Europe. It is to the Red Army in Europe, therefore, and not to ideologies, elections, forms of government, to socialism, to communism, to free enterprise, that a correctly conceived and soundly planned policy should be directed. . . .

We may now consider how we are to relate our role in the United Nations to our policy in the conflict with Russia. Mr. X does not deal with this question. But the State Department, in its attempt to operate under the Truman Doctrine, has shown where that doctrine would take us. It would take us to the destruction of the U.N. . . .

The U.N., which should be preserved as the last best hope of mankind that the conflict can be settled and a peace achieved, is being chewed up. The seed corn is being devoured. Why? Because the policy of containment, as Mr. X has exposed it to the world, does not have as its objective a settlement of the conflict with Russia. It is therefore implicit in the policy that the U.N. has no future as a universal society, and that either the U.N. will be cast aside like the League of Nations, or it will be transformed into an anti-Soviet coalition. In either event the U.N. will have been destroyed. . . .

REVIEW QUESTIONS

1. What did Lippmann mean by a "misuse of American power"?
2. Why did Lippmann contend that the objectives of Truman's containment doctrine conflicted with those of the United Nations?
3. Which analysis do you find more persuasive, Kennan's or Lippmann's? Why?

The Truman Doctrine (1947)

Although the catalyst for this speech was the crisis in Greece and Turkey, President Truman and his advisors seized the opportunity to delineate their broader concept of the postwar world and America's obligations. By pledging to resist communism anywhere and everywhere, Truman established a dangerous precedent.

From *Congressional Record*, 80th Cong., 1st sess., 12 March 1947, p. 1981.

The gravity of the situation which confronts the world today necessitates my appearance before a joint session of the Congress. The foreign policy and the national security of this country are involved.

One aspect of the present situation, which I wish to present to you at this time for your consideration and decision, concerns Greece and Turkey.

The United States has received from the Greek Government an urgent appeal for financial and economic assistance. Preliminary reports from the American Economic Mission now in Greece and reports from the American Ambassador in Greece corroborate the statement of the Greek Government that assistance is imperative if Greece is to survive as a free nation.

I do not believe that the American people and the Congress wish to turn a deaf ear to the appeal of the Greek Government. The very existence of the Greek state is today threatened by the terrorist activities of several thousand armed men, led by

Communists, who defy the Government's authority at a number of points, particularly along the northern boundaries. . . . Meanwhile, the Greek Government is unable to cope with the situation. The Greek Army is small and poorly equipped. It needs supplies and equipment if it is to restore the authority to the Government throughout Greek territory.

Greece must have assistance if it is to become a self-supporting and self-respecting democracy. The United States must supply this assistance. We have already extended to Greece certain types of relief and economic aid but these are inadequate. There is no other country to which democratic Greece can turn. No other nation is willing and able to provide the necessary support for a democratic Greek Government.

The British Government, which has been helping Greece, can give no further financial or economic aid after March 31. Great Britain finds itself under the necessity of reducing or liquidating its commitments in several parts of the world, including Greece.

We have considered how the United Nations might assist in this crisis. But the situation is an urgent one requiring immediate action, and the United Nations and its related organizations are not in a position to extend help of the kind that is required. . . .

Greece's neighbor, Turkey, also deserves our attention. The future of Turkey as an independent and economically sound state is clearly no less important to the freedom loving peoples of the world than the future of Greece. The circumstances in which Turkey finds itself today are considerably different from those of Greece. Turkey has been spared the disasters that have beset Greece. And during the war, the United States and Great Britain furnished Turkey with material aid. Nevertheless, Turkey now needs our support.

Since the war Turkey has sought additional financial assistance from Great Britain and the United States for the purpose of effecting the modernization necessary for the maintenance of its national integrity. That integrity is essential to the preservation of order in the Middle East.

The British Government has informed us that, owing to its own difficulties, it can no longer extend financial or economic aid to Turkey. As in the case of Greece, if Turkey is to have the assistance it needs, the United States must supply it. We are the only country able to provide that help.

I am fully aware of the broad implications involved if the United States extends assistance to Greece and Turkey, and I shall discuss these implications with you at this time.

One of the primary objectives of the foreign policy of the United States is the creation of conditions in which we and other nations will be able to work out a way of life free from coercion. This was a fundamental issue in the war with Germany and Japan. Our victory was won over countries which sought to impose their will, and their way of life, upon other nations.

To ensure the peaceful development of nations, free from coercion, the United States has taken a leading part in establishing the United Nations. The United Nations is designed to make possible lasting freedom and independence for all its members. We shall not realize our objectives, however, unless we are willing to help free peoples to maintain their free institutions and their national integrity against aggressive movements that seek to impose on them totalitarian regimes. This is no more than a frank recognition that totalitarian regimes imposed on free peoples, by direct or indirect aggression, undermine the foundations of international peace and hence the security of the United States.

The peoples of a number of countries of the world have recently had totalitarian regimes forced upon them against their will. The Government of the United States has made frequent protests against coercion and intimidation, in violation of the Yalta Agreement, in Poland, Rumania and Bulgaria. I must also state that in a number of other countries there have been similar developments.

At the present moment in world history nearly every nation must choose between alternative ways of life. The choice is too often not a free one.

One way of life is based upon the will of the majority, and is distinguished by free institutions, representative government, free elections, guarantees of individual liberty, freedom of speech and religion, and freedom from political oppression.

The second way of life is based upon the will of the minority forcibly imposed upon the majority. It relies upon terror and oppression, a controlled press and radio, fixed elections, and the suppression of personal freedoms.

I believe that it must be the policy of the United States to support free peoples who are resisting attempted subjugation by armed minorities or by outside pressures. I believe that we must assist free peoples to work out their own destinies in their own way.

I believe that our help should be primarily through economic and financial aid which is essential to economic stability and orderly political processes. The world is not static, and the status quo is not sacred. But we cannot allow changes in the status quo in violation of the charter of the United Nations by such methods as coercion, or by such subterfuges as political infiltration. In helping free and independent nations to maintain their freedom, the United States will be giving effect to the principles of the charter of the United Nations.

It is necessary only to glance at a map to realize that the survival and integrity of the Greek nation are of grave importance in a much wider situation. If Greece should fall under the control of an armed minority, the effect upon its neighbor, Turkey, would be immediate and serious. Confusion and disorder might well spread throughout the entire Middle East.

Moreover, the disappearance of Greece as an independent state would have a profound effect upon those countries in Europe whose peoples are struggling against great difficulties to maintain their freedoms and their independence while they repair the damages of war.

It would be an unspeakable tragedy if these countries, which have struggled so long against overwhelming odds, should lose that victory for which they sacrificed so much. Collapse of free institutions and loss of independence would be disastrous not only for them but for the world. Discouragement and possibly failure would quickly be the lot of neighboring peoples striving to maintain their freedom and independence.

Should we fail to aid Greece and Turkey in this fateful hour, the effect will be far reaching to the west as well as to the east. We must take immediate and resolute action.

I therefore ask the Congress to provide authority for assistance to Greece and Turkey in the amount of $400,000,000 for the period ending June 30, 1948.

In addition to funds, I ask the Congress to authorize the detail of American civilian and military personnel to Greece and Turkey, at the request of those countries, to assist in the tasks of reconstruction, and for the purpose of supervising the use of such financial and material assistance as may be furnished. I recommend that authority also be provided for the instruction and training of selected Greek and Turkish personnel.

Finally, I ask that the Congress provide authority which will permit the speediest and most effective use, in terms of needed commodities, supplies, and equipment, of such funds as may be authorized. . . .

The seeds of totalitarian regimes are nurtured by misery and want. They spread and grow in the evil soil of poverty and strife. They reach their full growth when the hope of a people for a better life has died. We must keep that hope alive. The free peoples of the world look to us for support in maintaining their freedoms.

If we falter in our leadership, we may endanger the peace of the world—and we shall surely endanger the welfare of this nation.

Great responsibilities have been placed upon us by the swift movement of events. I am confident that the Congress will face these responsibilities squarely.

REVIEW QUESTIONS

1. How was American national security affected by events in Greece and Turkey?
2. Truman outlined two alternative ways of life. What were they and which one corresponded to the United States? The Soviet Union?
3. Did Truman's speech imply American military as well as economic involvement in the affairs of other nations?

The Marshall Plan (1947)

Secretary of State George C. Marshall knew that the political stability of western Europe depended on its economic health. In this address to the Harvard University graduating class of 1947, he outlined the rationale for a massive infusion of American aid into the postwar recovery in Europe. He did not yet know the details of administering such a program, but he was confident of its necessity.

From *Congressional Record*, 80th Cong., 1st sess., 19 December 1947, pp. 11,749–11,751.

I need not tell you gentlemen that the world situation is very serious. That must be apparent to all intelligent people. I think one difficulty is that the problem is one of such enormous complexity that the very mass of facts presented to the public by press and radio make it exceedingly difficult for the man in the street to reach a clear appraisal of the situation. Furthermore, the people of this country are distant from the troubled areas of the earth and it is hard for them to comprehend the plight and consequent reactions of the longsuffering peoples, and the effect of those reactions on their governments in connection with our efforts to promote peace in the world.

In considering the requirements for the rehabilitation of Europe the physical loss of life, the visible destruction of cities, factories, mines, and railroads was correctly estimated, but it has become obvious during recent months that this visible destruction was probably less serious than he dislocation of the entire fabric of European economy.

For the past 10 years conditions have been highly abnormal. The feverish preparation for war and the more feverish maintenance of the war effort engulfed all aspects of national economies. Machinery has fallen into disrepair or is entirely obsolete. . . . Raw materials and fuel are in short supply. Machinery is lacking or worn out. The farmer or the peasant cannot find the goods for sale which he desires to purchase. So the sale of his farm produce for money which he cannot use seems to him an unprofitable transaction. He, therefore, has withdrawn many fields from crop cultivation and is using them for grazing. He feeds more grain to stock and finds for himself and his family an ample supply of food, however short he may be on clothing and the other ordinary gadgets of civilization.

Meanwhile people in the cities are short of food and fuel. So the governments are forced to use their foreign money and credits to procure these necessities abroad. This process exhausts funds which are urgently needed for reconstruction. Thus a very serious situation is rapidly developing which bodes no good for the world. The modern system of the division of labor upon which the exchange of products is based is in danger of breaking down.

The truth of the matter is that Europe's requirements for the next 3 or 4 years of foreign food and other essential products—principally from America—are so much greater than her present ability to pay that she must have substantial additional help, or face economic, social, and political deterioration of a very grave character.

The remedy lies in breaking the vicious circle and restoring the confidence of the European people in the economic future of their own countries and of Europe as a whole. The manufacturer and the farmer throughout wide areas must be able and willing to exchange their products for currencies the continuing value of which is not open to question.

Aside from the demoralizing effect on the world at large and the possibilities of disturbances arising as a result of the desperation of the people concerned, the consequences to the economy of the United States should be apparent to all. It is logical that the United States should do whatever it is able to do to assist in the return of normal economic health in the world, without which there can be no political stability and no assured peace. Our policy is directed not against any county or doctrine but against hunger, poverty, desperation, and chaos. Its purpose should be the revival of a working economy in the world so as to permit the emergence of political and social conditions in which free institutions can exist. Such assistance, I am convinced, must not be on a piecemeal basis as various crises develop. Any assistance that this Government may render in the future should provide a cure rather than a mere palliative.

Any government that is willing to assist in the task of recovery will find full cooperation, I am sure, on the part of the United States Government. Any government which maneuvers to block the recovery of other countries cannot expect help from us. Furthermore, governments, political par-

ties, or groups which seek to perpetuate human misery in order to profit therefrom politically or otherwise will encounter the opposition of the United States.

It is already evident that, before the United States Government can proceed much further in its efforts to alleviate the situation and help start the European world on its way to recovery, there must be some agreement among the countries of Europe as to the requirements of the situation and the part those countries themselves will take in order to give proper effect to whatever action might be undertaken by this Government.

It would be neither fitting nor efficacious for this Government to undertake to draw up unilaterally a program designed to place Europe on its feet economically. This is the business of the Europeans. The initiative, I think, must come from Europe. The role of this country should consist of friendly aid in the drafting of a European program and of later support of such a program so far as it may be practical for us to do so. The program should be a joint one, agreed to by a number, if not all European nations.

An essential part of any successful action on the part of the United States is an understanding on the part of the people of America of the character of the problem and the remedies to be applied. Political passion and prejudice should have no part. With foresight, and a willingness on the part of our people to face up to the vast responsibility which history has clearly placed upon our country, the difficulties I have outlined can and will be overcome.

REVIEW QUESTIONS

1. What was the most acute economic problem facing Europe after the end of World War II?
2. How do you think the Soviet Union would have responded to Marshall's speech?

JOSEPH MCCARTHY

Democrats and Communists (1950)

As suggested by the following speech delivered to a Republican women's club in Wheeling, West Virginia, Senator Joseph McCarthy from Wisconsin became a master at making outlandish charges about domestic subversion—and getting away with it. He declared that the United States was losing the cold war because the Truman administration was infested with scores of known communists; moreover, he claimed to have the names of 205 of them. Those who questioned his methods found themselves the subject of vicious attacks and smear campaigns. In July 1950 a Senate subcommittee chaired by Maryland Democrat Millard Tydings dismissed McCarthy's charges as "a fraud and a hoax." McCarthy thereupon turned on Tydings and helped undermine his reelection campaign.

From *Congressional Record*, 81st Cong., 2nd sess., 12 February 1950, pp. 1954–1957.

Today we are engaged in a final all-out battle between communistic atheism and Christianity. The modern champions of communism have selected this as the time, and ladies and gentlemen, the chips are down—they are truly down. . . .

Five years after a world war has been won, men's hearts should anticipate a long peace, and men's minds should be free from the heavy weight that comes with war. But this is not such a period—for this is not a period of peace. This is a time of the "cold war." This is a time when all the world is split into two vast, increasingly hostile camps—a time of a great armaments race. . . .

At war's end we were physically the strongest nation on earth—and at least potentially the most powerful intellectually and morally. Ours could have been the honor of being a beacon in the desert of destruction, a shining living proof that civilization was not yet ready to destroy itself. Unfortunately, we have failed miserably and tragically to arise to the opportunity.

The reason why we find ourselves in a position of impotency is not because our only powerful potential enemy has sent men to invade our shores, but rather because of the traitorous actions of those who have been treated so well by this Nation. It has not been the less fortunate or members of minority groups who have been selling this Nation out, but rather those who have had all the benefits that the wealthiest nation on earth has had to offer—the finest homes, the finest college education, and the finest jobs in Government we can give.

This is glaringly true in the State Department. There the bright young men who are born with silver spoons in their mouths are the ones who have been the worst. . . . In my opinion the State Department, which is one of the most important government departments, is thoroughly infested with Communists.

I have in my hand 205 cases of individuals who would appear to be either card carrying members or certainly loyal to the Communist party, but who nevertheless are still helping to shape our foreign policy.

One thing to remember in discussing the Communists in our Government is that we are dealing with spies who get 30 pieces of silver to steal the blueprints of a new weapon. We are dealing with a far more sinister type of activity because it permits the enemy to guide and shape our policy.

REVIEW QUESTIONS

1. According to McCarthy, what forces were arrayed against each other in 1950?

2. In what respects did McCarthy's remarks have a populist theme?
3. Why do you think McCarthy stressed the economic motivations of supposed communists working in the State Department? Did this contradict any of his earlier assertions?

WILLIAM O. DOUGLAS

The Black Silence of Fear (1952)

By 1952 a few prominent leaders began to criticize the excesses and dangers of the anti-communist movement led by Wisconsin senator Joseph McCarthy. Among the most articulate was Supreme Court Justice William O. Douglas (1898–1980). Born in Minnesota and raised in California and Washington state, Douglas graduated from Columbia University School of Law in 1925. He became a distinguished professor at the Yale University Law School before being appointed to the Supreme Court in 1939. Throughout his long career on the bench, he steadfastly defended civil liberties.

From *The New York Times Magazine*, 13 January 1952, pp. 7, 37–38. [Editorial insertions appear in square brackets—*Ed.*]

There is an ominous trend in this nation. We are developing tolerance only for the orthodox point of view on world affairs, intolerance for new or different approaches. . . .

. . . We have over the years swung from tolerance to intolerance and back again. There have been years of intolerance when the views of minorities have been suppressed. But there probably has not been a period of greater intolerance than we witness today. To understand this, I think one has to leave the country, go into the back regions of the world, lose himself there, and become absorbed in the problems of the peoples of different civilizations. When he returns to America after a few months he probably will be shocked. He will be shocked not at the intentions or purposes or ideals of the American people. He will be shocked at the arrogance and intolerance of great segments of the American press, at the arrogance and intolerance of many leaders in public office, at the arrogance and intolerance reflected in many of our attitudes toward Asia. He will find that thought is being standardized, that the permissible area for calm discussion is being narrowed, that the range of ideas is being limited, that many minds are closed. . . .

This is alarming to one who loves his country. It means that the philosophy of strength through free speech is being forsaken for the philosophy of fear through repression.

That choice [to limit free speech] in Russia is conscious. Under Lenin the ministers and officials were encouraged to debate, to advance new ideas and criticisms. Once the debate was over, however, no dissension or disagreement was permitted. But even that small degree of tolerance for free discussion that Lenin permitted disappeared under Stalin. Stalin maintains a tight system of control, permitting no free speech, no real clash in ideas, even in the inner circle. We are, of course, not emulating either Lenin or Stalin. But we are drifting in the direction of repression, drifting dangerously fast. . . .

The drift goes back, I think, to the fact that we carried over to days of peace the military approach to world affairs. . . .

. . . Today in Asia we are identified not with ideas of freedom, but with guns. Today at home we are thinking less and less in terms of defeating communism with ideas, more and more in terms of defeating communism with military might.

The concentration on military means has helped to breed fear. It has bred fear and insecurity partly because of the horror of atomic war. But the real reason strikes deeper. In spite of our enormous expenditures, we see that Soviet imperialism continues to expand and that the expansion proceeds without the Soviets firing a shot. The free world continues to contract without a battle for its survival having been fought. It becomes apparent, as country after country falls to Soviet imperialistic ambitions, that military policy alone is a weak one, that military policy alone will end in political bankruptcy and futility. Thus fear mounts.

Fear has many manifestations. The Communist threat inside the country has been magnified and exalted far beyond its realities. Irresponsible talk by irresponsible people has fanned the flames of fear. Accusations have been loosely made. Character assassinations have become common. Suspicion has taken the place of goodwill. Once we could debate with impunity along a wide range of inquiry. Once we could safely explore to the edges of a problem, challenge orthodoxy without qualms, and run the gamut of ideas in search of solutions to perplexing problems. Once we had confidence in each other. Now there is suspicion. Innocent acts become telltale marks of disloyalty. The coincidence that an

idea parallels Soviet Russia's policy for a moment of time settles an aura of suspicion around a person.

Suspicion grows until only the orthodox idea is the safe one. Suspicion grows until only the person who loudly proclaims that orthodox view, or who, once having been a Communist, has been converted, is trustworthy. Competition for embracing the new orthodoxy increases. Those who are unorthodox are suspect. Everyone who does not follow the military policymakers is suspect. Everyone who voices opposition to the trend away from diplomacy and away from political tactics takes a chance. Some who are opposed are indeed "subversive." Therefore, the thundering edict commands that all who are opposed are "subversive." Fear is fanned to a fury. Good and honest men are pilloried. Character is assassinated. Fear runs rampant. . . .

Fear has driven more and more men and women in all walks of life either to silence or to the folds of the orthodox. Fear has mounted: fear of losing one's job, fear of being investigated, fear of being pilloried. This fear has stereotyped our thinking, narrowed the range of free public discussion, and driven many thoughtful people to despair. This fear has even entered universities, great citadels of our spiritual strength, and corrupted them. We have the spectacle of university officials lending themselves to one of the worst witch-hunts we have seen since early days.

This fear has affected the youngsters. . . . Youth, like the opposition party in a parliamentary system, has served a powerful role. It has cast doubts on our policies, challenged our inarticulate major premises, put the light on our prejudices, and exposed our inconsistencies. Youth has made each generation indulge in self-examination.

But a great change has taken place. Youth is still rebellious; but it is largely holding its tongue. There is the fear of being labeled a "subversive" if one departs from the orthodox party line. That charge, if leveled against a young man or young woman, may have profound effects. It may ruin a youngster's business or professional career. No one wants a Communist in his organization nor anyone who is suspect. . . .

This pattern of orthodoxy that is shaping our thinking has dangerous implications. No one man, no one group can have the answer to the many perplexing problems that today confront the management of world affairs. The scene is a troubled and complicated one. The problems require the pooling of many ideas, the exposure of different points of view, the hammering out in public discussions of the pros and cons of this policy or of that. . . .

The great danger of this period is not inflation, nor the national debt, nor atomic warfare. The great, the critical danger is that we will so limit or narrow the range of permissible discussion and permissible thought that we will become victims of the orthodox school. If we do, we will lose flexibility. We will lose the capacity for expert management. We will then become wedded to a few techniques, to a few devices. They will define our policy and at the same time limit our ability to alter or modify it. Once we narrow the range of thought and discussion, we will surrender a great deal of our power. We will become like the man on the toboggan who can ride it but who can neither steer it nor stop it.

The mind of man must always be free. The strong society is one that sanctions and encourages freedom of thought and expression. . . . Our real power is our spiritual strength, and that spiritual strength stems from our civil liberties. If we are true to our traditions, if we are tolerant of a whole market place of ideas, we will always be strong. Our weakness grows when we become intolerant of opposing ideas, depart from our standards of civil liberties, and borrow the policeman's philosophy from the enemy we detest.

REVIEW QUESTIONS

1. Douglas claims that intolerance is bred by fear. What had generated such fear among Americans after World War II?
2. Why is he concerned about the forces of conformity and "orthodoxy" becoming so pervasive?
3. In what ways does he see the United States coming to resemble Soviet society?

HARRY S. TRUMAN

Statement on the Korean War (1950)

President Truman saw the North Korean invasion of South Korea as analogous with what German dictator Adolf Hitler had done in the 1930s—intimidating western democracies through bold aggressions. This time, he pledged, there would be no appeasement. Yet Truman also did not want the Korean conflict to escalate into another world war. This brought him into conflict with General Douglas MacArthur, who wanted to expand the fighting to mainland China. In April 1951 Truman made the difficult decision to remove MacArthur from his command.

From *Department of State Bulletin* 24 (16 April 1951):603–605.

... The Communists in the Kremlin are engaged in a monstrous conspiracy to stamp out freedom all over the world. If they were to succeed, the United States would be numbered among their principal victims. It must be clear to everyone that the United States cannot—and will not—sit idly by and await foreign conquest. The only question is: When is the best time to meet the threat and how?

In the simplest terms, what we are doing in Korea is this:

We are trying to prevent a third world war.

I think most people in this country recognized that fact last June. And they warmly supported the decision of the Government to help the Republic of Korea against the Communist aggressors. Now, many persons, even some who applauded our decision to defend Korea, have forgotten the basic reason for our action. . . .

The aggression against Korea is the boldest and most dangerous move the Communists have yet made.

The attack on Korea was part of a greater plan for conquering all of Asia. . . . They want to control all of Asia from the Kremlin. This plan of conquest is in flat contradiction to what we believe. We believe that Korea belongs to the Koreans. We believe that India belongs to the Indians. We believe that all the nations of Asia should be free to work out their affairs in their own way. This is the basis of peace in the Far East and it is the basis of peace everywhere else.

The whole Communist imperialism is back of the attack on peace in the Far East. It was the Soviet Union that trained and equipped the North Koreans for aggression. The Chinese Communists massed forty-four well-trained and well-equipped divisions on the Korean frontier. These were the troops they threw into battle when the North Korean Communists were beaten.

The question we have to face is whether the Communist plan of conquest can be stopped without general war. Our Government and other countries associated with us in the United Nations believe that the best chance of stopping it without general war is to meet the attack in Korea and defeat it there.

That is what we have been doing. It is a difficult and bitter task. But so far it has been successful. So far, we have prevented World War III. So far, by fighting a limited war in Korea, we have prevented aggression from succeeding and bringing on a general war. And the ability of the whole free world to resist Communist aggression has been greatly improved. . . .

But you may ask: Why can't we take steps to punish the aggressor? Why don't we bomb Manchuria and China itself? Why don't we assist nationalist Chinese troops to land on the mainland of China?

If we were to do these things we would be running a very grave risk of starting a general war. If that were to happen, we would have brought about the exact situation we are trying to prevent. . . .

I believe that we must try to limit the war to Korea for these vital reasons: to make sure that the precious lives of our fighting men are not wasted; to see that the security of our country and the free world is not needlessly jeopardized; and to prevent a third world war.

A number of events have made it evident that General MacArthur did not agree with that policy. I have therefore considered it essential to relieve General MacArthur so that there would be no doubt or confusion as to the real purpose and aim of our policy.

It was with the deepest personal regret that I found myself compelled to take this action. General MacArthur is one of our greatest military commanders. But the cause of world peace is more important than any individual.

The change in commands in the Far East means no change whatever in the policy of the United States. We will carry on the fight in Korea with vigor and determination in an effort to bring the war to a speedy and successful conclusion.

The new commander, Lt. Gen. Matthew Ridgway, has already demonstrated that he has the great qualities of military leadership needed for this task. We are ready, at any time, to negotiate for a restoration of peace in the area. But we will not engage in appeasement. We are only interested in real peace.

Real peace can be achieved through a settlement based on the following factors:

One: the fighting must stop.

Two: concrete steps must be taken to insure that the fighting will not break out again.

Three: there must be an end to the aggression.

A settlement founded upon these elements would open the way for the unification of Korea and the withdrawal of all foreign forces.

In the meantime, I want to be clear about our military objective. We are fighting to resist an outrageous aggression in Korea. We are trying to keep the Korean conflict from spreading to other areas. But at the same time we must conduct our military activities so as to insure the security of our forces. This is essential if they are to continue the fight until the enemy abandons its ruthless attempt to destroy the Republic of Korea.

That is our military objective—to repel attack and to restore peace. In the hard fighting in Korea, we are proving that collective action among nations is not only a high principle but a workable means of resisting aggression. Defeat of aggression in Korea may be the turning point in the world's search for a practical way of achieving peace and security. . . .

We do not want to widen the conflict. We will use every effort to prevent that disaster. And in so doing we know that we are following the great principles of peace, freedom, and justice.

REVIEW QUESTIONS

1. How did Truman link American security concerns with the situation in Korea?
2. Truman asserted that the United States should not appease aggressors, but at the same time he insisted that the fighting in Korea should remain limited. Was this possible?
3. Did the Korean War establish any important precedents for future American actions? If so, what were they?

DOUGLAS MACARTHUR

Address to Congress (1951)

General Douglas MacArthur was the consummate soldier. The son of a Civil War hero who won the Congressional Medal of Honor, he was born on an army base in 1880 and died at Walter Reed Naval Hospital eighty-four years later. He graduated first in his class from West Point and later designed the brilliant "island-hopping" strategy that Allied forces used against the Japanese in World War II. A proud man with a titanic ego, theatrical flair, and strong opinions, he grudgingly acceded to President Truman's decision to replace him as the commander of United Nations forces in Korea. But he remained convinced that the involvement of the Chinese in the Korean conflict warranted a change in strategy that would bring decisive victory in a region crucial to American interests. Upon his return to the United States after fourteen years abroad, MacArthur was invited to address a joint session of Congress. He did so in the dramatic fashion that always distinguished his career.

From *Congressional Record*, 82nd Cong., 1st sess., 19 April 1951, pp. 4123–4125.

. . . I do not stand here as an advocate for any partisan cause, for the issues are fundamental and reach quite beyond the realm of partisan consideration. They must be resolved on the highest plane of national interest if our course is to prove sound and our future protected. . . . I address you with neither rancor nor bitterness in the fading twilight of life with but one purpose in mind, to serve my country.

The issues are global and so interlocked that to consider the problems of one sector oblivious to those of another is but to court disaster for the whole.

While Asia is commonly referred to as the gateway to Europe, it is no less true that Europe is the gateway to Asia, and the broad influence of the one cannot fail to have its impact upon the other. . . .

The Communist threat is a global one. Its successful advance in one sector threatens the destruction of every other sector. You cannot appease or otherwise surrender to communism in Asia without simultaneously undermining our efforts to halt its advance in Europe. . . .

I now turn to the Korean conflict. While I was not consulted prior to the President's decision to intervene in the support of the Republic of Korea, that decision from a military standpoint proved a sound one . . . as we hurled back the invaders and decimated his forces. Our victory was complete and our objectives within reach when Red China intervened with numerically superior ground forces. This created a new war and an entirely new situation, a situation not contemplated when our forces were committed against the North Korean invaders, a situation which called for new decisions in the diplomatic sphere to permit the realistic adjustment of military strategy. Such decisions have not been forthcoming.

While no man in his right mind would advocate sending our ground forces into continental China—and such was never given a thought—the new situation did urgently demand a drastic revision of strategic planning if our political aim was to defeat this new enemy as we had defeated the old. . . .

I felt that military necessity in the conduct of the war made necessary:

First, the intensification of our economic blockade against China.

Second, the imposition of a naval blockade against the China coast.

Third, removal of restrictions on air reconnaissance of China's coastal areas and of Manchuria.

Fourth, removal of restrictions on the forces of the Republic of China on Formosa with logistical support to contribute to their effective operation against the Chinese mainland.

For entertaining these views . . . I have been severely criticized in lay circles, principally abroad, despite my understanding that from a military standpoint the above views have been fully shared in the past by practically every military leader concerned with the Korean campaign, including our own Joint Chiefs of Staff.

I called for reinforcements, but was informed that reinforcements were not available. I made clear that if not permitted to utilize the friendly Chinese force of some 600,000 men on Formosa; if not permitted to blockade the China coast to prevent the Chinese Reds from getting succor from without; and if there were to be no hope for major reinforcements, the position of the command from the military standpoint forbade victory. We could hold in Korea . . . but we could hope at best for only an indecisive campaign, with its terrible and constant attrition upon our forces if the enemy utilized his full military potential. I have constantly called for the new political decisions essential to a solution. Efforts have been made to distort my position. It has been said in effect that I was a warmonger. Nothing could be further from the truth. I know war as few other men now living know it, and nothing to me is more revolting. . . .

But once war is forced upon us, there is no other alternative than to apply every available means to bring it to a swift end. War's very object is victory—not prolonged indecision. In war, indeed, there can be no substitute for victory.

There are some who for varying reasons would appease Red China. They are blind to history's clear lesson. For history teaches with unmistakable emphasis that appeasement but begets new and bloodier war. It points to no single instance where the end had justified the means—where appeasement has led to more than a sham peace. Like blackmail, it lays the basis for new and successively greater demands, until, as in blackmail, violence becomes the only other alternative. Why, my soldiers asked of me, surrender military advantages to an enemy in the field? I cannot not answer. Some may say to avoid spread of the conflict into an all-out war with China; others, to avoid Soviet intervention. Neither explanation seems valid. For China is already engaging with the maximum power it can commit and the Soviet will not necessarily mesh its actions with our moves. Like a cobra, any new enemy will more likely strike whenever it feels that relativity in military or other potential is in its favor on a world-wide basis. . . .

I have just left your fighting sons in Korea. They have met all the tests there and I can report to you without reservation that they are splendid in every way. It was my constant effort to preserve them and end this savage conflict honorably and with the least cost of time and a minimum sacrifice of life. Its growing bloodshed has caused me the deepest anguish and anxiety. Those gallant men will remain often in my thoughts and in my prayers always.

I am closing my 52 years of military service.

When I joined the Army even before the turn of the century, it was the fulfillment of all my boyish hopes and dreams. The world has turned over many times since I took the oath on the plain at West Point, and the hopes and dreams have long since vanished. But I since remember the refrain of one of the most popular barrack ballads of that day which proclaimed most proudly that—"Old soldiers never die; they just fade away." And like the old soldier of that ballad, I now close my military career and just fade away—an old soldier who tried to do his duty as God gave him the light to see that duty.

Good-by.

REVIEW QUESTIONS

1. MacArthur claimed that there was "no substitute for victory." Do you agree? Why or why not?

2. What actions did MacArthur believe should have been taken against the Communist Chinese?

3. Compare MacArthur's remarks with those in the previous selection by Truman. Did they articulate the same foreign policy goals? If not, explain the differences.

32   THROUGH THE PICTURE WINDOW: SOCIETY AND CULTURE, 1945–1960

The dominant theme of American life after 1945 was unprecedented prosperity and spreading affluence coupled with persistent—if little noticed—poverty. Between 1945 and 1960 the economy soared, propelled by a boom in residential construction and by the high levels of defense spending spurred by the cold war. People weary of the sacrifices and rationing required by World War II eagerly purchased new consumer goods such as electric refrigerators, dishwashers, washing machines, television sets, high-fidelity phonographs, and transistor radios.

The postwar consumer culture was centered in the new suburban communities that sprouted like mushrooms across the landscape of American life. By 1960 some 60 million people, one-third of the total population, lived in suburban neighborhoods outside the cities that nurtured them. Suburban life revolved around the automobile and the new shopping centers as well as the fast-food restaurants that were invented to serve the retail needs of the expansive and mobile new middle class. In 1948, only 60 percent of families owned a car; by 1955 it had risen to 90 percent, and many households had two.

The prescribed role for women in this new suburban culture was focused on traditional domesticity. Women who worked in defense plants during the war were encouraged to return to the domestic circle and devote their attention to husbands and children. Even though the number of working women increased during the 1950s, the stereotypic image of the middle-class housewife remained that of a doting spouse who cooked the meals and transported the kids in her station wagon. Women who persisted in their efforts to lead independent lives outside the home were often denounced as deranged neurotics. A best-selling study of social psychology entitled Modern Woman: The Lost Sex *asserted that the very notion of an independent woman was "a contradiction in terms."*

Religious life also prospered in the postwar era. With the nation locked into an ideological battle with atheistic communism (which prohibited or suppressed religious expression), spiritual belief took on new political significance. In 1954

Congress saw fit to add the phrase "under God" to the Pledge of Allegiance, and the next year it required that the phrase "In God We Trust" be placed on all American currency. Attendance at churches and synagogues soared, movies with biblical themes were box office hits, and religious books were perennial best-sellers.

Yet not all observers were comforted by a religious revival animated by a "feel good" theology. Champions of more orthodox beliefs—theologians Reinhold Niebuhr and Will Herberg—criticized the superficiality associated with much of the era's religious enthusiasm.

FROM Up from the Potato Fields (1950)

Following World War II, returning military veterans and their families fueled an un-precedented demand for affordable housing. To meet this demand, the federal government and private industry collaborated in creating residential suburbs throughout America during the late 1940s and the 1950s. One of the first builders to take advantage of this informal partnership was William Levitt, often credited with being the father of modern suburbia.

On 1,200 flat acres of potato farmland near Hicksville, Long Island, an army of trucks sped over new-laid roads. Every 100 feet, the trucks stopped and dumped identical bundles of lumber, pipes, bricks, shingles and copper tubing—nearly as neatly packaged as loaves from a bakery. Near the bundles, giant machines with an endless chain of buckets ate into the earth, taking just 13 minutes to dig a narrow, four-foot trench around a 25-by-32 ft. rectangle. Then came more trucks, loaded with cement, and laid a four-inch foundation for a house in the rectangle.

After the machines came the men. On nearby slabs already dry, they worked in crews of two and three, laying bricks, raising studs, nailing lath, painting, sheathing, shingling. Each crew did its special job, then hurried on to the next site. Under the skilled combination of men & machines, new houses rose faster than Jack ever built them; a new one was finished every 15 minutes.

Three years ago, little potatoes had sprouted from these fields. Now there were 10,600 houses inhabited by more than 40,000 people, a community almost as big as 96-year-old Poughkeepsie, N.Y., Plainfield, N.J., or Chelsea, Mass. Its name: Levittown.

Levittown is known largely for one reason: it epitomizes the revolution which has brought mass production to the housing industry. Its creator, Long Island's Levitt & Sons, Inc., has become the biggest builder of houses in the U.S.

Super-Selling. The houses in Levittown, which sell for a uniform price of $7,990, cannot be mistaken for castles. Each has a sharp-angled roof and a picture window, radiant heating in the floor, 12-by-16 ft. living room, bath, kitchen, two bedrooms on the first floor, and an "expansion attic" which can be converted into two more bedrooms and bath. The kitchen has a refrigerator, stove and Bendix washer; the living room a fireplace and a built-in Admiral television set.

∗   ∗   ∗

The Great Change. To a man, Bill Levitt and all the other builders know exactly whom to thank for the boom and the steadily expanding market. Said one San Francisco builder last week: "If it weren't for the Government, the boom would end overnight."

At war's end, when the U.S. desperately needed 5,000,000 houses, the nation had two choices: the Federal Government could try to build the houses itself, or it could pave the way for private industry to do the job, by making available billions in credit. The U.S. wisely handed the job to private industry, got 4,000,000 new units built since the war, probably faster and cheaper than could have been done any other way.

The Government has actually spent little cash itself. But by insuring loans up to 95% of the value of a house, the Federal Housing Administration made it easy for a builder to borrow the money with which to build low-cost houses. The Government made it just as easy for the buyer by liberally insuring his mortgage. Under a new housing act signed three months ago, the purchase terms on low-cost houses with Government-guaranteed mortgages were so liberalized that in many cases buying a house is now as easy as renting it. The new terms: 5% down (nothing down for veterans) and 30 years to pay. Thus an ex-G.I. could buy a Levitt house with no down payment and installments of $56 a month.

The countless new housing projects made possible by this financial easy street are changing the way of life of millions of U.S. citizens, who are realizing for the first time the great American dream of owning their own home. No longer must young married couples plan to start living in an apartment, saving for the distant day when they can buy a house. Now they can do it more easily than they can buy a $2,000 car on the installment plan.

Fountain of Youth. Like its counterparts across the land, Levittown is an entirely new kind of community. Despite its size, it is not incorporated, thus has no mayor, no police force, nor any of the other traditional city officers of its own. It has no movies, no nightclubs and only three bars (all in the community shopping centers).

And Levittown has very few old people. Few of its more than 40,000 residents are past 35; of some 8,000 children, scarcely 900 are more than seven years old. In front of almost every house along Levittown's 100 miles of winding streets sits a tricycle or a baby carriage. In Levittown, all activity stops from 12 to 2 in the afternoon; that is nap time. Said one Levittowner last week, "Everyone is so young that sometimes it's hard to remember how to get along with older people."

The community has an almost antiseptic air. Levittown streets, which have such fanciful names as Satellite, Horizon, Haymaker, are bare and flat as hospital corridors. Like a hospital, Levittown has rules all its own. Fences are not allowed (though here & there a home-owner has broken the rule). The plot of grass around each house must be cut at least once a week; if not, Bill Levitt's men mow the grass and send the bill. Wash cannot be hung out to dry on an ordinary clothesline; it must be arranged on rotary, removable drying racks and then not on weekends or on holidays.

There are perquisites as well as rules. For the young children there are parks and countless playgrounds. For the old folks (the 5- to 35-year-olds) there are baseball diamonds, handball courts, six huge 75-by-125 ft. swimming pools, plus 25-by-75 ft. kiddy pools, shopping centers and 60-odd fraternal clubs and veterans' organizations.

"The Old Freeze." Actually, Levittown's uniformity is more apparent than real. Though most of the incomes are about the same (average: about $3,800), Levittowners come from all classes, all walks of life. Eighty percent of the men commute to their jobs in Manhattan, many sharing their transportation costs through car pools. Their jobs, as in any other big community, range from baking to banking, from teaching to preaching. Levittown

has also developed its own unique way of keeping up with the Joneses. Some Levittowners buy a new house every year, as soon as the new model is on the market. . . .

How Long? By 1951 Levitt & Sons expect to build another 10,000 Levittown houses. But whether the Levitts, or all of the other builders, will build as many houses as they plan depends on how long the housing shortage—and the housing boom—lasts. Last week, the Department of Commerce estimated that about two-thirds of the pent-up housing demand has already been filled. However, said the department, the "remaining backlog is still large and appears to be sufficient to warrant construction close to the recent yearly rates for [another] three years."

That seemed a conservative prediction, if the big builders like Levitt could keep on thinking up new mass-production tricks, and small merchant builders could adapt more of them to their operations, thus broadening the market for small, cheap houses. By stabilizing the construction industry, builders could offer more permanent work to labor, and thus eliminate the cause of the featherbedding that now adds so much to building costs. And as efficiency increased, the mass builders might also find they could economically supply some of the individuality that their houses now lack.

REVIEW QUESTIONS

1. From the perspective of this article, what seems most amazing about the development of suburbs? What role did the government play in making suburbs possible?
2. Suburbs were supposed to provide former city dwellers with greater "freedom." Does this article support that contention? Explain your response.
3. Think about the neighborhood you grew up in. Was it like Levittown? Why or why not?

FROM **What TV Is Doing to America (1955)**

Television emerged as the most popular form of entertainment after World War II. In the process it transformed leisure time and, some critics argued, degraded the quality of life. In 1955 U.S. News and World Report *magazine assessed the impact of the television industry.*

The biggest of the new forces in American life today is television. There has been nothing like it in the postwar decade, or in many decades before that—perhaps not since the invention of the printing press. Even radio, by contrast, was a placid experience.

The impact of TV on this country has been so massive that Americans are still wondering what hit them. Has the effect been good or bad? What permanent effects on the American way of life may be expected? These and other questions are considered in this survey.

Probably there are some people in the U.S. who have never seen a television program, but you would have to go into the hills to find them. Two out of three U.S. families now own their own sets, or are paying for them. In 32 million homes, TV dials are flicked on and off, from channel to channel, at least 100 million times between 8 a.m. and midnight.

Everywhere, children sit with eyes glued to screens—for three to four hours a day on the average. Their parents use up even more time mesmerized by this new marvel—or monster. They have spent 15 billion dollars to look since 1946.

Now, after nearly 10 years of TV, people are asking: "What hath TV wrought? What is this thing doing to us?"

Solid answers to this question are very hard to get. Pollsters, sociologists, doctors, teachers, the TV people themselves come up with more contradictions than conclusions whenever they start asking.

But almost everybody has an opinion and wants to air it.

What do these opinions add up to? People have strong views. Here are some widely held convictions, both against and for television:

That TV has kept people from going places and doing things, from reading, from thinking for themselves. Yet it is said also that TV has taken viewers vicariously into strange and fascinating spots and situations, brought distinguished and enchanting people into their living rooms, given them a new perspective.

That TV has interfered with schooling, kept children from learning to read and write, weakened their eyesight and softened their muscles. But there are those who hold that TV has made America's youngsters more "knowing" about life, more curious, given them a bigger vocabulary. Teaching by TV, educators say, is going to be a big thing in the future.

That TV arouses morbid emotions in children, glorifies violence, causes juvenile crime—that it starts domestic quarrels, tends to loosen morals and make people lazy and sodden. However, it keeps families together at home, provides a realm of cheap entertainment never before available, stimulates new lines of conversation.

That TV is giving the U.S. an almost primitive language, made up of grunts, whistles, standardized wisecracks and clichés—that it is turning the average American into a stereotype. Yet it is breaking down regional barriers and prejudices, ironing out accents, giving people in one part of the country a better understanding of people in other parts.

That TV is making politics "a rich man's game," turning statesmanship into a circus, handing demagogues a new weapon. But it is giving Americans their first good look at the inside of their Government, letting them judge the people they elect by sight as well as by sound and fury.

That TV has distorted and debased Salesmanship, haunting people with singing "commercials" and slogans. However, because or in spite of TV, people are buying more and more things they never before thought they needed or wanted.

These are just some of the comments that people keep on making about TV. The experts say that it probably will be another generation before there is a firm basis of knowledge about television's impact on America.

Today's TV child, the boy or girl who was born with a TV set in his home, is too young to analyze his feelings. Older people, despite their frequent vehemence about TV, are still far from sure whether they have all Aladdin's lamp or hold a bear by the tail,

Goliath with tubes. One thing you can be sure about. TV, a giant at 10, continues to grow like nobody's business. Here are some figures and comparisons: The 15 billion dollars that the U.S. people have invested in TV sets and repairs since the war is 15 per cent more than the country spent for new school and college buildings. About a billion more has gone into TV stations and equipment.

TV-viewing time is going *up*, not down, latest surveys show. This explodes the theory that people would taper off on television "once they got used to it."

"Pull" of popular TV programs is believed to be very effective. Pollsters report that three times as many people will leave a meal to answer questions at the door as will get up to abandon "Dragnet."

The number of families holding out against TV is declining to a small fraction. There still are 16 million families without sets, but most of these families either can't pay for sets or else live out of range of TV signals.

On an average evening, twice as many set owners will be watching TV as are engaged in any other form of entertainment or leisure activity, such as movie-going, card playing, or reading. Seven out of 10 American children watch TV between 6 and 8 o'clock most evenings.

Analysts are intrigued by the evidence that adults, not children, are the real television fans. The newest trend in viewing habits is a rise in the number of housewives who watch TV in the morning. One out of five with a set now watches a morning show with regularity.

What is it? Why do people want TV? A $67.50-per-week shoe repairman in San Francisco, puts it about as plainly as anyone can. "TV," he says, "is the only amusement I can afford." That was the reason he gave for paying four weeks' wages for his set.

The cobbler's comment explains TV's basic lure. It is free entertainment except for the cost of set, and repairs and electricity. It becomes so absorbing that a broken set is a family catastrophe. People will pay to have the set fixed before they will pay the milk bill, if necessary.

What does TV do to people? What do people do with TV? The researchers are digging into these questions all the time. In general, they come to theories, rather than conclusions. There are three main theories:

THEORY "A": This is widely held by people whose professions bring them into close contact with juveniles—judges, district attorneys, police officers, ministers. It assumes that TV is bound to be affecting the American mind and character because it soaks up one to five hours a day or more that used to be spent in outdoor play, in games requiring reasoning and imagination, or in reading, talking, radio listening, or movie-going.

Even the more passive of these pursuits, the theory runs, required more exercise of brain than does TV watching. Then, too, many TV programs, the theorists say, are violent or in questionable taste.

Net effect, according to these people, is a wasting away or steady decline in certain basic skills among American youngsters. Children lose the ability to read, forfeit their physical dexterity, strength and initiative.

Some see a definite connection between TV and juvenile delinquency. The Kefauver Subcommittee of the Senate Judiciary Committee has just explored this aspect. It stated:

"Members of the subcommittee share the concern of a large segment of the thinking public for the implications of the impact of this medium [television]. . . upon the ethical and cultural standards of the youth of America. It has been unable to gather proof of a direct casual relationship between the viewing of acts of crime and violence and the actual performance of criminal deeds. It has not, however, found irrefutable evidence that young people may not be negatively influenced in their present-day behavior by the saturated exposure they now receive to pictures and drama based on an underlying theme of lawlessness and crime which depict human violence."

THEORY "B": Mainly held by sociologists, communications economists, pollsters. This is that television is changing the American mind and character, although nobody knows for sure just how. The evidence is too fragmentary. The analysts are disturbed by some aspects of TV's effect on viewers. Some think TV is conditioning Americans to be "other directed," that is, getting their ideas from someone else. The early American, by contrast, is supposed to have been "inner directed," a man who thought things out for himself on the basis of his own reasoning.

A fancy name for this suspected effect of TV is "narcotic disfunction." This means that more and more men come home in the evening, drop into a chair in front of the TV set after supper and slip into a dream world of unreality.

However, the same researchers confess that TV can have a broadening influence, bringing to the masses a taste of the arts and sciences, a peek into government that they couldn't get any other way.

THEORY "C": This is what the TV people themselves like to think. It is that television is rapidly becoming "one more service" to the U.S. public, another medium such as newspapers, magazines, radio. Some people watch TV a lot, others very little. Most people want a set around, but some don't lean on it.

The TV people minimize the idea that TV is dominating American life. It is almost as if they were afraid their own baby is getting too big. What they usually say is that the people who allow their lives to be controlled by television were similarly dominated by radio and the movies—and that they are only a small minority.

The TV habit. What do the theorists base their theories on? What have they found out about the place of the TV set in American life?

Many studies have been made of the "TV habit." Latest of these indicates that TV viewing reaches a peak just after a set enters a home, then falls off rather sharply. Next, viewing begins to rise again in the average home, building up, evidently, toward a new peak that is not yet measured.

The A. C. Nielsen Company, a market research organization that attaches mechanical recorders to sets in private homes, finds this: During the 12 months ended in April, 1955, average use per day of TV sets was 4 hours and 50 minutes. That was up 4 per cent over the year before. . . .

Other studies indicate that women watch TV more than men do. Children, contrary to general impression, watch TV less than adults in the average home. Persons low in income, education or job status as a rule spend more time in front of TV sets than those with more money and education.

What's on TV. What do people get on TV? What do they want? Three out of every four TV programs are entertainment shows. . . . In a typical week of the peak TV season, in January of last year, crime, comedy, variety and Western shows accounted for 42.7 per cent of all TV program time on New York City screens. News accounted for 6.1 per cent of TV time—about the same share of time as was taken by quiz, stunt and contest shows. Other informational types of TV shows, such as interviews, weather reports, travelogues, children's instructional programs and cooking classes, got 16.2 per cent of the time.

Rating figures tend to show that people are getting just about what they want, in the opinion of the broadcasting industry. According to the "popularity" ratings of top shows, comedy and drama and straight entertainment are outpulling everything else.

What about information? The popularity cards seem to indicate the reaction is a stifled yawn. In a two-week period last June, when two comedy programs, the "George Gobel Show" and "I Love Lucy," were at the top of the list, each reaching more than 13 million homes, the top-ranking informational programs were way down the line. The "March of Medicine," for example, was No. 62, reaching 6.57 million homes; "Meet the Press" was No. 150, getting to 1.14 million families.

Studies also have been made of how long various programs hold their audiences. Love and adventure performances, it develops, will keep about 85 per cent of the audience to the end. By contrast, the most gripping historical sketches hold only 65 per cent, and many hold less than one third of their starting viewers. Informational programs, again, rank near the bottom in "holding power."

Television critics, who write about TV programs in newspapers and magazines, are frequently harsh in their remarks about violence, sadism, bad taste on the screen. However, Dallas W. Smythe, a professor of communications economics at the University of Illinois, analyzed New York City programs for 1955 and concludes that programs which critics liked best seldom drew the biggest audiences.

The public is fickle. Top rating is hard to hold. The viewers tire rapidly of a particular show unless the producers manage to come up with fresh material, new appeals.

REVIEW QUESTIONS

1. Summarize the supposedly negative effects of watching television.
2. What were the benefits of television?
3. Which concerns about television strike you as being equally relevant today?

BETTY FRIEDAN

FROM *The Feminine Mystique*

Born in 1921, Betty Friedan graduated with honors from Smith College and pursued a doctoral degree in psychology at the University of California at Berkeley before dropping out to marry. She raised three children during the 1950s and performed the role of the dutiful housewife and mother. In 1957, however, she experienced a revelation of sorts when she mailed an alumni questionnaire to her Smith classmates. The replies stunned her. Most of her classmates reported that while their lives were superficially successful they suffered from an aching "sense of dissatisfaction." This prompted Friedan to spend five years researching a book dealing with what she called the "problem with no name." Published in 1963, The Feminine Mystique *dissected the prevailing "mystique" of the blissful suburban housewife, and it helped launch the feminist movement.*

The suburban housewife—she was the dream image of the young American women and the envy, it was said, of women all over the world. The American housewife—freed by science and labor-saving appliances from the drudgery, the dangers of childbirth and the illnesses of her grandmother. She was healthy, beautiful, educated, concerned only about her husband, her children, her home. She had found true feminine fulfillment. As a housewife and mother, she was respected as a full and equal partner to man in his world. She was free to choose automobiles, clothes, appliances, supermarkets; she had everything that women ever dreamed of.

In the fifteen years after World War II, this mystique of feminine fulfillment became the cherished and self-perpetuating core of contemporary American culture. Millions of women lived their lives in the image of those pretty pictures of the American suburban housewife, kissing their husbands goodbye in front of the picture window, depositing their stationwagonsful of children at school, and smiling as they ran the new electric waxer over the spotless kitchen floor. . . .

Their only dream was to be perfect wives and mothers; their highest ambition to have five children and a beautiful house, their only fight to get and keep husbands. They had no thought for the unfeminine problems outside the home; they wanted the men to make the major decisions. They gloried in their role as women, and wrote proudly on the census blank: "Occupation: housewife."

For over fifteen years, the words written for women, and the words women used when they talked to each other, while their husbands sat on the other side of the room and talked shop or politics or septic tanks, were about problems with their children, or how to keep their husbands happy, or improve their children's school, or cook chicken or make slipcovers. . . .

But on an April morning in 1959, I heard a mother of four, having coffee with four other mothers in a suburban development fifteen miles from New York, say in a tone of quiet desperation, "the problem." And the others knew, without words, that she was not talking about a problem with her husband, or her children, or her home.

Suddenly they all realized they shared the same problem, the problem that has no name. . . .

The problem lay buried, unspoken, for many years in the minds of American women. It was a strange stirring, a sense of dissatisfaction, a yearning that women suffered in the middle of the twentieth century in the United States. Each suburban wife struggled with it alone. As she made the beds, shopped for groceries, matched slipcover material, ate peanut butter sandwiches with her children, chauffeured Cub Scouts and Brownies, lay beside her husband at night—she was afraid to ask even of herself the silent question—"Is this all?"

For over fifteen years there was no word of this yearning in the millions of words written about women, for women, in all the columns, books and articles by experts telling women their role was to seek fulfillment as wives and mothers. Over and over women heard in voices of tradition and of Freudian sophistication that they could desire no greater destiny than to glory in their own femininity. Experts told them how to catch a man and keep him, how to breastfeed children and handle their toilet training, how to cope with sibling rivalry and adolescent rebellion; how to buy a dishwasher, bake bread, cook gourmet snails, and build a swimming pool with their own hands; how to dress, look, and act more feminine and make marriage more exciting; how to keep their husbands from dying young and their sons from growing into delinquents. They were taught to pity the neurotic, unfeminine, unhappy women who wanted to be poets or physicists or presidents. They learned that truly feminine women do not want careers, higher education, political rights—the independence and the opportunities that the old-fashioned feminists fought for. Some women, in their forties and fifties, still remembered painfully giving up those dreams, but most of the younger women no longer even thought about them. A thousand expert voices applauded their femininity, their adjustment, their new maturity. All they had to do was devote their lives from earliest girlhood to finding a husband and bearing children. . . .

The feminine mystique says that the highest value and the only commitment for women is the fulfillment of their own femininity. It says that the great mistake of Western culture, through most of its history, has been the under-valuation of this femininity. It says this femininity is so mysterious and intuitive and close to the creation and origin of life that man-made science may never be able to understand it. But however special and different, it is in no way inferior to the nature of man; it may even in certain respects be superior. The mistake, says the mystique, the root of women's troubles in the past is that women envied men, women tried to be like men, instead of accepting their own nature, which can find fulfillment only in sexual passivity, male domination, and nurturing maternal love.

*　　*　　*

. . . The logic of the feminine mystique redefined the very nature of woman's problem. When woman was seen as a human being of limitless human potential, equal to man, anything that kept her from realizing her full potential was a problem to be solved: barriers to higher education and political participation, discrimination or prejudice in law or morality. But now that woman is seen only in terms of her sexual role, the barriers to the realization of her full potential, the prejudices which deny her full participation in the world, are no longer problems. The only problems now are those that might disturb her adjustment as a housewife. So career is a problem, education is a problem, political interest, even the very admission of women's intelligence and individuality is a problem. And finally there is the problem that has no name, a vague undefined wish for "something more" than washing dishes, ironing, punishing and praising the children. . . .

If an able American woman does not use her human energy and ability in some meaningful pursuit (which necessarily means competition, for there is competition in every serious pursuit of our society), she will fritter away her energy in neurotic symptoms, or unproductive exercise, or destructive "love."

It is time to stop giving lip service to the idea that there are no battles left to be fought for women in America, that women's rights have already been won. It is ridiculous to tell girls to keep quiet when they enter a new field, or an old one, so the men will not notice they are there. In almost every professional field, in business and in the arts and sciences, women are still treated as second-class citizens. It would be a great service to tell girls who plan to work in society to expect this subtle, uncomfortable discrimination—tell them not to be quiet, and hope it will go away, but fight it. A girl should not expect special privileges because of her sex, but neither should she "adjust" to prejudice and discrimination.

She must learn to compete then, not as a woman, but as a human being. Not until a great many women move out of the fringes into the mainstream will society itself provide the arrangements for their new life plan. . . .

REVIEW QUESTIONS

1. What did Friedan mean by the "problem with no name"?
2. What was the "feminine mystique" and what did it suggest about the historical causes of female unhappiness?
3. Describe how this excerpt might have helped inspire a new generation of feminist activists.

REINHOLD NIEBUHR

FROM Varieties of Religious Revival (1955)

Reinhold Niebuhr (1892–1971) was the foremost Christian theologian of the twentieth century. A graduate of Yale Divinity School, he pastored a church in Detroit during the 1930s before joining the faculty of Union Theological Seminary in New York City. In the midst of the surge of popular interest in Christianity during the cold war, he raised penetrating questions about the depth of spiritual commitment evident in the movement.

The New Republic 132 (6 June). Reprinted by permission of *The New Republic*, © 1955, The New Republic, Inc., pp. 13–16.

No one can question the fact that we are experiencing a marked increase of interest in religion if not a revival of religious faith. The interpretations of the causes and possible consequences of this phenomenon may differ. It may be viewed with contradictory emotions of satisfaction or alarm by those who rather too simply regard religion as *per se* either good or bad. But about the evidences of this revival there can be no doubt.

Both church statistics and public-opinion polls, as well as the sale of religious literature, can be regarded as telling evidence. Church membership in the three faiths of Catholicism, Judaism and Protestantism has reached the surprising percentage of 60 percent of the population. It is also significant that 15 percent more of the population actually claim to be members of congregations than the church statistics actually establish. . . .

The popularity of television and radio religious

broadcasts need not be numbered among the significant indices. . . . The sale of religious books, running into millions of copies for the "best sellers," may be a more important index, though this index immediately confronts us with the problem of gauging the inner significance of the current revival. For the most popular books on religion will be regarded by both the religious and the irreligious as evidence of the spread of a very dubious religion. Beginning with the best seller from the pen of the late Rabbi Joshua Liebman in 1946, and culminating in the phenomenal sale of the books by Norman Vincent Peale, this religious literature must be regarded as evidence of a rather frantic effort of the naturally optimistic American soul to preserve its optimism in the age of anxiety.

The themes of "peace of mind" and "positive thinking" either express a religion of self-assurance or they are pious guides to personal success. They can not be taken seriously by responsible religious or secular people because they do not come to terms with the basic collective problems of our atomic age, and because the peace which they seek to inculcate is rather too simple and neat. It is not like the "peace of God which passeth understanding." That peace passes understanding precisely because it is at peace with pain in it. The pain is caused by love and responsibility. In short, many of the indices of religiosity point to types of religion which are only remotely related to the main themes of the historic faiths. Interest in them can not, therefore, be attributed to a revival of these faiths.

The popularity of evangelists such as Billy Graham in Europe, as well as in America, is a quite different index of religious interest, but probably the interest is not as significant as usually assumed. Billy Graham expounds a fundamentalist version of the Christian faith. His faith is certainly superior to the success cults. It expresses some of the central themes of the Christian faith. He demands that men be confronted with God in Christ; and hopes that this confrontation will lead to conversion. Billy Graham carries on the traditions of our old frontier evangelistic piety, probably on a higher

level than Billy Sunday achieved a generation back. Such evangelism may discipline certain disordered individual lives. But the secular critics of religion do not have to take seriously a version of the Christian faith which suggests that the dilemma of our age is due to a "wickedness" which conversion can cure.

Billy Graham sincerely carries on the individualistic and perfectionist illusions of the evangelistic Christianity of the old "Bible Belt." The moral dilemmas of the atomic age are certainly among the causes of the decay of secular religious alternatives to the historic faiths. But this kind of simple religious moralism was ironically refuted on a recent week-end when Billy Graham preached to the President in the morning and appeared on a television program in the afternoon. On television he suggested that conversion to Christianity could solve the problem of the hydrogen bomb. He preached to a President whose loyalty board had eliminated a very high-minded scientist from our atomic energy program because *inter alia* he was not sufficiently "enthusiastic" about the production of the hydrogen bomb.

One wonders what the President thought about this curious juxtaposition of events. But at any rate, it is obvious that contemporary moral dilemmas refute both the secular and the religious moralists who think that we could solve our problems if either "evil" men would become "good" or "ignorant" men "intelligent." There is always validity in the religious challenge, which converts drunkards and adulterers from their evil ways, and which convicts all of us who regard ourselves as "normal" of really being quite self-centered. But any religious or secular interpretation of life which would solve our collective moral and political dilemmas simply either by conversion or enlightenment has obviously not measured the depth of the problem.

Reference to President Eisenhower's devotion to Billy Graham suggests another index of the religious revival which may well leave both the religious and the secularists somewhat apprehensive. I refer to the development of the idea that the religious faith is a part of the "American way of life." Foreign observers are baffled by this phenomenon in a nation which they regard as, in many respects, the most "secular" of all cultures and which certainly is, in the sense that it is more technocratic than any European culture, and reveals fewer evidences of religious influence upon its traditions. But we Americans have somehow combined good plumbing with religious faith in the "American way of life."

The Refutation of Secular Religions

But an analysis of the dubious and even dangerous manifestations of modern religiosity has not brought us closer to the real religious issue of our day, nor explained the real revival of interest in, if not adherence to, the historic Christian and Jewish faiths. One index of that genuine revival is the increased interest in religious courses in our colleges and universities and the increased sympathy for religious faith among "intellectuals." The fact is that the religious faith which was regarded as completely outmoded in the days when those of us who are not old were in college, has become a live option, not only for the "simple and the credulous" but for the sophisticated. How can we explain that startling change?

Perhaps one inclusive answer can be given: the secular alternatives to the historic faiths have been refuted by history. These secular alternatives were also "religions" in the sense that they answered the question about the meaning of human existence. They answered the question in terms of simple rational intelligibility rather than in terms of that paradoxical combination of mystery and meaning which characterizes the Biblical faiths. These Biblical faiths believe in a God who can not be quite comprehended, in the "mystery" of creation, and in the mystery of redemption and revelation. In the Christian faith, the crux of the revelation of the divine mystery is asserted to ban historical drama in which the relation between the divine justice and mercy is revealed in such a way that those who confront the divine through this revelation are at once convicted of their sin and

forgiven so that they can walk in the "newness of life."

. . . Will Herberg is probably right in asserting that the chief cause of the growth of the religious communities is the desire of "belonging" which men feel, particularly in the anonymity of our urban centers.

. . . The revival of religious faith today, despite the traditional and modern corruptions of religious faith proves that the enigmas of history, of man's freedom and responsibility and of his guilt, can not be solved as easily as modern culture assumed. The human being develops grace and wisdom by discerning the meaning of existence in a realm of mystery, and meaning by a commitment of faith. He is conscious of a responsible freedom which is not easily explained in any system of coherence elaborated by either the philosophies or the sciences; and he knows himself to be guilty, ultimately considered, and therefore in need of forgiveness. This mystery and meaning of freedom, sin, and grace are the perennial sources of the religious life. They have expressed themselves anew against the prejudices of a secular age.

It must, however, be recognized that the only religious faith which can be the source of charity and wisdom is one which knows the religious life itself to be as ambiguous as all human life is. The worship of God is claimed too simply as the ally of our cause against the foe.

This recognition of the ambiguity in the religious life itself must include an appreciation of the contributions which secular protests against religion have made and are making to the purification of religion; and of the necessity of all forms of rational discipline for the guidance of man in the moral and social complexities of our common life. This appreciation does not, however, invalidate the witness of a genuine religion against secular aberrations which deny the dignity of man and subordinate him to a social or political process, or which make the worship of reason the basis of a new fanatic unreasonableness, as grievous as the old religious fanaticism.

REVIEW QUESTIONS

1. Which indicators of religious revival were most reliable to Niebuhr?

2. What were some of the fundamental issues that religious life had to address?

3. Why does Niebuhr describe religious life as ambiguous?

33 ∞ CONFLICT AND DEADLOCK: THE EISENHOWER YEARS

Dwight D. Eisenhower was elected in 1952 in large part because voters believed he could end the stalemated war in Korea and lead the United States through the turbulent challenges of the cold war. Americans yearned for peace and stability, and "Ike" promised to provide both. As a hero of World War II and a political moderate who promised the nation a program of "dynamic conservatism," he perfectly suited the mood and needs of the time.

To satisfy the right wing of the Republican Party, Eisenhower tapped John Foster Dulles as his secretary of state. A dogmatic, humorless Calvinist descended from missionaries and diplomats, Dulles resolved to wage holy war against "atheistic communism." Impatient with the containment program of Truman and the Democrats, he advocated a more aggressive policy designed to "liberate" the "captive peoples" of Eastern Europe and China from communist tyranny. He threatened America's allies that if they did not support such a militant anticommunism he would undertake "an agonizing reappraisal" of American commitments. Moreover, Dulles believed that the Soviets responded only to force, and this sometimes required engaging in "brinkmanship," a willingness to take crises to the edge of war in order to stem communist aggression.

Dulles's crusading rhetoric pleased Republican conservatives, but Eisenhower preferred a less confrontational approach. To be sure, he, too, was a fervent anticommunist. But as a former general he also knew when and where to fight. For example, when the Hungarians and Poles revolted against Soviet rule in 1956, the United States did not intervene to help "liberate" them. Eisenhower realized that there was no feasible way to do so. He, more than Dulles, understood the limits of American power.

Eisenhower also understood the financial limits of a worldwide crusade against communism. The former general was determined to reduce military spending so as to maintain a balanced budget and a thriving economy. He and Dulles thus fastened on what came to be called a policy of "massive retaliation."

Instead of relying on expensive ground forces to provide national security and preserve international order, they decided to use the threat of massive nuclear retaliation to keep the Soviets in line and at the same time reduce defense spending. This would give the United States what Dulles called "a bigger bang for the buck."

The threatened use of nuclear weapons, however, made little sense in dealing with trouble spots in Southeast Asia. In Indochina, for example, the United States had provided France with $1.2 billion in military aid between 1950 and 1954 in its war against Ho Chi Minh and his Vietminh followers. Eisenhower adopted a rationale that later American presidents would repeat: if the communists gained control of Indochina, then the neighboring countries would soon fall like dominoes. In 1954 the French sought to draw the elusive Vietminh into the open for a single climactic battle at Dien Bien Phu. But the idea backfired, and the French found themselves surrounded and cut off. The French government issued a desperate plea for American air strikes, but Eisenhower refused. He did not want to involve the United States in another Asian war on the heels of the armistice in Korea.

The beleaguered French army at Dien Bien Phu surrendered in May 1954. At the Geneva Peace Conference the parties agreed to divide Indochina at the 17th parallel, creating the temporary states of North and South Vietnam. An election scheduled for 1956 would decide under what form of government the infant nation would be unified (though the United States subsequently refused to support the election because it feared that Ho Chi Minh would win by a large margin). Just as the United States had filled the breach created by the departure of the British from Greece, the American government now agreed to replace the French in Vietnam, offering its support to the new South Vietnamese leader, Ngo Dinh Diem.

Perhaps the greatest challenge associated with the cold war was that its ideological emphasis made every trouble spot in the world fertile ground for Soviet-American competition. The Middle East was roiling with tensions during the 1950s as Arab-Israeli hostility sparked violent confrontations and enhanced the appeal of communist rhetoric. To deal with the volatile situation, Eisenhower requested from Congress in 1957 a resolution empowering him to use military force in the Middle East against any manifestation of "international communism." This came to be known as the Eisenhower Doctrine, and it carried a significance beyond its immediate purposes: it effectively transferred the authority to wage war from Congress to the executive branch (a shift that had begun during the Korean War but had never received explicit recognition or approval). In the summer of 1957 Eisenhower invoked his new authority, dispatching 15,000 marines to Lebanon.

In the domestic arena the most important development during the 1950s involved civil rights and race relations. The social changes wrought by World

War II gave added impetus to the efforts to end racial segregation. The massive migration of blacks from the South to other regions of the country created new political dynamics that bolstered the efforts of the National Association for the Advancement of Colored People (NAACP) and other organizations to tear down racial barriers. Led by attorney Thurgood Marshall, the NAACP in 1950 decided to mount a legal challenge against the "separate but equal" doctrine that the Supreme Court had sanctioned in the case of Plessy v. Ferguson *(1896).*

Their opportunity arose when Oliver Brown, a resident of Topeka, Kansas, filed suit against the local school board. He objected to the requirement that his daughter be bused across town in order to attend an all-black school. Initially, a federal appeals court rejected Brown's suit because the segregated schools in Topeka satisfied the "equality test." But after two years of testimony and arguments, the Supreme Court overturned the lower court in its famous decision, Brown v. Board of Education of Topeka, Kansas *(1954). The resolution of the case did not itself end racial segregation, but it did set in motion a series of events that would give rise to a national civil rights movement dedicated to desegregation and true racial equality.*

JOHN FOSTER DULLES

Massive Retaliation (1954)

John Foster Dulles (1888–1959) was a prominent Wall Street lawyer before becoming secretary of state in 1953. He sharply criticized former president Truman's containment policy for being too complacent. Dulles viewed the conflict with the Soviet Union as a stark contrast between good and evil. He was convinced that the Soviets were intent upon dominating the world and that the United States was the epitome of democratic idealism. He wanted the United States not simply to contain the spread of communism but to defeat it. In practice, however, he sought to meet the Soviet threat without bankrupting the nation's economy or overtaxing its military resources. This led him to the concept of "massive retaliation," which he articulated in this 1954 address.

From *Department of State Bulletin* 30 (25 January 1954):107–110.

T he Soviet Communists are planning for what they call "an entire historical era," and we should do the same. They seek, through many types of maneuvers, gradually to divide and weaken the free nations by overextending them in efforts which, as Lenin put it, are "beyond their strength, so that they come to practical bankruptcy." Then, said Lenin, "our victory is assured"

Then, said Stalin, will be "the moment for the decisive blow."

In the face of this strategy, measures cannot be judged adequate merely because they ward off an immediate danger. It is essential to do this, but it is also essential to do so without exhausting ourselves.

When the Eisenhower administration applied this test, we felt that some transformations were needed. It is not sound military strategy permanently to commit U.S. land forces to Asia to a degree that leaves us no strategic reserves. It is not sound economics, or good foreign policy, to support permanently other countries; for in the long run, that creates as much ill will as good will. Also, it is not sound to become permanently committed to military expenditures so vast they lead to "practical bankruptcy."

Change was imperative to assure the stamina needed for permanent security. But it was equally imperative that change should be accompanied by understanding of our true purposes. Sudden and spectacular change had to be avoided. Otherwise, there might have been a panic among our friends and miscalculated aggression by our enemies. We can, I believe, make a good report in these respects.

We need allies and collective security. Our purpose is to make these relations more effective, less costly. This can be done by placing more reliance on deterrent power and less dependence on local defensive power.

This is accepted practice so far as local communities are concerned. We keep locks on our doors, but we do not have an armed guard in every home. We rely principally on a community security system so well equipped to punish any who break in and steal that, in fact, wouldbe aggressors are generally deterred. That is the modern way of getting maximum protection at a bearable cost.

What the Eisenhower administration seeks is a similar international security system. We want, for ourselves and the other free nations, a maximum deterrent at a bearable cost. Local defense will always be important. But there is no local defense which alone will contain the mighty land power of

the Communist world. Local defenses must be reinforced by the further deterrent of massive retaliatory power. A potential aggressor must know that he cannot always prescribe battle conditions that suit him. Otherwise, for example, a potential aggressor, who is glutted with manpower, might be tempted to attack in confidence that resistance would be confined to manpower. He might be tempted to attack in places where his superiority was decisive.

The way to deter aggression is for the free community to be willing and able to respond vigorously at places and with means of its own choosing.

So long as our basic policy concepts were unclear, our military leaders could not be selective in building our military power. If an enemy could pick his time and place and method of warfare— and if our policy was to remain the traditional one of meeting aggression by direct and local opposition—then we needed to be ready to fight in the Arctic and in the Tropics; in Asia, the Near East, and in Europe; by sea, by land, and by air; with old weapons and with new weapons. . . .

Before military planning could be changed, the President and his advisers, as represented by the National Security Council, had to make some basic policy decisions. This has been done. The basic decision was to depend primarily upon a great capacity to retaliate, instantly, by means and at places of our choosing. Now the Department of Defense and the Joint Chiefs of Staff can shape our military establishment to fit what is our policy, instead of having to try to be ready to meet the enemy's many choices. That permits of a selection of military means instead of a multiplication of means. As a result, it is now possible to get, and share, more basic security at less cost.

Let us now see how this concept has been applied to foreign policy, taking first the Far East.

In Korea this administration effected a major transformation. The fighting has been stopped on honorable terms. That was possible because the aggressor, already thrown back to and behind his place of beginning, was faced with the possibility that the fighting might, to his own great peril, soon spread beyond the limits and methods which he had selected.

The cruel toll of American youth and the non-productive expenditure of many billions have been stopped. Also our armed forces are no longer largely committed to the Asian mainland. We can begin to create a strategic reserve which greatly improves our defensive posture.

This change gives added authority to the warning of the members of the United Nations which fought in Korea that, if the Communists renewed the aggression, the United Nations response would not necessarily be confined to Korea. . . .

In the ways I outlined we gather strength for the longterm defense of freedom. We do not, of course, claim to have found some magic formula that insures against all forms of Communist successes. It is normal that at some times and at some places there may be setbacks to the cause of freedom. What we do expect to insure is that any setbacks will have only temporary and local significance, because they will leave unimpaired those free world assets which in the long run will prevail.

If we can deter such aggression as would mean general war, and that is our confident resolve, then we can let time and fundamentals work for us. . . .

REVIEW QUESTIONS

1. What is the essential reasoning behind Dulles's policy of deterrence?
2. Assess the strengths and weaknesses of using the threat of atomic weapons as the basis of a "massive retaliation" strategy.

DWIGHT D. EISENHOWER

A Letter to Ngo Dinh Diem (1954)

Following their catastrophic defeat at Dien Bien Phu in 1954, the French reluctantly granted independence to Vietnam. At the Geneva Peace Conference the new nation was "temporarily" divided into northern and southern states, with the communists in control in the north. The first premier in the south was Ngo Dinh Diem, a staunch anticommunist and devout Roman Catholic. As the nationwide elections to unify all of Vietnam under one government approached in 1956, Diem refused to participate because he sensed a communist victory. Even though this violated the Geneva Accords, the United States government endorsed Diem's action. By then, American officials were already propping up the Diem regime and were determined to maintain a separate, noncommunist South Vietnam. The following letter from Eisenhower to Diem reveals the depth of such a commitment.

From *Department of State Bulletin* 31 (15 November 1954):735–736.

Dear Mr. President:

I have been following with great interest the course of developments in Vietnam, particularly since the conclusion of the conference at Geneva. The implications of the agreement concerning Vietnam have caused grave concern regarding the future of a country temporarily divided by an artificial military grouping, weakened by a long and exhausting war, and faced with enemies without and by their subversive collaborators within.

Your recent requests for aid to assist in the formidable project of the movement of several hundred thousand loyal Vietnamese citizens away from areas which are passing under a *de facto* rule and political ideology which they abhor, are being fulfilled. I am glad that the United States is able to assist in this humanitarian effort.

We have been exploring ways and means to permit our aid to Vietnam to be more effective and to make a greater contribution to the welfare and stability of the Government of Vietnam. I am, accordingly, instructing the American Ambassador to Vietnam to examine with you in your capacity as Chief of Government, how an intelligent program of American aid given directly to your Government can serve to assist Vietnam in its present hour of trial, provided that your Government is prepared to give assurances as to the standards of performance it would be able to maintain in the event such aid were supplied.

The purpose of this offer is to assist the Government of Vietnam in developing and maintaining a strong, viable state, capable of resisting attempted subversion or aggression through military means. The Government of the United States expects that this aid will be met by performance on the part of the Government of Vietnam in undertaking needed reforms. It hopes that such aid, combined with your own continuing efforts, will contribute effectively toward an independent Vietnam endowed with a strong Government. Such a Government would, I hope, be so responsive to the nationalist aspirations of its people, so enlightened in purpose and effective in performance, that it will be respected both at home and abroad and discourage any who might wish to impose a foreign ideology on your free people.

REVIEW QUESTIONS

1. How did Eisenhower characterize the conflict in Vietnam?
2. What did Eisenhower mean by "a foreign ideology"?
3. Did Eisenhower specify what types of aid the United States should supply or what types of reform Diem should undertake?

The Eisenhower Doctrine (1957)

During the 1950s most of the newly independent nations in Africa and Asia refused to choose sides between the Soviet Union and the United States, preferring instead to remain neutral ("nonaligned"). In the view of Dulles and other policymakers, however, there could be no neutrality amid such an ideological conflict. Dulles often referred to such nonaligned status as "immoral." Concerns over the vulnerability of nonaligned nations in the Middle East to Communist subversion led Eisenhower and Congress to articulate a rationale for American intervention.

From *United States Statutes at Large*, 71:5–6.

*R*esolved, That the President be and hereby is authorized to cooperate with and assist any nation or group of nations in the general area of the Middle East desiring such assistance in the development of economic strength dedicated to the maintenance of national independence.

SEC. 2. The President is authorized to undertake, in the general area of the Middle East, military assistance programs with any nation or group of nations of that area desiring such assistance. Furthermore, the United States regards as vital to the national interest and world peace the preservation of the independence and integrity of the nations of the Middle East. To this end, if the President determines the necessity thereof, the United States is prepared to use armed force to assist any such nation or group of nations requesting assistance against armed aggression from any country controlled by international communism: *Provided,* That such employment shall be consonant with the treaty obligations of the United States and with the Constitution of the United States.

SEC. 3. The President is hereby authorized to use during the balance of the fiscal year 1957 for economic and military assistance under this joint resolution not to exceed $200,000,000 from any appropriation now available for carrying out the provisions of the Mutual Security Act of 1954. . . .

SEC. 4. The President should continue to furnish facilities and military assistance, within the provisions of applicable law and established policies, to the United Nations Emergency Force in the Middle East, with a view to maintaining the truce in that region.

SEC. 5. The President shall within the months of January and July of each year report to the Congress his action hereunder.

SEC. 6. This joint resolution shall expire when the President shall determine that the peace and security of the nations in the general area of the Middle East are reasonably assured by international conditions created by action of the United Nations or otherwise except that it may be terminated earlier by a concurrent resolution of the two Houses of Congress.

REVIEW QUESTIONS

1. Did the Eisenhower Doctrine place any limits on American assistance?
2. Did the resolution define "peace and security"?
3. The resolution focused on external threats posed by countries controlled by communism. What did this imply about the way policymakers viewed the spread of communism?

Brown v. Board of Education of Topeka (1954)

After trying for almost a half century, the National Association for the Advancement of Colored People (NAACP) finally succeeded in getting the Supreme Court to review the "separate but equal" principle articulated in the Plessy v. Ferguson *case of 1896. In the mid-1950s the vast majority of public schools, especially in the South, were racially separate but far from equal in resources or facilities. In the* Brown *case, however, the Court did not stress this fact; instead it advanced a different line of reasoning that ultimately invalidated racially based school segregation. While the decision did not transform school systems overnight, the unanimous Court provided the foundation for great advances over the next ten years.*

From *Supreme Court Reporter* (St. Paul, MN: West Publishing, 1954), 74:687–692. [Editorial insertions appear in square brackets—*Ed.*]

CHIEF JUSTICE WARREN: These cases come to us from the states of Kansas, South Carolina, Virginia, and Delaware. They are premised on different facts and different local conditions, but a common legal question justifies their consideration together in this consolidated opinion.

In each of the cases, minors of the Negro race, through their legal representatives, seek the aid of the courts in obtaining admission to the public schools of their community on a nonsegregated basis. In each instance, they have been denied admission to schools attended by white children under laws requiring or permitting segregation according to race. This segregation was alleged to deprive the plaintiffs of the equal protection of the laws under the Fourteenth Amendment. In each of the cases other than the Delaware case, a three-judge federal district court denied relief to the plaintiffs on the so-called "separate but equal" doctrine announced by this Court in *Plessy v. Ferguson* (1896).

Under that doctrine, equality of treatment is accorded when the races are provided substantially equal facilities, even though these facilities be separate. . . . The plaintiffs contend that segregated public schools are not "equal" and cannot be made "equal," and that hence they are deprived of the equal protection of the laws. Because of the obvious importance of the question presented, the Court took jurisdiction. . . .

Reargument was largely devoted to the circumstances surrounding the adoption of the Fourteenth Amendment in 1868. It covered exhaustively consideration of the Amendment in Congress, ratification by the states, then existing practices in racial segregation, and the views of proponents and opponents of the Amendment.

This discussion and our own investigation convince us that, although these sources cast some light, it is not enough to resolve the problem with which we are faced. At best, they are inconclusive. The most avid proponents of the post-[Civil] War Amendments undoubtedly intended them to remove all legal distinctions among "all persons born or naturalized in the United States." Their opponents, just as certainly, were antagonistic to both the letter and the spirit of the Amendments and wished them to have the most limited effect. What others in Congress and the state legislatures had in mind cannot be determined with any degree of certainty.

An additional reason for the inconclusive nature of the Amendment's history, with respect to segregated schools, is the status of public education at that time. In the South, the movement toward free common schools, supported by general taxation, had not yet taken hold. Education of white children was largely in the hands of private groups. Education of Negroes was almost nonexistent, and practically all of the race were illiterate. In fact, any education of Negroes was forbidden by law in some states.

Today, in contrast, many Negroes have achieved outstanding success in the arts and sciences as well as in the business and professional world. It is true that public education had already advanced further in the North, but the effect of the amendment on Northern States was generally ignored in the congressional debates. Even in the North, the conditions of public education did not approximate those existing today. The curriculum was usually rudimentary; ungraded schools were common in rural areas; the school term was but three months a year in many states; and compulsory school attendance was virtually unknown. As a consequence, it is not surprising that there should be so little in the history of the Fourteenth Amendment relating to its intended effect on public education.

In the first cases in this Court construing the Fourteenth Amendment, decided shortly after its adoption, the Court interpreted it as proscribing all stateimposed discriminations against the Negro race. The doctrine of "separate but equal" did not make its appearance in this Court until 1896 in the case of *Plessy v. Ferguson*, involving not education but transportation. . . .

In approaching this problem, we cannot turn the clock back to 1868 when the Amendment was adopted, or even to 1896 when *Plessy v. Ferguson* was written. We must consider public education in the light of its full development and its present place in American life throughout the Nation. Only in this way can it be determined if segregation in public schools deprives these plaintiffs of the equal protection of the laws.

Today, education is perhaps the most important function of state and local governments. Compulsory school attendance laws and the great expenditures for education both demonstrate our recognition of the importance of education to our democratic society. It is required in the performance of our most basic public responsibilities, even service in the armed forces. It is the very foundation of good citizenship. Today it is a principal instrument in awakening the child to cultural values, in preparing him for later professional training, and in helping him to adjust normally to his environment.

In these days, it is doubtful that any child may reasonably be expected to succeed in life if he is denied the opportunity of an education. Such an opportunity, where the state has undertaken to provide it, is a right which must be made available to all on equal terms.

We come then to the question presented: Does segregation of children in public schools solely on the basis of race, even though the physical facilities and other "tangible" factors may be equal, deprive the children of the minority group of equal educational opportunities? We believe that it does.

In *Sweatt v. Painter*, in finding that a segregated law school for Negroes could not provide them equal educational opportunities, this Court relied in large part on "those qualities which are incapable of objective measurement but which make for greatness in a law school." In *McLaurin v. Oklahoma State Regents*, the Court, in requiring that a Negro admitted to a white graduate school be treated like all other students, again resorted to intangible considerations: ". . . his ability to study, to engage in discussions and exchange views with other students, and, in general, to learn his profession."

Such considerations apply with added force to children in grade and high schools. To separate them from others of similar age and qualifications solely because of their race generates a feeling of inferiority as to their status in the community that may affect their hearts and minds in a way unlikely ever to be undone. The effect of this separation on their educational opportunities was well stated by a finding in the Kansas case by a court which nevertheless felt compelled to rule against the Negro plaintiffs:

"Segregation of white and colored children in public schools has a detrimental effect upon the colored children. The impact is greater when it has the sanction of the law; for the policy of separating the races is usually interpreted as denoting the inferiority of the Negro group. A sense of inferiority affects the motivation of a child to learn. Segregation with the sanction of law, therefore, has a tendency to retard the educational and mental development of Negro children and to deprive them of some of the benefits they would receive in a racially integrated school system."

Whatever may have been the extent of psychological knowledge at the time of *Plessy v. Ferguson*, this finding is amply supported by modern authority. Any language in *Plessy v. Ferguson* contrary to this finding is rejected.

We conclude that in the field of public education the doctrine of "separate but equal" has no place. Separate educational facilities are inherently unequal. Therefore, we hold that the plaintiffs and others similarly situated for whom the actions have been brought are, by reason of the segregation complained of, deprived of the equal protection of the laws guaranteed by the Fourteenth Amendment. . . .

REVIEW QUESTIONS

1. In reaching its decision, did the Court rely on the original intentions of the congressional framers of the Fourteenth Amendment? Why or why not?
2. According to the Court, were racially separate schools permissible as long as they were equal in quality and resources? Why or why not?

Southern Declaration on Integration (1956)

The Brown *decision provoked violent opposition in the South. Hastily formed White Citizens' Councils used economic pressure to coerce political leaders into opposing Court-ordered integration. State legislatures vowed to resist federal efforts to intervene in their schools, and some revived the rhetoric of nullification and secession. In 1956, 96 of the 128 southern senators and representatives signed a so-called Southern Manifesto castigating the Supreme Court's reasoning in the* Brown *case.*

From "Text of 96 Congressmen's Declaration on Integration," 12 March 1956. Copyright 1956 by *The New York Times.* Reprinted by permission. [Editorial insertions appear in square brackets—*Ed.*]

. . . We regard the decision of the Supreme Court in the school cases as clear abuse of judicial power. It climaxes a trend in the Federal judiciary undertaking to legislate, in derogation of the authority of Congress, and to encroach upon the reserved rights of the states and the people.

The original Constitution does not mention education. Neither does the Fourteenth Amendment nor any other amendment. The debates preceding the submission of the Fourteenth Amendment clearly show that there was no intent that it should affect the systems of education maintained by the states. . . .

When the amendment was adopted in 1868, there were thirty-seven states of the Union. Every one of the twenty-six states that had any substantial racial differences among its people either approved the operation of segregated schools already in existence or subsequently established such schools by action of the same law-making body which considered the Fourteenth Amendment.

As admitted by the Supreme Court in the public school case (*Brown v. Board of Education*), the doctrine of separate but equal schools "apparently originated in *Roberts v. City of Boston* (1849), upholding school segregation against attack as being violative of a state constitutional guarantee of equality." This constitutional doctrine began in the North—not in the South—and it was followed not only in Massachusetts, but in Connecticut, New York, Illinois, Indiana, Michigan, Minnesota, New Jersey, Ohio, Pennsylvania and other northern states until they, exercising their rights as states through the constitutional processes of local self-government, changed their school systems.

In the case of *Plessy v. Ferguson* in 1896 the Supreme Court expressly declared that under the Fourteenth Amendment no person was denied any of his rights if the states provided separate but equal public facilities. This decision has been followed in many other cases. It is notable that the Supreme Court, speaking through Chief Justice [William H.] Taft, a former President of the United States, unanimously declared in 1927 in *Lum v. Rice* that the "separate but equal" principle is ". . . within the discretion of the state in regulating its public schools and does not conflict with the Fourteenth Amendment."

This interpretation, restated time and again, became a part of the life of the people of many of the states and confirmed their habits, customs, traditions and way of life. It is founded on elemental humanity and common sense, for parents should not be deprived by Government of the right to direct the lives and education of their own children.

Though there has been no constitutional amendment or act of Congress changing this established legal principle almost a century old, the Supreme Court of the United States, with no legal basis for such action, undertook to exercise their naked judicial power and substituted their personal political and social ideas for the established law of the land.

This unwarranted exercise of power by the court, contrary to the Constitution, is creating chaos and confusion in the states principally affected. It is destroying the amicable relations between the white and Negro races that have been created through ninety years of patient effort by the good people of both races. It has planted hatred and suspicion where there has been heretofore friendship and understanding.

Without regard to the consent of the governed, outside agitators are threatening immediate and revolutionary changes in our public school systems. If done, this is certain to destroy the system of public education in some of the states.

With the gravest concern for the explosive and dangerous condition created by this decision and inflamed by outside meddlers:

We reaffirm our reliance on the Constitution as the fundamental law of the land.

We decry the Supreme Court's encroachments on rights reserved to the states and to the people, contrary to established law and to the Constitution.

We commend the motives of those states which have declared the intention to resist forced integration by any lawful means.

We appeal to the states and people who are not directly affected by these decisions to consider the constitutional principles involved against the time when they too, on issues vital to them, may be the victims of judicial encroachment.

Even though we constitute a minority in the present Congress, we have full faith that a majority of the American people believe in the dual system of government which has enabled us to achieve our greatness and will in time demand that the reserved rights of the states and of the people be made secure against judicial usurpation.

We pledge ourselves to use all lawful means to bring about a reversal of this decision which is contrary to the Constitution and to prevent the use of force in its implementation.

In this trying period, as we all seek to right this wrong, we appeal to our people not to be provoked by the agitators and troublemakers invading our states and to scrupulously refrain from disorder and lawless acts.

REVIEW QUESTIONS

1. According to the Declaration, why did the Court rule as it did in the *Brown* case?
2. What were the implications of the charge that "outside agitators" were trying to force changes in southern public schools?

DWIGHT D. EISENHOWER

The Situation in Little Rock (1957)

In the late summer of 1957 the school board of Little Rock, Arkansas, tried to implement the initial phase of its desegregation plan mandated by the federal government. Governor Orville Faubus, however, thwarted their efforts. Concerned that he would not be reelected if he did not oppose the racial integration of schools, he called out the National Guard to prevent the first African-American students from attending Central High School. After a three-week stalemate, a federal judge ordered the guardsmen off the school grounds. As the soldiers departed, they were replaced by an enraged white mob. The mayor appealed to President Eisenhower, who dispatched units of the 101st Airborne Division to disperse the mob, restore order, and protect the black students. Eisenhower was a reluctant participant in the Little Rock crisis, and he took pains to explain his actions.

From *Public Papers of the Presidents of the United States: Dwight D. Eisenhower, 1957,* no. 198 (Washington, DC, 1958), pp. 689–694.

*M*y Fellow Citizens. . . . I must speak to you about the serious situation that has arisen in Little Rock. . . . In that city, under the leadership of demagogic extremists, disorderly mobs have deliberately prevented the carrying out of proper orders from a federal court. Local authorities have not eliminated that violent opposition and, under the law, I yesterday issued a proclamation calling upon the mob to disperse.

This morning the mob again gathered in front of the Central High School of Little Rock, obviously for the purpose of again preventing the carrying out of the court's order relating to the admission of Negro children to that school.

Whenever normal agencies prove inadequate to the task and it becomes necessary for the executive branch of the federal government to use its powers and authority to uphold federal courts, the President's responsibility is inescapable.

In accordance with that responsibility, I have today issued an Executive Order directing the use of troops under federal authority to aid in the execution of federal law at Little Rock, Arkansas. This became necessary when my Proclamation of yesterday was not observed, and the obstruction of justice still continues. It is important that the reasons for my action be understood by all our citizens.

As you know, the Supreme Court of the United States has decided that separate public educational facilities for the races are inherently unequal and therefore compulsory school segregation laws are unconstitutional. . . .

During the past several years, many communities in our southern states have instituted public school plans for gradual progress in the enrollment and attendance of school children of all races in order to bring themselves into compliance with the law of the land.

They thus demonstrated to the world that we are a nation in which laws, not men, are supreme. I regret to say that this truth—the cornerstone of our liberties—was not observed in this instance. . . .

Here is the sequence of events in the development of the Little Rock school case. In May of 1955, the Little Rock School Board approved a moderate plan for the gradual desegregation of the public schools in that city. It provided that a start toward integration would be made at the present term in the high school, and that the plan would be in full operation by 1963. . . . Now this Little Rock plan was challenged in the courts by some who believed that the period of time as proposed in the plan was too long.

The United States Court at Little Rock, which has supervisory responsibility under the law for the plan of desegregation in the public schools, dismissed the challenge, thus approving a gradual rather than an abrupt change from the existing system. The court found that the school board had acted in good faith in planning for a public school system free from racial discrimination.

Since that time, the court has on three separate occasions issued orders directing that the plan be carried out. All persons were instructed to refrain from interfering with the efforts of the school board to comply with the law.

Proper and sensible observance of the law then demanded the respectful obedience which the nation has a right to expect from all its people. This, unfortunately, has not been the case at Little Rock. Certain misguided persons, many of them imported into Little Rock by agitators, have insisted upon defying the law and have sought to bring it into disrepute. The orders of the court have thus been frustrated.

The very basis of our individual rights and freedoms rests upon the certainty that the President and the Executive Branch of Government will support and insure the carrying out of the decisions of the federal courts, even, when necessary, with all the means at the President's command. . . .

Mob rule cannot be allowed to override the decisions of our courts.

Now, let me make it very clear that federal troops are not being used to relieve local and state authorities of their primary duty to preserve the peace and order of the community. . . .

The proper use of the powers of the Executive Branch to enforce the orders of a federal court is limited to extraordinary and compelling circumstances. Manifestly, such an extreme situation has been created in Little Rock. This challenge must be met and with such measures as will preserve to the people as a whole their lawfully protected rights in a climate permitting their free and fair exercise.

The overwhelming majority of our people in every section of the country are united in their respect for observance of the law—even in those cases where they may disagree with that law. . . . A foundation of our American way of life is our national respect for law.

In the South, as elsewhere, citizens are keenly aware of the tremendous disservice that has been done to the people of Arkansas in the eyes of the nation, and that has been done to the nation in the eyes of the world.

At a time when we face grave situations abroad because of the hatred that communism bears toward a system of government based on human rights, it would be difficult to exaggerate the harm that is being done to the prestige and influence, and indeed to the safety, of our nation and the world.

Our enemies are gloating over this incident and using it everywhere to misrepresent our whole nation. We are portrayed as a violator of those standards of conduct which the peoples of the world united to proclaim in the Charter of the United Nations. There they affirmed "faith in fundamental human rights" and "in the dignity and worth of the human person" and they did so "without distinction as to race, sex, language or religion."

And so, with deep confidence, I call upon the citizens of the State of Arkansas to assist in bringing to an immediate end all interference with the law and its processes. If resistance to the federal court orders ceases at once, the further presence of federal troops will be unnecessary and the City of Little Rock will return to its normal habits of peace and order and a blot upon the fair name and high honor of our nation in the world will be removed.

Thus will be restored the image of America and of all its parts as one nation, indivisible, with liberty and justice for all.

REVIEW QUESTIONS

1. Under what conditions did Eisenhower believe that intervention by the executive branch was justified?
2. How might the Soviet Union have exploited the controversy in Little Rock?
3. How would a proponent of segregation have rebutted Eisenhower's stance?

DWIGHT D. EISENHOWER

Farewell Address (1961)

After serving two full terms as president, Dwight D. Eisenhower retired from public life. Before turning the White House over to his Democratic successor, John F. Kennedy, he delivered a farewell address in which he expressed his hopes and fears for the nation and presented his personal disappointments and accomplishments. His speech turned out to be more prophetic than commentators at the time recognized.

From *Public Papers of the Presidents of the United States: Dwight D. Eisenhower, 1960–1*, no. 421 (Washington, DC, 1961), pp. 1035–1040.

My Fellow Americans:

Three days from now, after half a century in the service of our country, I shall lay down the responsibilities of office as, in traditional and solemn ceremony, the authority of the Presidency is vested in my successor. . . .

We now stand ten years past the midpoint of a century that has witnessed four major wars among great nations. Three of them involved our own country. Despite these holocausts America is today the strongest, the most influential and most productive nation in the world. Understandably proud of this preeminence we yet realize that America's leadership and prestige depend, not merely upon our unmatched material progress, riches and military strength, but on how we use our power in the interests of world peace and human betterment.

Throughout America's adventure in free government, our basic purposes have been to keep the peace; to foster progress in human achievement, and to enhance liberty, dignity and integrity among people and among nations. To strive for less would be unworthy of a free and religious people. Any failure traceable to arrogance, or our lack of comprehension or readiness to sacrifice would inflict upon us grievous hurt both at home and abroad.

Progress toward these noble goals is persistently threatened by the conflict now engulfing the world. It commands our whole attention, absorbs our very beings. We face a hostile ideology—global in scope, atheistic in character, ruthless in purpose, and insidious in method. Unhappily the danger it poses promises to be of indefinite duration. To meet it successfully, there is called for, not so much the emotional and transitory sacrifices of crisis, but rather those which enable us to carry forward steadily, surely, and without complaint the burdens of a prolonged and complex struggle—with liberty the stake. Only thus shall we remain, despite every provocation, on our charted course toward permanent peace and human betterment. . . .

A vital element in keeping the peace is our military establishment. Our arms must be mighty, ready for instant action, so that no potential aggressor may be tempted to risk his own destruction.

Our military organization today bears little relation to that known by any of my predecessors in peacetime, or indeed by the fighting men of World War II or Korea. Until the latest of our world conflicts, the United States had no armaments industry. American makers of plowshares could, with time and as required, make swords as well. But now we can no longer risk emergency improvisation of national defense; we have been compelled to create a permanent armaments industry of vast proportions. Added to this, three and a half million men and women are directly engaged in the defense establishment. We annually spend on military security more than the net income of all United States corporations.

This conjunction of an immense military establishment and a large arms industry is new in the American experience. The total influence—economic, political, even spiritual—is felt in every city, every state house, every office of the federal government. We recognize the imperative need for this development. Yet we must not fail to comprehend its grave implications. Our toil, resources, and livelihood are all involved; so is the very structure of our society.

In the councils of government, we must guard against the acquisition of unwarranted influence, whether sought or unsought, by the military-industrial complex. The potential for the disastrous rise of misplaced power exists and will persist. We must never let the weight of this combination endanger our liberties or democratic processes. We should take nothing for granted. Only an alert and knowledgeable citizenry can compel the proper meshing of the huge industrial and military machinery of defense with our peaceful methods and goals, so that security and liberty may prosper together.

Akin to, and largely responsible for the sweeping changes in our industrial-military posture, has been the technological revolution during recent decades.

In this revolution, research has become central; it also becomes more formalized, complex, and costly. A steadily increasing share is conducted for, by, or at the direction of, the federal government....

The prospect of domination of the nation's scholars by federal employment, project allocations, and the power of money is ever present—and is gravely to be regarded.

Yet, in holding scientific research and discovery in respect, as we should, we must also be alert to the equal and opposite danger that public policy could itself become the captive of a scientific-technological elite.

It is the task of statesmanship to mold, to balance, and to integrate these and other forces, new and old, within the principles of our democratic system—ever aiming toward the supreme goals of our free society.

Another factor in maintaining balance involves the element of time. As we peer into society's future, we—you and I, and our government—must avoid the impulse to live only for today, plundering, for our own ease and convenience, the precious resources of tomorrow. We cannot mortgage the material assets of our grandchildren without risking the loss also of their political and spiritual heritage. We want democracy to survive for all generations to come, not to become the insolvent phantom of tomorrow. Down the long lane of the history yet to be written America knows that this world of ours, ever growing smaller, must avoid becoming a community of dreadful fear and hate, and be, instead, a proud confederation of mutual trust and respect.

Such a confederation must be one of equals. The weakest must come to the conference table with the same confidence as do we, protected as we are by our moral, economic, and military strength. That table, though scarred by many past frustrations, cannot be abandoned for the certain agony of the battlefield. Disarmament, with mutual honor and confidence, is a continuing imperative. Together we must learn how to compose differences, not with arms, but with intellect and decent purpose.

Because this need is so sharp and apparent I confess that I lay down my official responsibilities in this field with a definite sense of disappointment. As one who has witnessed the horror and the lingering sadness of war—as one who knows that another war could utterly destroy this civilization which has been so slowly and painfully built over thousands of years—I wish I could say tonight that a lasting peace is in sight.

Happily, I can say that war has been avoided. Steady progress toward our ultimate goal has been made. But, so much remains to be done. As a private citizen, I shall never cease to do what little I can to help the world advance along that road....

REVIEW QUESTIONS

1. How did Eisenhower characterize the Soviet Union?

2. Given Eisenhower's description of communism, does his call for disarmament seem contradictory? Why or why not?

3. In light of the international environment during the 1950s, was Eisenhower's ability to keep the nation out of war a major or minor accomplishment? Explain.

34 ❧ NEW FRONTIERS: POLITICS AND SOCIAL CHANGE IN THE 1960s

The election of John F. Kennedy as president in 1960 ushered in a decade of energetic idealism that bore fruit in the founding of the Peace Corps, the War on Poverty, and Great Society programs of federal assistance to the poor. The 1960s also witnessed a dramatic new phase of the civil rights movement. Kennedy was one of the first political leaders to recognize the vast number of Americans not only mired in poverty but also hidden from public awareness. And, even though Kennedy himself was reluctant to assault racial injustice in the segregated South because of the political clout of southern Democrats, events eventually forced him and his successor, Lyndon B. Johnson, to make civil rights a primary concern.

During the 1950s Dr. Martin Luther King Jr., an ordained black minister, emerged as the heroic, charismatic leader of the national civil rights movement. He fastened upon a brilliant strategy—nonviolent civil disobedience—to gain the attention and sympathy of a complacent nation. Through boycotts, marches, sit-ins, and other forms of protest, King and the Southern Christian Leadership Conference (SCLC), which he founded, forced authorities to confront the injustices of racism. His passionate commitment and uplifting rhetoric helped excite national concern, and his efforts led directly to major new legislation such as the Civil Rights Act of 1964, which prohibited racial discrimination in employment and public facilities, and the Voting Rights Act of 1965, which outlawed literacy tests and other measures used by local registrars to deny blacks access to the ballot. In 1964 King was awarded the Nobel Peace Prize for his efforts.

Yet as time passed the civil rights movement began to fragment. The legal and political gains did not translate into immediate economic and social advances. Black neighborhoods continued to be plagued by crime and drug addiction, fatherless households, and intense frustration and alienation. On 11 August 1965, only five days after the passage of the Voting Rights Act, Watts, a black neighborhood in Los Angeles, erupted in a chaos of looting, arson, and violence. During the next three years, 300 more race riots occurred in inner-city communities across the nation. Over 200 people were killed, 7,000 injured, and 40,000 arrested. For many urban blacks outside the South, the mainstream civil rights movement had brought little tangible improvement in their lives. Most African Americans lived not in the rural South but in inner-city neighborhoods across the country, in major cities such as New York, Philadelphia, Detroit, Newark, Chicago, and Los Angeles. Blacks living in urban ghettos faced chronic poverty, unemployment, decaying housing and schools, and police brutality.

Young black activists outside the South grew impatient with Dr. King's leadership and his commitment to integration within the larger white society. Black militants such as Stokely Carmichael and H. Rap Brown rejected the nonviolent civil disobedience promoted by King and the SCLC. For them, "Black Power" became the rallying cry in the mid-1960s.

The concept of "Black Power" grew out of the tradition of black nationalism—the belief that people with African roots share a distinctive culture and destiny. It fed upon the seething discontent with the pace of social change within the black ghettos of urban America. Malcolm X was the most compelling proponent of black nationalism. A convert to the Black Muslim (the Nation of Islam) faith led by Elijah Muhammad, he urged African Americans to take control of their communities "by any means necessary," including violence. Unlike King and the other leaders of SCLC, Malcolm X was not interested in promoting integration. "Our enemy is the white man," he exclaimed. His goal was a separate, self-reliant black community within the United States. Yet during late 1964 Malcolm X began to moderate his stance. He broke with the Black Muslims and began to talk of racial cooperation. His defection cost him his life. On 21 February 1965, Malcolm X was shot and killed by three Black Muslim assassins.

The militance displayed by Malcolm X survived among the younger proponents of "Black Power." During the summer of 1966 Stokely Carmichael led the Student Nonviolent Coordinating Committee (SNCC) away from its original commitment to peaceful social change. His successor, H. Rap Brown, told the members of SNCC to grab their guns, burn the cities, and shoot the "honky to death." A group of young black militants in California led by Huey Newton and Bobby Seale shared these strong feelings and organized the Black Panther Party to engage in guerrilla violence against white authorities.

During each summer between 1965 and 1968, urban America was aflame with racial rioting. In 1967, for example, 87 people were killed and over 16,000 arrested. The violence prompted President Johnson in 1967 to appoint a special National Advisory Commission on Civil Disorders headed by Governor Otto Kerner of Illinois to determine the causes of the racial turmoil. The Kerner Commission Report appeared in 1968. It called for a "compassionate, massive and sustained" commitment to racial equality and social justice "backed by the re-sources of the most powerful and richest nation on this earth." Unfortunately, only a month after the report appeared, Martin Luther King Jr. was assassinated in Memphis. His tragic death sparked another outbreak of racial rioting across the country.

By the end of the 1960s the quest for racial equality had become interwoven with other powerful social currents, including the antiwar protests and the femi-nist movement. The combined energies of these and other crusades, coupled with the conservative backlash they provoked, threatened to unravel American society by the end of the 1960s.

John F. Kennedy

Inaugural Address (1961)

John Fitzgerald Kennedy (1917–1963) was the youngest president ever elected, and he self-consciously sought to inspire young adults to get more involved in politics and so-cial reform. Born into a wealthy Catholic Massachusetts family, a graduate of Harvard University and a World War II naval hero, he served in the Senate before gaining the Democratic nomination in 1960. He and his advisors viewed his victory over Republican vice president Richard Nixon as a mandate for change and an ac-tivist presidency. His inauguration occurred on a bitterly cold day, but Kennedy's up-lifting rhetoric caught the attention and imagination of the huge crowd.

From *Public Papers of the Presidents of the United States: John F. Kennedy, 1961*, no. 1 (Wash-ington, DC, 1962), pp. 1–3.

We observe today not a victory of party but a celebration of freedom—symbol-izing an end as well as a beginning—sig-nifying renewal as well as change. For I have sworn before you and Almighty God the same solemn oath our forebears prescribed nearly a century and three-quarters ago.

The world is very different now. For man holds in his mortal hands the power to abolish all forms of human poverty and all forms of human life. And yet the same revolutionary beliefs for which our forebears fought are still at issue around the globe—the belief that the rights of man come not from the generosity of the state but from the hand of God.

We dare not forget today that we are the heirs of that first revolution. Let the word go forth from this time and place, to friend and foe alike, that the torch has been passed to a new generation of Americans—born in this century, tempered by war, disciplined by a hard and bitter peace, proud of our ancient heritage—and unwilling to witness or permit the slow undoing of those human rights to which this nation has always been committed, and to which we are committed today at home and around the world.

Let every nation know, whether it wishes us well or ill, that we shall pay any price, bear any burden, meet any hardship, support any friend, oppose any foe to assure the survival and the success of liberty.

This much we pledge—and more.

To those old allies whose cultural and spiritual origins we share, we pledge the loyalty of faithful friends. United, there is little we cannot do in a host of cooperative ventures. Divided, there is little we can do—for we dare not meet a powerful challenge at odds and split asunder.

To those new states whom we welcome to the ranks of the free, we pledge our word that one form of colonial control shall not have passed away merely to be replaced by a far more iron tyranny. We shall not always expect to find them supporting our view. But we shall always hope to find them strongly supporting their own freedom—and to remember that, in the past, those who foolishly sought power by riding the back of the tiger ended up inside.

To those people in the huts and villages of half the globe struggling to break the bonds of mass misery, we pledge our best efforts to help them help themselves, for whatever period is required—not because the Communists may be doing it, not because we seek their votes, but because it is right. If a free society cannot help the many who are poor, it cannot save the few who are rich.

To our sister republics south of our border, we offer a special pledge—to convert our good words into good deeds—in a new alliance for progress—to assist free men and free governments in casting off the chains of poverty. But this peaceful revolution of hope cannot become the prey of hostile powers. Let all our neighbors know that we shall join with them to oppose aggression or subversion anywhere in the Americas. And let every other power know that this hemisphere intends to remain the master of its own house. . . .

In your hands, my fellow citizens, more than mine, will rest the final success or failure of our course. Since this country was founded, each generation of Americans has been summoned to give testimony to its national loyalty. The graves of young Americans who answered the call to service surround the globe.

Now the trumpet summons us again—not as a call to bear arms, though arms we need—not as a call to battle, though embattled we are—but a call to bear the burden of a long twilight struggle, year in and year out, "rejoicing in hope, patient in tribulation," a struggle against the common enemies of man: tyranny, poverty, disease, and war itself.

Can we forge against these enemies a grand and global alliance, North and South, East and West, that can assure a more fruitful life for all mankind? Will you join in that historic effort?

In the long history of the world, only a few generations have been granted the role of defending freedom in its hour of maximum danger. I do not shrink from this responsibility—I welcome it. I do not believe that any of us would exchange places with any other people or any other generation. The energy, the faith, the devotion which we bring to this endeavor will light our country and all who serve it—and the glow from that fire can truly light the world.

And so, my fellow Americans: ask not what your country can do for you—ask what you can do for your country.

My fellow citizens of the world: ask not what America will do for you, but what together we can do for the freedom of man. Finally, whether you are citizens of America or citizens of the world, ask of us here the same high standards of strength and sacrifice which we ask of you. With a good conscience our only sure reward, with history the final judge of our deeds, let us go forth to lead the land we love, asking His blessing and His help, but knowing that here on earth God's work must truly be our own.

REVIEW QUESTIONS

1. Kennedy asserted that America would "pay any price" to defend liberty. What kind of foreign policy commitments might this have entailed?

2. What did Kennedy identify as the "common enemies of man"? To defeat these enemies, would government power have to be expanded? Why?

3. Explain how the Soviet Union might have responded to this speech.

MICHAEL HARRINGTON

FROM *The Other America* (1962)

Throughout the 1950s public attention was focused on the amazing affluence generated by the American economy. Yet as social analyst Michael Harrington revealed in The Other America *(1962), 40 to 50 million Americans, some 20 percent of the total population, were in fact mired in poverty. This "underclass" was largely hidden from view. They included the elderly and the "unseen" residents of urban slums and rural hovels. President Kennedy read several reviews of Harrington's book and was so stunned by its revelations that he created a task force to design federal programs to address the nation's chronic pockets of poverty. Kennedy was assassinated before the programs could be implemented, but under Lyndon B. Johnson the government initiated a comprehensive—and ultimately ineffective—"war on poverty."*

There is a familiar America. It is celebrated in speeches and advertised on television and in the magazines. It has the highest mass standard of living the world has ever known.

In the 1950's this America worried about itself, yet even its anxieties were products of abundance. The title of a brilliant book was widely misinterpreted, and the familiar America began to call itself "the affluent society." There was introspection about Madison Avenue and tail fins; there was discussion of the emotional suffering taking place in the suburbs. In all this, there was an implicit assumption that the basic grinding economic problems had been solved in the United States. In this theory the nation's problems were no longer a matter of basic human needs, of food, shelter, and clothing. Now they were seen as qualitative, a question of learning to live decently amid luxury.

While this discussion was carried on, there existed another America. In it dwelt somewhere between 40,000,000 and 50,000,000 citizens of this land. They were poor. They still are.

To be sure, the other America is not impoverished in the same sense as those poor nations where millions cling to hunger as a defense against starvation. This country has escaped such extremes. That does not change the fact that tens of millions of Americans are, at this very moment, maimed in body and spirit, existing at levels beneath those necessary for human decency. If these people are not starving, they are hungry, and sometimes fat with hunger, for that is what cheap foods do. They are without adequate housing and education and medical care.

The Government has documented what this means to the bodies of the poor, and the figures will be cited throughout this book. But even more basic, this poverty twists and deforms the spirit. The American poor are pessimistic and defeated, and they are victimized by mental suffering to a degree unknown in Suburbia.

This book is a description of the world in which these people live; it is about the other America. Here are the unskilled workers, the migrant farm workers, the aged, the minorities, and all the others who live in the economic underworld of American life. . . . I would ask the reader to respond critically to every assertion, but not to allow statistical quibbling to obscure the huge, enormous, and intolerable fact of poverty in America. For, when all is said and done, that fact is unmistakable, whatever its exact dimensions, and the truly human reaction can only be outrage. . . .

The millions who are poor in the United States tend to become increasingly invisible. Here is a great mass of people, yet it takes an effort of the intellect and will even to see them. . . .

The other America, the America of poverty, is hidden today in a way that it never was before. Its millions are socially invisible to the rest of us. No wonder that so many misinterpreted Galbraith's[1] title and assumed that "the affluent society" meant that everyone had a decent standard of life. The misinterpretation was true as far as the actual day-to-day lives of two-thirds of the nation were concerned. Thus, one must begin a description of the other America by understanding why we do not see it.

There are perennial reasons that make the other America an invisible land. Poverty is often off the beaten track. It always has been. The ordinary tourist never left the main highway, and today he rides interstate turnpikes. He does not go into the valleys of Pennsylvania where the towns look like

movie sets of Wales in the thirties. He does not see the company houses in rows, the rutted roads (the poor always have bad roads whether they live in the city, in towns, or on farms), and everything is black and dirty. And even if he were to pass through such a place by accident, the tourist would not meet the unemployed men in the bar or the women coming home from a runaway sweatshop. . . .

If the middle class never did like ugliness and poverty, it was at least aware of them. "Across the tracks" was not a very long way to go. There were forays into the slums at Christmas time; there were charitable organizations that brought contact with the poor. Occasionally, almost everyone passed through the Negro ghetto or the blocks of tenements, if only to get downtown to work or to entertainment.

Now the American city has been transformed. The poor still inhabit the miserable housing in the central area, but they are increasingly isolated from contact with, or sight of, anybody else. Middle-class women coming in from Suburbia on a rare trip may catch the merest glimpse of the other America on the way to an evening at the theater, but their children are segregated in suburban schools. The business or professional man may drive along the fringes of slums in a car or bus, but it is not an important experience to him. The failures, the unskilled, the disabled, the aged, and the minorities are right there, across the tracks, where they have always been. But hardly anyone else is.

In short, the very development of the American city has removed poverty from the living, emotional experience of millions upon millions of middle-class Americans. Living out in the suburbs, it is easy to assume that ours is, indeed, an affluent society.

This new segregation of poverty is compounded by a well-meaning ignorance. A good many concerned and sympathetic Americans are aware that there is much discussion of urban renewal. Suddenly, driving through the city, they notice that a familiar slum has been torn down and that there are towering, modern buildings where once there had been tenements or hovels. There is a warm feeling of satisfaction, of pride in the way

---

[1] Economist John Kenneth Galbraith (1908–2006).

things are working out: the poor, it is obvious, are being taken care of.

The irony in this . . . is that the truth is nearly the exact opposite to the impression. The total impact of the various housing programs in postwar America has been to squeeze more and more people into existing slums. More often than not, the modern apartment in a towering building rents at $40 a room or more. For, during the past decade and a half, there has been more subsidization of middle- and upper-income housing than there has been for the poor. . . .

And finally, the poor are politically invisible. It is one of the cruelest ironies of social life in advanced countries that the dispossessed at the bottom of society are unable to speak for themselves. The people of the other America do not, by far and large, belong to unions, to fraternal organizations, or to political parties. They are without lobbies of their own; they put forward no legislative program. As a group, they are atomized. They have no face; they have no voice.

Thus, there is not even a cynical political motive for caring about the poor, as in the old days.

Because the slums are no longer centers of powerful political organizations, the politicians need not really care about their inhabitants. The slums are no longer visible to the middle class, so much of the idealistic urge to fight for those who need help is gone. Only the social agencies have a really direct involvement with the other America, and they are without any great political power. . . .

That the poor are invisible is one of the most important things about them. They are not simply neglected and forgotten as in the old rhetoric of reform; what is much worse, they are not seen.

REVIEW QUESTIONS

1. According to Harrington, America was commonly described as an "affluent society." What was implied by this phrase, and why did Harrington deny its validity?
2. Why were the poor so "invisible" to middle-class Americans?
3. Did the poor have political power? Why or why not?

MARTIN LUTHER KING JR.

FROM Letter from a Birmingham Jail (1963)

During the 1960 presidential campaign John F. Kennedy had promised to provide "moral leadership" to improve race relations in the United States. Once in office, however, he moved cautiously, fearful of alienating the powerful coalition of conservative southern Democrats in Congress. The mantle of "moral leadership" was instead taken up by Dr. Martin Luther King Jr., the inspirational black Baptist minister from Atlanta who helped found the Southern Christian Leadership Conference (SCLC) in 1957. In early 1963 King and the SCLC resolved to assault segregation in Birmingham, Alabama. They organized an economic boycott of white businesses and staged a series of protest marches. Birmingham police used dogs and fire hoses to break up the rallies, and they arrested King and many of his lieutenants. While in jail he used smuggled paper and pen to write a powerful response to criticism he had received from local white ministers.

While confined here in the Birmingham City Jail, I came across your recent statement calling our present activities "unwise and untimely."

. . . I am here, along with several members of my staff, because we were invited here. I am here because I have basic organizational ties here. Beyond this, I am in Birmingham because injustice is here. Just as the 8th-century prophets left their little villages and carried their "thus saith the Lord" far beyond the boundaries of their home town, and just as the Apostle Paul left his little village of Tarsus and carried the gospel of Jesus Christ to practically every hamlet and city of the Greco-Roman world, I too am compelled to carry the gospel of freedom beyond my particular home town. . . . Injustice anywhere is a threat to justice everywhere. . . .

You deplore the demonstrations that are presently taking place in Birmingham. But I am sorry that your statement did not express a similar concern for the conditions that brought the demonstrations into being. I am sure that each of you would want to go beyond the superficial social analyst who looks merely at effects, and does not grapple with underlying causes. I would not hesitate to say that it is unfortunate that so-called demonstrations are taking place in Birmingham at this time, but I would say in more emphatic terms that it is even more unfortunate that the white power structure of this city left the Negro community with no other alternative.

In any nonviolent campaign there are four basic steps: 1) collection of the facts to determine whether injustices are alive; 2) negotiation; 3) self-purification; and 4) direct action. We have gone through all of these steps in Birmingham. There can be no gainsaying of the fact that racial injustice engulfs this community. Birmingham is probably the most thoroughly segregated city in the United States. Its ugly record of police brutality is known in every section of this country. Its unjust treatment of Negroes in the courts is a notorious reality. There have been more unsolved bombings of Negro homes and churches in Birmingham than any city in this nation. These are the hard, brutal, and unbelievable facts. . . .

We know through painful experience that freedom is never voluntarily given by the oppressor; it must be demanded by the oppressed. Frankly I have never yet engaged in a direct action movement that was "well timed," according to the timetable of those who have not suffered unduly from the disease of segregation. For years now I have heard the word "Wait!" It rings in the ear of every Negro with a piercing familiarity. This "wait" has almost always meant "never." It has been a tranquilizing Thalidomide, relieving the emotional stress for a moment, only to give birth to an ill-formed infant of frustration. We must come to see with the distinguished jurist of yesterday that "justice too long delayed is justice denied." We have waited for more than 340 years for our constitutional and God-given rights. The nations of Asia and Africa are moving with jetlike speed toward the goal of political independence, and we still creep at horse and buggy pace toward the gaining of a cup of coffee at a lunch counter. . . .

You express a great deal of anxiety over our willingness to break laws. This is certainly a legitimate concern. Since we so diligently urge people to obey the Supreme Court's decision of 1954 outlawing segregation in the public schools, it is rather strange and paradoxical to find us consciously breaking laws. One may well ask, "How can you advocate breaking some laws and obeying others?" The answer is found in the fact that there are two types of laws: There are *just* laws and there are *unjust* laws. I would be the first to advocate obeying just laws. One has not only a legal but a moral responsibility to obey just laws. Conversely, one has a moral responsibility to disobey unjust laws. I would agree with Saint Augustine that "An unjust law is no law at all."

Now what is the difference between the two? How does one determine when a law is just or unjust? A just law is a man-made code that squares with the moral law or the law of God. An unjust law is a code that is out of harmony with the moral law. To put it in the terms of Saint Thomas Aquinas, an unjust law is a human law that is not rooted in eternal and natural law. Any law that uplifts human personality is just. Any law that degrades human personality is unjust.

All segregation statutes are unjust because segregation distorts the soul and damages the personality. It gives the segregator a false sense of superiority and the segregated a false sense of inferiority. . . . So segregation is not only politically, economically, and sociologically unsound, but it is morally wrong and sinful. Paul Tillich has said that sin is separation. Isn't segregation an existential expression of man's tragic separation, an expression of his awful estrangement, his terrible sinfulness? So I can urge men to obey the 1954 decision of the Supreme Court because it is morally right, and I can urge them to disobey segregation ordinances because they are morally wrong. . . .

Let me give another explanation. An unjust law is a code inflicted upon a minority which that minority had no part in enacting or creating because it did not have the unhampered right to vote. Who can say the legislature of Alabama which set up the segregation laws was democratically elected? Throughout the state of Alabama all types of conniving methods are used to prevent Negroes from becoming registered voters and there are some counties without a single Negro registered to vote despite the fact that the Negro constitutes a majority of the population. Can any law set up in such a state be considered democratically structured? . . .

We can never forget that everything Hitler did in Germany was "legal" and . . . it was "illegal" to aid and comfort a Jew in Hitler's Germany. But I am sure that, if I had lived in Germany during that time, I would have aided and comforted my Jewish brothers even though it was illegal. If I lived in a Communist country today where certain principles dear to the Christian faith are suppressed, I believe I would openly advocate disobeying these anti-religious laws. . . .

We will have to repent in this generation not merely for the vitriolic words and actions of the bad people, but for the appalling silence of good people. We must come to see that human progress never rolls in on wheels of inevitability. It comes through the tireless efforts and persistent work of men willing to be co-workers with God, and without this hard work time itself becomes an ally of the forces of social stagnation. . . .

You spoke of our activity in Birmingham as extreme. At first I was rather disappointed that fellow clergymen would see my nonviolent efforts as those of the extremist. I started thinking about the fact that I stand in the middle of two opposing forces in the Negro community. One is a force of complacency made up of Negroes who, as a result of long years of oppression, have been so completely drained of self-respect and a sense of "somebodiness" that they have adjusted to segregation, and of a few Negroes in the middle class who, because of a degree of academic and economic security, and because at points they profit by segregation, have unconsciously become insensitive to the problems of the masses. The other force is one of bitterness and hatred and comes perilously close to advocating violence. It is expressed in the various black nationalist groups that are springing up over the nation, the largest and best known being Elijah Muhammad's Muslim movement. This movement is nourished by the contemporary frustration over the continued existence of racial discrimination. It is made up of people who have lost faith in America, who have absolutely repudiated Christianity, and who have concluded that the white man is an incurable "devil."

I have tried to stand between these two forces saying that we need not follow the "donothingism" of the complacent or the hatred and despair of the black nationalist. There is the more excellent way of love and nonviolent protest. I'm grateful to God that, through the Negro church, the dimension of nonviolence entered our struggle. If this philosophy had not emerged I am convinced that by now many streets of the South would be flowing with floods of blood. And I am further convinced that if our white brothers dismiss us as "rabble rousers" and "outside agitators"—those of us who are working through the channels of nonviolent direct action—and refuse to support our nonviolent efforts, millions of Negroes, out of frustration and despair, will seek solace and security in black nationalist ideologies, a development that will lead inevitably to a frightening racial nightmare.

Oppressed people cannot remain oppressed forever. The urge for freedom will eventually come. This is what has happened to the American Negro. Something within has reminded him of his birthright of freedom; something without has reminded that he can gain it. . . .

So the question is not whether we will be extremist but what kind of extremist will we be. Will we be extremists for hate or will we be extremists for love? Will we be extremists for the preservation of injustice—or will we be extremists for the cause of justice? . . .

The contemporary Church is so often a weak, ineffectual voice with an uncertain sound. It is so often the arch-supporter of the *status quo*. Far from being disturbed by the presence of the Church, the power structure of the average community is consoled by the Church's silent and often vocal sanction of things as they are.

But the judgment of God is upon the Church as never before. If the Church of today does not recapture the sacrificial spirit of the early Church, it will lose its authentic ring, forfeit the loyalty of millions and be dismissed as an irrelevant social club with no meaning for the 20th century. . . . I

am thankful to God that some noble souls from the ranks of organized religion have broken loose from the paralyzing chains of conformity and joined us as active partners in the struggle for freedom . . . they have gone with the faith that right defeated is stronger than evil triumphant. These men have been the leaven in the lump of the race. Their witness has been the spiritual salt that has preserved the true meaning of the Gospel in these troubled times. They have carved a tunnel of hope through the dark mountain of disappointment. . . . But even if the Church does not come to the aid of justice, I have no despair about the future. I have no fear about the outcome of our struggle in Birmingham, even if our motives are presently misunderstood. We will reach the goal of freedom in Birmingham and all over the nation, because the goal of America is freedom. Abused and scorned though we may be, our destiny is tied up with the destiny of America. . . .

One day the South will recognize its real heroes. They will be the James Merediths, courageously and with a majestic sense of purpose, facing jeering and hostile mobs and the agonizing loneliness that characterizes the life of the pioneer. They will be old, oppressed, battered Negro women, symbolized in a seventy-two-year-old woman of Montgomery, Alabama,[1] who rose up with a sense of dignity and with her people decided not to ride the segregated buses, and responded to one who inquired about her tiredness with ungrammatical profundity: "My feets is tired, but my soul is rested." They will be young high school and college students, young ministers of the Gospel and a host of the elders, courageously and nonviolently sitting in at lunch counters and willingly going to jail for conscience's sake. One day the South will know that when these disinherited children of God sat down at lunch counters they were in reality standing up for the best in the American dream and the most sacred values in our Judeo-Christian heritage, and thus carrying our whole nation back to great wells of democracy which were dug deep by the founding fathers in the

---

[1] Rosa Parks (1913–2005).

formulation of the Constitution and the Declaration of Independence. . . .

I hope this letter finds you strong in the faith. I also hope that circumstances will soon make it possible for me to meet each of you, not as an integrationist or a civil rights leader, but as a fellow clergyman and a Christian brother. Let us all hope that the dark clouds of racial prejudice will soon pass away, that the deep fog of misunderstanding will be lifted from our fear-drenched communities, and that in some not too distant tomorrow the radiant stars of love and brotherhood will shine over our great nation with all of their scintillating beauty. . . .

REVIEW QUESTIONS

1. King describes two kinds of laws. What are they, and what criteria does King use in deciding when to obey them?
2. What were the two "opposing forces" in the "Negro community" according to King? What did each side advocate?
3. Do you think whites would have felt threatened by King's strategy of nonviolent civil disobedience? Explain.

GEORGE C. WALLACE

The Civil Rights Movement: Fraud, Sham, and Hoax (1964)

George Wallace served as the feisty governor of Alabama during the early 1960s. In 1958 he had lost the gubernatorial election to a rabid segregationist, and Wallace crudely vowed that he would "never be out-niggered again." He won the governorship in 1962 and pledged: "Segregation now! Segregation tomorrow! Segregation forever!" In June 1963 Wallace stood defiantly in a doorway at the University of Alabama to prevent the first black student from registering, only to step aside when federal marshals threatened his arrest. Wallace's theatrical defense of segregation and his opposition to civil rights legislation and related Supreme Court rulings, communism, and "left-wing" liberalism made him a hero among white conservatives. In 1964 he challenged Lyndon Johnson for the Democratic presidential nomination. Although unsuccessful, he displayed an ability to exploit the "white backlash" against political and social liberalism. This signaled an emerging conservative revolt that would flower in the 1970s and 1980s.

From George C. Wallace, "The Civil Rights Movement: Fraud, Sham, and Hoax," July 4, 1964. Alabama Department of Archives and History, Montgomery, Alabama. Reprinted with permission.

We come here today in deference to the memory of those stalwart patriots who on July 4, 1776, pledged their lives, their fortunes, and their sacred honor to establish and defend the proposition that governments are created by the people, empowered by the people, derive their just powers from the consent of the people, and must forever remain subservient to the will of the people.

Today, 188 years later, we celebrate that occasion and find inspiration and determination and courage to preserve and protect the great principles of freedom enunciated in the Declaration of Independence.

It is therefore a cruel irony that the President of the United States has only yesterday signed into law the most monstrous piece of legislation[1] ever enacted by the United States Congress.

It is a fraud, a sham, and a hoax.

This bill will live in infamy. To sign it into law at any time is tragic. To do so upon the eve of the celebration of our independence insults the intelligence of the American people.

It dishonors the memory of countless thousands of our dead who offered up their very lives in defense of principles which this bill destroys.

Never before in the history of this nation have so many human and property rights been destroyed by a single enactment of the Congress. It is an act of tyranny. It is the assassin's knife stuck in the back of liberty.

With this assassin's knife and a blackjack in the hand of the Federal force-cult, the left-wing liberals will try to force us back into bondage. Bondage to a tyranny more brutal than that imposed by the British monarchy which claimed power to rule over the lives of our forefathers under sanction of the Divine Right of kings.

Today, this tyranny is imposed by the central government which claims the right to rule over our lives under sanction of the omnipotent black-robed despots who sit on the bench of the United States Supreme Court.

This bill is fraudulent in intent, in design, and in execution. It is misnamed. Each and every provision is mistitled. It was rammed through the Congress on the wave of ballyhoo, promotions, and publicity stunts reminiscent of P. T. Barnum.

It was enacted in an atmosphere of pressure, intimidation, and even cowardice, as demonstrated by the refusal of the United States Senate to adopt an amendment to submit the bill to a vote of the people. . . .

It threatens our freedom of speech, of assembly, or association, and makes the exercise of these Freedoms a federal crime under certain conditions.

It affects our political rights, our right to trial by jury, our right to the full use and enjoyment of our private property, the freedom from search and seizure of our private property and possessions, the freedom from harassment by Federal police and, in short, all the rights of individuals inherent in a society of free men.

Ministers, lawyers, teachers, newspapers, and every private citizen must guard his speech and watch his actions to avoid the deliberately imposed booby traps put into this bill. It is designed to make Federal crimes of our customs, beliefs, and traditions.

Therefore, under the fantastic powers of the Federal judiciary to punish for contempt of court and under their fantastic powers to regulate our most intimate aspects of our lives by injunction, every American citizen is in jeopardy and must stand guard against these despots. . . .

I am having nothing to do with enforcing a law that will destroy our free enterprise system. I am having nothing to do with enforcing a law that will destroy neighborhood schools. I am having nothing to do with enforcing a law that will destroy the rights of private property.

I am having nothing to do with enforcing a law that destroys your right—and my right—to choose my neighbors—or to sell my house to whomever I choose. I am having nothing to do with enforcing a law that destroys the labor seniority system.

I am having nothing to do with this so-called civil rights bill.

---

[1] Civil Rights Act of 1964.

The liberal left-wingers have passed it. Now let them employ some pinknik social engineers in Washington, D.C., to figure out what to do with it. . . .

It has been said that power corrupts and absolute power corrupts absolutely. There was never greater evidence as to the proof of this statement than in the example of the present Federal Judiciary. . . .

I feel it important that you should know and understand what it is that these people are trying to do. The written opinions of the court are filled with double talk, semantics, jargon, and meaningless phrases. The words they use are not important. The ideas that they represent are the things which count.

It is perfectly obvious from the left-wing liberal press and from the left-wing law journals that what the court is saying behind all the jargon is that they don't like our form of government.

They think they can establish a better one. In order to do so it is necessary that they overthrow our existing form, destroy the democratic institutions created by the people, change the outlook, religion, and philosophy, and bring the whole area of human thought, aspiration, action and organization, under the absolute control of the court. Their decisions reveal this to be the goal of the liberal element on the court which is in a majority at present.

It has reached the point where one may no longer look to judicial decisions to determine what the court may do. However, it is possible to predict with accuracy the nature of the opinions to be rendered.

One may find the answer in the Communist Manifesto. The Communists are dedicated to the overthrow of our form of government. They are dedicated to the destruction of the concept of private property. They are dedicated to the object of destroying religion as the basis of moral and ethical values. . . .

I do not call the members of the United States Supreme Court Communists. But I do say, and I submit for your judgment the fact that every single decision of the court in the past ten years which related in any way to each of these objectives has been decided against freedom and in favor of tyranny. . . .

The Federal court rules that your children shall not be permitted to read the bible in our public school systems. Let me tell you this, though. We still read the bible in Alabama schools and as long as I am governor we will continue to read the bible no matter what the Supreme Court says. . . .

But yet there is hope.

There is yet a spirit of resistance in this country which will not be oppressed. And it is awakening. And I am sure there is an abundance of good sense in this country which cannot be deceived. . . .

Being a southerner is no longer geographic. It's a philosophy and an attitude. One destined to be a national philosophy—embraced by millions of Americans—which shall assume the mantle of leadership and steady a governmental structure in these days of crises.

Certainly I am a candidate for President of the United States. If the left-wingers do not think I am serious—let them consider this.

I am going to take our fight to the people—the court of public opinion—where truth and common sense will eventually prevail. . . . Conservatives of this nation constitute the balance of power in presidential elections.

I am a conservative.

I intend to give the American people a clear choice. I welcome a fight between our philosophy and the liberal left-wing dogma which now threatens to engulf every man, woman, and child in the United States.

I am in this race because I believe the American people have been pushed around long enough and that they, like you and I, are fed up with the continuing trend toward a socialist state which now subjects the individual to the dictates of an all-powerful central government.

I am running for President because I was born free. I want to remain free. I want your children and mine and our prosperity to be unencumbered by the manipulations of a soulless state.

I intend to fight for a positive, affirmative program to restore constitutional government and to stop the senseless bloodletting now being performed on the body of liberty by those who lead us willingly and dangerously close to a totalitarian central government.

In our nation, man has always been sovereign and the state has been his servant. This philosophy has made the United States the greatest free nation in history.

This freedom was not a gift. It was won by work, by sweat, by tears, by war, by whatever it took to be—and to remain free. Are we today less resolute, less determined and courageous than our fathers and our grandfathers?

Are we to abandon this priceless heritage that has carried us to our present position of achievement and leadership? I say if we are to abandon our heritage, let it be done in the open and full knowledge of what we do.

We are not unmindful and careless of our future. We will not stand aside while our conscientious convictions tell us that a dictatorial Supreme Court has taken away our rights and our liberties.

We will not stand idly by while the Supreme Court continues to invade the prerogatives left rightfully to the states by the constitution.

We must not be misled by left-wing incompetent news media that day after day feed us a diet of fantasy telling us we are bigots, racists and hate-mongers to oppose the destruction of the constitution and our nation.

A left-wing monster has risen up in this nation. It has invaded the government. It has invaded the news media. It has invaded the leadership of many of our churches. It has invaded every phase and aspect of the life of freedom-loving people.

It consists of many and various and powerful interests, but it has combined into one massive drive and is held together by the cohesive power of the emotion, setting forth civil rights as supreme to all.

But, in reality, it is a drive to destroy the rights of private property, to destroy the freedom and liberty of you and me. And, my friends, where there are no property rights, there are no human rights. Red China and Soviet Russia are prime examples.

Politically evil men have combined and arranged themselves against us. The good people of this nation must now associate themselves together, else we will fall one by one, an unpitied sacrifice in a struggle which threatens to engulf the entire nation.

We can win. We can control the election of the president in November. Our object must be our country, our whole country and nothing but our country.

If we will stand together—the people of this state—the people of my state—the people throughout this great region—yes, throughout the United States—then we can be the balance of power. We can determine who will be the next president. . . .

Let it be known that we will no longer tolerate the boot of tyranny. We will no longer hide our heads in the sand. We will reschool our thoughts in the lessons our forefathers knew so well.

We must destroy the power to dictate, to forbid, to require, to demand, to distribute, to edict, and to judge what is best and enforce that will of judgment upon free citizens. We must revitalize a government founded in this nation on faith in God.

I ask that you join with me and that together, we give an active and courageous leadership to the millions of people throughout this nation who look with hope and faith to our fight to preserve our constitutional system of government with its guarantees of liberty and justice for all within the framework of our priceless freedoms.

REVIEW QUESTIONS

1. According to Wallace, what were some of the freedoms endangered by the Civil Rights Act of 1964?
2. Why was Wallace especially critical of the Supreme Court?
3. Did Wallace direct his speech to appeal to the emotions or the intellect of his audience? Explain.

BARRY GOLDWATER

Extremism in the Defense of Liberty Is No Vice (1964)

In July 1964 Barry Goldwater, a Republican senator from Arizona, launched the modern conservative movement with a rousing speech in San Francisco accepting his party's nomination for the presidency. Goldwater had earlier written two books, The Conscience of a Conservative *(1960) and* Why Not Victory? *(1962), both of which sold millions of copies and established him as the nation's most prominent conservative leader. He lost the 1964 election to Lyndon B. Johnson, but his campaign set in motion the surge of political conservatism that reshaped the landscape of national politics. Goldwater was reelected to the Senate in 1968, 1974, and 1980. He died in 1998.*

New York Times, 17 July 1964, p. 10. [Editorial insertions appear in square brackets—*Ed.*]

. . . The good Lord raised this mighty Republic to be a home for the brave and to flourish as the land of the free—not to stagnate in the swampland of collectivism, not to cringe before the bullying of communism.

Now my fellow Americans, the tide has been running against freedom. Our people have followed false prophets. We must, and we shall, return to proven ways—not because they are old, but because they are true. We must, and we shall, set the tides running again in the cause of freedom. And this party, with its every action, every word, every breath, and every heartbeat, has but a single resolve, and that is freedom—freedom made orderly for this nation by our constitutional government; freedom under a government limited by the laws of nature and of nature's God; freedom balanced so that order lacking liberty will not become the slavery of the prison cell; balanced so that liberty lacking order will not become the license of the mob and of the jungle.

Now, we Americans understand freedom. We have earned it; we have lived for it, and we have died for it. This nation and its people are freedom's model in a searching world. We can be freedom's missionaries in a doubting world. But, ladies and gentlemen, first we must renew freedom's mission in our own hearts and in our own homes.

During four futile years, the Administration which we shall replace has distorted and lost that vision. It has talked and talked and talked and talked the words of freedom, but it has failed and failed and failed in the works of freedom.

Now failure cements the wall of shame in Berlin; failures blot the sands of shame at the Bay of Pigs [in Cuba]; failures mark the slow death of freedom in Laos; failures infest the jungles of Vietnam, and failures haunt the houses of our once great alliances and undermine the greatest bulwark ever erected by free nations, the NATO community. Failures proclaim lost leadership, obscure purpose, weakening will, and the risk of inciting our sworn enemies to new aggressions and to new excesses.

And because of this Administration we are

tonight a world divided. We are a nation becalmed. We have lost the brisk pace of diversity and the genius of individual creativity. We are plodding along at a pace set by centralized planning, red tape, rules without responsibility and regimentation without recourse.

Rather than useful jobs in our country, our people have been offered bureaucratic "make work"; rather than moral leadership, they have been given bread and circuses. They have been given spectacles, and, yes, they've even been given scandals.

Tonight there is violence in our streets, corruption in our highest offices, aimlessness amongst our youth, anxiety among our elders, and there's a virtual despair among the many who look beyond material success for the inner meaning of their lives. And where examples of morality should be set, the opposite is seen. Small men seeking great wealth or power have too often and too long turned even the highest levels of public service into mere personal opportunity.

Now, certainly simple honesty is not too much to demand of men in government. We find it in most. Republicans demand it from everyone. They demand it from everyone no matter how exalted or protected his position might be. The growing menace in our country tonight, to personal safety, to life, to limb and property, in homes, in churches, on the playgrounds, and places of business, particularly in our great cities, is the mounting concern, or should be, of every thoughtful citizen in the United States.

Security from domestic violence, no less than from foreign aggression, is the most elementary and fundamental purpose of any government, and a government that cannot fulfill this purpose is one that cannot long command the loyalty of its citizens.

History shows us, demonstrates that nothing, nothing prepares the way for tyranny more than the failure of public officials to keep the streets safe from bullies and marauders.

Now we Republicans see all this as more—much more—than the result of mere political differences or mere political mistakes. We see this as the result of a fundamentally and absolutely wrong view of man, his nature, and his destiny. Those who seek to live your lives for you, to take your liberties in return for relieving you of yours; those who elevate the state and downgrade the citizen, must see ultimately a world in which earthly power can be substituted for Divine Will, and this nation was founded upon the rejection of that notion and upon the acceptance of God as the author of freedom.

Now those who seek absolute power, even though they seek it to do what they regard as good, are simply demanding the right to enforce their own version of heaven on earth, and let me remind you they are the very ones who always create the most hellish tyranny. Absolute power does corrupt, and those who seek it must be suspect and must be opposed. Their mistaken course stems from false notions, ladies and gentlemen, of equality. Equality, rightly understood, as our founding fathers understood it, leads to liberty and to the emancipation of creative differences; wrongly understood, as it has been so tragically in our time, it leads first to conformity and then to despotism.

Fellow Republicans, it is the cause of Republicanism to resist concentrations of power, private or public—which enforce such conformity and inflict such despotism. It is the cause of Republicanism to ensure that power remains in the hands of the people—and, so help us God, that is exactly what a Republican President will do with the help of a Republican Congress.

It is further the cause of Republicanism to restore a clear understanding of the tyranny of man over man in the world at large. It is our cause to dispel the foggy thinking which avoids hard decisions in the delusion that a world of conflict will somehow mysteriously resolve itself into a world of harmony, if we just don't rock the boat or irritate the forces of aggression—and this is hogwash. It is, further, the cause of Republicanism to remind ourselves, and the world, that only the strong can remain free; that only the strong can keep the peace.

Now I needn't remind you, or my fellow Americans regardless of party, that Republicans have shouldered this hard responsibility and marched in this cause before. It was Republican leadership under Dwight Eisenhower that kept the peace, and passed along to this administration the mightiest arsenal for defense the world has ever known. And I needn't remind you that it was the strength and the believable will of the Eisenhower years that kept the peace by using our strength, by using it in the Formosa Straits, and in Lebanon, and by showing it courageously at all times.

It was during those Republican years that the thrust of Communist imperialism was blunted. It was during those years of Republican leadership that this world moved closer, not to war, but closer to peace, than at any other time in the last three decades.

And I needn't remind you, but I will, that it's been during Democratic years that our strength to deter war has been stilled and even gone into a planned decline. It has been during Democratic years that we have weakly stumbled into conflict, timidly refusing to draw our own lines against aggression, deceitfully refusing to tell even our people of our full participation, and tragically, letting our finest men die on battlefields unmarked by purpose, unmarked by pride or the prospect of victory.

Yesterday, it was Korea; tonight it is Vietnam. Make no bones of this. Don't try to sweep this under the rug. We are at war in Vietnam. And yet the President [Lyndon Johnson], who is the Commander in Chief of our forces, refuses to say, refuses to say mind you, whether or not the objective over there is victory, and his Secretary of Defense [Robert McNamara] continues to mislead and misinform the American people, and enough of it has gone by.

And I needn't remind you, but I will, it has been during Democratic years that a billion persons were cast into Communist captivity and their fate cynically sealed.

Today—today in our beloved country we have an Administration which seems eager to deal with Communism in every coin known—from gold to wheat, from consulates to confidences, and even human freedom itself.

Now the Republican cause demands that we brand Communism as the principal disturber of peace in the world today. Indeed, we should brand it as the only significant disturber of the peace. And we must make clear that until its goals of conquest are absolutely renounced, and its relations with all nations tempered, Communism and the governments it now controls are enemies of every man on earth who is or wants to be free.

Now, we here in America can keep the peace only if we remain vigilant, and only if we remain strong. Only if we keep our eyes open and keep our guard up can we prevent war. And I want to make this abundantly clear—I don't intend to let peace or freedom be torn from our grasp because of lack of strength or lack of will—and that I promise you Americans.

I believe that we must look beyond the defense of freedom today to its extension tomorrow. I believe that the Communism which boasts it will bury us will, instead, give way to the forces of freedom. And I can see in the distant and yet recognizable future the outlines of a world worthy of our dedication, our every risk, our every effort, our every sacrifice along the way. Yes, a world that will redeem the suffering of those who will be liberated from tyranny.

I can see, and I suggest that all thoughtful men must contemplate, the flowering of an Atlantic civilization, the whole of Europe reunified and freed, trading openly across its borders, communicating openly across the world.

This is a goal far, far more meaningful than a moon shot. It's a truly inspiring goal for all free men to set for themselves during the latter half of the twentieth century. . . .

I would remind you that extremism in the defense of liberty is no vice!

And let me remind you also that moderation in the pursuit of justice is no virtue!

By the—the beauty of the very system we Republicans are pledged to restore and revitalize, the beauty of this Federal system of ours is in its reconciliation of diversity with unity. We must not see malice in honest differences of opinion, and no matter how great, so long as they are not inconsistent with the pledges we have given to each other in and through our Constitution.

Our Republican cause is not to level out the world or make its people conform in computer regimented sameness. Our Republican cause is to free our people and light the way for liberty throughout the world. Ours is a very human cause for very humane goals. This party, its good people, and its unquenchable devotion to freedom, will not fulfill the purposes of this campaign, which we launch here and now, until our cause has won the day, inspired the world, and shown the way to a to-morrow worthy of all our yesteryears.

I repeat, I accept your nomination with humbleness, with pride, and you and I are going to fight for the goodness of our land.

Thank you.

REVIEW QUESTIONS

1. What was Goldwater's attitude toward the grow-ing conflict in Vietnam?
2. Like most acceptance speeches, Goldwater fo-cuses on the failures of the opposition and tends to speak in general terms. What specific initia-tives does he mention or imply?
3. Why did he feel the need to stress that "extrem-ism in the defense of liberty is no vice"?

FANNIE LOU HAMER

Why We Need the Vote (1964)

The African American civil rights activist Fannie Lou Hamer was a sharecropper who helped organize the Mississippi Freedom Democratic Party (MFDP). In 1964 it chal-lenged the regular Democratic delegation's authority to represent Mississippi at the party's national convention in Atlantic City, New Jersey. At the convention, which nominated Lyndon B. Johnson, Hamer delivered an impassioned address to the dele-gates that highlighted the need for federal voting rights legislation. A backroom deal at the convention gave the MFDP token participation among the Mississippi delega-tion, but Hamer rejected the compromise solution.

From Kay Mills, *This Little Light of Mine* (New York: Signet, 1993), pp. 119–121. [Editorial insertions appear in square brackets—*Ed.*]

Mr. Chairman, and the Credentials Com-mittee, my name is Mrs. Fannie Lou Hamer, and I live at 626 East Lafayette Street, Ruleville, Mississippi, Sunflower County the home of Senator James O. Eastland, and Senator [John] Stennis.

It was the 31st of August in 1962 that eighteen of us traveled twenty-six miles to the county court-house in Indianola to try to register to try to be-come first-class citizens. We was met in Indianola by Mississippi men, highway patrolmens, and they only allowed two of us in to take the literacy test at the time. After we had taken this test and started back to Ruleville, we was held up by the City Po-lice and the State Highway Patrolmen and carried back to Indianola, where the bus driver was charged that day with driving a bus the wrong color.

After we paid the fine among us, we continued on to Ruleville, and Reverend Jeff Sunny carried me four miles in the rural area where I had worked as a timekeeper and sharecropper for eighteen years. I was met there by my children, who told me the plantation owner was angry because I had gone down to try to register. After they told me, my husband came, and said the plantation owner was raising cain because I had tried to register, and before he quit talking the plantation owner came, and said, "Fannie Lou, do you know—did Pap tell you what I said?"

I said, "Yes, sir."

He said, "I mean that," he said. "If you don't go down and withdraw your registration, you will have to leave," he said. "Then if you go down and withdraw," he said. "You will—you might have to go because we are not ready for that in Mississippi."

And I addressed him and told him and said, "I didn't try to register for you. I tried to register for myself." I had to leave that same night.

On the 10th of September, 1962, sixteen bullets was fired into the home of Mr. and Mrs. Robert Tucker for me. That same night two girls were shot in Ruleville, Mississippi. Also Mr. Joe McDonald's house was shot in.

And on June the 9th, 1963, I had attended a voter-registration workshop, was returning back to Mississippi. Ten of us was traveling by the Continental Trailway bus. When we got to Winona, Mississippi, which is Montgomery County, four of the people got off to use the washroom, and two of the people—to use the restaurant—two of the people wanted to use the washroom. The four people that had gone in to use the restaurant was ordered out. During this time I was on the bus. But when I looked through the window and saw they had rushed out, I got off of the bus to see what had happened, and one of the ladies said, "It was a state highways patrolman and a chief of police ordered us out."

I got back on the bus and one of the persons had used the washroom got back on the bus, too. As soon as I was seated on the bus, I saw when they began to get the four people in a highway patrol-man's car. I stepped off the bus to see what was happening and somebody screamed from the car that the four workers was in and said, "Get that one there," and when I went to get in the car, when the man told me I was under arrest, he kicked me.

I was carried to the county jail, and put in the booking room. They left some of the people in the booking room and began to place us in cells. I was placed in a cell with a young woman called Miss Euvester Simpson. After I was placed in the cell I began to hear sounds of licks and screams. I could hear the sounds of licks and horrible screams, and I could hear somebody say, "Can you say, yes sir, nigger? Can you say yes, sir?"

And they would say other horrible names. She would say, "Yes, I can say yes, sir."

"So say it."

She says, "I don't know you well enough."

They beat her, I don't know how long, and after a while she began to pray, and asked God to have mercy on those people.

And it wasn't too long before three white men came to my cell. One of these men was a State Highway Patrolman and he asked me where I was from, and I told him Ruleville. He said, "We are going to check this." And they left my cell and it wasn't too long before they came back. He said "You are from Ruleville all right," and he used a curse word, and he said, "We are going to make you wish you was dead."

I was carried out of that cell into another cell where they had two Negro prisoners. The State Highway Patrolman ordered the first Negro to take the blackjack. The first Negro prisoner ordered me, by orders from the State Highway Patrolman for me, to lay down on a bunk bed on my face, and I laid on my face. The first Negro began to beat, and I was beat by the first Negro until he was exhausted, and I was holding my hands behind me at that time on my left side because I suffered from polio when I was six years old. After the first Negro had beat until he was exhausted, the State Highway Patrolman ordered the second Negro to take the blackjack.

The second Negro began to beat and I began to work my feet, and the State Highway Patrolman ordered the first Negro who had beat to set on my feet to keep me from working my feet. I began to scream and one white man got up and began to beat me in my head and tell me to hush. One white man—my dress had worked up high, he walked over and pulled my dress down—and he pulled my dress back, back up.

I was in jail when Medgar Evers[1] was murdered. . . .

All of this is on account we want to register, to become first-class citizens, and if the Freedom Democratic Party is not seated now, I question America, in this America, the land of the free and the home of the brave where we have to sleep with our telephones off the hooks because our lives be threatened daily because we want to live as decent human beings, in America?

Thank you.

REVIEW QUESTIONS

1. What echoes of slavery are evident in this excerpt?
2. What was the primary form of intimidation used against Hamer?
3. Speculate on the symbolic importance of the name "Freedom Democratic Party."

---

[1] A black civil rights leader.

MALCOLM X

FROM "The Black Revolution" Speeches (1964)

Born Malcolm Little in 1925, Malcolm X was the son of a Baptist preacher who promoted black separatism and was murdered by unknown assailants in Michigan. At age six, the fatherless Malcolm was taken to a foster home. He dropped out of school in the eighth grade and embarked upon a crime spree that landed him in a federal prison at age twenty-one. There he discovered the writings of Elijah Muhammad, leader of the Black Muslims. Muhammad portrayed whites as servants of the devil; blacks therefore had to separate themselves from the white community. Malcolm became a loyal disciple of Elijah Muhammad. Upon his release from prison, he became minister of a Black Muslim temple in Harlem, a black neighborhood in New York City. Clashes with the Black Muslim leadership over which tactics to use in fighting racism led to his suspension from the organization in late 1963. He then traveled to Mecca, where he adopted the beliefs of orthodox Muslims and founded the Organization of Afro-American Unity. In 1964 he delivered the following address.

Friends and enemies, tonight I hope that we can have a little fireside chat with as few sparks as possible being tossed around. . . . I hope that this little conversation tonight about the black revolution won't cause many of you to accuse us of igniting it when you find it at your doorstep. . . .

I'm still a Muslim but I'm also a nationalist, meaning that my political philosophy is black nationalism, my economic philosophy is black nationalism, my social philosophy is black nationalism. And when I say that this philosophy is black nationalism, to me this means that the political philosophy of black nationalism is that which is designed to encourage our people, the black people, to gain complete control over the politics and the politicians of our own community.

Our economic philosophy is that we should gain economic control over the economy of our own community, the businesses and the other things which create employment so that we can provide jobs for our own people instead of having to picket and boycott and beg someone else for a job.

And, in short, our social philosophy means that we feel that it is time to get together among our own kind and eliminate the evils that are destroying the moral fiber of our society, like drug addiction, drunkenness, adultery that leads to an abundance of bastard children, welfare problems. We believe that we should lift the level or the standard of our own society to a higher level wherein we will be satisfied and then not inclined toward pushing ourselves into other societies where we are not wanted.

*   *   *

Why is America in a position to bring about a bloodless revolution? Because the Negro in this country holds the balance of power and if the Negro in this country were given what the Constitution says he is supposed to have, the added power of the Negro in this country would sweep all of the racists and the segregationists out of office. It would change the entire political structure of the country. It would wipe out the Southern segregationism that now controls America's foreign policy, as well as America's domestic policy.

And the only way without bloodshed that this can be brought about is that the black man has to be given full use of the ballot in every one of the 50 states. But if the black man doesn't get the ballot, then you are going to be faced with another man who forgets the ballot and starts using the bullet.

Revolutions are fought to get control of land, to remove the absentee landlord and gain control of the land and the institutions that flow from that land. The black man has been in a very low condition because he has had no control whatsoever over any land. He has been a beggar economically, a beggar politically, a beggar socially, a beggar even when it comes to trying to get some education. So that in the past the type of mentality that was developed in this colonial system among our people, today is being overcome. And as the young ones come up they know what they want. And as they listen to your beautiful preaching about democracy and all those other flowery words, they know what they're supposed to have.

So you have a people today who not only know what they want, but also know what they are supposed to have. And they themselves are clearing another generation that is coming up that not only will know what it wants and know what it should have, but also will be ready and willing to do whatever is necessary to see that what they should have materializes immediately. Thank you.

REVIEW QUESTIONS

1. What were the economic and social philosophies of the Black Muslims?
2. According to Malcolm X, what would help prevent racial bloodshed from occurring? Was he optimistic about this? Explain.
3. Compare the views of Malcolm X and Dr. King. What were the essential differences?

STOKELY CARMICHAEL

FROM Black Power (1966)

Born in 1942 in the West Indies and raised in New York City, Stokely Carmichael joined the Student Nonviolent Coordinating Committee (SNCC) while enrolled at Howard University. In the mid-1960s, he emerged as the chairman of the organization and shifted its emphasis from voter registration to self-reliance and violent social change. His successor, H. Rap Brown, was even more militant, once asserting that "Violence is as American as cherry pie." Carmichael eventually changed his name to Kwame Ture and moved to the African nation of Guinea.

From Stokely Carmichael, "Black Power," *The New York Review of Books* 7 (22 September 1966):5–6, 8.

One of the tragedies of the struggle against racism is that up to now there has been no national organization which could speak to the growing militancy of young black people in the urban ghetto. There has been only a civil rights movement, whose tone of voice was adapted to an audience of liberal whites. It served as a sort of buffer zone between them and angry young blacks. None of its so-called leaders could go into a rioting community and be listened to. In a sense, I blame ourselves—together with the mass media—for what has happened in Watts, Harlem, Chicago, Cleveland, Omaha. Each time the people in those cities saw Martin Luther King get slapped, they became angry; when they saw four little black girls bombed to death, they were angrier; and when nothing happened, they were steaming. We had nothing to offer that they could see, except to go out and be beaten again. We helped to build their frustration.

For too many years, black Americans marched and had their heads broken and got shot. They were saying to the country, "Look, you guys are supposed to be nice guys and we are only going to do what we are supposed to do—why do you beat us up, why don't you give us what we ask, why don't you straighten yourselves out?" After years of this, we are at almost the same point—because we demonstrated from a position of weakness. We cannot be expected any longer to march and have our heads broken in order to say to whites: come on, you're nice guys. For you are not nice guys. We have found you out.

An organization which claims to speak for the needs of a community—as does the Student Nonviolent Coordinating Committee—must speak in the tone of that community, not as somebody else's buffer zone. This is the significance of black power as a slogan. For once, black people are going to use the words they want to use—not just the words whites want to hear. And they will do this no matter how often the press tries to stop the use of the slogan by equating it with racism or separatism.

An organization which claims to be working for the needs of a community—as SNCC does—must work to provide that community with a position of strength from which to make its voice heard. This is the significance of black power beyond the slogan.

Black power can be clearly defined for those who do not attach the fears of white America to their questions about it. We should begin with the basic fact that black Americans have two problems: they are poor and they are black. All other problems arise from this two-sided reality: lack of education, the so-called apathy of black men. Any program to end racism must address itself to that double reality.

Almost from its beginning, SNCC sought to address itself to both conditions with a program aimed at winning political power for impoverished Southern blacks. We had to begin with politics because black Americans are a propertyless people in a country where property is valued above all. We had to work for power, because this country does not function by morality, love, and nonviolence, but by power. Thus we determined to win political power, with the idea of moving on from there into activity that would have economic effects. With power, the masses could *make or participate in making* the decisions which govern their destinies, and thus create basic change in their day-to-day lives. . . .

SNCC today is working in both North and South on programs of voter registration and independent political organizing. In some places, such as Alabama, Los Angeles, New York, Philadelphia, and New Jersey, independent organizing under the black panther symbol is in progress. The creation of a national "black panther party" must come about; it will take time to build, and it is much too early to predict its success. We have no infallible master plan and we make no claim to exclusive knowledge of how to end racism; different groups will work in their own different ways. SNCC cannot spell out the full logistics of self-determination but it can address itself to the problem by helping black communities define their needs, realize their strength, and go into action along a variety of lines which they must choose for themselves. . . .

Ultimately, the economic foundations of this country must be shaken if black people are to control their lives. The colonies of the United States—and this includes the black ghettoes within its borders, north and south must be liberated. For a century, this nation has been like an octopus of exploitation, its tentacles stretching from Mississippi and Harlem to South America, the Middle East, southern Africa, and Vietnam; the form of exploitation varies from area to area but the essential result has been the same—a powerful few have been maintained and enriched at the expense of the poor and voiceless colored masses. This pattern must be broken. As its grip loosens here and there around the world, the hopes of black Americans become more realistic. For racism to die, a totally different America must be born.

This is what the white society does not wish to face; this is why that society prefers to talk about integration. But integration speaks not at all to the problem of poverty, only to the problem of blackness. Integration today means the man who "makes it," leaving his black brothers behind in the ghetto as fast as his new sports car will take him. It has no relevance to the Harlem wino or to the cotton-picker making three dollars a day. . . .

Integration, moreover, speaks to the problem of blackness in a despicable way. As a goal, it has been based on complete acceptance of the fact that *in order to have* a decent house or education, blacks must move into a white neighborhood or send their children to a white school. This reinforces, among both black and white, the idea that "white" is automatically better and "black" is by definition inferior. This is why integration is a subterfuge for the maintenance of white supremacy. It allows the nation to focus on a handful of Southern children who get into white schools, at great price, and to ignore the 94 percent who are left behind in unimproved all-black schools. Such situations will not change until black people have power—to control their own school boards, in this case. Then Negroes become equal in a way that means something, and integration ceases to be a one-way street. Then integration doesn't mean draining skills and energies from the ghetto into white neighborhoods; then it can mean white people moving from Beverly Hills into Watts. . . . Then integration becomes relevant. . . .

Whites will not see that I, for example, as a person oppressed because of my blackness, have common cause with other blacks who are oppressed because of blackness. This is not to say that there are no white people who see things as I do, but that it is black people I must speak to first. It must be the oppressed to whom SNCC addresses itself primarily, not to friends from the oppressing group.

From birth, black people are told a set of lies about themselves. We are told that we are lazy—yet I drive through the Delta area of Mississippi and watch black people picking cotton in the hot sun for fourteen hours. We are told, "If you work hard, you'll succeed"—but if that were true, black people would own this country. We are oppressed because we are black—not because we are ignorant, not because we are lazy, not because we're stupid (and got good rhythm), but because we're black.

*   *   *

The need for psychological equality is the reason why SNCC today believes that blacks must organize in the black community. Only black people can convey the revolutionary idea that black people are able to do things themselves. Only they can help create in the community an aroused and continuing black consciousness that will provide the basis for political strength. In the past, white allies have furthered white supremacy without the whites involved realizing it—or wanting it, I think. Black people must do things for themselves; they must get poverty money they will control and spend themselves, they must conduct tutorial programs themselves so that black children can identify with black people. This is one reason Africa has such importance: The reality of black men ruling their own nations gives blacks elsewhere a sense of possibility, of power, which they do not now have.

This does not mean we don't welcome help, or friends. But we want the right to decide whether anyone is, in fact, our friend. In the past, black Americans have been almost the only people whom everybody and his momma could jump up and call their friends. We have been tokens, symbols, objects—as I was in high school to many young whites, who liked having "a Negro friend." We want to decide who is our friend, and we will not accept someone who comes to us and says: "If you do X, Y, and Z, then I'll help you." We will not be told whom we should choose as allies. We will not be isolated from any group or nation except by

our own choice. We cannot have the oppressors telling the oppressed how to rid themselves of the oppressor. . . .

Black people do not want to "take over" this country. They don't want to "get whitey"; they just want to get him off their backs, as the saying goes. . . . The white man is irrelevant to blacks, except as an oppressive force. Blacks want to be in his place, yes, but not in order to terrorize and lynch and starve him. They want to be in his place because that is where a decent life can be had.

But our vision is not merely of a society in which all black men have enough to buy the good things of life. When we urge that black money go into black pockets, we mean the communal pocket. We want to see money go back into the community and used to benefit it. We want to see the cooperative concept applied in business and banking. We want to see black ghetto residents demand that an exploiting landlord or storekeeper sell them, at minimal cost, a building or a shop that they will own and improve cooperatively; they can back their demand with a rent strike, or a boycott, and a community so unified behind them that no one else will move into the building or buy at the store. The society we seek to build among black people, then, is not a capitalist one. It is a society in which the spirit of community and humanistic love prevail. The word love is suspect; black expectations of what it might produce have been betrayed too often. But those were expectations of a response from the white community, which failed us. The love we seek to encourage is within the black community, the only American community where men call each other "brother" when they meet. We can build a community of love only where we have the ability and power to do so: among blacks.

As for white America, perhaps it can stop crying out against "black supremacy," "black nationalism," "racism in reverse," and begin facing reality. The reality is that this nation, from top to bottom, is racist; that racism is not primarily a problem of "human relations" but of an exploitation maintained—either actively or through silence—by the society as a whole. . . .

We have found that they usually cannot condemn themselves, and so we have done it. But the rebuilding of this society, if at all possible, is basically the responsibility of whites—not blacks. We won't fight to save the present society, in Vietnam or anywhere else. We are just going to work, in the way we see fit, and on our goals we define, not for civil rights but for all our human rights.

1. What did Carmichael mean by "black power"?
2. Why did Carmichael reject the principle of racial integration?
3. What did he mean when he said that blacks should create a society that was not capitalist?

Report of the National Advisory Commission on Civil Disorders (1968)

Beginning in the mid-1960s the seething racial tensions in America's inner cities exploded. The Civil Rights Act of 1964 and the Voting Rights Act of 1965 provided new federal legal protections but did not resolve the culture of poverty that stripped people of hope for a better future. Each summer saw a rising number of race riots in major cities. The violence and destruction prompted President Johnson in 1967 to establish a multiracial national commission to investigate the causes of the unrest and to recommend ways to ease the tensions. Chaired by Governor Otto Kerner of Illinois, a year later the commission issued a report, which became known as the Kerner Report.

From *Report of the National Advisory Commission on Civil Disorders* (Washington, DC, 1968), pp. 1–2, 5, 225–236.

This is our basic conclusion: Our nation is moving toward two societies, one black, one white—separate and unequal.

Reaction to last summer's disorders has quickened the movement and deepened the division. Discrimination and segregation have long permeated much of American life; they now threaten the future of every American.

This deepening racial division is not inevitable. The movement apart can be reversed. Choice is still possible. Our principal task is to define that choice and to press for a national resolution.

To pursue our present course will involve the continuing polarization of the American commu-

nity and, ultimately, the destruction of basic democratic values.

The alternative is not blind repression or capitulation to lawlessness. It is the realization of common opportunities for all within a single society.

This alternative will require a commitment to national action—compassionate, massive and sustained, backed by the resources of the most powerful and the richest nation on this earth. From every American it will require new attitudes, new understanding, and, above all, new will.

The vital needs of the nation must be met;

hard choices must be made, and, if necessary, new taxes enacted.

Violence cannot build a better society. Disruption and disorder nourish repression, not justice. They strike at the freedom of every citizen. The community cannot—it will not—tolerate coercion and mob rule.

Violence and destruction must be ended—in the streets of the ghetto and in the lives of people.

Segregation and poverty have created in the racial ghetto a destructive environment totally unknown to most white Americans.

What white Americans have never fully understood—but what the Negro can never forget—is that white society is deeply implicated in the ghetto. White institutions created it, white institutions maintain it, and white society condones it.

It is time now to turn with all the purpose at our command to the major unfinished business of this nation. It is time to adopt strategies for action that will produce quick and visible progress. It is time to make good the promises of American democracy to all citizens—urban and rural, white and black, Spanish-surname, American Indian, and every minority group.

Our recommendations embrace three basic principles:

To mount programs on a scale equal to the dimension of the problems;

To aim these programs for high impact in the immediate future in order to close the gap between promise and performance;

To undertake new initiatives and experiments that can change the system of failure and frustration that now dominates the ghetto and weakens our society.

These programs will require unprecedented levels of funding and performance, but they neither probe deeper nor demand more than the problems which called them forth. There can be no higher priority for national action and no higher claim on the nation's conscience.

*   *   *

White racism is essentially responsible for the explosive mixture which has been accumulating in our cities since the end of World War II. Among the ingredients of that mixture are:

Pervasive discrimination and segregation in employment, education and housing, which have resulted in the continuing exclusion of great numbers of Negroes from the benefits of economic progress.

Black in-migration and white exodus, which have produced the massive and growing concentrations of impoverished Negroes in our major cities, creating a growing crisis of deteriorating facilities and services and unmet human needs.

The black ghettos where segregation and poverty converge on the young to destroy opportunity and enforce failure. Crime, drug addiction, dependency on welfare, and bitterness and resentment against society in general and white society in particular are the result.

At the same time, most whites and some Negroes outside the ghetto have prospered to a degree unparalleled in the history of civilization. Through television and other media, this affluence has been flaunted before the eyes of the Negro poor and the jobless ghetto youth.

Yet these facts alone cannot be said to have caused the disorders. Recently, other powerful ingredients have begun to catalyze the mixture:

Frustrated hopes are the result of unfulfilled expectations aroused by the great judicial and legislative victories of the Civil Rights Movement and the dramatic struggle for equal rights in the South.

A climate that tends toward approval and encouragement of violence as a form of protest has been created by white terrorism against nonviolent protest; by the open defiance of law and federal authority by state and local officials resisting desegregation; and by some protest groups engaging in civil disobedience who turn their backs on nonviolence, go beyond the constitutionally protected right of petition and free assembly, and resort to violence to attempt to compel alteration of laws and policies with which they disagree.

The frustrations of powerlessness have led some Negroes to the conviction that there is no effective alternative to violence as a means of achieving redress of grievances, and of "moving the system." These frustrations are reflected in alienation and hostility toward the institutions of law and government and the white society which controls them, and in the reach toward racial consciousness and solidarity reflected in the slogan "Black Power."

A *new mood* has sprung up among Negroes, particularly among the young, in which self-esteem and enhanced racial pride are replacing apathy and submission to "the system."

The police are not merely a "spark" factor. To some Negroes police have come to symbolize white power, white racism and white repression. And the fact is that many police do reflect and express these white attitudes. The atmosphere of hostility and cynicism is reinforced by a widespread belief among Negroes in the existence of police brutality and in a "double standard" of justice and protection—one for Negroes and one for whites.

*   *   *

Three critical conclusions emerge from this analysis:

1. The nation is rapidly moving toward two increasingly separate Americas.

Within two decades, this division could be so deep that it could be impossible to unite:

> a white society principally located in suburbs, in smaller central cities, and in the peripheral parts of large central cities; and a Negro society largely concentrated within large central cities.

The Negro society will be permanently relegated to its current status, possibly even if we expend great amounts of money and effort in trying to "gild" the ghetto.

2. In the long run, continuation and expansion of such a permanent division threatens us with two perils.

The first is the danger of sustained violence in our cities. The timing, scale, nature, and repercussions of such violence cannot be foreseen. But if it occurred, it would further destroy our ability to achieve the basic American promises of liberty, justice, and equality.

The second is the danger of a conclusive repudiation of the traditional American ideals of individual dignity, freedom, and equality of opportunity. We will not be able to espouse these ideals meaningfully to the rest of the world, to ourselves, to our children. They may still recite the Pledge of Allegiance and say "one nation . . . indivisible." But they will be learning cynicism, not patriotism.

3. We cannot escape responsibility for choosing the future of our metropolitan areas and the human relations which develop within them. It is a responsibility so critical that even an unconscious choice to continue present policies has the gravest implications.

That we have delayed in choosing or, by delaying, may be making the wrong choice, does not sentence us either to separatism or despair. But we must choose. We will choose. Indeed, we are now choosing.

Review Questions

1. What were the "ingredients" comprising the "explosive mixture" found in many cities? According to the commission, what was the primary cause of this mixture?

2. Summarize the report's conclusions. Do they remain valid today? Explain.

CASEY HAYDEN AND MARY KING

Feminism and the Civil Rights Movement (1965)

The Student Nonviolent Coordinating Committee (SNCC) attracted hundreds of idealistic young male and female activists, both black and white. Yet for all of the movement's commitment to racial equality, it failed to practice gender equality. The young men who led SNCC retained conventional notions of male superiority. They expected the women in the organization to cook meals, take notes, and defer to the men. Once, when asked about the role of women volunteers in SNCC, Stokely Carmichael replied that the "only position for women in SNCC is prone." Two white female activists, Casey Hayden and Mary King, wrote memos in 1964 and 1965 detailing their frustrations at the failure of the civil rights movement to recognize issues related to women's concerns. They and others would eventually leave the civil rights crusade and help organize the modern feminist movement.

From Mary King, *Freedom Song: A Personal Story of the Civil Rights Movement* (New York: Morrow, 1987), pp. 568–569, 571–574. Copyright 1987 by Mary Elizabeth King. With permission of Gerard McCauley Agency, Inc.

The average white person finds it difficult to understand why the Negro resents being called "boy," or being thought of as "musical" and "athletic," because the average white person doesn't realize that *he assumes he is superior*. And naturally he doesn't understand the problem of paternalism. So too the average SNCC worker[1] finds it difficult to discuss the woman problem because of the assumption of male superiority. Assumptions of male superiority are as widespread and deep-rooted and very much as crippling to the woman as the assumptions of white supremacy are to the Negro. Consider why it is in SNCC that women who are competent, qualified, and experienced are automatically assigned to the "female" kinds of jobs such as: typing, desk work, telephone work, filing, library work, cooking, and the assistant kind of administrative work but rarely the "executive" kind.

The woman in SNCC is often in the same position as that token Negro hired in a corporation.

The management thinks that it has done its bit. Yet, every day the Negro bears an atmosphere, attitudes, and actions which are tinged with condescension and paternalism, the most telling of which are seen when he is not promoted as the equally or less skilled whites are. . . .

It needs to be made known that many women in the movement are not "happy and contented" with their status. It needs to be made known that much talent and experience are being wasted by this movement, when women are not given jobs commensurate with their abilities. It needs to be known that just as Negroes were the crucial factor in the economy of the cotton South, so too in SNCC, women are the crucial factor that keeps the movement running on a day-to-day basis. Yet they are not given equal say-so when it comes to day-to-day decision making.

What can be done? Probably nothing right away. Most men in this movement are probably too threatened by the possibility of serious discussion on this subject. Perhaps this is because they have recently broken away from a matriarchal frame-

---
[1]I.e., male.

work under which they may have grown up. Then, too, many women are as unaware and insensitive to this subject as men, as there are many Negroes who don't understand they are not free or who want to be part of white America. They don't understand that they have to give up their souls and stay in their place to be accepted. So, too, many women, in order to be accepted by men, on men's terms, give themselves up to that caricature of what a woman is—unthinking, pliable, an ornament to please the man.

Maybe the only thing that can come out of this paper is discussion—amidst the laughter—but still discussion. . . . And maybe some women will begin to recognize day-to-day discriminations. And maybe sometime in the future the whole of the women in this movement will become so alert as to force the rest of the movement to stop the discrimination and start the slow process of changing values and ideas so that all of us gradually come to understand that this is no more a man's world than it is a white world.

*   *   *

We've talked a lot, to each other and to some of you, about our own and other women's problems in trying to live in our personal lives and in our work as independent and creative people. In these conversations we've found what seem to be recurrent ideas or themes. Maybe we can look at these things many of us perceive, often as a result of insights learned from the movement:

Sex and caste: There seem to be many parallels that can be drawn between treatment of Negroes and treatment of women in our society as a whole. But in particular, women we've talked to who work in the movement seem to be caught up in a common-law caste system that operates, sometimes subtly, forcing them to work around or outside hierarchical structures of power which may exclude them. Women seem to be placed in the same position of assumed subordination in personal situations too. It is a caste system which, at its worst, uses and exploits women.

This is complicated by several facts, among them: 1) The caste system is not institutionalized by law (women have the right to vote, to sue for divorce, etc.); 2) Women can't withdraw from the situation (à la nationalism) or overthrow it; 3) There are biological differences (even though those biological differences are usually discussed or accepted without taking present and future technology into account so we probably can't be sure what these differences mean). Many people who are very hip to the implications of the racial caste system, even people in the movement, don't seem to be able to see the sexual-caste system and if the question is raised they respond with: "That's the way it's supposed to be. There are biological differences." Or with other statements which recall a white segregationist confronted with integration.

Women and problems of work: The caste-system perspective dictates the roles assigned to women in the movement, and certainly even more to women outside the movement. Within the movement, questions arise in situations ranging from relationships of women organizers to men in the community, to who cleans the freedom house, to who holds leadership positions, to who does secretarial work, and to who acts as spokesman for groups. Other problems arise between women with varying degrees of awareness of themselves as being as capable as men but held back from full participation, or between women who see themselves as needing more control of their work than other women demand. And there are problems with relationships between white women and black women.

Women and personal relations with men: Having learned from the movement to think radically about the personal worth and abilities of people whose role in society had gone unchallenged before, a lot of women in the movement have begun trying to apply those lessons to their own relations with men. Each of us probably has her own story of the various results, and of the internal struggle occasioned by trying to break out of very deeply learned fears, needs, and self-perceptions, and of what happens when we try to replace them with concepts of people and freedom learned from the movement and organizing.

Institutions: Nearly everyone has real questions

about those institutions which shape perspectives on men and women: marriage, childrearing patterns, women's (and men's) magazines, etc. People are beginning to think about and even to experiment with new forms in these areas.

Men's reactions to the questions raised here: A very few men seem to feel, when they hear conversations involving these problems, that they have a right to be present and participate in them, since they are so deeply involved. At the same time, very few men can respond nondefensively, since the whole idea is either beyond their comprehension or threatens and exposes them. The usual response is laughter. That inability to see the whole issue as serious, as the straitjacketing of both sexes, and as societally determined often shapes our own response so that we learn to think in their terms about ourselves and to feel silly rather than trust our inner feelings. The problems we're listing here, and what others have said about them, are therefore largely drawn from conversations among women only—and that difficulty in establishing dialogue with men is a recurring theme among people we've talked to.

Lack of community for discussion: Nobody is writing, or organizing or talking publicly about women in any way that reflects the problems that various women in the movement come across and which we've tried to touch above. . . .

The reason we want to try to open up dialogue is mostly subjective. Working in the movement often intensifies personal problems, especially, if we start trying to apply things we're learning there to our personal lives. Perhaps we can start to talk with each other more openly than in the past and create a community of support for each other so we can deal with ourselves and others with integrity and can therefore keep working.

Objectively, the chances seem nil that we could start a movement based on anything as distant to general American thought as a sex-caste system. Therefore, most of us will probably want to work full time on problems such as war, poverty, race. The very fact that the country can't face, much less deal with, the questions we're raising means that the movement[2] is one place to look for some relief. Real efforts at dialogue within the movement and with whatever liberal groups, community women, or students might listen are justified. That is, all the problems between men and women and all the problems of women functioning in society as equal human beings are among the most basic that people face. We've talked in the movement about trying to build a society which would see basic human problems (which are now seen as private troubles), as public problems and would try to shape institutions to meet human needs rather than shaping people to meet the needs of those with power. To raise questions like those above illustrates very directly that society hasn't dealt with some of its deepest problems and opens discussion of why that is so. (In one sense, it is a radicalizing question that can take people beyond legalistic solutions into areas of personal and institutional change.) The second objective reason we'd like to see discussion begin is that we've learned a great deal in the movement and perhaps this is one area where a determined attempt to apply ideas we've learned there can produce some new alternatives.

REVIEW QUESTIONS

1. Hayden and King asserted that "this is no more a man's world than it is a white world." What did they mean by this statement?
2. What was the extent of the "sex-caste" system that they described?
3. Why did they believe that female equality should precede racial equality?

---

[2] Civil rights movement.

THE VIETNAM CONFLICT

During the 1960s the United States became mired in an expanding military conflict in Vietnam. It proved to be America's longest, most controversial, and least successful war. Some 2.5 million men and women served in Southeast Asia, and over 58,000 lost their lives. American intervention, which finally ended in 1973, cost billions of dollars and cost Lyndon B. Johnson the presidency. Discord over the war fractured the national consensus about foreign policy that had existed since 1945, eroded morale within the military, and spawned massive protests and violence at home. In the end South Vietnam fell to the North Vietnamese Communists in 1975. Yet for all of its controversy and tragedy, the Vietnam War seemed the logical, if problematic, course of action for American policymakers.

When John F. Kennedy assumed the presidency in 1961, he inherited an expanding American commitment in Indochina. His two predecessors, Presidents Truman and Eisenhower, had both insisted that the United States must help prevent the spread of communism in Vietnam. Otherwise, the rest of Asia would fall like "dominoes" to the communist menace. So the United States provided massive amounts of weapons, food, and money to prop up the corrupt regime of Ngo Dinh Diem in South Vietnam. Diem, in power since 1954, continued to resist American demands that he reform the political and economic structure to generate public support. By mid-1963, students and Buddhists were protesting in the streets in large numbers, and some monks were immolating themselves to draw world attention to the situation. Kennedy responded by sending American military "advisors" to shore up the government and the military. But the situation continued to deteriorate.

In the fall of 1963 Kennedy's advisors decided that Diem must go, and they encouraged South Vietnamese generals to stage a coup. In November the rebel officers killed Diem and his brother. Diem's successors, however, were no more effective in quelling public discontent. The Viet Cong (communist insurgents) took advantage of the political instability and stepped up their attacks. By the time Kennedy was shot and killed in Dallas on 22 November 1963, there were 16,000 U.S. military personnel in Vietnam.

Lyndon Johnson thus inherited a chaotic political and military situation in South Vietnam. His choices were daunting: either abandon the South Vietnamese to the communist insurgency or assume responsibility for the military defense of the country. He feared that a deepening American commitment in Southeast Asia would destroy the "woman I really loved—the Great Society." But he also did not want to be accused of "losing" Southeast Asia to communism as Truman had been accused of "losing" China. "I am not going to lose Vietnam," he resolved. "I am not going to be the president who saw Southeast Asia go the way China went."

In early 1965 Johnson and his advisors made the fateful decisions to initiate a major bombing campaign against communist North Vietnam and to send U.S. combat forces to South Vietnam. By the end of the year there were 200,000 troops in Vietnam, and the number steadily increased thereafter, reaching a peak of 536,000 by the end of 1968. The escalating war generated intense political criticism and social protests. People questioned both the integrity of the South Vietnamese government and the credibility of American military claims that the war was going well.

In late January 1968 the war effort suffered a major setback when the Viet Cong and their North Vietnamese allies launched the Tet offensive, a well-coordinated series of attacks on South Vietnamese and American installations throughout the country. Even though an American counterattack eventually devastated the communist forces, the Tet offensive's initial successes seemed to contradict the Johnson administration's claim that there was "light at the end of the tunnel."

In early 1968 antiwar Democrats, led by Senators Eugene McCarthy and Robert Kennedy, challenged Johnson for the Democratic nomination, and in March he announced his decision not to run for reelection. Vice President Hubert Humphrey eventually gained the nomination, but he was narrowly defeated by Republican Richard Nixon. Once in office, Nixon and his national security advisor, Henry Kissinger, instituted the "Vietnamization" of the war. This entailed a phased withdrawal of American ground forces coupled with an intensified bombing campaign to buy time so that the South Vietnamese military could assume greater responsibility for the fighting. At the same time, American diplomats began meeting in Paris with their Viet Cong and North Vietnamese counterparts to negotiate an end to the war. But the negotiations dragged on with little sign of progress, and the fighting continued unabated.

In January 1973, only days after Nixon unleashed a furious aerial bombardment of North Vietnamese cities, the negotiators in Paris reached an agreement to end the fighting and exchange prisoners. By March of that year the last remaining American forces left Vietnam. Nixon announced that the South Vietnamese would be able to defend themselves and maintain their independence as long as the American government continued to provide military supplies and financial assistance. Yet in April 1975 North Vietnamese tanks rolled into Saigon, the South Vietnamese capital, and the communists took complete control of the country. In the midst of defeat and the onset of totalitarian rule, hundreds of thousands of South Vietnamese "boat people" fled the country, seeking asylum wherever they could find it, with many of them eventually settling in the United States. America's longest and costliest war (over $150 billion) was over, but the wounds persisted for years.

FROM The Rusk-McNamara Report (1961)

Soon after taking office in March 1961, President John F. Kennedy dispatched a series of "fact-finding" missions to South Vietnam to assess the situation and to recommend a plan of action. One of the most important of these analyses was conducted by Secretary of State Dean Rusk and Secretary of Defense Robert McNamara.

From Neil Sheehan et al., eds., *The Pentagon Papers* (Boston: Beacon Press, 1971), pp. 150–153. [Editorial insertions appear in square brackets—*Ed.*]

1. United States' National Interests in South Viet-Nam.

The deteriorating situation in South Viet-Nam requires attention to the nature and scope of United States national interests in that country. The loss of South Viet-Nam to Communism would involve the transfer of a nation of 20 million people from the free world to the Communism bloc. The loss of South Viet-Nam would make pointless any further discussion about the importance of Southeast Asia to the free world; we would have to face the near certainty that the remainder of Southeast Asia and Indonesia would move to a complete accommodation with Communism, if not formal incorporation with the Communist bloc. The United States, as a member of SEATO,[1] has commitments with respect to South Viet-Nam under the Protocol to the SEATO Treaty. Additionally, in a formal statement at the conclusion session of the 1954 Geneva Conference, the United States representative stated that the United States "would view any renewal of the aggression . . . with grave concern and seriously threatening international peace and security."

The loss of South Viet-Nam to Communism would not only destroy SEATO but would undermine the credibility of American commitments elsewhere. Further, loss of South Viet-Nam would stimulate bitter domestic controversies in the United States and would be seized upon by extreme elements to divide the country and harass the Administration.

*　　*　　*

3. The United States' Objective in South Viet-Nam.

The United States should commit itself to the clear objective of preventing the fall of South Viet-Nam to Communist [sic]. The basic means for accomplishing this objective must be to put the Government of South Viet-Nam into a position to win its own war against the Guerrillas. We must insist that that Government itself take the measures necessary for that purpose in exchange for large-scale United States assistance in the military, economic and political fields. At the same time we must recognize that it will probably not be possible for the GVN to win this war as long as the flow of men and supplies from North Viet-Nam continues unchecked and the guerrillas enjoy a safe sanctuary in neighboring territory.

We should be prepared to introduce United States combat forces if that should become necessary for success. Dependent upon the circumstances, it may also be necessary for United States forces to strike at the source of the aggression in North Viet-Nam.

4. The Use of United States Forces in South Viet-Nam.

The commitment of United States forces to South Viet-Nam involves two different categories: (A) Units of modest size required for the direct support of South Viet-Namese military effort, such as communications, helicopter and other forms of airlift, reconnaissance aircraft, naval patrols, intelligence units, etc., and (B) larger organized units

[1] Southeast Asia Treaty Organization.

with actual or potential direct military mission. Category (A) *should be introduced as speedily as possible.* Category (B) units pose a more serious problem in that they are much more significant from the point of view of domestic and international political factors and greatly increase the probabilities of Communist block escalation. Further, the employment of United States combat forces (in the absence of Communist bloc escalation) involves a certain dilemma: if there is a strong South Viet-Namese effort, they may not be needed; if there is not such an effort, United States forces could not accomplish their mission in the midst of an apathetic or hostile population. Under present circumstances, therefore, the question of injecting United States and SEATO combat forces should in large part be considered as a contribution to the morale of the South Viet-Namese in their own effort to do the principal job themselves.
. . . In the light of the foregoing, the Secretary of State and the Secretary of Defense recommend that:

1. We now take the decision to commit ourselves to the objective of preventing the fall of South Viet-Nam to Communism and that, in doing so, we recognize that the introduction of United States and other SEATO forces may be necessary to achieve this objective. (However, if it is necessary to commit outside forces to achieve the foregoing objective our decision to introduce

United States forces should not be contingent upon unanimous SEATO agreement thereto.)
2. The Department of Defense be prepared with plans for the use of United States forces in South Viet-Nam under one or more of the following purposes:
(a) Use of a significant number of United States forces to signify United States determination to defend Viet-Nam and to boost South Viet-Nam morale.
(b) Use of substantial United States forces to assist in suppressing Viet Cong insurgency short of engaging in detailed counter-guerrilla operations but including relevant operations in North Viet-Nam.
(c) Use of United States forces to deal with the situation if there is organized Communist military intervention. . . .

REVIEW QUESTIONS

1. According to the report, what would happen if the communists took over South Vietnam? Why would this endanger American security interests?
2. What limits, if any, did Rusk and McNamara attach to American involvement in Vietnam? Explain.
3. In what respects did this report epitomize the premises of the cold war?

LYNDON B. JOHNSON

FROM Peace without Conquest (1965)

President Lyndon B. Johnson tried repeatedly to convince the public of the strategic importance of South Vietnam and to rally popular support for American military intervention. In this 1965 speech he presented themes and assumptions that would frequently reappear in his later pronouncements.

From U.S. Department of State, *Bulletin* 52 (26 April 1965):607. [Editorial insertions appear in square brackets—*Ed.*]

. . . Over this war, and all Asia, is the deepening shadow of Communist China. The rulers in Hanoi [North Vietnam] are urged on by Peking. This is a regime which has destroyed freedom in Tibet, attacked India, and been condemned by the United Nations for aggression in Korea. It is a nation which is helping the forces of violence in almost every continent. The contest in Vietnam is part of a wider pattern of aggressive purpose.

Why are these realities our concern? Why are we in South Vietnam? We are there because we have a promise to keep. Since 1954 every American President has offered support to the people of South Vietnam. We have helped to build, and we have helped to defend. Thus, over many years, we have made a national pledge to help South Vietnam defend its independence. And I intend to keep our promise.

To dishonor that pledge, to abandon this small and brave nation to its enemy, and to the terror that must follow, would be an unforgivable wrong.

We are also there to strengthen world order. Around the globe, from Berlin to Thailand, are people whose wellbeing rests, in part, on the belief that they can count on us if they are attacked. To leave Vietnam to its fate would shake the confidence of all these people in the value of American commitment, the value of America's word. The result would be increased unrest and instability, and even wider war.

We are also there because there are great stakes in the balance. Let no one think for a moment that retreat from Vietnam would bring an end to conflict. The battle would be renewed in one country and then another. The central lesson of our time is that the appetite of aggression is never satisfied. To withdraw from one battlefield means only to prepare for the next. We must say in Southeast Asia, as we did in Europe, in the words of the Bible: "Hitherto shalt thou come, but no further."

There are those who say that all our effort there will be futile, that China's power is such it is bound to dominate all Southeast Asia. But there is no end to that argument until all the nations of Asia are swallowed up.

There are those who wonder why we have a responsibility there. We have it for the same reason we have a responsibility for the defense of freedom in Europe. World War II was fought in both Europe and Asia, and when it ended we found ourselves with continued responsibility for the defense of freedom.

Our objective is the independence of South Vietnam, and its freedom from attack. We want nothing for ourselves, only that the people of South Vietnam be allowed to guide their own country in their own way.

We will do everything necessary to reach that objective. And we will do only what is absolutely necessary.

In recent months, attacks on South Vietnam were stepped up. Thus it became necessary to increase our response and to make attacks by air. This is not a change of purpose. It is a change in what we believe that purpose requires.

We do this in order to slow down aggression. We do this to increase the confidence of the brave people of South Vietnam who have bravely borne this brutal battle for so many years and with so many casualties.

And we do this to convince the leaders of North Vietnam, and all who seek to share their conquest, of a very simple fact:

We will not be defeated.

We will not grow tired.

We will not withdraw, either openly or under the cloak of a meaningless agreement. . . .

Once this is clear, then it should also be clear that the only path for reasonable men is the path of peaceful settlement.

Such peace demands an independent South Vietnam securely guaranteed and able to shape its own relationships to all others, free from outside interference, tied to no alliance, a military base for no other country.

These are the essentials of any final settlement.

We will never be second in the search for such a peaceful settlement in Vietnam.

There may be many ways to this kind of peace: in discussion or negotiation with the governments concerned; in large groups or in small ones; in the reaffirmation of old agreements or their strengthening with new ones. We have stated this position over and over again fifty times and more, to friend and foe alike. And we remain ready, with this purpose, for unconditional discussions.

And until that bright and necessary day of peace we will try to keep conflict from spreading. We have no desire to see thousands die in battle, Asians or Americans. We have no desire to devastate that which the people of North Vietnam have built with toil and sacrifice. We will use our power with restraint and with all the wisdom we can command. But we will use it. . . .

We will always oppose the effort of one nation to conquer another nation.

We will do this because our own security is at stake.

But there is more to it than that. For our generation has a dream. It is a very old dream. But we have the power and now we have the opportunity to make it come true.

For centuries, nations have struggled among each other. But we dream of a world where disputes are settled by law and reason. And we will try to make it so.

For most of history men have hated and killed one another in battle. But we dream of an end to war. And we will try to make it so.

For all existence most men have lived in poverty, threatened by hunger. But we dream of a world where all are fed and charged with hope. And we will help to make it so.

The ordinary men and women of North Vietnam and South Vietnam—of China and India—of Russia and America—are brave people. They are filled with the same proportions of hate and fear, of love and hope. Most of them want the same things for themselves and their families. Most of them do not want their sons ever to die in battle, or see the homes of others destroyed. . . .

Every night before I turn out the lights to sleep, I ask myself this question: Have I done everything that I can do to unite this country? Have I done everything I can to help unite the world, to try to bring peace and hope to all the peoples of the world? Have I done enough?

Ask yourselves that question in your homes and in this hall tonight. Have we done all we could? Have we done enough? . . .

REVIEW QUESTIONS

1. In what way did Johnson believe that American credibility was at stake in Vietnam? Why was such credibility so important?
2. Did Johnson make reference to domestic political concerns? How might partisan politics have affected his outlook on Vietnam?
3. How would the North Vietnamese have responded to this speech?

GEORGE BALL

FROM A Compromise Solution in South Vietnam (1965)

Undersecretary of State George Ball was one of the few members of the Johnson administration who was openly skeptical of the escalating U.S. military intervention in South Vietnam. In this 1965 memorandum he outlined his assessment of the situation and explained his opposition to a deepening American commitment.

From George W. Ball, "A Compromise Solution in South Vietnam," in Neil Sheehan et al., comp., *The Pentagon Papers* (Boston: Beacon Press, 1971), 2:615–617.

(1) A Losing War: The South Vietnamese is losing the war to the Viet Cong. No one can assure you that we can beat the Viet Cong or even force them to the conference table on our terms, no matter how many hundred thousand *white, foreign* (U.S.) troops we deploy.

No one has demonstrated that a white ground force of whatever size can win a guerrilla war—which is at the same time a civil war between Asians—in jungle terrain in the midst of a population that refuses cooperation to the white forces (and the South Vietnamese) and thus provides a great intelligence advantage to the other side. . . .

(2) The Question to Decide: Should we limit our liabilities in South Vietnam and try to find a way out with minimal long-term costs?

The alternative—no matter what we may wish it to be—is almost certainly a protracted war involving an open-ended commitment of U.S. forces, mounting U.S. casualties, no assurance of a satisfactory solution, and a serious danger of escalation at the end of the road.

(3) Need for a Decision Now: So long as our forces are restricted to advising and assisting the South Vietnamese, the struggle will remain a civil war between Asian peoples. Once we deploy substantial numbers of troops in combat it will become a war between the U.S. and a large part of the population of South Vietnam, organized and directed from North Vietnam and backed by the resources of both Moscow and Peiping.

The decision you face now, therefore, is crucial. Once large numbers of U.S. troops are committed to direct combat, they will begin to take heavy casualties in a war they are ill-equipped to fight in a noncooperative if not downright hostile countryside.

Once we suffer large casualties, we will have started a well-nigh irreversible process. Our involvement will be so great that we cannot—without national humiliation—stop short of achieving our complete objectives. *Of the two possibilities I think humiliation would be more likely than the achievement of our objectives*—even after we have paid terrible costs. . . .

REVIEW QUESTIONS

1. What did Ball mean when he said that the conflict in Vietnam was a "civil war between Asians"?
2. Why did he fear the injection of American military personnel into the Vietnam conflict?
3. Based on the information provided from this document, what specific recommendations do you think Ball would have made regarding American policy in Vietnam?

Le Duan

A North Vietnamese View of American Intervention (1965)

The North Vietnamese leaders engaged in their own analysis of the conflict in Vietnam and the prospect of massive American military intervention. In July 1965 Le Duan, a prominent official in the North Vietnamese Communist party, offered his assessment of America's growing involvement in the region to a group of Communist leaders.

From Gareth Porter, ed., *Vietnam: The Definitive Documentation of Human Decisions* (Stanfordville, NY: Earl M. Coleman Enterprises, Inc., 1979), 2:383–385. [Editorial insertions appear in square brackets—*Ed.*]

We know that the U.S. sabotaged the Geneva Agreement [1954] and encroached on South Vietnam in order to achieve three objectives:

1. To turn the South into a colony of a new type.
2. To turn the South into a military base, in order to prepare to attack the North and the Socialist bloc.
3. To establish a South Vietnam–Cambodia–Laos defensive line in order to prevent the socialist revolution from spreading through Southeast Asia.

At present, we fight the U.S. in order to defeat their first two objectives to prevent them from turning the South into a new-type colony and military base. We do not yet aim at their third objective, essentially to divide the ranks of the imperialist and to make other imperialists disagree with the U.S. in broadening the war in Vietnam and also to attract the support of other democratic and independent countries for our struggle in the South.

Our revolutionary struggle in the South has the character of a conflict between the two camps in fact, but we advocate not making that conflict grow but limiting it in order to concentrate our forces to resolve the contradiction between the people and U.S. imperialism and its lackeys, to complete the national democratic revolution in the whole country. It is for this reason that we put forward the slogan "peace and neutrality" for the South, a flexible slogan to win victory step by step. We are not only determined to defeat the U.S. but must know how to defeat the U.S. in the manner most appropriate to the relation of forces between the enemy and us during each historical phase. . . .

The U.S. rear area is very far away, and American soldiers are "soldiers in chains," who cannot fight like the French, cannot stand the weather conditions, and don't know the battlefield but on the contrary have many weaknesses in their opposition to people's war. If the U.S. puts 300,000–400,000 troops into the South, it will have stripped away the face of its neocolonial policy and revealed the face of an old style colonial invader, contrary to the whole new-style annexation policy of the U.S. in the world at present. Thus, the U.S. will not be able to maintain its power with regard to influential sectors of the United States. If the U.S. itself directly enters the war in the South, it will have to fight for a prolonged period with the people's army of the South,[1] with the full assistance of the North

---
[1] The Viet Cong.

and of the Socialist bloc. To fight for a prolonged period is a weakness of U.S. imperialism. The Southern revolution can fight a protracted war, while the U.S. can't, because American military, economic and political resources must be distributed throughout the world. If it is bogged down in one place and can't withdraw, the whole effort will be violently shaken. The U.S. would lose its preeminence in influential sectors at home and create openings for other competing imperialists, and lose the American market. Therefore at present, although the U.S. can immediately send 300,000 to 400,000 troops at once, why must the U.S. do it step by step? Because even if it does send many troops like that, the U.S. would still be hesitant; because that would be a passive policy full of contradictions; because of fear of protracted war, and the even stronger opposition of the American people and the world's people, and even of their allies who would also not support widening the war.

With regard to the North, the U.S. still carries out its war of destruction, primarily by its air force: Besides bombing military targets, bridges and roads to obstruct transport and communications, the U.S. could also indiscriminately bomb economic targets, markets, villages, schools, hospitals, dikes, etc., in order to create confusion and agitation among the people. But the North is determined to fight back at the U.S. invaders in a suitable manner, determined to punish the criminals, day or night, and determined to make them pay the blood debts which they have incurred to our people in both zones. The North will not flinch for a moment before the destructive acts of the U.S., which could grow increasingly with every passing day. The North will not count the cost but will use all of its strength to produce and fight, and endeavor to help the South. For a long time, the Americans have boasted of the strength of their air force and navy but during five to six months of directly engaging in combat with the U.S. in the North, we see clearly that the U.S. cannot develop that strength in relation to the South as well as in relation to the North, but revealed more clearly every day its weak-points. We have shot down more than 400 of their airplanes, primarily with ri-

fles, anti-aircraft guns; [but] the high level of their hatred of the aggressors, and the spirit of determination to defeat the U.S. invaders [are tenacious]. Therefore, if the U.S. sends 300,000–400,000 troops into the South, and turns special war into direct war in the South, escalating the war of destruction in the North, they still can't hope to avert defeat, and the people of both North and South will still be determined to fight and determined to win.

If the U.S. is still more adventurous and brings U.S. and puppet troops of all their vassal states to attack the North, broadening it into a direct war in the entire country, the situation will then be different. Then it will not be we alone who still fight the U.S. but our entire camp. First the U.S. will not only be doing battle with 17 million people in the North but will also have to battle with hundreds of millions of Chinese people. Attacking the North would mean that the U.S. intends to attack China, because the North and China are two socialist countries linked extremely closely with each other, and the imperialists cannot attack this socialist country without also intending to attack the other. Therefore the two countries would resist together. Could the American imperialists suppress hundreds of millions of people? Certainly they could not. If they reach a stage of desperation, would the U.S. use the atomic bomb? Our camp also has the atomic bomb. The Soviet Union has sufficient atomic strength to oppose any imperialists who wish to use the atomic bomb in order to attack a socialist country, and threaten mankind. If U.S. imperialism uses the atomic bomb in those circumstances they would be committing suicide. The American people themselves would be the ones to stand up and smash the U.S. government when that government used atomic bombs. Would the U.S. dare to provoke war between the two blocks, because of the Vietnam problem; would it provoke a third world war in order to put an early end to the history of U.S. imperialism and of the entire imperialist system in general? Would other imperialist countries, factions in the U.S., and particularly the American people, agree to the U.S. warmongers throwing them into suicide? Certainly, the U.S. could not carry out their intention, because U.S.

imperialism is in a weak position and not in a position of strength.

But the possibility of . . . broadening the direct war to the North is a possibility which we must pay utmost attention, because U.S. imperialism could be adventurous. We must be vigilant and prepared to cope with each worst possibility. The best way to cope, and not to let the U.S. broaden the direct warfare in the South or in the North, is to fight even more strongly and more accurately in the South, and make the puppet military units—the primary mainstay of the U.S.—rapidly fall apart, push military and political struggle forward, and quickly create the opportune moment to advance to complete defeat of U.S. imperialism and its lackeys in the South.

REVIEW QUESTIONS

1. Why did Le Duan predict that the United States would not be able to fight in Vietnam for "a prolonged period"?
2. How did he expect the Soviet Union and China to help oppose American military efforts in Vietnam?
3. In Le Duan's view, what were the American objectives in Vietnam? How did these differ from what American officials were saying?

CLARK M. CLIFFORD

FROM A Vietnam Reappraisal (1968)

Secretary of Defense Clark Clifford played a pivotal role in President Johnson's decision to stop the escalation of the Vietnam War. Soon after assuming his office in early 1968, he chaired a task force to consider a new request for additional combat forces. In the process, Clifford, a close personal friend of the president, grew skeptical that America's military intervention in Vietnam was succeeding. He then orchestrated an effort within the administration to convince Johnson to abandon the effort.

From Clark M. Clifford, "A Vietnam Reappraisal: The Personal History of One Man's View and How It Evolved." Reprinted by permission of *Foreign Affairs*, Vol. 47, July 1969. Copyright 1969 by the Council on Foreign Relations, Inc. www.ForeignAffairs.com.

I took office on March 1, 1968. The enemy's Tet offensive of late January and early February had been beaten back at great cost. The confidence of the American people had been badly shaken. The ability of the South Vietnamese Government to restore order and morale in the populace, and discipline and esprit in the armed forces, was being questioned. At the President's direction, General Earle G. Wheeler, Chairman of the Joint Chiefs of Staff, had flown to Viet Nam in late February for an on-the-spot conference with General Westmoreland.[1] He had just returned and presented the

---

[1] General William Westmoreland (1914–2005).

military's request that over 200,000 troops be prepared for deployment to Viet Nam. . . . I was directed, as my first assignment, to chair a task force named by the President to determine how this new requirement could be met. . . .

. . . Here are some of the principal issues and some of the answers as I understood them: "Will 200,000 more men do the job?" I found no assurance that they would.

"If not, how many more might be needed—and when?" There was no way of knowing.

"What would be involved in committing 200,000 more men to Viet Nam?" A reserve call-up of approximately 280,000, an increased draft call and an extension of tours of duty of most men then in service.

"Can the enemy respond with a build-up of his own?" He could and he probably would.

"What are the estimated costs of the latest requests?" First calculations were on the order of $2 billion for the remaining four months of that fiscal year, and an increase of $10 to $12 billion for the year beginning July 1, 1968.

"What will be the impact on the economy?" So great that we would face the possibility of credit restrictions, a tax increase and even wage and price controls. The balance of payments would be worsened by at least half a billion dollars a year.

"Can bombing stop the war?" Never by itself. It was inflicting heavy personnel and material losses, but bombing by itself would not stop the war.

"Will stepping up the bombing decrease American casualties?" Very little, if at all. Our casualties were due to the intensity of the ground fighting in the South. We had already dropped a heavier tonnage of bombs than in all the theaters of World War II. During 1967, an estimated 90,000 North Vietnamese had infiltrated into South Viet Nam. In the opening weeks of 1968, infiltrators were coming in at three to four times the rate of a year earlier, despite the ferocity and the intensity of our campaign of aerial interdiction.

"How long must we keep on sending our men and carrying the main burden of combat?" The South Vietnamese were doing better, but they were not ready yet to replace our troops and we did not know when they would be.

When I asked for a presentation of the military plan for attaining victory in Viet Nam, I was told that there was no plan for victory in the historic American sense. Why not? Because our forces were operating under three major political restrictions. The President had forbidden the invasion of North Viet Nam because this could trigger the mutual assistance pact between North Viet Nam and China; the President had forbidden the mining of the harbor at Haiphong, the principal port through which the North received military supplies; the President had forbidden our forces to pursue the enemy into Laos and Cambodia, for to do so would spread the war, politically and geographically, with no discernible advantage. These and other restrictions which precluded an all-out, no-holds-barred military effort were wisely designed to prevent our being drawn into a larger war. We had no inclination to recommend to the President their cancellation.

"Given these circumstances, how can we win?" We would, I was told, continue to evidence our superiority over the enemy; we would continue to attack in the belief that he would reach the stage where he would find it inadvisable to go on with the war. He could not afford the attrition we were inflicting on him. And we were improving our posture all the time.

I then asked, "What is the best estimate as to how long this course of action will take? Six months? One Year? Two Years?" There was no agreement on an answer. Not only was there no agreement, I could find no one willing to assert that he could see the "light at the end of the tunnel" or that American troops would be coming home by the end of the year.

After days of this type of analysis, my concern had greatly deepened. I could not find out when the war was going to end; I could not find out whether the new requests for men and equipment were going to be enough, or whether it would take more and, if more, when and how much; I could not find out how soon the South Vietnamese forces would be ready to take over. All I had was the statement, given with too little self-assurance to be comforting, that if we persisted for an indeterminate length of time, the enemy would choose not to go on.

And so I asked, "Does anyone see any diminution in the will of the enemy after four years of our having been there, after enormous casualties and after massive destruction from our bombing?"

The answer was that there appeared to be no diminution in the will of the enemy. . . .

And so, after these exhausting days, I was convinced that the military course we were pursuing was not only endless, but hopeless. A further substantial increase in American forces could only increase the devastation and the Americanization of the war, and thus leave us even further from our goal of peace that would permit the people of

South Viet Nam to fashion their own political and economic institutions. Henceforth, I was also convinced, our primary goal should be to level off our involvement, and to work toward gradual disengagement.

REVIEW QUESTIONS

1. Summarize the responses to Clifford's questions. Do you agree with his conclusions about such responses? Explain.
2. What were the three political restrictions American policymakers had to operate under? Why were they described as "political"?
3. How might President Johnson have responded to the information contained in this report?

RICHARD M. NIXON

Vietnamizing the War (1969)

During the 1968 presidential campaign, Republican candidate Richard Nixon pledged to end American military involvement in Vietnam and thereby defuse the mounting social unrest at home. To that end he announced in 1969 his plan to "Vietnamize" the war at the same time that negotiations with the North Vietnamese continued in Paris. What he could not announce was a specific timetable for the withdrawal of American forces.

From U.S. Department of State, *Bulletin* 61 (24 November 1969):437–438, 440–442.

Tonight I want to talk to you on a subject of deep concern to all Americans and to many people in all parts of the world—the war in Vietnam.

I believe that one of the reasons for the deep division about Vietnam is that many Americans have lost confidence in what their Government has told them about our policy. The American people cannot and should not be asked to support a

policy which involves the overriding issues of war and peace unless they know the truth about that policy. . . .

In January I could only conclude that the precipitate withdrawal of American forces from Vietnam would be a disaster not only for South Vietnam but for the United States and for the cause of peace.

For the South Vietnamese, our precipitate

withdrawal would inevitably allow the Communists to repeat the massacres which followed their takeover in the North fifteen years before. . . .

For the United States, this first defeat in our nation's history would result in a collapse of confidence in American leadership not only in Asia but throughout the world.

Three American Presidents have recognized the great stakes involved in Vietnam and understood what had to be done. . . .

For the future of peace, precipitate withdrawal would thus be a disaster of immense magnitude.

—A nation cannot remain great if it betrays its allies and lets down its friends.

—Our defeat and humiliation in South Vietnam without question would promote recklessness in the councils of those great powers who have not yet abandoned their goals of world conquest.

—This would spark violence wherever our commitments help maintain the peace—in the Middle East, in Berlin, eventually even in the Western Hemisphere. . . .

Ultimately, this would cost more lives. It would not bring peace; it would bring more war.

For these reasons I rejected the recommendation that I should end the war by immediately withdrawing all our forces. I chose instead to change American policy on both the negotiating front and the battlefront.

Let me briefly explain what has been described as the Nixon doctrine—a policy which not only will help end the war in Vietnam but which is an essential element of our program to prevent future Vietnams. . . .

—First, the United States will keep all of its treaty commitments.

—Second, we shall provide a shield if a nuclear power threatens the freedom of a nation allied with us or of a nation whose survival we consider vital to our security.

—Third, in cases involving other types of aggression, we shall furnish military and economic assistance when requested in accordance with our treaty commitments. But we shall look to the nation directly threatened to assume the primary responsibility of providing the manpower for its defense.

After I announced this policy, I found that the leaders of the Philippines, Thailand, Vietnam, South Korea, and other nations which might be threatened by Communist aggression welcomed this new direction in American foreign policy.

The defense of freedom is everybody's business—not just America's business. And it is particularly the responsibility of the people whose freedom is threatened. In the previous administration we Americanized the war in Vietnam. In this administration we are Vietnamizing the search for peace.

The policy of the previous administration not only resulted in our assuming the primary responsibility for fighting the war but, even more significantly, did not adequately stress the goal of strengthening the South Vietnamese so that they could defend themselves when we left. . . .

Let me now turn to our program for the future.

We have adopted a plan which we have worked out in cooperation with the South Vietnamese for the complete withdrawal of all U.S. combat ground forces and their replacement by South Vietnamese forces on an orderly scheduled timetable. This withdrawal will be made from strength and not from weakness. As South Vietnamese forces become stronger, the rate of American withdrawal can become greater.

*　　*　　*

My fellow Americans, I am sure you can recognize from what I have said that we really only have two choices open to us if we want to end this war:

—I can order an immediate, precipitate withdrawal of all Americans from Vietnam without regard to the effects of that action.

—Or we can persist in our search for a just peace, through a negotiated settlement if possible or through continued implementation of our plan for Vietnamization if necessary—a plan in which we will withdraw all of our forces from Vietnam on a schedule in accordance with our program, as the South Vietnamese become strong enough to defend their own freedom.

I have chosen this second course. It is not the easy way. It is the right way. It is a plan which will end the war and serve the cause of peace, not just in Vietnam, but in the Pacific and in the world.

In speaking of the consequences of a precipitate withdrawal, I mentioned that our allies would lose confidence in America.

Far more dangerous, we would lose confidence in ourselves. Oh, the immediate reaction would be a sense of relief that our men were coming home. But as we saw the consequences of what we had done, inevitable remorse and divisive recrimination would scar our spirit as a people.

We have faced other crises in our history and have become stronger by rejecting the easy way out and taking the right way in meeting our challenges. Our greatness as a nation has been our capacity to do what had to be done when we knew our course was right.

I recognize that some of my fellow citizens disagree with the plan for peace I have chosen. . . . I would be untrue to my oath of office if I allowed the policy of this nation to be dictated by the minority who hold that point and who try to impose it on the Nation by mounting demonstrations in the street. . . .

And now I would like to address a word, if I may, to the young people of this nation who are particularly concerned—and I understand why they are concerned—about this war.

I respect your idealism. I share your concern for peace. I want peace as much as you do. . . . I have chosen a plan for peace. I believe it will succeed.

If it does succeed, what the critics say now won't matter. If it does not succeed, anything I say then won't matter.

I know it may not be fashionable to speak of patriotism or national destiny these days. But I feel it is appropriate to do so on this occasion.

Two hundred years ago this nation was weak and poor. But even then, America was the hope of millions in the world. Today we have become the strongest and richest nation in the world. The wheel of destiny has turned so that any hope the world has for the survival of peace and freedom will be determined by whether the American people have the moral stamina and the courage to meet the challenge of freeworld leadership. Let historians not record that when America was the most powerful nation in the world we passed on the other side of the road and allowed the last hopes for peace and freedom of millions of people to be suffocated by the forces of totalitarianism. . . .

REVIEW QUESTIONS

1. Explain the essential elements of the so-called Nixon Doctrine.
2. How did Nixon plan to reduce the level and scope of American involvement in Vietnam?
3. Compare Nixon's assumptions about America's commitments in Vietnam to Lyndon Johnson's.

Thomas J. Vallely

The War Powers Act (1973)

In the fall of 1973 the Democratic majority in Congress passed what became known as the War Powers Act. It was intended to prevent future presidents from waging war without explicit congressional authorization. It read in part: "The President in every possible instance shall consult with Congress before introducing United States Armed Forces into hostilities or into situations where imminent involvement in hostilities is clearly indicated by the circumstances, and after every such introduction shall consult regularly with the Congress until United States Armed Forces are no longer engaged in hostilities or have been removed from such situations." The following excerpt details the act's additional requirements.

From *United States Legal Code*, 11 (1976):1926–1927.

n the absence of a declaration of war, in any case in which United States Armed Forces are introduced—

(1) into hostilities or into situations where imminent involvement in hostilities is clearly indicated by the circumstances;

(2) into the territory, airspace or waters of a foreign nation, while equipped for combat, except for deployments which relate solely to supply, replacement, repair or training of such forces; or

(3) in numbers which substantially enlarge United States Armed Forces equipped for combat already located in a foreign nation;

the President shall submit within 48 hours to the Speaker of the House of Representatives and to the President, pro tempore of the Senate a report, in writing, setting forth—

(A) the circumstances necessitating the introduction of United States Armed Forces;

(B) the constitutional and legislative authority under which such introduction took place; and

(C) the estimated scope and duration of the hostilities or involvement. . . . The President shall provide such other information as the Congress may request in the fulfillment of its constitutional responsibilities with respect to committing the Nation to war and to the use of United States Armed Forces abroad.

Whenever United States Armed Forces are introduced into hostilities . . . the President shall, so long as such armed forces continue to be engaged in such hostilities or situation, report to the Congress periodically on the status of such hostilities or situation as well as on the scope and duration of such hostilities or situation, but in no event shall he report to the Congress less often than once every six months.

1544. Congressional action . . . .

(b) *Termination of use of United States Armed Forces; exceptions; extension period.* Within sixty calendar days after a report is submitted or is required to be submitted pursuant to section 1543(a)(1) of this title, whichever is earlier, the President shall terminate any use of United States Armed Forces with respect to which such report was submitted (or required to be submitted), unless the Congress (1) has declared war or has enacted a specific authorization for such use of United States Armed Forces, (2) has extended by law such sixty-day period, or (3) is physically unable to meet as a result of an armed attack upon the United States. Such sixty-day period shall be extended for not more than an additional thirty days if the President determines and certifies to the Congress in writing that unavoidable military necessity respecting the safety of United States Armed Forces requires the continued use of such armed forces in the course of bringing about a prompt removal of such forces.

(c) *Concurrent resolution for removal by President of United States Armed Forces.* Notwithstanding subsection (b) of this section,

at any time that United States Armed Forces are engaged in hostilities outside the territory of the United States, its possessions and territories without a declaration of war or specific statutory authorization, such forces shall be removed by the President if the Congress so directs by concurrent resolution.

REVIEW QUESTIONS

1. Under the provisions of this resolution, what kinds of information must the president provide the Congress?
2. How long can troops be deployed without congressional authorization?
3. Does this resolution place too many constraints on the ability of the president to conduct foreign policy? Why or why not?

INTERPRETING VISUAL SOURCES: THE CIVIL RIGHTS MOVEMENT

The civil rights movement was one of the most important developments in the twentieth century. In 1900 state-mandated segregation was pervasive across the South, and racist violence against African Americans was widespread across the nation. Vigilante justice that often ended in the lynching of blacks was all too common.

Yet by the end of World War II, forces converged to spawn an organized crusade for civil rights and social justice. One of those factors was the war itself. Mobilization enabled a million African Americans to serve in the armed forces and broaden their horizons. Even more blacks were able to gain better jobs and working conditions in the defense industries. Waging a war against fascism and its theories of racial superiority led growing numbers of Americans to challenge racism in the United States. Blacks protested all kinds of discrimination, including social segregation. Membership in the National Association for the Advancement of Colored People (NAACP) soared.

After the war ended, the ideological conflict with the Soviet Union led many people to argue that racism was impeding the national effort in the cold war. In 1953, when Dwight D. Eisenhower assumed the presidency, he endorsed civil rights in principle, and during his first three years in office, public services in Washington, D.C., were desegregated, as were navy yards and veterans' hospitals. At the same time, challenges to segregated public schools were emerging across the nation.

When the Supreme Court in 1954 issued its pathbreaking decision in Brown v. Board of Education of Topeka, Kansas *outlawing segregated schools, it provided an essential catalyst to the civil rights movement. Equally influential was Rosa Parks's decision to violate the local ordinance in Montgomery, Alabama, requiring blacks to give up their seats to whites on public buses. Her courageous decision set in motion the Montgomery bus boycott. Its success convinced civil rights activists that the time was ripe for a sustained assault on all forms of racial discrimination. By the early 1960s the South was awash in civil disobedience, which in turn was met by "massive resistance." Demonstrators—women, men, and children—braved fire hoses, police dogs, beatings, and humiliation. Photographers, both black and white, captured on film the often horrific scenes, and the stunning images that appeared in newspapers and magazines helped prick consciences and galvanize national support for the struggle. The Civil Rights Act of 1964 and the Voting Rights Act of 1965 resulted largely from the grassroots movement for civil rights and social justice.*

THE LYNCHING OF RUBIN STACY   Picture History

Race relations in the United States took a decided turn for the worse after 1890. In the South whites grew concerned about a new generation of African Americans, born in freedom after the Civil War, who were reluctant to abide by traditional notions of white supremacy. By the early twentieth century, state after state had established laws to disenfranchise black voters; impose segregation in public facilities, schools, and transportation; and reinforce the sharecropping and tenantry systems that denied blacks social mobility and economic opportunity. Accompanying such legal and extra-legal efforts to impose racial subordination were increasing acts of violence designed to frighten and intimidate the African-American community.

Between 1882 and 1968, some 4,742 blacks were killed by lynch mobs. The victims were often accused of crimes against whites, but it mattered little to the vigilantes whether the charges were true. On occasion blacks were tortured, killed, and mutilated for no reason other than the color of their skin. Lynchings became so commonly accepted that they operated as a form of community recreation and social spectacle. They often were announced in local newspapers, and the spectators, many of them children, took grisly delight in the abuses meted out on blacks. "To kill the victim was not enough," one historian has written; "the execution became public theater, a participatory ritual of torture and death, a voyeuristic spectacle prolonged as long as possible (once for seven hours) for the benefit of the crowd."

This photograph shows the lynching of Rubin Stacy on 19 July 1935, in Ft. Lauderdale, Florida. He had been arrested for "assaulting" a white woman named Marion Jones. While six deputies were transporting Stacy to the Dade County jail in Miami, a mob of some 100 whites ran the police car off the road, overpowered the guard, and took control of the handcuffed Stacy. They riddled his body with bullets before hanging him. Later investigations revealed that Stacy, a homeless tenant farmer, had gone to the home of Mrs. Jones and had asked for food. She grew frightened and called police. There was no assault.

ROSA PARKS BEING FINGERPRINTED   AP Photo

The modern civil rights movement began with the refusal of Rosa Parks, a forty-three-year-old seamstress and officer in the local NAACP chapter, to give up her seat to a white man on a bus in Montgomery, Alabama, on 1 December 1955. The bus driver warned Parks that he would have her arrested if she did not move. "You may do that," she replied in a soft voice.

Her arrest led African American community leaders to organize a massive boycott of the city bus system. For months blacks in Montgomery formed carpools, hitchhiked, or simply walked. On 22 February 1956, Parks was indicted with the Reverend Martin Luther King Jr., and a hundred other blacks for violating the city's anti-boycott ordinance. But the boycott continued throughout 1956. The boycotters finally won a federal case they had initiated to protest the segregation ordinance, and in November 1956 the Supreme Court let stand a lower court opinion that "the separate but equal doctrine can no longer be safely followed as a correct statement of the law." Alabama's bus-segregation laws were deemed unconstitutional. On 21 December 1956, the first integrated bus rolled through the streets of Montgomery.

MARTIN LUTHER KING JR., ARRESTED ON A LOITERING CHARGE
Charles Moore/Black Star/Howard Greenberg Gallery

As the twenty-six-year-old minister at the Dexter Avenue Baptist Church, the Reverend Martin Luther King Jr. emerged as the courageous leader of the Montgomery bus boycott. After the boycott ended late in 1956, King became the nation's foremost champion of civil rights. On 3 September 1958, he attended a court hearing for his colleague Ralph David Abernathy. As he entered the courtroom, police officers told him to move on; King held his ground and was arrested. The officers marched King to police headquarters and shoved him against the receiving desk. The sergeant tossed the officers the keys to a cell while King's distraught wife, Coretta, looked on. Charles Moore, a newspaper photographer for the Montgomery Advertiser, *was at the courtroom when King was arrested and followed him to the police station. His photographs of the incident were reproduced across the world, and the powerful images helped galvanize public support for the civil rights movement.*

ELIZABETH BECKFORD BADGERED BY A MOB AS SHE ENTERS LITTLE ROCK HIGH SCHOOL

Bettmann/Corbis

In 1954 the Supreme Court issued its opinion in the landmark case of Brown v. Board of Education of Topeka, Kansas. *The justices unanimously declared that racially segregated public schools were unconstitutional. A year later the Court ordered that the process of integrating the nation's public schools occur "with all deliberate speed." Reaction among segregationists was swift and violent. Virginia senator Harry F. Byrd called upon southerners to use "massive resistance" to thwart the court ruling. By the end of 1956, in six southern states, not a single African American child attended school with whites. Arkansas governor Orville Faubus called out the National Guard to prevent nine black students, aged fourteen to sixteen, from entering Central High School in Little Rock.*

On 4 September 1957, Elizabeth Beckford rode a public bus to the high school. When soldiers prevented her entry to the school, she turned around to confront a hysterical white mob. "They moved closer and closer," Beckford recalled. "Somebody started yelling, 'Lynch her. Lynch her.'" A white woman finally led Beckford to the safety of a bus that took her home. Two weeks later a federal court order forced Faubus to remove the troops, and on September 23 the nine courageous black students entered a side door of the high school and began attending classes. The mob outside the school went berserk, forcing school officials to take the students home. The chaotic scene in Little Rock finally convinced President Dwight Eisenhower to dispatch federal troops to protect the black students.

SIT-IN AT F. W. WOOLWORTH'S COUNTER   AP Photo

After the Montgomery bus boycott of 1955–1956, Martin Luther King's philosophy of "militant non-violence" inspired others to challenge deeply entrenched patterns of racial segregation in the South. The momentum and energy of the broadening efforts spawned the first genuine mass movement in African-American history when four black college freshmen sat down and demanded service at a "whites-only" Woolworth's lunch counter in Greensboro, North Carolina, on 1 February 1960.

Within a week, the "sit-in" movement had spread to six more cities across the state, and within two months, demonstrations had occurred in fifty-four cities in nine states. In some locations the sit-in students, both black and white, were attacked, but they all followed the directions of student leader John L. Lewis: "Do show yourself friendly on the counter at all times. Do sit straight and always face the counter. Don't strike back, or curse if attacked." But above all, he concluded, "Remember the teachings of Jesus, Gandhi, Thoreau, and Martin Luther King Jr."

On 28 May 1963, a group of Tougaloo College students and professors organized a sit-in at the Woolworth's lunch counter in Jackson, Mississippi. After they sat down and requested service, the waitresses closed the counter. The sit-in continued, however, and soon scores of angry whites, including students from Jackson High School arriving for lunch, began taunting and assaulting them. A group of almost a hundred white policemen watched the melee from outside the store; they refused to intervene. For almost three hours, the demonstrators were kicked and beaten, burned with cigarettes, and covered with salt, pepper, sugar, ketchup, and mustard. Finally, the store owner succeeded in begging the police to end the fracas. This photograph shows students Anne Moody (far right) and Joan Trumpauer seated next to Professor John Salter Jr.

WILLIAM GADSDEN ATTACKED BY POLICE DOGS

AP Photo

In the spring of 1963 Martin Luther King and the SCLC launched a series of nonviolent demonstrations in Birmingham, Alabama, the most segregated city in the South. One of King's lieutenants, Fred Shuttlesworth, remembered that "we wanted confrontation, nonviolent confrontation, to see if it would work on a massive scale. Not just for Birmingham—for the nation. We were trying to launch a systematic, wholehearted battle against segregation which would set the pace for the nation." The Birmingham police commissioner, Eugene "Bull" Connor, served as the perfect foil for King's strategy of nonviolent civil disobedience. Connor ordered police to use attack dogs, tear gas, electric cattle prods, and fire hoses on the protesters while millions of outraged Americans watched the confrontations on television.

On 3 May 1963, hundreds of demonstrators, blacks and whites, assembled near the Sixteenth Street Baptist Church. Connor ordered them ousted and arrested. The shocking pictures of police dogs attacking demonstrators galvanized support for the civil rights movement around the nation—and the world. Congressman Peter Rodino was attending a conference in Geneva, Switzerland, when this photograph appeared in European newspapers. One of the conference delegates asked him, "Is this the way you practice democracy?" Rodino said he had no answer.

REVIEW QUESTIONS

1. Why did parents allow their children to attend lynchings?
2. Women played a central role in the civil rights movement. What impressions does the photograph portray of Rosa Parks?

3. Martin Luther King Jr. promoted the tactic of nonviolent civil disobedience for several reasons. What role did such photographic images play in his strategy?
4. What role do you think you would have played in the turmoil surrounding racial integration had you been a student in the late 1950s or early 1960s?

35 ᐒ REBELLION AND REACTION IN THE 1960s AND 1970s

During the decade and a half after John Kennedy entered the White House in 1961, the fabric of American society unraveled. A variety of social groups— middle-class white youth, racial and ethnic minorities, feminists, and others— challenged the consensus that had governed American society since the end of World War II. The tragic shootings of public figures—John and Robert Kennedy, Martin Luther King Jr., George Wallace—heightened the sense of chaos. Racial violence and the war in Vietnam fueled social tensions. Intense debates over the volatile issue of abortion further fragmented the nation. To be sure, the end of American involvement in Vietnam in 1973 removed a major source of controversy. But revelations of the Watergate scandal provided another wound to the body politic. The fact that American society survived such prolonged tensions and trauma testifies to the resilience of the Republic.

The civil rights and antiwar movements drew their energies from a youth revolt that began in the 1950s and blossomed in the 1960s and early 1970s. During the Eisenhower years, the baby boom generation began to enter high school. By the sixties they were enrolled in colleges in record numbers. While the vast majority of these young Americans entered the mainstream of social life, a growing minority grew alienated from the conformity and materialism they saw corrupting middle-class culture. Generational unrest appeared early in the 1950s with the emergence of the Beat poets and alienated teenagers personified by actor James Dean in films such as Rebel without a Cause *and by Holden Caulfield in J. D. Salinger's best-selling novel* Catcher in the Rye.

By the late 1960s a full-fledged cultural rebellion was under way, and all forms of authority were being questioned. The so-called counterculture celebrated personal freedom at the expense of traditional social mores. Youthful rebels— dubbed hippies—defied parental authority and college officials. In "dropping out" of conventional society, they grew long hair, wore eccentric clothes, gathered in urban or rural communes, used mind-altering drugs, relished "hard" rock music, and engaged in casual sex.

Other young rebels chose to change society rather than abandon it. During the late 1950s small groups of college students began to explore the promise of radical politics, and people began to refer to the emergence of a "New Left." Unlike the Old Left of the 1930s that had relied upon Marxist theory and presumed that the contradictions inherent in capitalism would eventually bring about its own collapse, the leaders of the New Left asserted that fundamental social and political changes had to be initiated by well-organized young intellectuals.

The most prominent of the groups representing the New Left was the Students for a Democratic Society (SDS). In 1962 the organization distributed the Port Huron Statement, a manifesto that promoted "participatory democracy"—rather than the traditional political parties as the vehicle for social change—and envisioned universities as the locus of the new movement. SDS was not willing to wait decades for the dialectic of materialism to run its course. They wanted to effect changes immediately. The Port Huron Statement thus decried the apathy on college campuses and urged young people to take collective action against racism, poverty, and the military-industrial complex. Thereafter, members of SDS and other like-minded college students fanned out across the country, seeking to organize poor people into political action groups and to help southern blacks register to vote.

During the mid-1960s the youth revolt spread from the inner cities and rural South to college campuses across the nation. As student activists returned from working as volunteers in the civil rights movement or in anti-poverty programs, they brought with them a militant idealism that initially manifested itself in protests against university regulations and later focused its energies on opposition to the Vietnam War and the draft.

Beginning with the start of the American bombing campaign in 1965 and fueled by the rising numbers of ground forces fighting and dying in Vietnam, organized antiwar protests and teach-ins occurred at hundreds of universities across the country. Such domestic dissent seemed only to harden the commitment of the Johnson and Nixon administrations to the war in Vietnam and produced a social backlash against the protesters. By the end of the 1960s militants were resorting to violence to draw attention to their cause. Dozens of bombings rocked college campuses in 1969 and 1970. One such explosion killed a student at the University of Wisconsin.

President Nixon's announcement of the "incursion" of South Vietnamese and American troops into Cambodia in the spring of 1970 unleashed dozens of antiwar demonstrations on college campuses. At Kent State University in Ohio, students set fire to the ROTC building. The governor dispatched National Guard units to quell the unrest, and the next day a confrontation occurred at the com-

mons in the center of the campus. As demonstrators hurled rocks and epithets at the troops, the Guardsmen panicked and opened fire, killing four students and wounding many others.

After the American withdrawal from Vietnam in 1973, the antiwar movement subsided. But youthful activism persisted and quickly found new causes to promote. The idealism and energy generated by the civil rights movement and antiwar activities helped inspire organized efforts to gain equality and benefits for other groups: women, Native Americans, gays and lesbians, migrant workers, and the elderly. Still other idealists focused their attention on the degradation of the environment and sought to promote an ecological consciousness.

TOM HAYDEN

FROM The Port Huron Statement (1962)

In 1962 sixty members of the Students for a Democratic Society (SDS) gathered at a conference center at Port Huron on the southern shore of Lake Huron, about fifty miles north of Detroit. Led by Tom Hayden, a graduate student at the University of Michigan and editor of the campus newspaper, they drafted a statement of principles and objectives that came to be known as the Port Huron Statement.

From Tom Hayden, "The Port Huron Statement" from *Democracy Is in the Streets: From Port Huron to the Siege of Chicago*, ed. J. Miller, pp. 329–345. Reprinted by permission of the author.

We are people of this generation, bred in at least modest comfort, housed now in universities, looking uncomfortably to the world we inherit. When we were kids the United States was the wealthiest and strongest country in the world; the only one with the atom bomb, the least scarred by modern war, an initiator of the United Nations that we thought would distribute Western influence throughout the world. Freedom and equality for each individual, government of, by, and for the people—these American values we found good, principles by which we could live as men. Many of us began maturing in complacency.

As we grew, however, our comfort was penetrated by events too troubling to dismiss.

First, the permeating and victimizing fact of human degradation, symbolized by the Southern struggle against racial bigotry, compelled most of us from silence to activism. Second, the enclosing fact of the Cold War, symbolized by the presence of the Bomb, brought awareness that we ourselves, and our friends, and millions of abstract "others" we knew more directly because of our common peril, might die at any time. We might deliberately ignore, or avoid, or fail to feel all other human problems, but not these two, for these were too immediate and crushing in their impact, too challenging in the demand that we as individuals take the responsibility for encounter and resolution.

While these and other problems either directly oppressed us or rankled our consciences and became our own subjective concern, we began to see complicated and disturbing paradoxes in our surrounding America. The declaration "all men are created equal . . ." rang hollow before the facts of Negro life in the South and the big cities of the North. The proclaimed peaceful intentions of the United States contradicted its economic and military investments in the Cold War status quo.

We witnessed, and continue to witness, other paradoxes. With nuclear energy whole cities can easily be powered, yet the dominant nation-states seem more likely to unleash destruction greater than that incurred in all wars of human history. Although our own technology is destroying old and creating new forms of social organization, men still tolerate meaningless work and idleness. While two-thirds of mankind suffers undernourishment, our own upper classes revel amidst superfluous abundance. Although the world population is expected to double in forty years, the nations still tolerate anarchy as a major principle of international conduct and uncontrolled exploitation governs the sapping of the earth's physical resources. Although mankind desperately needs revolutionary leadership, America rests in national stalemate, its goals ambiguous and tradition-bound instead of informed and clear, its democratic system apathetic and manipulated rather than "of, by, and for the people."

Not only did tarnish appear on our image of American virtue, not only did disillusion occur when the hypocrisy of American ideals was discovered, but we began to sense that what we had originally seen as the American Golden Age was actually the decline of an era. The world-wide outbreak of revolution against colonialism and imperialism, the entrenchment of totalitarian states, the menace of war, overpopulation, international disorder, supertechnology—these trends were testing the tenacity of our own commitment to democracy and freedom and our abilities to visualize their application to a world in upheaval.

Our work is guided by the sense that we may be the last generation in the experiment with living. But we are a minority—the vast majority of our people regard the temporary equilibriums of our society and world as eternally functional parts. In this is perhaps the outstanding paradox: we ourselves are imbued with urgency, yet the message of our society is that there is no viable alternative to the present. Beneath the reassuring tones of the politicians, beneath the common opinion that America will "muddle through," beneath the stagnation of those who have closed their minds to the future, is the pervading feeling that there simply are no alternatives, that our times have witnessed the exhaustion not only of Utopias, but of any new departures as well.

Feeling the press of complexity upon the emptiness of life, people are fearful of the thought that at any moment things might be thrust out of control. They fear change itself, since change might smash whatever invisible framework seems to hold back chaos for them now.

For most Americans, all crusades are suspect, threatening. The fact that each individual sees apathy in his fellows perpetuates the common reluctance to organize for change. The dominant institutions are complex enough to blunt the minds of their potential critics, and entrenched enough to swiftly dissipate or entirely repel the energies of protest and reform, thus limiting human expectancies. Then, too, we are a materially improved society, and by our own improvements we seem to have weakened the case for further change.

Some would have us believe that Americans feel contentment amidst prosperity—but might it not better be called a glaze above deeply felt anxieties about their role in the new world? And if these anxieties produce a developed indifference to human affairs, do they not as well produce a yearning to believe there *is* an alternative to the present, that something *can* be done to change circumstances in the school, the work-places, the bureaucracies, the government?

It is to this latter yearning, at once the spark and engine of change, that we direct our present appeal. The search for truly democratic alternatives to the present, and a commitment to social experimentation with them, is a worthy and fulfilling human enterprise, one which moves us and, we hope, others today.

On such a basis do we offer this document of our convictions and analysis: as an effort in understanding and changing the conditions of humanity in the late twentieth century, an effort rooted in the ancient, still unfulfilled conception of man attaining determining influence over his circumstances of life.

*   *   *

Values

Making values explicit—an initial task in establishing alternatives—is an activity that has been devalued and corrupted. The conventional moral terms of the age, the politician moralities—"free world," "peoples democracies"—reflect realities poorly, if at all, and seem to function more as ruling myths than as descriptive principles. But neither has our experience in the universities brought us moral enlightenment. Our professors and administrators sacrifice controversy to public relations; their curriculums change more slowly than the living events of the world—, their skills and silence are purchased by investors in the arms race: passion is called unscholastic. The questions we might want raised—what is really important? can we live in a different and better way? if we wanted to change society, how would we do it?—are not thought to be questions of a "fruitful, empirical nature," and thus are brushed aside.

*   *   *

. . . It has been said that our liberal—and socialist—predecessors were plagued by vision without program, while our own generation is plagued by program without vision. All around us there is astute grasp of method, technique—the committee, the ad hoc group, the lobbyist, the hard and soft sell, the make, the projected image—but, if pressed critically, such expertise is incompetent to explain its implicit ideals. It is highly fashionable to identify oneself by old categories, or by naming a respected political figure, or by explaining "how we would vote" on various issues.

Theoretic chaos has replaced the idealistic thinking of old—and, unable to reconstitute theoretic order, men have condemned idealism itself. Doubt has replaced hopefulness and men act out a defeatism that is labeled realistic. The decline of utopia and hope is in fact one of the defining features of social life today. The reasons are various: the dreams of the older left were perverted by Stalinism and never re-created; the congressional stalemate makes men narrow their view of the possible; the specialization of human activity leaves little room for sweeping thought; the horrors of the twentieth century, symbolized in the gas ovens and concentration camps and atom bombs, have blasted hopefulness. To be idealistic is to be considered apocalyptic, deluded. To have no serious aspirations, on the contrary, is to be "tough-minded."

In suggesting social goals and values, therefore, we are aware of entering a sphere of some disrepute. Perhaps matured by the past, we have no sure formulas, no closed theories—but that does not mean values are beyond discussion and tentative determination. A first task of any social movement is to convince people that the search for orienting theories and the creation of human values is complex but worthwhile. We are aware that to avoid platitudes we must analyze the concrete conditions of social order. But to direct such an analysis we must use the guideposts of basic principles. Our own social values involve conceptions of human beings, human relationships, and social systems.

We regard *men* as infinitely precious and possessed of unfulfilled capacities for reason, freedom, and love. In affirming these principles we are aware of countering perhaps the dominant conceptions of man in the twentieth century: that he is a thing to be manipulated, and that he is inherently incapable of directing his own affairs. We oppose the depersonalization that reduces human beings to the status of things—if anything, the brutalities of the twentieth century teach that means and ends are intimately related, that vague appeals to "posterity" cannot justify the mutilations of the present. We oppose, too, the doctrine of human incompetence because it rests essentially on the modern fact that men have been competently manipulated into incompetence—we see little reason why men cannot meet with increasing skill the complexities and responsibilities of their situation, if society is organized not for minority, but for majority, participation in decision-making.

Men have unrealized potential for self-cultivation, self-direction, self-understanding, and creativity. It is this potential that we regard as crucial and to which we appeal, not to the human potentiality for violence, unreason, and submission to authority. The goal of man and society should be human independence: a concern not with image or popularity but with finding a meaning in life that is personal and authentic; a quality of mind not compulsively driven by a sense of powerlessness, nor one which unthinkingly adopts status values, nor one which represses all threats to its habits, but one which has full, spontaneous access to present and past experiences, one which easily unites the fragmented parts of personal history, one which openly faces problems which are troubling and unresolved; one with an intuitive awareness of possibilities, an active sense of curiosity, an ability and willingness to learn.

This kind of independence does not mean egotistic individualism—the object is not to have one's way so much as it is to have a way that is one's own. Nor do we deify man—we merely have faith in his potential.

Human relationships should involve fraternity and honesty. Human interdependence is contemporary fact; human brotherhood must be willed, however, as a condition of future survival and as the most appropriate form of social relations. Personal links between man and man are needed, especially, to go beyond the partial and fragmentary bonds of function that bind men only as worker to worker, employer to employees, teacher to student, American to Russian.

Loneliness, estrangement, isolation describe the vast distance between man and man today.

These dominant tendencies cannot be overcome by better personnel management, nor by improved gadgets, but only when a love of man overcomes the idolatrous worship of things by man. As the individualism we affirm is not egoism, the selflessness we affirm is not self-elimination. On the contrary, we believe in generosity of a kind that imprints one's unique individual qualities in the relation to other men, and to all human activity. Further, to dislike isolation is not to favor the abolition of privacy; the latter differs from isolation in that it occurs or is abolished according to individual will.

We would replace power rooted in possession, privilege, or circumstance by power and uniqueness rooted in love, reflectiveness, reason, and creativity. As a *social system* we seek the establishment of a democracy of individual participation, governed by two central aims: that the individual share in those social decisions determining the quality and direction of his life; that society be organized to encourage independence in men and provide the media for their common participation.

In a participatory democracy, the political life would be based in several root principles: that decision-making of basic social consequence be carried on by public groupings; that politics be seen positively, as the art of collectively creating an acceptable pattern of social relations; that politics has the function of bringing people out of isolation and into community, thus being a necessary, though not sufficient, means of finding meaning in personal life; that the political order should serve to clarify problems in a way instrumental to their solution; it should provide outlets for the expression of personal grievance and aspiration; opposing views should be organized so as to illuminate choices and facilitate the attainment of goals; channels should be commonly available to relate men to knowledge and to power so that private problems—from bad recreation facilities to personal alienation—are formulated as general issues.

The economic sphere would have as its basis the principles: that work should involve incentives worthier than money or survival. It should be educative, not stultifying; creative, not mechanical;

self-directed, not manipulated, encouraging independence, a respect for others, a sense of dignity, and a willingness to accept social responsibility since it is this experience that has crucial influence on habits, perceptions, and individual ethics; that the economic experience is so personally decisive that the individual must share in its full determination; that the economy itself is of such social importance that its major resources and means of production should be open to democratic participation and subject to democratic social regulation.

Like the political and economic ones, major social institutions—cultural, educational, rehabilitative, and others—should be generally organized with the well-being and dignity of man as the essential measure of success.

In social change or interchange, we find violence to be abhorrent because, it requires generally the transformation of the target, be it a human being or a community of people, into a depersonalized object of hate. It is imperative that the means of violence be abolished and the institutions—local, national, international—that encourage nonviolence as a condition of conflict be developed. These are our central values, in skeletal form. It remains vital to understand their denial or attainment in the context of the modern world.

*   *   *

Tragically, the university could serve as a significant source of social criticism and initiator of new modes and molders of attitudes. But the actual intellectual effect of the college experience is hardly distinguishable from that of any other communications channel—say, a television set—passing on the stock truths of the day. Students leave college somewhat more "tolerant" than when they arrived, but basically unchallenged in their values and political orientations. With administrators ordering the institution, and faculty the curriculum, the student learns by his isolation to accept elite rule within the University, which prepares him to accept later forms of minority control. The real function of the educational system—as opposed to its more rhetorical function of "searching for truth"— is to impart the key information and styles that will help the student get by, modestly but comfortably, in the big society beyond. . . .

The very isolation of the individual—from power and community and ability to aspire— means the rise of a democracy without publics. With the great mass of people structurally remote and psychologically hesitant with respect to democratic institutions, those institutions themselves attenuate and become, in the fashion of the vicious circle, progressively less accessible to those few who aspire to serious participation in social affairs. The vital democratic connection between community and leadership, between the mass and the several elites, has been so wrenched and perverted that disastrous policies go unchallenged time and again. . . .

REVIEW QUESTIONS

1. According to Hayden, what two phenomena disrupted the complacency of his generation?
2. What factors did Hayden cite as impeding the formulation of new values and a larger social vision?
3. How did Hayden define the concept of participatory democracy?

GLORIA STEINEM

Women's Liberation (1970)

The social turbulence of the 1960s gave new momentum to the women's rights movement. Prominent feminists such as writer Gloria Steinem focused their efforts on passage of the Equal Rights Amendment (ERA) to the Constitution. In 1970 the Senate Judiciary Committee held hearings on the ERA, which passed in Congress but failed to gain ratification by the required three-fourths of the states. The following transcript comes from Steinem's testimony before the committee.

From U.S. Senate, *"The Equal Rights" Amendment: Hearings before the Subcommittee on Constitutional Amendments of the Senate Committee on the Judiciary*, 91st Cong., 2d sess., 5–7 May 1970, pp. 331–335.

During 12 years of working for a living, I have experienced much of the legal and social discrimination reserved for women in this country. I have been refused service in public restaurants, ordered out of public gathering places, and turned away from apartment rentals; all for the clearly-stated, sole reason that I am a woman. And all without the legal remedies available to blacks and other minorities. I have been excluded from professional groups, writing assignments on so-called "unfeminine" subjects such as politics, full participation in the Democratic Party, jury duty, and even from such small male privileges as discounts on airline fares. Most important to me, I have been denied a society in which women are encouraged, or even allowed to think of themselves as first-class citizens and responsible human beings.

However, after 2 years of researching the status of American women, I have discovered that in reality, I am very, very lucky. Most women, both wage-earners and housewives, routinely suffer more humiliation and injustice than I do.

As a freelance writer, I don't work in the male-dominated hierarchy of an office. (Women, like blacks and other visibly different minorities, do better in individual professions such as the arts, sports, or domestic work; anything in which they don't have authority over white males.) I am not one of the millions of women who must support a family. Therefore, I haven't had to go on welfare because there are no day-care centers for my children while I work, and I haven't had to submit to the humiliating welfare inquiries about my private and sexual life, inquiries from which men are exempt. I haven't had to brave the sex bias of labor unions and employers, only to see my family subsist on a median salary 40 percent less than the male median salary.

I hope this committee will hear the personal, daily injustices suffered by many women-professionals and day laborers, women housebound by welfare as well as by suburbia. We have all been silent for too long. But we won't be silent anymore.

The truth is that all our problems stem from the same sex based myths. We may appear before you as white radicals or the middle-aged middle-class or black soul sisters, but we are all sisters in fighting against these outdated myths. Like racial myths, they have been reflected in our laws. Let me list a few.

That woman are biologically inferior to men. In fact, an equally good case can be made for the reverse. Women live longer than men, even when the men are not subject to business pressures. Women survived Nazi concentration camps better, keep cooler heads in emergencies currently studied by disaster-researchers, are protected against heart attacks by their female sex hormones, and are so much more durable at every stage of life that nature must conceive 20 to 50 percent more males in order to keep the balance going.

Man's hunting activities are forever being pointed to as tribal proof of superiority. But while he was hunting, women built houses, tilled the fields, developed animal husbandry, and perfected language. Men, being all alone in the bush, often developed into a creature as strong as women, fleeter of foot, but not very bright.

However, I don't want to prove the superiority of one sex to another. That would only be repeating a male mistake. English scientists once definitively proved, after all, that the English were descended from the angels, while the Irish were descended from the apes; it was the rationale for England's domination of Ireland for more than a century. The point is that science is used to support current myth and economics almost as much as the church was.

What we do know is that the difference between two races or two sexes is much smaller than the differences to be found within each group. Therefore, in spite of the slide show on female inferiorities that I understand was shown to you yesterday, the law makes much more sense when it treats individuals, not groups bundled together by some condition of birth.

*   *   *

Another myth, that women are already treated equally in this society. I am sure there has been ample testimony to prove that equal pay for equal work, equal chance for advancement, and equal training or encouragement is obscenely scarce in every field, even those—like food and fashion industries—that are supposedly "feminine."

A deeper result of social and legal injustice, however, is what sociologists refer to as "Internalized Aggression." Victims of aggression absorb the myth of their own inferiority, and come to believe that their group is in fact second class. Even when they themselves realize they are not second class,

they may still think their group is, thus the tendency to be the only Jew in the club, the only black woman on the block, the only woman in the office.

Women suffer this second class treatment from the moment they are born. They are expected to be, rather than achieve, to function biologically rather than learn. A brother, whatever his intellect, is more likely to get the family's encouragement and education money, while girls are often pressured to conceal ambition and intelligence. . . .

Teachers, parents, and the Supreme Court may exude a protective, well-meaning rationale, but limiting the individual's ambition is doing no one a favor. Certainly not this country; it needs all the talent it can get.

Another myth, that American women hold great economic power. Fifty-one percent of all shareholders in this country are women. That is a favorite male-chauvinist statistic. However, the number of shares they hold is so small that the total is only 18 percent of all the shares. Even those holdings are often controlled by men.

Similarly, only 5 percent of all the people in the country who receive $10,000 a year or more, earned or otherwise, are women. And that includes the famous rich widows.

The constantly repeated myth of our economic power seems less testimony to our real power than to the resentment of what little power we do have.

Another myth, that children must have full-time mothers. American mothers spend more time with their homes and children than those of any other society we know about. In the past, joint families, servants, a prevalent system in which grandparents raised the children, or family field work in the agrarian systems—all these factors contributed more to child care than the labor-saving devices of which we are so proud.

The truth is that most American children seem to be suffering from too much mother, and too little father. Part of the program of Women's Liberation is a return of fathers to their children. If laws permit women equal work and pay opportunities, men will then be relieved of their role as sole breadwinner. Fewer ulcers, fewer hours of meaningless work, equal responsibility for his own children: these are a few of the reasons that Women's Liberation is Men's Liberation too.

As for psychic health of the children, studies show that the quality of time spent by parents is more important than the quantity. The most damaged children were not those whose mothers worked, but those whose mothers preferred to work but stayed home out of the role-playing desire to be a "good mother."

Another myth, that the women's movement is not political, won't last, or is somehow not "serious." When black people leave their 19th century roles, they are feared. When women dare to leave theirs, they are ridiculed. We understand this; we accept the burden of ridicule. It won't keep us quiet anymore.

Similarly, it shouldn't deceive male observers into thinking that this is somehow a joke. We are 51 percent of the population; we are essentially united on these issues across boundaries of class or race or age; and we may well end by changing this society more than the civil rights movement. That is an apt parallel. We, too, have our right wing and left wing, our separatists, gradualists, and Uncle Toms. But we are changing our own consciousness, and that of the country. . . . Women's bodies will no longer be owned by the state for the production of workers and soldiers; birth control and abortion are facts of everyday life. The new family is an egalitarian family.

Gunnar Myrdal[1] noted 30 years ago the parallel between women and Negroes in this country. Both suffered from such restricting social myths as: smaller brains, passive natures, inability to govern themselves (and certainly not white men), sex objects only, childlike natures, special skills, and the like. When evaluating a general statement about women, it might be valuable to substitute "black people" for "women"—just to test the prejudice at work.

And it might be valuable to do this constitutionally as well. Neither group is going to be content as a cheap labor pool anymore. And neither is going to be content without full constitutional rights.

Finally, I would like to say one thing about this time in which I am testifying.

I had deep misgivings about discussing this topic when National Guardsmen are occupying our campuses, the country is being turned against itself in a terrible polarization, and America is enlarging an already inhuman and unjustifiable war. But it seems to me that much of the trouble in this country has to do with the "masculine mystique;" with the myth that masculinity somehow depends on the subjugation of other people. It is a bipartisan problem; both our past and current Presidents seem to be victims of this myth, and to behave accordingly.

Women are not more moral than men. We are only uncorrupted by power. But we do not want to imitate men, to join this country as it is, and I think our very participation will change it. Perhaps women elected leaders—and there will be many of them—will not be so likely to dominate black people or yellow people or men; anybody who looks different from us.

After all, we won't have our masculinity to prove.

REVIEW QUESTIONS

1. What were some of the "myths" that stifled women's progress?
2. Why was "Internalized Aggression" so pernicious?
3. Has the condition of women changed much since Steinem's testimony? Explain.

---

[1] Swedish sociologist.

The Report of the President's Commission
on Campus Unrest (1970)

President Nixon's effort to "Vietnamize" the war and thereby reduce American involvement initially defused the antiwar movement, but his decision in the spring of 1970 to send troops into Cambodia to destroy Viet Cong sanctuaries unleashed a new round of demonstrations and riots. The worst incident occurred at Kent State University in Ohio. Over 750 National Guard troops were called in to quell the violence. During a tense confrontation, the poorly trained and nervous Guardsmen fired on student protesters, killing four. The tragic incident prompted the creation of an investigative commission.

From President's Commission on Campus Unrest, *Report* (Washington, DC, 1970), pp. 272–277.

On May 2, the ROTC building at Kent State was set afire. On May 4, Kent State students congregated on the university Commons and defied an order by the Guard to disperse. Guardsmen proceeded to disperse the crowd. The students then began to taunt Guard units and to throw rocks. . . .

Many guardsmen said they had hard going as they withdrew up the hill. Fassinger said he was hit six times by stones, once on the shoulder so hard that he stumbled.

Fassinger had removed his gas mask to see more clearly. He said the guardsmen had reached a point between the Pagoda and Taylor Hall, and he was attempting to maintain them in a reasonably orderly formation, when he heard a sound like a shot, which was immediately followed by a volley of shots. He saw the troops on the Taylor Hall end of the line shooting. He yelled, "Cease-fire!" and ran along the line repeating the command.

Major Jones said he first heard an explosion which he thought was a firecracker. As he turned to his left, he heard another explosion which he knew to be an M-1 rifle shot. As he turned to his right, toward Taylor Hall, he said he saw guardsmen kneeling and bringing their rifles to their shoulders. He heard another M-1 shot, and then a volley of them. He yelled, "Cease-fire!" several times, and rushed down the line shoving rifle barrels up and away from the crowd. He hit several guardsmen on their helmets with his swagger stick to stop them from firing.

General Canterbury stated that he first heard a single shot, which he thought was fired from some distance away on his left and which in his opinion did not come from a military weapon. Immediately afterward, he heard a volley of M-1 fire from his right, the Taylor Hall end of the line. The Guard's fire was directed away from the direction from which Canterbury thought the initial, nonmilitary shot came. . . .

Canterbury, Fassinger, and Jones—the three ranking officers on the hill—all said no order to fire was given.

Twenty-eight guardsmen have acknowledged firing from Blanket Hill. Of these, 25 fired 55 shots from rifles, two fired five shots from .45 caliber pistols, and one fired a single blast from a shotgun. Sound tracks indicate that the firing of these 61 shots lasted approximately 13 seconds. The time of the shooting was approximately 12:25 PM. Four persons were killed and nine were wounded. . . .

REVIEW QUESTIONS

1. Why were college students so active in protesting American involvement in the Vietnam War?

2. In what respects might it be accurate to say that America was embroiled in a civil war during the late 1960s?

3. What role do you think you would have played in the college protests against the war?

TOM GRACE

The Shooting at Kent State (1970)

Tom Grace, one of the students wounded at Kent State, provided the following account of the incident.

From Tom Grace, *From Camelot to Kent State* by Joan Morrison and Robert K. Morrison, pp. 329–335. Copyright © 1987 by Joan Morrison and Robert K. Morrison. Currently available in paperback from Oxford Univ. Press. Reprinted by permission.

My first class of the day was at nine-fifty-five and my girlfriend was in the same class. Because of all the tumultuous disorder that had gone on for the preceding days, the professor, being an understanding man, gave people the option of leaving and taking the exam at another time if the events had interfered with their studying, or going ahead and taking the test. My girlfriend chose to make an exit; history was not her strong point. As far as I was concerned, I had no problem taking the test. So she left and I stayed. . . .

Toward the end of the class, I recall a student standing and saying that there was going to be a rally on the commons as soon as the class was over. I sat there for a few minutes deliberating as to whether I should go or not, and I remembered my earlier assurances to my girlfriend.

Then I thought to myself, this is too momentous; it's too important for me to stay away. Certainly I couldn't see any harm in my going over just to watch. So I went over there really with the intention of more or less surveying the scene, not knowing what I was going to find.

It was only a short five-minute walk to the commons. I found several hundred students, and some of my roommates, Alan Canfora and Jim Riggs, had flags, black flags, I believe. Alan had spray-painted "KENT" on it, and the other one was just a black flag, and they were waving these things about. So I was drawn to them right away. There was some chanting going on: "One, two, three, four, we don't want your fucking war" and "Pigs off campus."

The crowd had grouped around the victory bell, which had been historically used to signal victories in Kent State football games, and the bell was being sounded to signal students to congregate. There were at the very least another thousand or so observers and onlookers ringing the hills that surround this part of the commons.

At that point, a campus policeman in a National Guard jeep ordered the crowd, through the use of a bullhorn, to disperse and go to their homes. The policeman was riding shotgun, and I believe a National Guardsman was driving the jeep. "All you bystanders and innocent people go to your homes for your own safety," is what we heard. I think he had the best intentions in terms of asking the crowd to disperse, but it did nothing but whip the crowd into a further frenzy. We have to remember here the mind-set of people and everything that had gone on. A very adversarial atmosphere existed, and we felt that this was our campus, that we were doing nothing wrong, and that they had no right to order us to disperse. If anyone ought to leave, it's them, not us. That's how I felt.

I was standing there yelling and screaming along with everyone else, and then someone flung either a rock or a bottle at the jeep, which bounced harmlessly off the tire. I don't think it was necessarily meant to bounce off the tire; fortunately the person was not a very good shot. That, of course, alarmed the occupants of the jeep. I think they realized at that point because of the crescendo the chants had reached, and also the fact that people were pitching objects in their direction—that we weren't going to leave.

So the jeep drove back to the National Guard lines which had formed on the other side of the commons in front of the remains of the burned ROTC building. Then the National Guardsmen leveled their bayonets at us and started to march across the commons in our direction, shooting tear gas as they came.

I was teargassed along with perhaps a thousand other people. Unlike some of the students, who delayed to throw rocks or tear-gas canisters back in the direction of the National Guard, I chose to leave the area as fast as I could. I retreated to a girls' dormitory where there were some first-floor restrooms. The female students had opened up the windows and were passing out moistened paper towels so people could relieve the effects of the tear gas. So I went and I cleansed my eyes to the best of my ability, and that seemed to take care of me at the moment.

In the meantime, one group of National Guardsmen had advanced the same way that I had retreated, but they did not chase the students further. But another troop of the National Guard had gone right past and proceeded downhill onto the practice football field. There was a rather abrupt drop-off and a chain-link fence where some construction had been going on, and on the other three sides the National Guardsmen were ringed by students.

I cautiously moved a little closer and watched. Some students were throwing rocks at the National Guard, and some of the National Guard were picking up the rocks and throwing them back at the students. I didn't see any National Guardsmen hit by rocks. They seemed to be bouncing at their feet.

Then I remember that the National Guard troop seemed to get into a little huddle before leaving the practice football field. They reformed their lines and proceeded back up the hill. It was almost like the parting of the Red Sea. The students just moved to one side or the other to let the National Guardsmen pass, because no one in their right mind would have stood there as bayonets were coming.

A lot of people were screaming, "Get out of here, get off our campus," and in the midst of all this were some students, oddly enough, who were still wandering through the area with their textbooks, as if they were completely unaware of all that was taking place. I felt that I was still keeping a safe distance. I was 150, 165 feet away. I know that because it's since been paced off.

When the National Guardsmen got to the top of the hill, all of a sudden there was just a quick movement, a flurry of activity, and then a crack, or two cracks of rifle fire, and I thought, Oh, my God! I turned and started running as fast as I could. I don't think I got more than a step or two, and all of a sudden I was on the ground. It was just like somebody had come over and given me a body blow and knocked me right down.

The bullet had entered my left heel and had literally knocked me off my feet. I tried to raise myself, and I heard someone yelling, "Stay down, stay down! It's buckshot!" I looked up, and about five or ten feet away from me, behind a tree, was my roommate Alan Canfora. That was the first time I had seen him since we were down on the other side of the commons, chanting antiwar slogans.

So I threw myself back to the ground and lay as

prone as possible to shield myself as much as I could, although like most people I was caught right in the open. I couldn't run, because I had already been hit. There was no cover. I just hugged the ground so as to expose as little of my body as possible to the gunfire. It seemed like the bullets were going by within inches of my head. I can remember seeing people behind me, farther down the hill in the parking lot, dropping. I didn't know if they were being hit by bullets or they were just hugging the ground. We know today that it only lasted thirteen seconds, but it seemed like it kept going and going and going. And I remember thinking, When is this going to stop?

So I was lying there, and all of a sudden this real husky, well-built guy ran to me, picked me up like I was a sack of potatoes, and threw me over his shoulder. He carried me through the parking lot in the direction of a girls' dormitory. We went by one body, a huge puddle of blood. Head wounds always bleed very badly, and his was just awful.

The female students were screaming as I was carried into the dormitory and placed on a couch, bleeding all over the place. A nursing student applied a tourniquet to my leg. I never really felt that my life was in danger, but I could look down at my foot and I knew that I had one hell of a bad wound. The bullet blew the shoe right off my foot, and there was a bone sticking through my green sock. It looked like somebody had put my foot through a meatgrinder.

The ambulances came. Some attendants came in, put me on a stretcher, and carried me outside. The blood loss had lessened because of the tourniquet that was on my leg. I remember having my fist up in the air as a sign of defiance. They put me into the top tier in the ambulance rather than the lower one, which was already occupied. I remember my foot hitting the edge of the ambulance as I went in. From that moment on, until the time that I actually went under from the anesthesia at Robinson Memorial Hospital, I was probably in the most intense pain that I've ever experienced in my life.

They had the back doors closed by this time, and the ambulance was speeding away from the campus. I looked down and saw Sandy Scheuer. I had met Sandy about a week or two beforehand for the first and only time. She had been introduced to me by one of the guys who lived downstairs in my apartment complex. They were casual friends, and she struck me as being a very nice person. She had a gaping bullet wound in the neck, and the ambulance attendants were tearing away the top two buttons of her blouse and then doing a heart massage. I remember their saying that it's no use, she's dead. And then they just pulled up the sheet over her head.

The ambulance got to the hospital, and it was a scene that's probably been played out any number of times when you have a big disaster. There were people running around, stretchers being wheeled in, and I was just put out in a hallway because the medical personnel were attending to the more severely wounded. I had the tourniquet on my leg, so I wasn't bleeding all over the place, but the pain kept getting more excruciating. I was screaming by that time, "Get me something for this pain!" Then I was wheeled into an elevator and brought up to one of the other floors. I remember receiving some anesthesia and being told to count backward from ten. I didn't get very far, and then I was out.

The next thing I remember was waking up in a hospital bed. I looked up at the ceiling and then all of a sudden it came to me what had occurred. I didn't know how long I had been out, and I sat up as quickly as I could and looked down to see if my foot was still there. I could see the tips of my toes sticking out of a cast. I just lay back, and I breathed a big sigh of relief. . . .

Today, if I engage in any strenuous exercise, I'll have a noticeable limp for a couple of days afterward. But on the whole, I consider myself to be rather fortunate. I could have lost my foot; I could have been killed. Four people had been shot to death: Sandy Scheuer, Jeff Miller, Allison Krause, and Bill Schroeder. My roommate Alan Canfora was struck by gunfire. He was among the least injured of the thirteen people who were either mortally wounded or recovered.

Eventually federal indictments against enlisted

men and noncommissioned officers in the Ohio National Guard were handed down. But, as it turned out, the judge ruled that the Justice Department failed to prove a case of conspiracy to violate our civil rights and dismissed the case before it was ever sent to the jury. That was the end of criminal proceedings against the Ohio National Guard. They got off scot-free.

But I think there are some guardsmen who are sorry for what happened. One guy in particular seemed to be genuinely remorseful. I remember his testimony. He has very poor eyesight, and on May 4 he couldn't get the gas mask on over his glasses, so he had to wear the gas mask without glasses. He was blind as a bat without them, and he admitted he just knew he was shooting in a certain direction. That was a startling admission. There was a guy out there who could hardly see, blasting away with an M-1.

. . . Every year from May 1971, which was the first anniversary of the killings, there has been a commemorative ceremony at Kent State that has attracted anywhere from one thousand students to eight thousand. So the issue has been kept alive there, and I'd say that the main focus now is to erect a proper and suitable memorial to the people who were killed there. The university has finally agreed to do that. They have commissioned a study as to what the memorial should look like, and what it should say.

I'm more concerned about what it says than what it looks like. Ever since I was young, I've been an avid reader of history, with a particular focus on the American Civil War, and for that reason I have more than the usual interest in the subject. When I go down to the Gettysburg battlefield or Antietam, I can read on those monuments about what took place there, what the casualty figures were, and I can try to envision what took place. Somebody should be able to do that at Kent State as well.

I think the memorial should state: "On May 4, 1970, units of the Ohio National Guard—Company H, 107th Armored Cavalry (Troop G) and Company A, 145th Infantry Regiment—shot and killed four student protesters and wounded nine others during a demonstration against the U.S. invasion of Cambodia." Straight-out, simple facts.

REVIEW QUESTIONS

1. How did this student view the presence of the Guardsmen on campus?
2. Did you find Grace's account of the events convincing?
3. What would you suggest as the appropriate inscription on the memorial? Explain.

36 ❧ A CONSERVATIVE INSURGENCY

During 1979 President Jimmy Carter and his Democratic administration grew impotent. The stagnant economy remained sluggish, double-digit inflation continued unabated, and failed efforts to free the American hostages in Iran prompted critics to denounce the administration as indecisive and incapable of bold action. Complicating matters was the chronic bickering among the president's key advisors. Carter's inability to mobilize the nation behind his ill-fated energy program revealed mortal flaws in his reading of the public mood and his understanding of legislative politics.

While the lackluster Carter administration was foundering, Republican conservatives were forging a plan to win the White House in 1980. Those plans centered on the popularity and charisma of Ronald Reagan, the Hollywood actor turned California governor and political commentator. He was not a deep thinker, but he was a superb analyst of the public mood, an unabashed patriot, and a committed advocate of conservative principles. Reagan was also charming, cheerful, and funny, a likable politician renowned for his relentless anecdotes and deflecting one-liners. Where the moralistic Carter denounced the evils of free enterprise capitalism and tried to scold Americans into reviving long-forgotten virtues of frugality, a sunny Reagan promised a "revolution of ideas" designed to unleash the capitalist spirit, restore national pride, and regain international respect. As a true believer and an able compromiser, Reagan combined the fervor of a revolutionary with the pragmatism of a diplomat. One commentator recognized that he was unique in "possessing the mind of both an ideologue and a politician."

Reagan credited Calvin Coolidge and his treasury secretary, Andrew Mellon, with demonstrating that by reducing taxes and government regulations, the elixir of free-market capitalism would revive the economy. Like his Republican predecessors of the 1920s, he wanted to unleash entrepreneurial energy as never before. By cutting taxes and domestic spending, he claimed, a surging economy would produce more government revenues that would help reduce the budget deficit. As it turned out, the Reagan administrations failed to cut government spending—indeed, the federal budget deficit increased dramatically during his presidency. But inflation and unemployment subsided, and public confidence returned.

At the same time that Reagan was promoting his domestic agenda he was pursuing an aggressive foreign policy. He sent American marines into war-torn Lebanon, launched a bombing raid on terrorist Libya, provided massive aid to the anticommunist Contra rebels in Nicaragua, authorized a marine invasion of Cuban-controlled Grenada, and authorized the largest peacetime defense budget in American history.

In 1983 Reagan escalated the nuclear arms race by authorizing the Defense Department to develop a Strategic Defense Initiative (SDI). It involved a complex anti-missile defense system using super-secret laser and high-energy particle weapons to destroy enemy missiles in outer space. To Reagan its great appeal was the ability to destroy weapons rather than people, thereby freeing defense strategy from the concept of mutually assured destruction that had long governed Soviet and American attitudes toward nuclear war. Journalists quickly dubbed the program "Star Wars" in reference to the popular science-fiction film. Despite skepticism among the media and many scientists that such a "foolproof" celestial defense system could be built, SDI forced the Soviets to launch an expensive research and development program of their own to keep pace.

Reagan easily won reelection in 1984, and his personal popularity helped ensure the election of his vice president, George H. W. Bush, in 1988. Just how revolutionary the Reagan era was remains a subject of intense partisan debate. What cannot be denied, however, is that during the 1980s Ronald Reagan became the most dominant—and beloved—political leader since Franklin Roosevelt. His actions and his beliefs set the tone for the decade and continue to affect American political and economic life.

Yet Reagan's policies did not actually constitute a revolution. Although he had declared in his 1981 inaugural address his intention to "curb the size and influence of the federal establishment," the New Deal welfare state remained intact when Reagan left office. Neither the Social Security system nor Medicare was dismantled or overhauled, and the federal agencies that Reagan threatened to abolish, such as the Department of Education, not only remained intact in 1989, but their budgets had grown.

Reagan's administration did bring inflation under control and in the process helped stimulate the longest sustained period of peacetime prosperity in history. Such economic successes, coupled with the nuclear disarmament treaty as well as Reagan's efforts to light the fuse of freedom in eastern Europe and set in motion forces that would soon cause the collapse of Soviet Communism, put the Demo-

cratic Party on the defensive, and forced conventional New Deal "liberalism" into a panicked retreat. The fact that Reagan's tax policies widened the gap between the rich and poor and created huge budget deficits for future presidents to confront did not seem to faze many voters. Most observers, even Democrats, acknowledged that Reagan's greatest success was in renewing America's soaring sense of possibilities. As columnist George Will recognized, what the United States needed most in 1981, when Reagan was sworn in, was to recover "the sense that it has a competence commensurate with its nobilities and responsibilities."

George Gallup Jr. and D. Michael Lindsay

Surveying the Religious Landscape (1999)

Public-opinion polls and surveys are valuable primary sources for historians. During the twentieth century, George Gallup Jr. emerged as the nation's leading pollster and analyst of public opinion. At the end of the century, he and an associate conducted a survey of religious life. It documented the growing diversification of American religious practices. In the 1950s, for example, 67 percent of Americans listed themselves as Protestants. By 1999, that percentage had dropped to barely 50 percent. The Catholic population increased from 24 percent in the 1950s to 29 percent in 1999— an increase primarily caused by the rapid growth of the Hispanic population. The number of Americans claiming a religious affiliation other than Protestantism, Catholicism, or Judaism more than tripled between the 1950s and the 1990s. Most of the growth occurred within the Buddhist, Hindu, and Islamic faiths. Overall, the data revealed that the United States remained one of the most religious nations in the world. Nine out of ten Americans reported that they pray, with 75 percent doing so daily.

From George Gallup, Jr. and D. Michael Lindsay, "Religion and Practice" from *Surveying the Religious Landscape: Trends in U.S. Beliefs* (New York: Morehouse Publishing, 1999), pp. 43–45. Reprinted by permission of George Gallup, Jr. and D. Michael Lindsay.

Religion and Practice

Although 95% of Americans claim some religious tenets, a much smaller segment of the population practices their religious faith on a consistent basis. Three prevalent forms of spirituality include prayer, study of Scripture, and charitable acts of service. As Benjamin Franklin once remarked, "Serving God is doing good to man, but praying is thought an easier service and therefore more generally chosen." Indeed, prayer is the spine that holds up all other forms of American spirituality.

Over 90% of Americans today pray, and three in four U.S. adults pray on a daily basis. Most often they pray silently and alone, and nearly one-third of the population always prays before a meal (29%). Common subjects of these prayers involve the well-being of an individual's family, giving thanks, asking for strength or guidance, or asking for forgiveness. Americans also pray for very specific requests such as getting good grades, attaining victory in athletic events, or winning the lottery. Although some might denounce these types of prayers as self-serving or petty, they also reveal the prevailing American notion that prayer is a means by which humans acquire. For most Americans, prayer is petition. Nearly all who pray contend that their petitions have been answered in the past (95%); consequently, a number of Americans trust the power of prayer.

A robust majority of people in this country pray on a daily basis (75%), but only 15% read the Bible with the same frequency. Another 20% of the population read the Bible at least once a week. Most of them (69%) read the Bible alone. Individuals claim that the primary benefit of Scripture reading is that it makes them feel closer to God. Seventy-six percent of the nation says that reading the Bible helps them commune to a greater extent with God. Adults also cite the feeling of peace and finding meaning in life as primary benefits of reading Scripture.

The Chinese characters for "crisis" stand for both "danger" and "opportunity." Many Americans believe times of crisis provide good opportunities for deeper religious growth and spiritual development. Nearly everyone (94%) believes that more time spent in prayer, meditation, or reading the Bible is an effective way to allay personal depression. Almost nine out of ten U.S. adults (87%) think a pastor or religious leader can offer effective support and encouragement during bouts of depression. Not nearly the same number of people actually pursue these activities during the melancholy seasons of life. For example, the percentage of Americans who seek the help of a pastor during times of discouragement plummets a dramatic sixty points from those who think it would be a good idea (87% think it is a good idea; 27% actually do it). Eight out of ten Americans do find solace in prayer during times of crisis. Women are more inclined to seek spiritual solutions (such as prayer or Bible reading) to crises. Likewise, non-Whites respond to troubles by seeking spiritual solutions much more often than Whites do.

Almost four out of five adults (79%) received some form of religious training as children. An even higher percentage of society's most educated members, individuals with postgraduate education, experienced some form of religious training. Nearly all Americans—regardless of their own experience—would want their children to receive some form of religious instruction. Eighty-nine percent of adults express this desire. Generally, the strongest consensus on this matter arises from the Midwestern and Southern states of the Union. Strong majorities of both Protestants and Catholics wish for some form of religious education for their children.

For many Americans personal piety manifests itself through charitable giving. Gallup research reveals that three-fourths of Americans contributed food, clothing, or other property within the twelve months prior to the survey. Seventy percent contributed monetarily to non-church organizations, and 60% gave money to churches. People are much more willing to contribute material goods than they are to offer their time. Only 42% of the nation reported serving as unpaid volunteer workers for some charity within the last twelve months. Americans clearly prefer to give to charities that benefit the local community—59% compared to 11% benefiting the nation and 12% helping the world.

Involvement in small groups greatly bolsters the likelihood of an individual's practicing his or her personal faith. Princeton University sociologist Robert Wuthnow calls the small group movement in this nation a "quiet revolution." With almost half of the nation's population participating in small groups of some type, many faith communities are employing them as a means to develop greater spiritual disciplines within their congregations. Two members in three of all small groups—not just those that are church-related—say their groups lead them closer to God. For a majority of them (57%), the Bible has become more meaningful to them as a result of their group experience. Many—but not all—church-related small groups center around study of Scriptures and prayer. Wuthnow's landmark study estimates that there are more than 900,000 Bible study groups and 800,000 adult Sunday school classes in the United States today, and more are beginning every year.

In his 1948 text, *The Shaking of the Foundations*, theologian Paul Tillich declared the following:

> People sometimes say, "This is right in theory, but it doesn't work in practice." They ought to say, "This is wrong in theory and consequently it is wrong in practice." There is no true theory which could be wrong in practice. This contrast between theory and practice is contrived by people who want to escape hard and thorough thinking. . . . This is true of the history of science, morals and religion."

Certainly, American pragmatists have driven a wedge between theory and practice in the minds of many people. Within the religious arena, this wedge represents the distinction between religious belief and spiritual practice. Gallup research would indicate that the greatest chink in the bulwark of American religion is the lack of spiritual practices and disciplines actively exercised by religious adherents. Consider, for instance, the following statistic: 93% of Americans have a copy of the Bible or other Scriptures in their household, yet only 42% of the nation can name even five of the Ten Commandments. Spirituality in America may be three thousand miles wide, but it remains only three inches deep.

REVIEW QUESTIONS

1. Do you trust the reliability of public opinion polls? What are their strengths and weaknesses?
2. Why do you think fewer Americans identify with mainstream religious denominations than was the case in the 1950s?

RONALD REAGAN

The "Evil Empire" (1983)

Ronald Reagan skillfully courted the Religious Right during his presidency. In a speech to the Annual Convention of the National Association of Evangelicals in Orlando, Florida, he outlined his crusade against atheistic communism.

From *Public Papers of the Presidents of the United States: Ronald Reagan, 1983* (Washington, DC, 1984) 1, pp. 359–364.

. . . There are a great many God-fearing, dedicated, noble men and women in public life, present company included. And, yes, we need your help to keep us ever mindful of the ideas and the principles that brought us into the public arena in the first place. The basis of those ideals and principles is a commitment to freedom and personal liberty that, itself, is grounded in the much deeper realization that freedom prospers only where the blessings of God are avidly sought and humbly accepted.

The American experiment in democracy rests on this insight. Its discovery was the great triumph of our Founding Fathers voiced by William Penn when he said: "If we will not be governed by God, we must be governed by tyrants." Explaining the inalienable rights of men, Jefferson said, "The God who gave us life, gave us liberty at the same time." And it was George Washington who said that "of all the dispositions and habits which lead to political prosperity, religion and morality are indispensable supports."

And finally, that shrewdest of all observers of American democracy, Alexis de Tocqueville, put it eloquently after he had gone on a search for the secret of America's greatness and genius—and he said: "Not until I went into the churches of America and heard her pulpits aflame with righteousness did I understand the greatness and the genius of America. . . . America is good. And if America ever ceases to be good, America will cease to be great."

Well, I'm pleased to be here today with you who are keeping America great by keeping her good. Only through your work and prayers and those of millions of others can we hope to survive this perilous century and keep alive this experiment in liberty, this last, best hope of man.

I want you to know that this administration is motivated by a political philosophy that sees the greatness of America in you her people, and in your families, churches, neighborhoods, communities—the institutions that foster and nourish values like concern for others and respect for the rule of law under God. Now, I don't have to tell you that this puts us in opposition to, or at least out of step with, a prevailing attitude of many who have turned to a modern-day secularism, discarding the tried and time-tested values upon which our very civilization is based. No matter how well intentioned, their value system is radically different from that of most Americans. And while they proclaim that they're freeing us from superstitions of the past, they've taken upon themselves the job of superintending us by government rule and regulation. Sometime their voices are louder than ours, but they are not yet a majority. . . .

Freedom prospers when religion is vibrant and the rule of law under God is acknowledged. When our Founding Fathers passed the first amendment, they sought to protect churches from government interference. They never intended to construct a wall of hostility between government and the concept of religious belief itself.

The evidence of this permeates our history and our government. The Declaration of Independence mentions the Supreme Being no less than four times. "In God We Trust" is engraved on our coinage. The Supreme Court opens its proceedings with a religious invocation. And the Members of Congress open their sessions with a prayer. I just happen to believe the schoolchildren of the United States are entitled to the same privileges as Supreme Court Justices and Congressmen.

Last year, I sent the Congress a constitutional amendment to restore prayer to public schools. Already this session, there's growing bipartisan support for the amendment, and I am calling on the Congress to act speedily to pass it and to let our children pray.

Perhaps some of you read recently about the Lubbock school case, where a judge actually ruled that it was unconstitutional for a school district to give equal treatment to religious and nonreligious student groups, even when the group meetings were being held during the students' own time. The first amendment never intended to require government to discriminate against religious speech. . . .

More than a decade ago, a Supreme Court decision literally wiped off the books of 50 states statutes protecting the rights of unborn children. Abortion on demand now takes the lives of up to one and a half million unborn children a year. Human life legislation ending this tragedy will some day pass the Congress, and you and I must never rest until it does. Unless and until it can be proven that the unborn child is not a living entity, then its right to life, liberty, and the pursuit of happiness must be protected. . . .

America's goodness and greatness

One recent survey by a Washington-based research council concluded that Americans were far more religious than the people of other nations; 96 percent of those surveyed expressed a belief in God and a huge majority believed the Ten Commandments had real meaning in their lives. And another study has found that an overwhelming majority of Americans disapprove of adultery, teenage sex, pornography, abortion, and hard drugs. And this same study showed a deep reverence for the importance of family ties and religious belief.

I think the items that we've discussed here today must be a key part of the Nation's political agenda. For the first time the Congress is openly and seriously debating issues—and that's enormous progress right there. I repeat: American is in the midst of a spiritual awakening and a moral renewal. And with your Biblical keynote, I say today, "Yes, let justice roll on like a river, righteousness like a never-failing stream."

Now, obviously, much of this new political and social consensus I've talked about is based on a positive view of American history, one that takes pride in our country's accomplishments and record. But we must never forget that no government schemes are going to perfect man. We know that living in this world means dealing with what philosophers would call the phenomenology of evil or, as theologians would put it, the doctrine of sin.

There is sin and evil in the world, and we're enjoined by Scripture and the Lord Jesus to oppose it with all our might. Our nation, too, has a legacy of evil with which it must deal. The glory of this land has been its capacity of transcending the moral evils of our past. For example, the long struggle of minority citizens for equal rights, once a source of

disunity and civil war, is now a point of pride for all Americans. We must never go back.

There is no room for racism, anti-Semitism, or other forms of ethnic and racial hatred in this country.

I know that you've been horrified, as have I, by the resurgence of some hate groups preaching bigotry and prejudice. Use the mighty voice of your pulpits and the powerful standing of your churches to denounce and isolate these hate groups in our midst. The commandment given us is clear and simple; "Thou shalt love thy neighbor as thyself."

But whatever sad episodes exist in our past, any objective observer must hold a positive view of American history, a history that has been the story of hopes fulfilled and dreams made into reality. Especially in this century, America has kept alight the torch of freedom, but not just for ourselves but for millions of others around the world.

And this brings me to me final point today. During my first press conference as President, in answer to a direct question, I pointed out that, as good Marxist-Leninists, the Soviet leaders have openly and publicly declared that the only morality they recognize is that which will further their course, which is world revolution. I think I should point out I was only quoting Lenin, their guiding spirit, who said in 1920 that they repudiated all morality that proceeds from supernatural ideas—that's their name for religion—or ideas that are outside class conception. Morality is entirely subordinate to the interests of class war. And everything is moral that is necessary for the annihilation of the old, exploiting social order and for uniting the proletariat.

Well, I think the refusal of many influential people to accept this elementary fact of Soviet doctrine illustrates an historical reluctance to see totalitarian powers for what they are. We saw this phenomenon in the 1930's. We see it too often today.

This doesn't mean we should isolate ourselves and refuse to seek an understanding with them. I intend to do everything I can to persuade them of our peaceful intent, to remind them that it was the

West that refused to use its nuclear monopoly in the forties and fifties for territorial gain and which now proposes 50-percent cut in strategic ballistic missiles and the elimination of an entire class of land-based, intermediate range nuclear missiles.

At the same time, however, they must be made to understand we will never compromise our principles and standards. We will never give away our freedom. We will never abandon our belief in God. And we will never stop searching for a genuine peace. . . .

Yes, let us pray for the salvation of all of those who live in that totalitarian darkness—pray they will discover the joy of knowing God. But until they do, let us be aware that while they preach the supremacy of the state, declare its omnipotence over individual man, and predict its eventual domination of all peoples on the Earth, they are the focus of evil in the modern world. . . .

While America's military strength is important, let me add here that I've always maintained that the struggle now going on for the world will never be decided by bombs or rockets, by armies or military might. The real crisis we face today is a spiritual one; at root, it is a test of moral will and faith.

Whittaker Chambers, the man whose own religious conversion made him a witness to one of the terrible traumas of our time, the Hiss-Chambers case, wrote that the crisis of the Western World exists to the degree in which the West is indifferent to God, the degree to which it collaborates in communism's attempt to make man stand alone without God. And then he said, for Marxism-Leninism is actually the second oldest faith, first proclaimed in the Garden of Eden with the words of temptation, "Ye shall be as gods." The Western World can answer this challenge, he wrote, "but only provided that it's faith in God and the freedom He enjoins is as great as communism's faith in Man." I believe we shall rise to the challenge. I believe that communism is another sad, bizarre chapter in human history whose last pages even now are being written. I believe this because the source of our strength in the quest for human freedom is not material, but spiritual. And because it knows no limitation, it must terrify and ultimately triumph over those who would enslave their fellow man. For in the words of Isaiah: "He giveth power to the faint; and to them that have no might He increased strength. . . . But they that wait upon the Lord shall renew their strength; they shall mount up with wings as eagles; they shall run, and not be weary. . . ."

Yes, change your world. One of our Founding Fathers, Thomas Paine, said, "We have it within our power to begin the world over again." We can do it, doing together what no one church could do by itself.

God bless you, and thank you very much.

REVIEW QUESTIONS

1. Do you agree with Reagan's interpretation of the separation between church and state in American history?
2. How do you feel about the incorporation of prayers in public schools?
3. Do you accept Reagan's characterization of the Soviet Union as the source of evil in world affairs?

RONALD REAGAN

"Tear Down This Wall" (1987)

Ronald Reagan spent much of his political career crusading against communism. As president, he referred to the Soviet Union as the "evil empire" and steadfastly sought to exert diplomatic and financial pressure against global communism. On 12 June 1987, he stood in front of the Berlin Wall, which separated East and West Berlin, and delivered a stirring speech calling for the Soviet ruler Mikhail Gorbachev to end the Communist domination of Eastern Europe. Less than three years later, on 9 November 1989, East Germany removed the Berlin Wall in the aftermath of the transformation (and disintegration) of the Soviet Union as a result of Gorbachev's reforms.

http://www.reagan.utexas.edu/archives/speeches/1987/061287d.htm [Editorial insertions appear in square brackets—*Ed.*]

. . . Twenty-four years ago, President John F. Kennedy visited Berlin, speaking to the people of this city and the world at the city hall. Well, since then two other presidents have come, each in his turn, to Berlin. And today I, myself, make my second visit to your city. . . .

Our gathering today is being broadcast throughout Western Europe and North America. I understand that it is being seen and heard as well in the East. To those listening throughout Eastern Europe, I extend my warmest greetings and the goodwill of the American people. To those listening in East Berlin, a special word: Although I cannot be with you, I address my remarks to you just as surely as to those standing here before me. For I join you, as I join your fellow countrymen in the West, in this firm, this unalterable belief: *Es gibt nur ein Berlin.* [There is only one Berlin.]

Behind me stands a wall that encircles the free sectors of this city, part of a vast system of barriers that divides the entire continent of Europe. From the Baltic south, those barriers cut across Germany in a gash of barbed wire, concrete, dog runs, and guardtowers. Farther south, there may be no visible, no obvious wall. But there remain armed guards and checkpoints all the same—still a restriction on the right to travel, still an instrument to impose upon ordinary men and women the will of a totalitarian state. Yet it is here in Berlin where the wall emerges most clearly; here, cutting across your city, where the news photo and the television screen have imprinted this brutal division of a continent upon the mind of the world. Standing before the Brandenburg Gate, every man is a German, separated from his fellow men. Every man is a Berliner, forced to look upon a scar.

President von Weizsäcker has said: "The German question is open as long as the Brandenburg Gate is closed." Today I say: As long as this gate is closed, as long as this scar of a wall is permitted to stand, it is not the German question alone that remains open, but the question of freedom for all mankind. Yet I do not come here to lament. For I find in Berlin a message of hope, even in the shadow of this wall, a message of triumph.

*   *   *

Where four decades ago there was rubble, today in West Berlin there is the greatest industrial output of any city in Germany—busy office blocks, fine homes and apartments, proud avenues, and the spreading lawns of parkland. Where a city's culture seemed to have been destroyed, today there are two great universities, orchestras and an opera, countless theaters, and museums. Where there was want, today there's abundance—food, clothing, automobiles. . . . From devastation, from utter ruin, you Berliners have, in freedom, rebuilt a city that once again ranks as one of the greatest on Earth. The Soviets may have had other plans. . . .

In the 1950s, Khrushchev predicted: "We will bury you." But in the West today, we see a free world that has achieved a level of prosperity and well-being unprecedented in all human history. In the Communist world, we see failure, technological backwardness, declining standards of health, even want of the most basic kind—too little food. Even today, the Soviet Union still cannot feed itself. After these four decades, then, there stands before the entire world one great and inescapable conclusion: Freedom leads to prosperity. Freedom replaces the ancient hatreds among the nations with comity and peace. Freedom is the victor.

And now the Soviets themselves may, in a limited way, be coming to understand the importance of freedom. We hear much from Moscow about a new policy of reform and openness. Some political prisoners have been released. Certain foreign news broadcasts are no longer being jammed. Some economic enterprises have been permitted to operate with greater freedom from state control. Are these the beginnings of profound changes in the Soviet state? Or are they token gestures, intended to raise false hopes in the West, or to strengthen the Soviet system without changing it? We welcome change and openness; for we believe that freedom and security go together, that the advance of human liberty can only strengthen the cause of world peace.

There is one sign the Soviets can make that would be unmistakable, that would advance dramatically the cause of freedom and peace. General Secretary Gorbachev, if you seek peace, if you seek prosperity for the Soviet Union and Eastern Europe, if you seek liberalization: Come here to this gate! Mr. Gorbachev, open this gate! Mr. Gorbachev, tear down this wall!

I understand the fear of war and the pain of division that afflict this continent—and I pledge to you my country's efforts to help overcome these burdens. To be sure, we in the West must resist So-

viet expansion. So we must maintain defenses of unassailable strength. Yet we seek peace; so we must strive to reduce arms on both sides. Beginning ten years ago, the Soviets challenged the Western alliance with a grave new threat, hundreds of new and more deadly SS-20 nuclear missiles, capable of striking every capital in Europe. The Western alliance responded by committing itself to a counterdeployment unless the Soviets agreed to negotiate a better solution; namely, the elimination of such weapons on both sides. For many months, the Soviets refused to bargain in earnestness. As the alliance, in turn, prepared to go forward with its counterdeployment, there were difficult days—days of protests like those during my 1982 visit to this city—and the Soviets later walked away from the table.

But through it all, the alliance held firm. And I invite those who protested then—I invite those who protest today—to mark this fact: Because we remained strong, the Soviets came back to the table. And because we remained strong, today we have within reach the possibility, not merely of limiting the growth of arms, but of eliminating, for the first time, an entire class of nuclear weapons from the face of the Earth. As I speak, NATO ministers are meeting in Iceland to review the progress of our proposals for eliminating these weapons. At the talks in Geneva, we have also proposed deep cuts in strategic offensive weapons. And the Western allies have likewise made far-reaching proposals to reduce the danger of conventional war and to place a total ban on chemical weapons.

While we pursue these arms reductions, I pledge to you that we will maintain the capacity to deter Soviet aggression at any level at which it might occur. . . .

*   *   *

In Europe, only one nation and those it controls refuse to join the community of freedom. Yet in this age of redoubled economic growth, of information and innovation, the Soviet Union faces a choice: It must make fundamental changes, or it will become obsolete. Today thus represents a moment of hope. We in the West stand ready to cooperate with the East to promote true openness, to break down barriers that separate people, to create a safer, freer world.

And surely there is no better place than Berlin, the meeting place of East and West, to make a start. . . .

And I invite Mr. Gorbachev: Let us work to bring the Eastern and Western parts of the city closer together, so that all the inhabitants of all Berlin can enjoy the benefits that come with life in one of the great cities of the world. To open Berlin still further to all Europe, East and West, let us expand the vital air access to this city, finding ways of making commercial air service to Berlin more convenient, more comfortable, and more economical. We look to the day when West Berlin can become one of the chief aviation hubs in all central Europe.

*   *   *

In these four decades [since the end of World War II], as I have said, you Berliners have built a great city. You've done so in spite of threats—the Soviet attempts to impose the East-mark [a uniform German currency], the blockade. Today the city thrives in spite of the challenges implicit in the very presence of this wall. What keeps you here? Certainly there's a great deal to be said for your fortitude, for your defiant courage. But I believe there's something deeper, something that involves Berlin's whole look and feel and way of life—not mere sentiment. No one could live long in Berlin without being completely disabused of illusions. Something, instead, that has seen the difficulties of life in Berlin but chose to accept them, that continues to build this good and proud city in contrast to a surrounding totalitarian presence, that refuses to release human energies or aspirations. Something that speaks with a powerful voice of affirma-

tion, that says yes to this city, yes to the future, yes to freedom. In a word, I would submit that what keeps you in Berlin is love—love both profound and abiding.

Perhaps this gets to the root of the matter, to the most fundamental distinction of all between East and West. The totalitarian world produces backwardness because it does such violence to the spirit, thwarting the human impulse to create, to enjoy, to worship. . . .

As I looked out a moment ago from the Reichstag, that embodiment of German unity, I noticed words crudely spray-painted upon the wall, perhaps by a young Berliner: "This wall will fall. Beliefs become reality." Yes, across Europe, this wall will fall. For it cannot withstand faith; it cannot withstand truth. The wall cannot withstand freedom.

And I would like, before I close, to say one word. I have read, and I have been questioned since I've been here about certain demonstrations against my coming. And I would like to say just one thing, and to those who demonstrate so. I wonder if they have ever asked themselves that if they should have the kind of government they apparently seek, no one would ever be able to do what they're doing again.

Thank you and God bless you all.

REVIEW QUESTIONS

1. How does Reagan compare and contrast the capitalist and communist systems?
2. In what ways does Reagan use the symbolism of the Berlin Wall to represent the human ideal of freedom?

NEW YORK TIMES

The Cold War Is Over (1989)

The dramatic changes instituted by Mikhail Gorbachev in the Soviet Union provoked considerable discussion among analysts in the United States. In April 1989 the New York Times *summarized the opinions of leading experts in international relations.*

The cold war of poisonous Soviet-American feelings, of domestic political hysteria, of events enlarged and distorted by East-West confrontation, of almost perpetual diplomatic deadlock is over.

The we-they world that emerged after 1945 is giving way to the more traditional struggles of great powers. That contest is more manageable. It permits serious negotiations. It creates new possibilities—for cooperation in combating terrorism, the spread of chemical weapons and common threats to the environment, and for shaping a less violent world.

True, Europe remains torn in two; but the place where four decades of hostility began is mending and changing in complicated patterns. True, two enormous military machines still face each other around the world; but both sides are searching for ways to reduce the burdens and risks. Values continue to clash, but less profoundly as Soviet citizens start to partake in freedoms.

The experts who contributed to a two-month series on the Op-Ed page called "Is the Cold War Over?" agreed, with variations in emphasis and definition, that Soviet-American relations are entering a new era. They differed over whether Mikhail Gorbachev can last and whether his policies can outlast him, and over how much the West can or should do to help him and what to ask in return. But these questions are the stuff of genuine policy debate, not grist for old ideological diatribes.

In his four years of power, what has Mikhail Gorbachev done to bring about this reconsideration of the cold war?

A great deal, as Jeremy Stone of the Federation of American Sciences rightly pointed out. Mr. Gorbachev has pushed Yasir Arafat[1] toward renouncing terrorism and accepting Israel, supported political settlements in Angola and Cambodia, pulled out Soviet troops from Afghanistan, agreed to vastly disproportionate cuts in medium-range missiles and pledged significant unilateral reductions in Soviet forces in Central Europe.

At home, Mr. Stone said properly, the Soviet leader is introducing economic decentralization, allowing Soviet nationalities to assert their separate identities, encouraging free speech and experimenting with elections. These measures give hope for a more open Soviet society and Government. And, as Graham Allison of Harvard's Kennedy School pointed out, this has been the very goal of America's containment policy.

But what if Mr. Gorbachev is ousted? Couldn't his successors readily reverse his actions?

Frank Carlucci argued that it's too early to foretell Mr. Gorbachev's fate or judge whether he or his successors might not simply change policies. The former Defense Secretary argued that Soviet policy is in a transitional phase.

Dimitri Simes of the Carnegie Endowment for

---

[1] Head of the Palestine Liberation Organization (PLO).

International Peace, on the other hand, convincingly made the case that the changes occurring in the Soviet Union are of a more fundamental nature. Whoever leads the Soviet Union, he argued, would have little choice but to respond to Moscow's current economic and political weaknesses and follow the Gorbachev path.

Mr. Simes rightly argued that the debate in the Soviet Union revolves around the scope and pace of change, not the need for change. And there is little evidence that Mr. Gorbachev's foreign and military policies are under attack. Moscow simply does not have the resources for costly global challenges.

If the Soviet Union is in such bad shape, why not squeeze hard for concessions?

William Luers, a former U.S. diplomat, offered one reason. He warned against humiliating Mr. Gorbachev in ways that would unite a proud nation against the West. Ed Hewitt of the Brookings Institution provided another: Soviet leaders still have sufficient economic strength and foreign policy options to make life easier or harder for the West.

These cautions have to be kept in mind. But the West should not shy away from driving hard bargains. That can be done, as Ronald Reagan demonstrated, without destroying relations.

What should Western policy be?

Zbigniew Brzezinski correctly argued that the West needs a strategy to deal with "the gravity of the challenge and the magnitude of the opportunity." But the West would tie itself in knots if it followed his advice to "insist that any substantial assistance be reciprocated by reforms that institutionalize economic and political pluralism."

On the contrary, the West cannot manage Soviet reforms any more than it can "save" Mr. Gorbachev. It can reinforce and encourage reforms when Western interests are also at stake— by providing credits and technology on a modest and safe scale and by easing restrictions on trade. The point is for the West to rid itself of self-made restraints on expanding economic relations so that decisions can be made on a case-by-case basis.

The prospect of such economic openings and the diminishing Soviet threat are likely to give freer play to conflicts among Western industrialized powers, according to Edward Luttwak of the Center for Strategic and International Studies. He was exactly right in urging Western leaders to "act now to construct a new system of economic cooperation that would stand on its own and not lean on the imperatives of resisting" Moscow.

No one seems to have a good answer about the division of Europe, always the most dangerous East-West question. Michael Mandelbaum of the Council on Foreign Relations offered as good a prescription as anyone. He looked toward superpower talks to bring about sovereign nations in Eastern Europe and special arrangements for the two Germanys.

The Bush Administration seems less attentive to these issues and more preoccupied with Mr. Gorbachev's seizing headlines worldwide. It would do better to think of him as part of the solution, not the problem, as Richard Ullman of Princeton University counseled. "Who takes the initiative," he wrote, "matters less than the result."

The Administration now nears the completion of its East-West policy review. Hints dribble out about senior officials worrying that Mr. Reagan was too friendly with Mr. Gorbachev and too eager for arms control. That's self-defeating talk. The treaty eliminating medium-range missiles in Europe represents a substantial victory for the West. Similarly, Mr. Bush and the country would gain by early completion of a treaty to cut intercontinental-range missiles and bombers.

None of the contributors recommended cosmic disarmament agreements, and Mr. Bush would be right to avoid them. But he would be flat wrong not to exploit Moscow's willingness to compromise on cutting troops in Europe and otherwise reduce the costs and risks of security.

It would also be unfortunate if the Bush team worried too much about its right flank and tried to prove that it can out-tough Mr. Reagan.

That would drain them of the imagination and boldness necessary to go beyond the cold war. Presidents Bush and Gorbachev have the opportunity of the century to refocus energies and resources from sterile conflicts onto common threats to mankind.

REVIEW QUESTIONS

1. What contributions did Gorbachev make to the thawing of East-West relations?
2. How did economic issues contribute to the rapprochement between the United States and the Soviet Union?
3. What concerns did the analysts have about Bush administration actions?

COLIN L. POWELL

The Powell Doctrine (1992)

After the end of Persian Gulf War in 1991, General Colin Powell, then chairman of the Joint Chiefs of Staff, outlined his vision for efficient, decisive military action. His plan is now referred to as the Powell Doctrine. The Doctrine essentially says that military force should be used only as a last resort and only if there is a clear risk to national security. In addition, Powell insisted that if forces are deployed, their firepower should be overwhelming. Finally, he stressed the need for policymakers to generate widespread public support for the use of military force and to develop a clear exit strategy from the conflict.

From Colin Powell, "U.S. Forces: Challenges Ahead." Reprinted by permission of *Foreign Affairs*, Vol. 71, Winter 1992/1993. Copyright 1992 by the Council on Foreign Relations, Inc. www.ForeignAffairs.com.

*   *   *

To help with the complex issue of the use of "violent" force, some have turned to a set of principles or a when-to-go-to-war doctrine. "Follow these directions and you can't go wrong." There is, however, no fixed set of rules for the use of military force. To set one up is dangerous. First, it destroys the ambiguity we might want to exist in our enemy's mind regarding our intentions. Unless part of our strategy is to destroy that ambiguity, it is usually helpful to keep it intact.

Second, having a fixed set of rules for how you will go to war is like saying you are always going to use the elevator in the event of fire in your apartment building. Surely enough, when the fire comes the elevator will be engulfed in flames or, worse, it will look good when you get in it only to fill with smoke and flames and crash a few minutes later. But do you stay in your apartment and burn to death because your plans call for using the elevator to escape and the elevator is untenable? No, you run to the stairs, an outside fire escape or a window. In short, your plans to escape should be governed by the circumstances of the fire when it starts.

When a "fire" starts that might require committing armed forces, we need to evaluate the circumstances. Relevant questions include: Is the political objective we seek to achieve important, clearly defined and understood? Have all other nonviolent policy means failed? Will military force achieve the objective? At what cost? Have the gains and risks been analyzed? How might the situation that we seek to alter, once it is altered by force, develop further and what might be the consequences?

As an example of this logical process, we can examine the assertions of those who have asked why President Bush did not order our forces on to Baghdad after we had driven the Iraqi army out of Kuwait. We must assume that the political objective of such an order would have been capturing Saddam Hussein. Even if Hussein had waited for us to enter Baghdad, and even if we had been able to capture him, what purpose would it have served? And would serving that purpose have been worth the many more casualties that would have occurred? Would it have been worth the inevitable follow-up: major occupation forces in Iraq for years to come and a very expensive and complex American proconsulship in Baghdad? Fortunately for America, reasonable people at the time thought not. They still do.

When the political objective is important, clearly defined and understood, when the risks are acceptable, and when the use of force can be effectively combined with diplomatic and economic policies, then clear and unambiguous objectives must be given to the armed forces. These objectives must be firmly linked with the political objectives. We must not, for example, send military forces into a crisis with an unclear mission they cannot accomplish—such as we did when we sent the U.S. Marines into Lebanon in 1983. We inserted those proud warriors into the middle of a five-faction civil war complete with terrorists, hostage-takers and a dozen spies in every camp, and said, "Gentlemen, be a buffer." The results were 241 dead Marines and Navy personnel and a U.S. withdrawal from the troubled area.

When force is used deftly—in smooth coordination with diplomatic and economic policy—bullets may never have to fly. Pulling triggers should always be toward the end of the plan, and when those triggers are pulled all of the sound analysis I have just described should back them up.

Over the past three years the U.S. armed forces have been used repeatedly to defend our interests and to achieve our political objectives. In Panama a dictator was removed from power. In the Philippines the use of limited force helped save a democracy. In Somalia a daring night raid rescued our embassy. In Liberia we rescued stranded international citizens and protected our embassy. In the Persian Gulf a nation was liberated. Moreover we have used our forces for humanitarian relief operations in Iraq, Somalia, Bangladesh, Russia and Bosnia.

All of these operations had one thing in common: they were successful. There have been no Bay of Pigs, failed desert raids, Beirut bombings or Vietnams. Today American troops around the world are protecting the peace in Europe, the Persian Gulf, Korea, Cambodia, the Sinai and western Sahara. They have brought relief to Americans at home here in Florida, Hawaii and Guam. Ironically enough, the American people are getting a solid return on their defense investment even as from all corners of the nation come shouts for imprudent reductions that would gut their armed forces.

The reason for our success is that in every instance we have carefully matched the use of military force to our political objectives. We owe it to the men and women who go in harm's way to make sure that this is always the case and that their lives are not squandered for unclear purposes.

Military men and women recognize more than most people that not every situation will be crystal clear. We can and do operate in murky, unpredictable circumstances. But we also recognize that military force is not always the right answer. If force is used imprecisely or out of frustration rather than clear analysis, the situation can be made worse.

Decisive means and results are always to be preferred, even if they are not always possible. We should always be skeptical when so-called experts suggest that all a particular crisis calls for is a little surgical bombing or a limited attack. When the "surgery" is over and the desired result is not obtained, a new set of experts then comes forward with talk of just a little escalation—more bombs, more men and women, more force. History has not been kind to this approach to war-making. In fact this approach has been tragic—both for the men and women who are called upon to implement it and for the nation. This is not to argue that the use of force is restricted to only those occasions where the victory of American arms will be resounding, swift and overwhelming. It is simply to argue that the use of force should be restricted to occasions where it can do some good and where the good will outweigh the loss of lives and other costs that will surely ensue. Wars kill people. That is what makes them different from all other forms of human enterprise.

When President Lincoln gave his second inaugural address he compared the Civil War to the scourge of God, visited upon the nation to compensate for what the nation had visited upon its slaves. Lincoln perceived war correctly. It is the scourge of God. We should be very careful how we use it. When we do use it, we should not be equivocal: we should win and win decisively. If our objective is something short of winning—as in our air strikes into Libya in 1986—we should see our objective clearly, then achieve it swiftly and efficiently.

I am preaching to the choir. Every reasonable American deplores the resort to war. We wish it would never come again. If we felt differently, we could lay no claim whatsoever to being the last, best hope of earth. At the same time I believe every American realizes that in the challenging days ahead, our wishes are not likely to be fulfilled. In those circumstances where we must use military force, we have to be ready, willing and able. Where we should not use force we have to be wise enough to exercise restraint. I have infinite faith in the American people's ability to sense when and where we should draw the line.

REVIEW QUESTIONS

1. Why does Powell argue that there should not be "fixed rules" for deciding when the United States should go to war?
2. Why does Powell deem it essential to give the armed forces "clear and unambiguous" military and political objectives?

37 òò TRIUMPH AND TRAGEDY: AMERICA AT THE TURN OF THE CENTURY

The United States during the last decade of the twentieth century ricocheted be-tween extremes in search of a stable center. In politics, as an editorial in Business Week *stressed in 1996, "voters want their leaders to govern from the center." In 1992 Bill Clinton defeated George H. W. Bush by portraying himself as a new type of Democrat, a centrist and a Washington outsider committed to reducing the size and cost of government. Once in office, however, he fell under the sway of old-style liberals who convinced him to focus on apportioning government jobs to minorities, promoting gay rights within the military, and allowing his wife Hillary to design a government-run health-care reform package that smacked of New Dealism.*

The results were catastrophic for the Democrats. Republicans scored a major victory in the 1994 elections. For the first time in forty years, they seized control of both houses of Congress and announced that their "Contract with America" involved nothing less than the dismantling of the welfare state. "It's the Russian revolution in reverse," said Republican strategist Bill Kristol. Newt Gingrich, the outspoken new Speaker of the House, declared that "We are at the end of an era." Tom DeLay, Gingrich's lieutenant in the House, brazenly stressed that "we are ideologues."

Yet the radical Republicans soon found themselves the victims of their own hubris. Middle-of-the-road Americans balked at the idea of shutting down the federal government, and the ever-resilient Bill Clinton surprised his opponents by moving decisively toward the political center. He hired a new stable of advisors and began stressing that the "era of Big Government is over." He used his State of the Union address in 1995 to co-opt the Republicans on key issues such as welfare reform and balancing the budget. Clinton now insisted that the Democratic Party had allowed itself to be seduced by "identity politics"—self-interested groups pre-occupied with race, ethnicity, gender, and sexual orientation. He promised to abandon such factionalism by moving the party to the center of American values.

He began talking about the need to curb teen pregnancy and underage smoking as well as improve the quality of TV programs.

By 1996 the editor of U.S. News and World Report *could remark that Clinton had stopped the Republican "revolution and successfully placed himself in the political center, uniting his own party and widening his appeal to independents." His victory over Bob Dole in the 1996 presidential election confirmed his successful makeover. One of Clinton's top aides declared after the election that "We're going to see government from the center."*

The same conservative forces steering Bill Clinton toward the center were also affecting racial attitudes during the 1990s. People in both political parties began to question the affirmative action policies that had given preferential treatment to women and minorities. When the Supreme Court ruled in Adarand Constructors v. Pena *(1995) that the government required a "compelling interest" to justify affirmative action mandates, efforts spread across the country to set aside race- and gender-based preferences. In 1996 the state of California eliminated affirmative action programs in employment, contracting, and university admissions. Democratic senator Joseph Lieberman of Connecticut expressed the widespread view that racial and gender preferences were "patently unfair."*

A new generation of conservative African American intellectuals agreed. Thomas Sowell, Shelby Steele, Glen Loury, and Ward Connerly, among others, stressed that affirmative action and social welfare programs had backfired. Instead of liberating and uplifting blacks, they had made them dependent on government assistance and undercut individual initiative. Connerly, a member of the board of regents of the University of California, asked, "Are we going to continue to believe that blacks by definition are disadvantaged? As a black man, I say no."

Another widespread concern during the 1990s was the erosion of civic virtue and public involvement. Between 1960 and 1990, a quarter of the electorate lost interest in voting. In 1994 only 39 percent of the registered voters cast ballots. Apathy at the polls was indicative of a larger trend toward declining participation in community affairs. A dramatic rise in people registering as "independents" rather than Democrats or Republicans, a sharp decline in membership in voluntary associations, and a growing cynicism toward politicians, the political process, and others prompted social scientists to analyze the reasons for a diminishing sense of civic engagement. The Harvard University political scientist Robert Putnam declared in 1995 that the "social fabric is becoming visibly thinner, our connections among each other are becoming visibly thinner. We don't trust one another as much, and we don't know one another as much. And, of course, this is behind the deterioration of the political dialogue, the deterioration of public debate."

Putnam blamed television, VCRs, and computers for distracting people from their social responsibilities; others cited the sharp increase in working wives and the self-absorbed hedonism of the "baby boom" generation and their children—

"Generation X." Whatever the case, Americans headed toward the twenty-first century with an uncertain confidence that the center would hold.

But the center did not hold. The presidential election of 2000 was one of the most controversial in American history. After the votes were tallied on election night, victory hinged on the state of Florida, where the results were so close that a recount was ordered. For days the outcome remained uncertain as each party accused the other of vote fraud. The Supreme Court finally decided the matter, and it awarded the state's electoral votes and therefore the presidency to Republican George W. Bush. He was the first president since John Quincy Adams to follow his father in the White House. He was also the fifth president to have been elected with fewer popular votes than his opponent, former vice president Al Gore.

Bush not only arrived in the White House amid the controversy of a disputed election, but he also inherited a sputtering economy and a falling stock market. By the spring of 2000, the high-tech companies that had led the soaring stock market during the 1990s had begun to stall. Stock values collapsed, stealing over $2 trillion from household wealth. Consumer confidence and capital investment plummeted with the stock market. By March 2001 the economy was in recession for the first time in over a decade. "These are times of shattered illusions," said economist Robert Samuelson. "The mythology of the 'New Economy' is receding before the reality of declining jobs and profits."

With the collapse of the Soviet Union and the end of the Cold War, world politics grew even more unstable during the 1990s. The basic premise of American foreign policy was "unipolar"—to maintain the nation's leadership role in global affairs. Yet the very preponderance of American military power and economic influence created instability. A simmering mistrust of America's geopolitical dominance festered throughout the world at the same time that traditional diplomatic relations were being fractured by growing competition among the world's major civilizations. Where ideologies such as capitalism and communism had earlier been the cause of conflict and tension in foreign relations, issues of religion, ethnicity, and clashing cultural values now divided peoples. "Most important," wrote Harvard University scholar Samuel Huntington, "the efforts of the West to promote its values of democracy and liberalism as universal values, to maintain its military predominance, and to advance its economic interests engender countering responses from other civilizations."

As the twenty-first century unfolded, nations were no longer the sole actors on the stage of world politics. Instead, nebulous multinational groups inspired by religious fanaticism and anti-American rage began to use sophisticated methods of terrorism to gain notoriety and to attack the allies of Israel. The very rootlessness of such zealots—they were alienated from their native societies and able to move around at will in order to infiltrate other countries and cultures—proved to be an ironic strength. Well-financed and well-armed terrorists flourished in the cracks of foundering nations such as Sudan, Somalia, Pakistan, Yemen, and Afghanistan. Throughout the 1990s, the United States fought a losing, secret war against organized terrorism. The ineffectiveness of intelligence agencies in tracking the movements and intentions of militant extremists became tragically evident in 2001.

At 8:45 on the morning of September 11, 2001, a hijacked commercial airliner slammed into the north tower of the World Trade Center in New York City. As people on the streets and in front of television screens watched the famous skyscraper burning, a second jet, traveling at 500 miles per hour, hit the south tower. The fuel-laden planes tore gaping holes in the buildings and turned them into infernos. But worse was to come. The twin towers, both 110 stories tall and filled with thousands of employees, collapsed from the intense heat. Surrounding buildings also collapsed. The entire southern end of Manhattan—"Ground Zero"—became a hellish scene of twisted steel, suffocating smoke, and wailing sirens.

While the catastrophic drama in New York was unfolding, a third hijacked plane crashed into the Pentagon in Washington, D.C. The fourth airliner, thought to be headed for the White House, missed its mark when passengers, who had heard reports, via cell phones, of the earlier hijackings, assaulted the terrorists to prevent the plane from being used as a weapon. During the struggle in the cockpit, the plane went out of control and plummeted into the Pennsylvania countryside, killing all on board.

Within hours of the hijackings, officials identified the nineteen terrorists as members of Al Qaeda ("the base"), a well-financed worldwide network of Islamic extremists led by a wealthy Saudi renegade, Osama bin Laden. For several years, bin Laden had been using remote bases in war-torn Afghanistan as his personal refuge and terrorist training centers. Afghanistan's ruling Taliban regime collaborated with bin Laden's terrorist agenda.

The September 11 terrorist assault on America changed the course of a new presidency, a nation, and the world. The economy, already in decline, went into a free fall. President Bush, who had never professed to know much about international relations or world affairs and had shown only disdain for Clinton's "multilateralism" policy, was suddenly thrust onto center stage as commander-in-chief of a wounded nation.

The Bush administration immediately forged an international coalition to fight terrorism worldwide. On 7 October, after the Taliban defiantly refused to turn over bin Laden, the United States and its allies launched a military campaign—Operation Enduring Freedom—to locate and punish terrorists or "those harboring terrorists." On 9 December, only two months after the American-led military campaign in Afghanistan had begun, the Taliban regime collapsed entirely.

In the fall of 2002 President Bush unveiled a new national security doctrine that marked a distinct shift from previous administrations. Containment and deterrence had been the guiding strategic concepts of the cold war years. In the war against terrorism, however, such cold-war policies were bankrupt. Fanatics willing to become suicide bombers would not be deterred. President Bush declared that the growing menace posed by "shadowy networks" of terrorist groups and unstable rogue nations with weapons of mass destruction required a new doctrine of preemptive military action. "If we wait for threats to fully materialize," he explained, "we will have waited too long. In the world we have entered, the only path to safety is the path of action. And this nation will act."

The new policy, however short on specifics, made sense to many Americans. But to many outside the United States it reinforced fears of American interventionism and unilateralism. As the French foreign minister explained, "We cannot accept either a politically unipolar world, nor a culturally uniform world, nor the unilateralism of a single hyperpower." The ultimate test of the Bush Doctrine would be whether the United States could convert its overwhelming global power into an international consensus for preemptive action.

The Bush Doctrine made sense to many Americans traumatized by the threat of global terrorism. But to many outside the United States it reinforced fears of American arrogance, interventionism, and unilateralism. As the French foreign minister explained, "We cannot accept either a politically unipolar world, nor a culturally uniform world, nor the unilateralism of a single hyperpower." The ultimate test of the Bush Doctrine would be whether the United States could convert its overwhelming global power into an international consensus for dealing with terrorism and the proliferation of weapons of mass destruction.

Contract with America (1994)

On 27 September 1994, over 300 Republican candidates for Congress, led by Representatives Newt Gingrich of Georgia and Dick Armey of Texas, pledged themselves to a "Contract with America." The document represented their shared platform for the upcoming election. The "contract" struck a responsive chord with the voters, who gave the Republicans a stunning victory at the polls. For the first time in forty years, Republicans gained control of both houses of Congress (230 to 205 in the House and 53 to 47 in the Senate). After being elected the Speaker of the House, Gingrich began transforming the elements of the Contract with America into legislation.

From Republican National Committee, *Contract with America: The Bold Plan by Representative Newt Gingrich, Representative Dick Armey, and the House Republicans to Change the Nation*, Ed Gillespie and Bob Schellhas, eds. (New York: Times Books, 1994), pp. 7–11.

As Republican Members of the House of Representatives and as citizens seeking to join that body we propose not just to change its policies, but even more important, to restore the bonds of trust between the people and their elected representatives.

That is why in this era of official evasion and posturing, we offer instead a detailed agenda for national renewal, a written commitment with no fine print.

This year's election offers the chance, after four decades of one-party control, to bring to the House a new majority that will transform the way Congress works. That historic change would be the end of government that is too big, too intrusive, and too easy with the public's money. It can be the beginning of a Congress that respects the values and shares the faith of the American family.

Like Lincoln, our first Republican president, we intend to act "with firmness in the right, as God gives us to see the right." To restore accountability to Congress. To end its cycle of scandal and disgrace. To make us all proud again of the way free people govern themselves.

On the first day of the 104th Congress, the new Republican majority will immediately pass the following major reforms, aimed at restoring the faith and trust of the American people in their government:

FIRST, require all laws that apply to the rest of the country also apply equally to the Congress;

SECOND, select a major, independent auditing firm to conduct a comprehensive audit of Congress for waste, fraud or abuse;

THIRD, cut the number of House committees, and cut committee staff by one third;

FOURTH, limit the terms of all committee chairs;

FIFTH, ban the casting of proxy votes in committee;

SIXTH, require committee meetings to be open to the public;

SEVENTH, require a three-fifths majority vote to pass a tax increase;

EIGHTH, guarantee an honest accounting of our Federal Budget by implementing zero base-line budgeting.

Thereafter, within the first 100 days of the 104th Congress, we shall bring to the House Floor the following bills, each to be given full and open debate, each to be given a clear and fair vote and each to be immediately available this day for public inspection and scrutiny.

1. THE FISCAL RESPONSIBILITY ACT

A balanced budget/tax limitation amendment and a legislative line-item veto to restore fiscal responsibility to an out-of-control Congress, requiring them to live under the same budget constraints as families and businesses.

2. THE TAKING BACK OUR STREETS ACT

An anti-crime package including stronger truth-in-sentencing, "good faith" exclusionary rule exemptions, effective death penalty provisions, and cuts in social spending from this summer's "Crime" bill to fund prison construction and additional law enforcement to keep people secure in their neighborhoods and kids safe in their schools.

3. THE PERSONAL RESPONSIBILITY ACT

Discourage illegitimacy and teen pregnancy by prohibiting welfare to minor mothers and ending increased AFDC (Aid to Families with Dependent Children) for additional children while on welfare, cut spending for welfare programs, and enact a tough two-years-and-out provision with work requirements to promote individual responsibility.

4. THE FAMILY REINFORCEMENT ACT

Child support enforcement, tax incentives for adoption, strengthening rights of parents in their children's education, stronger child pornography laws, and an elderly dependent care tax credit to reinforce the central role of families in American society.

5. THE AMERICAN DREAM RESTORATION ACT

A $500 per child tax credit, begin repeal of the marriage tax penalty, and creation of American Dream Savings Accounts to provide middle class tax relief.

6. THE NATIONAL SECURITY RESTORATION ACT

No U.S. troops under U.N. command and restoration of the essential parts of our national security funding to strengthen our national defense and maintain our credibility around the world.

7. THE SENIOR CITIZENS FAIRNESS ACT

Raise the Social Security earnings limit which currently forces seniors out of the work force, repeal the 1993 tax hikes on Social Security benefits and provide tax incentives for private long-term care insurance to let Older Americans keep more of what they have earned over the years.

8. THE JOB CREATION AND WAGE ENHANCEMENT ACT

Small business incentives, capital gains cut and indexation, neutral cost recovery, risk assessment/cost-benefit analysis, strengthening the Regulatory Flexibility Act and unfunded mandate reform to create jobs and raise worker wages.

9. THE COMMON SENSE LEGAL REFORM ACT

"Loser pays" laws, reasonable limits on punitive damages and reform of product liability laws to stem the endless tide of litigation.

10. THE CITIZEN LEGISLATURE ACT

A first-ever vote on term limits to replace career politicians with citizen legislators.

REVIEW QUESTIONS

1. Summarize how Republicans wanted to change the operations of the House of Representatives.
2. Which groups did the Contract favor? Which did it slight?
3. Did the Contract's proposed changes constitute reforms or a revolution? Explain.

SHELBY STEELE

The New Segregation (1992)

A senior fellow at the Hoover Institute at Stanford University and a professor of literature at San Jose State University, Shelby Steele has emerged as one of the most persuasive African American critics of affirmative action.

From Shelby Steele, "The New Segregation," *Imprimus* 21 (August 1992):1–4.

The Civil Rights Movement of the 1950s–1960s culminated in the 1964 Civil Rights Act and the 1965 Voting Rights Act—two monumental pieces of legislation that have dramatically altered the fabric of American life. During the struggle for their passage, a new source of power came into full force. Black Americans and their supporters tapped into the moral power inspired by a 300-year history of victimization and oppression and used it, to help transform society, to humanize it, to make it more tolerant and open. They realized, moreover, that the victimization and oppression that blacks had endured came from one "marriage"—a marriage of race and power. They had to stop those who said, "merely because we are white, we have the power to dominated, enslave, segregate and discriminate."

Race should not be a source of power or ad-

vantage or disadvantage for anyone in a free society. This was one of the most important lessons of
the original civil rights movement. The legislation
it championed during the 1960s constituted a new
"emancipation proclamation." For the first time
segregation and discrimination were made illegal.
Blacks began to enjoy a degree of freedom they had
never experienced before.

Delayed Anger

This did not mean that things changed
overnight for blacks. Nor did it ensure that their
memory of the past injustice was obliterated. I hesitate to borrow analogies from the psychological
community, but I think this one does apply:
Abused children do not usually feel anger until
many years after the abuse has ended, that is, after
they have experienced a degree of freedom and
normalcy. Only after the civil rights legislation had
been enacted did blacks at long last begin to feel
the rage they had suppressed. I can remember that
period myself. I had a tremendous sense of delayed
anger at having been forced to attend segregated
schools. (My grade school was the first school to be
involved in a desegregation suit in the north.) My
rage, like that of other blacks, threatened for a time
to become all consuming.

Anger was both inevitable and necessary. When
suppressed, it eats you alive; it has got to come out,
and it certainly did during the 1960s. One form
was the black power movement in all of its many
manifestations, some of which were violent. There
is no question that we should condemn violence,
but we should also understand why it occurs. You
cannot oppress people for over three centuries and
then say it is all over and expect them to put on
suits and ties and become decent attaché-carrying
citizens and go to work on Wall Street.

Once my own anger was released, my reaction
was that I no longer had to apologize for being
black. That was a tremendous benefit and it helped
me come to terms with my personal development.
The problem is that many blacks never progressed
beyond their anger.

The Politics of Difference

The black power movement encouraged a permanent state of rage and victimhood. An even
greater failing is that it rejoined race and power—
the very "marriage" that civil rights had been designed to break up. The leaders of the original
movement said, "Anytime you make race a source
of power, you are going to guarantee suffering,
misery and inequity." Black power leaders declared:
"We're going to have power because we're black."

Well, is there any conceivable difference between black power and white power? When you
demand power based on the color of your skin,
aren't you saying that equality and justice are
impossible? Somebody's going to be in, somebody's going to be out. Somebody's going to win,
somebody's going to lose, and race is once again a
source of advantage for some and disadvantage for
others. Ultimately, black power was not about
equality or justice; it was, as its name suggests,
about power.

And when blacks began to demand entitlements based on their race, feminists responded
with enthusiasm, "We've been oppressed too!" Hispanics said, "We're not going to let this bus pass us
by," and Asians said, "We're not going to let this
pass us by either." Eskimos and American Indians
quickly hopped on the bandwagon, as did gays, lesbians, the disabled and other self-defined minorities. By the 1970's, the marriage of race and power
was once again firmly established. Equality was
out: the "politics of difference" was in. From then
on, everyone would rally around the single quality
that make them different from the white males and
pursue power based on that quality. It is a very
simple formula. All you have to do is identify that
quality, whatever it may be, with victimization.
And victimization is itself, after all, a tremendous
source of moral power.

The politics of difference demanded shifting
the entire basis of entitlement in America. Historically, entitlement was based on the rights of citizenship elaborated in the Declaration of Independence and the U.S. Constitution. This was the kind
of entitlement that the original civil rights move-

ment leaders claimed for blacks: recognition of their rights as American citizens to equal treatment under the law. They did not claim, "We deserve rights and entitlements because we are black," but, "We deserve them because we are citizens of the United States and like all other citizens are due these rights." The politics of difference changed all that. Blacks and other minorities began demanding entitlement solely based on their history of oppression, their race, their gender, their ethnicity, or whatever quality that allegedly made them victims.

Grievance Identities

By the 1980's, the politics of difference had, in turn, led to the establishment of "grievance identities." These identities are not about such things as the great contributions of women throughout history or the rich culture of black Americans. To have a strong identity as a woman, for example, means that you are against the "oppressive male patriarchy"—period. To have a strong identity as a black means that you are against racist white America—period. You have no choice but to fulfill a carefully defined politically correct role: (1) you must document the grievance of your group; (2) you must testify to its abiding and ongoing alienation; and (3) you must support its sovereignty. As a black who fails any of these three requirements you are not only politically incorrect, you are a traitor, an "Uncle Tom." You are blaming the victim, you are letting whites off the hook, and you are betraying your people.

In establishing your grievance identity, you must turn your back on the enormous and varied fabric of life. There is no legacy of universal ideas or common human experience. There is only one dimension to your identity: anger against oppression. Grievance identities are thus "sovereignties" that compete with the sovereignties of the nation itself. Blacks, women, Hispanics and other minorities are not even American citizens anymore. They are citizens of sovereignties with their own right to autonomy.

The New Segregation on Campus

The marriage of race and power, the politics of difference, and grievance identities—these are nurtured by the American educational establishment. They have acted on the establishment and affected it in significant ways. After a talk I gave recently at a well-known university, a woman introduced herself as the chairperson of the women's studies department. She was very proud of the fact that the university had a separate degree granting program in women's studies and stressed that I had always been very much in favor of teaching students about the contributions of women. But I asked her what it was that students gained from segregated women's studies that could not be gained from studying within the traditional liberal arts disciplines. Her background was in English, as was mine, so I added, "What is a female English professor in the English department doing that is different from what a female professor in the women's studies department is doing? Is she going to bring a different methodology to bear? What is it that academically justifies a segregated program for women or for blacks, or any group? Why not incorporate such studies into the English department, the history department, the biology department or into any of the other regular departments?"

As soon as I began to ask such questions, I noticed a shift in her eyes and a tension in her attitude. She began to see me as an enemy and quickly made an excuse to end the conversation. This wasn't about a rational academic discussion of women's studies. It was about *the sovereignty of the feminist identity* and unless I tipped my hat to that identity by saying, "Yes, you have the right to a separate department," no further discussion or debate was possible. Meanwhile, the politics of difference is overtaking education. Those with grievance identities demand separate buildings, classrooms, offices, clerical staff—even separate XEROX machines. They all want to be segregated universities within the universities. They want their own space—their sovereign territory. Metaphorically, and sometimes literally, they insist that not only the university but society at large must pay tribute to their sovereignty.

Today, there are some 500 women's studies departments. There are black studies departments, Hispanic studies departments, Jewish studies departments, Asian studies departments. They all have to have space, staff, and budgets. What are they studying that can't be studied in other departments? They don't have to answer this question, of course, but when political entitlement shifted away from citizenship to race, class and gender, a shift in cultural entitlement was made inevitable.

Those with grievance identities also demand *extra* entitlements far beyond what should come to us as citizens. As a black, I am said to "deserve" this or that special entitlement. No longer is it enough just to have the right to attend a college or university on an equal basis with others or to be treated like anyone else. Schools must set aside special money and special academic departments just for me, based on my grievance. Some campuses now have segregated dorms for blacks students who demand to live together with people of their "own kind." Students have lobbied for separate black student unions, black yearbooks, black Homecomings dances, black graduation ceremonies—again, all so that they can be comfortable with their "own kind." One representative study at the University of Michigan indicates that 70 percent of the school's black undergraduates have never had a white acquaintance. Yet, across the country, colleges and universities like Michigan readily and even eagerly continue to encourage more segregation by granting the demands of every vocal grievance identity.

White Guilt

A great contributing factor is, of course, white guilt—specifically a knowledge of ill-gotten advantage. Ignorance is innocence, knowledge is guilt. Whites in America generally know that there is at least a slight advantage in being white. If a white person walks into a department store, chances are he or she is not going to be followed by the security guard as I am. This kind of knowledge makes whites vulnerable. (Incidentally, I do not mean to deride all forms of guilt. Guilt can be a wonderful thing, a truly civilized emotion. Prisons are full of people incapable of feeling guilt.) A member of a grievance identity points a finger and says, "Hey whitey, you've oppressed my people! You have had generations to build up wealth and opportunity while I've had nothing." Almost automatically, the white person's first reaction is, "Am I guilty? Am I a racist?"

The second reaction is escapism. "All right, what do you want? What is it going to take to prove to you that I am not racist?" White college and university administrators say, "You want a black student lounge? You got it. We have a little extra money, so we can pay for a black yearbook. We can hold a separate graduation just for you. What else do you want?"

The third reaction is blindness. Obviously, when you are preoccupied with escaping your own feeling of guilt, you are utterly blind to the people causing it. So college and university administrators blindly grant black students extra entitlements, from dorms to yearbooks, and build an entire machinery of segregation on campus while ignoring the fact that 72 percent of black American college students are dropping out. Black students have the lowest grade point average of any student group. If whites were not so preoccupied with escaping their own guilt, they would see that the real problem is not racism; it is that black students are failing in tragic numbers. They don't need separate dorms and yearbooks. They need basic academic skills. But instead they are taught that extra entitlements are their due and that the greatest power of all is that power that comes to them as victims. If they want to get anywhere in American Life, they had better wear their victimization on their sleeve, they had better tap into white guilt, making whites want to escape by offering money, status, racial-preferences—something, anything—in return. Is this the way for a race that has been oppressed to come into its own? Is this the way to achieve independence?

A Return to a Common Culture

Colleges and universities are not only segregating their campuses, they are segregating learning. If only for the sake of historical accuracy, we should teach all students—black, white, female, male—about many broad and diverse cultures. But those with grievance identities use the multicultual approach as an all-out assault on the liberal arts curriculum, on the American heritage, and on Western culture. They have made our differences, rather than our common bonds, sacred. Often they do so in the name of building the "self-esteem" of minorities. But they are not going to build anyone's self-esteem by condemning our culture as the product of "dead white males."

We *do* share a common history and a common culture, and that must be the central premise of education. If we are to the end the new segregation on campus, and everywhere else it exists, we need to recall the spirit of the original civil rights movement, which was dedicated to the "self evident truth" that all men are created equal.

Even the most humble experiences unite us. We have all grown up on the same sitcoms, eaten the same fast food, and laughed at the same jokes. We have practiced the same religions, lived under the same political system, read the same books, and worked in the same marketplace. We have the same dreams and aspirations as will as fears and doubts for ourselves and for our children. How, then, can our differences be so overwhelming?

REVIEW QUESTIONS

1. In Steele's opinion, what resulted when the politics of difference replaced the politics of equality?
2. How did "grievance identities" affect the demands made by certain groups?
3. Why did Steele criticize the "new segregation" that emerged on college campuses?

JOHN LEWIS GADDIS

Setting Right a Dangerous World (2002)

The September 11, 2001, terrorist assaults on the World Trade Center in New York City and the Pentagon outside Washington, D.C., transformed national security policy and prompted a reexamination of America's role in the world. In the following essay, the distinguished diplomatic historian John Lewis Gaddis assesses the new geopolitical environment and suggests a new approach for American foreign policy.

From John Lewis Gaddis, "And Now This: Lessons from the Old Era for the New One," *Age of Terror: America and the World After September 11*, edited by Strobe Talbott and Nayan Chanda. Copyright © 2001 by Strobe Talbott and Nayan Chanda. Reprinted by permission of Basic Books, a member of Perseus Books Group.

We've never had a good name for it, and now it's over. The post–cold-war era—let us call it that for want of any better term—began with the collapse of one structure, the Berlin Wall on November 9, 1989, and ended with the collapse of another, the World Trade Center's twin towers on September 11, 2001. No one, apart from the few people who plotted and carried out those events, could have anticipated that they were going to happen. But from the moment they did, everyone acknowledged that everything had changed.

It's characteristic of such turning points that they shed more light on the history that preceded them than on what's to come. The fall of the Berlin Wall didn't tell us much about the post–cold-war world, but it told us a lot about the Cold War. It suddenly became clear that East Germany, the Warsaw Pact, and the Soviet Union itself had long since lost the authority with which the United States and its NATO allies had continued to credit them right up to the day the wall came down. The whole history of the cold war looked different as a result. Having witnessed the end, historians could never again see the middle, or even the beginning, in the same way they once had.

Something similar seems likely to happen now to the post–cold-war era. For whatever we eventually settle on calling the events of September 11—the Attack on America, Black Tuesday, 9/11—they've already forced a reconsideration, not only of where we are as a nation and where we may be going, but also of where we've been, even of who we are. Our recent past, all at once, has been thrown into sharp relief, even as our future remains obscure. To paraphrase an old prayer, it's obvious now that we have done some things that we ought not to have done, and that we have not done other things that we ought to have done. How much health there is in us will depend, to a considerable degree, on how we sort this out.

But first things first. No acts of commission or omission by the United States can have justified what happened on September 11. Few if any moral standards have deeper roots than the prohibition against taking innocent life in peacetime. Whatever differences may exist in culture, religion, race, class, or any of the other categories by which human beings seek to establish their identities, that rule transcends them.

The September 11 attacks violated it in ways that go well beyond all other terrorist attacks in the past: first, by the absence of any stated cause to be served; second, by the failure to provide warning;

and finally, by the obvious intent to time and configure the attack in such a manner as to take as many lives as possible—even to the point, some have suggested, of the airplanes' angle of approach, which seemed calculated to devastate as many floors of the twin towers as they could. Let there be no mistake: This was evil, and no set of grievances real or imagined, however strongly felt or widely held, can excuse it.

At the same time, though, neither our outrage nor the patriotic unity that is arising from it relieves us of the obligation to think critically. Would anyone claim, in the aftermath of September 11, that the United States can continue the policies it was following with respect to its national defense, or toward the world, before September 11? Americans were not responsible for what happened at Pearl Harbor, but they would have been irresponsible in the extreme if they had not, as a consequence of that attack, dramatically altered their policies. Nobody given the opportunity to rerun the events leading up to that catastrophe would have handled things again in just the same way.

It's in that spirit, I think, that we need a reconsideration of how the United States has managed its responsibilities in the decade since the cold war ended, not with a view to assigning blame, indulging in recrimination, or wallowing in self-pity, but rather for the purpose—now urgent—of determining where we go from here. Patriotism demands nothing less.

The clearest conclusion to emerge from the events of September 11 is that *the geographical position and the military power of the United States are no longer sufficient to ensure its security.* . . .

In the aftermath of September 11, we have not only adopted the concept of "homeland security" —it has become synonymous with national security. Such is the revolution in our thinking forced upon us by the events of that day. It means that Americans have entered a new stage in their history, in which they can no longer take security for granted: It is no longer free—anywhere, or at any time. . . .

Security, therefore, has a new meaning, for which little in our history and even less in our planning has prepared us. That leads to a second conclusion, which is that *our foreign policy since the cold war ended has insufficiently served our interests.*

National security requires more than just military deployments or intelligence operations. It depends ultimately upon creating an international environment congenial to the nation's interests. That's the role of foreign policy. Despite many mistakes and diversions along the way, the United States managed to build such an environment during the second half of the 20th century. The Soviet Union's collapse stemmed, in no small measure, from its failure to do the same.

As a consequence, the world at the end of the cold war was closer to a consensus in favor of American values—collective security, democracy, capitalism—than it had ever been before. President George H. W. Bush's talk of a "new world order" reflected a convergence of interests among the great powers that, while imperfect, was nonetheless unprecedented. Differences remained with the European Union, Russia, China, and Japan over such issues as international trade, the handling of regional conflicts, the management of national economies, the definition and hence the protection of human rights; but those were minor compared with issues that had produced two world wars and perpetuated the cold war. Americans, it seemed, had finally found a congenial world.

What's happened since, though? Can anyone claim that the world of 2001—even before September 11—was as friendly to American interests as it had been in 1991? It would be silly to blame the United States alone for the disappointments of the past decade. Too many other actors, from Saddam Hussein to Slobodan Milosevic to Osama bin Laden, have helped to bring them about. But the question that haunted Americans after Pearl Harbor is still worth asking: Given the opportunity to rerun the sequence, what would we want to change in our foreign policy, and what would we leave the same?

The question is not at all hypothetical. The administration of George W. Bush has already undertaken, in the wake of September 11, the most sweeping reassessment of foreign-policy priorities

since the cold war ended. Its results are not yet clear, but the tilt is far more toward change than continuity. That is an implicit acknowledgment of deficiencies in the American approach to the world during the post–cold-war era that are clearer now than they were then.

One of those, it seems, was unilateralism, an occupational hazard of sole surviving superpowers. With so little countervailing power in sight, such states tend to lead without listening, a habit that can cause resistance even among those otherwise disposed to follow. The United States managed to avoid that outcome after its victory in World War II because we had, in the Soviet Union, a superpower competitor. Our allies, and even our former adversaries, tolerated a certain amount of arrogance on our part because there was always "something worse" out there; we, in turn, fearing their defection or collapse, treated them with greater deference and respect than they might have expected given the power imbalances of the time.

With our victory in the cold war, though, we lost the "something worse." American ideas, institutions, and culture remained as attractive as ever throughout much of the world, but American policies began to come across as overbearing, self-indulgent, and insensitive to the interests of others. . . .

A second problem, too, arose largely as a result of unilateralism: We neglected the cultivation of great-power relationships. We seemed to have assumed, perhaps because we were the greatest of the great powers, that we no longer needed the cooperation of the others to promote our interests. We therefore allowed our relations with the Russians and the Chinese to deteriorate to the point that by the end of the 1990s we were barely on speaking terms with Moscow and Beijing. We failed to sustain one of the most remarkable achievements of American foreign policy during the cold war—the success of Richard Nixon and Henry Kissinger in creating a situation in which our adversaries feared each other more than they feared us. . . .

That happened chiefly as the result of a third characteristic of our post–cold-war foreign policy: a preference for justice at the expense of order. We had never entirely neglected the demands of justice during the cold war, but we did tend to pursue those goals by working with the powerful to get them to improve their treatment of the powerless. We sought to promote human rights from the inside out rather than from the outside in: Sometimes we succeeded, sometimes we did not.

With the end of the cold war, however, we changed our approach. We enlarged NATO against the wishes of the Russians, not because the Poles, the Czechs, and the Hungarians added significantly to the alliance's military capabilities, but rather because those states had suffered past injustices and therefore "deserved" membership. We then used the expanded alliance to rescue the Kosovars and bomb the Serbs, despite the fact that in doing so we were violating the sovereignty of an internationally recognized state without explicit United Nations approval. Unsurprisingly, that angered not just the Russians but also the Chinese, both of whom had discontented minorities of their own to worry about. Our intentions were praiseworthy in both of those episodes, but our attention to the larger geopolitical implications was not what it might have been.

A fourth aspect of our post–cold-war foreign policy followed from the third: It was the inconsistency with which we pursued regional justice. We were, as it turned out, by no means as adamant in seeking justice for the Chechens or the Tibetans as we were for the Kosovars; Moscow and Beijing, despite their nervousness, had little to fear. But by applying universal principles on a less than universal basis, Washington did open itself to the charge of hypocrisy. . . .

Meanwhile, in the Middle East, we tolerated the continuing Israeli dispossession and repression of Palestinians, even as we were seeking to secure the rights of the Palestinians; and we did nothing to adjust policy in response to the fact that an old adversary, Iran, was moving toward free elections and a parliamentary system, even as old allies like Saudi Arabia were shunning such innovations. There was, in short, a gap between our principles and our practices: We proclaimed the former without linking them to the latter, and that

invited disillusionment. There are several reasons that the rantings of Osama bin Laden resonate to the extent that they do in so many parts of North Africa, the Middle East, and Asia; surely that is one of them.

A fifth problem was our tendency to regard our economic system as a model to be applied throughout the world, without regard to differences in local conditions and with little sense of the effects it would have in generating inequality. This was particularly evident in Russia, where we too easily assumed a smooth transition to market capitalism. Our efforts to help came nowhere near the scope and the seriousness of the programs we'd launched to rebuild the economies of our defeated adversaries after World War II.

Meanwhile, Washington officials were less sensitive than they should have been to the extent to which American wealth and power were being blamed, throughout much of the world, for the inequities that the globalization of capitalism was generating. Capitalism would have expanded after the cold war regardless of what the United States did. By linking that expansion so explicitly to our foreign-policy objectives, however, we associated ourselves with something abroad that we would never have tolerated at home: the workings of an unregulated market devoid of a social safety net. Adam Smith was right in arguing that the pursuit of self-interest ultimately benefits the collective interest; but Karl Marx was right when he pointed out that wealth is not distributed to everyone equally at the same time, and that alienation arises as a result. The United States and most other advanced societies found ways to reconcile those competing truths with the emergence of the regulatory state during the first half of the 20th century. Capitalism might not have survived had that not happened. No such reconciliation was sought, however, as a foreign-policy priority during the post–cold-war era.

Finally, and largely as a consequence, the United States emphasized the advantages, while neglecting the dangers, of globalization. There was a great deal of talk after the cold war ended of the extent to which that process had blurred the boundary between the domestic and the international: It was held to be a good thing that capital, commodities, ideas, and people could move more freely across boundaries. There was little talk, though, of an alternative possibility: that danger might move just as freely. That's a major lesson of September 11: The very instruments of the new world order—airplanes, liberal policies on immigration and money transfers, multiculturalism itself, in the sense that there seemed nothing odd about the hijackers when they were taking their flight training—can be turned horribly against it. It was as if we had convinced ourselves that the new world of global communications had somehow transformed an old aspect of human nature: the tendency to harbor grievances and sometimes to act upon them.

What connects these shortcomings is a failure of strategic vision: the ability to see how the parts of one's policy combine to form the whole, and to avoid the illusion that one can pursue particular policies in particular places without their interacting with one another. It means remembering that actions have consequences: that for every action there will be a reaction, the nature of which won't always be predictable. It means accepting the fact that there's not always a linear relationship between input and output: that vast efforts can produce minimal results in some situations, and that minimal efforts can produce vast consequences in others. It means thinking about the implications of such asymmetries for the relationship between ends and means, always the central problem of strategy. Leverage is important, and our adversaries have so far proved more successful than we in using it. Finally, it requires effective national leadership, a quality for which American foreign policy during the post–cold-war era is unlikely to be remembered.

Where do we go from here? Will the events of September 11 bring our policies back into line with our interests? Can we regain the clarity of strategic vision that served us well during the cold war, and that seemed to desert us during its aftermath? Shocks like this do have the advantage of concentrating the mind. . . .

What's emerging is the prospect, once again, of "something worse" than an American-dominated world—perhaps something much worse. The appalling nature of the attacks on New York and Washington forged a new coalition against terrorism overnight. The great-power consensus that withered after 1991 is back in place in expanded form: The United States, the European Union, Russia, China, and Japan are all on the same side now—at least on the issue of terrorism—and they've been joined by unexpected allies like Pakistan, Uzbekistan, and perhaps even, very discreetly, Iran. Terrorism can hardly flourish without some state support; but September 11 brought home the fact that terrorism challenges the authority of all states. Everybody has airplanes, and everything that lies below them must now be considered a potential target. So just as fear of the Soviet Union built and sustained an American coalition during the cold war—and just as the prospect of nuclear annihilation caused the Soviets themselves ultimately to begin cooperating with it—so the sudden appearance of "something much worse" is a paradoxical but powerful ally in the new war that now confronts us.

Maintaining this coalition, however, will require tolerating diversity within it. . . . If the global coalition against terrorism is to survive, it will demand even greater flexibility on the part of Americans than our cold-war coalition did. We'll have to give up the unilateralism we indulged in during the post–cold-war era. The Bush administration, prior to September 11, had seemed particularly to relish that bad habit. We'll have to define our allies more in terms of shared interests and less in terms of shared values. We'll have to compromise more than we might like in promoting human rights, open markets, and the scrupulous observance of democratic procedures. We'll have to concentrate more than we have in the past on getting whatever help we can in the war against terrorism, wherever we can find it. Our concerns with regional justice may suffer as a result. . . . The compensation, one hopes, will be to secure justice on a broader scale, for terrorism will offer little justice for anyone. . . .

The era we've just entered—whatever we decide to call it—is bound to be more painful than the one we've just left. The antiterrorist coalition is sure to undergo strains as its priorities shift from recovery to retaliation. Defections will doubtless occur. Further terrorist attacks are unavoidable, and are certain to produce demoralization as well as greater resolve.

But it does seem likely, even at this early stage in the war they have provoked, that the terrorists have got more than they bargained for. "What kind of a people do they think we are?" Winston Churchill asked of the Japanese in the aftermath of Pearl Harbor. It's worth asking the same of our new enemies, because it can hardly have been their purpose to give the United States yet another chance to lead the world into a new era, together with the opportunity to do it, this time, more wisely.

REVIEW QUESTIONS

1. Do you agree that nothing the United States had done warranted the terrorist attacks of September 11, 2001? Explain.
2. What are the drawbacks of a "unilateralist" foreign policy?
3. In what ways has the "globalization" of American capitalism and culture generated international tension and animosity?

BARACK OBAMA

Victory Speech (2008)

Illinois senator Barack Obama launched a remarkable presidential campaign in 2007. A first-term senator, he developed a superb campaign organization, raised incredible amounts of money from grassroots supporters, and used brilliant oratory centered on the themes of "hope" and "change" to catapult himself to the Democratic nomination and eventual victory in the 2008 presidential election. He was the first African American to win the presidency. After his victory on 4 November, the new president-elect addressed a huge crowd at Grant Park in Chicago.

http://my.barackobama.com/page/community/post/stateupdates/gGx3Kc. [Editorial insertions appear in square brackets—*Ed.*]

If there is anyone out there who still doubts that America is a place where all things are possible; who still wonders if the dream of our founders is alive in our time; who still questions the power of our democracy, tonight is your answer.

It's the answer told by lines that stretched around schools and churches in numbers this nation has never seen; by people who waited three hours and four hours, many for the very first time in their lives, because they believed that *this* time must be different; that their voice could *be* that difference.

It's the answer spoken by young and old, rich and poor, Democrat and Republican, black, white, Latino, Asian, Native American, gay, straight, disabled and not disabled—Americans who sent a message to the world that we have never been a collection of red states and blue states: we are, and always will be, the *United* States of America.

It's the answer that led those who have been

told for so long by so many to be cynical, and fearful, and doubtful of what we can achieve to put their hands on the arc of history and bend it once more toward the hope of a better day.

It's been a long time coming, but tonight, because of what we did on this day, in this election, at this defining moment, change has come to America.

*   *   *

. . . I will never forget who this victory truly belongs to—it belongs to you.

I was never the likeliest candidate for this office. We didn't start with much money or many endorsements. Our campaign was not hatched in the halls of Washington—it began in the backyards of Des Moines and the living rooms of Concord and the front porches of Charleston.

It was built by working men and women who dug into what little savings they had to give five dollars and ten dollars and twenty dollars to this cause. It grew strength from the young people who rejected the myth of their generation's apathy; who left their homes and their families for jobs that offered little pay and less sleep; from the not-so-young people who braved the bitter cold and scorching heat to knock on the doors of perfect strangers; from the millions of Americans who volunteered, and organized, and proved that more than two centuries later, a government of the people, by the people and for the people has not perished from this earth. This is your victory.

I know you didn't do this just to win an election and I know you didn't do it for me. You did it because you understand the enormity of the task that lies ahead. For even as we celebrate tonight, we know the challenges that tomorrow will bring are the greatest of our lifetime—two wars, a planet in peril, the worst financial crisis in a century. Even as we stand here tonight, we know there are brave Americans waking up in the deserts of Iraq and the mountains of Afghanistan to risk their lives for us. There are mothers and fathers who will lie awake after their children fall asleep and wonder how they'll make the mortgage, or pay their doctor's

bills, or save enough for college. There is new energy to harness and new jobs to be created; new schools to build and threats to meet and alliances to repair.

The road ahead will be long. Our climb will be steep. We may not get there in one year or even one term, but America—I have never been more hopeful than I am tonight that we will get there. I promise you—we as a people will get there.

There will be setbacks and false starts. There are many who won't agree with every decision or policy I make as president, and we know that government can't solve every problem. But I will always be honest with you about the challenges we face. I will listen to you, especially when we disagree. And above all, I will ask you join in the work of remaking this nation the only way it's been done in America for two hundred and twenty-one years—block by block, brick by brick, calloused hand by calloused hand.

What began twenty-one months ago in the depths of winter must not end on this autumn night. This victory alone is not the change we seek—it is only the chance for us to make that change. And that cannot happen if we go back to the way things were. It cannot happen without you.

So let us summon a new spirit of patriotism; of service and responsibility where each of us resolves to pitch in and work harder and look after not only ourselves, but each other. Let us remember that if this financial crisis taught us anything, it's that we cannot have a thriving Wall Street while Main Street suffers—in this country, we rise or fall as one nation; as one people.

Let us resist the temptation to fall back on the same partisanship and pettiness and immaturity that has poisoned our politics for so long. Let us remember that it was a man from this state [Abraham Lincoln] who first carried the banner of the Republican Party to the White House—a party founded on the values of self-reliance, individual liberty, and national unity. Those are values we all share, and while the Democratic Party has won a great victory tonight, we do so with a measure of humility and determination to heal the divides that have held back our progress. As Lincoln said to a nation far more divided than ours, "We are not enemies, but friends . . . though passion may have strained it must not break our bonds of affection." And to those Americans whose support I have yet to earn—I may not have won your vote, but I hear your voices, I need your help, and I will be your president too.

And to all those watching tonight from beyond our shores, from parliaments and palaces to those who are huddled around radios in the forgotten corners of our world—our stories are singular, but our destiny is shared, and a new dawn of American leadership is at hand. To those who would tear this world down—we will defeat you. To those who seek peace and security—we support you. And to all those who have wondered if America's beacon still burns as bright—tonight we proved once more that the true strength of our nation comes not from the might of our arms or the scale of our wealth, but from the enduring power of our ideals: democracy, liberty, opportunity, and unyielding hope.

For that is the true genius of America—that America can change. Our union can be perfected. And what we have already achieved gives us hope for what we can and must achieve tomorrow.

This election had many firsts and many stories that will be told for generations. But one that's on my mind tonight is about a woman who cast her ballot in Atlanta. She's a lot like the millions of others who stood in line to make their voice heard in this election except for one thing—Ann Nixon Cooper is 106 years old.

She was born just a generation past slavery; a time when there were no cars on the road or planes in the sky; when someone like her couldn't vote for two reasons—because she was a woman and because of the color of her skin.

And tonight, I think about all that she's seen throughout her century in America—the heartache and the hope; the struggle and the progress; the times we were told that we can't, and the people who pressed on with that American creed: Yes we can.

At a time when women's voices were silenced and their hopes dismissed, she lived to see them stand up and speak out and reach for the ballot. Yes we can.

When there was despair in the dust bowl and depression across the land [in the 1930s], she saw a nation conquer fear itself with a New Deal, new jobs and a new sense of common purpose. Yes we can.

When the bombs fell on our harbor and tyranny threatened the world, she was there to witness a generation rise to greatness and a democracy was saved. Yes we can.

She was there for the buses in Montgomery, the hoses in Birmingham, a bridge in Selma, and a preacher from Atlanta who told a people that "We Shall Overcome." Yes we can.

A man touched down on the moon, a wall came down in Berlin, a world was connected by our own science and imagination. And this year, in this election, she touched her finger to a screen, and cast her vote, because after 106 years in America, through the best of times and the darkest of hours, she knows how America can change. Yes we can.

America, we have come so far. We have seen so much. But there is so much more to do. So tonight, let us ask ourselves—if our children should live to see the next century; if my daughters should be so lucky to live as long as Ann Nixon Cooper, what change will they see? What progress will we have made?

This is our chance to answer that call. This is our moment. This is our time—to put our people back to work and open doors of opportunity for our kids; to restore prosperity and promote the cause of peace; to reclaim the American Dream and reaffirm that fundamental truth—that out of many, we are one; that while we breathe, we hope, and where we are met with cynicism, and doubt, and those who tell us that we can't, we will respond with that timeless creed that sums up the spirit of a people:

Yes We Can. Thank you, God bless you, and may God bless the United States of America.

REVIEW QUESTIONS

1. What are the prevailing themes of Obama's speech?
2. Why do you think Obama chose to compare the themes of his campaign and his new presidency with the themes expressed by Abraham Lincoln?
3. Both Obama and Ronald Reagan interspersed stories about "common" people in their speeches. Why are such anecdotes so effective rhetorical devices?